# Brotherhood of Kings

# Brotherhood
*of*
# Kings

*How International Relations*
*Shaped the Ancient Near East*

AMANDA H. PODANY

OXFORD
UNIVERSITY PRESS

2010

# OXFORD
## UNIVERSITY PRESS

Oxford University Press, Inc., publishes works that further
Oxford University's objective of excellence
in research, scholarship, and education.

Oxford   New York
Auckland   Cape Town   Dar es Salaam   Hong Kong   Karachi
Kuala Lumpur   Madrid   Melbourne   Mexico City   Nairobi
New Delhi   Shanghai   Taipei   Toronto

With offices in
Argentina   Austria   Brazil   Chile   Czech Republic   France   Greece
Guatemala   Hungary   Italy   Japan   Poland   Portugal   Singapore
South Korea   Switzerland   Thailand   Turkey   Ukraine   Vietnam

Published by Oxford University Press, Inc.
198 Madison Avenue, New York, New York 10016

www.oup.com

Oxford is a registered trademark of Oxford University Press

Library of Congress Cataloging-in-Publication Data
Podany, Amanda H.
Brotherhood of kings: how international relations
shaped the ancient Near East /
Amanda H. Podany.
p.   cm.
Includes bibliographical references and index.
ISBN 978-0-19-531398-7
1. Middle East—History—To 622.   2. Middle East—Foreign relations.
3. International relations—History—To 1500.   4. Middle East—Commerce—History.
5. Middle East—Kings and rulers—History.   6. Ambassadors—Middle East—History—
To 1500.   7. Alliances—History—To 1500.
I. Title.
DS62.23.P64 2010
939'.4—dc22      2009049011

*For Jerry, Emily, and Nicholas*

# Contents

*A Word about Chronology and Translation*, xi
*Cast of Characters*, xiii
*Time Line*, xvii
*Acknowledgments*, xxiii

Introduction, 3


PART I  THE EARLY DYNASTIC PERIOD AND AKKADIAN EMPIRE,
2500–2000 BCE

CHAPTER ONE  The First Evidence for Diplomacy
(*"I am your brother and you are my brother"*), 19

CHAPTER TWO  Traders and Ships from Distant Lands
(*"At the wharf of Akkad he made moor ships"*), 37


PART II  THE OLD BABYLONIAN PERIOD, 2000–1595 BCE

CHAPTER THREE  War and Allegiance
(*"I have always done good things for him and his heart
knows the good deeds that I have done for him"*), 63

CHAPTER FOUR  Long Journeys Away from Home
(*"Who is there who would sell lapis lazuli?"*), 93


PART III  A TIME OF CRISIS AND CHANGE, 1595–1400 BCE

CHAPTER FIVE  Attack on Babylon by a Distant Enemy
(*"I sent to a far-off land"*), 119

CHAPTER SIX  A Clash between Expanding Empires
(*"Prepare yourselves! Make your weapons ready! For one will engage
in combat with that wretched foe in the morning"*), 131

CHAPTER SEVEN  Diplomatic Overtures between the Great Powers
(*"A notable event! The like of this occurrence had not been
heard of since the time of the demigods"*), 163


PART IV  THE AMARNA AGE, 1400–1300 BCE

CHAPTER EIGHT  Brother Kings United and at Peace
(*"My brother, whom I love and who loves me"*), 191

CHAPTER NINE  Diplomatic Marriages
(*"We, between us, are one, the Hurrian land
and the land of Egypt"*), 217

CHAPTER TEN  Luxury Goods from Everywhere
(*"The gold is much. Among the kings there are brotherhood,
amity, peace, and good relations"*), 243

CHAPTER ELEVEN  A Crisis in the Brotherhood
(*"My father became hostile"*), 265

CHAPTER TWELVE  The End of an Empire
and the Restoration of Peace
(*"My ancestors and your ancestors made a mutual
declaration of friendship"*), 291

Epilogue, 305

*Abbreviations*, 311
*Notes*, 313
*Further Reading*, 359
*Bibliography*, 363
*Index*, 379

# A Word about Chronology and Translation

In most history books, one can count on the dates given by the author to be correct. This is unfortunately not the case for ancient history before around 1000 BCE. No one knows the true dates; all scholars use educated guesses. Since each of the ancient civilizations used its own dating system, each one of them has to be correlated to the BCE/CE (traditionally BC/AD) system of dates that we use now. There is no continuous record of the ancient year names and numbers, so one has to find ways to bridge gaps in the documentation and to find synchronisms between civilizations. Carbon 14 dating, dendrochronology (tree-ring dating), and some ancient astronomical observations have helped a lot, but many questions still remain.

The dates I am using in this book are based on what is known as the Middle Chronology, which sets the reign of Hammurabi of Babylon at 1792–1750 BCE. It was developed from ancient observations of the planet Venus, and is widely used by historians and archaeologists, although most think it is inaccurate. Nonetheless, it is convenient to have a common set of dates and it works well enough until a consensus emerges around a more accurate chronology. (Some believe that dates in the third and second millennia BCE may eventually prove to be off by as much as one hundred years.) Even among scholars who agree to use the Middle Chronology, there is disagreement about the dates of specific reigns, especially for the kings of Hatti and Mittani. On the other hand, the sequence of kings and events is generally agreed upon.

Another peculiarity of ancient history is that it is based on incomplete and broken source material. Clay cuneiform tablets are rarely found in pristine condition. Often they are broken, with whole sections of the text missing or

scratched and abraded beyond legibility in places. The same is true with papyrus scrolls, which sometimes crumble with age or turn dark brown or black,
making the script difficult to read. Most scholarly translations are careful to
note where the original is broken or illegible. This makes for disjointed reading sometimes, but it's accurate. I have followed established practice and the
published translations in this. The rules are as follows:

- A break in the text is indicated with square brackets [ ].
- Any words (or parts of words) inside the square brackets have been
  reconstructed based on context or parallel texts.
- Words that have to be added in English to make sense of the text, though
  they are missing in the original, are in parentheses ( ).
- An ellipsis (…) in a quotation shows that words found in the original
  have been omitted.
- A question mark between parentheses (?) after a word indicates that the
  reading of the word is not entirely certain.
- A word in italics is in the original language, usually because it represents a technical term and the exact translation is unknown.

In translating ancient texts, scholars usually use a number of letters that
are not in our alphabet to represent sounds not used in English. For ease of
reading, I have changed these, both in my own narrative and in quoted passages, as follows.

š is rendered as sh
ṣ is rendered as s (it's usually read as "ts")
ṭ is rendered as t (it's usually read just like a normal t)
ḫ is rendered as h (it's usually read as the "ch" in Scottish "loch")

Many of the personal and place names in this book have two or more vari-
ant spellings in modern works. One finds, for example, Suppiluliuma, Shup-
piluliuma, and Suppiluliumas in modern works to refer to the same Hittite
king. For consistency I have chosen one spelling in each case and have used it
throughout, even when quoting scholars whose original publications spelled
the name differently.

What often surprises modern readers is that the ancient languages are
very well understood; decipherment of both cuneiform and hieroglyphs was
completed well over a century ago. Scholars may debate the meaning of a few
technical terms or unusual verb forms, but the translations of ancient texts
can be counted on to be accurate.

# Cast of Main Characters

*Gods*

Amen, Egyptian god of Thebes
Aten, Egyptian god of the disk of the sun
Baal, chief god of the Canaanites
Dagan, Syrian god of the Middle Euphrates region
Enlil, king of the Mesopotamian gods
Hathor, Egyptian goddess
Hepat, Hurrian goddess
Inanna/Ishtar, Mesopotamian goddess of love
Kura, Syrian god of Ebla
Marduk, Mesopotamian god of Babylon
Nanna/Sin, Mesopotamian moon god
Ra, Egyptian sun god
Sarpanitum, Mesopotamian goddess of Babylon, divine wife of Marduk
Shamash, Mesopotamian sun god
Shaushka, Hurrian goddess of love and war
Shimige, Hurrian sun god
Storm-god of Hatti, Hittite god
Sun Goddess of Arinna, chief deity of the Hittites
Teshup, Hurrian storm god

*Individuals (all dates are approximate)*

Agum-Kakrime, Kassite king of Babylonia (sixteenth century BCE)

Ahmose, king of Egypt (early New Kingdom, 1550–1525 BCE)

Akhenaten, king of Egypt (Amarna Period, 1353–1336 BCE)

Aki-Teshup, Mittanian leader (Amarna Period, fourteenth century BCE)

Amenhotep II, king of Egypt (early New Kingdom, 1427–1400 BCE)

Amenhotep III, king of Egypt (Amarna Period, 1391–1353 BCE)

Amenhotep IV, original name of King Akhenaten

Amminaia, queen of Arrapkha (probably fifteenth century BCE)

Ankhesenpaaten/Ankhesenamen, wife of King Tutankhamen, daughter
of King Akhenaten (Amarna Period, fourteenth century BCE)

Artashumara, King of Mittani (Amarna Period, 1372 BCE)

Artatama I, king of Mittani (1400–1382 BCE)

Artatama II, king of Mittani (Amarna Period, 1326–1325 BCE)

Ashur-uballit I, king of Assyria (Amarna Period, 1363–1328 BCE)

Burna-buriash II, king of Babylonia (Amarna Period, 1359–1333 BCE)

Ea-nasir, Dilmun trader (Old Babylonian Period, nineteenth century
BCE)

Eanatum, king of Lagash (Early Dynastic Period, mid-twenty-fifth century
BCE)

Enmetena, king of Lagash (Early Dynastic Period, late twenty-fifth century
BCE)

Gudea, king of Lagash (twenty-second century BCE)

Hammurabi, king of Babylon (Old Babylonian Period, 1792–1750 BCE)

Hani, ambassador from Egypt (Amarna Period, fourteenth century BCE)

Hatshepsut, king of Egypt, daughter of King Thutmose I (early New
Kingdom, 1479–1458 BCE)

Hattusili I, king of Hatti (1650–1620 BCE)

Haya-Sumu, king of Ilan-Sura (Old Babylonian Period, eighteenth century BCE)

Ibubu, steward of King Irkab-damu (Early Dynastic Period, twenty-third
century BCE)

Idrimi, vassal king of Mittani, king of Alalakh (fifteenth century BCE)

Irkab-damu, king of Ebla (Early Dynastic Period, early twenty-third century BCE)

Ishar-damu, king of Ebla, son of King Irkab-damu (Early Dynastic Period,
early twenty-third century BCE)

Ishhi-Addu, king of Qatna (Old Babylonian Period, eighteenth century BCE)

Ishme-Dagan, king of Ekallatum, son of King Shamshi-Adad (Old Babylonian Period, 1775–1762 BCE)

Kadashman-Enlil I, king of Babylonia (Amarna Period, 1374–1360 BCE)

Keliya, ambassador from Mittani (Amarna Period, fourteenth century BCE)

Kilu-Hepa, princess of Mittani, daughter of Shuttarna II, wife of Amenhotep III (Amarna Period, fourteenth century BCE)

Kirum, daughter of King Zimri-Lim, wife of King Haya-Sumu of Ilan-Sura (Old Babylonian Period, eighteenth century BCE)

Kurigalzu I, king of Babylonia (d. 1374 BCE)

Kurigalzu II, king of Babylonia (1332–1308 BCE)

Lu-Enlilla, seafarer (Ur III period, twenty-first century BCE)

Mane, ambassador from Egypt (Amarna Period, fourteenth century BCE)

Manishtusu, king of Akkad (Akkadian Empire Period, 2269–2255 BCE)

Mursili I, king of Hatti (1620–1590 BCE)

Mursili II, king of Hatti, son of Suppiluliuma (Amarna Period, 1321–1282 BCE)

Naram-Sin, king of Akkad (Akkadian Empire Period, 2254–2218 BCE)

Nefertiti, wife of King Akhenaten (Amarna Period, fourteenth century BCE)

Ninmetabarri, princess of Mari (Early Dynastic Period, twenty-third century BCE?)

Niqmaddu II, king of Ugarit (Amarna Period, fourteenth century BCE)

Parattarna I, king of Mittani (1500–1480 BCE)

Piyassili, king of Carchemish, son of Suppiluliuma (Amarna Period, fourteenth century BCE)

Ramesses II, king of Egypt (late New Kingdom, 1279–1213 BCE)

Rim-Sin, king of Larsa (Old Babylonian Period, 1822–1763 BCE)

Samsuditana, king of Babylon (Old Babylonian Period, 1625–1595 BCE)

Sargon, king of Akkad (Akkadian Empire Period, 2334–2279 BCE)

Shamshi-Adad, king of Upper Mesopotamia (Old Babylonian Period, 1808–1776 BCE)

Sharrukin, original spelling of Sargon

Shattiwaza, king of Mittani, son of Tushratta (Amarna Period, 1325–1300 BCE)

Shaushtatar II, king of Mittani (1440–1410 BCE)

Shilwa-Teshup, prince of Arrapkha (fifteenth century BCE?)

Shimatum, daughter of King Zimri-Lim, wife of King Haya-Sumu of Ilan-Sura (Old Babylonian Period, eighteenth century BCE)

Shulgi, king of Ur (Ur III period, 2094–2047 BCE)

Shuttarna II, king of Mittani (1382–1372 BCE)

Shuttarna III, king of Mittani, son of Artatama II, (Amarna Period, 1326–1325 BCE)

Sinuhe, Egyptian official (Middle Kingdom, twentieth century BCE)

Smenkhare, king of Egypt (Amarna Period, 1336 BCE)

Suppululiuma, king of Hatti (Amarna Period, 1344–1322 BCE)

Tadu-Hepa, princess of Mittani, daughter of King Tushratta, wife of King Amenhotep III and King Akhenaten (Amarna Period, fourteenth century BCE)

Tarhundaradu, king of Arzawa (Amarna Period, fourteenth century BCE)

Telipinu, king of Hatti (1525–1500 BCE)

Thutmose I, king of Egypt (early New Kingdom, 1504–1492 BCE)

Thutmose III, king of Egypt, stepson of Hatshepsut (early New Kingdom, 1479–1425 BCE)

Thutmose IV, king of Egypt, son of Amenhotep II (early New Kingdom, 1400–1391 BCE)

Tiy, wife of King Amenhotep III, queen of Egypt (Amarna Period, fourteenth century BCE)

Tudhaliya I, king of Hatti (c. 1425 BCE)

Tudhaliya II, king of Hatti (Amarna Period, 1360–1344 BCE)

Tushratta, king of Mittani (Amarna Period, 1372–1326 BCE)

Tutankhaten/Tutankhamen, king of Egypt (Amarna Period, 1336–1327 BCE)

Ur-Namma, king of Ur (Ur III period, 2112–2095 BCE)

Zannanza, prince of Hatti, son of Suppululiuma (Amarna Period, fourteenth century BCE)

Zimri-Lim, king of Mari. (Old Babylonian Period, 1775–1761 BCE)

Time Line (all dates are BCE, and all are approximate)

| | Syria | Mesopotamia | Egypt | Anatolia | Mediterranean | Indus, Dilmun, Magan |
|---|---|---|---|---|---|---|
| 3500–3400 | | First cities<br>Uruk colonies | Mesopotamian objects in Egypt | | | |
| 3399–3300 | | | | | | |
| 3299–3200 | | | First kings | | | |
| 3199–3100 | | Cuneiform writing invented | Hieroglyphic writing invented | | | |
| 3099–3000 | | | | | Minoan communities founded | |
| 2999–2900 | Mari founded | First kings, beginning of Early Dynastic period | | | | |
| 2899–2800 | | | | | | |
| 2799–2700 | Ebla and other cities founded | | | | | |
| 2699–2600 | | | Cedar from Lebanon imported | First cities | | Cities founded in Meluhha (Indus valley) |

| | Syria | Mesopotamia | Egypt | Anatolia | Mediterranean | Indus, Dilmun, Magan |
|---|---|---|---|---|---|---|
| 2599–2500 | | | Great pyramids constructed | | | |
| 2499–2400 | | Royal tombs of Ur<br>**Eanatum of Lagash 2454**<br>Treaty with Umma<br>**Enmetena of Lagash 2400**<br>Alliance with Uruk | | | | |
| 2399–2300 | **Irkab-damu of Ebla 2300**<br>Alliances between Ebla and Mari, Hamazi | **Sargon of Akkad 2334–2279**<br>Ships from Magan, Meluhha, Dilmun in Akkad<br>Conquest of Mesopotamia and Syria | **Pepi I 2321–2287** | Possible arrival of Hittite speakers in Anatolia | | |
| 2299–2200 | **Ishar-damu of Ebla 2285**<br>Gift from Egypt<br>Lapis imported from Afghanistan<br>Treaty with Mari<br>Ebla/Kish marriage<br>Destruction of Ebla 2250 | **Manishtusu of Akkad 2269–2255**<br>Attack on Magan<br>**Naram-Sin of Akkad 2254–2218**<br>Expansion of Akkadian Empire<br>Akkad/Urkesh marriage<br>Treaty with Elam | **Pepi II 2278–2184**<br>Trading mission to Punt | Naram-Sin invaded Anatolia? | | City founded in Bahrain (Dilmun) |

| Date | | | | | | |
|------|---|---|---|---|---|---|
| 2199–2100 | | **Gudea of Lagash** / Imports from Meluhha, Magan / **Ur-Namma of Ur, 2112–2095** / Ur/Elam marriages | | | | Gold sent from Magan to Ur |
| 2099–2000 | | **Shulgi of Ur 2094–2047** / Ur/Elam marriages / Ur traders went to Magan / End of Ur III 2004 | | | First cities on Crete | "Meluhha village" in Mesopotamia |
| 1999–1900 | | | Beginning of Twelfth Dynasty 1985 / **Senusret I, 1956–1911** / Sinuhe lived in Canaan | Assyrian trading colonies founded, treaties between merchants and local authorities | | Decline of Indus civilization |
| 1899–1800 | | Hammurabi's ancestors ruled Babylon from 1894 | | | Minoan trade with Egypt | |
| 1799–1700 | **Shamshi-Adad of Upper Mesopotamia 1808–1776** / Sent envoys to Dilmun / **Zimri-Lim of Mari, 1775–1761** / Mari/Babylon alliance / Mari/Eshnunna alliance / Destruction of Mari 1761 | **Rim-Sin of Larsa 1822–1763** / Dilmun traders / **Hammurabi of Babylon 1792–1750** / Hammurabi built empire / **Ishme-Dagan of Ekallatum, 1775–1762** / Ekallatum/Qatna gifts / Various diplomatic marriages | | End of Assyrian colonies, 1750 | Crete bought tin from Mari, Minoan artists decorated some palaces in the Levant / Alashiya (Cyprus) sold copper to Mari Cities in Alashiya | |

| | Syria | Mesopotamia | Egypt | Anatolia | Mediterranean | Indus, Dilmun, Magan |
|---|---|---|---|---|---|---|
| **1699–1600** | Hana subject to Babylon | **Samsuditana of Babylon, 1625–1595** Conquest of Babylon by Hittites 1595 | | **Hattusili I, 1650–1620** Attacks on N. Syria Adoption of cuneiform writing **Mursili I, 1620–1590** Attack on Babylon | Peak of Minoan civilization | |
| **1599–1500** | Hana independent Mittani founded 1560 | Arrival of Kassite dynasty **Agum-Kakrime of Babylon** Negotiations with Hittites **Burna-buriash I of Babylon** Treaty with Assyria | Hyksos ruled northern Egypt, 1630–1539 Beginning of Eighteenth Dynasty 1550 **Ahmose 1550–1525** Expulsion of Hyksos 1539 | **Telipinu 1525–1500** Hatti/Kizzuwatna treaty | | |
| **1499–1400** | **Parattarna I of Mittani 1500–1480** Vassal treaty with Alalakh  **Shaushtatar II 1440–1410** Mittani conquered Assyria Treaty with Egypt | **Kara-indash of Babylon, 1413** Treaties with Assyria, Egypt | **Thutmose I 1504–1492** Attack on Mittani **Hatshepsut and Thutmose III 1479–1458** Trade mission to Punt **Thutmose III 1458–1425** Attack on Mittani Egypt/Canaan marriages Envoys from Assyria, Babylonia, Hatti **Amenhotep II 1427–1400** Treaties with Mittani, Hatti, Babylonia | **Tudhaliya I 1425** Treaties with Egypt, Kizzuwatna | Minoan artists decorated palace in Egypt Destruction of cities on Crete 1450 | |

| 1399–1300 | Artatama I 1400–1382 Egypt/Mittani marriage **Shuttarna II 1382–1372** Egypt/Mittani marriage and treaty **Artashumara 1372** **Tushratta 1372–1326** Marriage and alliance with Egypt **Artatama II and Shuttarna III 1326–1325** Allied with Assyria **Shattiwaza 1325–1300** Treaty and marriage with Hatti | **Kurigalzu I of Babylon died 1374** Babylonia/Elam marriage **Kadashman-Enlil I of Babylon 1374–1360** Egypt/Babylonia marriages **Burna-buriash II of Babylonia 1359–1333** Egypt/Babylonia marriage Babylonia/Assyria marriage **Ashur-uballit of Assyria 1363–1328** Assyrian independence from Mittani **Kurigalzu II of Babylonia 1332–1308** **Enlil-nirari of Assyria 1328–1321** | **Thutmose IV 1400–1391** Egypt/Mittani marriage **Amenhotep III 1391–1353** Marriages with Mittani, Babylonia, Arzawa **Akhenaten 1353–1336** Marriage with Mittani **Smenkhare 1336** **Tutankhamen 1336–1327** **Haremhab 1323–1295** Battles against Hittites in Canaan | **Tudhaliya II 1360–1344** Expansion of Hittite empire **Suppiluliuma 1344–1322** Hatti/Egypt alliance Hatti/Babylonia marriage and alliance War against Mittani, Canaan Treaty and marriage with Mittani **Mursili II 1321–1282** Battles against Egypt in Canaan Uluburun shipwreck 1300 | Mycenaeans dominant in Greece and Crete Alashiya sold copper to Egypt and elsewhere |
|---|---|---|---|---|---|
| 1299–1200 | End of Mittani, annexed into Assyria | | **Seti I 1290–1279** **Ramesses II 1279–1213** Battle of Kadesh against Hatti 1275 Treaty and marriage with Hatti 1258 | Battle of Kadesh against Egypt, 1275 Treaty and marriage with Egypt 1258 Alliance with Babylonia | |

# Acknowledgments

I am indebted to my university, Cal Poly Pomona, for supporting my research with a sabbatical in 2005–06 when I began working on this book and a later research grant in summer 2007. My gratitude is also extended to the late Ray Westbrook, Giorgio Buccellati, Paul Collins, Jack Sasson, Julian Hills, and Nancy Toff for their assistance at various points during the writing and editing of the book, and particularly to Daniel Fleming and the anonymous external reviewer for Oxford University Press for their many detailed comments and suggestions. I also have benefited from the support of my colleagues in the history department at Cal Poly Pomona. Susan Ferber has been an extraordinary editor. I very much appreciate her detailed edits and her congenial, understated manner; she has kept my colloquialisms in check and pushed me to think more clearly. All the other editors who have worked with me at Oxford University Press have also been tremendously helpful. My parents, Margaret and Brian Hills, and my friend Vicki Cowsill have encouraged me throughout, for which I am very grateful.

The picture credits are listed in the captions to the illustrations. I also would like to thank the following publishers for granting me permission to quote primary sources from their books (please see the bibliography for full citations for those publishers who have not requested a specific wording of the citation):

Eisenbrauns (for passages from *Letters to the King of Mari* by Wolfgang Heimpel, 2003).

SBL (for passages from *Hittite Diplomatic Texts* by Gary M. Beckman, 1999).

Koninklijke Brill NV (for passages from *The Context of Scripture* by William W. Hallo and K. Lawson Younger, 2003).

Princeton University Press (for passages from *Ancient Near Eastern Texts* by James B. Pritchard, 1969).

Éditions du Cerf and Johns Hopkins University Press (for passages from *Les Lettres d'El-Amarna: Correspondance diplomatique du pharaon.* Translation by William L. Moran with the collaboration of V. Haas and G. Wilhelm. French translation by Dominique Collon et Henri Cazelles. 640 pages. Collection « Littérature Ancienne du Proche-Orient » N° 13, © Editions du Cerf, 1987, appearing in English as *The Amarna Letters* by William L. Moran, 1992).

University of California Press (for passages from Miriam Lichtheim, *Ancient Egyptian Literature Volume 2.* © 1976 by the Regents of the University of California. Published by the University of California Press).

Most of all I want to thank my husband Jerry and children, Emily and Nicholas, to whom this book is dedicated. They have been very sweet and understanding about the amount of time it has consumed. Jerry has supported me endlessly (including giving me, as a generous series of birthday and Christmas presents, many of the books I needed to work from). At one point, when I thought the book might never be done, it was his encouragement that inspired me to put my full energies back into it and to finish. I could not have written it without them.

# Brotherhood of Kings

# Introduction

*A Letter*

On the second floor of the British Museum, Gallery 55 attracts fewer visitors than the cathedral-like halls of Egyptian and Assyrian statuary downstairs. It is an unassuming gallery, recently redesigned, full of small objects from the later years of ancient Mesopotamian history. Those visitors who haven't been seduced by the nearby rooms of mummies and objects from Egyptian tombs sometimes stop to admire the tiny Mesopotamian cylinder seals with their intricate designs, or to take in the fine workmanship of some Assyrian ivories and glass vases, and then wander on. In past years, on days when guards were in short supply, the gallery was sometimes roped off. It's not one that many tourists clamor to see.

Yet object E 29793, in Gallery 55, is worth a special visit. It's under a glass cover, tucked next to some cylinder seals: an almost square tablet of baked clay, about three inches on each side. Its slightly shiny reddish-brown surface is covered in cuneiform writing. It has survived the three thousand years that have passed since it was written without so much as a scratch. The label says that it was found in El-Amarna in Egypt, and that "it is addressed to Amenhotep III from Tushratta, king of Mitanni (centred in modern Syria)." The date of the letter is about 1350 BC.

This object has had a fascinating history. Its recent quiet years in a display case were preceded by thousands of years lost in the ground in Egypt. But before that were its days of glory. Tracing its history takes us to the heart of an era of international cooperation unlike anything seen before or, until quite

EA 29793, the letter from Tushratta of Mittani to Amenhotep III of Egypt in the British Museum. (©Trustees of the British Museum)

recently, since. We can't be sure of all the details, but can imagine some of its history.

The setting is a room in a brick palace in the kingdom of Mittani in Syria. It's around 1350 BCE, but at the time the year is dated in the reign of King Tushratta. The kingdom is at peace, at least for the moment. A well-dressed man—a literate official of the court—has taken some fine, slightly hardened clay from a container and has formed it into an almost square tablet. He must have done this same activity thousands of times, forming a tablet ready to be written on. This tablet will eventually become E 29793, but for now it is still blank. Perhaps the man smooths the clay and sharpens his reed stylus as he waits for his audience with the king.

At last, the official walks into the presence of King Tushratta, for whom he has worked for many years. Tushratta has an extensive staff of advisors and officials. This official is named Keliya, and he is much more than a scribe; he enjoys a prestigious position near the top of the administration and often serves as Tushratta's ambassador to Egypt. Tushratta tells Keliya that he has had a revelation: the goddess Shaushka wants to visit Egypt. Possibly this is because Shaushka is a goddess of healing and the pharaoh is suffering from bad toothaches. Or perhaps it's because the pharaoh has recently married Tushratta's daughter and the goddess wishes to bless the marriage.[1] In any event, her journey must be explained in a letter that will accompany the goddess to the court of the pharaoh, which Keliya must write. Tushratta speaks in Hurrian, the common language of Mittani, giving Keliya a double task. First he has to capture both the intent and spirit of the king's words as best he can, and then he has to translate the king's message into the international language of Akkadian. His stylus flies across the tablet, forming tidy lines of script as he writes.

Keliya probably reads the message back to the king and then asks about arrangements for the journey of the goddess. It's one thing for a group of men to travel to Egypt, as they have done regularly, and quite another for a goddess to join them. Usually the ambassadors to Egypt take expensive presents with them to the pharaoh—chariots and horses and lapis lazuli—but a goddess will be much more demanding. Presumably she will need a priest to attend to her needs, such as for food and drink. Shaushka may be a cult statue, but she still requires all the same comforts that a queen might desire. And since she is probably fashioned of gold and other precious materials, she will need soldiers to guard her. The goddess has been to Egypt before, a generation ago, and now it is time for a return visit.

Keliya leaves the presence of the king and surveys his tablet. Is the writing neat enough? Does he need to recopy it? This time, perhaps not. He takes the tablet to the archive room to prepare it to be baked. Royal letters must be treated in the kiln before they are carried, not just left out in the sun to dry. The baking process gives the smooth tablet a slight shine and the hardness of a brick. It is now unlikely to be damaged on its long journey.

When all the arrangements are finally made for Shaushka's care, the Mittanian expedition sets off. They will walk for hundreds of miles over the next six weeks before reaching Egypt. Throughout the journey, the tiny letter to the Egyptian king will be held safely in a bag or pouch, perhaps around Keliya's neck.

For days they walk over the plains of Syria, toward the coast, then turn down the road that leads through the Jordan Valley, across to the Mediterranean coast, along the northern edge of the Sinai Peninsula, and eventually into Egypt. The journey is probably slower than usual because of the special care needed in transporting the goddess, who rides in a litter of her own with men to carry it on their shoulders the whole way. They take a well-traveled road, but few of the people they meet along the way have ever been anywhere near Egypt.

Keliya and his companions must find themselves repeating stories about the great riches of Egypt almost every time they stop for the night. You are traveling for the king of Mittani? people ask. With a message for the pharaoh? And a goddess? Have you ever seen the Egyptian king? What is he like? And his land, is it as rich as they say? Is there gold on the streets simply to be taken? One of the envoy's companions is an Egyptian messenger; messengers from the two lands usually traveled together. This man must relish telling strangers of the greatness of his native land. All the time, the letter is safely enclosed in its pouch, and soldiers guard the goddess night and day. It wouldn't do for either the letter or the goddess to be damaged or stolen en route.

After a journey south up the Nile by boat, the men finally reach Thebes. It's a busy city, thronged with people. As they climb off the boat, the vast temple to the god Amen can be seen to the south, brightly colored pennants flying from its walls, and across the river the distant white colonnade of the mortuary temple of Queen Hatshepsut gleams in the sun. The messengers are greeted warmly and taken to comfortable quarters in the palace.

Finally comes the moment when the letter is to be delivered to the Egyptian king, Amenhotep III. Keliya, the Mittanian envoy, probably approaches the king in the long, pillared throne room of his palace. The blazing Egyptian sun shines in narrow beams through high windows, lighting millions of dancing dust particles. Keliya holds the tablet as he prepares to read it aloud in the presence of the king himself. The king, a living god who is dressed in white linen and seated on a gold throne, listens attentively. His chief wife probably sits next to him, dressed in an elaborately pleated robe and a braided black wig. Keliya looks quite different from the Egyptians in the room. With his short beard, his hair tied in a chignon at the back of his head, and his Mittanian clothes—a long wool robe with a fringed hem that falls below his knees and a round hat on his head—he could not be mistaken for an Egyptian.[2] Not so the man standing next to him, the Egyptian messenger who has traveled with him from Mittani, who is no doubt happy to be breathing the warm, dry Egyptian air again after months away.

Keliya clears his throat and reads his king's letter, using the formal name for Amenhotep III—Nimmureya (the III in his name is a modern addition to distinguish him from the other three Amenhoteps who ruled Egypt):

Nimmureya, the king of Egypt, my brother, my son-in-law, whom I love and who loves me: Thus Tushratta, the king of Mittani, who loves you, your father-in-law. For me all goes well. For you may all go well. For your household, for Tadu-Heba, my daughter, your wife, whom you love, may all go well. For your wives, for your sons, for your magnates, for your chariots, for your horses, for your troops, for your country and for whatever else belongs to you, may all go very, very well.[3]

Perhaps the Mittanian envoy is trilingual and is able to translate from Akkadian into Egyptian as he reads. Or perhaps he uses an Egyptian translator. If so, the translator will stay not just for the reading of the letter but also for the conversation that will no doubt follow it.

Of course, the two messengers have brought more than just the letter with them. They are also accompanied in the audience hall by Shaushka, dressed in her finest robes and jewels. The letter explains her presence:

Thus Shaushka of Nineveh, mistress of all lands: "I wish to go to Egypt, a country that I love, and then return." Now I herewith send her, and she is on her way.[4]

Although Shaushka is currently taking the form of a statue, to the scribe from Mittani she is real and powerful. It is rare for a goddess to travel like this. Keliya must be very relieved to have delivered her safely to the king of Egypt, and he will, perhaps, worry for her city of Nineveh until she returns home. The Mittanian king's words continue:

Now, in the time, too, of my father … [the goddess] went to this country, and just as earlier she dwelt there and they honored her, may my brother now honor her 10 times more than before. May my brother honor her, (then) at (his) pleasure let her go so that she may come back. May Shaushka, the mistress of heaven, protect us, my brother and me, 100,000 years, and may our mistress grant both of us great joy. And let us act as friends.[5]

The message is received warmly. The kings of Egypt and Mittani are related by marriage, after all. The king's youngest and most recent wife, Tadu-Hepa, daughter of the king of Mittani, may be in the audience hall too in order to hear her father's words. She will need to wait for the letter to be read in Hurrian, as she is probably not yet fluent in Egyptian. The messages that regularly come from her father, Tushratta, to her husband, Amenhotep III, are always friendly, and sometimes fulsome in their protestations of love, even though the two kings have never met.

Tushratta has added a postscript to his letter, posing a question to the pharaoh: "Is Shaushka for me alone my goddess, and for my brother not his goddess?" He does not seem to be doubting that the pharaoh would believe in the goddess (in this era everyone, Egyptians and Mittanians alike, would have believed in the power of the gods of all civilizations), but wondering, perhaps, whether Amenhotep III would have the same close relationship with Shaushka that he himself feels.[6]

After the letter has been read aloud, the pharaoh probably has questions for Keliya and for his own messenger. Perhaps he asks about the appropriate treatment of the goddess or the health of his brother the king of Mittani, or about any presents that he was anticipating receiving from Tushratta. Here the envoys have a certain amount of autonomy. Although the Mittanian king has prepared them for the discussion, he is far away now, and it is up to them to keep the relationship between their two lands on an even keel. At last the pharaoh is satisfied, and he dismisses the envoys from his presence.

This account is based on abundant evidence from the archives at Amarna and other sources; we can be fairly certain that this took place. But what happened next? Presumably Amenhotep III eventually summoned the envoys back and dictated a message to be sent to King Tushratta, though we don't have a copy of it. This reply would have ended up in the Mittanian archives, where it may still lie—the capital city of Mittani hasn't been found yet.

And what happened to the original tablet after it had played the important role of announcing the arrival of Shaushka and reaffirming the close relationship between the two kings? The pharaoh must have gone off to attend to other matters, and the envoys, happy to have completed their long journey and to have delivered their message, would have retired to their quarters, thinking about the feast they would be attending that night, a banquet that was traditionally held in honor of visiting dignitaries. They would be receiving gifts from the pharaoh too.

Some Egyptian official wrote on the back of the tablet in ink, using the Egyptian hieratic script, giving the date on which the tablet had been received.[7] He then must have taken Tushratta's letter and filed it in the king's archive room, stored in a basket or jar. Most of the documents stored in the palace were written in the Egyptian script and language on papyrus scrolls, which have long since disintegrated, but international letters, written on clay in cuneiform script and baked hard, didn't decompose.

Years later, when the Egyptian capital city was moved north to Amarna, someone must have packed up the tablets that constituted the royal correspondence—letters not just from Mittani but from many kings—and moved them to the new palace. This city, known at the time as Akhetaten, was the capital city of Egypt for just a few years during the reign of the pharaoh Akhenaten,

son of Amenhotep III, and during a few years in the short reigns of two of his
successors. Akhenaten thought the letters were important enough to keep,
and they may have been consulted for reference occasionally, but mostly they
gathered dust as world events unfolded. Those events were pretty dramatic;
the Egyptian king attempted to change the religion of his land, and neglected
his relationships with other kings, such as Tushratta. He alienated many people, and not long after his death almost all his reforms were abandoned. So
was his capital city. And when Amarna was abandoned, the royal letters were
abandoned with it.

The letter from Tushratta, forgotten by Akhenaten's successors, still lay in
a room in the palace that was called "place of the pharaoh's correspondence"
according to an inscription stamped on bricks that made up the walls. Tushratta was dead by now, and his kingdom had soon fallen apart. The city at
Amarna was no longer the center of the Egyptian kingdom. It was occupied
by a few remaining villagers who must have passed the gradually crumbling
ruins and told stories about the heretic king who had once lived there. In
time the walls fell, weeds grew in the piles of debris, and Tushratta's letter
was buried. For thousands of years it lay there. Every year the Nile flooded
and receded, every year fields were planted, but the remains of the palace at
Amarna were safe from being covered by the muddy silt, having been built
above the flood plain.

Children were born, grew up, married, had children of their own, grew
old and died, generation after generation. Once-powerful Egypt fell under the
control of successive waves of foreigners: Libyans, Nubians, Assyrians, and
Persians. Hellenistic Greeks were later followed by Romans, then Byzantines.
Egypt became predominantly Christian, then Muslim. Still Tushratta's letter
lay in the ground. And then, in 1887, some peasants digging in the ground in
Amarna found some tablets with cuneiform writing on them. The tablets were
unceremoniously packed into bags and carted around on the backs of donkeys
and camels as they were sent from one dealer to another to see if anyone had
an interest in buying them. Many of them broke in the process and, tragically,
some were lost altogether, crumbled to dust.[8] Once scholars saw these tablets,
though, they caused a stir—why would cuneiform documents with Babylonian writing on them be found in such numbers in Egypt?

The hundreds of tablets that had lain together in the ground were split
up, some going to London, some to Berlin, some to Cairo. Epigraphists copied
the cuneiform texts, provided translations, and attempted to figure out the
order in which they had been written. Ultimately, Tushratta's letter ended
up in Gallery 55 of the British Museum. It has been studied and published in
many languages, having a far bigger impact than Tushratta could ever have

guessed over 3,300 years ago. What would the ancient kings have thought of the British Museum visitors walking past the letter, with their audio guides and blue jeans?

## The First International Community

One thing might have made them proud. Although they had no word for diplomacy, these kings, their contemporaries, and their ancestors had helped invent it. What the kings forged, as they saw it, was a relationship of friends—brothers—across hundreds of miles. This brotherhood included not only the kings of Egypt and Mittani but the other great powers of Babylonia (in modern Iraq) and Hatti (modern Turkey) as well. They did not use the term "brother" lightly. These men saw one another as family and expected the kind of loyalty that real brothers would show to one another. Their ambassadors could expect to travel safely and regularly to one another's capitals. The kings followed formal rules of interaction and shared a set of strategies to work out disagreements. They negotiated peace treaties, agreed to uphold them, and (for the most part) abided by them. And their efforts paid off with the exchange of luxury goods that each king wanted from the others. They also became relatives in a concrete way as marriages were negotiated and concluded between their royal dynasties.

The kings agreed to communicate in a single language—Akkadian, the language of Mesopotamia—even when (as in the case of Tushratta writing to Amenhotep III) it was the native language of neither the sender nor the recipient. This fact attests, perhaps, to how important writing had become in the creation of alliances, in spite of the illiteracy of the kings (only scribes could read and write). Kings sometimes referred to hearing the words of a letter read from a tablet or to confirming that a messenger had spoken the words as they were written; it was important to them to have the written record of the message.

Any one of the great powers of the time could have tried to take over the others through warfare, but diplomacy usually prevailed and provided a respite from bloodshed. Instead of fighting, the kings learned from one another, and cooperated in peace.

The focus of this book is, then, on the ties and interactions between ancient peoples, who often lived at great distances from one another, and how those contacts gave shape to a shared international community spread over a vast area. The expression "international community" is often used in modern times in reference to the United Nations. Kofi Annan, former Secretary-General of the UN, wrote of the international community that

In the broadest sense there is a shared vision of a better world for all people, as set out, for example in the founding Charter of the United Nations.... There is the framework of international law, treaties and human rights conventions. There is equally our sense of shared opportunity, which is why we build common markets and joint institutions such as the United Nations. Together, we are stronger.[9]

The ancient kings did not have our modern conceptions of human rights, but those men who belonged to the brotherhood of kings observed international treaties and shared an understanding of acceptable behaviors which, though not written out as international law, were agreed upon by all. They, too, were stronger together than apart.

King Tushratta and his contemporaries did not invent the complex and sophisticated diplomatic system. It had been in use for over a thousand years by their time, gradually spreading a wider and wider net across the Near East. Although the details of the interactions among the ancient kings are unfamiliar to most people today, many ancient Near Eastern scholars and Egyptologists have devoted their careers to the study of international contacts between civilizations.[10] This book represents an attempt to bring their remarkable findings together in a single narrative and, in the process, to recreate an ancient world.

Throughout the millennium from 2300 to 1300 BCE, theirs was a world led by kings, some of them powerful leaders who ruled large kingdoms and viewed themselves as forming the "brotherhood," others lesser men who lived in the shadows of the great kings. Each king spent his life surrounded by administrators and advisors, along with scribes to record their words. Many of the texts written by these scribes survive, like Tushratta's letter to the pharaoh, baked hard, lost for millennia in the ground, and rediscovered. It has been estimated that over half a million cuneiform tablets have been found in the Near East, and hundreds of thousands (maybe millions) more surely await excavation. The vast majority of them are administrative texts: lists of taxes, rations, workers, animals, anything the administration might have needed to keep track of. These can on rare occasions give us glimpses into international relations, but they tend to be frustratingly terse. Other documents are more expansive: the royal letters, of course, which sometimes paint vivid portraits of the kings who dictated them; royal inscriptions in which the kings boasted of their successes; treaties of equality between great kings; vassal treaties between great and lesser kings; even cooking recipes and dowry lists have something to tell us. Not all writing was in cuneiform. In Egypt records were kept in hieroglyphs (or the more cursive hieratic script) on papyrus or stone.

There, most administrative records have disintegrated, but some wonderful tales remain, such as the story of Sinuhe, an Egyptian official who took up residence in Canaan, or the autobiographies of soldiers who campaigned with the pharaoh. Royal inscriptions that were carved on stone have also survived in Egypt.

As much as possible, the words of the ancient men and women themselves will be quoted in this book. Their words are often much more colorful than any retelling might be. They also show just how deeply the people felt about events and ideas in their own era. It is sometimes hard to see the ancient past as anything but dry and distant, but then one reads the speech of a king or the plea of a messenger, and one senses the passion behind his words, frozen in time, just as anguished or angry, just as affectionate or pompous as when they were spoken thousands of years ago.

In the minds of many, the words "ancient history" bring to mind the Greeks and the Romans, along with, perhaps, the Egyptians. They tend to be the starring attractions of most video documentaries, college courses, and popular books about ancient history. One can understand why. Egypt had mummies, along with all-powerful pharaohs and huge pyramids. Greece had beautiful temples, arresting artwork, and brilliant philosophers. Rome had gladiators, scheming emperors, and soaring architecture. The ancient Mesopotamians and Syrians don't register so quickly in the public mind. Their buildings have almost entirely returned to the mud from which they were made. Their art doesn't have the same instantly recognizable quality of Egyptian art, or the naturalism of Classical Greek or Roman art. Sargon and Hammurabi are perhaps the best-known Mesopotamian kings, but are not nearly as familiar as King Tut or Julius Caesar. And yet the ancient Syrian and Mesopotamian civilizations were every bit as rich, varied, and fascinating as those of Egypt, Greece, or Rome. This book will introduce readers not only to the brotherhood of kings, but also to ancient Near Eastern religion, family life, food, clothing, etiquette, travel, and any number of particulars that gave life to past events. They will meet not just the kings but also many others: ambassadors, messengers, traders, princesses, soldiers, translators, and seafarers (a "cast of characters" is included for assistance in keeping all their names straight).

## Three Syrian Kings

Although this book ranges over a thousand years and thousands of miles, one place is almost always at the center, and three kings dominate our story.

The place is Syria, which was at the geographic heart of ancient Near Eastern civilization. Anyone traveling by land from Anatolia (modern Turkey) to Egypt or vice versa had to journey through Syria; the same was true of anyone traveling from Mesopotamia (modern Iraq) to the Mediterranean coast, or from Mesopotamia to Anatolia or Egypt. Ships from Cyprus and the Aegean docked in Syria. So Syria's cities and kingdoms were open to influences from across the Near East and beyond, and its peoples incorporated those influences into their own culture. Perhaps for this reason, Syria played a crucial role in the spread of diplomacy and the creation of an international community.

For a few of the centuries covered in this book, the history of Syria is less well known than those of its neighbors because of a shortage of documentation, so there are some unavoidable gaps in this story. For much of the time, however, the record is abundant and vivid. The surrounding lands of Babylonia, Assyria, Hatti, Canaan, Egypt, and Cyprus had trade or diplomatic contacts with Syria and with one another at various times and will show up often in the narrative. More distant lands like Greece, Crete, Nubia (Sudan), Dilmun (Bahrain), Magan (Oman), Meluhha (the Indus Valley), Afghanistan, and even Southeast Asia and China sometimes played a role as well.

The three Syrian kings who feature most prominently in this narrative are King Irkab-damu, who ruled the kingdom of Ebla in western Syria in the twenty-third century BCE; King Zimri-Lim, who ruled the kingdom of Mari on the Euphrates River in the eighteenth century BCE; and King Tushratta (author of the letter in Gallery 55), who ruled Mittani from his capital in northern Syria in the fourteenth century BCE. None of them are household names, and they were not even necessarily the most influential kings of their time. We do, however, know a great deal about them, and their three eras mark the high points of international activity in ancient Near Eastern history. These are known as the Early Dynastic period (the time of Irkab-damu), the Old Babylonian period (Zimri-Lim), and the Amarna period (Tushratta). By looking at the experiences of the three kings, one can explore the whole world in which they lived. Three of the four parts of this book explore those eras. In each of these parts, at least one chapter addresses how the kings interacted diplomatically and one chapter addresses their trade relationships. These spread over a wide area and often served as a precursor to later diplomatic ties.

### Changes over a Thousand Years

This book focuses on international relations that evolved over a long span of time—a thousand years—but the story starts when civilization was already many centuries old. Diplomacy only becomes visible to us when people began to write about it, which was long after they began living in cities, building monumental architecture, and obeying kings. The millennium from 2300 to 1300 BCE, the focus of this book, saw the steady development of interstate relations from a local phenomenon to an international community that encompassed almost the whole known world (that is, the world as the people of the Near East knew it).

Part I is devoted to the time of King Irkab-damu of Ebla in the Early Dynastic period. Already in his era, the twenty-third century BCE, kings sent ambassadors to foreign courts with gifts and letters, negotiated peace treaties, and cemented their alliances with marriages. Diplomatic contacts were, as far as we know, all within Syria and Mesopotamia, and allies shared a common culture. Although the diplomatic ties between states that these early kings forged sometimes delayed wars, they do not seem to have prevented them (except when the cities were far away from one another). The alliances had the dual benefits of creating peace and making a king stronger in times of war.

The kings of the Early Dynastic period did maintain some important connections beyond the Tigris and Euphrates Rivers. They wanted luxuries that set them apart from their subjects and that showed off their wealth and power: materials like gold, lapis lazuli (a deep blue stone), and carnelian (a red stone). They also needed copper and tin in order to make bronze, which had increasingly become a necessity since its invention a few centuries earlier. These metals and semiprecious stones could only be obtained from distant lands like Afghanistan, Egypt, Oman, and India, which lay far beyond the kings' immediate circle of allies and enemies. At this time, goods seem mostly to have come from those lands in the hands of foreign traders. Mesopotamians and Syrians didn't venture far away from home.

Part II focuses on the time of King Zimri-Lim of Mari and his more famous ally, King Hammurabi of Babylon. Diplomacy had become more sophisticated over the five centuries that had passed since the time of Irkab-damu, with detailed treaties drawn up between allies and a regular flurry of letters carried by innumerable messengers between the many courts. Still, though, diplomatic contacts seem to have stayed within Syria and Mesopotamia, and diplomacy assisted in the preparation for war as often as it delayed or prevented it. Things were changing in relationships with the outside world, however. More Mesopotamian and Syrian traders were making difficult journeys out to the places from which luxury goods could be obtained. Traders from southern Mesopotamia traveled by boat to Bahrain and Oman, traders from northern Mesopotamia traveled with donkeys on the long overland trip to Anatolia. They brought ideas from home with them and, when they returned, must have expanded their own people's conception of the world, its size and variety.

Part III explores a time of great change. Although this period, the sixteenth and fifteenth centuries BCE, isn't usually seen as marking a time of significant international exchange, in fact it made possible the truly international community of the subsequent Amarna period. Two violent episodes severely threatened the established diplomatic system: attacks by the Hittites (a new power based in Turkey) on Syria and Mesopotamia at the beginning of the sixteenth century BCE, and attacks by the Egyptians on Syria in the fifteenth century BCE. These wars, promulgated by aggressive kings with huge military strength, must have shocked and terrified the Syrians and Mesopotamians. To them, the lands from which the armies came were distant and foreign, and their cultures and languages thoroughly unfamiliar. Previously these regions had posed no threat at all, but suddenly they were raiding and conquering in the valley of the Euphrates and Tigris Rivers.

Remarkably, both these lands—Hatti and Egypt—ended up joining the diplomatic brotherhood. The former aggressors ultimately became formal allies of the Syrians and Mesopotamians, adopting all of the elements of the established diplomatic system, even to the extent of writing their letters in the Akkadian language on cuneiform tablets.

Part IV brings us to the time of Tushratta of Mittani, who was one of the great kings of the Amarna period in the fourteenth century BCE. Tushratta inherited peaceful relationships with Babylonia and Egypt from his father and grandfather. The Amarna letters written between the great kings, unlike those of the Old Babylonian era of Zimri-Lim, don't even hint at warfare. International diplomacy had little if anything to do with military action. Theirs was a time when the most pressing international issues were the value of the gifts that passed between the kings and the etiquette of marriage preparations for foreign princesses. The brotherhood of great kings extended right across the Near East and might even, for a while, have included Greece. In this era, trade can sometimes be hard to distinguish from the exchange of luxury gifts between kings, because all but the most distant of the trading partners had become members of the international community. Peace facilitated the transfer of vast amounts of wealth from one kingdom to another.

Partway through Tushratta's reign, a particularly belligerent king of Hatti named Suppiluliuma came close to disrupting the international community through his attacks on the neighboring empires of Mittani and Egypt. But even he was unable to destroy the spirit of brotherhood that marked international relations in this remarkable age.

The diplomatic system developed in the ancient Near East was forgotten for millennia; there's no collection of marble busts of ancient kings in the entrance hall to the United Nations in honor of their contribution to the history of humankind, no requirement that children study the ancient peace treaties as founding documents, the way they might study the Magna Carta or the United States Constitution. There's a good reason for this: We can find no direct link between the ancient practice of diplomacy and that used today.

But it is edifying, even inspiring, to know that, right from the earliest centuries of civilization, ancient kings and statesmen of distinct and different lands were often willing, even eager, to find alternatives to war and to see one another as brothers rather than enemies.

# PART I

# The Early Dynastic Period and Akkadian Empire,
## 2500–2000 BCE

CHAPTER ONE

# The First Evidence
# for Diplomacy

*"I am your brother and you are my brother."*

*The Kingdom of Ebla around 4,300 Years Ago*

A thousand years before the reign of Tushratta of Mittani, another powerful kingdom had thrived in Syria. It provides the earliest evidence for the type of diplomacy that had become so routine by Tushratta's time. The kingdom was centered in the city of Ebla, which during the reign of King Irkab-damu was about as prosperous as a Syrian town could be in the twenty-third century BCE. Its 15,000 or 20,000 inhabitants must have thought that they lived in the best place on earth.[1] Past the city wall that encircled Ebla were groves of olive trees and vineyards. The city produced wine from the grapes and oil from the olives.[2] And beyond that were lush fields growing barley, which was made into bread and beer, and stands of flax, which produced linen. The Eblaites lived not far from the steppes, where they could often see, in the distance, groups of sheep from their city's vast herd of over 80,000.[3] These resources contributed to Ebla's main source of wealth: elaborate textiles of linen and wool that were made by hundreds of spinners, weavers, and embroiderers.[4]

Not everyone worked in the textile business, though. The people of Ebla held many other jobs as well. Many of them were farmers, while others made pots, baked bread, brewed beer, or took on innumerable other responsibilities that helped the city run smoothly. Thousands of them received pay, in the form of rations, directly from the king himself, so that, in one way or another, most of the households in Ebla were closely tied to, or even dependent on, the palace.[5] This seems to have been normal for the time; kings required their subjects to work for them in many different ways.

One tends to think of the twenty-third century BCE—almost 4,300 years ago—as close to the beginning of civilization. To get a sense of just how long ago this was, look at it this way: more time passed between the lifetimes of Irkab-damu and Julius Caesar (around 2,200 years) than has passed from Caesar's death to the present (less than 2,100 years). But the civilization wouldn't have seemed at all primitive or newly created to the Eblaites. Their city had been in existence for almost 600 years already, such a long time that the level of the streets and buildings had slowly risen with respect to the plain around them so that Ebla sat on a high mound, or "tell," about 124 acres in extent.[6] No doubt a local could point out the oldest buildings still standing, their mud-brick walls decaying and soon ready to fall and be rebuilt anew; these structures had been constructed long before the lifetimes of any of its then residents. In the center, at the highest point of the city, was the citadel, where the king's palace rose above the homes of his subjects.[7]

King Irkab-damu's palace at Ebla has been partially excavated, revealing some of its grandeur. At its heart was a large courtyard with columned porticos along at least two sides that would have provided welcome shade in the hot Syrian summer.[8] Under one portico a platform probably supported a throne where the king could receive visitors. A letter from a later era describes a similar scene; Irkab-damu might well have appeared to his visitors just like this. While seated under his portico, he "was decked out in gold and lapis-lazuli. He sat on a throne which was set up on a high-quality cloth cover (and) had his feet set on a golden footstool."[9] A scribe would have stood near him, keeping track of administrative affairs, reading letters, and organizing the king's agenda.

The walls of some rooms in the palace were decorated with elaborate mosaic inlays made of limestone, depicting fantastic animals and soldiers in battle, each five or six inches high, arranged in rows.[10] Some of the limestone relief figures sparkled with gold leaf, or had added wigs or belts in stone of varying colors. Even the furniture in the palace was opulent, with delicate shell inlay and open-worked wood carvings of lions and bulls.[11]

No statues survive of Irkab-damu, but he probably dressed somewhat like a king named Ishqi-Mari, who ruled about fifty years later and whose statue was found at the ancient Syrian city of Mari, around 190 miles to the east of Ebla.[12] Ishqi-Mari wore his hair long, parted in the middle, and tied up in the back in a complicated bun-like knot. Around his head he wore a braided headband, which seems to have been a type of "crown" reserved for kings, and over his left shoulder and around his body hung a tasseled cape. He left his feet bare. Men throughout Mesopotamia and Syria at this time seem to have gone barefoot, even in battle, if we are to believe the evidence of their artwork. King Ishqi-Mari shaved his upper lip, but grew his beard almost to his waist.

Beards were, however, surprisingly rare among the depictions of men at Ebla and Mari; King Irkab-damu of Ebla might well have been clean-shaven. If so, he must have truly trusted his barber—the man who perhaps daily held a razor-sharp bronze blade right next to his neck. A small limestone figure from a wall at Ebla shows a helmeted man with no beard, wearing a cape similar to that of Ishqi-Mari—perhaps a representation of the king himself.[13]

Irkab-damu had four "main wives," of whom his favorite was a woman named Dusigu.[14] Like her husband, she would have parted her long hair in the middle, and she wore tufted or tasseled gowns that stretched from her neck to her ankles.[15] She lived in the palace with the king and his other wives and children, including her own young son, Ishar-damu, who would eventually come to the throne.

One of the most remarkable features of Ebla is that we can read its daily records. Thousands of fragments of documents, constituting 1,727 clay tablets

A limestone inlay from Ebla, showing a soldier with a spear fighting an enemy. The style of the spotted cloak worn by the soldier suggests that this might be a representation of the king of Ebla. (Erich Lessing/Art Resource, NY)

when they were complete, were found in the palace, in archive rooms near the porticoed courtyard. They had been placed there by the palace scribes, organized into categories, and neatly stacked on the floor and on shelves.[16] Most of them were administrative, written to keep track of the complicated functions of the palace and the kingdom, and filed away for future reference. Some were big, square blocks of clay as much as ten inches on a side and two or three inches thick, covered in meticulous cuneiform words and numbers that often recorded the minutiae of textile manufacture and distribution and other details of the palace economy. But not all the documents in the archive room were administrative. The king had his scribes keep other tablets as well, including some that were drawn up in the course of diplomatic encounters with other kingdoms.

When the Ebla palace burned down around 2250 BCE, about thirty-five years after Irkab-damu's death, the archives were left in the abandoned building, baked by the fire and lying in the places where they had fallen when the shelves collapsed.[17] There they stayed for over 4,000 years. Thanks to these tablets, a great deal is known about the kingdom of Ebla; more, in fact, than about any other state from such an early date.

What the tablets reveal is that Ebla was rich not just because of its fields and its flocks of sheep, but also because it controlled a considerable territory, a kingdom perhaps 125 miles from east to west and about the same from north to south. Within the kingdom were hundreds of towns and villages.

Beyond the kingdom's borders lay other states, each dominated by a major city at its center that gave its name to the kingdom. This era of Syrian and Mesopotamian history is known as the Early Dynastic period, and it was characterized by the independent states that dotted the landscape. To the kings of Ebla, the most important of the other kingdoms were, to the east, Mari on the Euphrates; to the northeast, Nagar on the Khabur River; and to the south, in Mesopotamia, the ancient city of Kish. Remarkably, it turns out that King Irkab-damu of Ebla was regularly in touch with these distant places.[18]

Mari and Kish had much the same culture as Ebla. The languages spoken in each were similar enough that they would probably have been mutually intelligible. All were of the Semitic family of languages (which later came to include Hebrew and Arabic). Each city had a king and an organized system of government.[19] They used the same weights and measures and the same system of dating their years and months, and they worshiped many of the same gods. Even the fashions and hairstyles were similar in all the cities: men wore long kilts made of a tasseled fabric; women donned floor-length tunics of the same material, leaving one shoulder exposed. Perhaps most importantly for us, the kingdoms had all adopted a common writing system—cuneiform— that had been invented in southern Mesopotamia hundreds of years before, around 3100 BCE.[20] For the first 600 or so of those years it had been used pretty much exclusively for making lists—lists of commodities, taxes, workers, and words—but by the twenty-fifth century BCE, southern scribes had started using cuneiform to write letters, royal inscriptions, and other useful documents.[21]

By 2400 BCE, scribes in Ebla had learned to write in cuneiform, but we don't know exactly how the transmission of the script to Syria took place.[22] It wasn't haphazard, though—that is certain. Scribes in Ebla were trained using almost exactly the same curriculum taught in Mesopotamian schools; the word lists that they memorized were preserved on the top shelf in the main archive room in the palace, and they include standard "textbooks" of words that were studied by aspiring scribes across Mesopotamia.[23] Presumably, the first Eblaites who learned to write were taught directly by Mesopotamian teachers. Perhaps a Mesopotamian scribe came to Ebla at the request of an earlier king, specifically to train a new bureaucratic class. Or perhaps an Eblaite, or several of them, traveled to a Mesopotamian city to attend a local school and to learn there, coming home afterwards with all the knowledge needed to keep records for their own king. Either way, there does seem to have been some continuing interaction with southern schools. One eminent Mesopotamian scribe might even have lived in Ebla; a learned mathematical list found at Ebla was composed by a man described as a "scribe of Kish."[24]

It's no mystery *why* the kings would have wanted to have literate scribes to attend them. Writing was obviously a good idea, and earlier, preliterate peoples who encountered literate Mesopotamians—travelers, perhaps, or traders—would no doubt have been transfixed by them. Here were men who could stare at a dumb object, a piece of clay, and could learn from it, just as though it spoke. They didn't have to carry all the information they needed in their heads, but could rely on a rectangular tablet. It must have seemed magical to anyone unfamiliar with the new invention. Once they mastered this new tool, the king's administrators would be able to keep track of thousands of mundane statistics, such as which of their subjects had paid their silver or gold to the palace, which workers had received rations for the month, how many cows were needed for a particular temple, and so on.

It is probable that literacy spread to the neighboring kingdom of Mari at around the same time that it came to Ebla, though many fewer documents have been found from the Early Dynastic period in Mari. Scribes in both kingdoms adapted the writing system to the peculiarities of their own language. The Ebla scribes even added columns to some of their Sumerian word lists, giving translations of the Sumerian words into Eblaite.[25] These very practical texts are the earliest known dictionaries in the world. In the documents they produced in Ebla the scribes switched between Sumerian and Eblaite, depending on the context, often using Sumerian as shorthand for words that they no doubt read aloud in Eblaite.

## King Irkab-damu's World

One might have hoped that the Ebla tablets would include plenty of details about the politics of the kingdom, the kings' victories, building projects, and other achievements. (They were unlikely to record their defeats or disappointments on any palace-authorized document.) Unfortunately, though, the kings of Ebla do not seem to have adopted the somewhat bombastic habit, common to their Mesopotamian contemporaries, of creating royal inscriptions proclaiming their great deeds.[26] Instead, glimpses of political events tend to come in the form of short explanations in administrative texts. For example, one tablet includes the statement that Irkab-damu performed a purification ceremony for a god "in the year (in which) Mari was vanquished by [the locality] Atini."[27] Another victory over Mari that took place during the reign of Irkab-damu (or perhaps it was the same one) is mentioned in passing when a man received a cloth as thanks for "the news (that) Mari was defeated."[28]

The political events of Irkab-damu's reign are therefore shadowy (as are those of all the other Ebla kings). And yet it is important, not just to ancient Near Eastern history but, in some ways, to the history of the world, to determine as much as we can about this Syrian kingdom. This is because Ebla provides us with some of the first evidence for the ways in which early states and their rulers dealt with one another. Some of these interactions were, not surprisingly, belligerent. Men certainly fought one another long before anyone invented a writing system to record the fact. But the stakes were higher once a city-based government could arm and organize its men to launch an attack on a neighboring community. City-dwellers in Syria and Mesopotamia began protecting themselves behind fortification walls at right around the same time that writing was invented.[29]

Not all, in fact far from all, of the contacts between Ebla and other states were at dagger's point, however. The Ebla scribes created a record of their world as they listed the commodities that went in and out of the palace, and it was a world in which many kingdoms, local and more distant, were at peace with one another—not accidentally but deliberately at peace. These peaceful episodes were not necessarily long-lasting (though the farther away an allied city was located, the less likely it was to go to war against Ebla). But even the fact that peace was a goal is noteworthy. The ways in which the kings maintained their alliances were wisely constructed and are worth our attention.

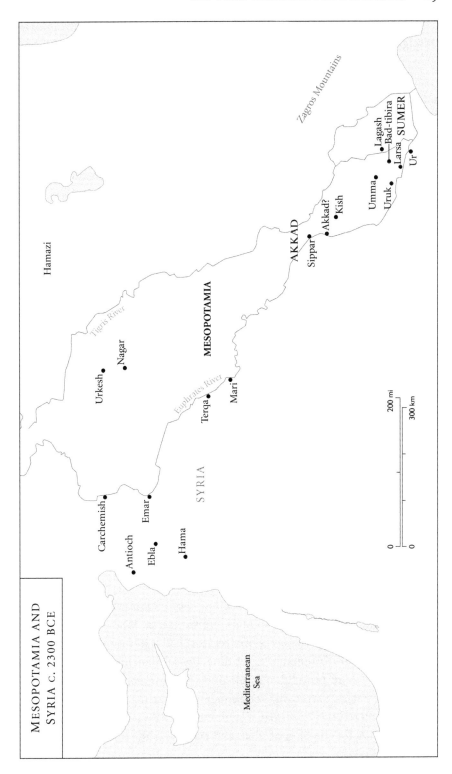

MESOPOTAMIA AND
SYRIA C. 2300 BCE

Irkab-damu seems to have extended the kingdom of Ebla, presumably through warfare, west to the plain of Antioch, northeast to the city of Carchemish on the Euphrates, and south to the city of Hama.[30] At one point during his reign he granted some fields to his ally to the east, the king of Emar, probably fields that fell between their two kingdoms, and he brought that city into Ebla's realm.[31] Emar would have been important to Irkab-damu because, when heading east from Ebla, it was the first city one would reach on the Euphrates. From there, one could journey on to Mari and to Mesopotamia beyond, along the southeast course of the river. An alternate road from Emar went northeast, hugged the foothills going east, then headed south along the Tigris River, only to rejoin the Euphrates near the city of Sippar in Mesopotamia.[32]

The kings of Ebla were not always on good terms with other kingdoms and didn't shy away from warfare with their neighbors when it became necessary. The relationship with Mari was particularly fraught at times. A letter from a king of Mari to the king of Ebla, almost certainly Irkab-damu, recalled earlier generations of border disputes between their two lands and seems to have been designed to intimidate Irkab-damu.[33] It included references to the Mari king heaping up burial mounds, presumably of the dead killed in battle.[34] In the letter, the Mari king listed the cities won and lost and the kings who ruled during these times. Mari seems initially to have held the upper hand. Perhaps in order to keep Mari from invading directly, Ebla paid vast amounts of gold and silver to Mari as tribute—according to one text, a total of 2,267 pounds of silver and 139 pounds of gold had been delivered from Ebla to Mari.[35] One can imagine the relief of the Eblaites when they managed to put an end to this obligation and to keep the wealth for their own uses. Perhaps the defeats of Mari, mentioned in passing in other documents, resulted in an end to the expensive tribute that Ebla had been paying.

### The First Known Diplomatic Letter

Despite this warfare, right from the beginning of Irkab-damu's reign, official delegations traveled from Ebla to Mari and vice versa. When a king of Mari died, Irkab-damu (or perhaps his predecessor) had sent four high officials to Mari with gifts for his funeral.[36] Over time, the relationship between the two cities became more peaceful and remained that way for thirty years.[37] The kings seemed at last to recognize one another as equals. Every year, and sometimes even more often than that, a high-ranking steward would arrive from Mari with gifts for the king of Ebla, and every year the king of Ebla would reciprocate.[38]

The stewards probably brought more than just gifts; they almost certainly carried letters with them as well. No such diplomatic letters survive between Ebla and Mari, but the Ebla archives contained one missive that Irkab-damu had sent to another ally, the king of Hamazi, probably located in northeastern Mesopotamia, hundreds of miles east of Ebla.[39] This letter provides the sole testimony for the relationship between Ebla and Hamazi—in fact, it is the only diplomatic letter of its kind found at Ebla and the only mention of Hamazi in the archives—but it represents what must have been a hoard of such letters.[40] It doesn't reflect a fumbling stab at diplomacy but provides clear evidence of the existence of a well-oiled diplomatic machine, one in which both partners knew the rules of the system.[41]

The letter was written not by King Irkab-damu himself but by a high official, the steward of his palace, whose name was Ibubu, and it was written to the envoy of the king of Hamazi.[42] After identifying the sender and recipient, Ibubu wrote "I am (your) brother and you are (my) brother." Ibubu was saying that he viewed the foreign envoy as his equal and ally. This phrase was characteristic of diplomatic correspondence for centuries after this letter was written. (Recall that Tushratta referred to Amenhotep III as "my brother" a thousand years later when he sent the goddess statue from Mittani to Egypt.) Ibubu continued, "What is (appropriate) to brother(s): whatever desire you express, I shall grant you, (whatever) desire (I express), you shall grant." Such "desires," at least in diplomatic letters from later eras, were always for material goods, usually luxuries that were unavailable in their homelands. And, indeed, the next words of this letter reflected a request for horses, or some other kind of equid, of "finest quality." Hamazi's steeds must have been particularly desirable, perhaps like Arabian horses today. Just in case there was any doubt, Ibubu then reiterated his assurance that "You are (my) brother and I am (your) brother." But he didn't expect the equids to simply be sent as gifts; there was a protocol to this, and a gift had to be sent in anticipation of a return gift. He sent with his letter "ten (wagon) ropes, and two boxwood wagons." The letter ended with more assurances of brotherhood, this time not between the officials but between the kings they represented, and with the note that King Irkab-damu of Ebla and his scribe Tira-Il had dispatched the goods.

Although this letter is often heralded as the earliest known diplomatic document, it does not mark the first invention of diplomacy.[43] These men knew what they were doing and must have learned the ropes from diplomats who had come before them. Obviously the two kings (or at least their envoys) had been in contact before; this wasn't a letter wondering whether the two kingdoms might set up an alliance but an exchange between established "brothers."

One wonders at the peaceful, orderly relationship between these two lands. Yet, if Hamazi was a distant place, which seems likely, a military campaign there would have been almost impossible to mount, and peace would have been a given between them. But how did the kings find one another in the first place? Which of them sent the first delegation of visitors to his "brother"? What did they hope to achieve through their alliance?

The first two questions have no answers, just intriguing possibilities. The third is easier to address. Almost certainly the gifts that they sent one another were the chief reward for maintaining contact. This would have been an ideal way to acquire luxury goods, such as those prized equids from Hamazi.[44] Irkab-damu would presumably have craved many things that weren't available locally in Ebla and that would have showed off his wealth and importance to everyone he came in contact with.

Why pay traders for expensive items if you could deal directly with the kings in whose lands they were found, and perhaps even identify something they wanted from you in exchange? It's possible that Irkab-damu had no idea where Hamazi was located or how far away it was. He might not have known what language was spoken there, and he might never have met his "brother" the king of Hamazi (they certainly were not true brothers). His messengers and stewards would have taken care of all the details. They presumably knew the way to Hamazi, the layout of its town, and the appropriate ways to behave when they got there. And so we are left to imagine the mechanisms behind the relationship: the rest stops along the long journey, the guards who presumably accompanied the messengers and envoys, the grooms who took care of the animals pulling the two "boxwood wagons," the translator who read the letter aloud in the language of Hamazi, and all the arrangements by which the messengers were accommodated in the foreign land.

### Imagining Family Ties

Perhaps there was even a formal treaty between Ebla and Hamazi in which these arrangements were laid out. This is a guess, but not an unwarranted one. In the letter, the word "brother" came up seven times, and this was a term that was later commonly used in treaties between allies.[45] In later eras great kings were referred to as "fathers" and their vassals as "sons"; this may have already been true in the Early Dynastic period. The terms were fitting because family was all-important to the Mesopotamians and Syrians. They saw much of the universe, in both the divine and human realms, as in some way taking its cues from relationships within the family. For example, their gods and goddesses were married and had children, and the loyalties and fights among the gods echoed those of human families. One's own family was, of course, the first bastion of social order, and the Mesopotamians and Syrians always wanted life to be orderly. Their idea of chaos was a world in which sons disobeyed their fathers, or brothers turned against one another. In one poem a curse read "May brother not recognize his brother."[46]

People saw in their parents models for the other authority figures that dominated their towns and kingdoms. The term for father in Akkadian, the Semitic language of northern Mesopotamia, was *abum*, but it was used for other men as well. An expert in any field was known as *abum* by his subordinates. The sheikh, someone who oversaw the activities of a town in much the same way that a father might supervise his wife and children, was a bigger *abum* still. Even the most distant and powerful leader—one whom most of his subjects had never seen—styled himself as *abum* of his vassals and servants.[47]

Projecting family relationships onto larger and larger arenas, the whole state came to be viewed as an extended household, with the king at its head.[48] Expectations of behavior within the family, such as obedience to one's parents, extended to one's superiors. Fatherhood came to stand in for any hierarchical relationship; the man in the higher position was the father, the lower man was his son.

But Irkab-damu was neither the "father" nor the "son" of the king of Hamazi. Their relationship as "brothers" had its own set of expectations. The Akkadian word for brother, *ahum,* had another meaning as well: "arm" or "side."[49] And, fittingly, the Mesopotamians saw a brother as someone who would reliably be at one's side. Where a father inspired awe and respect, a brother was ideally an equal, a reliable partner, and a true friend. Here, too, the term expanded beyond real biological connections to encompass many relationships marked by friendship and equality: an *ahum* could be a colleague, a fellow member of a tribe, or a business partner. So when Irkab-damu of Ebla thought of his counterpart in Hamazi—a man who, like himself, ruled a kingdom, to whom he sent letters and expensive presents, and from whom he expected letters and presents in return—it was as a brother.

If a treaty did exist between Ebla and Hamazi, it might have resembled one that was found in the Ebla palace. This remarkable document, the earliest known treaty anywhere (of the over forty that have been found in Mesopotamia and Syria from all eras), was drawn up between Ebla and a city named Abarsal during the early years of Irkab-damu's reign.[50] The tablet on which it was written down is imposing—over nine inches by eight inches—and packed with 623 lines of tiny script in thirty-one columns.[51] As with the diplomatic letter to Hamazi, it doesn't look like a first attempt but rather seems to follow a formula, as though such treaties were commonplace and this simply happens to be the earliest that has yet been excavated. That said, it's not an easy document to make sense of, and translators differ in their interpretations of many of the clauses.

Whereas Hamazi was distant and probably largely unknown, Abarsal was evidently closer to home, apparently reached by "waterways" from Ebla.[52] Perhaps the armies of Ebla fought against those of Abarsal prior to the creation of the treaty. The concerns expressed in it are different from those that would have arisen between two distant lands connected only by trade and diplomacy.

The treaty begins with a detailed listing of the lands of Ebla and a much vaguer description of Abarsal's possessions. No personal names appear on the treaty at all, unlike in later treaties, which tend to be very specific about the kings who drew them up and even the exact historical circumstances in which they were formulated. Perhaps this one was kept generic on purpose so that it would be valid beyond the lifetimes of the kings who signed on to it (though not literally, since this was long before anyone had come up with the idea of a "signature"). The clauses of the treaty follow, and the document ends with a colorful, though not particularly terrifying, curse against "all...who assemble for evil" purposes, and against someone, perhaps the king of Abarsal, should he "go on an evil expedition."[53] In response to these infractions, the gods were called on to ensure that the words of the evildoers (though not the evildoers themselves) would "perish in bile" and that their couriers would get no drinking water.

The gods played a crucial role in all ancient treaties from this one onwards. This was a world without any international body to impose sanctions if a treaty were to be broken. Who, then, would punish the offender in such cases? Each party to the treaty could, hypothetically, threaten to attack the other in such a situation, but this was not necessarily practical. And who was to judge when the treaty had been broken? Could it be left to the interested parties themselves? They couldn't be expected to be impartial. Only the gods could play this role, and of course the gods of both parties needed to be called on. The gods were absolutely real to the ancients, and they believed in everyone's gods, not just their own. If someone broke an oath he could expect that the gods would punish him.

As for the clauses in the Abarsal treaty, they vary from such practical matters as calling on the cities to protect one another against attack to an obscure injunction that seems to be addressed to anyone who "lies with the wife of a worker."[54] For the most part, the treaty favors Ebla, giving the city the right to trade with Abarsal by waterways but denying this right to Abarsal, and even apparently stating that "The sons of Abarsal as well as the daughters of Abarsal shall be slaves to Ebla."[55] It's unlikely that this clause was to be taken literally; instead, it seems that Abarsal had become a protectorate or vassal to the kingdom of Ebla.

Few of the clauses in the Abarsal treaty would have applied to a treaty with distant Hamazi, if one existed. It's unlikely that the kings would have been in a position to protect one another militarily, for example, and no one in Hamazi could conceivably have been a "slave" to Ebla. But a whole section of the Abarsal treaty deals with the needs of messengers who traveled between the kingdoms, and here we might glimpse some concerns of a more international nature.

The Abarsal treaty shows that messengers traveled regularly from Ebla to Abarsal, presumably bringing letters from their king. Such a messenger was expected to stay in Abarsal for around ten days before being released to go home. The messengers would consume their own provisions at their own king's expense for ten days, but if the Abarsal king wanted them to stay longer, he had to support them and provide food: "Arriving messengers will stop as long as ten days and will eat their travel provisions. But if you want them to stay (longer), you (Abarsal) will give them travel provisions."[56] This suggests that there was a well-established set of expectations and behaviors with respect to other kingdoms.

The treaty provided protection not just for messengers but also for merchants traveling between the two lands: "As concerns the merchants of Ebla, Abarsal will let them come back (safely). As concerns the merchants of Abarsal, Ebla will let them come back (safely)." Safe travel would have been a crucial concern for merchants traveling within and beyond the Ebla kingdom, who no doubt worried about being robbed or kidnapped, given the value of the goods they carried with them.

Long before the invention of written law (which took place in southern Mesopotamia over 300 years later), some clauses in the Ebla-Abarsal treaty strikingly resemble laws: "If anyone among the ten overseers (?) pronounces a curse, he shall give fifty rams as fine," and "If...someone from Abarsal has a fight with someone from Ebla (and) kills him, he shall give fifty rams as fine. If someone [from Ebla has a fight with someone from Abarsal] (and) kills him, he shall give fifty rams as fine."

These clauses follow exactly the form of the later laws. They are conditional: "if" a certain misdeed takes place, then a particular punishment will be meted out. These rudimentary laws seem to have been agreed upon by both kings, and they required officials and other travelers to behave in a civilized way while venturing abroad.

After the death of Irkab-damu, his son and successor, Ishar-damu, drew up another peace treaty, this time with the king of Mari.[57] The treaty marked a break in the normally tense relationship between the two kingdoms, one that must have taken considerable diplomatic talent to achieve. At this point both kings decided that peace, and a treaty-bound alliance, was preferable to war. Mari and Ebla were equals, so their kings would have been "brothers." The treaty might have been similar to the one with Abarsal, though neither would have agreed to it unless the provisions treated their kingdoms equally. Sadly, it's not preserved in the Ebla archives. We know about the treaty because the Mari representatives who came to Ebla for the ceremony were rewarded with gifts of silver, which were, of course, recorded in the meticulous records of the Ebla palace. The names and amounts of silver were followed by the note that they came "for the oil offering (of) Mari." More silver was required on the same occasion—fifty shekels for "a sheet (for covering) one tablet: that of the oath of Ebla and Mari (for) the temple of [the god] Kura."[58] The treaty was referred to as an "oath" because this was such a crucial part of it—calling on the gods for their support.

One can envision the scene: the Mari delegation had traveled for days in order to reach Ebla. The group included three powerful men, whose names were Aha-arshe, Asha, and Ila; a lesser official named Dutum; and some other representatives.[59] They would have been welcomed at the palace, presumably by King Ishar-damu (who was probably only a child at the time), his influential mother Dusigu, and the king's minister, along with other high officials. They progressed, perhaps walking and talking together, or perhaps in a formal silence, to the main temple of the city, dedicated to Kura, the chief god of Ebla. Confirmation of the treaty would have been a solemn ceremony, perhaps in the dark of the sanctuary itself. An oil offering was presented, and Kura was no doubt called upon to witness the oath sworn by the representatives of the two lands.[60] Then the tablet on which the clauses of the treaty had been recorded was placed under a silver sheet and deposited in some safe spot within the temple.

The Mari delegation then received gifts of silver. The three highest officials were given about ten pounds between them, whereas lowly Dutum received just a fraction, around two and a half ounces of silver, and the unnamed other representatives split one pound of silver.[61] What happened next? Did the men feast together? Almost certainly a parallel ceremony also took place in a temple at Mari, with delegates from Ebla receiving comparable gifts from the king of Mari.

### Brother Kings and Warriors in Sumer

The kings of Ebla and Mari were not the only ones in this Early Dynastic era to commit themselves to a relationship as brothers. Some kings in southern Mesopotamia apparently had similar arrangements (though their treaty is also lost).[62]A king of the city of Uruk with the delightful name of Lugalkigi-nedudu managed to conquer nearby Ur, upon which he titled himself (with some hyperbole) "king of all the lands."[63] This inspired the king of another nearby city, Lagash, to negotiate a treaty with Lugalkiginedudu, presumably because he didn't want his city to be the next one to fall to Uruk. He referred to this treaty proudly in a number of his royal inscriptions by the Sumerian term *nam-shesh* or "brotherhood."[64] This king of Lagash, Enmetena, also had similar arrangements with the kings of the Sumerian city-states of Larsa and Bad-tibira.[65] They were allies, and this was something to be vaunted.

A generation or two before the reign of King Enmetena, another king of Lagash, Eanatum, had forged an agreement with his former enemy, the king of the neighboring (and much hated) state of Umma. There was no mention of brotherhood here. Eanatum had won a victory over Umma and took the opportunity to make his enemy agree to an oath not to cause any more problems for Lagash. The king of Umma would no longer "transgress the territory [of Lagash]....shift the course of its irrigation channels and canals...[or] smash its monuments."[66] If he were to back out on the agreement and to do any of these things, his oath called upon the great god Enlil to punish his own city of Umma. This was not a treaty between equals, though it had some of the same characteristics, such as the clear provisions and the oath to abide by them. Some sort of negotiation must have preceded it. The agreement was written out on a stone monument known as "Stela of the Vultures." The text is illustrated with relief sculptures showing Eanatum proudly leading his massed infantrymen into war in one scene and riding in his chariot in another. The other side of the monument depicts a giant god holding a net, in which are seen the dead and dying men of Umma.

The Mesopotamian cities of the south recognized their shared culture, and treaties like the one between Enmetena and Lugalkiginedudu might have been common, even though the royal inscriptions of the Early Dynastic kings tended to dwell more on warfare. Enmetena did not renounce war. Like his predecessor Eanatum, he was a fighter, still warring against, and defeating, the city of Umma. He commissioned an inscription that described his victory: "Enmetena...defeated him. [The king of Umma] escaped, but was killed in Umma itself." The battle scene must have been terrible to see, with "the bones

of their personnel (the Ummaites) strewn over the plain."[67] Enmetena claimed
that the bodies of the enemy dead required five separate burial mounds.


### Allies and In-Laws

We know, therefore, that the early Syrian kings in Ebla conducted diplomatic
relationships in what must have been successful, and already time-honored,
ways that they shared with other Syrian and Mesopotamian kingdoms. They
wrote diplomatic letters, sent ambassadors to distant courts, exchanged gifts
with allied kings (both of neighboring states such as Mari and of distant
states such as Hamazi), and drew up formal treaties to govern their relationships with vassals and allies. But these strategies seem not to have been quite
enough. They also, just like King Tushratta a millennium later, married their
daughters off to other kings, some of them local vassals and some more distant allies, in both Syria and Mesopotamia.[68]

These are the earliest known examples of the types of diplomatic marriages
that came to dominate Near Eastern diplomacy.[69] Clearly, the kings of Ebla were
not alone in this practice. In fact, the Ebla archives even mention princesses of
other cities married to kings of yet different cities.[70] The tradition must have
been quite widespread by the twenty-third century BCE, having developed in preliterate times, and it must have been reasonably effective in cementing relationships between kings. If not, the tradition would surely have died out.

When Princess Keshdut of Ebla married the son of the king of the great
Mesopotamian city of Kish, the event was so auspicious that a year was named
after it in the Ebla calendar.[71] (The Mesopotamians and Syrian kings named
the years rather than numbering them, a practice that permitted them to boast
of their greatest achievements.) When a princess left Ebla for her new home,
many servants and officials accompanied her, and she took clothes, jewelry,
and other personal items.[72] In Keshdut's case, she was sent off with tremendous wealth; her dowry included "3,290 bovines, 1,680 sheep, 159 mules, one
ass, five pigs, nineteen bisons, fourteen bears."[73] One wonders why she and
her new husband wanted fourteen bears, but the other animals would have
constituted a valuable addition to her husband's herds. The Ebla princesses
presumably all received substantial dowries from their fathers, which would
have functioned much like the luxury goods traded between allied kings, just
on a grander scale.

Once the princess arrived in her new home, the ceremonies that took place
might have been much like those enacted for royal weddings in Ebla itself. In
these the king "indeed brings the queen to His Father's House. And, on the day

of the queen's wedding, (the king) indeed puts olive oil on the queen's head."[74] There were elaborate processions and ceremonies in the temple to the city god to celebrate and formalize the occasion. Princess Keshdut probably went through all this, then settled into the palace at Kish and began to learn the differences in etiquette between the two kingdoms. As it turns out, her timing was lucky; her marriage took place just a year before Ebla was destroyed, so she presumably was safely ensconced in Kish when her family faced that disaster.[75]

The kings of Ebla not only supplied their daughters with dowries, they also continued to send gifts after the marriage. When the king of the city of Nagar was passing through Ebla at one point, he was given various textiles to take to his wife, who was a daughter of the king of Ebla.[76] She had perhaps even asked him for some items from home. Keshdut might have done the same.

One's tendency is, perhaps, to assume that humans have progressed a long way since the beginning of civilization. So it might come as a surprise to find much that is familiar so early in human history. The earliest preserved written documents reveal not a barbarous world of constant warfare but the records of very well organized government offices, letters to foreign leaders,

The Babylonian conception of the world: a disk of land with the Euphrates River flowing through the center and a sea surrounding it. Foreign lands are marked as circles and triangles extending beyond the sea. (©Trustees of the British Museum)

dictionaries of foreign words, and peace treaties. The Syrian kingdoms were obviously in close and regular contact with one another, using a code of behavior that must have developed long before, and following rules that provided what must have been a reassuring sense of order.

In addition to the lands mentioned in the tablets, objects found in the palace testify to the fact that Ebla maintained relationships, whether directly or indirectly, right across the Near Eastern world, from Egypt to what is now the western border of China. This is counterintuitive; one imagines that people in the ancient world knew little of the world beyond their homes. This instinct isn't unfounded; it's borne out by an ancient cuneiform "map" of the world created in Mesopotamia over 1,500 years after Ebla was destroyed. By the time the map was made, Babylon was the greatest city of southern Mesopotamia, so it lies at the center of the map, with the Euphrates River running through it, and local lands are labeled. Around the circular territory of Mesopotamia lies a "Salt-Sea" beyond which are eight apparently mythical lands. This is a small world, with Mesopotamia comfortably at its center. The Eblaites might have had a similar conception of the world, though of course Ebla would have been at the center of their map (had they drawn one). They would have included the cities mentioned in their records—Mari, of course, and distant Kish and Nagar, and smaller towns and villages nearby. And yet could they have been entirely ignorant of other much more distant lands with which they were connected by trade? Were these, too, in contact with Ebla, or did only the goods from those lands arrive, disconnected from any memory of their origins? Whether directly or through middlemen, both Ebla and Mari were in touch with lands thousands of miles away.

CHAPTER TWO

# Traders and Ships from Distant Lands

*"At the wharf of Akkad he made moor ships"*

*Luxury Goods in Syria and Mesopotamia*

Many of the archival records in the palace at Ebla listed gold and silver, and lots of it. This is quite unexpected. Ebla was a kingdom of limited extent, with what would today seem a small population, in an area with no mineral ores or other intrinsically valuable resources. And yet many documents record the payment of gold and silver to the palace by rich subjects, or the distribution of gold and silver objects, along with bronze objects, to palace dependents.[1] They also record ceremonial gifts that passed between Ebla and its allies, cementing existing ties and helping to forge new ones.[2] Some of these gifts were of textiles made locally, but some were objects of precious metals. Jewelry was sometimes offered (bracelets, pendants, or earrings), or ceremonial weapons (daggers and sabers), or even statues.[3] And there were the thousands of pounds of silver that Ebla paid to Mari, at least until King Irkab-damu's time. Excavators also found objects of silver and gold when they dug up the palace.[4]

What is it about gold and silver? Why were (and are) they so prized? Gold must have attracted human attention early on, since it occasionally was discovered in the form of a shining nugget, not needing any sort of smelting or purifying. The nugget could be hammered into shape, into something that one could wear, like a bracelet. And then it shone forever. Gold, alone among the metals, doesn't tarnish. The Sumerians called silver *ku-babbar*, meaning "pure white." The sign used for the word *babbar*—white—was the same sign used for the word *utu*—the sun. Silver might have seemed like a piece of sunlight miraculously turned solid.

In a village of stone tools and mud-brick houses, gold and silver must have seemed otherworldly. In the ancient world, unlike today, no object that shone or sparkled was inexpensive. The farther the gold and silver had traveled from their original sources, the more of a statement a king made in having command of vast quantities of them.

Other precious materials also materialized in the excavation at Ebla: statues of steatite and many pounds of unworked lapis lazuli, a deep blue stone that was prized by peoples across the Near East.[5] The lapis lazuli, according to archival records, had been sent from Mari, though it must have come originally from elsewhere, since there is no source of it near Mari.[6]

The kings of Ebla weren't alone in their wealth. Mari kings also enjoyed luxury goods. It seems that right before the palace at Mari was destroyed (some time after the destruction of Ebla), someone placed a whole collection of treasures in a jar for safekeeping and buried it beneath a courtyard floor.[7] The objects, which were crammed together, included fine small artworks made of copper, ivory, lapis lazuli, and gold; seventy beads made of red carnelian, lapis lazuli, and gold; jewelry of silver and gold; and seals. One of the beads was inscribed with the name of a king from southern Mesopotamia, Mesanepadda of Ur, so the collection has been dubbed the "Treasure of Ur." Although some of the objects are now thought to have come to Mari from elsewhere, the fact that some of them came from wealthy Ur is not surprising.[8]

Ur was situated in the far south of Mesopotamia in the region known as Sumer, right near the shores of what the locals called the Lower Sea (the Persian Gulf). Presumably some traders or ambassadors from Mari had visited Ur and brought these objects back. Indeed, a fragment of a calcite vase found in Ur was inscribed with the name of Ninmetabarri, a princess of Mari who lived during this era.[9] It must have been taken there either by the princess herself (some speculate that she was married to a king of Ur or served as a high priestess there), or perhaps by messengers.[10]

Ur and Mari had closer ties than might be supposed, given that they were over 400 miles apart. A later Mesopotamian tradition even credited the kings of Mari with having had some kind of authority over Ur and the other southern lands for a while. This tradition was recorded in a document called the Sumerian King List. It begins in the realm of fairy tale, giving the names of kings who were said to have enjoyed reigns lasting tens of thousands of years. Gradually the reigns grew shorter (though still fantastically long)—just hundreds of years. The way the King List tells it, the major cities of Mesopotamia took it in turn to be the seat of true kingship. After a couple of hundred (or thousand) years in each place, "kingship was taken" to another city, one of which was Mari.[11] Scholars don't give this tale much credence, but the King List does at least tell us that Mari was considered by the southern Sumerian kingdoms to be "one of us," so to speak.

Let us suppose that it was Princess Ninmetabarri herself who traveled to Ur. What kind of a world would she have found when she got there? In some ways, it probably would not have seemed terribly foreign to her. As at her home in Mari, during the Early Dynastic period the kingdoms in the south each centered on a major city. Each was surrounded by fields, and by smaller towns and villages. The clothing of the people she would have met was not that different from at home, nor, probably, was the food. Each city boasted a palace for the king and a temple to its local god or goddess, who watched over the city. Some of these gods were also worshiped in Syria, others would have been less familiar. Being a polytheist, Ninmetabarri would not have doubted the existence of the local deities and would have willingly paid them homage. To her, like all Syrians and Mesopotamians, there was no such thing as a false god.

A few aspects of the place would have seemed alien, however. Whereas in Ninmetabarri's homeland of Mari land could be bought and sold, in the south the temples to the gods dominated the kingdom and are believed to have controlled much of its land. Land didn't belong to the people, so they couldn't buy or sell it.[12]

Another difference was in the language. Sumerian, the main language of the south at this time, was completely different from the Semitic languages of Mari and Ebla, and quite unrelated to them. In Semitic tongues, the form of a verb was often changed by adding vowels between the consonants (just as forms of "sing" can be "sang" or "sung" in English). In Sumerian, the core of the verb never changed, but innumerable prefixes or suffixes had to be added in order to clarify the meaning. It can not have been easy to learn for speakers of a Semitic language. Fortunately, though, if Ninmetabarri came to marry the king of Ur, she no doubt was joined by a retinue of many attendants from home, along with a translator who could help her understand her Sumerian-speaking husband. Besides, many of the southerners spoke Akkadian, which was closely related to her native language.[13]

The landscape around Ur would have struck Ninmetabarri as strange, too. Near Mari, the flat river valley was closely bounded by cliffs that led up to the rolling hills of the steppe. In places, the steep cliffs came right to the banks of the Euphrates. The region around Ur was as flat as the sea, a dry sea, stretching in all directions. The flatness of the landscape was relieved only by the levees of the rivers and canals and by the palm trees and tells that marked the places where villages and towns had been located since before the beginning of history. The land was rich in some ways, rich in fertile soil and river water, but poor in others. Like the area around Mari, it had no mineral deposits or ores. Southern Mesopotamia didn't even have building stone or timber for construction.

The weather was also much dryer than it was to the northwest in Syria. Mari too was built near the Euphrates, but here in the south the river was all that made it possible to live in what would otherwise have been a forbidding land of scorching heat and sandstorms. Water from the rivers irrigated the crops of barley and wheat and the orchards of date palms.

The city of Ur itself was home to the moon god, Nanna, whose temple stood on a raised platform. Near that platform was an area that perhaps Ninmetabarri visited—an extensive cemetery of about 2,000 graves.[14] It was here that, thousands of years later, the true wealth of Ur was discovered, eclipsing that of any other ancient Mesopotamian city.

From 1922 to 1934, Sir Leonard Woolley, an Englishman given to wearing a felt hat and sports jacket while excavating in the blazing heat of southern Iraq, dug at Ur, and it was his good fortune to find the cemetery. Among all the graves, sixteen stood out. They were the tombs, apparently, of royalty, both men and women. These kings and queens (if that is what they were) were not buried alone. In a macabre discovery, Woolley found that each was accompanied by youthful attendants, in some cases dozens of them, presumably there to serve their lord or lady in the afterlife. The attendants wore fine jewelry and ornaments, and each had been put to death at the time of the burial, killed by a sharp blow to the head.[15] One of the tombs even included wagons and oxen, all outfitted as though ready to carry their master whenever he called. This was a surprise; human sacrifice was not mentioned in Mesopotamian documents, and no later examples are known of this type of mass sacrifice in a royal tomb. On the other hand, very few other royal tombs have been found in Mesopotamia, not even robbed ones.

The riches that Woolley and his team uncovered in the tombs were staggering. The *New York Times* ran many stories about the finds in 1927 and 1928, following Woolley's amazing discoveries. Headlines exclaimed, "Ur's Culture Rivaled Egypt's"; "Find Queen's Tomb and Rich Art in Ur"; "Royal Tombs of Ur Rich in Treasure." The treasure consisted of almost anything one might imagine a royal tomb should contain: vessels made of precious metals, jewelry, headdresses, musical instruments, furniture, weapons, statues, even board games (perhaps to relieve the boredom of the hereafter).[16] The same luxury materials found at Ebla and Mari—gold, silver, copper, lapis lazuli, carnelian, and ivory—were used to make these objects, but in far larger amounts.[17] The workmanship was extraordinary, with detailed mosaics of lapis and shell inlaid on the lyres and harps, fine granulation on the gold, and perfectly drilled beads by the thousands.

A lapis lazuli cylinder seal with gold caps, and its impression. The seal was found in the Royal Tombs of Ur. The design includes a master of animals, a traditional Mesopotamian motif. (©Trustees of the British Museum)

Although the relationship between Ur and Mari can be seen concretely (in the mention of a king of Ur on a bead at Mari and of a Mari princess on a vessel at Ur), Ebla too seems to have had a connection with the city of Ur, if only indirectly through Mari.[18] It's seen in subtle clues—a piece of lapis sculpted as a lock of hair found in Ebla was identical to (though less well made than) a detail on a lyre from a royal tomb at Ur, and stone bowls in similar designs have been found at both sites, along with inlaid panels from furniture.[19] It seems that some luxury objects from Ur did make it as far as Ebla, where they were copied by local craftsmen, and perhaps some inlaid furniture from Ebla was traded as far away as Ur. But Ur isn't mentioned in the Ebla archives, so the people there may not have known of the connection. In fact, the records at Ebla are stubbornly silent about the ultimate sources for all the exotic luxury goods that were in circulation. No traders are named who went out on behalf of the king to acquire gold, silver, lapis lazuli, or carnelian.[20] These materials simply seem to have existed in the Ebla economy, unquestioned. And yet, of course, they had to have come from somewhere.

## A Long Tradition of Trade

Where did the gold and silver, lapis and carnelian come from? Nowhere in Mesopotamia or Syria could these materials have been mined out of the ground. The diplomatic relationships among the Syrian and Mesopotamian

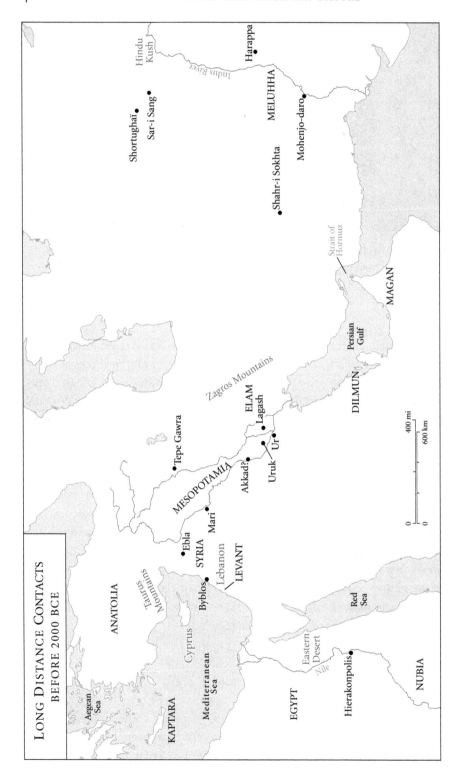

LONG DISTANCE CONTACTS
BEFORE 2000 BCE

kings might well have helped distribute the luxuries from place to place, but how did they reach the region at all?

The silver, along with some of the copper (for bronze), may have come from Anatolia (modern Turkey), to the north of Ebla and Mari, at the end of a long journey through the Taurus Mountains.[21] This was virtually in Mesopotamia's backyard compared to the distances to the sources of gold, lapis, and carnelian. Such materials had, in some cases, traveled over a thousand miles in order to reach Ebla, Mari, and Ur: the carnelian from India, the gold perhaps from Egypt or Afghanistan, and the lapis lazuli from the Hindu Kush mountains in what is now Afghanistan, almost at the modern border with China.[22]

It's clear, therefore, that the Mesopotamian and Syrian kingdoms like Ebla, Mari, and Ur were not just in contact with the neighboring states within their region. Each kingdom had access to goods from what must have seemed, to the people living there, impossibly remote and foreign lands.

How was this trade possible, so many thousands of years before the kinds of structures that we see as essential for international trade, like shipping companies and long-distance communication? Traveling over long distances at that time must have been arduous, time-consuming, and dangerous. The distant horizon, viewed from Ebla, would have taken days to reach on foot. Even if one walked fifteen miles a day (which the ancient Mesopotamians viewed as typical), neighboring Mari was a two-week journey from Ebla.[23] Had a man from Ebla got it into his head to visit India or Afghanistan, it would have taken him months on foot (or perhaps in part by boat), and he would have had to travel many through foreign lands with different languages, customs, gods, and foods in order to get there.

Archaeologists have found that during the Early Dynastic period in the later third millennium BCE, when Ebla, Mari, and Ur were thriving, a string of oasis towns connected Mesopotamia to the Indus valley.[24] Some of the people in these towns might have been friendly enough, others were almost certainly hostile. There were no paved roads anywhere, no hotels, and no easy way of contacting either home or the place one was traveling to. And yet people did travel, and they were far from being the first to do so.

Traders had been moving around Asia for thousands of years by the time Irkab-damu was ruling in Ebla. Way back in 8000 BCE, long before the development of cities or writing, when humans were only just beginning to plant crops and herd animals, craftsmen in Syria already fashioned tools from obsidian, a glassy stone that had to be imported from hundreds of miles away.[25]

We have little idea how this earliest trade took place, since no records survive—it was long before the invention of writing. Perhaps initially the transactions did not involve any one person going very far; the items might have been traded from one village to a neighboring village, to another, and so on, until they ended up hundreds of miles from their places of origin.


*Sargon's Boasts*


By the time of Irkab-damu's kingdom, traders almost certainly traveled directly from the sources of the goods to the markets where they wanted to sell or exchange them. Although the objects from Ebla are mute, contemporary records from Mesopotamia help us to glimpse this world of long-distance connections.

Just a few years after the time that Irkab-damu ruled in Ebla, an ambitious young man usurped the throne of the city of Kish in Mesopotamia; created a new capital city, which he called Akkad; and gave himself a fitting new name: "True King."[26] His name was pronounced Sharrukin in the local language, Akkadian, but we refer to him as "Sargon" for a slightly convoluted reason. A much later king took the same name, in tribute to the first mighty Sharrukin, and this later king was vilified in the Hebrew Bible—he was one of the hated rulers of the enemy Assyrians. The Biblical authors spelled the names of their contemporaries the way they heard them, not the way they were spelled in cuneiform, so Sharrukin became Sargon. His earlier namesake, though not mentioned in the Bible, has been given the same name by scholars.

Whereas Irkab-damu seems to have been promptly forgotten soon after his death (his existence wasn't rediscovered until recently), Sargon was remembered for thousands of years. More than remembered, he was idolized by the Mesopotamians. His exploits were told and retold, and of course exaggerated. According to a legend written down over a thousand years after his reign, Sargon had a near-miraculous origin. He was born in secret, placed by his mother in a basket and set adrift on a river, and found and adopted by a humble man who drew irrigation water from the river for a living. Sargon became a gardener alongside his adoptive father, and might have seemed destined for the most ordinary of lives. But the gods intervened, or so the Mesopotamians believed, and a goddess, Ishtar, loved him and made him king.[27] There's no telling if any detail of this tale is true. The basket part seems particularly suspicious, since he shared this mode of infant transportation with Moses in Egypt, Krishna in India, and Romulus and Remus in Rome.

The legend, which purports to be in Sargon's own words, portrays Sargon, once he had become king, as some kind of superhero: "Humankind I ruled... With copper pickaxes I cut through the mighty mountains.... I sailed around the sea[lands] three times. Dilmun [submitted to me]." But this part of the later legend was not all fiction. An inscription written in Sargon's own time records that he conquered all of Mesopotamia and Syria "from the Lower Sea to the Upper Sea"—that is, from the Persian Gulf to the Mediterranean—and most historians believe him.[28] Once he had made these conquests, no longer could the city-states of Mesopotamia and Syria trade and create treaties with some neighbors, wage war with others, and periodically form confederations for mutual defense. They were under the thumb of Sargon, who seems to have been the first person to come up with the goal of ruling the whole world (or what he knew of the world). In order to try to do so, he conquered all these city-states and brought in Akkadian governors to rule them. In fact, Sargon claimed to have been "given" the city of Ebla, among other cities, by the local Syrian god Dagan. This would have been soon after Irkab-damu's reign. One guesses that the "gift" entailed no small amount of destruction and bloodshed. Sargon's realm is known as the Akkadian Empire, and it was the first empire in history.

It seems, though, that Sargon probably did not give up on diplomacy, at least with those parts of the world that he was unable to conquer. His grandson, King Naram-Sin, later made a treaty with the king of Elam, whose land was to the east of the Akkadian empire.[29] In it, the two leaders agreed to support one another in war and to return any fugitives who might flee to one another's lands. Like the Early Dynastic kings, they invoked the gods to enforce the treaty. The agreement must have been drawn up as a result of negotiations, with envoys traveling between Akkad and Elam. One unusual clause was that the king of Elam had to put up statues of Naram-Sin in temples in his land, whereas the reverse was not required.[30] (Naram-Sin was not a humble man; he was one of the few Mesopotamian kings to proclaim that he was, in fact, a god.) Presumably the tradition of making treaties with neighboring lands had continued through the reign of Sargon, even though none of his treaties have been found.

Sargon is important to this tale for another reason, not just because he violently united the Mesopotamian and Syrian lands into an unwilling and apparently resentful empire., Sargon mentioned, in one of his inscriptions, the names of some of the distant lands with which he traded for precious goods, and he claimed that traders from those places came all the way to Akkad. He had his scribes write the following: "At the wharf of Akkad he made moor ships from Meluhha, ships from Magan, (and) ships from Dilmun."[31] At a later date, after the end of Sargon's empire, another writer recalled a similar scene in Akkad: "The Meluhhaites, the people of the black land, brought up to her the (exotic) wares of foreign lands," including elephants, monkeys, and water buffalo.[32]

These ships that Sargon invited to come to Akkad were from very far away. Dilmun was southeast of Mesopotamia in the Persian Gulf: it comprised the island of what is now Bahrain and the mainland opposite.[33] Farther southeast still, beyond the Strait of Hormuz, lay Magan, in the land that is now Oman. Meluhha lay across the Arabian Sea from Magan, in the region of the Indus Valley.[34] These were, indeed, important and rich places in the late third millennium BCE. Archaeologists have worked for decades in all three regions and have found plenty of evidence that Sargon was right to brag about his ties to their lands.

### Ships of Dilmun and Black Stone from Magan

During most of the Early Dynastic period, the settlements in Dilmun seem to have been largely on the mainland of Arabia opposite Bahrain; only later did the island dominate the land of Dilmun.[35] Archaeologists have found that the communities were initially small, but a much larger city was founded on the island around 2300 BCE, right around the time when Sargon was on the throne in Akkad.[36] Something had boosted the economy of Dilmun to help make this city thrive.

Some Sumerian kings who ruled before Sargon's conquests acquired copper from Dilmun in exchange for wool, silver, and some foods made of milk and grain.[37] One Early Dynastic king of the city of Lagash repeated in many of his royal inscriptions that he "had ships of Dilmun transport timber from foreign lands" to him.[38] These "ships of Dilmun" were perhaps the key to the land's economic success, as Dilmun was almost as devoid of valuable resources as Mesopotamia. By building ships and conveying goods from place to place, the Dilmunites prospered, and their land became a central meeting place where people from south of the Gulf could sell copper, ivory, tin, and timber. Near Dilmun, the island of Tarut might have been the source of distinctive vessels made of chlorite, a greenish gray stone, which were fashionable in the Early Dynastic and Akkadian periods across a vast area. They have been found as far west as Mari and as far east as the Hindu Kush mountains.[39] The people of Dilmun could have shipped all these goods north, no doubt making a healthy profit on the transactions.

The Indus Valley—known as Meluhha—had a profound influence on Dilmun in the third millennium. By the twenty-first century BCE, the traders in Dilmun mostly used the Indus Valley system of weights and measures and carried square Indus Valley seals to mark their property rather than Mesopotamian cylinder seals.[40]

Magan, modern Oman, was less urbanized than Dilmun, but it was home to extensive copper mines—it was apparently one of Mesopotamia's chief sources for copper in the Early Dynastic period.[41] The people of Magan also quarried a hard black stone called diorite that the Mesopotamian kings valued for statues.[42]

The attraction of these abundant and expensive resources was powerful. After Sargon's death, his son Manishtusu put an end to the peaceful trading relationship that Sargon had promoted. Instead, he attacked Magan, using warships.[43] The Magan cities, thirty-two of them, "assembled for war, and he vanquished (them) and smote their cities. He felled their rulers and captured their fugitives as far as the silver mines."[44] But Manishtusu doesn't seem to have been interested in bringing Magan into his empire. He was interested in bringing home riches: "He quarried the black stone of the mountains...and loaded (it) into the boats and moored (them) at the wharf of Akkad."[45] This was not an empty boast; stone objects have been found at Ur and Nippur inscribed with their place of origin—they were booty from Magan.[46] King Naram-Sin also later claimed a victory in Magan. He too had his eye on its diorite. He "captured Manium, the 'lord' of Magan; he quarried blocks of diorite in their mountains, [and] transported (them) to his city Akkad."[47]

### Red Carnelian Beads from Meluhha

The extent and wealth of the land of Meluhha were on a different scale altogether. Stretching along the Indus River, this civilization, which flourished from around 2600 BCE, was on a par, in terms of its sophistication, with those of Mesopotamia and Egypt at the same time. In fact, the land of Meluhha was much more extensive than either—it stretched over double the area of either Mesopotamia or Egypt—and the well-planned cities were grand and orderly.[48] The largest of these, Harappa and Mohenjo Daro, have been extensively excavated. They were built of baked bricks on top of platforms designed to protect the cities from floods, with wide, arrow-straight streets, well-engineered drainage systems, and plenty of evidence of an impressively organized government. The Meluhhan people had a writing system that they used for writing short inscriptions on stone seals. They probably also used it to write on other, less stable materials, which have long since disintegrated. Unfortunately, their writing system has not yet been deciphered (and those short inscriptions might include little more than names), so we know very little about the people, their government, their religion, or their culture.

We do know, though, that they produced long, thin, carnelian beads of astonishing quality. It may be a little hard for us to appreciate these beads. Factories could mass-produce them now, but imagine the skill involved in making a hole several centimeters in length but of minuscule diameter in a hard stone, without a diamond drill bit and with only one's own muscles to power the drill. If the drill strayed to the side, the bead would break. It has been estimated that a single bead could take as many as eight days to drill. Elite members of societies all over the Near East, including Central Asia, Mesopotamia, and Iran, acquired and treasured these beads during the Early Dynastic period.[49] Some of the beads even graced the bodies of the dead in the royal tombs at Ur. The largest four of these were an astonishing six inches (fifteen centimeters) long.[50]

Pearls and silver came from Meluhha too, especially during the height of the Early Dynastic period.[51] It's likely that the shell used to make some objects in the royal tombs at Ur was Meluhhan in origin.[52] No one had yet figured out how to cut and polish precious stones like diamonds, sapphires, emeralds, or rubies, so pieces of jewelry made from carnelian, pearls, and shell from Meluhha were the most extravagant and valuable of ornaments.

In the reign of Sargon, boats from Meluhha probably hugged the coast as they headed to Mesopotamia, sailing west along the southern shores of what are now Pakistan and Iran and perhaps stopping in Magan before entering the Strait of Hormuz and sailing north on to Dilmun. When they reached the mouth of the Euphrates River, the wind and the current would both have been against them. Perhaps they had to tow their boats up the river to Akkad. Their journey stretched for almost 2,000 miles each way, taking months. Finally they reached Sargon's capital, and we have evidence of them there, proudly featured by the king in his inscription.

It's a tantalizing image—boats from such distant places all roped to the quay in Akkad, their crews trying to make themselves understood as they unloaded their cargoes, which were destined, presumably, for the palace. The boats would have been loaded with carnelian, shell, and pearls, along with ivory and precious black wood, and perhaps animals such as water buffalo, zebu, monkeys, and even Indian elephants (though it would have been a challenge to transport such large animals by boat).[53] Perhaps the traders then milled among the Mesopotamians in the streets, sampling the local foods and staring up at the impressive city walls and temples, like visitors anywhere. The earlier carnelian and shell objects found at Mari and Ur had probably arrived in the same way. Admittedly, there is no reference to Meluhha before Sargon's inscription, but carnelian beads from the region had been imported for some time before.[54] Not all the beads were necessarily imported as finished

objects; Meluhhan craftsmen might even have lived and worked at Ur in previous centuries, crafting some of the beads found in the royal tombs.[55]

The Indus Valley goods didn't have to come by boat, though. There was
a land route as well, one that went north from the Indus into the forbidding
Hindu Kush Mountains before turning west, across the Iranian Plateau,
through the Zagros Mountains, and down into Mesopotamia. The people of
Meluhha had set up a colony in a valley in the Hindu Kush at a place now
called Shortughaï. Excavations show that a community of Meluhhans lived
there and prospered from around 2500 to 1800 BCE.[56] This must have been a
crossroads, where miners brought lapis lazuli from nearby in the Hindu Kush
and Indus Valley peoples brought carnelian, ivory, and pearls. The merchants
of Shortughaï then transported the goods to the west. Some of the oasis settlements in southeastern Iran that connected Shortughaï and the Indus Valley
to Mesopotamia were impressive cities. One of them, Shahr-i Sokhta, was
almost 375 acres in extent.[57] By 2500 BCE, as many as 15,000–20,000 people
may have lived there.[58] Another nearby city was more than two square kilome-
ters in extent, with an imposing stepped platform and citadel. Rich people in
these cities were buried with hundreds of carnelian, lapis lazuli, and turquoise
beads as well as fine copper and chlorite vessels, all imported from far away.[59]
Clearly, some people in the society made a good living from the merchants
and messengers who traveled through. But this was more than a way station
for trade; it was a major civilization in its own right.

At least one man living in Mesopotamia during Sargon's time made
a career of helping the Meluhhans from South Asia. He had a solid Akkadian name—Sin-ilishu—and he listed his profession on his cylinder seal as
"Meluhha interpreter."[60] Perhaps the king employed him to negotiate with the
foreign traders and to translate their words. It's intriguing to wonder how he
learned to speak the Meluhhan language. Did he travel to Meluhha himself,
or did he pick up the language from the merchants? We know nothing of him
but the brief inscription on his seal—"Sin-ilishu, Meluhha interpreter"—but
we can guess that an interesting and perhaps adventurous life gave him the
right to that title.

Sin-ilishu was certainly not alone. Other Mesopotamians must have
worked in the business of trade with Meluhha, Magan, and Dilmun. People
from those lands in turn may have settled in Mesopotamia, even during the
Early Dynastic and Akkadian periods. Their presence is seen in the discovery,
at various Mesopotamian sites, of over thirty stamp seals in the Indus Valley
style, some of them with inscriptions in the Indus script.[61] Images of Indus
Valley animals such as the water buffalo and the zebu, with its huge horns,
begin to appear in Mesopotamian art during Sargon's time as well.[62] There

are even a few images of people who seem to be Central Asian or Meluhhan in Akkadian art.[63]

Influence in the other direction is harder to spot. No Mesopotamian objects have materialized in Indus Valley excavations, so it seems that fewer Mesopotamians made the long journey to Meluhha than vice versa.[64] But some images from Mesopotamian art did begin to be used on Indus Valley stamp seals. A few of them featured a favorite Mesopotamian image, a nude hero standing in a contest with one, or more often two, ferocious animals.[65] The animals stand on their hind legs as though about to attack, but the hero has them under control, often with a powerful hand on each.[66] In Mesopotamia the attacking animals were often lions, but the Indus people transformed them into their local big cats—tigers.[67]

A few cylinder seals have been found in the Indus Valley, though they were of local manufacture, not imports, perhaps made by artisans who had seen them used when visiting Mesopotamia.[68] Cylinder seals are certain evidence of contact with Mesopotamia at this time. Wherever the Mesopotamians went, they took their cylinder seals with them, using them to impress designs on clay lumps stopping up containers of traded wares, on doors that were supposed to remain sealed, or on tablets recording transactions. Most seals were no bigger than the face on a modern wristwatch, and they were sometimes worn in the same way—on a bracelet. Incised designs covered the tube-shaped stones, each one distinct. The simplest seals bore geometric patterns, but more complex examples revealed a frieze of delicately carved images of gods, animals, people, and symbols when rolled on a clay surface (see figure on page 41).[69] In the late third millennium BCE, a traveler would have encountered people using cylinder seals all the way from Egypt in the west, across the Levant, Syria, Mesopotamia, and Iran, to the Indus Valley in the east.[70]

### Blue Lapis Lazuli from Aratta

Lapis lazuli was one of the types of stone that was sometimes used to make cylinder seals, though probably only for the richest people in society, given its value.[71] Its deep blue surface can sparkle with golden flecks (so-called fool's gold), giving the appearance of a miniature starry sky. Most scholars agree that lapis lazuli was mined in just one place during ancient times: a forbidding mountain location now called Sar-i Sang in an almost inaccessible gorge in the far northeastern ranges of the Hindu Kush mountains.[72] One wonders how anyone ever discovered it there in the first place. Yet already at the end of the fifth millennium BCE, over 1,500 years before Irkab-damu or the royal tombs at Ur, lapis lazuli from this region had been imported into Mesopotamia and was being used at a place now called Tepe Gawra in northeastern Iraq.[73] Some sort of trade network must have developed that transported the beautiful stone from its barren place of origin to the growing communities of Mesopotamia. Back then, the traders probably traveled with their goods overland rather than by boat, since lapis is not found in southern Mesopotamia until later. From the fifth millennium BCE onwards, countless generations participated in the trade that brought lapis lazuli to the west. By the time of Irkab-damu and his contemporaries, Shortughaï, the Meluh-han colony in the Hindu Kush Mountains, was a principal station near the start of this land route, and the lapis lazuli trade was a well-established business.[74]

The Sumerians had their own legend to explain the source of lapis. They believed that it came from a very distant place known as Aratta, which was "seven mountain ranges" away.[75] At the beginning of the legend, which was set in a long-ago mythical time, there was no trade between Aratta and Sumer.[76] The king of the Sumerian city of Uruk set about to change this. It took the intervention of a goddess (of course), the invention of writing, and a willing messenger who traveled from Uruk to Aratta to meet its king, along with the posing of impossible puzzles and all sorts of posturing by the kings of the two lands, before a deal was reached between the two kings. In the end, the king of Aratta agreed to provide precious goods, including gold and lapis lazuli, to Uruk in exchange for figs and grapes.[77] The figs and grapes don't make much sense, since they didn't grow in Uruk, but this was a legend, after all. What is interesting is that the legend shows that the Sumerians had at least a vague sense of just how far the lapis lazuli had to travel before it reached them. Where exactly was the ancient land of Aratta, if it existed at all? No one is sure. It could have been in the Hindu Kush Mountains, or at some point along the trade route from which the Mesopotamians obtained the lapis lazuli.[78]

What did the Mesopotamians and Syrians produce that could possibly have paid for the wealth that they acquired? Chances are, they used fine textiles as at least part of their payment. This would account for the archival texts at Ebla that record, with so much attention to detail, a vast output of manufactured cloth. It would also account for why archaeologists find no evidence of Mesopotamian or Syrian goods in Afghanistan or in the Indus region, beyond adopted artistic motifs. The textiles would have disintegrated long ago.

### Stone Jars from Egypt

Trade at Ebla did not just extend to the east. The kings also had contact with places to the west of their land, many of which were mentioned in the archives.

Regular roads had long connected the Mediterranean coast with the area of Ebla and, beyond that, the Euphrates and Northern Mesopotamia. By Irkab-damu's time, there were even communities spaced about thirteen miles apart so that a caravan could stop after a day's journey and find food and a place to sleep.[79]

The western kingdoms included Byblos, which was perched on the Mediterranean coast to the southwest of Ebla. Byblos had uniquely strong ties with Egypt during this era, the Egyptian Old Kingdom, the time when the pyramids were built and the kings had godlike power over their subjects. The leaders of Byblos sent shiploads of cedar (for construction), along with cedar oil (which was used in mummification), to Egypt. So many Egyptian artifacts and royal inscriptions have been found at Byblos that some speculate it might even have been under direct Egyptian control.[80] It was a beautiful spot. From the walled city, a gate led right down to the harbor with the deep blue of the Mediterranean as its backdrop. People had lived there for eons; by the time that Irkab-damu was ruling at Ebla, Byblos had already been occupied for over 3,000 years, and it remained important for thousands of years afterwards.[81]

At the very end of Egypt's New Kingdom, hundreds of years after Irkab-damu's time, we get a glimpse of Byblos in an Egyptian story. An Egyptian official went to visit the local king of Byblos and related that "I found him sitting in his upper chamber, with his back turned toward a window, while behind his head were breaking the waves of the great Syrian sea."[82] When one walks through archaeological sites in this region, strolling on dusty pathways between weed-strewn stone foundations, it's almost impossible to conjure up in one's mind the aspect of the places when they were occupied—the grandeur of a palace in which a king sat in an upper chamber, with white breakers against the blue of the Mediterranean framed in a window behind him. It's too bad that the ancient scribes so rarely included such descriptions of the world they lived in.

Perhaps because of the Egyptian presence in Byblos, Irkab-damu seems to have had some contact with the mighty kings of Egypt. Two stone vessels found in the palace at Ebla bear inscriptions in Egyptian hieroglyphs, though with no mention of how they got there.[83] One is a fragmentary diorite oil lamp inscribed with the name of King Khafra.[84] He was an immensely powerful Egyptian king who had ruled in the twenty-sixth century BCE, the builder of one of the Great Pyramids at Giza and the man whose portrait was used for the head of the Sphinx. The other is a fragment of the circular lid of a fine alabaster jar giving the name and titles of Pepi I, who reigned more than two centuries after Khafra and would have been a contemporary of perhaps the last of the Ebla kings, Irkab-damu's son Ishar-damu. Pepi's inscription, when it was complete, read: "The Horus Beloved of the Two Lands, the King of Upper and Lower Egypt and son of Hathor, mistress of Dendera, Pepi, given life, stability, and dominion."[85]

It's tempting to see this jar as a generous gift from Pepi I to the king of Ebla; it perhaps originally contained perfumed ointment. One could fancy that Pepi I and Ishar-damu had a similar relationship to that which Tush-ratta of Mitanni and Amenhotep III later enjoyed. Perhaps the king of Egypt sent letters, messengers, and gold (along with the alabaster jar), and the king of Ebla reciprocated by shipping off textiles and other manufactured goods in exchange, just as he communicated with the king of Hamazi. Egypt later became the main source of gold for the Near East; it might already have been playing this role to some extent.[86] Such a scenario is remotely possible, but there's no mention of Egypt in the Ebla archives. Perhaps more likely is that Pepi I simply traded with the king of Ebla for lapis lazuli and textiles, or that the objects arrived at Ebla indirectly, having been dedicated first at Byblos.[87]

Byblos and Ebla were among the very few Near Eastern cities where Egyptian Old Kingdom goods have been found. Other than this, though, Egypt was surprisingly shut off from most of the ancient Near East during the closing centuries of the third millennium BCE, even though so much communication seems to have been taking place across much of Asia. It's particularly odd because Egypt was enjoying a time of enormous wealth and prosperity. The kings seem to have had almost boundless riches and unprecedented control over their subjects, whom they conscripted to work on construction projects, the most conspicuous of which were the pyramids.

The Egyptians did look outwards to other regions besides Byblos, though. To the south, Egyptian expeditions ventured all the way to the land of Punt, which was probably located in the region of Somalia.[88] The trade with Byblos was regular, perhaps almost routine, but expeditions to Punt were much less common. Getting to Punt was a much bigger production; it involved carrying boats, in pieces, more than sixty miles across the harsh Eastern Desert, then assembling them on the shores of the Red Sea in order to sail south.

Like their contemporaries in Ebla, Mari, Ur, and other Near Eastern kingdoms, the Egyptian kings explored beyond their own borders primarily because they wanted to find resources that weren't available at home. As it happens, Egypt was naturally rich—it had fertile soil that was replenished every year by the annual flood, and it had abundant building stone, along with sources of turquoise, copper, and gold in the deserts nearby. Over the centuries, these treasures gave Egypt a big advantage in its dealings with the outside world. But Egypt, like Mesopotamia, was too hot for the types of trees that were needed in construction, such as cedars and firs, which grew so well near

Byblos. Punt was their source for other goods they couldn't acquire at home: incense, ivory, and exotic woods and animals.


### Mesopotamians in Egypt Long before the Early Dynastic Period

Curiously, *before* the time of the pyramids, and before Egypt was unified under a single king, it seems that the Egyptians had much more contact with Mesopotamia than they had during the Old Kingdom. The evidence for the early contact is all archaeological—writing wasn't developed enough in either civilization to have left records of their relationship.

The clues are intriguing, though: by about 3400 BCE, the Egyptians were using lapis lazuli, which, like all lapis, must have made the long journey from distant Afghanistan. They prized it for its brilliance and shine—the Egyptian word for lapis lazuli means "glittery-bright."[89] The Mesopotamians probably had a hand in getting the lapis to Egypt, perhaps as middlemen.[90] At a northern site in Egypt, occupied around the same time, archaeologists have found distinctive decorative clay cones of a kind that Mesopotamians used to create geometric mosaics on the walls of their temples.[91]

A century or so later (but still about 800 or 900 years before the time of Irkab-damu), some very Sumerian-looking images began to turn up in Egyptian art, such as rows of animals sculpted in registers.[92] Most dramatic is an Egyptian ivory knife handle that shows, on one side, a classic Mesopotamian contest scene with a man between two lions, and on the other, what seems to be a naval battle between what are recognizably Egyptian boats and other boats that look as though they had been lifted straight from a Mesopotamian cylinder seal.[93]

If this is a representation of an actual event—a moment when Mesopotamian and Egyptian boats could be seen side by side—what were Mesopotamian boats doing in Egypt so early? For that matter, how could they have got there? No waterways connected Mesopotamia and Egypt; a Mesopotamian who wanted to go by boat to Egypt would have had to carry his boat from the Euphrates in Syria to the Mediterranean. The other option, to sail south to the Persian Gulf and right around Arabia and north up the Red Sea, would still have required that the boat be carried across the desert from the Red Sea to the Nile. The knife handle is a mystery. A few scholars have even claimed that it is a fake. It's true that it was not found during an organized excavation but was purchased in Cairo.[94] But most believe it to be authentic: it is similar to other prehistoric Egyptian knives in minute points of detail, and it is not the only evidence for Mesopotamian contact at this early date.[95] For example, a tomb in the ancient Egyptian city of

Hierakonpolis was decorated with a scene that includes a Mesopotamian-style hero subduing two animals, along with a lone high-prowed Mesopotamian boat sailing alongside five crescent-shaped Egyptian boats.[96]

At around the same time, Egyptians began building some of their monumental mud-brick structures with niches and buttresses on the exterior walls, in a fashion very much like that of Mesopotamian temples. The Mesopotamians left an even clearer marker behind of their early contacts with Egypt— cylinder seals, which show up in the graves of a few wealthy Egyptians from around 3500–3000 BCE.[97]

So contact certainly took place between the two lands in the fourth millennium BCE. At the very least, some Egyptian artists obtained Mesopotamian cylinder seals, perhaps through trade, and copied some of the motifs they saw on them in their own artwork.[98] But this would not account for the appearance of Mesopotamian clay cones in Egypt, nor of the style of mud-brick architecture. The contact seems to have been more extensive than that. Perhaps some Egyptian merchants traveled to Mesopotamia and saw the boats there, along with the niched walls and clay cone mosaics on the public buildings, and they admired the animal contest scenes in the art. They then acquired some Mesopotamian luxuries, cylinder seals and lapis lazuli (imported from farther afield) and some decorative clay cones, and returned home. It's just as possible, however—maybe a little more so—that Mesopotamians visited Egypt.

This was a time, known in Mesopotamia as the Uruk period, when any number of innovations were transforming people's lives, from metallurgy to urbanism to writing to cylinder seals to the wheel. It was also a time of expansion. People from southern Mesopotamia established what seem to have been colonies in many places far from home, in what were later Syria and Assyria and even in what is now southeastern Turkey and southwestern Iran. These cities boasted Mesopotamian pottery and architecture.[99] Perhaps settlers from one of the colonies in Syria visited Egypt and were responsible for the Mesopotamian influences there. It's even possible that some Mesopotamian settlers set up a colony near the Red Sea or in the delta region in Egypt, bringing with them the same artifacts and architectural styles found in other colonies closer to home.[100]

One wishes that the Mesopotamians had used their writing system, invented towards the end of this period, to record the thinking behind these colonies. Unfortunately, the documents they were writing at the time are all utilitarian, all lists of commodities. This was before there were even kings ruling the cities, long before Mesopotamia was unified, and yet the people apparently had the wherewithal to send settlers hundreds of miles away to build grand cities patterned on the ones at home. Perhaps they were motivated by a desire to control the resources that Mesopotamia was so sorely lacking—timber, building stone, and minerals—rather than trading with the local peoples who lived in the regions where such materials could be found.

In any event, the influence on Egypt from Mesopotamia didn't last long, and Egypt seems to have cut off most of her connections with her neighbors to the north and east. Some Mesopotamian cylinder seals were still being used in Egypt in the third millennium BCE, and cedar from Lebanon shows up in Egyptian tombs around 2650 BCE as a result, no doubt, of the close ties to Byblos.[101] But no references to Egypt appear in Mesopotamian records for centuries. Beyond the Egyptian objects at Ebla and Byblos, communication between the two great civilizations seems to have been very limited in the third millennium BCE.

## Minoan Beginnings

Way across the Mediterranean Sea to the west from Syria, a civilization was developing in the Aegean region on the island of Crete. We call it Minoan, but the people there probably referred to their land as Keftiu or Kaptara. When the islanders first arrived, they could only have reached Crete by boat, and they continued to be profoundly tied to the sea over the centuries. Although no imports from Crete are found at Ebla in the Early Dynastic period, art from Crete and other Aegean lands somehow influenced the Syrian artists. The Aegean peoples loved the image of a running spiral that captured the form of waves on the sea, as well as a continuous looping line, which shows up on a gold bowl in Ebla.[102] A few cylinder seals even found their way into towns in the Aegean region, though whether they were brought there in person by Syrians or Mesopotamians is impossible to know.[103]

So step back now for a moment to look over this region extending from Egypt and Crete to the Indus Valley and what is now the far eastern border of Afghanistan. In what was the Early Dynastic period in Mesopotamia, populations across this area spoke very different languages and worshiped different gods. Some built temples to their gods and others did not. Some buried their dead in separate tombs and some in mass graves. No doubt other customs varied just as widely. But all the lands of this region were in contact with one another through trade, even if only indirectly, and the luxury goods that leaders and other rich men and women acquired must have made the long journeys worth all the hardship. It had become very important to kings to distinguish themselves from their populations. What better way to do this than

with the ostentatious display of goods that less affluent people in their kingdom couldn't possibly acquire: objects made of colorful and exotic materials
that came from hundreds or even thousands of miles away.

### The Destruction of Ebla

After examining the limits of Ebla's trading world, we return now to Ebla and
to the reign of Irkab-damu's son, Ishar-damu. How did that peace treaty with
Mari work out? Not too well, it seems. Both kingdoms still saw one another
as rivals rather than allies. Throughout the thirty-five years of Ishar-damu's
reign, the kings of Ebla and Mari maneuvered constantly to get the upper
hand against one another. On one occasion they renewed their peace treaty,
but both kings frequently led their armies on military campaigns within their
realms, and eventually Ishar-damu turned against the kingdom of Mari.[104] He
didn't try to defeat his enemy alone; in preparation for battle, Ishar-damu used
diplomacy with other kingdoms to strengthen his hand. He met with ambassadors from the Mesopotamian city of Kish on several occasions in order to
gain southern support, and he received pledges of loyalty from a number of
Syrian cities. He even sent thousands of bronze spearheads to his allies in
distant Nagar and Kish and in more local cities, probably to convince them to
join in his campaign against Mari.[105]

King Ishar-damu's army met up with their reinforcements near the city
of Terqa, north of Mari, where the battle was probably fought.[106] After the
battle, Ebla's allies received many gifts from the palace, which were dutifully
recorded in the archive—hence our knowledge of the events.

One can draw on images in the artwork of the time to imagine the scene
as Ebla launched its offensive against Mari.[107] The foot soldiers, as they
marched into battle, wore identical cap-shaped helmets, knee-length tunics
and long spotted capes that hung over their left shoulders. The troops were
well trained, taught to march in phalanx formation, and protected by the wall
of shields that they held in their left hands, their long spears pointing out in
front. Archers fired arrows with barbed shafts from behind the protection of
thick assault shields with curved tops that protected their heads. Other men
rode in four-wheeled chariots, each drawn by four donkeys or onagers (domesticated horses had not yet arrived in Syria or Mesopotamia). One man held the
reins and controlled the chariot while his partner had a spear at the ready. As
the forces from Ebla crashed into the forces from Mari, the quiet fields and
orchards around Terqa would have resounded with cries and with the clangs
and thuds of their weapons.

A scene from the Standard of Ur, found in one of the Royal Tombs, showing soldiers on a chariot. (©Trustees of the British Museum)

The clash of the two sides on the battlefield must have been bloody; the dead and dying fell beneath the hooves of the donkeys and the wheels of the chariots. Those who survived were stripped naked by the victors (their armor, weapons, and capes were all valuable), and the victors roped their captives' arms together behind their backs before marching them away.

The outcome of Ebla's victory in battle was not the domination of Mari by Ebla, however. Instead the kings drew up yet another peace treaty—it was a "year of the offering of oil of Ebla and Mari."[108] The victorious general from Ebla was rewarded with a ceremonial dagger decorated in gold for "having taken part in the expedition (against) Mari, (and for) the oil offering."[109] He also received garments, a gold plate, a set of reins, and a chariot with wheels decorated in gold.

Only three years after the victory over Mari, Ebla itself was destroyed. It's unclear from the excavations who was responsible. It might have been Sargon of Akkad, who claimed that the god Dagan gave him the city of Ebla. It might have been Sargon's grandson, King Naram-Sin, who denied that Sargon had been successful there. He wrote that "since the creation of mankind, no king whosoever had destroyed Armanum and Ebla," but that he, "Naram-Sin, the mighty, conquered Armanun and Ebla."[110] It's possible, however, that Ebla had been destroyed before either Sargon or Naram-Sin got there, perhaps by its old rival, Mari, in retribution for its humiliating loss to Ebla.[111]

It seems, then, that the diplomatic efforts of the kings of Ebla were not entirely successful. The treaties with Mari did not result in a long-lasting peace between them. To judge from the archives, attempts at alliances between neighboring kingdoms were not based on any pacifist ideal but came out of pragmatic concerns. Each king was presumably always strategizing: What would be best for his kingdom? How could he prevail over his rivals?

## The Arbitrary Nature of Our Evidence

We should not be surprised by the fairly constant military campaigns of the kings of the Early Dynastic period. What *is* surprising is that a king had an alternative if he did not want to be at war with a neighbor, or if he wanted to establish a formal relationship with a distant trading partner. He could make sure his messengers traveled regularly to that king's court, bearing gifts and friendly letters, and he could expect that king to reciprocate. He referred to his ally as a member of his family, a "brother," and he could choose to create real family ties between their two royal houses by negotiating a marriage. With neighboring kings, and perhaps more distant ones as well, he could negotiate a peace treaty, offering oil to the gods of both their lands.

With each message sent, each gift received, each child born to the princess and king of the two "brother" states, perhaps war between them became less likely. Or perhaps it simply was postponed. In either case, the Syrian and Mesopotamian kings who lived around 2350 BCE looked out beyond the confines of their small kingdoms and saw not just an array of enemies and foreigners but a world with which they could communicate, negotiate, and trade.

Ebla is sometimes credited with being home to the earliest known evidence of diplomacy. This is true, but it doesn't mean that the Ebla kings are to be thanked for thinking up the whole diplomatic system. One of the odd outcomes of archaeology is that we focus not necessarily on the places that were the most important in their own time but on the ones that have been excavated and have produced the most dramatic finds. This often means, for Syria or Mesopotamia at least, that we know most about the cities that were burned down. The conqueror who put the torch to the palace at Ebla (whether he was from Akkad, Mari, or some other city) inadvertently baked the bricks and the clay tablets and sealed them under debris, creating a time capsule for archaeologists to uncover. Ebla has become the most informative city for our understanding of late third-millennium Syria. But this doesn't mean that it was the most important city at the time, or that diplomacy started there. For all we know, most of the Early Dynastic kingdoms in Syria and Mesopotamia were ruled by kings who had alliances with one another, married one another's daughters, sent one another gifts, and exchanged letters and envoys. Perhaps treaties governed all these relationships.

Once the scribes started writing letters, treaties, inscriptions, contracts, and so on, our temptation is to think that these documents reflect institutions that had just been invented. The apparently "new" institutions included long-distance communication, a judicial system, and diplomacy. But it's entirely possible that the people of Syria and Mesopotamia had been sending messengers (with oral messages) over long distances, entering into formal relationships (with witnesses, rather than written documents, as evidence), and setting up alliances with distant kingdoms long before they thought to write anything down about them.

In any event, we are faced with the frustrating truth that it is not possible to closely examine the origins of diplomacy, because the earliest diplomatic documents available to us are not from the time when diplomacy began. What we can look at is the increasing scope, effectiveness, and sophistication of diplomacy as kingdoms grew larger and more powerful over subsequent centuries.

# PART II

# The Old Babylonian Period, 2000–1595 BCE

### CHAPTER THREE

# War and Allegiance

*"I have always done good things for him and his heart
knows the good deeds that I have done for him"*

### Hammurabi Discovered

The Early Dynastic and Akkadian Empire kings seem to have been fascinated by lands beyond their own, making alliances, diplomatic marriages, treaties, trading relationships, and (especially in the cases of Sargon and Naram-Sin) conquests. The next great era of international contact was the Old Babylonian period, from around 2000 to 1595 BCE, when kings in Syria and Mesopotamia used the diplomatic system to promote their own interests and build up their own power. At the same time, traders began moving out into the areas from which valuable resources could be acquired, rather than waiting for the goods to come to them.

The figure who looms over all others in this era is King Hammurabi, who ruled the kingdom of Babylon from 1792 to 1750 BCE. Curiously, he is famous in the minds of many for something that he didn't do: inventing law. This is an understandable mistake, though. When Hammurabi's laws were first excavated in 1902 and translated soon thereafter, they made international news. The *New York Times* reported in 1903 that "King Hammurabi...must be regarded as the 'Father of Laws,' as the man who, before the dawn of history as it has until lately been known, tabulated a system which in many respects is similar to the most elaborate and carefully thought out codes of modern times."[1] His laws were unlike anything else known to have developed before the writing of the Bible and, as far as anyone could tell in 1903, Hammurabi had invented the whole concept of law, and perhaps had influenced Moses himself. Besides, Hammurabi's laws were found on a massive stone monolith with an image of the king at the top, praying before the god of justice, which suggested a correspondence, in the imagination of an excited journalist, "to the story of Moses receiving the Ten Commandments from Jehovah."[2]

This analogy to the Bible is typical of the news reports from the early twentieth century; Hammurabi's fame came mostly from the similarities in his laws to those of the Bible, as well as from a charismatic speaker, Professor Friedrich Delitzsch, who traveled around the U.S. and Europe lecturing about his finds.[3] Delitzsch's talks galvanized audiences, as he drew attention to a whole world that existed before the Greeks and Romans. (Unfortunately, Delitzsch proved to be an unsavory and bigoted person; he grew increasingly anti-Semitic in his views as the years went by, and tried to claim that the West owed more to Babylon than to the Bible.[4]) Already in 1903, only a year after the laws had been discovered, they had been published in a book called *The Oldest Code of Laws in*

The relief sculpture from the top of the stela containing Hammurabi's laws. Hammurabi stands on the left, receiving symbols of authority from Shamash, the god of the sun and of wisdom, who is seated on a throne. (Réunion des Musées Nationaux/Art Resource, NY)

*the World* by C. H. W. Johns.[5] The idea stuck. Hammurabi is still often called (by nonspecialists) the author of the "oldest surviving collection of laws."[6]

The scholars, however, had dated Hammurabi far too early—in the third millennium BCE instead of the second—and already by 1915 scholars knew that other lawgivers had preceded Hammurabi.[7] The earliest laws that we know of now were written by a king of Ur, over 300 years before Hammurabi drew up his code.[8] Subsequent collections of laws, put together by kings of the kingdoms of Isin and Eshnunna among others, also predate those of Hammurabi.[9] But these kings didn't enjoy the public relations blitz that accompanied the discovery of Hammurabi's Code.

Although Hammurabi was not the inventor of law, he is nonetheless a king deserving of attention. He reunited southern Mesopotamia under his rule on a scale not seen since the time of Sargon of Akkad almost five hundred years earlier. And, of course, he was king of a city that has its own allure: Babylon.

Babylon dominated Mesopotamia for over a thousand years and eventually came to be associated with extravagance and decadence in the Bible and in classical sources. But for the first couple of decades of Hammurabi's reign, Babylon was not a particularly impressive or famous place.[10] Around 1765 BCE it was at the center of one of about seven states in Mesopotamia and Syria of more or less equal size and importance. In the south, near the Gulf, was Larsa; in central Mesopotamia were Babylon and Eshnunna; to the north, the kingdom of Ekallatum; to the northwest, the kingdom of Mari; and in the Syrian west, Yamhad (centered on Aleppo) and its southern neighbor Qatna. As in the time of Irkab-damu of Ebla, each major city dominated the lands around it. One difference was that the kingdoms were larger now and included smaller cities, each of which had its own king. A letter written to the king of Mari summarized the situation outside his own kingdom (which was, no doubt, similar): "There is no king who is strong on his own: Hammurabi of Babylon has a following of ten or fifteen kings, Rim-Sin of Larsa the same, Ibal-pi-El of Eshnunna the same, Amut-pi-El of Qatna the same, and Yarim-Lim of Yamhad has a following of twenty kings."[11]

At this point, Hammurabi was simply a regional overlord. If he had died young, he would be no more familiar to the average person today than Ibal-pi-El or Yarim-Lim. Because he later became a great conqueror and, at the end of his reign, proclaimed his famous laws, he finds a place in the history books.

It is, however, the early period of his reign that interests us in our search for evidence of diplomacy. If, at this time, Hammurabi was itching to rule beyond the traditional bounds of his kingdom, he didn't show it, and he managed to get along reasonably well with a number of the neighboring kings.

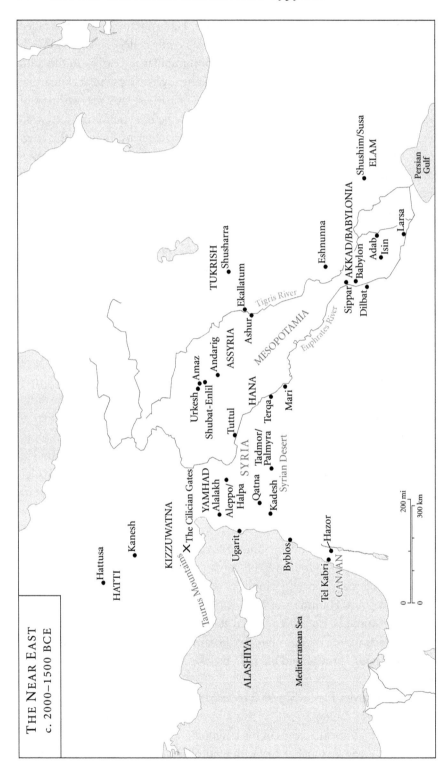

THE NEAR EAST
c. 2000–1500 BCE

Hattusa
HATTI
Kanesh

KIZZUWATNA
X The Cilician Gates
Taurus Mountains

Ugarit
Byblos
Tel Kabri
Hazor
CANAAN

ALASHIYA

Mediterranean Sea

YAMHAD
Aleppo/
Halpa
Alalakh
Qatna
Kadesh
Tadmor/
Palmyra
SYRIA
Syrian Desert

Urkesh
Amaz
Shubat-Enlil
Andarig
ASSYRIA
Tuttul
HANA
Terqa
Mari

TUKRISH
Shusharra
Ekallatum
Ashur
MESOPOTAMIA

Tigris River
Euphrates River

Eshnunna

Sippar
Dilbat
AKKAD/BABYLONIA
Babylon
Adab
Isin
Larsa

Shushim/Susa
ELAM

Persian
Gulf

200 mi
300 km

Given that Hammurabi went on to rule for forty-two years, he was probably relatively young when his father died and he took the throne—in his twenties, perhaps. Mesopotamian artists never tried to create portraits of the kings; they were always idealized. Was Hammurabi tall or short? Fat or thin? Did his hairline recede as he aged? Was his expression worried, intense, or friendly? The best-known sculpture of him, which appears at the top of his law code, was carved when he was elderly, but it shows the king as handsome and youthful, his face impassive. Still, his dress seems right. He wore the broad-rimmed round cap that was reserved for kings. His hair seems to have been cut short beneath his cap, but he grew his beard long. He wore a wide necklace and bracelet, perhaps of gold, and a long cape that wrapped around his chest under his right arm and fell from his left shoulder across his left arm. His feet were bare.

### Before Hammurabi

The five hundred years that separated Hammurabi from Sargon had seen many kingdoms rise and fall in Syria and Mesopotamia. Sargon's empire had splintered after the reign of his grandson Naram-Sin. The chaotic sequence of monarchs who tried to claim the throne immediately thereafter was summed up by the author of the Sumerian King List with the words, "Then who was king?" After which he added, resignedly, "Who was not king?"[12]

Towards the end of the third millennium BCE, a new family of leaders from Ur, the third dynasty to take power there, managed to reunify and restore order to Mesopotamia. Modern scholars refer to this era by the somewhat clumsy name of the Ur III period. These kings, especially Ur-Namma and his son Shulgi, created standard weights and measures that applied across their kingdom, wrote down laws, and built the first monumental stepped towers, known as ziggurats, adjoining the great temples of the major Mesopotamian cities. They also created a stunningly elaborate bureaucratic system that produced mountains of administrative records, thousands of which can now be found in museums and collections around the world. Like the Early Dynastic kings before them, the kings of Ur sent ambassadors to distant lands carrying letters and gifts, and they contracted diplomatic marriages for their daughters. The Ur princesses tended to be married off to kings in the powerful kingdom of Elam, to the east of Mesopotamia in what is now western Iran.[13]

The Elamites made their mark on Mesopotamia in other ways, beyond marrying Ur princesses. At many times in history they played the role of stereotypical enemy to the Mesopotamians. But at the start of the second millennium BCE, Elam was an ally of Babylon and a more powerful kingdom than any in the valley of the Tigris and Euphrates rivers. As far as Hammurabi was concerned (at least at the start of his reign), the king of Elam was greater than him—he was his "father."

Just to the south of the kingdom of Babylon lay its rival Larsa, where an elderly king named Rim-Sin had already ruled for decades before Hammurabi came to power. Rim-Sin's ancestors were Elamites. Hammurabi wasn't Elamite, but he wasn't Akkadian or Sumerian either; he would have described himself as being Amorite. Historians used to think of the Amorites as somewhat uncouth invaders who rode into Mesopotamia from the Syrian desert after the Ur III period and who had to learn the arts of civilization from their new subjects. An ancient writer seems to have thought of the Amorites as complete barbarians:

> Their hands are destructive and their features are those of monkeys....They never stop roaming about....Their ideas are confused." An Amorite, he wrote, "is clothed in sack-leather..., lives in a tent, exposed to wind and rain, and cannot properly recite prayers. He...eats raw flesh. He has no house during his life, and when he dies he will not be carried to a burial place.[14]

This description needs to be taken with a grain of salt. It was included in a myth about a god and wasn't intended to be an accurate account. The real Amorites weren't as rugged or uncivilized as the myth suggests. Some of them had worked as pastoralists, seasonally traveling with their flocks of sheep and goats in search of fodder, while others had long been farmers and city-dwellers.[15] These people already shared the same basic culture and ideals as the southern Mesopotamians, but they spoke a slightly different language. Amorite was related to Akkadian, but it is poorly known because the Amorite scribes chose to write in Akkadian and Sumerian rather than in their own language.

Two centuries before Hammurabi came to power, the kingdom of the Ur III period, which had stretched right across Mesopotamia and into Elam, had been replaced by smaller kingdoms, many of which, like Babylon, were ruled by Amorite dynasties. The Old Babylonian era (so named because of the central role that Babylon came to play in it) was dominated by these Amorite kings.

For the first two decades of Hammurabi's reign, his kingdom was overshadowed by those of Larsa to the south and Elam to the east, and especially by that of an imperialistic neighbor to the north, a king named Shamshi-Adad. Shamshi-Adad ruled a land that stretched from the Zagros Mountains to the

Euphrates, having taken over the kingdoms of Ekallatum and Mari. In an innovative move, he placed one son, Ishme-Dagan, as his viceroy in Ekallatum and another son, Yasmah-Addu, as his viceroy in Mari. Shamshi-Adad himself ruled from a capital city between the two, a place called Shubat-Enlil. Letters passed back and forth between the three rulers as they coordinated their government. The letters reveal that Ishme-Dagan was competent and warlike, whereas his younger brother Yasmah-Addu was weak and indecisive, and was even mocked sometimes by his father. One can imagine Yasmah-Addu's humiliation when a scribe read aloud the words of one his father's letters: "Is there no beard on your chin? How long will you neglect the administration of your house? Don't you see that your brother is heading vast armies? So, as for you, lead your palace and your house!"[16] Shamshi-Adad's kingdom didn't survive long after the death of its founder. Ishme-Dagan took over, but he was unable to hold onto the land of Mari, which soon fell back into the hands of a local leader, King Zimri-Lim.

Mari holds the key to much of our knowledge of this era. The site of Babylon has physically sunk over the years so that now the palace and archives of Hammurabi are below the water table and, presumably, reduced to mud (though later levels at Babylon can still be seen).[17] But we know quite a bit about Hammurabi's diplomatic efforts because they are memorialized in letters by and about him, some of which were found in the palace of his ally, King Zimri-Lim of Mari.

### Zimri-Lim, Hammurabi's Ally

Zimri-Lim lived in a sprawling palace of over 250 ground-floor rooms (more would have been located on the second, missing, story), a labyrinth of passageways, apartment suites, kitchens, workshops, offices, and public audience halls.[18] The palace even had a luxurious bathroom for the king, with bathtubs and a toilet, flushed by a stream beneath the seat. The walls of many rooms were painted with brightly colored murals of processions and fantastic animals. The rooms were probably also decorated with wall hangings, rugs, and inlaid wooden furniture, now all disintegrated. As easy as it must have been to get lost in this veritable rabbit warren, one tended to end up back in one of two large courtyards. The larger one was a public space, the smaller one (planted with palm trees for shade) was only open to visitors to the king—his throne room lay right beside it. The palace employed a workforce of hundreds—from slaves who worked in spinning and weaving all the way up to high officials and advisors to the king.

As in the case of Ebla, the vast archive of thousands of documents from eighteenth-century Mari is preserved because the palace burned down.[19] Surprisingly, the man who burned it was Hammurabi himself, Zimri-Lim's erstwhile ally. Because of this, it is possible to read, in some of the letters baked and buried in the conflagration, about Hammurabi's relations with Mari in happier times.

Although Zimri-Lim and Hammurabi held the same title, "king," and were avowed allies (through most of Zimri-Lim's reign, at least), their kingdoms were different in a fundamental way. Where Hammurabi was an urban king, ruling people who defined themselves in terms of where they lived, Zimri-Lim was a tribal leader.[20] His tribe is known as the Sim'alites. Many of its members lived in towns, just like the Babylonians in the south, but they formed communities that sometimes acted collectively, and whole groups of them would sometimes attend talks with Zimri-Lim's officials.[21] In such an environment, alliances could shift quickly and radically. Even before Hammurabi turned against Zimri-Lim, war was a fact of life for both of them, as it had always been; the Amorite kingdoms of Syria and Mesopotamia fought one another regularly, then formed alliances, changed their alliances, and then changed them again.

The kings each occupied a specific spot in the pecking order; a man was "brother" to kings who were equal in status to himself (just like Irkab-damu and the king of Hamazi so many years before), but he could also be a "son" to the greater kings and a "father" to lesser kings. When he came to the throne, a young king initially, and respectfully, referred to himself as the "son" of his father's allies. When the older men recognized him as an equal he switched to being their "brother."[22] The etiquette for addressing one another was complicated but important to them, and they seem to have worried about it quite a bit. This was in part because the pecking order also shifted frequently.[23] A powerful king, a "brother" of the major kings, might see a change in his fortunes and be demoted to a "son." Other kings longed to join the brotherhood of high-ranking kings, wanting to change their status as "son" to that of "brother" or "father."[24] Vassals switched allegiance too, moving from one overlord to another. All this caused frequent movements of troops and urgent letters requesting more soldiers, along with intrigue in courts about vassals and their intentions.

### Envoys and Protocol

Among allies (at least as long as they *were* allies) and between overlords and vassals, the trappings of diplomacy continued in the Old Babylonian period, just as they had in the time of Irkab-damu of Ebla and in the Ur III period. The kings sent one another ambassadors and letters and married one another's daughters. Vassals sent tribute to their overlords, while allies exchanged luxury gifts and got angry when they felt snubbed. They also relied on peace treaties, sworn in the presence of the gods, to secure their relationships.[25]

When we were looking at the Early Dynastic period in the third millennium BCE for evidence of diplomacy we had only fragments to work with, and this was true not only in Ebla but right across Syria and Mesopotamia. A few passing references to oath-making in a text that was devoted to keeping track of silver, a single diplomatic letter, two treaties, a few lines in a poem—it was like having a few sherds from a pot and trying to reconstruct the whole. For Hammurabi's time, the evidence is much more extensive.

The letters that passed between Zimri-Lim and his vassals and allies, including Hammurabi, include few formalities; these were mostly practical notes about troops, vassals, and military engagements.[26] Occasionally, the kings wrote directly to one another (though scribes wrote down their words, since both kings were, like almost all Mesopotamian and Syrian kings, illiterate), but more often an ambassador would report back to his king, quoting the other king's words. A typical letter begins "To my lord (Zimri-Lim) speak! Your servant Ibal-pi-El says, 'Some time ago, Hammurabi spoke a word as follows: "There is peace between Mari and Babylon...."'"[27] One gets the sense that Hammurabi and Zimri-Lim were not unalike; they wanted to be on the move, keeping their kingdoms intact, sending off messengers to learn all they could about their neighbors—friends for now, but wily enough to not show all their cards.

Messengers weren't the only travelers. Some of Hammurabi's sons visited Mari as well, and lived in houses there.[28] Perhaps this was how the kings knew about the lands of their allies and enemies; they had visited them before taking the throne.

We know a lot about the relationship between Hammurabi and Zimri-Lim thanks to the very observant messengers who reported back, in their letters to Zimri-Lim, even the slightest details of what they experienced. As in earlier times, there were no permanent ambassadors at the foreign courts, so the messengers not only carried letters and wrote reports, they also took on the main role of representing their king.[29]

Hammurabi could be stubborn and quick to anger, especially when dealing with messengers who brought bad news or less than civil messages from their kings. One messenger was put in the difficult position of being required to read a letter accusing Hammurabi of backing out on a commitment. This letter came from Ishme-Dagan, the son and successor of Shamshi-Adad. Quoting

Ishme-Dagan, the messenger read, "And I wrote you for troops, but you did not give me troops. And you gave troops to another place."[30] Hammurabi must have fairly roared his response: "To [whom] did I give troops? Speak up! Speak up!" He repeated this command "5, 6 times" and then demanded: "indeed there is (another) message that you carry." The messenger and other envoys were worried now. As it happened, they did have another message, but they must have feared how Hammurabi would take it. Instead they pleaded, "Do not be so very hard on us." Although the king raged at them, it's clear that he didn't harm them—it was their king with whom he was really angry. He finally extracted the contents of the additional letter from his own messenger.

On the other hand, Hammurabi had a generous side. On one occasion he was particularly pleased with the work of some troops from Mari who had assisted him on campaign, and he rewarded them—all 650 of them—with gifts of silver, each man receiving one-fifth of a shekel.[31] One shekel was about a quarter of an ounce, and this amount of silver represented approximately a month's salary for a laborer.[32] Thus an extra fifth of a shekel would have been reason to celebrate for these soldiers.

Messengers traveled regularly down the Euphrates from Zimri-Lim in Mari to Hammurabi in Babylon, bringing gifts with them from their own king. They made the long journey in groups, accompanied by armed guards.[33] It would have been dangerous to travel alone, as they feared nomads might rob them.[34] They were also accompanied by someone from Hammurabi's court, returning home from Mari; he would protect them as they traveled through the kingdom of Babylon and vouch for them. But he could also report to his king about the messages they were bringing.[35] He was, in some ways, a spy in their midst.[36]

When the envoys reached Babylon, they were well treated by their host. Hammurabi and Zimri-Lim were allies, after all. Hammurabi knew that the messengers would report back to their king on just what happened in Babylon; any mistreatment of them could be interpreted as a slight against Zimri-Lim himself. So they were given quarters in a specific building set aside to accommodate foreign messengers, known as the *bit naptarim*, where they could rest. Like other Mesopotamian houses, this would have been a mud-brick structure, with the doors to the rooms opening inward onto a courtyard. The rooms for the messengers were no doubt decorated comfortably with rugs and cushions. The thick walls kept out the worst of the summer heat. Without window glass (it hadn't been invented yet), windows were kept small and high up, so the rooms were dim and shady even during the day.

The messengers received extravagant rations of grain, oil, wool, meat, clothes, and silver—more for the highest-ranking members of the party, less for others.[37] They were also given gifts of silver, beyond their rations, though they may have been required to hand these over to their king when they got home.[38]

Once settled in, the envoys started paying attention to the other people sharing the messenger house with them. Delegations from other kingdoms were sometimes there at the same time, and the letters show they were all very touchy about how they were treated. Anything that might be interpreted as favoritism to another city could send a messenger into a rage. The Mari messengers were usually among the most favored in Babylon. One king lamented that the Mari delegation received much better food than he had received himself—"pork, fish, birds, and pistachios."[39] Indeed, the delegates could expect to dine with King Hammurabi. This meal was a festive affair, with musicians, dancers, and acrobats to entertain the guests, and elaborate rules about who was allowed to sit closest to the king.[40]

But on one occasion the men from Mari were thoroughly annoyed. The envoys from the kingdom of Yamhad, who were in Babylon at the same time, had all been given special formal robes to wear for their meal with the king. So too had the top three diplomats from Mari, but not the lesser members of the delegation. Yamhad delegates of the same status had been given them. Where, these Mari men wondered, were *their* robes? They protested to Hammurabi's official: "Why do you set us apart as if we were criminals?...Are we not all servants of our lord?" They should, they thought, get the same treatment as the Yamhad men. And then the men from Mari "got angry, and stormed out of the palace's chamber."[41] The incident was reported to Hammurabi and the men duly received the formal robes. But Hammurabi was annoyed by the whole scene and later proclaimed to a Mari official, "Do you imagine you can control my palace in the matter of formal wear? I provide and deny clothing at will! I won't come back to this affair; I will not provide clothing to the messengers at dinner!"[42]

The formal audience with Hammurabi, when the main diplomat presented the letter from Zimri-Lim, did not happen at dinner. It might have taken place beforehand or perhaps the day after, depending on the circumstances.

A vivid description of this moment comes from a letter written by a man named Yansib-Addu, who traveled to the city of Sippar, where Hammurabi was staying, with a message from Zimri-Lim.[43] He wrote back to his own king with a blow-by-blow account of his audience with Hammurabi. Unfortunately, he didn't describe the setting—did he meet with the king in a room in the palace there? Such details were unimportant to him, and presumably to Zimri-Lim. (Had the audience taken place in Babylon, it would have been in a particular room in Hammurabi's palace set aside for the purpose.[44]) What he does show us is just how much authority an envoy such as himself commanded in the presence of an allied king.

Yansib-Addu was brought into Hammurabi's presence, but they probably wouldn't have been alone. Any number of officials had a claim to be there—people from Hammurabi's court, other foreign ambassadors, even diviners.[45] The other ambassadors would have been expected to report back to their own kings on what was said between Hammurabi and the envoy from Mari. Only on rare occasions did the king meet in secret, with just a handful of advisors present.

Yansib-Addu would have greeted the king formally and presented him with the gifts that he had brought from Zimri-Lim. The clay envelope protecting Yansib-Addu's letter was then broken open, and Yansib-Addu began to read.[46] It seems that Hammurabi was an attentive listener as Yansib-Addu read aloud the letter he had brought: "[while] Yansib-Addu delivered the message of my lord," meaning Zimri-Lim, "Hammurabi [kept listening to] him throughout the delivery of the message. And he did not open his mouth, until he (Yansib-Addu) had finished his message. He (Hammurabi) paid close attention."[47] One can envision the Babylonian king weighing the words of the letter in his mind, thinking through the proposal that Zimri-Lim had put forward in it. Unfortunately, in his letter describing the scene, Yansib-Addu didn't mention what had been the exact purpose of his visit, though it had something to do with some cities that had been given to Mari by the king of Elam and which Hammurabi seems to have been disputing. The king of Mari would, of course, have known all the details, so he didn't need them repeated in the letter sent back to him.

Then Hammurabi replied. Perhaps Yansib-Addu took quick notes as the king spoke, or perhaps he recalled the words afterwards when writing to his own king. But Hammurabi's first words must have pleased Zimri-Lim when he eventually heard them: "The city of Mari and Babylon have always been one house and one finger that does not lend itself to be split." As usual, the terminology used to express alliance was that of the household.

Hammurabi was evidently satisfied with this state of affairs, and felt that he was blameless in the relationship: "Since the day on which Zimri-Lim turned his face towards me and started communicating with me, there has been no wrongdoing…on my part against him. I have always done good things for him and his heart knows the good deeds that I have done for him." With that, Hammurabi was apparently finished.

One might have expected this to be the end of the audience; Yansib-Addu might have been led out to wait until the king of Babylon had decided on a formal reply to the letter. But instead, Yansib-Addu recorded that he answered Hammurabi in a speech of his own, which he recalled in his letter to Zimri-Lim. Obviously the envoy wasn't constrained to just read what was in the original message, although he had to do that first; later he could do negotiating on his own as well.[48]

He did more than simply restate Zimri-Lim's message in his own words. First he emphasized just how helpful Zimri-Lim had been to Hammurabi, reminding the Babylonian king of things Zimri-Lim had done on his behalf, including sending troops to support Babylon. Zimri-Lim was, indeed, a good ally. But then Yansib-Addu presumed to get tough with Hammurabi, complaining forcefully about the Babylonian king's failure to address the issue at hand. Yansib-Addu's voice must have risen as he said "But beware of what I have been telling you again and again, once, five times, many times..." after which he accused Hammurabi of not paying attention: "Have you in all this time not understood the words of my lord?" Yansib-Addu must have had enough clout that he didn't fear retribution from Hammurabi for what might have been seen as insubordination in a lesser official. Finally he commanded the Babylonian king: "Commit yourself about the cities that the Vizier of Elam, your father, gave my lord...!"[49]

Of course, Yansib-Addu was not only the speaker but also the author of the description. He might have exaggerated his role a little. But given the practical nature of the communication, the essence of it must have been accurate. Other witnesses to the scene—and there were probably a lot of them—could have let Zimri-Lim know if Yansib-Addu had misrepresented the discussion.

Perhaps at this point Hammurabi paused a moment to consider his options. Yansib-Addu had made a good case. Zimri-Lim was an important ally—a "brother"—whose assistance he often needed. When Hammurabi spoke, his words were reassuring: "In view of his (Zimri-Lim's) goodness I will answer him forthrightly, and the hem shall be knotted among us forever." Knotting the hem was symbolic of marriage and was also a ritual used between allies. The two kings were brothers, and therefore members of the same family (even if they weren't connected by marriage), so they would "knot the hem" and be bound together.[50] Zimri-Lim seems to have won the argument this time.

Yansib-Addu, on finishing his long letter, sent it quickly to Zimri-Lim, using two other messengers and asking for a response: "My lord must quickly write me a full report, and I shall do whatever my lord writes me." Yansib-Addu presumably stayed put in Sippar in order to speak again with Hammurabi if he got the chance. This type of diplomacy was well suited to kingdoms that shared a border. Sippar was about 250 miles downstream from Mari; a messenger could travel by boat on the river on the return journey. The current and the wind together made the trip downstream much faster than the long walk north to Mari—Zimri-Lim's response would presumably have arrived in a few short weeks, rather than months.

## An Unappreciated Gift

Although Yansib-Addu didn't mention it in this letter, he almost certainly delivered a gift to Hammurabi at the same time that he read the letter.[51] Just as Irkab-damu had sent gifts to the king of Hamazi in anticipation of receiving luxuries in exchange, so the contemporaries of Hammurabi during the Old Babylonian period did the same.[52] In this era it's clear—much more so than in the Early Dynastic period—that the kings followed specific rules surrounding gift exchange; most importantly, the gifts had to be equivalent in value.

This could become a problem for kings who weren't as affluent as their overlords. One destitute vassal wrote to Zimri-Lim, begging him not to give any gifts to his envoy, because he wasn't able to reciprocate. He had found himself in the embarrassing position of having his gift rejected by Zimri-Lim's envoys. He had tried giving them just two shekels of silver, "but they didn't accept, saying 'It is (too) little!' "[53]

Even among the major kings, misunderstandings and hurt feelings could result over the value of the presents that were sent. A painfully honest letter written during the time of Hammurabi from one king to another reveals this very clearly. The recipient of the letter was Ishme-Dagan, the king of Ekal-latum, and the letter reached him after he had taken over from his father Shamshi-Adad, but before he lost control of Mari. He had probably been on the throne only a short time. The sender was an older king, Ishhi-Addu, ruler of the land of Qatna, about 400 miles from Ishme-Dagan's kingdom, to the west in Syria.[54]

Ekallatum and Qatna were both important kingdoms. But whereas Ekal-latum had been losing prestige since the death of Shamshi-Adad, Qatna was at the height of its power. The city covered almost 250 acres and was square in plan, with an imposing high rampart right around it.[55] The waters of a lake lapped the base of the tell on two sides, almost like a moat, reflecting the soft golden brown hills of the Orontes Valley.[56] Ishhi-Addu's palace, which was built on top of a cliff over forty feet above the lower city, dominated the skyline.[57]

Qatna lay at the crossroads of three major highways. One originated in Babylonia, wound up the Euphrates, crossed the Syrian desert (with a welcome respite at the green oasis city of Tadmor, later called Palmyra), passed through Qatna, and went on through a pass in the mountains to the ancient city of Byblos on the Mediterranean. A second passed from the northern Mediterranean port of Ugarit through Qatna to Emar on the Euphrates. And the third was a north-south route between Anatolia and Egypt. Ishhi-Addu was able to get rich from the taxes on the goods that passed along all these roads.

To judge from a pair of almost life-size statues found at Qatna from this time, Ishhi-Addu would have worn distinctive clothes, somewhat different from those worn in Mesopotamia. His royal robes fell to his ankles, with a thick rope-like hem on the shawl around his shoulders. His beard was short, and he wore a broad band around his hair, a headdress reserved for kings.[58]

The two kings were "brothers"—equals in the royal hierarchy—and they were also related through marriage. Ishme-Dagan's brother, who was still the viceroy at Mari, was married to Ishhi-Addu's daughter.

Ishme-Dagan seems to have been feeling his way through the confusing world of diplomatic relationships at this time, and he had reached out—clumsily as it turned out—to his brother king in Qatna. He apparently had written to Ishhi-Addu asking for two horses. The horses were duly delivered, and Ishme-Dagan responded by sending back twenty minas (approximately twenty pounds) of tin. When Ishhi-Addu's messengers appeared again in Ishme-Dagan's court, some weeks later, perhaps Ishme-Dagan expected thanks for the tin. He didn't get it.

Instead, Ishhi-Addu sent a blistering letter back to Ishme-Dagan, telling him right at the beginning that he was going to broach a subject that was usually taboo: "Right now, just to relieve my feelings, I must speak about this matter which should not be spoken about."[59] Perhaps he felt that he had to correct the new king in matters of protocol before Ishme-Dagan made any other egregious errors, but he also wanted to blow off some steam. He continued "You are a great king; you made a request to me for two horses, and I had them conducted to you." This was apparently normal behavior for two great kings; nothing was wrong yet. "But you sent me twenty minas of tin!" Here was Ishme-Dagan's big mistake; perhaps he wildly overestimated the value of the tin in Qatna, or perhaps horses were worth much less in Assyria than in Qatna, or perhaps he hadn't realized that he was expected to send back a gift of equal value.

Ishhi-Addu then pointed out how generous he had been, in spite of not having any treaty with Ishme-Dagan: "Without any formal agreement with me you have not gone wanting (what you requested, and yet) you sent me this bit of tin! Had you simply not sent me (anything), by the name of the god of my father my feelings would not have been hurt." It seems that he would have been less insulted had his gift been simply accepted with no exchange attempted; the two horses could have been seen as a very expensive present and his generosity would have been lauded. But no: "The price of these horses over here by us in Qatna was six hundred shekels of silver, yet you sent me twenty minas (that is, twelve hundred shekels) of tin!" The cost of tin was a fraction of the cost of silver; twelve hundred shekels of tin were not even close to the value of the horses.

It seems that kings were usually circumspect and polite in their dealings with one another; they avoided coming right out and elucidating the rules that governed their interactions. But Ishhi-Addu, in this letter, blew the cover off normal polite behavior, and what he wrote shows us that the gifts were not simply expressions of friendship; the goods sent and received needed to be equal in the eyes of both kings.[60]

Ishhi-Addu wasn't just upset that he had been cheated of wealth. His feelings were more complicated than that. "What will the one who hears of this say? Will he not vilify us?" This was a big part of the gift exchange as well: the public display of the goods received. Kings wanted to be able to show off what they had received from their brother kings, almost as though it were tribute. With a good exchange, each king gained not only in wealth but also in prestige in the eyes of his vassals, allies, and subjects. Twenty minas of tin was not an amount worth displaying; in fact, Ishhi-Addu may have tried to cover up that he had received it at all. But over in Assyria, Ishme-Dagan was parading around in a chariot drawn by his two fine new Qatna horses. No wonder Ishhi-Addu was fuming.

In the next line he expressed his complete confusion about the exchange; after all, Ishme-Dagan wasn't poor and they were joined in the same "house" as brothers: "This house is your house. What is missing in your house (that) a brother does not grant a request to a brother?" Apparently Ishhi-Addu had in fact sent a "request" and asked for something specific in exchange for the horses, making the receipt of twenty minas of tin more humiliating still; perhaps he thought that Ishme-Dagan had treated him as he would a vassal or inferior. He repeated his assertion that he would rather have just given the horses as a straightforward gift: "Had you not sent me the tin, my feelings would not have been hurt at all." Brother kings were supposed to behave like true brothers, sharing the wealth of their houses and granting one another's requests.

How could Ishhi-Addu make it any clearer to Ishme-Dagan that he had blundered catastrophically? He could tell him that he wasn't worthy of his throne: "You are not a great king!" he raged. Imagine Ishme-Dagan's feelings when these words were read aloud to him. Finally, though, in the last couple of lines Ishhi-Addu seems to have calmed down a little: "Why have you acted so? This house is your house."[61]

We don't know how Ishme-Dagan reacted. He couldn't charge off in anger and fight against Ishhi-Addu; not only was that king his brother's father-in-law, but Qatna was a long way off and Ishme-Dagan had enough to worry about at home—his vassals were rebelling. Perhaps he quickly sent off a gift of silver with an excuse that some servant must have switched the silver for tin and that he had meant to send silver all along. It does seem likely that he wrote to his brother in Mari, though, and this would have been a good plan, since the brother could have consulted his wife and asked her how to appease her father. This might be the reason why Ishhi-Addu's furious letter wasn't found at Ishme-Dagan's palace but at his brother's palace at Mari.

In the end, Ishme-Dagan's career didn't improve, his kingdom shrank, and he ended up being demoted to a "son" of the great kings instead of continuing as a brother. Hammurabi wrote to Ishme-Dagan: "To those kings that write me as sons you [write] as brother," meaning that Ishme-Dagan was now equal with the kings who were vassals of Hammurabi, not with the Babylonian king himself.[62] The ultimate humiliation was that Zimri-Lim, the king who took over control of Mari when Ishme-Dagan couldn't hold onto it, was also higher up in the pecking order than he was, according to Hammurabi's instructions: "To Zimri-Lim who writes me as a brother, you write as son." Ishme-Dagan was incensed by this. He had begun his reign as the master of Mari. He wrote angrily, "You made me write Zimri-Lim as son. Is [that man] not my servant? He is not sitting on a throne of his (own) majesty." But his appeal was in vain. He was a minor king now. Perhaps Ishme-Dagan's political instincts had remained bad, even after the tongue-lashing he received from Ishhi-Addu.

It wasn't just kings who exchanged gifts of items that they desired from one another's households; it was apparently expected of siblings at all levels of society. Gift exchange was indeed, as noted in the Ebla letter to Hamazi, "[w]hat is (appropriate) to brother(s)" and to sisters.[63]

Two sisters who lived around the same time as Ishme-Dagan and Ishhi-Addu corresponded about a gift exchange, though about more prosaic goods than silver and horses. One woman wrote that she had received from her sister "in the last caravan ... 100 liters of barley semolina, fifty liters of dates, and one and a half liters of oil; and they've just delivered ten liters of sesame seeds, and ten liters of dates." She needed to compensate her sister, so she wrote, "In return, I'm sending you twenty liters of coarse flour, thirty-five liters of bean flour, two combs, a liter of *shiqqu*-brine."[64] And, just like the kings, she had a request: "There isn't any *ziqtu*-fish here. Send some to me so that I can make you some of that brine and can have it brought to you."

There must have been messengers who regularly transported goods between family members, probably from one town to another. The "caravan" that the woman referred to would not have been necessary had the women lived near one another; they could have sent a servant or male family member to make the delivery. The fact that messengers were usually familiar is seen in one letter wherein a man assured his brother that the messenger bringing the letter was "not a stranger, he is my son-in-law, he will hand you the letter."[65]

Just as the kings saw matching gifts as a sign of affection, so too did average people. One woman complained to her sister that she had not yet received a present from her, even though the woman had offered to send her sister five logs. She sent a messenger to the sister and wrote, "Send by him one hundred locusts and food worth one-sixth of a shekel of silver. In this I will see your sisterly attitude toward me."[66] (Locusts were considered to be a delicious delicacy.) As with the kings, these women expected that siblings who lived apart would send regular gifts, and took the absence of these gifts as a snub. A large number of personal letters between siblings written during the time of Hammurabi's dynasty pertain to just this issue. This happens to be the era for which we have the most personal letters, but the same was probably true in other eras as well.

### Killing a Donkey and Swearing an Oath

Ishhi-Addu had underlined in his letter the fact that there was no formal treaty between himself and Ishme-Dagan and yet he had always treated him well. Most relationships among Old Babylonian period kings do seem to have been formalized in treaties.[67] From earliest times, the Mesopotamians had a particular obsession—they wanted every transaction, every relationship, to be witnessed and therefore to be formal and dependable. If a man bought a house or a field or a slave during Hammurabi's reign, he always brought along witnesses to attest to the transaction between himself and the seller. Thousands of such contracts have been found in private houses that were occupied during this era. The laws that Hammurabi later drew up specified that anyone who bought "silver, a slave, a slave woman, an ox, a sheep, a donkey, or anything else whatever...without witnesses or a contract...that man is a thief."[68] That would be the only explanation for such behavior in their world—the need for witnesses was so pervasive and ingrained that if you didn't have them, it could only be because you stole the item. A similar idea was true for marriage: "If a man marries a wife but does not draw up a formal contract for her, that woman is not a wife."[69] So perhaps an alliance without a treaty was not really an alliance. The gods needed to witness the commitment. Contracts didn't have to be written down so long as they were witnessed, and the same seems to have been true of treaties.[70]

So how did two kings go about making a treaty? If they lived close enough to one another, they chose a meeting place where they could come together to work out the stipulations and swear an oath to the gods. A treaty between two of Zimri-Lim's vassals provides a good example of how this worked.[71] The kings decided to meet at a place near the border of their two kingdoms. Each of them arrived with a large entourage, and word had been sent out to Zimri-Lim and many of his allies as well—representatives from Mari, Babylon, and two other major kingdoms joined the group there. It's likely that it took several days for the envoys to all gather in one place. Did they stay in houses in the town? The scribes didn't say. Instead they noted that "they all congregated and started talking of the matters between them."[72] One of the vassal kings who was party to the treaty turned at one point to the gathered assembly, including delegations from the major powers who were there, and enthusiastically, though perhaps ill-advisedly, praised his overlord in almost godlike terms: "Besides Zimri-Lim, our father, our elder brother, and our guide, there is no other king."[73] We don't know how the men might have voiced their approval to this, but it sounds like a line designed to get the crowd of Mari dependents cheering.

But the diplomats from Babylon and one other major kingdom "were displeased" by the comment "and withdrew to the side." They took it as a direct insult to their own kings. The air grew tense. The Mari envoy who wrote the letter describing the scene was determined to find out what would happen next, even though he was convalescing at the time: "I was ill, and two men were holding me on carrying poles, but I stood up for the purpose of listening to the negotiations, facing the kings." The other vassal quickly covered up for his ally's gaffe by noting that other kings were also great, and "appeasement issued from his mouth." The affronted diplomats seem to have been mollified by this.

Negotiations continued between the two kings, along with some powerful elders, on details of the treaty. There was some question as to a particular field: which of the two kingdoms did it belong to? One king proposed that they should wait until harvest time. The field was already planted, and after harvesting, the gods would be consulted: "let them find out the true owner of the field." This seems to have been a satisfactory solution to both parties. The gods would give their decision through oracles, and no one doubted that their answer would be valid. To them, the gods were as real as anyone else present at the negotiations.

Both kings expressed to one another their worry that the other would ally himself with a particular enemy king, in which case "I will become your enemy." But they seem to have resolved this as well, and negotiations were finally complete.

Then the two men "tied the ties," which might have been a formal gesture (perhaps actually knotting their garments together), and a donkey was sacrificed. This was an essential feature of a peace treaty negotiation in this region, and must have been dramatic.[74] The blood would have flowed from the dying animal. Was it a gift to the gods? They don't say. But only a donkey would do; one king tried substituting a goat and a puppy, which was not at all acceptable; only the donkey had the nobility necessary for the moment.[75]

At last, it was time to take an oath in the names of the gods of both the cities: "brother made brother declare a sacred oath." The statues of the gods, or perhaps their symbols, would have been brought to the negotiating ground. This was a solemn moment when each man swore to uphold his pledge to his ally and each heard the curses that would be called down upon him if he broke his promises.

The solemnity of the occasion was brought to a close with a festive ceremony during which "they sat down to drink. After they consorted and drank, brother brought a gift to brother."[76] They presumably all went home well satisfied with the results.

Other treaties that have survived from this time echo the treaty between Ebla and Abarsal of so many centuries before; like that one, they were drawn up between vassals and their overlords. The language of the later treaties is easier for modern scholars to understand than that of the Abarsal treaty, and the clauses therefore make more sense to us. The basic goal was the same, though, in both eras: to create a formalized and orderly relationship.

One of Zimri-Lim's vassals swore "by the sun in heaven...from this day forth, so long as I live, I will commit no misdeed against Zimri-Lim...nor against his city, his army, nor his land....I swear that I will follow closely and act wholeheartedly in the best interests of Zimri-Lim."[77] This type of lifelong allegiance might have been a worthy goal, but many of the vassals seem to have had a hard time living up to it. This could be infuriating for an overlord. One wrote in complete exasperation about a particularly fickle vassal:

> Previously he followed the ruler of Shimurrum. He left the ruler of Shimurrum, and followed the ruler of the Tirukkeans. He left the ruler of the Tirukkeans, and followed Ya'ilanum. He left Ya'ilanum, and followed me. He left me, and now follows the ruler of Kakmum. And to all these kings he has sworn an oath! Within just three years he made alliances with these kings and broke them![78]

As far as the overlord was concerned, this vassal "does not know his own words and he does not know the oath he swears. As if he swears an oath in his dream, he disregards (it). He is a madman, and his statement is false!"[79] And yet it seems that the overlord was often powerless to force his vassals to stay true to him, especially if it would involve the expense of going to war against the vassal's new overlord. So the kings could only hope that the gods would enforce their own order by cursing the defiant vassal.

The kings of the major powers also wanted their alliances to be formalized in treaties, but they rarely if ever met one another, so their treaties had to be negotiated by their envoys. These men traveled back and forth from one court to the other carrying what they referred to as "small tablets," which presumably included specific clauses of the treaty.[80] An ancient king would wait weeks or months to hear the verdict of his ally on just one provision, so the whole process of finalizing a treaty could have taken years.

The final version of the treaty was written out on a "big tablet," a few of which have survived. Neither king seems to have had a copy of all the obligations in the agreement; each retained a copy that included the clauses pertaining just to him, though the two versions were probably very similar.[81] Such treaties included three main parts: first, a list of the gods invoked from both kingdoms to witness the event; second, a list of clauses; and finally, a curse on anyone who might break the treaty.[82] The clauses show a preoccupation with mutual defense; for example, the kings swore to have the same friends and enemies, to help one another if either one were to be attacked, and not to sign separate peace agreements with other kings.[83]

When it came time to swear to these treaties, the kings each sent their gods (that is, statues or symbols of their gods) all the way to their ally's capital so that the oaths would be witnessed by the deities of both sides. The oaths took place in both cities, with an envoy standing in for the missing king in each case.[84] And then each king "touched his throat" and did something that involved blood.[85] Perhaps, some scholars think, the allies exchanged samples of their blood, which they touched when taking the oath.[86] If so, what a job this would be for a messenger! He might have been asked to carry a small sample of blood drawn from his own king (perhaps dried on a piece of cloth) all the way to the distant home of the ally. After this, the kings referred to the "blood relations and strong ties" that existed between them.[87] It was, once again, all about family.

## One Big (If Sometimes Contentious) Family

It's entirely possible that the allied kings at this time really did form one huge extended family. When a treaty was concluded, the ideal outcome was for one of the kings to marry the daughter of the other, with expensive gifts passing between the two courts in the form of dowry, bride-price, and wedding gifts. Shamshi-Adad sent valuable gold statues of himself and his ally on such an occasion, and gave a dowry of an entire vassal kingdom: "I will have a statue of you and a statue of me made in gold, and brother will embrace brother. I will give you my daughter, and as dowry for my daughter I will give you the country of Shusharra."[88] Under similar circumstances, Zimri-Lim married a daughter of the king of Yamhad as well as a princess of Qatna.[89] Hammurabi was married to a daughter of the king of Eshnunna and perhaps also to a Mari princess. Ishme-Dagan, the unlucky king of Ekallatum, married his son to the daughter of another powerful king.[90] We don't know much about other Old Babylonian royal wives, but their stories might well have been similar—whenever their origins are mentioned, the women were almost always princesses from other kingdoms. After all, who would have the appropriate status to serve as a royal wife other than a woman who had grown up as a princess? And given that the Mesopotamian and Syrian kings didn't marry their sisters, the only choice was to look to their allies and overlords.[91] Between allies, it apparently didn't matter much which king became the groom and which the father-in-law; one wrote, "Either give me your daughter or let me give you my daughter." In either case, the kings hoped for the same thing: "may the family ties between us not be dissolved."[92] On the other hand, the kings generally don't seem to have had much interest in marrying the daughters of their vassals.

The Mesopotamians and Syrians put a great deal of faith in family—one sees it repeatedly. They don't seem even to have had a conception of a "state" or "government." They had no words for these ideas. In their places they thought of families and fathers and brothers.[93] By creating marriage ties between themselves, the relationships were not just fictive but real. Many of the vassals who called themselves "sons" of an overlord were indeed his sons, or at least his sons-in-law.[94]

Marriages like these had been a fact of life since Irkab-damu's time, of course. Naram-Sin of Akkad, who bragged about conquering Ebla (though someone else had probably beaten him to it), had sent one of his daughters to the far northern city of Urkesh, probably to marry the local king there.[95] At the very end of the third millennium BCE, the Ur III kings had also sent their daughters hundreds of miles from home to marry foreign kings.[96]

Hammurabi and Zimri-Lim were following in the footsteps of all these previous kings as they strategized. Whom should they marry? Which princes would be most useful as sons-in-law? A daughter was a valuable asset to a major king; he could marry her off to one of his vassals and, in so doing, ideally secure a loyal spy in the vassal's court and hope that a son born of the marriage might become king of the vassal realm. A king could also dedicate a daughter to a god as a priestess. The role of such a woman was important, too; she was obligated to pray to the gods for the health and prosperity of her father and his kingdom. The more daughters a king had, the better.

Zimri-Lim had at least two sisters and eleven daughters, and many of them, perhaps almost all, played these roles.[97] The women selected for diplomatic marriage would have been married young, probably only in their teens, but they were not viewed simply as a particularly valuable gift, as some have suggested. In a sense, upon marriage they joined the diplomatic corps. Not surprisingly, the negotiations leading up to a royal marriage took time and involved high officials, though the vassal king receiving the bride might not have met his wife until after the wedding ceremony.

Messengers would have traveled between the cities of the bride's father and her future husband many times, negotiating the conditions of the marriage, just as they did when negotiating a peace treaty.[98] The groom, like all grooms, had to provide a gift known as a *terhatum* to the bride's father. This is sometimes translated as "bride-price," but the bride wasn't being bought. The arrival of the *terhatum* was an important moment; it signified that the marriage really was going ahead. In turn, the bride's father provided her with a dowry that she would take with her to her new home. For most women this would have included practical items like utensils and furniture. A richer family might provide silver jewelry, fields, farm animals, or slaves.[99] The princesses received considerable riches from their fathers; this was a way in which the overlord could demonstrate his wealth and power. The dowry of one princess from Mari included 117 items and ten servants (one of whom was a scribe).[100] Among the dowry items were many necklaces, bracelets, earrings, and other pieces of jewelry, along with twenty-seven bronze vessels, nineteen items of clothing, two litters, eighteen seats and stools, a tray, and four tables. The weight of the gold and silver items alone was almost six and a half pounds.

The envoys from the groom's court seem to have gone through some of the formalities of the marriage ceremony on their lord's behalf in the bride's city, placing a veil on the bride's head before she was brought back to their kingdom.[101] Special boats seem to have been constructed for the occasion (for the part of the journey that could be done on the river), and troops traveled ahead of the new bride on her first trip to her new home. One can envision a Mari princess taking leave of her father, Zimri-Lim, to go to her new husband's city. The letters show that the royal men and women of this time were willing to show their emotions, so the girl might well have shed tears as she left. Special gowns had been made for the occasion, and the princess must have looked quite stunning in them. She probably wore a long, straight, dress that draped around her to create a V-neckline, and a shawl wrapped around her shoulders.[102] The shawl had a wide beaded hem on one side and a neat row of tassels on the other. Around her neck lay a seven-strand necklace, probably of gold, and she wore several bracelets on both wrists. Her long hair was braided, with the braids looped together at the back.[103]

Some of the princesses took the title "queen" once they were married. Only one of a king's wives could hold this title, and she had a surprising amount of power, at least in Old Babylonian Syria.[104] In one instance a queen proposed taking a trip with her husband, to which he responded "I and you are going together? And to whom will we leave the city? Stay over here until I return from Mari!"[105] It was her responsibility to take charge of the city when he was absent. The same was true of Zimri-Lim's wife Shiptu when her husband was away.

Zimri-Lim's married daughters wrote to their father in letters that were surprisingly uncensored; they seem to have sent messengers quite independently of their husbands. One Mari princess, Inbatum, was married to the king of Andarig, a vassal kingdom of Mari that was strategically important to Zimri-Lim. On one occasion her father had sent her a messenger with

Bust of a princess from Mari from the time of Zimri-Lim,
showing the elaborate clothing and jewelry worn by royal
women. (Réunion des Musées Nationaux/Art Resource, NY)

a question about affairs in the city of Amaz, apparently asking her what she knew. She described the scene: "I listened to the tablet that my lord (Zimri-Lim) sent me. My lord wrote me many things at length about the city of Amaz."[106] She continued with a short history of what she had learned about Amaz: "For many years, the city of Amaz was following the lead of the land of my lord (her husband). And as that city separated from the side of my lord (her husband), your (Zimri-Lim's) servant…went and returned that city to the city of my lord and subdued that land." Inbatum continued with political details; she was very clear about what had happened in the past regarding the city of Amaz. Then she had some advice. Her husband was away, she said, but she suggested to her father that he confer with him later: "When my lord (her husband) has come back, you and [he] talk among yourselves!" Somewhat confidentially she added, "If that city [is your city], my lord (her husband) will certainly give it to you."

Zimri-Lim must have been grateful for this advice. Inbatum was doing exactly what he needed her to do: providing him with information about the kingdom in which she lived and with insights into how her husband—Zimri-Lim's vassal—was likely to behave.

Other marriages were less successful. One was nothing short of a disaster. Zimri-Lim chose to marry off two of his daughters to the same king, Haya-Sumu of Ilan-Sura. (Kings, unlike ordinary Syrians and Mesopotamians, often took multiple wives.[107]) Haya-Sumu was the overlord of some lesser kings, but was subject to Mari. On the other hand, he seems to have had thoughts of defecting to the king of Elam.[108] Haya-Sumu was a violent and impulsive man, periodically threatening to kill his enemies. "Let a god hand two or else three of my enemies over to me and then I shall cut off their heads," he said on one occasion.[109] This type of inflammatory language was rare in the world of the Mari letters, where, even though kings often grew impatient, they rarely threatened violence.

The two princesses reacted to their unpredictable husband in very different ways. Shimatum, the first to marry him, was initially enthusiastic about her new position in Ilan-Sura. She wrote to her father in almost girlish tones when she first arrived: "Since the day on which [I arrived] from Mari, I have been on the run much. And I saw all their cities."[110] Over time, though, she seems to have become involved in politics, and she was accused of turning against her own father, even to the point of using witchcraft. A worried official told Zimri-Lim: "About the herbs of sorcery that Shimatum sent my lord—that matter is true, not false. My lord must watch that matter closely."[111] She also said "insulting words about my lord (Zimri-Lim)." All this must have made Zimri-Lim despair—his daughter was supposed to be his assistant in Ilan-Sura, not his enemy—so he went to ask the gods for help. When Shimatum suffered an injury, the assumption was that the gods were punishing her for her treachery: "and the god caught her and mutilated her fingers—and (still) seizures befall her."[112]

Perhaps Zimri-Lim thought he would have more luck with the second princess, Kirum, who was sent off as a bride to Haya-Sumu, joining her sister in Ilan-Sura. Kirum was entirely loyal to her father, and she did end up giving birth to a son, so it seemed as though this diplomatic marriage might work well.[113]

But Kirum's situation turned out to be even worse than Shimatum's. She was absolutely miserable in Ilan-Sura. She sent messages through couriers to let Zimri-Lim know that her husband was inattentive—"Haya-Sumu never cares about me"—that her maids had all been taken away from her, and that her sister (and fellow wife) was no support at all. In fact, the sister had treated her badly, saying "I [shall] do to you whatever [I] wish."[114] Kirum grew more and more miserable, complaining that "my life has become short through hearing again and again the word of Shimatum."[115] But as hard as it was for her to live with Shimatum, her sister wasn't Kirum's main problem. She began to fear for her life.

For some reason, Haya-Sumu's explosive temper came to be directed at Kirum. She wrote to Zimri-Lim, perhaps taking a considerable risk when she did so, telling her father that her husband "rose to my face and said.... In the end I will kill you."[116] Zimri-Lim must have been terrified for his daughter, especially when one of his officials witnessed the same threat on a visit to Ilan-Sura. This man heard Haya-Sumu say to Kirum, "If you do not come with me, I will kill you with a bronze dagger and go." The official knew of Haya-Sumu's violent streak and begged Zimri-Lim not to mention this incident to his messenger in case it was reported back to Haya-Sumu: "Now I am afraid my lord will mention that story to his messenger without paying attention and he (Haya-Sumu) will kill, will not let her live."[117]

Kirum saw only one solution to her disastrous marriage: she had to be allowed to return home to Mari. "And he (Zimri-Lim) must send me a trusted person from among his servants, and they must quickly conduct me (to Mari)."[118] Zimri-Lim seems to have agreed; a number of letters refer to various plans for bringing Kirum home. In the meantime, she was growing ever more desperate; anything, she thought, even death, would be better than her current situation. "If my lord does not conduct me to Mari, I will not hesitate to throw myself from the roof," she wrote, then pleading, "You are my only hope."

In the meantime, Haya-Sumu had divorced the miserable Kirum, who was still probably only in her late teens or early twenties. He did this using the traditional gesture, referred to as "severing the hem" in front of witnesses. Kirum described it: "He severed the hem (of) my (garment) before the kings. He (said), 'Go to the house of your father. In the end, I have seen the (real) face of my wife.'"[119] It must have been a wrenching moment for her. She had been humiliated and now divorced, and all she could think about was home: "My lord must dispatch a chariot and a bed...and I shall come to my father and my lord and offer an offering to the gods of my father." Her voice grew wistful as she added, "And there (in Mari) I shall be well."[120]

Probably the chariot did finally arrive to accompany her, along with a wagon for her own transportation, and she gratefully left behind the city of Ilan-Sura and the husband whom she despised and feared. The letters don't mention her again, probably because she was safely back in Mari. Had Haya-Sumu actually killed her, it would surely have provoked some retaliation, or at least a mention in the letters.

Nevertheless, the advantages that came with a good diplomatic marriage seem to have outweighed the risks of a disaster like the union of Haya-Sumu and Kirum.

### A Shared Culture

The immediate diplomatic world of Hammurabi and Zimri-Lim extended throughout Syria and Mesopotamia, and even into Elam. The people who lived there during the Old Babylonian period probably thought that there was little more to the world than these lands. All the scribes across the region wrote in cuneiform, and all of them knew Akkadian, no matter what their native tongue might have been. Akkadian had replaced Sumerian as the dominant language of Mesopotamia by this time, and it served as the international language of diplomacy.[121] These peoples also worshiped most of the same gods and shared a common culture.[122] With so much in common, it is hardly surprising that they were able to find common ground and to agree on principles of diplomatic engagement.[123]

Perhaps more than in earlier times, though, diplomacy was now an accessory to war, rather than an alternative. The Syrian and Mesopotamian kingdoms jostled for power over a finite area; one king's gain in territory was inevitably another king's loss. Each recognized that he could not thrive alone in this environment; he needed allies from the Upper Sea to the Lower Sea, and he needed, as much as he could, to enforce the loyalty of his vassals. Allies might be friendly enough to one another, like Hammurabi and Zimri-Lim, but they used their alliances to strategize in wars against other kingdoms.

### Hammurabi's Empire and the End of Mari

Throughout Zimri-Lim's reign, Hammurabi had been a fixture in his life. His ally had already been on the throne in Babylon for decades when Zimri-Lim became king. Through the early years of Hammurabi's reign, the Babylonian king had seemed content to continue the traditions of his ancestors, ruling wisely, digging new irrigation canals, making alliances with other kings or fighting with them over territory, and venerating the gods by improving their temples and providing for their welfare.[124] But after many years on the throne, he seems to have started dreaming of greater things, changing the whole diplomatic world of his time.

The change began with battles against neighboring kingdoms. Initially, these battles were in self-defense, his borders having been attacked by a former ally, the great eastern kingdom of Elam.[125] But gradually a larger goal seemed to take hold of him: he would be king not just of Babylon, but of the whole world. Ultimately, his conquests took him all the way south to the Lower Sea and north to Mari. In his thirty-fifth year on the throne of Babylon, Hammurabi attacked that city, home to Zimri-Lim, to whom he had formerly vowed brotherhood. Mesopotamians continued to refer to their years by names, not numbers, and Hammurabi named the thirty-fifth year of his reign after the conquest.[126] He burned Zimri-Lim's palace, but not, it seems, until after his soldiers had robbed the place of all its riches (though we can be thankful that they left many of the cuneiform tablets in the archive room).[127]

The empire that Hammurabi created extended throughout much of what is now Iraq. Perhaps he hoped to be seen as a true successor to Sargon. But having united Mesopotamia into a single realm, Hammurabi took a different turn from Sargon. The earlier king had filled his royal inscriptions with accounts of his military might; Sargon "was victorious in thirty-four campaigns and dismantled (all) the cities, as far as the shore of the sea."[128] Hammurabi, although he too noted that he was a "peerless warrior," seems to have wanted more to be seen as "the judicious one," the one who "shows mercy," and "provides abundant waters" for the people, "the pious prince" who was "the shepherd of the people," someone who brought them peace, prosperity, and justice.[129] This may have been one reason why, in the closing years of his reign, he set out his collection of laws and had them inscribed on public monuments.

These monuments not only included the laws—over 280 of them—they also featured a prologue and an epilogue in which Hammurabi extolled his own brilliance and benevolence as king. He had done many good things for his people and their cities. He restored the city of Eridu, enriched the city of

Ur, established the foundations of the city of Sippar, revitalized Uruk, showed mercy to Larsa, Mari, and Tuttul, enlarged Kutu, enlarged the fields of Dilbat, gave life to the city of Adab, and on and on.[130] But in defining the peace that he had brought about, he made it clear that war had been a necessary part: "I annihilated enemies everywhere," he wrote, and in so doing, "I put an end to wars, I enhanced the well-being of the land....I held the people of Sumer and Akkad safely on my lap. They prospered under my protective spirit, I maintained them in peace."[131] In the mind of Hammurabi, and probably in those of the other kings who had formerly been his allies, it seems that war was still necessary in order to create peace.[132]

CHAPTER FOUR

# Long Journeys away from Home

*"Who is there who would sell lapis lazuli?"*

*Far from Mari*

In the 500 years that had passed between the times of Irkab-damu and Zimri-Lim, diplomacy had clearly become a fact of life. The region over which messengers regularly traveled had grown, and the letters sent between kings had become much more detailed. Expressions of "brotherhood" had become more nuanced (and more loaded with the potential to offend) and peace treaties more regular. The system worked, but wars still broke out on a regular basis.

The scribes at Mari mentioned the names of hundreds of cities, towns, and villages in the records that have been found there. The archives reflect only about thirty years of the kingdom's history, and yet some 160 men were identified in the documents as kings—160![1] These were all men with various sorts of ties to the Mari king, men who were categorized as "brother," "son," or "father" (or sometimes "elder brother," if more clarification were needed). One wonders, with so many kings to remember, whether the messengers sometimes had to remind Zimri-Lim about which man was which. Did he, for example, look blankly at his envoy when told that Yumras-El, king of Abi-ili was on his way to Mari to meet with him? Remind me, he might have said, is this the one who has been accused of plotting with his neighboring king? Was his father that man who was so hard of hearing? No, the envoy would have responded, he's the one who came to Mari last time with 300 men.[2] Of course the letters never reveal any such memory lapses on the king's part, but it's a safe guess that the messengers filled their king in about all the details.

Some of the 160 kings must have ruled over tiny realms, but others were as powerful as Zimri-Lim himself. Among the most distant (and powerful) were the kings of Elam and Babylonia—far away, but still within the same cultural world as Mari. They belonged in a shared universe. All the diplomatic relationships described in the previous chapter took place within the realm that included Syria, Mesopotamia, and Elam. No king of Meluhha appears in the records, no king of Crete or Egypt.

But even Zimri-Lim knew that the world extended beyond the lands of his brother kings. Just as in the time of King Irkab-damu at Ebla so many years before, objects and raw materials arrived in Mari from far beyond the lands with which Zimri-Lim had alliances or enmities, peace treaties or wars. Now the contacts with the world beyond that of the brother kings were growing more organized and regular. Increasingly, Mesopotamian and Syrian men traveled to these places, to the sources of valuable goods. Some of these goods were luxuries—such as gold, lapis lazuli, and carnelian—but no great king could do without them. His prestige depended in part on the ostentatious display of objects made from the rarest materials, and gifts he dedicated to the gods had to include them.

Other valuable goods from distant lands had become necessary to the economy. Bronze would have been seen everywhere, in weapons, armor, tools, vessels, and utensils. All the copper and tin used to make it had to be imported. Silver was, by the Old Babylonian period, much more than a beautiful metal for luxury objects; it had become the standard medium of exchange, the basis of the money system. So vastly more copper and silver needed to be imported than gold or semiprecious stones.

Just as changes had taken place in Mesopotamia and Syria since the time of Irkab-damu, so too had changes taken place in the lands of their trading partners, both those that had sent ships to Sargon's port at Akkad and the others whose products arrived there indirectly. Some such changes might even have resulted from the trade and gift exchange. Looking at each of the lands in turn, one sees that connections among some of them had grown closer by the time of Zimri-Lim and Hammurabi, while others had collapsed or had ceased having regular contact with Mesopotamia and Syria.

### Meluhhan Immigrants

A visit to the ancient Indus Valley land of Meluhha in Zimri-Lim's reign would have revealed a profoundly changed place. The great Meluhhan cities

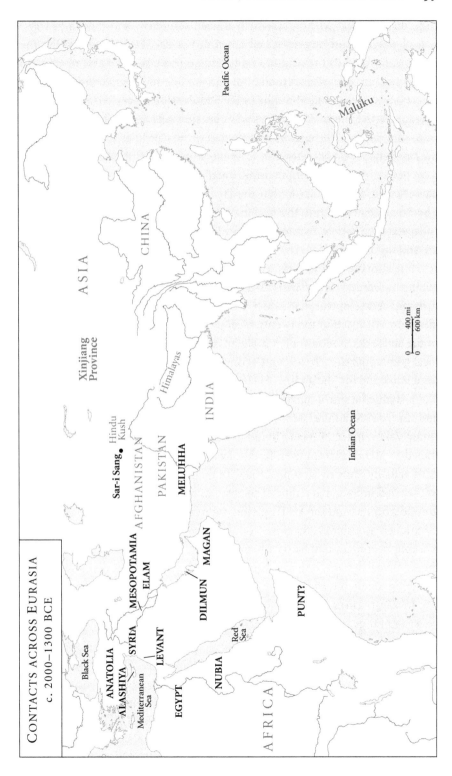

CONTACTS ACROSS EURASIA
c. 2000–1300 BCE

Pacific Ocean

Maluku

CHINA

ASIA

Xinjiang
Province

Hindu
Kush

Sar-i Sang

Himalayas

INDIA

Indian Ocean

0    400 mi
0    600 km

AFGHANISTAN

PAKISTAN

MELUHHA

MESOPOTAMIA

ELAM

MAGAN

DILMUN

PUNT?

SYRIA

LEVANT

Red
Sea

NUBIA

Black Sea

ANATOLIA

ALASHIYA

Mediterranean
Sea

EGYPT

AFRICA

were in ruins, the writing system had been forgotten, and the unified system of weights and measures had fallen out of use. Each region within the Indus Valley had its own culture now, and no more seafaring merchants set off for Dilmun and Mesopotamia.[3] In fact, no one in Mesopotamia seems to have even written about Meluhha in the Old Babylonian period, at least not in documents that survive.[4] No one knows for sure why this brilliant civilization went into decline. Perhaps wars broke out or new peoples arrived. Whatever the case, after 1900 BCE a traveler to some of the old Meluhhan capitals would have been greeted with empty ruins. Small settlements and towns might still have carried on some trade, but the civilization had changed dramatically.[5] The urban centers in Iran that had marked the land route to Mesopotamia had collapsed even earlier. By 2100 BCE, they had been abandoned, for reasons that are still unknown.[6]

But suppose one had visited earlier—in the twenty-second century BCE, about a hundred years after Irkab-damu and Sargon. Then, Meluhha was still thriving. A Mesopotamian leader named Gudea, who ruled the Sumerian kingdom of Lagash in the twenty-second century, used riches from Meluhha in the lavish decorations of a temple he constructed that was dedicated to the local god Ningirsu: "He brought ebony wood from the land of Meluhha and used it to build for [the god].... He brought gold ore from the land of Meluhha and fashioned it into a quiver for him."[7] Gudea also acquired carnelian, lapis, and tin from Meluhha.[8] Most of these goods didn't actually originate in the Indus Valley; in fact, tin isn't found in South Asia at all. They must have been traded to Meluhha from even farther away. According to Gudea, the Meluhhans actually came to Mesopotamia with the luxury goods for his temple, just as they had in Sargon's reign.[9] It seems that some of them even settled there; around 2060 BCE, in the Ur III period, men from the "Meluhha village" were mentioned (in some otherwise routine administrative records) living and working next to local Mesopotamians.[10] The Meluhhan foreigners still spoke their native language, but, to judge from the inscriptions on their seals, it was changing. By then they probably had no direct contact with their homeland.[11]

In Zimri-Lim's time and throughout the Old Babylonian period, Mesopotamian kings still managed to acquire carnelian, and it still probably came from South Asia, but Meluhhan ships were no longer moored at Mesopotamian wharfs. The trade that brought the carnelian west must have been more circuitous.

Lapis lazuli was also still available, finding its way from the Hindu Kush Mountains, but it didn't come through Meluhha anymore either, and it could be hard to acquire. One of Zimri-Lim's officials went to the Mesopotamian city of Larsa in search of lapis lazuli at one point. Zimri-Lim had asked the official to "Turn everything upside down, and lapis-lazuli, be it a lapis-lazuli necklace, be it a lapis-lazuli frog—take silver from a merchant (for it), and I will send you the purchase price of silver from here."[12] But the official had no luck, as he explained to Zimri-Lim: "Not only is there no silver for (buying) lapis-lazuli to be seen in anybody's hand—who is there who would sell lapis-lazuli?" He had been told the reason, though: "Not [one] man comes from Shushim."[13] Shushim was Susa, in Elam. Apparently the lapis traders traveled that way.

Another option, for someone in search of precious stones, was to do a little strategic digging—probably tomb robbing. A young man asked his father to "get me a fine string full of beads, to be worn around the head.... If you have none at hand, dig it out of the ground wherever (such objects) are (found) and send it to me."[14] The son was pretty demanding: "It should be full (of beads) and should be beautiful. If I see it and dislike (?) it, I shall send it back!"

### Gudea's Magan Connection

To the west of Meluhha was Magan in Oman. Here, the copper mines were still active and the towns still occupied in the eighteenth century BCE.[15] Vast amounts of copper were being mined to meet the growing demand across the Near East.

Surprisingly, direct contact with Mesopotamia was minimal; nothing like Manishtusu's earlier invasion of Magan disturbed the peace there. Few, if any, Mesopotamians were in Magan at all, and ships from Magan don't seem to have traveled to Mesopotamia. By the Old Babylonian period, the people of Magan sent their copper to Dilmun, and it was from Dilmun that the Mesopotamians acquired it.[16]

Things here too had changed a lot over the four hundred years since Gudea's time. Back then, Magan, like Meluhha, still had direct ties with his kingdom, as it had with the earlier kingdom founded by Sargon. In fact, Gudea must have had a special relationship with the place, since he had commissioned any number of statues of his portrait carved out of shiny black diorite from Magan. These statues all show him the same way; a squat, muscular man, usually wearing a round cap. His face was beardless and his bald pate was usually invisible under his cap. Sometimes he was seated, sometimes standing with his hands folded. In one statue he had a tablet on his lap inscribed with a plan of a temple, to highlight his achievements as a builder.[17] Gudea was oddly proud of the fact that his statues were made of stone, without inlay or other precious attachments. He wrote that he had "brought a diorite stone from Magan (and) shaped it into this stone statue.... The statue is (made of) neither precious metal nor lapis lazuli; from neither copper nor tin nor bronze did the man sculpt it."[18] This may, in fact, be the reason why more of his statues survive than of any other leaders in the third and second millennia BCE. If other kings were fond of forging gold or copper statues of themselves (as Gudea implies), it's no wonder that theirs are long gone, having been melted down for other uses. There's not much that can be done to destroy a diorite statue.

The Ur III kings had an even closer relationship with Magan, one that might have brought it into the diplomatic world, even though Magan was so far away. An administrative text shows that King Shulgi received a gift of gold dust from the king of Magan. A later leader of Magan sent a messenger to the king of Ur in 2042; the arrival was noted of "Wedum, the courier of Nadu-beli, *ensi* (governor) of Magan."[19] Perhaps the Ur kings sent messengers back, with the usual letters and gifts.

A visitor to Magan around 2000 BCE would have been rewarded with the sight of Mesopotamian traders bartering wool, textiles, sesame oil, and leather goods in exchange for copper.[20] One such man was named Lu-Enlilla, whose job title specified that he was a "seafarer." When not on a trading expedition, he lived in the city of Ur. The temple of Nanna (the moon god) employed Lu-Enlilla to sell woolen textiles in Magan in order to buy copper.[21] He came home not only with the copper but also with beads, ivory, and special (and presumably delicious) "Magan onions."[22] His must have been an exciting, though perhaps somewhat hazardous, career. The Persian Gulf through which he sailed regularly was blazing hot and humid in summer, even hotter than his native Ur, and in the fall, sudden gales would blow up out of nowhere, buffeting the boats and no doubt capsizing some.

But after Lu-Enlilla's time, the Mesopotamian traders seem to have stopped traveling all the way to Magan for their copper. By the nineteenth century BCE, the sailors who set out in their boats on the Persian Gulf in search of copper headed not for Magan but for the closer shores of Dilmun (Bahrain).[23]

### Ea-nasir, Dilmun Trader

In the early second millennium BCE, the Old Babylonian period in Mesopotamia, Dilmun was booming. It seems to have grown in importance almost in proportion to the decline of Meluhha and the loss of direct Mesopotamian trade with Magan. In place of the small communities that had thrived there in the third millennium was a large city surrounded by an impressive stone wall. Enormous mounds, some of them as much as eighty feet high, housed the burials of Dilmun's powerful leaders.[24] The Dilmunites still didn't have much in the way of local resources—pearls are the only precious item native to the island—but they did a brisk business as brokers. Copper ingots poured in from Magan, and everyone in the Near East needed copper for their bronze weapons and utensils.

As in the case of Magan in the twenty-first century BCE, the ships that passed between Dilmun and Mesopotamia now seem to have been Mesopotamian in origin. On the island of Bahrain, archaeological finds show that the influence of Mesopotamia had come to eclipse that of the Indus Valley—no longer were Indus Valley weights and measures used, no longer were Indus inscriptions found, and the few documents that have been excavated in Dilmun were written in cuneiform.[25] A successor to Lu-Enlilla continued trading on behalf of Ur's temple of the moon god Nanna, but he traveled to Dilmun rather than Magan. His name was Ea-nasir, and he was not just a "seafarer"; he bore a more specific title than that of Lu-Enlilla. Ea-nasir was a "Dilmun trader." We know quite a bit about him from Sir Leonard Woolley's excavations in the city of Ur.

Ea-nasir lived in a neighborhood of medium-sized houses in Ur, about a hundred years before Hammurabi came to the throne. In his house Ea-nasir kept some of the letters that had been written to him when he was in Dilmun, and they were still there on the floors when Woolley excavated.[26] Woolley (somewhat idiosyncratically) named the streets of Ea-nasir's neighborhood after the streets in England; according to him, the Dilmun trader lived at No. 1, Old Street.[27]

The roads in Ur were narrow and labyrinthine. Some led to public squares and busy crossroads, others dead-ended into the doors of the houses at the end. No street signs marked the way, and houses were not identified with names or numbers (signs would have been of little use, anyway, since the vast majority of the population was illiterate). People defined where they lived by the names of their neighbors.[28] No spaces marked where one house ended and another began; all a pedestrian on the street would have seen was a long, high mud-brick wall interrupted here and there by a front door. The ends of the beams supporting the roofs probably jutted out at the top of the walls. There were no front or back yards to houses, no sidewalks, no windows onto the streets that we know of, and almost no visible clues about the homes that lay beyond the closed wooden doors.

It was probably loud in the streets—the Mesopotamians were forever worrying about upsetting the gods with all their noise. The gods needed their sleep, and the din of people and animals in the streets around the temples threatened to keep them awake.[29] During the days, the streets were crowded

10    5    0         10         20         30         40         50
S C A L E    O F    M E T R E S

Plan of an Ur neighborhood in the time of King Rim-Sin of Larsa. Ea-nasir, the
trader, lived in the highlighted house at No. 1 Old Street. (©Trustees of the British
Museum)

with men, women, and children, along with donkeys and carts. The smells
were, no doubt, pungent as well—smells of cooking, sweat, and waste (human
and animal) all mingled together.

The front door to Ea-nasir's house didn't open directly onto Old Street but
was reached by a very narrow alleyway, no wider than a doorway. This would
have made the house especially difficult to find. But once inside, a visitor
would have been impressed. Ea-nasir's was a comfortable house, with a shady
courtyard surrounded by five rooms on the ground floor and probably a similar number on an upper floor as well. All next-door neighbors shared walls—
there was no space at all between the houses—and sometimes a homeowner

would purchase just a couple of rooms from a neighbor, rooms that would then be walled off on one side and opened up with doors into the new owner's house. That is what Ea-nasir (or some previous owner of the house) had done at some earlier time—he had blocked off two rooms and sold them to his neighbor, who had added a door to make them part of his own house.[30]

But Ea-nasir wasn't in Ur all the time. Like Lu-Enlilla before him, he seems to have traveled regularly, taking his boat to Dilmun, loaded with textiles and silver to pay for vast quantities of copper.[31] One tablet mentions a shipment of 13,000 minas (pounds) of it.[32] He also brought back other items, such as small objects made of carnelian, lapis lazuli, white coral, gold, and ivory that he could easily sell in Ur; the ivory and carnelian probably came to Dilmun all the way from South Asia.[33]

Ea-nasir traded not only on behalf of the temple but also for private individuals, and the letters that he kept show that they weren't always happy with the copper that he procured for them. One man wrote in a fury to complain that Ea-nasir had shown his messenger poor-quality copper and had then refused to show him anything better. The writer was incensed: "Who am I that you are treating me in this manner and offending me?...Who is there among the Dilmun traders who has ever acted against me in this way?"[34] Those "Dilmun traders"—a whole group of merchants who shared Ea-nasir's specialized knowledge of boats, sea travel, copper trading, and finance, and who, presumably, had a familiarity with the language of Dilmun—provided an important resource for the Mesopotamians. They seem also to have made a good living.[35]

Ea-nasir's neighbors included a scribe, a metalworker, and a cook; they no doubt heard from Ea-nasir about his travels. Dilmun would not have seemed quite so exotic or distant when he regaled them with his tales. In fact, for a brief time it seemed that Dilmun might become part of the diplomatic world of Syria and Mesopotamia.

### Dilmun Ambassadors Visit Mesopotamia

Around the same time that Ea-nasir was making his trading journeys, King Shamshi-Adad did more than support trade with Dilmun. He seems to have wanted to know more about the distant land, so he sent envoys to visit the king of Dilmun, as perhaps the Ur III kings had previously done in Magan.

Shamshi-Adad (the father of Ishme-Dagan) had no doubt about his own importance to the world. Instead of using the title "king of Assyria" or "king of Ekallatum" (either of which might have been the name of his realm), he referred to himself as "king of the universe."[36] His ambition was reminiscent of Sargon of Akkad. Shamshi-Adad not only controlled a vast stretch of the Near East, he also claimed to have "received the tribute of the kings of Tukrish and the king of the upper land"—that is, lands to the east and north of his kingdom. Although he might have wanted his subjects to think that this "tribute" was an outright gift, it is more likely to have been one half of an exchange of goods. To the west he set up "memorials in the land of Lebanon on the shore of the Great Ocean."[37] How much more of the universe could there be? Shamshi-Adad must have wanted people to believe that there wasn't much that he didn't control. But in fact he must have known that his claim to be "king of the universe" was a wild exaggeration and that many lands lay beyond his grasp; Dilmun was one of them, as were the other lands from which luxury goods could be obtained.

One of Shamshi-Adad's capitals was at the city of Ashur on the Tigris River. This was later to become the spiritual center for the huge and powerful Neo-Assyrian Empire, but when Shamshi-Adad reigned, that was still over 900 years in the future. Nevertheless, Ashur was already an important city in Shamshi-Adad's time.[38] One highlight of the city was its temple to the god Enlil. Shamshi-Adad boasted in an inscription about how elaborately he had rebuilt this temple. He provided it with a cedar roof—the cedar probably came from the forests in Lebanon—and the walls were coated with a particularly extravagant "plaster of silver, gold, lapis lazuli, carnelian, cedar oil, fine oil, honey and butter."[39] Besides the oil, honey, and butter, all those ingredients came from beyond his empire. It's hard to imagine just how this plaster worked—perhaps the precious stones and metals were set in the plaster to create designs. The walls would have sparkled in the light from the lamps that illuminated the sacred space. Even the cedar doors to the temple were studded with silver and gold stars. Anyone setting foot in the temple would have known exactly how rich Shamshi-Adad was, which was just as he wanted it.

Shamshi-Adad needed goods from the south for building projects like this one, and he might well have sponsored traders who headed for Dilmun to acquire them. His diplomatic mission to the king of Dilmun was something different, though. We know about it because, at Mari, among Zimri-Lim's own records, were found many earlier letters from the time of Shamshi-Adad, when Mari was part of his empire.

The letters relating to the Dilmun expedition start when his envoys had already visited the island and, accompanied by some high officials from Dilmun, were back in Mesopotamia. These men probably traveled with many attendants, befitting their status. Shamshi-Adad wanted to stay informed about their progress as they made their way north toward his kingdom, so his messengers sped on ahead from the expedition to report back to him.

One messenger brought a letter to let the king know that the members of the diplomatic expedition would soon be passing through Babylon. Another letter noted that they continued their journey to Mari. For some reason, one of the Dilmun men decided to stay put in Mari rather than venturing on north to Shamshi-Adad's capital, and this annoyed the king greatly. The rest of the Dilmun delegation did eventually arrive at Shamshi-Adad's palace, but the meeting between them isn't recorded in any of the letters. One administrative document records that an ornate jar of some sort of special oil was provided for the king of Dilmun.[40] This must have been an expensive present for the envoys to take back home to their king; perhaps it was presented during the audience.

Dilmun doesn't seem to have remained a part of the diplomatic world of the Mesopotamian and Syrian states after this one expedition—trade was the glue that tied it to Mesopotamia, not diplomacy—but Shamshi-Adad's expedition marks an intriguing attempt at extending that world. One wonders what the Dilmun officials thought of the Mesopotamian cities they traveled through and what sort of reception they received. Did the kings exchange letters? Had the Dilmun king sent any sort of gift for Shamshi-Adad? If so, this exchange might have been comparable to Shamshi-Adad's relationship with those kings of Tukrish and the upper lands that he mentioned receiving "tribute" from.

Later, Hammurabi seems to have disrupted the Dilmun copper trade when he took control of Ur.[41] He might have moved the "Dilmun traders" to a different town, or perhaps another neighborhood in Ur. In any event their documents, if they existed, haven't been found. Dilmun's heady days of prosperity seem to have been coming to an end by this time. The Mesopotamians increasingly turned away from their old southern partners when seeking luxury goods, and toward the north and west.

### Assyrian Traders in Anatolia

While visiting the city of Ashur in the time of Shamshi-Adad, one might have seen, in the streets outside some of the private houses, many black donkeys, each being loaded with about 150 pounds of goods—large textiles (probably in rolls) and ingots of tin.[42] This scene marked the preparations of some prosperous traders for a remarkable mission. They regularly took whole caravans of these donkeys on a trip of over 600 miles. First they traveled to the west, right across northern Mesopotamia, then through a pass in the Taurus Mountains, and then northwards, up onto the Anatolian Plateau, ending at the city of Kanesh. Once there, the goods (along with the donkeys) were traded for silver and gold, which would be brought back to Ashur. The people of Ashur—Assyrians—controlled this very lucrative trade, and had done so since around 1900 BCE.

This might sound, at first glance, like an overland version of Ea-nasir's trips to Dilmun, and it might indeed have been similar. But whereas only a few cuneiform tablets attest to the Dilmun traders' lives, around 23,000 tablets have been found that were written to expedite the Assyrian trade in Anatolia.[43] And whereas Ea-nasir seems to have worked for the temple in Ur, the Assyrian traders were independent entrepreneurs, beholden neither to their king nor to a particular temple. The southern cities were, by now, powerfully dominated by their kings, but power in Ashur had traditionally been held by the city itself, as a collective authority. This gave entrepreneurs an opportunity to work much more autonomously than would have been possible in Babylonia.

The trade network between Ashur and Anatolia was the work of a number of businessmen who had found, in creating this connection, a clever way to obtain silver and gold, which were highly valued back home in Mesopotamia. One could pay for most things with pieces of silver; they could be cut off a coil (perhaps wrapped around a man's wrist) and weighed by a merchant against a set of standard weights. Even though coinage wasn't invented until a thousand years after this, the silver was used as money.

Kanesh, their destination, was an impressive place, the biggest of all the Anatolian cities in the early second millennium, built on a tell that rose sixty-five feet above the surrounding fields. A large three-acre palace for the local king stood in the center of the city.[44] Nearby were a number of temples for the gods, and a high wall surrounded the city for defense.

At the end of their long journey, the Assyrian traders would have headed first for the palace. A local official broke the seals on the tin and the textiles, making sure that no one had removed (or sold) anything along the way. The traders then had to pay taxes on the goods they had brought.[45] They also had a formal agreement whereby the local authorities could purchase up to 10 percent of each shipment for a set price.[46] The Assyrians promised, in these same treaties with the local kings, not to smuggle goods into the land.[47] The arrangement suited the Assyrians, since in exchange the local administration kept the roads safe for the merchants and even reimbursed them if they were robbed.[48] (The letters show, though, that smuggling wasn't unheard of, and that the Anatolian kings threw smugglers in jail.)

After visiting the palace, the traders could leave the city center and drive their donkeys down into a sprawling community at the base of the tell, the *karum*, or commercial quarter. The journey from Ashur took over a month, and, understandably, men who traveled to Kanesh didn't necessarily turn right around and go home again.[49] Some of them stayed in the *karum.* Some, indeed, bought houses and settled down there. This was no shantytown. The mud-brick buildings were built on sturdy stone foundations along paved streets.[50] In the summers the shade of the densely packed buildings might have provided some relief from the intense heat, and they would also have helped people survive the bitter cold of the Anatolian winter. Not many locals lived in this part of town; the houses were largely home to Assyrians who had settled in Kanesh in order to do business.

A number of other Anatolian cities had their own *karums* of Assyrian traders, who monopolized business in this region, but the one at Kanesh was the biggest.[51] On the other hand, there were areas where, apparently according to international agreements, the Assyrians weren't allowed to trade, such as in the coastal plain south of the Taurus Mountains that later came to be called Kizzuwatna. Although the Assyrians had to pass through the area in order to get to Kanesh, long-distance trade there was in the hands of another city, possibly Ebla.[52]

Over seventy of the houses in Kanesh, when excavated, were found to contain the cuneiform archives of Assyrian businessmen—letters, lists, notes, memos, loan contracts, and court records—that provide an astounding level of detail about the trade. Curiously enough, though, if it weren't for the cuneiform tablets, archaeologists would not necessarily have guessed that this was a settlement of foreigners.[53] The Assyrians had adopted the house styles, pottery, and utensils of their Anatolian neighbors, even though they were in regular contact with their families and business partners back home.

The Anatolians with whom the Assyrians traded were a sophisticated bunch. The communities in this region had been rich for thousands of years, benefiting from the bountiful resources in the very rocks that surrounded their communities—first, volcanic obsidian, which made the finest stone tools, and then silver and gold. This was a region that had perhaps been reached by Sargon of Akkad when he forged his empire from the Lower Sea to the Upper Sea (though he didn't conquer Anatolia), but it hadn't depended on Mesopotamia to provide the impetus for urbanization. The rocky highlands of the Anatolian plateau were dotted with fortified cities on tall tells, some of which had been occupied since the fourth millennium BCE. The one thing the Anatolians seem not to have invented was a system of writing. Somehow the administrations of these early cities managed without one.

The Anatolians welcomed the Assyrian traders. Their presence in the communities was not the result of a hostile invasion, nor did it represent the harsh hand of a colonial power. Instead, the Assyrians provided valuable goods and sometimes served as bankers. Some of the Assyrians married local women.[54] The traders became respected members of the community. Occasionally, Anatolians even traveled in the opposite direction, to Ashur. The letters tell of a woman of Kanesh named Kunnaniya who had married a trader from a rich Assyrian family.[55] Kunnaniya helped him with his business, and they had children together. Her husband wrote to her when on his travels. After he died, though, she needed to settle matters with her in-laws, so she took the long trip to meet with them in Ashur. She made it there and managed to return home again, months later. But in the meantime, her own sister had moved into her house.[56] Perhaps the sister didn't believe that Kunnaniya would ever come home again.

Over about forty years, the Assyrian traders brought phenomenal quantities of goods to Anatolia, textiles by the tens of thousands and hundreds of tons of tin.[57] The Assyrians were middlemen, though; neither the tin nor the most of the fabrics came directly from Assyria.[58] The finest textiles that they sold originally came from southern Mesopotamia, and the traders asked a far higher price in Anatolia than they had paid the weavers.[59] Sometimes, though, they had difficulties in acquiring the textiles, for example when southern Mesopotamia (which they referred to as Akkad) was experiencing a political crisis. A man in Assyria wrote to his partner in Anatolia: "as to the purchase of Akkadian textiles, about which you wrote me, since you left, the Akkadians have not entered the City [Ashur]; their country is in revolt."[60] But he would do what he could: "If they arrive before the winter, and there is the possibility of a purchase which allows you profit, we will buy (the textiles) for you and we will pay the silver from our own means." But of course this would be a loan, not a gift: "You should take care to send the silver."

The tin that the traders took to Anatolia probably came from Afghanistan, near the source of lapis lazuli, and again, they charged much more for it than they originally paid.[61] It's been estimated that the traders could make as much as a 200 percent profit (though their expenses would have come out of that amount).[62]

The journeys of these traders, their sales, interactions with the locals, smuggling attempts, and sometimes strained relationships with family members back home are all recorded on the cuneiform documents that they left in their houses in Anatolian cities.[63] As in the case of Dilmun, by the early second millennium BCE Mesopotamians were moving out into the areas with which they traded most extensively and influencing the people with whom they came in contact.

The Assyrian traders introduced literacy to the Anatolian civilization, and a few Anatolians may have learned to write in cuneiform. Surprisingly, though, writing didn't spread, and the local people didn't adopt cuneiform just yet.[64]

No one knows exactly why, but the extensive trade between Assyria and Anatolia collapsed around 1750 BCE, right around the time that Hammurabi died. Probably traders continued to travel back and forth, since silver would still have been needed in Mesopotamia and tin in Anatolia, but perhaps it took place on a smaller scale, without the necessity for Mesopotamians to continue to reside in Anatolian towns. At any rate, their cuneiform tablets are no longer found.

Another change was taking place around this same time in Anatolia: the increasing dominance of a group of people who spoke a language we call Hittite (their land came to be known as Hatti). The Hittite language was Indo-European and is therefore related to most modern European languages; it was the earliest Indo-European language to be written down, but far from the earliest to be spoken. It was quite distinct from the earlier Hattic language that had been spoken in Anatolia. Hittite-speaking peoples seem to have arrived in Anatolia in the third millennium BCE, bringing with them their gods and traditions.[65] Later they came to dominate the land.

### Zimri-Lim Travels to the Mediterranean

The traders and messengers who took to the roads in this era would often have encountered military contingents on the march, and sometimes even royal caravans. Zimri-Lim of Mari once took an entourage of his officials and servants west all the way to the Mediterranean coast.[66]

He wasn't just on a sightseeing vacation; the journey to the coast was, in part, to accompany troops who would be serving there for the king of Yamhad. But it also gave Zimri-Lim a chance to pay a state visit to Aleppo, to see the king of Yamhad himself. This king was Zimri-Lim's father-in-law, and might have played a role in his rise to power—the king of Yamhad claimed to have put Zimri-Lim on the Mari throne. Over 4,000 people traveled with Zimri-Lim on this expedition, most of them soldiers, but he also took many members of his court, including wives, officials, artisans, servants, and a diplomatic corps of one hundred envoys and sixty-four runners.[67] They set out in April and didn't return to Mari until around October.

The king and his entourage must have been quite a sight to see as they traveled the land. The first part of his journey took well over a month, as Zimri-Lim went out of his way to visit towns in his kingdom and vassals who owed him allegiance. This wasn't a military campaign, but it no doubt had a similar effect in intimidating vassals who might have been thinking about rebellion. It's not surprising that he made a stop at the court of Haya-Sumu, his mercurial son-in-law who made Princess Kirum's life so difficult. The vassals gave Zimri-Lim presents that assured him of their continued support. By the time he got to Aleppo, it was time for Zimri-Lim to do the gift-giving. He had brought over 1,000 pounds of tin along with him (probably loaded on donkeys or in wagons) to give to his allies, the kings and other important persons in the western lands of Yamhad, Ugarit, Qatna, and Hazor.[68] He spent several weeks in Aleppo, no doubt enjoying the hospitality of his host, while his envoys traveled to nearby kingdoms to present and receive gifts. Then, in July, he journeyed on to the city of Ugarit on the coast.[69]

Perhaps Zimri-Lim had never seen the sea before. What must he have thought on first glimpsing the crisp deep blue line that marked the meeting of sea and sky? His people believed that this sea surrounded the earth, so one would have thought that the horizon marked the edge of the world, right there within sight. But Zimri-Lim knew already that this was not the edge—there were people who lived beyond the horizon on islands called Kaptara (now Crete) and Alashiya (Cyprus).[70] In fact, his officials sold some of the tin that Zimri-Lim had brought with him to the chief merchant from Kaptara. They also paid twenty shekels of tin to a translator who helped with the transaction.[71]

Zimri-Lim might have come across people from Crete in other places during his stay. He visited a village called Alahtum (probably later called Alalakh) during his month-long vacation in Ugarit, and there he might have seen artists from Kaptara decorating the walls with frescoes in the Aegean style.[72] (This style, and the whole Bronze Age civilization on Crete, is known as Minoan because the British excavators who first encountered it saw a connection to the mythical King Minos of Greek legend.)

Such wall paintings (and even floor paintings) were all the rage in the Levant at the time. The rulers at Qatna and at a place now called Tel Kabri had some too—beautiful landscapes with palm trees, papyrus plants, and wild animals, and seascapes with leaping dolphins. The artists used a distinctly Minoan style, with the paint initially being applied while the plaster was still wet.[73] This might be evidence of something more than just a trade connection; perhaps the web of gift exchanges and diplomatic relationships that spread across Syria and Mesopotamia might by now have even extended to Crete.[74] In this case, it's possible that the services of Minoan artists were offered as a gift by the king on Crete to his counterparts at Alalakh, Qatna, and Kabri. This wouldn't be unusual for the time. The tablets from Mari record all kinds of professionals and artists being sent from one city to another: musicians, physicians, gymnasts, diviners, barbers, translators, and on and on.[75] They weren't slaves being presented as gifts by one king to another, but well-regarded specialists whose expertise was needed wherever they went. After their services had been rendered, most seem to have been allowed to return home.

After about a month in Ugarit, Zimri-Lim took the road back to Mari, back to dealing with the intrigues and skirmishes with enemies that dominated his reign.[76] But he had a reminder, right there on the walls of his palace, of his visit to the coast. The artists who painted the walls at Zimri-Lim's own palace at Mari had been influenced by the same Aegean style that he had seen in Alalakh. Although most of the scenes at Mari were of a more sober, Mesopotamian type (showing, for example, stately processions of tribute bearers and the king being invested by a goddess), the borders around the paintings exploded with Aegean running spirals and colorful imitation marble.[77] Zimri-Lim must have talked quite a bit about the marvels of his palace at Mari while he was away. His friend, the king of Ugarit, expressed a desire to come and visit Mari just in order to see the palace, and may have done so.[78]

## Seafarers from Kaptara and Alashiya

The urban civilization that was flourishing in Crete had been developing from the time that Hammurabi's ancestors first began to rule in Babylon, around 2000 BCE.[79] The towns in Crete were not fortified, unlike those in Mesopotamia and Syria, and they were centered around extensive monumental structures that were probably palaces. The uncertainty on this point, and many others, comes from the fact that the Minoans on Crete—just like the Meluhhans in the Indus Valley region—wrote in a script that has not yet been deciphered. Actually, they used two. The earlier script was hieroglyphic; the later one, which was invented around the time that Hammurabi was creating his empire, was relatively simple and nonpictorial (it's known as Linear A), but not much has survived of either.[80] Only around 2,000 characters—not documents, 2,000 individual written signs—survive in the hieroglyphic script, and only about 7,500 characters in Linear A, on about 1,500 (mostly broken) clay tablets and other objects.[81] That means that each Linear A inscription averages just five signs. Almost certainly the Minoans wrote most of their texts on some organic substance that is long lost. With so little evidence remaining, perhaps it's no wonder that neither script has been deciphered yet. (Later Greeks who adopted the Minoan linear script used it to write their own language; this script—Linear B—has been deciphered.)

Without texts, we are at a loss to make many definitive statements about the Minoan culture. Perhaps they had kings. No monumental statues of kings have been found, but then that's true of Zimri-Lim's palace at Mari as well, and there's no doubt that Mari had a tradition of kingship. No monumental temples were found on Crete either, whereas every Mesopotamian city had multiple temples, but the Minoans were certainly religious.

We do know that the Minoans were seafarers, trading their wares across the Mediterranean. They needed metals, which were not native to their island, so they obtained tin from Mari and copper from Cyprus, and they probably got gold from Egypt. With these raw materials they created highly sophisticated metal vessels, figurines, and swords.[82] This raises the question, what did the Minoans provide in exchange? They had plenty of olive trees and vines from which to produce oil and wine, and analysis of some Minoan pottery has revealed that they manufactured perfumed oils that would have been valued not just as perfume but also in medicine and religious ceremonies.[83] They probably also traded other goods that leave few archaeological traces, like expensive purple dye (from crushed murex shells), spices, honey, and textiles. Although any group of people could make textiles, those from foreign lands like Crete might have been highly valued and appreciated because of their quality (as was the case for the textiles from southern Mesopotamia), or simply because of their rarity. Objects made in Crete from metal and semiprecious stones (the raw materials having been first imported to Crete) would have been valuable trade goods as well.[84] Texts from Mari mention leather shoes, clothing, metal vases, and weapons from Crete, though no such objects were found in the palace.[85] The shoes and clothing would long since have disintegrated, and the metal objects might well have been melted down and reused.

Archaeological evidence confirms that the Minoans had ties to both the Eastern Mediterranean region and Egypt.[86] The Minoan relationship with Egypt seems to have been strong, to judge from the extent of the finds. Some fragments of Minoan pots even showed up in a village in Egypt built in the 1870s BCE for workmen who were constructing a pyramid.[87] It's an odd place for them to be, so far from the halls of power, and the pots were ordinary ones, not luxury vessels. Perhaps they belonged to some Minoan workers who were helping to build the pyramid (though one wonders what role they might have played, and how they might have been recruited), or perhaps to a Minoan wife of an Egyptian workman.[88] The land of Keftiu (the Egyptian spelling for Kaptara) is mentioned in just one known text from Egypt at this time, though it was named many more times later.[89] Many Egyptian objects have been found in Crete as well—all manner of jars, stone bowls, amulets, statuettes, scarabs and beads—far outnumbering objects from the Levant, Cyprus, Anatolia, or Mesopotamia.[90] Many scholars also detect Egyptian influences in Minoan art.[91]

A few dozen objects from the Levant have been found in Crete, and, in the opposite direction, several hundred pots from Crete have been found in the Levant.[92] Many of these weren't storage pots that might have been used to transport liquids but cups and jars used for drinking. Were they trade goods? It seems unlikely, because they're not especially finely made. Perhaps the vessels were used by Minoans living away from home in the cosmopolitan centers of Ugarit, Byblos, and other coastal towns. If only a cuneiform letter from, say, the ruler of Alalakh were to materialize on an excavation in Crete, we would know much more about how Crete fit into the international world of the time.

Oddly enough, not a single Minoan object has shown up anywhere in Mesopotamia proper, even though Mesopotamian cities were trading with the same coastal Mediterranean ports as the Minoans. A lone Mesopotamian seal and a separate seal impression found in Crete provide the sole evidence of any direct connection between the Minoans and the Mesopotamians.[93]

Not only did Mari sell tin to Crete, it also obtained copper from Cyprus, which was known as Alashiya. Alashiya was becoming an important alternative to Magan and Dilmun when Mesopotamian and Syrian kingdoms sought copper for their bronzes. Alashiya had other contacts in Syria as well. A cuneiform list from a site near the Syrian coast mentions objects that came from Alashiya.[94] Archaeological finds on the island of Cyprus show that this was just when the earliest towns began to be built there and the first copper mines began to be worked.[95] Zimri-Lim might well have met some Alashiyan merchants in Ugarit during his visit, and seen their boats setting out across the Mediterranean.

These islands seem, though, to have been beyond the reach of Syrian or Mesopotamian boats at this time. No groups of Mesopotamian- or Syrian-based "Kaptaran traders" are mentioned in the documents who might have taken on the role that Ea-nasir enjoyed in Dilmun, and no cuneiform tablets have been found on Crete or Cyprus from this era; there was nothing (so far as we know) like the *karum* communities in Anatolian cities.

But perhaps this was not true of Egypt. Amenemhet II, of the powerful Twelfth Dynasty, claimed to have conquered Cyprus during his reign.[96] This seems impossibly unlikely. The Egyptians had no navy, and all other indications suggest that Alashiya was independent. But perhaps Egyptian trading boats did venture to the island.

### An Egyptian Official in Exile in the Levant

This brings us to a strange fact: not only were the Kaptarans close to invisible in finds from Mesopotamia during the Old Babylonian period, so too were the Egyptians. Throughout this era, not a single mention of the land of Egypt has yet been found on any tablet from Mesopotamia, from the beginning of the second millennium to the end of the sixteenth century BCE.[97] And yet, at the beginning of the Old Babylonian period, Egypt was enjoying one of its zeniths, under the kings of the Middle Kingdom. It was also in close contact with the Levant.

Right around the same time that Amorite kings were coming to power in Mesopotamian and Syrian cities, the Twelfth Dynasty arose in Egypt (it began in 1985 BCE). During the same two centuries that the Amorite kingdoms vied with one another and created their whole web of alliances, the kings of the Twelfth Dynasty (all of them named either Amenemhet or Senusret) oversaw innumerable projects that strengthened Egypt and its economy. They reclaimed land from a lake to add to Egypt's agricultural wealth, they sponsored expeditions and opened up copper and turquoise mines, and they traded with coastal cities in the Levant, especially with Byblos.[98] The vizier of Egypt was in charge of preparing the boats that undertook this trade. According to one story from the time, a boat destined for Byblos docked near the king's palace (the "Residence"), at a field owned by the vizier, and the vizier "loaded a Byblos-boat of the palace...with every good thing...from his house."[99] Not everyone was working hard, though. In an aside, the author noted that: "They spent the whole day (working) while his son [made holi]day." Byblos was more Egyptian than ever by this time. The rulers there even wrote their inscriptions in Egyptian hieroglyphs, using cartouches for their names, just like the Egyptian kings.[100]

A compelling story was written down during the Twelfth Dynasty, purportedly an autobiography of an Egyptian official. It may or may not be the story of a real man, but that doesn't really matter, since it gives us a vivid picture of relations between Egypt and the Levant that must have been based on fact. The official's name was Sinuhe. He was an honest man, someone who served his king and queen loyally and would have done anything for them. But he found himself in a tough spot. He worked for the queen during the reign of Amenemhet I. The king was assassinated by members of his own bodyguard while sleeping, and women in the court were in some way implicated. Sinuhe was horror-struck when he overheard this news. He was innocent of any wrongdoing, but he knew that he was in danger. He saw no option but to flee. In secrecy, he headed north, out of Egypt, to Canaan in the Levant. He had to crouch behind bushes when he came to the wall at the border of Egypt; it was hardly a dignified moment for such an important man. From there, his journey was a nightmare as he crossed the desert. Sinuhe was so thirsty that he groaned, "This is the taste of death!"[101]

Sinuhe initially headed for Byblos, but didn't end up there. Instead, he traveled inland to a rural area called Yaa, where the local leader took him in and took pity on him. He gave him not only food and drink but a place to live, along with land to farm. Yaa must have been on the road to Egypt, because the leader assured Sinuhe, when he first arrived, that "you will hear the language of Egypt." This proved to be true. Sinuhe's new home became a regular stop for messengers traveling to and from Egypt. Sinuhe confided that "the envoy who came north or went south to the residence (the Egyptian capital) stayed with me. I let everyone stay with me." The Egyptian travelers must have been relieved to find a countryman living so far from home. Sinuhe didn't just invite these Egyptians in, he gave them directions if they needed them, gave them something to drink, and even rescued people who had been robbed. In his conversations, he no doubt learned a lot about what was going on in Egypt.

In turn, he probably told the Egyptians quite a bit about his life in Yaa. He had a good life there. He had married the eldest daughter of his mentor, and she had borne them children. He owned a large herd of cattle, and his orchards were planted with fig trees, olive trees, and grapevines. "Abundant was its honey," he wrote of Yaa, "plentiful its oil. All kinds of fruit were on its trees. Barley was there, and emmer, and no end of cattle of all kinds." He gave up looking like an Egyptian, instead growing his beard long like the Canaanites. He probably wore the brightly colored and boldly patterned clothes that Canaanites loved rather than the plain white linen garments of Egypt. He must have learned to speak the local language, and perhaps people came to be surprised to hear him speak Egyptian.

Although Sinuhe looked and lived like a Canaanite he never stopped hoping that he might return to Egypt. Some of the messengers who stayed with him when journeying through Yaa must have told the king about him, because eventually Sinuhe received the message he had been waiting for. The king, Senusret I, sent a formal royal decree, inviting Sinuhe to return home.

Sinuhe didn't hesitate. He put his grown son in charge of his land and went back to Egypt immediately, accompanied by the Egyptian messengers who had summoned him. Senusret I, who had not seen Sinuhe in decades, could scarcely believe that this Canaanite chief was the same official who had served his father. He remarked to the queen: "Here is Sinuhe, come as an Asiatic, a product of nomads!" She was astounded. "She uttered a very great cry, and the royal children shrieked all together. They said to his majesty: 'Is it really he, O king, our lord?' Said his majesty: 'It is really he!'" Sinuhe spent the rest of his life as a guest of the palace, giving up his Canaanite clothing, "clothed in fine linen" and "anointed with fine oil."

Sinuhe's tale must have been popular. Many copies of it have been found in Egypt. It reminded the Egyptians, like some sort of Middle Kingdom Wizard of Oz tale, that there's no place like home (as long as home was in Egypt). But it also told them that the world beyond the Nile wasn't all that bad. It wasn't chaotic or barbaric, as the Egyptians had generally believed non-Egyptian lands to be. The people there had treated Sinuhe well and he had been happy there. "It was a good land," Sinuhe said.

Not all Twelfth-Dynasty literature was so open-minded about the outside world, though. The kings don't seem to have always shared Sinuhe's respect for foreigners. Their treatment of the Nubians to the south and some of the Canaanites to the north of Egypt was sometimes brutal. One king called himself "the throat-slitter of Asia."[102] Another described the Nubians as "not people to be respected—they are wretches," and went on to brag about how he had treated them: "I have plundered their women, and carried off their underlings, gone to their wells, driven off their bulls, torn up their corn, and put fire to it."[103]

At about the same time that Hammurabi began to conquer lands to the north and south of Babylon, unifying Mesopotamia under his rule, Egypt experienced the opposite—it began suffering a decline that ended up with the land divided. One mace head found in Ebla seems to be from Egypt at this time, the Thirteenth Dynasty, providing a clue to some sort of contact with Syria.[104] It bears a name in golden Egyptian hieroglyphs, Hotepibre, which is the name of an obscure Egyptian king.[105] But scholars can't agree on almost anything about this object; the more they study it, the less it seems to say. The hieroglyphs in the king's name are not all the right way up or in the right order. Some scholars believe the object itself may not even be Egyptian, with only the hieroglyphic inscription having been imported (and muddled). Others think that it was a real object, damaged and repaired in Ebla by artisans who couldn't read hieroglyphs.[106] The slightly underwhelming conclusion about this object is that someone at Ebla during the Old Babylonian period had access to some hieroglyphic characters that were produced in Egypt. But given how little Egyptian contact of any kind can be proven with Syria or Mesopotamia in the Old Babylonian period, this is perhaps noteworthy anyway.

Of course it's possible that the relevant documents just haven't been found yet and that the Mesopotamians were, in fact, aware of the existence of Egypt in the Middle Kingdom. A single fragment of a Babylonian letter, found at a site in the Egyptian delta, shows that by the end of the Old Babylonian period the Babylonians had some diplomatic contact with Egypt.[107] But northern Egypt was, by then, in the grip of a foreign dynasty.

### Southeast Asian Spices in a Syrian Pantry

There is one more piece of evidence of trading relationships to consider, and it's a very strange one. In the city of Terqa, to the north of Mari, archaeologists have excavated a neighborhood not unlike the one where Ea-nasir lived in Ur. It was occupied a couple of centuries after Ea-nasir's time, though, and after Hammurabi had conquered Mari. Terqa, which lay beyond the limits of Hammurabi's empire, had replaced Mari as the most important city in the region. In this neighborhood of the city, houses were lined up along a narrow lane opposite a small shrine, and one of these unassuming homes held a remarkable, almost unbelievable, piece of evidence for long-distance trade. The house belonged to a farmer and landowner named Puzurum.[108] He was not especially wealthy and he was not a foreign trader, but he was affluent enough to have bought and sold a few fields in his lifetime. In his pantry were found dozens of pots, which the archaeologists cleaned carefully, looking for any evidence of what they might have contained. At the bottom of one they discovered a few cloves.[109] This might seem unimpressive—a jar of cloves could be found in almost any kitchen today, after all. But their presence in Syria in the eighteenth century BCE is remarkable. These cloves, if that is what they are, could be from only one place: the islands in northern Maluku in Indonesia.[110] This reflects by far the earliest contact between the Near East and Southeast Asia, the earliest by about 1700 years. But it's just so strange. Why would an ordinary citizen like Puzurum have access to such an exotic spice unless cloves were fairly widely available? And if they were widely available, why haven't more been found? Have other archaeologists been less meticulous in cleaning out excavated pots? If they are real, how did the cloves make it all the way to Terqa at such an early date?

Perhaps future finds will show that desired goods were traded, from person to person, thousands of miles farther than we now suspect, even if no one from Mesopotamia had even the vaguest notion that the Southeast Asian islands existed.

One puzzling question is whether any Near Eastern influence can be detected in ancient China, where the earliest urban civilizations began to appear around the time of the Old Babylonian kings of Mesopotamia. Most scholars view the Chinese developments as independent. The writing system, bronzes, and cities might well have grown out of local predecessors; there's nothing notably foreign about them. On the other hand, the Chinese did begin cultivating wheat and herding sheep and goats, none of which are indigenous to the area.

Excavations in what is now the far northwest of China, in the region of Yanghai in Xinjiang province, are uncovering evidence of a people who might have helped bring Near Eastern innovations to China and Chinese innovations to the Near East. Between 2000 and 1500 BCE, this region, which is now a desert, was apparently much wetter, and was home to a people who made jewelry and accessories in bronze and gold, and shared many traits in common with Central Asian peoples of the same time.[111] Some of them lived along the now-dry Peacock River. A woman who died around 2000 BCE was naturally mummified (as were many of the people buried in this region). Her skin and auburn hair survive, along with her wool and fur clothing and a feather that had been placed in her bonnet. Buried with her were a basket and winnowing tray, along with grains of wheat like those she must have carried, winnowed, and ground into flour during her life.[112]

Her people might have helped bring bronze technology and wheat, along with perhaps domesticated cattle, sheep, and goats, from the Near East to China. Earlier inhabitants of this region might also have been instrumental in introducing a Chinese idea to the peoples who lived to the west of them. Domesticated millet was cultivated in China as early as 8000 BCE, much earlier than its use by farmers in the Near East or Europe. Its earliest known Western use was near the Black Sea around 5000 BCE.[113]

The ancient people of Yanghai lived as far away from the ocean as it is possible to be on earth, and far distant from all the major civilizations of the time. They were over 2,000 miles east of Mesopotamia, and hundreds of miles east even of the Hindu Kush Mountains, where the Mesopotamians and Egyptians got their lapis lazuli, hundreds of miles north of the Indus Valley, and well over 1,000 miles west of the cities that first developed in China. But this was land that was, much later, traversed by the Silk Road, when trade in luxury goods across Asia had become almost routine. Some scholars think that future finds will reveal an earlier incarnation of the Silk Road, with much closer connections between western and eastern Asia during the early millennia of civilization than we currently imagine.

# PART III

# A Time of Crisis
# and Change,
# 1595–1400 BCE

CHAPTER FIVE

# Attack on Babylon
# by a Distant Enemy

*"I sent to a far-off land"*

*Hammurabi's Successors*

Up to the time of Hammurabi, diplomacy in the Near East had changed little and slowly. The players were known to one another, they shared a common culture and worshiped many of the same gods, and they understood the roles of messengers, diplomats, dynastic marriages, peace treaties, and gift exchange in their relationships. Except for the Ur III kings' possible diplomatic involvement with Magan and Shamshi-Adad's brief overture to the land of Dilmun, all the diplomatic partners were kings who ruled in the broad arc that stretched from Qatna (in western Syria) east and then south to the Persian Gulf. Their interactions resembled a vast chess game, as each player tried to gain an advantage over his rivals, but they all followed the same rules when it came to war and peace. Even when Hammurabi had upset the system by forging his empire, he was following a precedent; he would have been well aware of Sargon's conquests and those of the Ur III kings hundreds of years before. In the years that followed his death, new forces and powers began to form in the Near East that threatened to destroy the ancient diplomatic system. In the end, though, it was the diplomatic system that prevailed, transforming the new great powers and in turn being transformed by them into a true international community.

After Hammurabi's death, his empire continued to be ruled by his successors—five generations of them, son following father to the throne. But as time went by, their realm came to look less and less like an empire. Almost all the cities of southern Mesopotamia seem to have been abandoned between 1738 and 1720, though the region was not completely depopulated. People probably moved into the countryside, away from the cities.[1] This was a dramatic change; the south had always been a center for culture and religion. The disaster might have started with a drastic flood that resulted in the Euphrates shifting its course away from the cities. The southern fields might also have been growing less productive over time as the soil became more and more salty as a result of water evaporating in the hot sun and pulling salts to the surface.[2]

It wasn't just nature that was a problem. A new enemy also appeared, one that was alien to the diplomatic world of Babylon—a people known as the Kassites, who would ultimately play a major role in Mesopotamian history. Hammurabi's successors recorded several battles against them in the names they gave to the relevant years.[3]

By the time that Hammurabi's great-great-grandson Samsuditana came to the throne in 1625, Babylon's kingdom extended along the Euphrates from Babylon north to the area around Mari and Terqa.[4] Perhaps because modern scholars know that the land was about to be conquered from outside, it's tempting to see Babylon as limping toward ruin, but that's not how its residents would have seen things. Toward the beginning of his reign, Samsuditana probably was still pretty secure in his power. No obvious enemies presented themselves (the Kassites seem to have been laying low at the time), and he commemorated the events of each year in year names that mostly recalled his pious activities for the gods.[5]

In contrast with the epic deeds of his ancestor Hammurabi, Samsuditana seems to have been a self-absorbed, stay-at-home king. His year names mention no kingly activities such as wars or building projects, new canals, or debt cancellations; instead, all thirty-one of the years mention the giving of extravagant gifts for the gods or the setting up of statues of himself in various poses, such as marching, holding a scepter, and presenting a lamb as a gift.[6] These statues—ten of them—were mostly described as being for the gods and were placed in temples, but a certain amount of self-promotion was surely involved as well.[7] Samsuditana was following the lead of his father and grandfather, who had also set up many statues of themselves in temples, but those kings had been more like Hammurabi; they had found time to build cities, dig canals, and cancel debts as well. Sadly, in spite of Samsuditana's efforts, all of the statues have gone missing.

He considered himself to have been chosen by the god Marduk to rule Babylon (his first year was named "Samsuditana, the king, at the supreme command of Marduk, the king who established his reign"), just as Hammurabi and all the intervening Babylonian kings had done.[8] Not that he probably

knew all that much about his famous ancestor; there was no tradition of narrative history in Mesopotamia, and Hammurabi had kept no annals or chroni-
cles of his reign that we know of. Samsuditana may not even have been aware
of how much larger the Babylonian kingdom had been 150 years before. But
he ruled uneventfully for thirty-one years and, as he approached old age, probably thought his own son would soon take over from him.

### Babylon Attacked

Then, suddenly, in 1595 BCE, an enemy appeared outside the walls of Babylon,
an enemy so unexpected that it seems to have barely registered in the minds
of the Babylonian kings up to that time. The enemy forces were commanded
by a king named Mursili. (One form of his name was Mursilis, which sounds
like the word "merciless," a coincidence that fits the personality of this king
well.) The Babylonian kings had fought Kassites, Elamites, and many others,
but this new enemy was apparently unknown to them: Hittites, from the faraway Anatolian land of Hatti, about 700 miles northwest of Babylon, beyond
the Taurus Mountains.

The textbook image of the Hittites descending on Babylon casts them as
"barbarians," but that's a mistake. Their civilization had a long pedigree by the
time Mursili took the throne. The Hittites had started appearing in Anatolia
hundreds of years earlier and had adopted the culture of the local peoples of
Kanesh and other major cities.[9] They worked gold and silver into beautiful
jewelry and vessels, they forged strong weapons out of bronze, and they made
elegant, long-necked pitchers of a fine, gleaming red ceramic.[10]

After the end of the period of the Assyrian colonies, Mursili's predecessors had set up a capital city at Hattusa, on the Anatolian plateau, and quite
soon began expanding their domain. They were not much interested in the
niceties of diplomacy, it seems. Like Sargon so many centuries before, the
early Hittite kings were conquerors.

Mursili's predecessors, Kings Hattusili and Labarna of Hatti, were both
proud of the destruction they wrought.[11] A proclamation by a later monarch,
Telipinu, sums up the reigns in the following way, repeating the same phrase
verbatim about both kings: "Wherever he went on campaign, he held the enemy
country subdued by his might. He destroyed the lands one after the other,
stripped the lands of their power and made them the borders of the sea."[12]

It was in the reign of Hattusili I, Mursili's grandfather, that the Hittites
first adopted the cuneiform script (to write Akkadian as well as their own language of Hittite).[13] Hattusili made good use of the new writing system; he had

an account, known as his annals, written of his campaigns. To hear him tell it, Hattusili I seems to have fought constantly, bringing lands right across Anatolia under his control. More ambitiously, he led his troops twice out of Anatolia and into northern Syria, the realm of the king of Yamhad, Babylon's northern neighbor. To get there, his troops had to march through a narrow pass in the Taurus Mountains known as the Cilician Gates. The Taurus Mountains formed a very clear barrier at the southeastern edge of Anatolia, but Hattusili wanted to go farther.

He boastfully described his surprise attack on a Syrian city named Zippasna: "I entered Zippasna, and I ascended Zippasna in the dead of night. I entered into battle with them and heaped dust upon them... Like a lion I... destroyed Zippasna. I took possession of its gods and brought them to the temple of the Sun Goddess of Arinna."[14] Taking the statues of the gods away was the crowning insult to the conquest of the city; it deprived the citizens of their main source of divine support. By taking those gods to the temple of his high goddess he ensured that they too symbolically submitted to the Hittites. Although Hattusili seems to have had his heart set on the conquest of Aleppo, he was unsuccessful.[15]

Hattusili I inspired a fierce response from the Syrians, specifically from a population known as the Hurrians who had borne the brunt of the Hittite conquest. Hurrian-speaking peoples had occupied northern Syria since at least the third millennium BCE.[16] They shared the culture of the other Syrians and Mesopotamians in many ways but spoke a completely distinct language, unrelated to either Sumerian or Akkadian. The angry Hurrian forces followed the Hittites back into Anatolia, attacking them on their own ground.[17]

But in his annals Hattusili presented his reign as a complete success. He had, after all, succeeded in fighting far into Syria, and he depicted himself as a latter-day Sargon in having crossed the Euphrates (though in the opposite direction): "No one had crossed the Mala [Euphrates], but I the Great King... crossed it on foot, and my army crossed it on foot. Sarrugina (Sargon) (also) crossed it."[18] Hattusili doesn't seem to have been interested in maintaining any control in Syria; he had sacked a number of cities and withdrawn back to Anatolia.

Hattusili must have been a hard act to follow. When Mursili took the throne he first reasserted Hittite influence in Syria by campaigning there once again, and he was finally able to conquer Aleppo.[19] Unlike his grandfather, he left no annals; the terse description in Telipinu's proclamation provides all our information: "He went to the city of Halpa (Aleppo), destroyed Halpa and brought Halpa's deportees (and) its goods to Hattusa."[20]

Perhaps then Mursili visited the lands near Aleppo, gazed south down the Euphrates River and asked the local people what lay that way. He might have known, even before asking, that it was a rich land, on the basis of the stories that had survived about Sargon, who had lived seven centuries earlier. He also might have heard tales of the rich Assyrian traders and the Babylonian textiles and tin they had brought to his land two centuries before. The trading colonies were long gone, but perhaps a memory of them had lived on and helped inspire the king's desire to take Babylon.

Like Zimri-Lim visiting the Mediterranean coast, Mursili standing on the banks of the Euphrates was at the edge of the area previously familiar to his people, and he knew that there was a whole world lying beyond. Perhaps it occurred to him that if he could conquer wealthy Babylon he would leave an even grander legacy than that of his grandfather.

His army didn't have to march far from Aleppo before reaching the northern border of the Babylonian kingdom, near the city of Terqa in a region known as Hana.[21] A local king, Kuwari, named one of his years after a struggle against the soldiers of Hatti—perhaps this was that fight.[22] On the other hand, the local people in Hana had no great love for Babylon; they had resisted Babylon before, and perhaps ended up seeing Mursili's campaign as a chance to regain their independence.

In any event, Mursili and his troops seem to have encountered little resistance as they marched south. Perhaps they also rode in boats down the river. One can imagine the wonder of the Hittite soldiers as they ventured so far beyond their familiar homeland. They came from a rocky land of high plateaus and winter snow, quite unlike this flat plain with its tawny mud-brick towns.

Unfortunately, no contemporary description survives of the battle for Babylon. It seems likely that messengers from the north carried word to King Samsuditana of the invaders' march. A single courier could travel much faster than a whole army and its entourage even if that army didn't have to fight along the way, and they probably did meet at least some resistance. Did Samsuditana call up his troops and those of his allies and meet the Hittite army on the battlefield? Or did he and his people retreat within the walls of the city and withstand a long hungry siege before capitulating? Did the Babylonians stand on the city walls and watch in horror as the Hittites destroyed or consumed all their crops and burned the villages round about?

Telipinu's inscription tells us very little: "Now, later he [Mursili] went to Babylon and fought the Hurrian [troops]. Babylon's deportees (and) its goods he kept in Hat[tusa]."[23] From this we know that Hurrians, the enemies of the Hittites since their attack on Hatti, either fought with the Babylonians to defend their city or impeded the way of the Hittites as they passed through Syria on their way to or from Babylon.[24] Kuwari, the king of Terqa who mentioned his struggle against the Hittites, bore a Hurrian name; he might have led one of the regiments of "Hurrian" troops that Telipinu recalled.

So we know from Telipinu that the Hittites raided Babylon and took hostages. Then they turned around and marched hundreds of miles home again with their loot, not even leaving a governor in place to control the conquered land. The Hittites seem to have had no interest in ruling an empire (though their descendants did later). Two of the hostages that they carried back to Hatti weren't even human, but they were the most valuable individuals the Hittites could have taken: the statues of the city god of Babylon, Marduk, and of his wife, Sarpanitum.[25] Those Babylonians who were left in the city to pick up the pieces of their lives must have been devastated. The temple of Marduk, called Esagila, was deserted; the gods were gone. Even the king seems to have died or gone into exile—Samsuditana and his dynasty disappeared from the records.

## A Turning Point

The sack of Babylon marked a turning point in Mesopotamian history. Samsuditana's dynasty had come to an end, but the Hittites had left. Unlike the Hurrians, the Babylonians seem not to have wanted to retaliate—as far as we know, they mounted no counterattack against the Hittites. The people must have been demoralized. Perhaps, after so many years of safety and prosperity the Babylonians had come to believe that their kingdom was immune to attack and impregnable; now they knew otherwise. The days when Samsuditana's greatest concern was the creation of yet another statue of himself were long gone. Now Babylon had no king and its god was missing.

No doubt the Babylonians wondered: Who would rule their land? And how could Marduk and Sarpanitum be retrieved from the enemy? It wasn't an option simply to make a new statue of each of the deities; the statues were irreplaceable homes to the gods. If the statues were in Hatti, then the gods were there too. And a city without its city god was a place without a soul, orphaned and unprotected.

Perhaps another shift took place in the thinking of the Babylonians, one that was vague and hard to express and yet unnerving. What to make of a world in which another civilization, one at the far edge of the world, with which their own king had apparently had no previous diplomatic contact, seemed to have as much power as, or perhaps more than, the Babylonians did? Worse yet, this new enemy was aggressive and unpredictable. The old conception of the world had included local powers with which one corresponded and periodically quarreled or warred, and faraway lands with which one traded. Here was a faraway land that didn't seem to follow the rules at all.

No one alive would have been able to remember a time when Babylon had ever been conquered before. If the attack had come from a relatively local enemy such as the Elamites or the Kassites, the impact would have been just as devastating, but at least the villains would have been familiar. Until now it seems that the Hittites, if they had registered in the minds of the Babylonians at all, had been distant and provincial people who lived beyond the cedar mountains and who had supplied silver in exchange for textiles and tin.

The Hittites, in turn, might have experienced a similar culture shock. They wouldn't have thought of themselves as provincial or as living on the fringes of civilization. In their minds, no doubt, it was the Anatolian Plateau that lay at the center of the universe. And yet they discovered enormous wealth in Babylon—these were people from whom they might not just steal but perhaps learn as well.

As we have seen, they had already adopted the Mesopotamian writing system; the earliest local Anatolian cuneiform inscription came from before the reign of Hattusili and had probably been learned from Syrian scribes.[26] Schools must have been set up in Hatti so that scribes could learn to write in cuneiform.[27] They had adapted the script so as to be able to write Hittite using the characters. But they also learned Sumerian and Akkadian, and use of the cuneiform writing system came to be a royal prerogative in Hatti. They preserved many of the royal records, including both the Annals of Hattusili and the Proclamation of Telipinu, in both Hittite and Akkadian versions.

### The Kassite Kings

The century that followed the attack on Babylon, from 1595 to 1500 BCE, is obscure right across the Near East because very little that was written (if much of anything was written at all) has been found. The south came under the control of what is known as the First Sealand Dynasty. The kings there bore old-fashioned Sumerian names, Ayadaragalama and Peshgaldaramesh (in spite of the fact that Sumerian had long been a dead language), and they probably maintained diplomatic contacts with Arabia.[28] Meanwhile, to the northwest, kings who ruled the kingdom of Hana on the Euphrates enjoyed a period of independence. These two are among the few Syrian or Mesopotamian kingdoms from which any written records survive for this time period.[29]

When the smoke cleared around 1500 BCE, there was a new dynasty ruling Mesopotamia, a dynasty of Kassites.[30] These kings were destined to play a large part in the story of the international community that developed during the next two centuries, but their origins and homeland are unknown. Although they had fought the Babylonian kings periodically after Hammurabi's time, and probably even had their own kingdom back then, it hasn't been found yet. Curiously, after arriving in Mesopotamia, they apparently never chose to write a single document in their own language; not one royal inscription or letter or contract in Kassite has been found.[31] It's almost as though it didn't occur to them that their language could be expressed in writing, as though writing was only designed to record Akkadian and Sumerian. The same had been true of the Amorites, who were similarly uninspired to write in their native tongue, and, as with the Amorites, the main evidence for the Kassites' foreign origin is in their names. But whereas the Amorite names reveal them to have been speakers of a Semitic language, Kassite names are like no other known language.

Wherever they came from, the Kassites must have arrived in Babylon after the Hittite attack led by Mursili, but unlike the Hittites, they chose not to leave. They settled and then took over. It's a curious fact that from the arrival of the Amorites onward, Babylonia was almost never ruled by native Babylonians, but every dynasty was full of Babyloniaphiles, and the Kassites were no exception. The Kassite kings absorbed local Babylonian culture thoroughly. They dressed as Babylonians, venerated Babylonian gods, celebrated Babylonian festivals, and wrote in Akkadian. They even began to give Babylonian names to some of their children.[32]

### The Return of Marduk and Sarpanitum—Long-Distance Diplomacy

We know that Mesopotamian life settled down again after the Kassites took over in the early sixteenth century, though we don't know how soon things got back to normal. The first texts found from Kassite times come from much later, the late fifteenth century.[33] But, thanks to a later copy of a royal inscription, we do know that at least one of the early Kassite kings, a man named Agum-Kakrime, adopted the same worry that must have tormented the locals ever since the Hittites disappeared up the river: how to convince these enemies to send the gods Marduk and Sarpanitum home. Presumably the Kassite kings hadn't been particularly devoted to Marduk before they arrived in Babylon, but Marduk was the god of this place, and he needed to return to his temple.

Perhaps Agum-kakrime thought his subjects would see him as more legitimate if he proved his devotion toward Marduk and Sarpanitum by bringing them back. Or perhaps he believed that the city could never be secure without its god and goddess in residence. Whatever the case, Agum-kakrime was successful, and he seems to have used diplomacy rather than warfare in order to reach his goal—in this case diplomacy with a distant and very foreign state.

The royal inscription that he set up to commemorate his achievement is long and boastful, but frustratingly short on details of his negotiations.[34] Agum-kakrime started the inscription with several lines about his own greatness, then turned to the issue of the missing gods. Needless to say, he never suggested that Marduk and Sarpanitum were taken captive or forced to do anything against their wills. Rather, Marduk had apparently left voluntarily and now had decided for himself, along with the other great gods, that it was time to return to his home in the Esagila temple in Babylon. He revealed this to Agum-kakrime: "When Marduk, lord of Esagila and Babylon, (and) the great gods ordered with their holy command his [ret]urn to Babylon, (and?) Marduk had set his face towards Babylon, [I prayed to?] Marduk..."[35]

Agum-kakrime must have met with his advisors to plan how to fulfill Marduk's wish. Perhaps he toyed with the idea of sending troops to Hatti to force the Hittite king to give up the god and goddess. But there was a simpler way— the same technique used in Mesopotamia for gaining the release of human hostages taken during warfare: negotiation and ransom. Hammurabi had even put forward a law to cover the ransoming of hostages in wartime. It starts by stating that when a soldier was taken captive by an enemy, then, routinely, "a merchant redeems him and helps him get back to his city."[36] The merchant was expected to use his own wealth to start with, to pay the ransom, and to use his knowledge of the journey involved in order to bring the soldier home safely. At that point, someone had to repay the merchant. If he could afford it, the soldier "shall redeem himself." If not, then the cost would be absorbed by the temple in his city, and "if there are not sufficient means in the city's temple to redeem him, the palace shall redeem him."[37] There was no question; a ransom would certainly be paid. In war, men on the losing side faced either being killed or taken captive, and often it was more lucrative for the victors to capture a prisoner and to hold him for ransom than to kill him. Marduk and Sarpanitum were in a similar situation now. Perhaps the Hittite king even expected the Babylonian king to start negotiations for their return, just as though they had been rich hostages.

Agum-kakrime probably sent a messenger, perhaps a high-ranking ambassador, north to Hatti to find out where Marduk and Sarpanitum were being kept and what might be the terms of their release. It's possible that a merchant who had traded in Hatti helped out as well, just as in the case of a human hostage. Such a man might have a decent knowledge of the Hittite land and its language and could be of assistance to an official from the Babylonian court, especially if the two kings had never been in direct contact before.

None of this is recorded, but the exchange couldn't have taken place without negotiations. Agum-kakrime was probably pretty certain that Marduk had been well cared for. The god and his wife Sarpanitum were prisoners of war, but the kidnappers would have believed that their victims had divine power and wouldn't have wanted to incur their wrath. The gods were probably comfortably housed, like the gods that Hattusili had earlier stolen from Zippasna, residing in another god's temple and receiving regular meals and offerings, as though they were enormously powerful houseguests.

Agum-kakrime wrote, "I carefully planned to fetch Marduk, and towards Babylon did I set his face. I went to the assistance of Marduk, who loves my reign."[38] This "assistance" might well have included a hefty ransom payment, but Agum-kakrime would have had no desire to let on about this in his inscription.

Another land Agum-kakrime seems to have negotiated with was the land of Hana in Syria, midway between Hatti and Babylon. He wrote that "I asked of king Shamash by divination(?), I sent to a far-off land, to the land of the Haneans, and Marduk and Sarpanitum did they conduct to me." It's unclear why the gods would have come from Hana rather than Hatti. Possibly they had already made half the journey home, and it was indeed the Haneans who conducted the gods on the last leg of their travels. In any event, the Babylonians must have been very relieved, and very grateful to King Agum-kakrime, when the gods were back in Babylon.

Much of the rest of Agum-kakrime's long inscription recalls in loving detail the refurbishing of the statues of the deities (though they were not, of course, referred to as statues). For this he hired the best craftsmen and provided them with four talents—around 240 pounds!—of gold, and all manner of imported semiprecious stones such as lapis lazuli, agate, alabaster, and chalcedony. The gods were given beautiful new gold clothes along with horned crowns of lapis and gold. The king also spruced up the gods' home—the Esagila temple—with cedar doors bearing scenes of fantastic creatures in the same brightly colored precious materials that were used for the gods' clothes.[39]

This moment—the successful return of the gods to the Esagila—was a diplomatic triumph. Nothing in the text suggests that Agum-kakrime had to fight to win back the gods. Instead he "carefully planned" and "sent to a far-off land," and the people of that land brought the gods back to Babylon. Two states that could well have been enemies, given the history of hostilities between them, instead found a way to cooperate.

The story of Marduk's journey to and from Hatti wasn't forgotten. Not only was Agum-kakrime's inscription preserved, but later storytellers wove another tale to explain that the god's absence from Babylon had been his own decision.

He hadn't been captured; instead (and the author used Marduk's own words), "I gave the command that I go to Hatti, I put Hatti to the test, there I set up the throne of my supreme godhead. For twenty-four years I dwelt there."[40] The god noted that during those twenty-four years he was busy helping Babylonians to set up commercial expeditions and to market the goods from Hatti in their own cities. It's quite possible that this was indeed an outcome of the Hittite attack; with a new knowledge of the wealth of one another's lands, people began wanting the exotic goods that they couldn't get at home, and Babylonian merchants began traveling back and forth to facilitate the trade. Like the Assyrian traders before them, they probably took textiles to Hatti and brought silver and gold home.

This tale of Marduk's visit to Hatti agrees with that of Agum-kakrime in that when Marduk returned, he came in style and was restored. With this explanation, the Babylonians both saved face and waved away their misfortune: the gods, Marduk and his wife, hadn't been stolen; they had benevolently gone to Hatti of their own accord.

As a result of all this, Agum-kakrime must have seen the benefit of using diplomacy on a wider scale, not just with familiar partners but with a strange and previously hostile foreign power, and it had worked. The Hittites learned something from the encounter as well. Soon thereafter, the Hittite kings began to formulate peace treaties with their vassals and allies, treaties with a clear Syrian or Mesopotamian influence behind them.[41]

The Kassites themselves started formalizing their relationships with the outside world at around the same time. At a later point in the sixteenth century BCE, the Kassite king Burna-buriash I negotiated an agreement with the Assyrian king to the north, a man named Puzur-Ashur III, establishing the location of the boundary between their lands.[42] Behind the terse mention of this agreement in a later list we have to imagine all the diplomatic effort involved and the essential optimism that a treaty represented, with its promise of peace and brotherhood. But already the kings of Babylonia and Assyria might have had a more pragmatic reason for their agreement—the appearance of a new and aggressive kingdom on their borders in Syria. It was known as Mittani.

CHAPTER SIX

# A Clash between
# Expanding Empires

*"Prepare yourselves! Make your weapons ready! For
one will engage in combat with that wretched foe
in the morning"*

### Egyptian Forces Venture North

In 1504 BCE, right around the same time the Dark Age was ending in Mesopotamia and almost seventy years after Agum-kakrime had brought the statues of the gods Marduk and Sarpanitum back to Babylon from Hatti, a king came to power in Egypt who was to launch his kingdom into the international world of the Near East.[1] His name was Thutmose I, and his goals were neither diplomatic nor peaceable; he was interested in war. He led his newly formed army on a march right across the Levant and all the way to the Euphrates, to regions that, as far as we know, no Egyptian king had ever visited before. The Egyptian kings before him had focused their aggression on Nubia to the south, keeping their distance—whether consciously or inadvertently—from Syria and Mesopotamia. Now these ancient lands—Egypt on the one hand, and Syria and Mesopotamia on the other—would have to figure out what to make of one another. Initially, at least, they seem to have felt nothing but hostility. Eventually, though, Egypt became a vital member of the diplomatic world of the Near East.

The first leg of Thutmose's expedition might have been by boat. It would have been easy enough to bring Egyptian troops in to the port at Byblos, Egypt's ancient outpost. From there, they struck out overland into new territory.[2] So much in western Syria would have been strange and a little unnerving to the Egyptians: green hills, forests, cloudy skies, frequent rain showers. The soldiers came from the flat expanse of the Nile Valley with its red desert cliffs to the east and west; no forests grew there, and rain was almost unheard of south of the delta. A later pharaoh referred to the unfamiliar phenomenon of rainfall as "a Nile in the sky" that had been divinely created for the foreign lands "that it may descend for them...to irrigate the fields in their towns," just as the Egyptians' own Nile came from the ground for the same purpose.[3] Another Egyptian writer was amazed, and perhaps a little claustrophobic, when he discovered that in some places in Syria "the sky is dark by day. [The road] is overgrown with junipers and...cedars (that) have reached the sky."[4] The Egyptians would have been used to the huge blue sky in their own land that extended, unobstructed, from one horizon to the other.

The kingdom the Egyptians encountered as they pressed on with their offensive was the same new and powerful land that might have inspired the Babylonians and Assyrians to make an alliance. The people who lived there called their land Mittani, but the Egyptians often referred to it as Naharin. A later Egyptian scribe described a soldier's experiences as he campaigned in Syria:

> Come, (let me relate) to you his journey to Khor [that is, the land of the Hurrians, yet another name for Mittani] and his marching upon the hills. His rations and his water are upon his shoulder like the load of an ass, while his neck has been made a backbone like that of an ass. The vertebrae of his back are broken, while he drinks of foul water. He stops work (only) to keep watch.[5]

One can imagine the heavy loads of food, water, and arms that the men had to carry; the dirt that crusted their legs; the noise and commotion of the marching troops; the nights spent sleeping in the open or in tents, or keeping watch and then marching on, unrested.

Unfortunately, no official account by Thutmose I of his campaign into Syria is preserved. There are, however, records written by several of his soldiers, including two autobiographies of men who served together, both of whom were named Ahmose.[6] These autobiographies were engraved on the men's tombs for posterity, so they might have exaggerated their accomplishments a little. Nevertheless, they provide us with a few vivid, if brief, snapshots of the campaign.

One of the Ahmoses wrote just one sentence about the battle against Mittani in his autobiography: "again I acted on behalf of the king of Upper and Lower Egypt Okheperkare (Thutmose I), deceased, when I captured for him, in the land of Naharin, twenty-one hands, and a horse and chariot."[7] A "hand" was chopped off the body of a fallen soldier and taken as a trophy to prove that an enemy had been killed.[8] King Thutmose I no doubt took the horse and chariot from Ahmose as booty from the battle.

The second Ahmose began by explaining why Thutmose fought in Mittani; according to him the king went on "the subsequent campaign to Retjenu (the Levant) to slake his desire throughout the foreign lands."[9] According to Ahmose, the king fought simply because he wanted to. And Ahmose credited much of the victory to Thutmose alone: "His Majesty reached Naharin, and found that the fallen one (the king of Mittani) had mustered his troops. Then His Majesty made a great slaughter among them, there was no end to the living captives His Majesty took in his victory."[10] Ahmose himself also played a role in the victory, as he noted: "Now I was at the head of our army, and His Majesty saw my bravery, for I brought off a chariot and its horses which were with it as captives, dispatched to his Majesty."[11] From this account, it's clear that Thutmose I and his army were successful in at least some of their battles, killing soldiers, taking booty, and seizing enemies as captives.

As proof of his victory there in Mittani, so very far from home, Thutmose I had a stela carved and set up right on the banks of the Euphrates. Monuments like these were erected by Egyptian kings at what they considered to be the ends of the world. The very act of visiting a land and setting up a stela somehow, to Egyptian eyes, brought that land into the known world.[12] What a strange sight it must have been to the locals, none of whom would have been able to read it. It hasn't been found, but it was probably covered with lines of intricate hieroglyphs (which would have looked to the Mittanians just like pictures—birds, snakes, eyes, and men among them) with an image of the king at the top, frozen in that stiff Egyptian posture, shoulders and torso facing the viewer, head and legs in profile.

Like the Hittites attacking Babylon a century earlier, the Egyptians seem to have had no plans to rule Mittani. They attacked, plundered, and left.[13] No treaties were drawn up, no governors installed. Thutmose I's goal might simply have been to intimidate the foreigners and to capture booty. The king perhaps looked forward to boasting of his victories when he returned home, and to showing off all the horses, chariots, and other wealth that he had looted from Mittani. He even seems to have taken some time to hunt elephants (which were still found in the wild in Syria) on his way back.[14]

The soldiers were perhaps less enthusiastic, however, at the prospect of the march home. The scribe who recounted a soldier's life described the travails of the exhausted troops who returned from a campaign, ill and poor: "He proceeds to return to Egypt, and he is like a stick which the worm has devoured. He is sick, prostration overtakes him. He is brought back upon an ass, his clothes taken away by theft."[15]

Obviously the scribe who wrote this had a bias—he thought that being a scribe was superior to any other profession and wanted to make other careers look unappealing—but his account probably had more than a grain of truth to it. The campaign to Syria would have been grueling for the troops.

### Parattarna I: A Syrian Match for Thutmose I

The land of Mittani, Thutmose I's adversary, flourished in Syria for around 300 years, starting around 1560 BCE.[16] The kingdom had gradually expanded throughout the sixteenth-century Dark Age, spreading west and later east from its heart in the area around the Khabur River. At its height, the kingdom stretched almost 500 miles across Upper Mesopotamia, from Kizzuwatna in the west, at the northeast corner of the Mediterranean, all the way to the foot of the Zagros Mountains beyond the Tigris in the east, and south to the city of Kadesh in northern Canaan.[17] It included the area that had previously been home to the kingdom of Irkab-damu of Ebla 750 years before, along with many other Early Dynastic city-states, and to what had been the Old Babylonian kingdoms of Qatna, Yamhad, Mari, and Ekallatum 250 years earlier.

The capital city of Mittani was at Washshukkanni. This city lay somewhere in or near the triangle of fertile land bounded by the rivers that flow south into the Khabur River, which in turn flows into the Euphrates. The area is now near Syria's border with Turkey, considerably to the north of Mari. The ancient capital hasn't been excavated yet—it's one of the great, undiscovered cities that will one day undoubtedly transform our understanding of the era. For decades, archaeologists and historians have thought that it may lie beneath later occupation levels in the huge tell at a place called Tell Fakhariyah.[18] Chemical analysis of the clay used for tablets written in Washshukkanni confirms that they came from somewhere in the area of Tell Fakhariyah.[19] But it may be decades before the excavations there turn up anything from the time of Mittani.

Without Washshukkanni, we have no archives belonging to the kings of Mittani, and unfortunately there's no other city that might be equivalent to the excavations at Ebla or Mari to provide details of the Mittani kings and their administrations. Here's a sobering fact: across all of Mittani, from a town called Nuzi in the far east to Alalakh, hundreds of miles away near the Mediterranean coast, only sixteen cuneiform documents have been found that include the names of kings of Mittani and that were written during their reigns (some other documents have been found outside Mittani).[20] Just sixteen. And these weren't royal inscriptions or annals or diplomatic letters.

Most of them were contracts that include the seal of a king and a brief reference to the king. Think of the thousands of tablets at Mari that mentioned Zimri-Lim alone and you get a sense of just how scarce the evidence is for the Mittani kings. Mittani was huge and powerful, so it's odd that so few documents have been found within its borders. It's not that texts weren't being written, just that archaeologists have so far been unlucky in finding them. The biggest and best-preserved archives for any era were sealed together and abandoned when the walls around them collapsed, often when the buildings burned (as at Ebla and Mari). This tended to happen when a town was invaded, so one hopes that later cataclysms in Mittanian history might have caused a few archives to have been burned and forgotten. They may still lie in wait for archaeologists.

Historians don't know the identity of the king of Mittani who was described as the "fallen one" by one of the Ahmoses, but it might well have been Parattarna I.[21] Parattarna, like Thutmose I, was a warlike king, referred to by one of his contemporaries as "the strong king, the king of the Hurrian troops,"[22] who expanded his kingdom into an empire through long years of battle. A minor local king, Idrimi, wrote an autobiography in which he described how he ultimately became a vassal of Parattarna I. (Another man named Sharruwa was cited as the author of this autobiography of Idrimi.[23] Maybe Sharruwa was an ancient equivalent of a modern ghostwriter or speech writer, hired to put a sparkle in Idrimi's words.[24])

The text was inscribed on a statue of Idrimi to commemorate his achievements. Unfortunately, to modern eyes his statue is one of the most unprepossessing works of art ever found in the Near East. The king's head is huge in comparison with his seated rectangular body; he looks a bit like one of the playing-card soldiers in an *Alice in Wonderland* illustration. His facial expression is that of a pouty child about to burst into tears. Perhaps an ancient Syrian might have seen it differently, but the statue looks more cartoonish than awe-inspiring.

Idrimi explained in his autobiography how, many years before, he had fled from an attack on his homeland of Aleppo and gone into exile. In fairy-tale fashion, he left with only a groom for company: "I took my horse, my chariot, and my groom and I went into the desert."[25] He didn't say who attacked Aleppo, but it could have been forces from Mittani.[26]

He lived in exile for seven years, constantly checking various omens and oracles for signs from the gods that now was a propitious time for him to try to regain his power. Finally he assembled an army and "caused them to board the ships and proceed by sea" back to his own land near Aleppo. In typical Near Eastern fashion, just as Zimri-Lim would have done a few centuries

Statue of Idrimi, the king of Alalakh. His
autobiography, describing his battles and
eventual treaty with King Parattarna I of
Mittani, is engraved on the statue. (©Trustees
of the British Museum)

before, he drew up treaties with several lands in order to strengthen his force:
"My allies heard and came before me. When they made a treaty with me,
I established them as my allies." Idrimi's enemy in this war was King Parat-
tarna I of Mittani: "Now for seven years Parattarna...was hostile toward me."
Seven seems to have been a symbolic number in this tale; the war might well
have been shorter.[27]

Idrimi seems to have fared poorly against the formidable king of Mittani,
and they eventually found a face-saving way of bringing the war to an end.
He agreed to become Parattarna's vassal. Idrimi cited a historical precedent
for this: his ancestors had been vassals to Hurrian kings before and, more

importantly, had sworn oaths and drawn up treaties. These earlier treaties might well have been arrangements for mutual defense made when Hattusili I and Mursili I of Hatti had terrorized Syria in the early sixteenth century.[28] Idrimi believed that he and Parattarna need not be enemies if the kings who had come before them had been "father" and "son": "The mighty king heard of the vassal service of our predecessors and the agreement between them, and he had respect for the oath because of the words of the agreement and because of our vassal service."

Now, of course, a new treaty was needed. Idrimi and Parattarna must have agreed to the terms and sworn to uphold their agreement in front of the gods of their lands: "I swore a binding oath to him concerning my position as a loyal vassal and I was king in Alalakh." Alalakh was a city on the Orontes River near Idrimi's original home of Aleppo (it was there that Zimri-Lim would have seen the wall paintings by Minoan artists when he visited three centuries earlier). Parattarna had, through this treaty, secured Alalakh as a faithful vassal kingdom of Mittani and won the support (and tribute) of a former enemy. In return, Idrimi gained a throne and was allowed to turn his attention to other battles, in which he could pillage cities and gain some wealth for himself.

So Idrimi once again began to fight, but this time it was on behalf of Parattarna rather than against him. Idrimi "took troops and went against Hatti." He conquered a number of cities that had previously belonged to Hatti and were "under their treaty protection." Hatti was weak at this time and unable to respond to the Syrian aggression.[29]

Through his conquests, perhaps Idrimi was able to expand Parattarna's empire, but that wasn't his principal reason for fighting. What he bragged about was "destroying cities," raiding and taking loot, just as Thutmose I did when he attacked Mittani. "I did as I pleased," wrote Idrimi; "I took them as captives; I took their goods, their possessions and their valuables and divided (them) among my auxiliaries.... I entered my city Alalakh with captives."[30]

It was a violent time. People inhabiting Levantine towns might well have lived in fear. Their crops might be seized by the troops either of their own overlord or of another king. Their overlord—whether it was the king of Hatti, Mittani, or Egypt—might come to their defense, or he might not, if another king attacked. Their houses might be burned, and they might find themselves taken as hostages to some distant capital. And yet, in spite of this, the Mittanian Empire prospered. Idrimi obviously had considerable autonomy; he was able to build himself a palace and to build houses for some of his citizens who "formerly did not dwell in buildings."[31]

Idrimi also swore to an alliance with another of Parattarna's vassal kingdoms, Kizzuwatna.[32] Later known as Cilicia, Kizzuwatna was centered on a flat plain, benefiting from the rich silt of three rivers that flow through the kingdom from the Taurus, and was surrounded by mountains. One pass led to Mittani in the east; another (the Cilician Gates) provided the only passage northwest up onto the Anatolian Plateau, the heartland of Hatti. Anyone traveling from Mittani to Hatti had to go through Kizzuwatna.

This area was something of a prize, sought by both empires.[33] In the words of the Hittite king Tudhaliya I, writing in the late fifteenth century BCE: "Formerly, in the time of my grandfather, Kizzuwatna came into the possession of Hatti, but afterwards the land of Kizzuwatna freed itself from Hatti, and turned to the land of Hurri (Mittani)."[34] Kizzuwatna's king had originally been bound to a treaty with the king of Hatti, but had switched allegiance to King Parattarna of Mittani before making the agreement with Idrimi.[35] But that wasn't the end of the story; later, "the people of the land of Kizzuwatna…freed themselves from the ruler of Hurri (Mittani) and turned to My Majesty [the Hittite king]."[36]

The vassals of Mittani all seem to have had quite a lot of power, at least locally, just like Idrimi. For example, at Terqa, which was now subject to Mittani, people who agreed to a contract had to swear an oath in the names not only of Parattarna and the gods, but also in the name of the local vassal king.[37]

In excavations in Syria, archaeologists have found no evidence for Thutmose I's campaign. Given the amount of warfare that seems to have been taking place in the region at the time—with small kings like Idrimi fighting against Parattarna and then the Hittite cities—perhaps the Egyptian raid didn't make much of an impression. Its impact was probably stronger on the Egyptians than on the Mittanians, in spite of the Egyptian claims of victory. The Egyptians now knew about Mittani—and must have found it to be an unexpectedly rich and impressive adversary. A couple of generations later, another Egyptian king, Thutmose I's grandson, Thutmose III, set out to try to conquer it.

### Egypt before Thutmose I

Why was Thutmose I so aggressive when earlier kings had paid no attention to the Near East at all, beyond Canaan? For thousands of years the Egyptian kings had been mostly content to stay within their fertile, isolated river valley.[38] Egyptians viewed their own land as perfect and orderly. Like the Mesopotamians, they believed they lived at the center of the universe, but their sense of superiority to the lands around them was more pronounced. If Egypt was the model of perfection, as of course it was in their eyes, then foreign lands were closer to (and perhaps in league with) a violent force at the chaotic edges of the universe, a destructive being they called Isfet.[39] When an Egyptian artist wanted to represent disorder, he often symbolized it by depictions of foreigners.[40]

In earlier centuries, the Egyptian kings had periodically conquered their neighbors to the south—the unfortunate Nubians whom the Egyptians looked down upon and disparaged, calling them "vile Nubians" and their land "miserable Kush"—because they wanted control of Nubia's gold.[41] Their relationship with lands to the north had been much less antagonistic. Trade with the seaside cities of the Levant, particularly with Byblos, was well established, and groups of Canaanites had periodically moved into the Egyptian Delta and settled there. In years when rainfall was scarce in Canaan, Egypt always had crops, because the Nile wasn't dependent on local rain. But the Levantine cities had been free from Egyptian rule, and Egypt had, until the seventeenth century BCE, been blissfully free from outside invasion of any kind.

In most of the ancient Near East, men were regularly called up for military service, and big walls were constructed around cities for defense. Not so in Egypt; throughout the Old and Middle Kingdoms, the Egyptians hadn't needed to worry about such things. Egypt was both physically and psychologically isolated from the lands around it, the deserts and seas forming a formidable barrier to any invaders (though not to immigrants). But then, around 1630 BCE, a century and a half before the reign of Thutmose I, a group of foreigners known as the Hyksos had changed all that. They had been able to come to power as kings and to rule the area of the Delta during a time of internal weakness.

The period of Hyksos rule is full of mystery—who were these people and where did they come from? Did they invade or just immigrate? Did they instigate a period of chaos or was the land largely unaffected? Did the economy collapse or thrive during their era?[42] The Hyksos were almost certainly from the Levant, and perhaps were related to the Amorites. To hear the later kings tell it, the time of Hyksos rule had been disastrous; the foreign rulers were barbarians who had destroyed buildings and monuments. One later pharaoh wrote, "I have raised up what was dismembered from the first time when the Asiatics were in Avaris of the North Land [the Hyksos capital] (with) roving hordes in the midst of them overthrowing what had been made, while they ruled in ignorance of Ra."[43] But these words were written at the command of a king, and all kings wanted to prove that they had brought order out of chaos, even if it meant exaggerating the chaos. Another Egyptian writer, Manetho (who wrote over 1,300 years later), reinforced this stereotype of the Hyksos. In summing up this period, he wrote, "By main force they easily overpowered the rulers of the land, they then burned our cities ruthlessly, razed to the ground the temples of the gods, and treated all the natives with a cruel hostility, massacring some and leading into slavery the wives and children of others."[44]

It's unlikely that things were as bad under the Hyksos as the later kings and writers wanted people to believe. Archaeologists have found little evidence for invasion or destruction, and, although Egypt was divided under different kings (the Hyksos in the north and local rulers in the south), their subjects' lives probably changed little. The Hyksos even seem to have been in contact with Mesopotamia. It was during their time that a letter was received from Babylon and kept in the palace at Avaris—the earliest evidence for correspondence between Mesopotamia and Egypt.[45] Most indications suggest that it was a relatively peaceful era. The Egyptian accounts probably exaggerated the brutality of the Hyksos in order to justify the foreign dynasty's eventual demise.

Nonetheless, it's clear that the Hyksos kings were seen as thoroughly unwelcome. After almost a hundred years of their rule in the north, Egyptian leaders from the southern Egyptian city of Thebes mounted an offensive, marched down the Nile, successfully besieged Avaris, the Hyksos' capital city in the Delta, and claimed control of the whole land.

The pharaoh who was able to finalize the reunification of Egypt in 1539 was named Ahmose. This was evidently a popular name around this time for both men and women; in addition to the two soldiers named Ahmose who later served in Thutmose I's army, King Ahmose's wife—who was also his sister—was also named Ahmose, and they had a daughter, also named Ahmose (who married Thutmose I), along with another daughter—Ahmose again—who had married his predecessor. An earlier king in this family had named all his children, a son and four daughters, Ahmose. (Fortunately, almost all these men and women also had alternative names, which must have cleared up some of the confusion.[46]) King Ahmose founded a new dynasty—the splendid Eighteenth—and a new era, which modern historians refer to as the New Kingdom.

The foreign dynasties had a lasting impact: once the Hyksos kings were expelled, the Egyptian kings changed their conception of their kingdom and its relationship to the outside world in a fundamental way. Later kings repeatedly made the case that it was necessary to attack lands beyond Egypt in order to combat foreigners who might possibly be interested in ruling Egypt, as the Hyksos had done. These threatening figures were described by a number of kings as being "on the march against" them or "intending to destroy Egypt."[47] If natural geographical isolation wasn't going to be enough to keep foreign rulers out, as it had been in the past, then Egypt needed an empire, in part to control any potential invaders who might be close at hand, and in part to create a big buffer between the Nile Valley and the rest of the world. The tribute that could be exacted from imperial holdings would, of course, be welcome too. Ultimately, the desire for an empire brought Egypt into the international Near Eastern community in ways that the kings never anticipated.

### A Woman in Charge: Hatshepsut

The Eighteenth Dynasty had started with warfare when King Ahmose expelled the Hyksos, and Thutmose I was continuing that militaristic tradition when he invaded Mittani. But for around thirty years after Thutmose I's Syrian expedition, the Egyptian rulers stayed out of the Levant; they were preoccupied with domestic matters. For one thing, the kings had a spell of bad luck in coming up with legitimate heirs.[48] Thutmose I's claim to the throne had been somewhat suspect—he was the brother-in-law of the king who came before him—but his marriage to a princess (Ahmose, daughter of Ahmose and Ahmose) ensured that his sons were of the royal line. Unfortunately, the two sons born to Queen Ahmose and Thutmose I died before their father, and only a daughter, Hatshepsut, survived.[49] The son who ultimately took the throne, Thutmose II, had been born to a minor wife, and wasn't directly related to the original royal family. Not to worry—he could marry his half-sister, Hatshepsut, and produce a son who had royal blood from his mother. He did marry her, and they had…a daughter. And then Thutmose II died after just a few years on the throne, leaving his very royal wife, their royal daughter, and a son who had been born to a woman who doesn't even seem to have been one of the king's wives.

What to do? This boy had almost no blood connection to the original royal family, and was just a young child at the time. But he was designated Thutmose III and in 1479 was appointed king. Like his father, he may also have been "married" to his half-sister (Hatshepsut's daughter), although they were initially both far too young for the marriage to mean much.[50]

In fact, Thutmose was so young when he took the throne that there was no way for him to actually rule, so Hatshepsut served as regent in his place. The job evidently suited her; after less than seven years, she took all the titles and responsibilities of being pharaoh upon herself while Thutmose III cooled his heels, served as her coregent, and presumably waited for her to die (which she eventually did after sharing the throne with him for over fifteen years).[51]

Hatshepsut proved to be a remarkable pharaoh. Not only was she one of the very few women to rule Egypt, but she was also responsible for rebuilding major structures that had fallen into disrepair (she of course blamed the Hyksos for much of the devastation) and for constructing many new buildings.[52] She ran the Egyptian state very efficiently. She doesn't seem to have been engaged much with the lands to the north of Egypt; instead, her focus was on the African states to the south. She personally led troops south into Nubia at least once, and mounted a second campaign in her twelfth year on the throne.[53]

She also sponsored what seems to have been a spectacularly successful trading expedition to Punt, an African land whose location has not been conclusively determined, though it might have been in the region of Somalia.[54] This venture was one of Hatshepsut's proudest accomplishments. Although she didn't go there herself, she had scenes carved on her mortuary chapel showing the various stages of the expedition. The boats, with all their rigging and cargo, were carefully depicted, as were the Puntite houses built on stilts, safe from flooding; the foreign plants and animals; and the extensive wealth obtained there. The rulers of Punt—a remarkably corpulent queen and a regal king—were depicted greeting the Egyptians, arms raised, ready to provide the Egyptians with valuable gifts. The caption to this image read, "The coming of the chiefs of Punt, doing obeisance, with bowed head, to receive this army of the king."[55] (Hatshepsut was regularly referred to as "the king.")

The Egyptians set up a tent for Hatshepsut's royal ambassador in what must have been a picturesque setting, "in the myrrh-terraces of Punt, on the side of the sea." There, he received what the Egyptians referred to as "tribute" from Punt. The people loaded the Egyptian ships with "all goodly fragrant woods...heaps of myrrh resin, with fresh myrrh trees, with ebony and pure ivory, with green gold of Emu, with cinnamon wood," and with various other types of exotic woods and incense, along with bars and rings of electrum, a naturally occurring alloy of gold and silver. Manufactured goods were also included: "eye cosmetic; (and) throw-sticks of the Puntites." The Egyptians also took animals—apes, monkeys, dogs, and "a southern panther alive, captured for her majesty" (which presumably needed a strong cage on board ship)—and people: "natives and their children," though it's unclear whether these were being taken as slaves or guests. The "heaps of myrrh in great quantities" and myrrh trees seem to have been the biggest prize of this mission, mentioned time and again in the inscriptions.

Hatshepsut wanted her Egyptian audience to think that Punt was paying tribute to Egyptian greatness when they sent the luxury gifts, but the Egyptians certainly paid for the goods, or exchanged them for "presents" of equal value. The items that they mentioned bringing as offerings to the Puntite chiefs were mostly foodstuffs: "bread, beer, wine, meat, fruit," which presumably could not have matched the value of the riches they received in return. The scribe added coyly, though, that they also brought "everything found in Egypt" to Punt, which might have included more valuable items such as gold, turquoise, and copper.

The benefits of the mission were primarily economic; Punt doesn't seem to have posed any sort of military threat to Egypt, and Egypt seems to have had no practical plans to bring Punt into an Egyptian empire as a vassal state (though Hatshepsut did claim to rule there in some of her more hyperbolic inscriptions). By sponsoring the mission, Hatshepsut reaped many rewards, gaining access to treasures that she couldn't have obtained within Egypt. She wasn't interested in profit. She wasn't about to sell the goods from Punt; they were items that she specifically needed for her own purposes.[56] But there might have been another side to the venture as well, and it would be fascinating to know if diplomatic efforts contributed to the success of the trade expedition. Did Egyptian envoys travel to Punt ahead of the trading ships to negotiate the items to be obtained and the cost to the Egyptians? Did Hatshepsut send a letter to the king and queen of Punt, and if so, what language did she use and what did she say? It's possible that there was no advance warning, because she claimed that the Puntites were surprised at the arrival of the Egyptians. The chiefs of Punt asked, "Why have you come thither unto this land, which the people [of Egypt] know not?"[57] Presumably, if Hatshepsut had sent a messenger ahead of the expedition, the chiefs would have known why they came.

Hatshepsut wasn't breaking new ground with this trading mission; Punt had been a trading partner of Egypt almost 800 years before, during the Sixth Dynasty, when a very young King Pepi II had anxiously awaited the arrival of the treasures from Punt. He had been particularly keen to see a dancing man who had been captured from a tribe of pygmies. He wrote to tell his representative on the boat coming north that the man should be treated with utmost care. As his words show, Pepi II was just a child and was not yet interested in Punt for its material wealth: "Take care lest he [the pygmy dancer] fall in the water! When he sleeps at night, get capable persons sleeping around him in his cabin. Inspect ten times during the night, for My Majesty desires to see this pygmy more than the produce of the mining country of Punt."[58]

## Death by Toothache

Through all Hatshepsut's trading and building activity, Thutmose III played only a supporting role. Although he might have been anxious to rule alone and to escape the shadow of his stepmother, he did not have her murdered. To judge from a mummy that has recently been identified as that of Hatshepsut, she suffered from a painful abscess in her mouth that became infected. The infection that spread throughout her body was what killed her.[59]

The appearance of her mummy, if indeed DNA studies prove it to be the queen, is a bit of a surprise. In art from her reign, Hatshepsut was portrayed as a classic beauty, with delicate facial features and a slim physique, eternally youthful, staring out at the viewer with resolution and intelligence. The intelligence was certainly real, but her middle-aged mummy shows her to have been obese, balding, and probably suffering from diabetes and liver cancer by the time she died. Her dental problems didn't just include the deadly abscess; she was also missing a front tooth. (The tooth was buried separately, marked with her name—it proved to be the key to identifying her body.[60])

### Thutmose III Faces Rebellion in Canaan

Once Thutmose III took the throne alone in 1458, some twenty-two years after he had first been proclaimed king, he was immediately confronted with opposition in Canaan. The city of Kadesh took the lead in mustering forces for an attack on Egypt. This was an ominous sign, and the Egyptians might well have experienced a certain amount of déjà vu—they certainly did not want another group of foreign rulers taking over in Egypt as had happened during the Hyksos period.[61]

Thutmose III organized quickly and marched his army of about 10,000 men across the northern Sinai and into Canaan.[62] It was midsummer and probably brutally hot, but at least the barley and wheat in the fields were ripe and the army could pillage enough to eat.[63] Warfare continued to be less than glorious for the troops. A gritty account written some time later described a soldier's life on such a campaign:

> He is called up for Syria. He may not rest. There are no clothes, no sandals. The weapons of war are assembled at the fortress of Sile. His march is uphill through the mountains. He drinks water every third day; it is smelly and tastes of salt. His body is ravaged by illness.[64]

Thutmose III described his first campaign in detail in numerous accounts; he seems to have viewed it as one of the most glorious moments of his long reign. The king wrote that along the route his army reached a town called Yehem. The king stopped there to consult with his military leaders. One can imagine them gathered around him as he thought through their options based on the intelligence that he had received.

"That wretched foe of Kadesh has come and entered into Megiddo and is there at this moment," the king said to his assembled men. "He has gathered to him the princes of all the foreign lands that had been loyal to Egypt, as well as those from as far as Naharin (Mittani), consisting of Khor and Kedy, their horses, their armies, their people. And he says—it is reported—'I shall wait and fight his majesty here in Megiddo.' Now tell me what you think."[65]

Thutmose's advisors were worried. The pass that they had to travel through to get to Megiddo, which was called the Aruna road, was narrow. They would be vulnerable to attack if they went that way, with the troops strung out one behind the other. Other roads might be longer, but they seemed safer. The advisors pleaded with the king: "Do not make us go on that difficult road!"

But Thutmose III was undaunted, convinced that he had the gods' support. "I swear, as Ra loves me, as my father Amen (god of Thebes) favors me, as my nostrils are refreshed with life and dominion, my majesty shall proceed on this Aruna road! Let him of you who wishes go on those roads you spoke of. Let him of you who wishes come in my majesty's following. Or will they say, those foes whom Ra abhors: 'Has his majesty gone on another road because he is afraid of us?' So they will say."

The king, of course, prevailed, and his decision proved to be a good one. The army made it through the pass and "a camp was laid out for his majesty" on the banks of a stream to the south of Megiddo. Word went out to the soldiers as they settled down for the night: "Prepare yourselves! Make your weapons ready! For one will engage in combat with that wretched foe in the morning."

On the next morning, the Egyptian troops must have been inspired by the sight of their king "on a chariot of fine gold, decked in his shining armor" as they marched onto the battlefield. The soldier's tale gives us a glimpse of the confusion and exhaustion that they might have experienced there: "The enemy comes, surrounds him with missiles, and life recedes from him. He is told 'Quick, forward, valiant soldier! Win for yourself a good name!' He does not know what he is about. His body is weak, his legs fail him."[66]

The battle resulted in a decisive victory for Egypt, at least according to Thutmose III. The Canaanites fled back to Megiddo, "abandoning their horses, their chariots of gold and silver," only to find the city gate locked. Some of them had to be hauled up over the city wall on ropes made of clothing in order to escape the Egyptians.

The Egyptians then besieged Megiddo, and even the king did his part: "his majesty himself was on the fort east of town, guarding (it day and night)." Their efforts ultimately proved successful; the Canaanites surrendered "on their bellies to kiss the ground to the might of his majesty, and to beg breath for their nostrils." The vanquished princes also brought extensive tribute with them: "silver, gold, lapis lazuli, and turquoise" for the king himself, along with "grain, wine, and large and small cattle for his majesty's army." Generously, Thutmose III spared their lives.

The pharaoh returned to Egypt with vast amounts of wealth: not just the tribute, but much more that he had captured in Canaan. Some of this must have been tough (and slow) to transport—207,300 sacks of wheat and 20,500 sheep, for example.[67] Other objects were so valuable they would have needed their own guards, like the items that were richly inlaid with gold, including two chariots, six carrying chairs, an elaborate bed, and a statue of the enemy. Thutmose listed in his battle accounts everything he had seized, ranging from 892 regular army chariots and 502 bows to six footstools. He also marched home with an additional 3,400 prisoners of war and 2,503 other people, including Canaanite warriors, male and female servants, pardoned persons who had surrendered, and dozens of children.[68] The care of some of these individuals probably fell to the soldiers, who were already weakened themselves. Sometimes a man could even end up carrying one of the hostages. This was a difficult situation for the gloomy soldier whose expedition to Syria was recalled later: "When victory is won, the captives are handed over to his majesty, to be taken to Egypt. The foreign woman faints on the march; she hangs herself (on) the soldier's neck. His knapsack drops, another grabs it while he is burdened with the woman.... If he comes out alive, he is worn out from the marching."[69]

In the early years of his sole reign after this first campaign, Thutmose III continued to focus on Canaan, leaving Mittani alone for now. He enforced Egyptian control throughout the region, taking the children of Canaanite princes back to Egypt for education so that they would be loyal to Egypt when they returned, as adults, to their homelands.[70] He also took over some Canaanite port cities and stored the harvests of their fields as rations to feed his troops during future campaigns.

### The Expanding Empires Clash Again

A few years later, Thutmose III decided to emulate his namesake and predecessor, Thutmose I, and to fight his way north to the Euphrates and into the heart of Mittani. Thutmose III seems to have been determined to prove that the gods had put, not just Egypt and Canaan, but the whole world under his command. In one inscription he quoted Amen-Ra (a god with the combined characteristics of the two greatest Egyptian gods—Amen, the god of Thebes, and Ra, the god of the sun): "I gave you valor and victory over all lands. I set your might, your fear in every country, the dread of you as far as heaven's four supports.... For I bestowed on you the earth, its length and breadth, westerners and easterners are under your command."[71] Thutmose III was responsible for what was a new idea in Egypt—he was determined to build and control an empire, including Canaan in the north and Nubia and Sudan in the south.[72] Thanks to his military genius and his long reign, he was able to achieve this goal.

Of course, the "earth, its length and breadth," which Amen-Ra had given him, was a big place, as had become apparent in the time of Thutmose I. But perhaps the king thought that Mittani marked one edge of the earth, and he was determined to take the army back and to conquer it. He called it "wretched Naharin," and its king was "the feeble enemy."[73] We can't be sure of the identity of this king of Mittani, but he wasn't so feeble that Thutmose felt assured of victory.[74] He spent years preparing for his campaign, even creating prefabricated boats that could be assembled when needed.[75]

The campaign against Mittani involved Egyptian troops not only traveling over land but by sea as well. It seems, remarkably, that Thutmose III was able to surprise the king of Mittani and to force him to flee downstream and to the east.[76] He couldn't, though, force the Mittanian king to do battle with him.[77] Unfortunately we have only Thutmose's account, which presents the war as a huge victory for the Egyptians (the king of Mittani, who seems to have survived, no doubt told the story very differently). Thutmose III wrote that "there was no one to protect them in that land of Naharin because its lords had fled out of fear. I hacked up his cities and villages and set fire to them, my majesty having reduced them to mounds."[78] Not content with this victory and destruction of the cities, in one of his inscriptions Thutmose asserted that the towns "will not be repopulated, my majesty having carried off all their people as prisoners of war and their cattle without limit and their property as well." He even "cut down all their orchards and all their fruit trees." This is obviously hyperbole; had he taken the entire population of Mittani as prisoners of war he would have had nowhere to put them all.

But there must be a grain of truth to his war tales. He claimed that he "crossed the Euphrates after the one who had attacked him, at the head of his armies." Crossing the Euphrates would have been a symbolic coup, since the heartland of Mittani lay to the east of the great bend of the Euphrates. Thutmose III also carved a monument there, at the border of his empire: "Now my majesty set up my stela on that mountain of Naharin being hewn from the mountain on the western side of the Euphrates." This stela was not alone— his grandfather Thutmose I had been there before; Thutmose III set his one up "beside the stela of his (grand)father, the King of Upper and Lower Egypt, Okheperkare (Thutmose I)."[79] Thutmose III must have put his scribes and masons to work on this impressive monument (which, regrettably, and like that of Thutmose I, has not been found), showing that he too had been there.

Two years later, Thutmose III was again at war with Mittani, which was perhaps now ruled by a new king, but this campaign seems to have been less successful, with neither side emerging victorious.[80] It received much less coverage in the pharaoh's inscriptions; Thutmose wanted his subjects to think that Mittani had been annihilated. The truth was different, though. The Egyptian campaigns must have been a setback, but Mittani actually grew in strength and power after this time.[81]

### Aegean Painters Working for the Pharaoh

During the early years of the Eighteenth Dynasty, through the reigns of the various Thutmoses and of Hatshepsut, the kings put the old Hyksos capital city at Avaris in the Delta to good use. They used it in part as a military camp; it was dotted with grain silos to hold rations for the troops, and some soldiers were buried there.[82] But the city was most important for its harbor, where ships from around the Mediterranean could dock, giving Egypt more access to international goods.[83]

The kings built three elegant palaces at Avaris, featuring courtyards, shady colonnades, stone bathing basins, and shiny white plastered walls. One palace even had a toilet—with two stone slabs on which the king could sit. Archaeologists found that one of the seat slabs of the toilet had fallen into the pit below during the early occupation of the palace. Manfred Bietak, the director of the excavation, conjured up a less-than-dignified image of the pharaoh when he commented dryly that "one can only hope this was not connected to a royal misfortune."[84]

It's possible that one of the palaces was built for a princess who came from Crete to marry King Thutmose III.[85] Although this marriage is not mentioned in Thutmose's records, he did marry foreign princesses—the tombs of his three Canaanite wives have been found—and it's hard to explain this palace any other way.[86]

The palace was decorated with beautiful wall paintings, rendered in reds, blues, greens, blacks, and browns on a white background. The artists who painted them were clearly not Egyptian but Minoan. They had come from Crete, perhaps with the specific commission of decorating this palace at Avaris. Their art seems joyous somehow; they painted running spirals and half-rosette friezes, loose-limbed athletes leaping over charging bulls, and griffins with wings spread wide, just as though they were decorating a palace in

Crete rather than Egypt. The artists used all the techniques they had learned at home, from the way they polished the plaster base to the use of a cord to impress the initial design, the application of color before the plaster dried, and the particular patterns they chose.[87] The designs on the walls have no parallels anywhere but the Minoan capital city of Knossos. The brightly painted griffins at Avaris may well have flanked a stone throne, just as they did at Knossos. The excavator believes that a Minoan princess might have received visitors while seated on the throne.[88]

Thutmose III or Hatshepsut must have authorized ships from Keftiu (Crete) to tie up at the port of Avaris—they're mentioned in the dockyard records of the city.[89] Minoan "chiefs" were sending gifts to Egyptian kings at around this time; they're depicted carrying vessels in familiar Minoan shapes in paintings on the walls of some tombs of high officials.[90] Just as in the case of Punt, the Egyptians described the gifts from Keftiu as "tribute," but Keftiu was an ally, not a vassal state.[91]

Minoan artists had decorated Canaanite palaces in the eighteenth and seventeenth centuries BCE, but this seems to have been their first work in Egypt.[92] Under Thutmose III, Egypt was gradually becoming more involved with the outside world. Some of this involvement was military, but the presence of foreign wives and craftsmen signals a greater openness to foreign culture as well.

*Gifts from Foreign Kings*

Some of the most intriguing comments in Thutmose III's royal annals are found after his first Mittani campaign, when three very distant lands sent gifts, presumably carried by ambassadors who also brought letters from their kings (though the letters haven't been found): these were Assyria, Babylonia, and Hatti.[93] Babylonia and Hatti were beyond the southeastern and northwestern borders of Mittani respectively, and Assyria was to the east. They must have been cheered by news of Thutmose's victories over their imperialistic neighbor. Gifts and messages also came from Assuwa (in Anatolia), Alalakh (in the Levant), and Tanaja (probably in Greece).[94] The leaders of all six of these lands, large and small, must have been watching Thutmose III's moves carefully. All of them had reasons to be worried about the growing strength and imperial ambitions of Mittani, so they had perhaps appreciated the Egyptian attempt to weaken that land. Some scholars see their gift-giving as a request for an alliance with Egypt against Mittani.[95] But perhaps they initially just wanted Thutmose to know that they were on his side and that they would rather not experience an Egyptian invasion of their own lands.

The gifts the foreign leaders sent to Thutmose were generous, but still relatively small, nothing like the amount of tribute that the subjected rulers in Canaan and Nubia were required to contribute.[96] The Assyrian leader, for example, sent Thutmose III about twelve pounds of lapis lazuli, along with "wide bowls of silver on low feet," horses, and various kinds of wood as a gift.[97] The first gift from the Hittite king included ninety-seven pounds of silver in eight rings and a large block of white stone.[98] So although Thutmose III may have appreciated the luxuries he received, he perhaps viewed the gifts as tribute from relatively unimportant, faraway countries.

Did Thutmose even know where these lands were? He had certainly never journeyed to Babylonia, Assyria, or Hatti, and there were no maps that could help him envision the layout of the region. In his mind, they all would have been in the same category—places at the edge of the world that sent presents and therefore acknowledged his power.[99] But the ambassadors from Babylonia, Hatti, and Assyria knew better, and they probably returned to their native lands wide-eyed and astounded at the wonders of the place they had visited: they would have seen the pyramids and the Sphinx, the temple of Karnak with its gold-plated obelisks, and the riches of Thutmose III's palace. The palaces of their own great kings might have seemed just a little less impressive on their return.

Babylon only sent gifts to Thutmose III once, but in Thutmose III's fortieth year another messenger appeared from Hatti with a gift for the pharaoh.[100] Perhaps a new Hittite king had just come to power and wanted to continue his predecessor's good relationship with Egypt.[101] At some point during these early years of the Eighteenth Dynasty, the kings of the Hittites and Egyptians drew up a treaty and became formal allies, but it probably wasn't quite this early.[102] Still, the two kingdoms were friendly, and they had every reason to be. They shared a common enemy, the formidable and expanding kingdom of Mittani. Conspicuously, there is no mention in Thutmose III's records of any gifts from Mittani. The rivalry between them seemed to be growing as they each scrambled for control of the northwestern Syrian kingdoms. The Mittanian king would have had no reason to voluntarily send any more wealth than Thutmose III had already seized.

After his forty-second year, Thutmose III apparently lost interest in campaigning; at least, no records survive of any military activity that can be reliably dated after then, though he ruled for another decade.[103] This was a boon for at least one Near Eastern kingdom. During the quiet last years of Thutmose III's reign, Mittani's king lost no time in expanding both west and east. Another change took place in the same year—Thutmose seems to have altered his opinion of the years in which he had ruled as coregent with Hatshepsut. Twenty years had passed since he had taken over as sole ruler, but suddenly Thutmose wanted to write her out of history.[104] He had his officials systematically carve her image from relief sculptures, erase her name from inscriptions (sometimes replacing it with the name of Thutmose I or II), and dump her statues out of her mortuary temple, but it's not clear why.[105] He wasn't successful, though. If anything, his malicious campaign against her has made her reign all the more intriguing, and today she eclipses Thutmose III among the big names of the New Kingdom. A 2005 exhibit at the Metropolitan Museum of Art in New York that explored their coregency was titled "Hatshepsut: From Queen to Pharaoh"; Thutmose III would hardly have been happy to know that he would ultimately be overshadowed by his aunt.

### Shaushtatar II of Mittani

Like his grandfather, Thutmose III didn't mention the names of the kings of Mittani whom he attacked, but the man he fought in his thirty-fifth year was probably a powerful leader named Shaushtatar II, whose reign seems to have marked the height of Mittanian power.[106] The only royal inscription that survives from Shaushtatar II's reign is found on the impression of his cylinder seal. It reads, somewhat unhelpfully, "Shaushtatar, son of Parsatatar, king of Maitani."[107] This seal was impressed on the one document that we know was written during his reign—or at least on the only one that has been found. This contract recorded a gift of land that the king donated to a "son of the town of Basiru."[108]

Of the sixteen tablets from Mittani that mention the kings, nine of them were written before the time of Shaushtatar II. But of the six that were written during and after his reign, all—every one of them, no matter where they were found, at four different sites scattered over hundreds of miles—were sealed with the very same seal.[109] What are the chances of that? Shaushtatar II's personal cylinder seal was so treasured by his successors that it became a dynastic heirloom used generation after generation, through the reigns of at least five Mittanian kings. Shaushtatar II must have been deeply revered by his subjects and descendents, even after his death, probably because of his role in establishing his kingdom as a great power.

We can piece together a few facts about Shaushtatar's reign from clues in sundry documents. For one thing, he seems to have traveled from place to place across his empire and to have given out plots of land as gifts to friends and valued officials—this would account for his presence in the city of Basiru and the land donation that was found there.[110]

Also, he expanded the empire to the east. A treaty, written a century later, mentions a "door of silver and gold" that Shaushtatar "took by force from the land of Assyria as a token of his glory and set up in his palace in the city of Washshukkanni."[111] The value of the door shouldn't be underestimated; it must have been a rare prize—perhaps it was a magnificent door of a temple or a palace. Assyrian kings a few generations later filled long sections of their royal inscriptions with accounts of their improvements to temples; gold and silver doors were probably among the great treasures of the land.

So Shaushtatar must have conquered Assyria, to the east of Mittani, and brought it within his empire. Assyria wouldn't be sending any more independent emissaries to Egypt (as it had done earlier) for quite a while.[112] One suspects that when (and if) royal inscriptions and archives of Shaushtatar II are found, he will prove to have been one of the great leaders of this period and easily the match of Thutmose III: a powerful military commander and adept administrator.

### The Land of Mittani

The heart of Shaushtatar II's kingdom, in Syria near the Khabur River, was a land of gentle hills and wild grasslands. Barley and wheat grew thickly in the fields, nourished by the warm sunshine and ample rainfall, and in the spring, wildflowers erupted over the landscape. Looking out from the gates of Washshukkanni, King Shaushtatar could have seen the walls and temple towers of many other cities scattered across the landscape, all under his control. Each town sat on top of a tell that had built up over centuries of occupation, and each was surrounded by hundreds of acres of farmland. Shaushtatar's land experienced none of the fierce extremes of climate that marked the lands of his neighbors. Mittani did not suffer from the dry desert heat of summers in Egypt and Babylonia, or the intense cold of the winters in the high plateaus of Hatti to the north. Shaushtatar no doubt believed that the gods had blessed this land.

The one shortfall in Mittani, though the king probably didn't view it that way, was the same one that had been true for all the earlier kings in this region: a dearth of valuable natural resources. When the king wanted gold or silver, lapis or carnelian for his jewelry, he had to import them. When he wanted copper and tin for making weapons and tools, those had to come in from outside too. The heartland of Mittani was also short on forests; few trees there were suitable for construction. So he couldn't isolate himself from the world beyond his borders, even if he had wanted to; like all his predecessors in this region, he needed to obtain many goods from other lands.

But it's unlikely that Shaushtatar lost much sleep over his country's economy. It was a wealthy place. The area near the capital city was a bread-basket (as it still is for Syria) and could export wheat, barley and beer. Sheep and goat herding had always been important in this region, the wool from the sheep being processed into textiles. Mittanian horses were famous and sought after, as were her chariots. In fact, the development of the war chariot in Mittani and the strict training of horses to pull them might have been two decisive factors in Mittani's rise to power.[113] But perhaps the land was best known for the fine craftsmanship of objects made there. Glass was a brand-new Mittanian invention—not plates of glass, which didn't develop until much later, but small, elegant, multicolored glass vessels.[114] The melted glass was looped around a core and wound into patterns, with different metal ores providing bright colors. Once the glass cooled and hardened, the core was chipped away and removed, leaving a small jar or vase with jewel-like colors and transparency. The Mittanians also figured out how to create shiny glazed pottery and colorful faience.[115] Glazed cylinder seals could be made much more cheaply and easily than stone-carved seals, making them accessible to many more people in society than could previously have afforded them. They're found in large numbers in Mittani.

Artisans also manufactured beautiful objects from the metals and precious stones that the kings of Mittani imported. A list of thousands of items in the dowry that a later Mittanian king assembled for his daughter includes little that was formed from materials native to Mittani, other than perhaps the clothing, blankets, horses, and leather items. Most of the objects were of gold, silver, iron, bronze, lapis, alabaster, and ebony, all of which had been imported and worked into fine objects, such as necklaces, earrings, daggers, bowls, and armor.[116]

Most of the Mittanian population seems to have been made up of farmers of wheat and barley, herders of sheep and goats, and craftsmen.[117] Many of them may have lived in small settlements near their fields and herds; this was an era in Syria when fewer people lived in cities than had done so in the Old Babylonian period before it. The society was stratified—one can see that in the different sizes of houses and the luxury goods found in some of the mansions. Some people were very wealthy, while others were quite poor. In some towns, archaeologists have found evidence for just a few large houses of elite families, almost alone on the tell, with few other inhabitants.[118] Above the peasants and craftsmen in power was an aristocratic class of men who dominated the military. They were chariot warriors, known as the *maryanni,* adept at controlling the nimble new two-wheeled chariots that had recently revolutionized warfare and become an essential part of any army. *Maryanni* is a curious term. The last part, -anni, is a normal Hurrian suffix, but *maryu* was not a local word. Its origin seems to be related to the Sanskrit word *marya* meaning "young soldier."[119]

This might seem to be no more than a coincidence. After all, Sanskrit was a language of ancient India, and India was over a thousand miles away from Mittani. Yet many features of the Mittani ruling class show that they were probably descended from an Indo-Aryan group related to the Sanskrit speakers of India.[120] The names of Kings Shaushtatar and Parattarna wouldn't have been out of place in ancient India, and they make sense in Sanskrit. The same was true of the name of every king in the Mittani dynasty: Shuttarna, Artatama, Tushratta, Artashumara, Shattiwaza.[121] When, at a later time, a Mittanian king listed the gods of his people, he included not only the local Hurrian gods but also "the Mitra-gods, the Varuna-gods, Indra and the Nasatya-gods," all of which are familiar from Indian sources.[122] A few other words in the Hurrian vocabulary came from the same roots—words for horse training, numbers, and colors, and some technical terms.[123]

How did kings with what seem to be South Asian names, who worshiped Vedic gods, end up ruling in Syria? The most widely accepted theory is that they were descendants of a group of migrants who spoke a language closely related to Sanskrit and who had arrived from Central Asia and unified the region by the mid-sixteenth century.[124] Some of them moved on to South Asia. During this same era, other related peoples, known collectively as Indo-European speakers, were traveling throughout Europe and the Middle East. The Hittite language was also Indo-European, as was Greek. Between the lands of Mittani and India, another wave of Indo-Europeans brought Persian speakers to Iran.

By this time, though, one shouldn't envision a Sanskrit-speaking (or so-called Indo-Aryan) elite ruling the Hurrian-speaking masses in Mittani. Aside from their throne names and their high status, almost nothing about the kings seems to have set them apart from rest of the population. Their native language was by now Hurrian, and some, if not all, of the kings seem to have had Hurrian names before they took the throne.[125] Most of the names of their sons and daughters were in the Hurrian language as well. Ancient personal names had more meaning than do our modern names. They didn't just give a clue as to the person's ethnicity or nationality; most were sentences, often expressing piety. One might spend one's life being called "(the god) Shamash is great" or "Gift of (the god) Sin." Many of the Hurrian names in the Mittanian royal family included mention of the Hurrian gods.

So the kings probably thought of themselves as Hurrian in both language and culture, even though they maintained a tradition of using Sanskrit-related throne names. Their own words show that Hurrian gods were more important to them by this time than were the Vedic gods. Shaushka was a Hurrian goddess of love and war, and Shimige was the Hurrian god of the sun. The kings were also devoted to another great Hurrian deity, the goddess Hepat. Most important of all, though, was Teshup, the traditional storm god of the Hurrians. He was believed to live in the temple in Urkesh, an ancient Hurrian capital.

The storm god (under several names) prevailed over the pantheons of many lands in the north and west; the Canaanites, Hittites, and Hurrians all believed that he was among the most powerful of the gods. These were lands without major rivers for irrigation, where people were dependent on the rain that the storm god blessed them with but where they also feared the damage that he could inflict on their lands. Storms were fairly frequent in the fall and spring in these areas, and they were wild and awe-inspiring; a storm swept across the plains like an invading army.

An oncoming storm in ancient times must have been much like storms in the region today. Even with a modern understanding of weather systems, one still can't help but be awed by them. The sky grows heavy and menacing, blades of lightning shooting down towards earth in the distance. The wind is warm and seems to blow in every direction at once. Trees shake and bend towards the ground. The dark undersides of the clouds billow and swirl, and the approaching rain looks like a moving wall charging across the farmland. Thunder cracks constantly—the ancients would have thought that surely this was the roar of Teshup's voice—and as the storm grows nearer there is no break between lightning and thunder. The rain arrives like the opening of a floodgate. Between the constant roars of thunder one hears the rush of water pouring from rooftops, as though the sky had cracked open and a river was pouring down. At night, each lightning flash momentarily silhouettes the landscape and then blows out again, leaving everything in darkness. The wind whips and howls through the trees and the buildings, eerily animating objects as though they had their own life force, banging the wooden doors against their frames. In ancient times, when homes were lit by the flickering flames of oil lamps, the lights would have blown out in the gusts of wind, leaving just the lightning to illuminate the night. Teshup was a war god as well as a storm god, and his army drenched the land, pulled up trees by their roots, and forced the population indoors. No one who has experienced a Syrian storm could wonder why the storm god reigned supreme there in ancient times.

The kings of Mittani seem to have been hungry for land and power right from the start, much more so than their predecessors in that same region. The Hurrian attack on the Hittites during the reign of Hattusili I, all the way back in the seventeenth century BCE, showed that the Hurrian-speaking peoples had no qualms about fighting back when attacked, and Mursili also had to fight Hurrians on his campaign to Babylon.[126] Even before Parattarna I's rule in Mittani, his predecessors seem to have been in a position to expand the kingdom during the sixteenth century BCE, when all their neighbors were weak. At that time, the Kassites were just establishing themselves in Babylonia, the Hyksos still ruled half of a divided Egypt, and the Hittites in Anatolia were suffering through the reigns of a series of weak kings.

This imperialistic approach apparently didn't initially appeal to Mittani's neighbors. The Kassites seem to have had no designs on the states that surrounded them at all, and the Hittites' idea of conquest, so far, was to attack, loot, and leave. Thutmose I was aggressive, but didn't have a successful system for imposing his rule over foreign lands just yet. Mittani kings, by contrast, clearly wanted to control an empire, allowing vassal kings to stay on the throne while controlling—and rewarding—these vassals through formal treaties.

These lesser kings presumably pledged their allegiance to Shaushtatar II, paid tribute, and supplied troops, just as vassals had done during the Old Babylonian period. In exchange, they not only got protection, they also seem to have been awarded land. Shaushtatar II provided the "son of the city of Basiru" with a domain (as recorded in the contract from his reign), and another letter sealed with Shaushtatar's seal (but otherwise undated) refers to lands that a king of Mittani—perhaps Shaushtatar II—had given to a vassal in the past.

### The Household of a Vassal Prince in the East

This second letter with Shaushtatar's seal has quite a tale to tell. It arrived, perhaps from Shaushtatar II himself, at the court of the king of the vassal state of Arrapkha, probably brought by a messenger from Washshukkanni.[127] Arrapkha was hundreds of miles to the east of Washshukkanni in an area of low rolling hills near the Zagros Mountains, an area that traditionally belonged to Assyria. But Shaushtatar had brought the region into his empire when he conquered the city of Ashur.

The letter from the Mittanian king was a practical one. Apparently he had previously given a region within his vassal state of Arrapkha to the local queen, whose name was Amminaia. Now he wanted to change the terms of his gift a little, taking away a town within the region in order to assign it to someone else, and giving her another town in exchange. The letter didn't invite a response; there were no polite pleasantries or questions that begged an answer. He was simply notifying his vassal of the decision that he had made. He wrote "With regard to (the place called) Paharrashe which I gave to (Queen) Amminaia, now, from its confines, I have assigned a town to (a man named) Ugi."[128] He then continued with the details. The vassal king to whom the letter was addressed didn't file the letter in his own archives—had he done so, the letter would be lost to us (as are all the rest of the letters he must have received), since his own palace has not been found. Instead, he gave the letter to Queen Amminaia for her records, and it was in the house where she lived, away from the capital, that it was discovered.[129]

Queen Amminaia resided about eight miles from the capital of Arrapkha in a mansion outside the walls of the agricultural town of Nuzi. She owned land in at least six different cities in the kingdom and must have been wealthy and influential in her own right. The letter from the king of Mittani refers to just one of her holdings. The villa where she lived (and where the letter was found) belonged to her son, Prince Shilwa-Teshup. The house has been excavated and found to contain about 730 cuneiform tablets that had been abandoned there by Shilwa-Teshup and his family.[130] Unfortunately, none of the other tablets mention the kings of Mittani at all. But they, and the house in which they were found, do tell us a lot about the lives of an elite provincial family within the empire.

Shilwa-Teshup's villa was, like so many ancient Mesopotamian houses, centered around a courtyard. But it was much larger than a normal dwelling, with over thirty-five rooms, some of them tiled, some boasting terracotta pipes to carry away wastewater.[131] The walls of Shilwa-Teshup's house had been decorated by an artist familiar with motifs borrowed from as far away as Egypt and the Aegean.[132] The paintings included panels of red and gray, decorated with delicate designs such as palmette trees, the head of the Egyptian goddess Hathor, and the Aegean symbol of bulls' horns.[133] Egypt and Greece were hundreds of miles away, of course, but artists at Nuzi had adopted the foreign artistic motifs into their own style. Shilwa-Teshup and his family must have taken pride in the spacious rooms of their house, decorated as they were in the height of fashion. Nuzi may have been a relatively small and provincial place, but it was still connected to the wider international world.

Queen Amminaia was mentioned often in the cuneiform tablets that were excavated from Shilwa-Teshup's house, but the mother and son did not live alone there—far from it. The prince, along with his principal wife Shashuri, headed a large household. Many ration lists were found, showing that Shashuri received substantial amounts of grain, oil, and wool from the family storage rooms—much more than she needed just to eat. She probably used the extra as an allowance with which to purchase other items.[134] Queen Amminaia also received rations, though it's hard to see why she needed them, given her large landholdings. Lower in status than Shashuri and Amminaia, Shilwa-Teshup's seven lesser wives lived in the mansion as well, probably with their children. They too received rations (though less than those of Shashuri), as did a grown son of Shilwa-Teshup and the son's wife. This was a big family, but Shilwa-Teshup could afford to support them all.[135] He also paid rations to dozens of slaves and hired men who farmed his land, took care of his herds, and created textiles in his workshops.[136]

The texts found in Shilwa-Teshup's house include much more than ration lists (and the letter from the Mittanian king); among them were contracts, marriage documents, declarations in court, loan records, and lists of sheep, goats, oxen, and horses.[137] They show that Shilwa-Teshup was a rich man, the crown prince of Arrapkha, who used his wealth judiciously and kept meticulous records.[138] He made large loans of grain, wood, and silver, but he did not charge interest on the loans.[139] Instead, he profited from foreclosing on the loans when the debtors couldn't pay. Although, as we have seen, Shilwa-Teshup's household occasionally had reasons to be in touch with the great king of Mittani, for the most part Shilwa-Teshup busied himself with matters closer to home.

His situation may have been typical of a vassal prince of this time. The vassal kings of Mittani were allowed quite a lot of freedom in ruling their domains, as long as they remained loyal to the great king (and presumably paid their taxes or tribute to him). The affluence of the vassal kings and their families (like that of Shilwa-Teshup) made possible the affluence of the whole Mittanian empire.

Shilwa-Teshup's father, the king of Arrapkha, vassal to the king of Mittani, must have lived in the provincial capital, which, unfortunately, lies under the modern city of Kirkuk, inaccessible to archaeologists. His palace might, though, have resembled a palace at Nuzi, not far from Shilwa-Teshup's house. Nuzi had only about 1,600 inhabitants, and this palace, within the city walls, wasn't home to a king but to a mayor. Still, it was an impressive building. It had over 100 rooms, with a bakery, wells for fresh water, toilets, and offices for government officials. The private apartments were luxurious; their walls were painted in much the same international style found in Shilwa-Teshup's house, with brightly colored bands of triangles and other geometric patterns and panels showing stylized plants and bull's heads.[140] These rooms boasted imported marble floors and even marble seats on the toilets, which were flushed using water from a pot on an adjacent stand.[141] The mayor, the members of the royal family, and other wealthy people in Nuzi, ate and drank from luxury vessels made in a very finely decorated style called "Nuzi ware." The goblets and cups made in this style were elegant and distinctive, with a black or reddish brown background and fine white geometric patterns and plant forms forming the decoration in bands around the vessels. Pottery in this style wasn't limited to Nuzi—it almost certainly didn't even develop there—but is found at sites right across Mittani.[142] Travel must have been relatively easy within the empire, allowing traders and other travelers to bring objects in the latest styles to the provinces.

The town was also home not only to farmers but also to scribes, judges, craftsmen of all kinds, and many textile workers, who produced fabrics for the palace. As in so many Mesopotamian and Syrian cities, locally manufactured textiles helped drive the economy. The townspeople paid their taxes, and the town in turn paid taxes to Arrapkha. The king of Arrapkha no doubt sent on a lot of this in tribute to the king of Mittani. The economy of Nuzi flourished, allowing imports of luxury goods from far away, some of which were resold at a profit.[143]

And yet Nuzi was not a particularly remarkable place, just one of hundreds of towns within the Mitannian empire. It's important to us only because the excavations there have been so thorough and have included areas of private housing as well as public buildings like the palace, and because the town was burned late in the fourteenth century, leaving almost 7,000 cuneiform documents in the ruins (regrettably, none of them mention any of the kings of Mittani).[144]

In a way, Nuzi is important for its very ordinariness. One gets a sense of the general wealth and prosperity of the time if such an average town could boast such a strong economy and such amenities.

### A Vassal Kingdom in the West

A couple of tablets found in excavations show that another small town at the opposite end of the empire had also been visited by a messenger from the king of Mittani, or perhaps by the great king himself. This was Alalakh, the town that had been ruled by Idrimi a few generations before. It lay towards the western end of the empire, on the Orontes River, not far from the Mediterranean coast. Two tablets found there were sealed with Shaushtatar II's seal (though during the reigns of later kings). Like Nuzi, Alalakh was burned when it was conquered, preserving the cuneiform tablets right where they were lying at the moment of the conflagration. The destruction probably took place around 1425 BCE, possibly as a result of a Hittite attack, but the city remained in the Mittanian empire for many more years.[145]

A messenger arriving in Alalakh with a message from the king would have noticed some similarities with other Mittanian towns like Nuzi. For one thing, he would have heard the same languages spoken around him—mostly Hurrian and Akkadian—and the names of the people he met on the street were mostly Hurrian as well.[146] If he had a message for the local king, he would have been directed to the palace. Its layout wasn't much like that of the palace at Nuzi, though it was equally grand. The messenger would have approached the palace up a short flight of stone steps that led to a shaded portico supported by two huge columns. To his right and left, the lower parts of the walls were ornamented with blocks of polished basalt. Beyond the anteroom, in place of the open courtyard he might have expected, was a large room with a hearth.[147]

Alalakh was more the equivalent of Arrapkha than of Nuzi; it was the capital of a Mittanian vassal kingdom and home to a dynasty of local kings.[148] As in Arrapkha, these kings seem to have been largely left alone by their Mittanian overlord; the vassals took censuses of their people, distributed rations, and decided legal disputes. They even made treaties with other vassal kings.[149] In one such treaty, drawn up with another king and sealed by the king of Alalakh, the two kings were particularly concerned with fugitives escaping from one land into the other:

> If anyone from my country approaches your land to live there, if you hear of it, you must report it. If he lives in your country, you must seize him and give him up. If there are captives from my country whom they sell in your country you must seize them along with the one who sold them, and give them to me.[150]

In creating this treaty, the vassals were participating in a tradition that had its roots way back in Ebla and the Early Dynastic period. The two partners knew what to expect from one another, and they would have honored their reciprocal obligations.

### The Value of Swearing an Oath as a Vassal

The Mitannian kings must have drawn up treaties with each of their vassals as well, as the earlier king Parattarna I had done with Idrimi of Alalakh. These treaties were witnessed by the local gods, and would have included all the usual clauses and curses. In each case, both the vassal and the overlord swore to uphold the agreement.[151] Near Eastern kings knew that treaties were a simple necessity if one wanted an empire to run smoothly.

In Mittani, as in the kingdoms of Mari and Ebla so many centuries before, the great king gave his vassals reasons to want to stay in the empire. He pledged to help them if they were attacked, he confirmed them on their thrones, he sometimes gave them land, and he took them on as his "sons." They sent him tribute in return and contributed their troops to his campaigns.

The Egyptian kings don't seem to have been familiar with this system. Their idea of a relationship with a vassal was much more one-sided. An Egyptian vassal was required to swear an oath of loyalty to the king, but the king didn't have to swear to the oath at all.[152] The vassal would send tribute not as part of a contractual arrangement, but because the Egyptian king could force him to.[153] The pharaoh didn't feel that he needed to do anything in return.[154] But Thutmose III might have started learning a thing or two from his Syrian neighbors. At some point during his reign, he decided to install a vassal king in the land of Nuhashe in Syria. In the ceremony associated with this, the pharaoh "put oil on his (the vassal's) head."[155] Some sort of ritual involving oil had been performed in treaty ceremonies in Syria ever since the kings of Ebla and Mari had formed their alliance in the twenty-third century BCE. Brides were also anointed with oil before their weddings, which makes sense—in both a wedding and a vassal treaty ceremony, new family ties (whether real or symbolic) were being created between people.[156] In Mesopotamia and Syria, the kings would not have felt threatened or weakened by bringing their vassals into the extended family that was their state.[157] It made them stronger, in fact. The Egyptian kings took a long time to grasp this idea.

In the sixty years between 1504 BCE, when Thutmose I first came to the throne, and 1444, when Thutmose III launched his second attack on Mittani, both Egypt and Mittani had grown in strength and aggressiveness. The international diplomatic system of earlier centuries, with its ambassadors, gift exchanges, treaties of alliance, and dynastic marriages, had gone into decline. Mittani's kings don't seem, at first, to have been interested in collaborating with their equals; they were hostile towards both Hatti and Egypt, having swallowed up Assyria and Kizzuwatna. Egypt, in turn, had imposed imperial control on Nubia and Canaan and was looking hungrily at the lands controlled by Mittani. This was a time of war; neither Mittani nor Egypt recognized any absolute borders, and the Egyptian king, at least, claimed the right to rule the whole world. One might have thought that they would fight to the death.

On the other hand, each power might well have initially underestimated the other, having had little previous contact. Now, in the contemporary reigns of Tuthmose III and Shaushtatar II, they had seen one another's armies and knew that they were well matched. Perhaps both kings sat up late with their advisors in their separate capitals wondering if it might be possible to completely annihilate the other, and if not, what their options might be. Hatti and Babylon had both sent gifts to Egypt; they didn't pose a threat at this point. To Egypt the immediate problem was Mittani, and that problem was to be solved just a few years later.

### CHAPTER SEVEN

# Diplomatic Overtures between the Great Powers

*"A notable event! The like of this occurrence had not been heard of since the time of the demigods"*

### An Athletic and Aggressive King: Amenhotep II

Pharaoh Amenhotep II, who came to power in 1427 BCE, was one of the great warrior kings of Egypt's New Kingdom, a man who prided himself on his military ruthlessness and athletic prowess. So it is perhaps surprising that it was during his reign that Egypt finally was brought into the system of alliances that had for so many centuries helped to create stability in Syria and Mesopotamia.

It's unfortunate for us, in a way, that so many of the kings of the Eighteenth Dynasty in Egypt were named either Amenhotep or Thutmose (there were four of each). Amenhotep II tends to be overshadowed by his more famous descendents, Amenhotep III and IV. In fact, the Amenhoteps and Thutmoses weren't often called by these names during their own lifetimes—during his reign, Amenhotep II was almost universally referred to as Aakherperure, his "king of Lower and Upper Egypt name" (the name that was enclosed in a cartouche).

Amenhotep II was the son of Thutmose III, the great fighter who had built the Egyptian empire, and in many ways he was the image of his father. He came to the throne at the age of eighteen, already strong and athletic, and happy to brag about it.[1] He excelled (according to his own inscriptions) at rowing, running, horsemanship, and archery. Three separate inscriptions described the king as having superhuman strength when he fired multiple arrows at metal targets. In one, the king

> found erected for him four targets of Asiatic copper of one palm in thickness.... His Majesty appeared in his chariot.... He took up his bow and grabbed four arrows at once. He rode northward shooting at them...his arrows coming forth from their back-sides as he shot another post. Now it was a deed that had never been done before, nor heard of by report: shooting at a target of copper an arrow that came forth from it and landed on the ground.[2]

Could anyone fire an arrow with such strength that it would go right through a thick copper target and land on the ground? The target shown in a sculpture of Amenhotep II firing his arrows was not a sheet of copper on a wooden structure, as one might expect. It was a solid block of copper cast in the traditional "oxhide" shape of copper ingots. Amenhotep II was, of course, making the case that he wasn't just anyone.

In this inscription, set up next to the Great Sphinx (which was already a very ancient monument), everything that Amenhotep was said to have done emphasized his athleticism. Whereas his men, after just half a mile of rowing,

Amenhotep II, king of Egypt, shown riding his chariot and shooting arrows right through a copper target. The target is in the form of a solid copper "oxhide"-shaped ingot. (Foto Marburg/Art Resource, NY)

"were weak, limp in body, and breathless," the manly king "had done three miles of rowing without interrupting his stroke."[3]

Could he really have been so physically imposing, or was this just pharaonic rhetoric? The tomb of Amenhotep II was found in 1898 with, to the joy of the archaeologists, a mummy lying in the sarcophagus. After the discovery of innumerable tombs that were empty, robbed in antiquity, this was the first tomb in which the body of the pharaoh was still there. (The discovery of Tutankhamen's tomb came over twenty years later.[4]) The mummy is of a tall man; he stood over six feet and would have towered over most contemporary Egyptians, who were considerably shorter than modern people from the same region—he was someone who looked quite capable of the feats ascribed to him.[5]

Amenhotep II's bravado was not just based on his athletic skill. It continued in his descriptions of his military engagements. He bragged in a letter that he was "without opponent in any land."[6] Not surprisingly, though, opponents sprang up almost as soon as Thutmose III died.[7]

### More Egyptian Attacks on Mittani

In Amenhotep II's seventh year, he set out to put down the rebellions and to fight against Mittani.[8] In a monumental inscription that he set up in his capital city of Memphis, Amenhotep II's first boast (after a list of all his epithets and titles) was that "His mace struck Naharin (Mittani), while his bow trampled Nubia."[9]

Thutmose III, in his earlier inscriptions, had admitted that his armies played a major role in his victories. Not so his son. Amenhotep II wrote his war accounts as though he had accomplished every victory single-handedly: "There was no one with his majesty except himself with his valiant, powerful arm. His majesty slew them (the enemy) with arrows." His army is almost never mentioned, except to note that they were of no help at all: "His majesty watched over them (a group of prisoners) until the break of day, his battle axe being in his right hand, he being alone with no one with him. At that time, the army was far from him, except for the personal servants of pharaoh."

Amenhotep II described the stages of his journey through western Syria in his seventh-year campaign, but nowhere does he seem to have encountered the king of Mittani himself.[10] Shaushtatar II did not bring his armies out to meet Amenhotep, and the pharaoh doesn't seem to have ventured far into Mittanian territory.[11] In fact, in spite of mentioning that he struck Mittani, Amenhotep II seems to have avoided including in his inscriptions the types of hostile references to Mittani that his father had relished.

The pharaoh was successful in his first campaign, bringing home almost unbelievable amounts of gold and silver as booty: 1,643 pounds of gold and 120,833 pounds of silver.[12] He also outdid his predecessors in his brutal treatment of the enemy, especially in how he punished seven rebel princes from Canaan. They were first "placed head downward at the prow of his majesty's barge," apparently while still alive. When Amenhotep II got back to the temple of Amen in Thebes, "with joy of heart to his father, Amen, he slew with his own weapon the seven princes."[13] One wonders how he did this; did the king cut their heads off with his ax or crush them over the head with his mace? The latter was an image that had been popular with Egyptian kings since the third millennium BCE. Amenhotep II himself referred to this execution method in another stela: "The southerners come to him bowed down, the northerners on their bellies. He has gathered them all into his fist, his mace has crushed upon their heads."[14] But he also used decapitation at times: "His heart is satisfied when he sees them after he decapitated the trouble makers."[15]

It is hard to understand the "joy of heart" that Amenhotep II felt in dispatching his enemies in these ways. As if the rebels had not suffered enough indignities, six of their bodies were then hung up in front of the wall of Thebes. How did the Thebans feel about this grisly addition to their beautiful city? The body of the last prince was taken south to Nubia "and hanged on the wall of Napata, in order to cause to be manifest the victories of his majesty."

Amenhotep II's second northern campaign, in his ninth year, didn't get as far as Mittani; he stuck to his Canaanite territories.[16] He claimed to have been greeted with open arms and given presents in some cities (perhaps because the residents feared what he might do if they resisted). The people of the city of Aphek, for example, "came out with gifts because of the great victories of the pharaoh."[17] Other cities resisted and were plundered. This time, though, the king seems to have been less interested in killing the rebels and more interested in taking captives. He listed an astounding 101,128 prisoners taken in the second campaign, along with "all their herds and all their endless cattle, sixty gold and silver chariots, 1,032 painted chariots, including all their weapons of war being 13,500."[18] Scholars debate whether the huge numbers represent an exaggeration or a combined account from several campaigns.[19] But perhaps his army did capture this much wealth. What they did with over 101,000 prisoners is another question. It's unlikely that they all ended up as slaves in Egypt; even in the New Kingdom, slavery didn't play a big role in the Egyptian economy. Perhaps they were resettled somewhere within the Egyptian empire. This tactic was used many centuries later by the Neo-Assyrian kings to remove hostile peoples from their homeland (and the source of their rebellion) and set them to work farming land that could be made productive—and could therefore be a source of taxes. It may be that Amenhotep II had the same idea.

### Foreign Delegations Appeal to Egypt

Amenhotep II was, according to his propaganda, king not just of Egypt but of the whole world: "All countries are under his fear.... All countries have his protection; his borders reach the rim of heaven, the lands are in his hand in a single knot.... His portion is that on which Ra shines, to him belongs what Ocean encircles."[20] The overall impression one gets is of a heartless world ruler and superhero, undefeated, and (at least in his own eyes) infinitely superior to the rest of the human race. He doesn't seem a likely candidate for the role of peacemaker; he scarcely even conceded that there was anyone left outside his empire with whom he would need to make peace.

But the very last section of his Memphis inscription, recording the culmination of his achievements in his Asiatic campaigns, was not about hunting, or campaigning, or shooting arrows through targets, or decapitating enemies, or bringing home prisoners and loot, but about the respect the king had gained from his powerful (though distant) neighbors:

> Now at that time the chieftain of Naharin (Mittani), the chieftain of Hatti, and the chieftain of Sangar (Babylonia) heard of the great victories which [his majesty] had accomplished. Each one tried to outdo his counterpart with gifts of every foreign land. They thought on account of their grandfathers to implore his majesty, to go that the breath of life be given to them. 'We shall carry our taxes to your palace, Son of Ra, Amenhotep, divine ruler of Heliopolis, ruler of rulers, a panther who rages in every foreign land and in this land forever.'[21]

As Amenhotep II saw it (or at least as he presented it to his Egyptian audience), the great kings of these lands sent elaborate gifts because they were so impressed by his conquests. Of course, this also makes it sound as though they were far from being his equals. The words were not unlike those that his father, Thutmose III, used when foreign delegations from Hatti, Assyria, and Babylonia had sent him gifts. Hatti and Babylonia had every reason to continue to be supportive of Egypt if the pharaoh was going to keep Mittani in check.[22] But now Mittani was involved in sending gifts as well, and that was something new.

Amenhotep II also mentioned a visit from the "chiefs of Mittani" alone in another inscription from Karnak, this time leaving out any mention of

Babylonia or Hatti.[23] Here the pharaoh elaborated more, noting that the Mittanians came "their tribute upon their backs, to seek the peace of His Majesty, desirous of his sweet breath of life. A notable event! [The like of this occurrence] had not been heard of since the time of the demigods: this land which knew not Egypt was supplicating the Good God!"[24]

The ruler of Mittani at the time was probably still Shaushtatar II.[25] It seems highly unlikely, however, that he was one of the "chiefs of Mittani" who actually visited Egypt in person, because doing so would have required leaving his capital for months. The chiefs mentioned by Amenhotep II were probably high officials and ambassadors.

Asking the pharaoh to grant "the breath of life" was a phrase used in Egyptian royal inscriptions when lesser kings appealed to the pharaoh for his favor. So was the pharaoh implying that Mittani, Hatti, and Babylonia were simply his vassals? He might have wanted his subjects to think so, but he would have known that in reality they were great kings themselves and not within his grasp. Of course, until the beginning of the New Kingdom, no pharaoh had encountered another king that he would have viewed, by any stretch of the imagination, as his equal, so the Egyptians didn't have a set of phrases to denote this. The fact, though, that the chiefs of Mittani were said to have come "to seek the peace from his Majesty" marks a new development. "Seeking peace" was not a phrase used with respect to vassals, and it is a telling sign of the new way in which these great kings were seeing one another—as partners in peace rather than as enemies in war.[26] And even Amenhotep II couldn't help but comment on how remarkable it was that he found himself talking with representatives from Mittani; it was indeed "a notable event!"

If only we knew more about this moment. After it, things seem to have radically changed between the kings of Mittani and Egypt and, in fact, across the whole Near East. The formerly bellicose Amenhotep II didn't send his armies back out again into Syria at all after that second campaign in his ninth year.[27] In a dramatic transformation, his reign became remarkably peaceful, notable for the many buildings he constructed.[28] He seems to have agreed to a peace treaty with Mittani, surprising though that may seem given the history of hostilities between the two lands.

Unfortunately, the documentation that we have from other eras of Near Eastern history for this type of peace agreement is simply missing in this case. There are no preserved letters between the kings or their officials, no text of a peace treaty, no administrative documents listing the oil or silver required for the ceremony, nothing but the pompous statements by the Egyptian king about the foreign kings bringing tribute. But peace did break out between the kings of Egypt and Mittani, and it continued into the reigns of their sons and grandsons.

## Why the King of Mittani Sought Peace

It seems likely that it was Shaushtatar II who made the first gesture of friendship towards Amenhotep II, rather than vice versa.[29] The diplomatic alliance that ended up flourishing between their two lands was entirely Syro-Mesopotamian in its conception. It was something that only a king of Mittani, or perhaps Babylonia, could have brought to the table. He clearly proposed to the pharaoh the system that was so familiar to him: ambassadors would travel between the courts of the great kings carrying letters; the kings would refer to one another as "brother"; they would write on clay tablets in Akkadian cuneiform; they would send one another lavish gifts of equal value; they would agree to regard one another as equals; their families would intermarry; and they would abide by treaties to which they both agreed. All these aspects of the diplomatic system came to be adopted in the relationships between Egypt and the other great powers of the time. Over a thousand years of tradition lay behind these ideas in Syria—in the very lands where Shaushtatar ruled—whereas almost none of this had any history in Egypt. And yet the Egyptian king agreed to it.

As to whether it was the Babylonians or the Mittanians who introduced the ideas, Mittani was almost certainly the one. Amenhotep II singled out Mittani in his inscription as the land seeking peace, and the kings of Mittani and Egypt had locked horns for decades. Babylonia had not been involved, except to send gifts to first Thutmose III and later Amenhotep II. Mittani was much more engaged with Egypt than were either Babylonia or Hatti.

So the obvious question is why? Assuming that Shaushtatar II proposed an alliance, and Amenhotep II agreed—what inspired them both?

Shaushtatar was in a tough position after Amenhotep II's second campaign. He would have seen clearly that the pharaoh was aggressive, and the execution of Canaanite princes and all those deportations of Canaanites to Egypt must have come as a shock to Mittani. Amenhotep II was using tactics that were designed to terrify populations into submission to Egypt, tactics that no king is known to have used before him.[30] And Egypt wasn't the only threat. Hatti, to the northwest, was also becoming aggressive towards Mittani. Shaushtatar II was in the position of possibly having to fight enemies on two fronts.[31]

The years since the Hittite attack on Babylon in 1595 BCE had initially been troubled ones for the kings of Hatti. Mursili I, the king who had led the Babylonian attack, had been assassinated by two of his in-laws. His sister's husband then seized the throne, but when that man died, his sons (and heirs) were killed by Mursili's other assassin, who in turn took the throne.[32] It only got worse: this new king was killed by his own son, and the assassinations continued, all the time weakening the kingdom. Stability didn't return to Hatti until about three generations after Mursili's death, when a king named Telipinu (whose vague claim to legitimacy was that he was married to the sister of a king whose claim was equally dubious) decided to break the cycle of assassinations.[33] He proclaimed "From now on in Hattusa, let nobody do evil to a son of the family and draw a dagger on him." He also spoke wisely to future kings: "Do not kill anybody of your family. It (is) not right."[34]

Once Telipinu had pulled the Hittite kingdom back together, he acknowledged the king of Kizzuwatna (located directly between Hatti and Mittani) as a "great king" and drew up a treaty with him.[35] Kizzuwatna was taken over by Mittani under Telipinu's weaker successors, but the treaty with Hatti was renewed (though this time with Kizzuwatna in an inferior position) under a later king, Tudhaliya I, who was probably a contemporary of Shaushtatar II of Mittani.

In this treaty, Mittani was cast as a potential enemy of Hatti.[36] The Hittite king wrote: "If any cities of the land of Hurri (Mittani) interfere with the cities of (the king of Kizzuwatna), we will fight side by side against the ruler of Hurri."[37] This sounds defensive, as though the allies were planning for the future, when the king of Mittani might "interfere" in Kizzuwatna. That was probably a pretty safe bet, given how Kizzuwatna had bounced back and forth between its two powerful neighbors in the past. But later the Hittite king wrote, in the same treaty, "in regard to whatever cities of the land of Hurri we defeat—I, My Majesty, will take all that I, My Majesty, desire." He seemed to relish the idea of defeating Mittanian cities and taking booty.

This must have worried Shaushtatar II. The Hittite king, Tudhaliya I, wasn't just full of words. He had already taken his armies all the way to the Aegean in the west, fighting in Anatolian kingdoms along the way.[38] He had campaigned in Syria and managed to convince the rich city of Aleppo to switch its allegiance to Hatti from Mittani. He had also put down a rebellion within his territory that might have been instigated by Mittani.[39] After these intrusions so close to home, Shaushtatar II probably expected an outright war with Hatti.

Interestingly, though, it seems that the two kingdoms—Hatti and Mittani—were still in communication through their diplomats, even when posturing as though they were preparing for war. In the introduction to his treaty with Kizzuwatna, Tudhaliya provided informative quotes from letters that he had written to the king of Mittani. In one he was complaining about some refugees from a contested city, who had fled to Mittani: "I, My Majesty, sent to the ruler of Hurri (Mittani): 'Return my subjects!'" One suspects that his letter was longer than this, that it included the usual introductory greetings and plenty of arguments for the return of the subjects. But he credited the king of Mittani with being even more succinct in his response: "the ruler of Hurri sent back to My Majesty thus: 'No!'"

The ambassadors continued to go back and forth between the capital cities, even as Mittanians plundered the contested territory that both kingdoms claimed. The Hittite king posed a question to the Mittanian king in his next letter, asking him what he would think if the tables were turned: "I ... sent as follows to the ruler of Hurri: 'If some land were to free itself from you and turn to Hatti, then how would this matter be?' The ruler of Hurri sent to me as follows: 'Exactly the same!'"

So now, the two kingdoms had reached a crisis point. The Hittites felt that the king of Mittani had broken an old treaty, making it void: "We will certainly erase the tablet of the oath which had been made previously. We will indeed discard the word of the ruler of Hurri." The treaty he referred to erasing and discarding probably had governed Kizzuwatna's relationship as a vassal of Mittani, since the Hittite king added that the king of Kizzuwatna "is no longer [the subject] of the ruler of Hurri." A new treaty was in order, probably the very one in which this account was written, but this one would be between Kizzuwatna and Hatti, not Mittani: "We will make another tablet," Tudhaliya wrote. And once this new treaty was in place, the exchange of diplomats would come to an end, at least between Mittani and Kizzuwatna. The king of Kizzuwatna "must not send his messenger to the ruler of Hurri, and he must not allow the messenger of the land of Hurri into his land." The Hittite king probably feared that the king of Kizzuwatna might be convinced to defect again to Mittani if the persuasive Mittanian ambassadors were allowed to visit his court. He also anticipated that the Mittanian king might try to win Hittite favor with extravagant gifts, but he was determined not to be bribed: "if on account of (the king of Kizzuwatna) the King of Hurri prepares some diplomatic gift, for the sake of (the king of Kizzuwatna) I ... will not accept his gift." This suggests that gift giving might have been a way of avoiding war, and was recognized as such.

Shaushtatar II seems, therefore, to have lost Kizzuwatna, and was facing the prospect of an attack by Tudhaliya I of Hatti on his lands. Given all this aggression, Shaushtatar might have reasoned, it would be better to be on the same side as Egypt than to have Egypt and Hatti join forces against him. He might well have heard about the gifts that the king of Hatti had sent to Egypt during the reign of Thutmose III, and perhaps also about gifts that were being sent to Amenhotep II. He would have stood little chance of defeating both his enemies together. Also, Shaushtatar might have thought about the possible future of his relationship with Egypt. With his strong military he had been able to keep Egypt at bay for now, and probably could continue to do so, but he couldn't possibly invade Egypt. It was simply too far away and too powerful. The best he could hope for was to keep fending off the pharaoh's forces if they continued to attack.

Shaushtatar might also have considered the situation from an economic perspective. He wouldn't have thought of it in those terms, of course—the ancient languages don't even have a word for "economics"—but he must have seen where his interests lay. Fighting against nearby cities, conquering and looting them, and bringing them into the Mittani empire was one thing; fighting the Egyptian army was another. It was expensive both in terms of arms and personnel, and since the fighting would take place in Shaushtatar's own territory, there was little chance of gaining wealth through looting, except in taking weapons and armor from the Egyptians.

The other side of the equation was that Egypt was very rich. If the Egyptians continued to fight Mittani, Shaushtatar probably couldn't obtain luxury goods from Egypt. If they were at peace, he could hope for access to Egyptian gold.

Shaushtatar wouldn't have had to come up with any radical new ideas in order to imagine an alliance with Egypt; such alliances were almost as old as civilization itself in his area. And all those centuries of diplomatic relationships between cities had demonstrated the many advantages, including wealth from the exchange of luxury gifts, good feelings from frequent letter-writing, and kinship ties from marrying one's daughters to foreign kings.

Shaushtatar's (probably) pragmatic mind might have also checked off other reasons to propose this alliance, and he would have considered the gods. Would they approve? Ancient Near Eastern gods were in many ways perceived by the population as very self-centered. They didn't care about big issues like human salvation or suffering, and they didn't have any special plans for the future, whether for bringing on the end of the world or for converting nonbelievers. They wanted meals at the right times and roofs over their heads. Prayers and hymns were appreciated, as were fancy clothes and jewelry. They didn't approve of being taken out of their temples and sent into exile (which usually only happened when a city was conquered), though they did travel, in times of peace, to the capital cities of allies.[40] Although they were sometimes said to have directed the kings to go to war, peace suited most of the gods just fine. In times of peace, the temple estates prospered and the gods were wealthy landowners. Besides, Syrian and Mesopotamian gods had been witnessing and enforcing peace treaties for centuries. Of course they approved.

One of the king's traditional roles in Mesopotamia and Syria had been to maintain order, and to create order where it was lacking. Egypt had become a source of disorder for the Mittanians. Its forces were powerful and unpredictable. What could be more disorderly than for the populations of whole cities to be deported en masse far from their beloved homes? Egypt couldn't be conquered, but it could perhaps be tamed. If the king of Egypt would participate in the time-honored practice of diplomacy, he would be less likely to wreak havoc beyond his empire. Send him gifts and ask for gifts in exchange; send ambassadors to his court; regale him with friendly letters; make him agree that he is your equal; make him behave in ways you can predict—then order will take the place of chaos.

And, above all, make him a brother. This is what Shaushtatar and his advisors must have decided. A man who recognized the ties of family would no longer be a stranger or an enemy or a barbarian.

## How the King of Mittani Sought Peace

Once the decision had been reached to try to get the king of Egypt to agree to an alliance, the Mittanian king must have acted fairly quickly. We know from Amenhotep II's inscriptions that a "chieftain of Naharin" arrived in Egypt with gifts not long after the pharaoh had returned to Memphis from his campaign to Canaan (accompanied by his vast horde of prisoners).

A Mittanian messenger had been to Egypt before this, though, after Amenhotep II's first Syrian campaign in his seventh year. According to the pharaoh's Memphis inscription, Amenhotep had been traveling "south within the Valley of Sharon" on his way home when he "discovered a messenger of the chieftain of Naharin (Mittani) carrying a document around his neck. He carried him off as a prisoner-of-war at the rear of the chariot."[41] One wonders where this Mittanian messenger had been heading. Was his message for one of the Canaanite leaders? Or was he perhaps intercepted on his way to Egypt with an early message for Amenhotep II from Shaushtatar II about a possible alliance?

This messenger must have feared for his life as he was transported to Egypt in the chariot, traveling with the Egyptian army and all their booty from the campaign. He would have known of Amenhotep II's reputation for brutality and perhaps wondered whether he would be killed and his body hung up as a warning, alongside those unfortunate Canaanite princes. But that document that hung in a pouch around his neck must have intrigued Amenhotep II, enough to warrant a mention in the inscription and, perhaps, enough to spare the life of the messenger. At least, Amenhotep didn't mention having killed him. If the messenger was bringing a first letter from Shaushtatar, though, it's odd that he seems to have been traveling alone.

The first formal embassy sent by Mittani to Egypt to start negotiations for an alliance almost certainly involved more than one lone messenger. Shaushtatar II would have sent one or more high-ranking officials, a guard (as in Old Babylonian times), and gifts. They no doubt took a letter from their king to the pharaoh with them, probably in a pouch around the neck of one of the men.

What would Shaushtatar II have written in his letter? Although we can read none of the first missives that passed between Mittani and Egypt, because they have not yet been found, we do have a letter that might have resembled that first one. When Assyria gained its independence from Mittani, some years later, the Assyrian king sent a letter to the pharaoh in Egypt to try to precipitate diplomatic relations. It's a very short, straightforward note:

> Say to the king of E[gypt]: Thus Ashur-ubal[lit, the king of As]syria. For you, your household, for your [coun]try, for your chariots and your troops, may all go well. I send my messenger to you to visit you and to visit your country. Up to now, my predecessors have not written; today I write to you. [I] send you a beautiful chariot, two horses, [and] one date-stone of genuine lapis lazuli, as your greeting gift. Do [no]t delay the messenger whom I send to you for a visit. He should visit and then leave for here. He should see what you are like and what your country is like, and then leave for here.[42]

In the same way, the first letter sent from the Mittanian king would probably have started off with wishes for the pharaoh's well-being. When the Assyrian king wrote his letter, long after Shaushtatar's reign, the diplomatic community (which included not just Egypt and Mittani but also Hatti and Babylonia) was long established, and he didn't presume to ask for friendship, let alone brotherhood—these were by then seen as privileged terms only used among the great kings. On the other hand, Shaushtatar II from Mittani might have done so right away in a letter to Amenhotep II. Shaushtatar's goal would have been brotherhood.

In the later Assyrian letter, the king didn't ask for anything in exchange when he sent the chariot, horses, and lapis to the Egyptian king. Perhaps the Mittanian king didn't either when he first approached Egypt. (This would have made it even easier for the Egyptian king to claim in his inscription that the Mittanian representatives arrived "with their tribute upon their backs to seek the peace of His Majesty."⁴³)

The Assyrian king just wanted his messenger to be allowed to look around and to return home safely (which he reiterated in three of the eight sentences in the letter). In spite of the man's long journey, the king claimed that he wanted the messenger only to "see what you are like and what your country is like." He was to be the eyes and ears for his king, who no doubt wanted to hear about the appearance of this Egyptian pharaoh, how big his palace might be, and whether his land was rich and fertile (and if gold was strewn all over the ground, a common legend about Egypt).⁴⁴ The Mittanian king might well have made the same request for his messenger to be sent back quickly after delivering the gifts and the letter. But he wanted more than just for the delegation to be sent home. He might have proposed right away that the two kings enter into a formal, oath-bound relationship.

It's possible that Amenhotep II was astounded at the presumptuousness of the letter he received, once the Mittanian delegation had been granted an audience in order to read it to him. The king of Mittani wouldn't have groveled in the way that an Egyptian or a vassal would in writing a letter to the pharaoh. The standard greeting, at least in later years, from such a person was "I fall at the feet of my Lord, my Sun, seven times and seven times."⁴⁵ Shaushtatar II certainly didn't fall at anyone's feet, in person or in writing, and would have opened the letter with a greeting that assumed his equal standing with the pharaoh.

Shaushtatar's letter (like later such letters) must have been in Akkadian, written in the cuneiform script on a clay tablet, not in Egyptian hieroglyphs on papyrus. How did the Egyptian king understand the words when they were read to him? He didn't speak Akkadian. It could be that one of the Mittanian messengers spoke both Akkadian and Egyptian and translated as he read, or perhaps a translator had been sent along as well. This might have been someone who spoke Egyptian, perhaps a merchant from Mittani, who had been summoned by the king for the job. It's unlikely that Shaushtatar assumed that someone in Egypt would be able to read Akkadian.

Was the pharaoh thrown off guard by this visit and the letter? Mittani was a recent enemy, and the fact that its king had made direct contact was obviously astonishing to Amenhotep II. As he put it in his inscription, something like this "had not been heard of since the time of the demigods: this land which knew not Egypt was supplicating the Good God!"⁴⁶ The pharaoh had a number of options. He could have had the diplomatic delegation killed on the spot. Or he could have sent back an angry response demanding more gifts—seeing them as tribute—or objecting to what he might have viewed as the unwarranted and disrespectfully friendly tone of the letter. The pharaoh seems, however, to have done neither. Instead, he accepted the overture and probably returned the delegation back to Mittani with a letter (presumably written down in Akkadian by the Mittanian scribe) in reply. His enthusiastic mention of the Mittani chieftains in his inscription suggests that he was pleased with the idea of an alliance.[47]

One can imagine the tales told by the Mittanian travelers, when they returned home, of what they had seen in Egypt. Their descriptions of the riches of the kingdom—the immense temples, gold statues, magnificent state-rooms—might have further inspired Shaushtatar II to pursue the alliance.

Presumably it took several more visits back and forth between the ambassadors of the two lands before they reached any sort of formal agreement. In Old Babylonian Mesopotamia this had been true even between kings who understood the diplomatic system well—they had sent one another many notes arguing about specific terms and clauses. It must have been all the more complicated to agree on terms when one party was presumably completely new to the idea of treaties of alliance.

In order to convince the pharaoh to sign on as a diplomatic partner, the Mittanian ambassadors would first have had to explain clearly how it would benefit him to do so. Only after that could they draw up the specific clauses of the treaty. It might have been a hard sell; an ally was a "brother" and an equal. Without agreement on that point, one didn't have an alliance at all. But the Egyptian kings had never been the equals of anyone. After all, the pharaoh wasn't just an earthly king, he was the Good God, someone who, after death, would join the cosmic gods. How could Amenhotep II agree to be seen as the equal of the king of Mittani, who only a few years earlier had been called "the fallen one" by Amenhotep's father?

Incredibly, though, the pharaoh did end up agreeing to the alliance. In letters between the later kings of Mittani and Egypt they called one another loving brothers and friends and they looked back to their fathers and grandfathers as the founders of their alliance. Not only that, the pharaoh ended up in the same type of relationship with all the "great kings"—the kings of Hatti and Babylonia as well. Which all raises the question, what did the pharaohs stand to gain from these alliances?

## Why Amenhotep II Agreed

We have no direct evidence for why Amenhotep II agreed to the plan. Nothing he wrote or commissioned in his lifetime (at least nothing that is preserved) even hinted that he had conceded that he was the equal of any other king, let alone that he believed in that equality.

But some of the features of international diplomacy would have appealed to Amenhotep II. The Mittanian ambassador no doubt got the pharaoh's attention when he told the pharaoh that, if he agreed to the alliance, he would marry daughters of each of his "brother" kings. This wouldn't have sounded like a signal of equality to the pharaoh. His father Thutmose III had been married to three Canaanite princesses and perhaps to a Minoan princess as well; a harem of foreigners was a sign of strength.[48] What better way to show his subjects that he was the lord of these supposed allies than to present a parade of women arriving from the foreign powers, like so much living tribute? And of course each of the women would arrive with a huge dowry. But Amenhotep II must have made one thing perfectly clear from the start: he would never reciprocate by sending his own daughters to marry his allies. A later pharaoh put it succinctly: "From time immemorial no daughter of the king of Egy[pt] is given to anyone."[49]

So the access to foreign princesses would have been a plus for the pharaoh, but on the other hand, Egypt wasn't physically threatened by Mittani. The pharaoh's vassal states that stretched from the Sinai to the border of Mittani assured that no foreign army could venture even close to the Nile. Raids into the borderlands around Mittani had produced plenty of wealth, and probably would continue to do so. Why would Amenhotep II have accepted a peace if he had little to fear from the enemy?

Besides which, he might have thought, wasn't Egypt divinely ordained to control all the lands in the world? According to Amenhotep II's own inscription—the one set up near the Great Sphinx—he had been instructed to rule the world by the great god Amen himself. The god "commanded him to conquer all lands without fail."[50] Amenhotep might have taken this very seriously, and it might well have motivated his campaigns. And perhaps, when he was a young man, it might even have seemed possible. If he could just conquer Mittani, then he would have been that much closer to fulfilling the god's command. But then there were Hatti, Babylonia, Keftiu, and Punt. Each of them had sent embassies to Egypt, and each of them was well defended and a long way away. Perhaps Amenhotep II had even heard of lands that were farther away still—the places from which lapis lazuli and tin came, for instance. The gods might have decreed it to be the destiny of Amenhotep II that "To him belongs what the Ocean encircles,"[51] that is, all lands on earth, but realistically he must have known he could spend his whole life fighting and would never bring every one of these lands under the kind of direct control he enjoyed in Canaan and Nubia.

If Amenhotep II agreed to a formal peace with Mittani, what other benefits (besides a new royal wife) might there be from a close connection with its king? The ambassadors from Mittani, in explaining the diplomatic system, would have highlighted the exchange of luxury goods. They had probably brought some of the country's finest offerings with them as part of that "tribute" the pharaoh mentioned. To judge from later letters, these gifts would have included chariots, horses, lapis lazuli, finely worked jewelry, perhaps containers of a perfume known as "sweet oil," and some garments.[52]

A ready supply of lapis lazuli was something the Egyptian king might have appreciated: pharaohs had long loved a combination of gold and lapis in their jewelry and furniture. And Mittanian horses were among the best— Amenhotep II would have wanted more. He had raised and trained horses since his childhood (needless to say, given the king's all-around perfection, "They did not tire when he held the reins; they did not drip sweat in the gallop").[53] The ambassadors from Mittani might well have flattered the pharaoh about his athletic skill and other achievements during their negotiations, recognizing that this might help win him over.[54]

Perhaps the economic argument occurred to Amenhotep II as he weighed his options. Military conquest of Mittani must have seemed increasingly unlikely as Shaushtatar II built up his army and extended his empire into Assyria. It was expensive for Egypt to campaign in Syria, but there was not much hope of big gains in future conflicts; the pharaoh's army and Shaushtatar's were evenly matched. With an alliance, he could obtain Mittanian wealth and women in exchange for gold, which would cost him much less than another war against Mittani.

The pharaoh must have agreed to diplomatic marriages and gift exchanges. He would also have agreed to send his letters in Akkadian, to dispatch messengers regularly and not detain foreign messengers for too long, and even to use the usual format for diplomatic letters, with the traditional salutations at the beginning.[55] This was a system that worked, and all the parts of it had to be in place. But one wonders whether the pharaoh initially rejected the whole notion—why should he obey rules imposed by some other king?

There was also the tricky fact that Amenhotep II would have to agree to become a "brother" of the king of Mittani, and he would have to agree that they shared the same title: "great king." How did the Egyptian king, the Good God, reconcile himself to this?

Perhaps it helped that the correspondence was to be carried on in Akkadian cuneiform on clay tablets. The expressions of equality and brotherhood would be in a foreign language and incomprehensible to most Egyptians. The king could even present this new alliance to his own people as evidence of his greatness: Look at this! It's never happened before! Even distant kings, ones who hadn't even heard of Egypt before, send ambassadors who bow down before Amenhotep II and bring him gifts!

Just the appearance of the gifts from the foreign land, carried in processions of boats up the Nile by emissaries of the king of Mittani, would seem to provide public evidence of the pharaoh's upper hand in this relationship. The Egyptians need not see the gold that he would send in exchange for these things; they need not know that he sent anything in exchange at all.

All of which is to say that the kings on both sides entered into their new peaceful relationship probably not as a result of any idealism or commitment to peace in principle, but because, in a pragmatic way, peace suited them. They could be richer and more comfortable as allies than as enemies, and each king could use the agreement to his own advantage in the way he presented it to his people.

### Possible Treaty Provisions

Although no formal treaty has survived recording this new arrangement, one was probably drawn up at the end of the negotiations.[56] Written treaties had, after all, been associated with alliances ever since the third millennium. We can guess that the treaty between Egypt and Mittani might have been similar to the one that was created at around the same time between King Tudhaliya I of Hatti and the king of Kizzuwatna.[57] After a historical introduction, this one began with two parallel clauses, in which each king was identified as a "great king" and each agreed that he would "not stir up revolt...nor be hostile" against his new ally. Each king was also required to "protect the person and land" of the other and "protect for kingship whichever son" of the allied king "he designates...as his successor."[58] This set the stage: the great kings were equals, they would protect one another, they would be at peace, and whoever lived longer would support the other's chosen successor.

In subsequent paragraphs they laid out in detail a defensive alliance: in the case of either a revolt within one of their lands or of an invasion from outside, each kingdom would come to the assistance of the other. Each provision was written in parallel form—the lands had exactly the same obligations to one another. The goal of this treaty was for the lands to "be at peace" and to be friendly with one another: The two lands "shall be united. They must certainly maintain friendly relations with one another." All these same clauses probably were to be found in the treaties drawn up between Egypt and its new ally. They would be "united" and "at peace" and would "maintain friendly relations."

Other clauses in the Hatti/Kizzuwatna treaty, though written later, when Hatti had become the overlord of Kizzuwatna, still reflected the mechanisms of the diplomatic world of the time. They mentioned "diplomatic gift exchange," which was clearly a formal indication of alliance, because no such exchange could take place with an enemy. They also agreed not to send messengers to their enemies or to allow messengers from enemy lands to come to their own courts. On the other hand, it was assumed in the treaty that letters would pass between the allies: "In regard to a tablet which I…send you—a tablet on which words have been set down—and the words [of] the messenger, which he speaks orally in response to you—if the words of the messenger are in agreement with the words of the tablet, trust that messenger." Obviously, this required each king to employ a scribe who could check the contents of the letter against what had been said by the foreign envoy to make sure that they agreed. An earlier treaty between the same two lands also indicated that they should treat one another's messengers with respect; if either king sent "either his son or his subject" to the other, that king "shall not harm him."[59] With the great powers, it was even more important that the messengers be well treated.

The treaty between Egypt and Mittani might have included an agreement about which cities fell within the boundaries of each of their empires. Amenhotep was able to hold on to almost the entire Mediterranean coast, from the border of Egypt in the south all the way to the city of Ugarit far to the north.[60] The king of Mittani controlled the country inland in Syria and the city of Alalakh, north of Ugarit and close to the coast. The subsequent Egyptian agreement with Hatti would have carved up the rest of northern Syria.

### Treaties Proliferate

Babylonia was the only one of the great powers of the time that had no territorial arguments with the rest, and yet the Babylonian king seems to have joined the trend and negotiated with Egypt as well. A later Babylonian king referred to such a treaty, and its renewal, sworn in his own time, when he wrote that "My brother (the king of Egypt) and I made a mutual declaration of friendship, and this is what we said: 'Just as our fathers were friends with one another, so will we be friends with one another.' "[61] The king in Babylonia at the time of Amenhotep II was probably named Kara-indash. This man is almost completely obscure to us, known mostly from a dedication text that he had inscribed on bricks in a temple to the goddess Inanna in the southern Mesopotamian city of Uruk.[62]

A later text recalled, though, that Kara-indash of Babylon made a treaty with the king of Assyria (presumably before Shaushtatar annexed Assyria into Mittani), so it seems likely that he agreed to a treaty with Egypt as well.[63] One of his descendants wrote to the king of Egypt, "From the time of Kara-indash, since the messengers of your ancestors came regularly to my ancestors, up to the present, they (the ancestors in the two lands) have been friends."[64] It seems that treaties were considered important even between states that were too far away from one another to fear military action.

Perhaps Amenhotep II's mention of the delegation from Hatti meant that he drew up a treaty with the Hittites around this time as well.[65] It's not impossible; a treaty between Hatti and Egypt certainly existed in this era. It was mentioned about a century later, when a Hittite king wrote about having consulted it. The treaty told "how the Storm-god of Hatti took the people of Kurushtama to Egyptian territory, and how the Storm-god of Hatti made a treaty concerning them with the Hittites. Furthermore, they were put under oath by the Storm-god of Hatti...the Hittites and the Egyptians had been put under oath by the Storm-god of Hatti."[66] Kurushtama was in the northern part of Hatti. For some reason, the pharaoh seems to have requested men from this area to come to Egypt, perhaps for some kind of labor service, and this brought about the need for a treaty. In spite of the way it is phrased, some learned and skillful diplomats (not the Storm God) drew up the treaty. They no doubt invoked the Storm God of Hatti, as well as the great gods of Egypt, in the blessings and curses that came at the end of such treaties. This might still have been during the reign of Tudhaliya I of Hatti.[67] Once he heard of Mittani's alliance with Egypt he might have feared their combined strength (and possible animosity towards him) and thought it better to join the brotherhood.

### Cementing the Ties

When negotiations concerning each of the treaties were complete, the final copies were incised onto sheets of copper or bronze and presented by the kings to one another. The kings then would have sworn an oath, though separately, of course.[68] In Hatti, the final copy of each of the kings' treaties was placed in the temple of the main deity, the Sun Goddess of Arinna.[69] The same was probably true in Mittani and Egypt; the treaties might have resided in the temple of Amen in Egypt and of Teshup in Mittani.

Once the treaties had been drawn up and agreed to, the ambassadors probably were delighted to find that they were to receive elaborate gifts from Amenhotep II. Providing gifts to messengers had been a tradition in Mesopotamia since at least the twenty-fourth century, when it was described on the treaty between Ebla and Abarsal and mentioned in innumerable administrative texts. Egyptian kings adopted this practice by the mid-fourteenth century; perhaps this was when they first did so. On each of their trips to Egypt during the alliance negotiations, one imagines that the ambassadors of the great kings took mental notes about Egyptian etiquette so that they could advise future visitors. For example, you should always wash your hands before seeing the king.[70] When invited into the pharaoh's presence, you should raise your arms in praise, as described in this later text: "(They) were immediately ushered in before the Good God, their arms were (raised) in praise to his *ka* (soul), jubilating and paying homage to his fair countenance."[71]

The ambassadors must have been proud of their work; their kings were evidently happy with the outcome. If and when any royal inscriptions are found from the reign of Shaushtatar II, it will be interesting to see whether he mentioned this transformation in his relationship with Egypt, and how he explained it. Even more interesting would be to find the letters between these first allies. Perhaps they are still in the ground, some in Egypt and some in Syria, Babylonia, or Hatti, awaiting excavation.

In his twenty-third year, during what seems to have been an unguarded moment—he was relaxing in his harem and drinking wine—Amenhotep II dictated a letter to his viceroy in Nubia, in which he described his relationship to the foreign lands that had become his allies.[72] What he wrote about Mittani is broken (only the word "Naharin" appears), but he referred to himself as one "who gives orders to the Hittite."[73] Perhaps so, but only as one might give "orders" to a brother; the Hittite king was not compelled to obey.

The pharaoh went on in the same letter to refer to himself as "the [possessor of a wo]man from Babylon, and a servant from Byblos, of a young maiden from Alalakh and an old lady from Arrapkha."[74] He probably was referring to real women—quite possibly women who surrounded him in his harem as he was dictating the letter. His successors married princesses from Mittani and Babylon, so Amenhotep II might have done the same. The young maiden from Alalakh and old lady from Arrapkha both would have come from cities within Mittani. Only the "servant from Byblos" grew up within the Egyptian empire. (This letter, incidentally, survives because the viceroy was so pleased to have received it, he had it carved onto a stone monument.)

From around the end of the fifteenth century BCE, when the alliances between Egypt, Mittani, Hatti, and Babylonia might have been forged, for almost a century, the Near East enjoyed a respite from war between the great powers, and every land prospered. Even when wars later erupted between Hatti and Mittani, the diplomatic institutions continued to work, and peace largely was maintained among the other great powers, right up until around 1200 BCE.

## A New Generation of Allies

Amenhotep II died after a long reign and was succeeded, around 1400 BCE, by one of his many sons, Thutmose IV.[75] His contemporary in Mittani, who came to the throne perhaps in the same year, was named Artatama I.[76]

Thutmose described himself as being a carbon copy of his father in some ways. He liked hunting and archery and speeding around in his chariot: "Now he passed time amusing himself...shooting copper targets and hunting [lions] and wild goats, and traveling on his chariot, his horses being faster than the wind."[77] Like his father, he also campaigned at least once in Syria, even attacking some kingdoms that were vassals of his ally, the king of Mittani, and bringing home some captives. He might, though, have simply been flexing his muscles during the renegotiation of the alliance treaty with Mittani.[78] Soon enough, gifts were coming to Egypt from their land, and no doubt gold was flowing in the opposite direction.

One inscription written in the reign of Thutmose IV described the "chiefs of Naharin" waiting around near the Egyptian palace with their gifts "that they might behold Menkheperurue (Thutmose IV) when he proceeds from his house and that they might hear his voice."[79] This certainly makes the Mittanians sound as though they were in awe of the pharaoh, longing just to see him and to hear him speak. The Mittanians saw their relationship somewhat differently, though, and just as much to their own advantage. A later king remembered the pharaoh Thutmose IV begging repeatedly for a favor from King Artatama, who strung him along before finally agreeing: "When [Thutmose IV], the father of Nimmureya, wrote to Artatama, my grandfather, he asked for the daughter of [my grandfather, the sister] of my father. He wrote five, six times, but he did not give her. When he wrote my grandfather seven times, then only under such pressure did he gi[v]e [her]."[80]

If the pharaoh really did plead for a Mittanian bride, it might have been because he had concluded that a wife was the most valuable item he could request from Mittani. And perhaps Artatama I held out for a large bride-price from Egypt before agreeing. This was one occasion when the gifts from Egypt would have been truly magnificent—though he would have had to reciprocate with a huge dowry as well. On the other hand, it's unlikely that Artatama I was quite as stubborn as he was depicted by his grandson in the letter describing this transaction, and some scholars assert that the whole idea that the

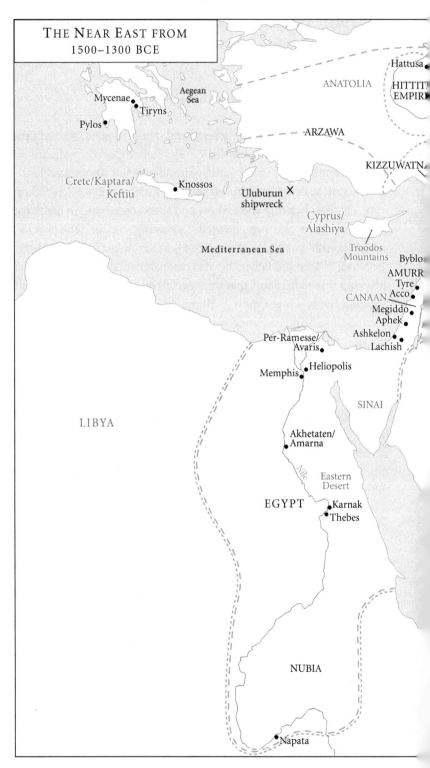

THE NEAR EAST FROM
1500–1300 BCE

ASKA

Arassantiya River

MITTANI
EMPIRE
Irrite
rchemish                    ALSHI
Washshukkanni
MUKISH                    •Urkesh
alakh  •Aleppo  Umm
    el-Marra
Jgarit                ASSYRIA
                    Ashur•    •Arrapkha
    NUHASHI              •Nuzi
•Kadesh
    SYRIA        MESOPOTAMIA

Damascus

                    Babylon•
                    BABYLONIA

                                Persian
                                Gulf

Khabur River
Tigris River
Euphrates River

d
a

- - - - Kingdoms of Egypt, Hatti, Mittani
        and Babylonia around 1500 BCE

- - -   Kingdoms of Egypt, Hatti, Assyria
        and Babylonia around 1300 BCE

0                              400 mi
0                              600 km

pharaoh had to ask many times before Artatama agreed was a wild exaggeration.[81] Artatama probably assented long before seven requests were made. Syrian and Mesopotamian kings had an established tradition of marrying their daughters off to other kings, so the idea might even have occurred to the king of Mittani first. In fact, since in their region it tended to be the higher-ranking king who gave a princess and the lower-ranking king who received one, it's more likely that, far from resisting, the king of Mittani couldn't believe his luck when the Egyptian king consented to marry his daughter.

Both kings could therefore boast about the marriage: Thutmose IV because a growing collection of foreign wives seemed to be proof of his power over distant lands, and Artatama I because he was now the father-in-law of the pharaoh, which put him in what would have seemed to him to be the superior position.[82]

The marriage was also proof of the continued alliance between the two lands. Since the kings always thought of their relationship as being one of brothers, it had to be renewed when either of the kings died; the alliance was not really between states at all. Once the first diplomatic marriages had taken place among the great kings, they seem to have become the norm.

### The Amarna Letters

The letter mentioning the marriage between Thutmose IV and the daughter of Artatama I was one of the group called the Amarna letters, which were found in the late nineteenth century at the site of Amarna in Egypt.[83] Just forty-four of them pertain to international interactions, mostly between the great powers; the other 306 had passed between the pharaoh and his vassals in Canaan.[84] Of the forty-four international letters, three are almost completely illegible, thirteen are from kings of Mittani to kings of Egypt, eleven are from Babylonia to Egypt, seven are from Alashiya (Cyprus) to Egypt, three are from Hatti to Egypt, two are from Assyria to Egypt, and one is from Arzawa (a kingdom near Hatti) to Egypt. Just four are copies of letters that the pharaoh sent to other kings (one to Arzawa, three to Babylon).

This cache happened to survive, but many, many more such tablets must have been written. In one letter the king implied that it was normal for messengers to travel between home and Egypt once a year, so the archives should have included at least one letter for each of the fifteen to thirty years of the Amarna period from each of the foreign kings.[85] Most of them are missing. This is clear even from the letters themselves, which sometimes referred back to other letters that haven't been recovered. Also, there would have been

earlier letters—ones sent to Amenhotep II and Thutmose IV from their contemporaries. There were letters from the Egyptian kings that would have been
archived (and conceivably might eventually show up) in palaces in Babylonia, Mittani, Hatti, Assyria, Arzawa, and Alashiya, and there were no doubt
other letters that had nothing to do with Egypt—from Babylonia to Mittani,
for example, or from Hatti to Alashiya. A later archive of documents has been
found at Hattusa, the Hittite capital city, with exactly these types of letters,
and an additional group comes from Ugarit, on the Syrian coast. These later
letters can help us understand the mechanisms of diplomacy among the international community, but tell us little about its founding.

Here is one of the great innovations of human history—diplomacy on
a truly international scale, when major kings chose not to fight but to seek
peace, and created all the necessary protocols and instruments for diplomatic
solutions to international problems—and all that we have is an almost ran-
dom selection of forty-four of the documents that passed between the kings
who benefited from this new idea. They are documents that don't even come
from the beginning of the era, letters without answers, pregnant with implications but short on political history.

And yet, taken along with other contemporary evidence—including
inscriptions, treaties, contracts, and archaeological sites—they make it possible to peer into the world that created them. They show that the diplomatic
system that had been developing ever since the time of the kings of Ebla found
its greatest realization in this new brotherhood of great kings. No longer were
the alliances designed to strengthen a king's hand as he prepared for war, or
even to help him find a way to avoid war. The alliances and the close connections they created between brother kings had become an end in themselves.[86]

# PART IV

# The Amarna Age,
## 1400–1300 BCE

### CHAPTER EIGHT

# Brother Kings United
# and at Peace

*"My brother, whom I love and who loves me"*

Thutmose IV died young. He had ruled for only about a decade, so his son and successor, Amenhotep III, was only about twelve years old when he came to power in 1391 BCE.[1] The era that encompassed Amenhotep III's reign and that of his son Akhenaten is known as the Amarna period. It was a time of unprecedented international cooperation.

The brotherhood of great kings, through much of Amenhotep III's reign, probably only included Egypt, Mittani, and Babylonia.[2] Hatti had been a great power before and would become one again, but it was going through a period of weakness. No letters were found at Amarna that had been sent between the king of Hatti and Amenhotep III, and the pharaoh wrote at one point, "I have heard that everything is finished and the country Hattusa is shattered."[3] Amenhotep III also corresponded with kings in Alashiya (Cyprus) and Arzawa (in western Anatolia), but they were not at the same level of power and importance as Babylonia and Mittani.

Toward the end of the Amarna period, though, Mittani fell into decline, lost its status as a great power, and lost control of Assyria. The king of Assyria promptly joined the kings of Egypt and Babylonia, becoming a new member of the great king brotherhood, along with the king of a revived Hatti. The international system was flexible enough to accommodate changes in the fortunes of its member states without disintegrating. It survived for over two centuries, until around 1200 BCE, when almost all the major powers collapsed.

The relationship between Egypt and Mittani was perhaps the oldest of the alliances among great kings, and it is the best understood. In the letters that passed between the two courts, we can see all of the structures that made the international system work. Babylonia continued to be powerful and rich, but the focus of the diplomatic community had moved westward with Egypt's involvement. Babylonia did not represent a potential threat in the way that Egypt, Mittani, and Hatti sometimes did to one another.

### Amenhotep III: A Peaceable Man

When Amenhotep III came to power, Artatama I was still on the throne in Mittani and Artatama's daughter would still have been living at the young pharaoh's court, so Amenhotep III seems to have been thoroughly familiar and comfortable with his northern ally. There was no need for him to ceremonially troop through the Levant as his father had done in preparation for the renewal of their alliance. Their relationship was secure.

Amenhotep III, who was known to his allies by his alternate name, Nebmaatra, revealed himself to be an impressive character almost as soon as he took the throne.[4] In spite of his youth, he immediately set about establishing his household. He married Tiy, his "great wife" (the highest ranking of his wives), before he had been on the throne for even two years. Tiy, a strikingly beautiful woman (to judge from the sculptures of her), was not his sister, or a relative of any kind. They seem to have been very fond of one another throughout their lives. Amenhotep thought up a novel way to introduce his subjects to Tiy: he had a short inscription about her impressed onto the flat bottom of a large faience model of a beetle, called a scarab (it was about the size of the palm of a man's hand), and had many copies made of it. The scarabs have been found throughout Egypt and even in the distant areas controlled by Egypt, so they seem to have been sent out, almost like newspapers, to inform the people about his wife.[5]

By the fifth year of his reign, Amenhotep III was leading his first military campaign. He must have been about seventeen, fighting at the head of his army in "vile Kush" to the south of Egypt. "His Majesty led on to victory; he completed it in his first campaign of victory…Nebmaatra was the fierce-eyed lion whose claws seized vile Kush, who trampled down all its chiefs in their valleys, they being cast down in their blood, one on top of the other."[6] One might think from this that he took to military campaigning like a duck to water. It looked as though he was destined to follow the lead of his great-grandfather Thutmose III and to spend much of his reign fighting. But it didn't happen. This campaign to Nubia was apparently his one and only military venture.

Perhaps Amenhotep III didn't fight because he didn't need to. The Egyptian empire in the Levant was relatively stable. Mittani, Babylonia, and Hatti, along with the lesser states of Arzawa and Alashiya, were Egyptian allies. None of the major powers of the time had any reason or even inclination to fight against Egypt. Every one of the great kings benefited from this peace, Amenhotep perhaps most of all. Instead of expending time and wealth on arms and chariots and training soldiers, he spent his days hunting wild bulls, overseeing huge building projects (many of which featured immense statues of himself), and enjoying the company of his wives, especially Tiy.

Where earlier New Kingdom kings had emphasized their military prowess in their inscriptions, Amenhotep III took pride in his building works and his patronage of the arts. The buildings he constructed were described lovingly in his inscriptions; one monument, built for "receiving the produce of all foreign countries," was "a place of relaxation," landscaped with ponds and "planted with all kinds of flowers."[7] Most of the other buildings were "worked with gold throughout," and many had "pavements of silver." Silver and gold seem to have been the standard floor and wall treatments of every room Amenhotep commissioned, some with gold doors and inlays of lapis and "costly stone" for better effect. Here was a king who wanted to be surrounded by an ostentatious display of his wealth all the time. Egypt was transformed over the course of his reign, with innumerable grand new buildings and monuments dotting the landscape. Many of them still stand today.

Amenhotep III also was deeply devoted to the sun god. The god of Thebes, Amen, who was the patron of the Eighteenth Dynasty, was increasingly seen as one and the same as the sun god, Ra. Amenhotep III sometimes claimed that Amen-Ra had briefly assumed human form in order to conceive him.[8] The disk of the sun, the Aten, was an important part of the sun god, and Amenhotep, as king, believed that he was chosen by, and even made in the image of, Aten. The king referred to himself as "the dazzling Aten."[9] It was a small step from that to the idea that the king actually *was* the god. Amenhotep took that step in his thirty-fifth year on the throne. He had images carved showing himself wearing headdresses that were reserved for Amen-Ra, and had a temple built in Nubia for the worship not just of Amen-Ra but of the king himself.[10]

In his inscriptions, though, he was remarkably measured in his descriptions of neighboring lands, compared to the belligerent tones of his grandfather and great-grandfather. Although he referred, as did almost all the Egyptian kings, to "wretched Kush" or "vile Kush" when mentioning the neighbors to the south, he recognized the value of nurturing foreign princes so that they would become loyal vassals. Some of these princes, from Canaan as well as Kush, were brought from their homes and settled in Egypt. One fort was "enclosed by a great wall that reaches heaven, and settled with the princes' sons of Nubia's Bowmen," and Amenhotep's mortuary temple was "surrounded by Syrian settlements, inhabited by the children of the princes."[11] After living in Egypt, and presumably being educated there (at least in the arts and skills they would need to run their lands), these princes probably felt as Egyptian as they did Nubian or Syrian.

Another side of Amenhotep III's personality came through in his later letters, which, although designed to impress his fellow kings, were not written for either the gods or posterity and are more or less free of propaganda. They show him to have been imperious and stubborn. Only three letters found at Amarna are clearly "signed" by Amenhotep, in that he names himself as the sender, and one of them is unlike any of the other Amarna letters. Amenhotep composed it entirely in response to statements by his correspondent, King Kadashman-Enlil I of Babylon. He started each section of the letter with a quote from a previous letter that had been sent by the Babylonian king, usually introduced by "And as for your writing me...." He then shot down Kadashman-Enlil's argument, or used sarcasm to belittle him ("It is a fine thing that you give your daughters in order to acquire a nugget of gold from your neighbors!"), or maligned the Babylonian messengers ("Your messengers keep telling you what is not true").[12] One might have thought the two men were adversaries, rather than allies, if not for his statement "Now, we are brothers, you and I."[13] Brothers could argue, but their ties of kinship were unaffected. Amenhotep was not defensive in the letter, nor apologetic; he seemed perfectly assured that he was in the right.

This letter pertained to one of his wives, a sister of the Babylonian king, and the possibility that the Babylonian king might refuse to send the pharaoh another wife. Amenhotep seemed to have had an insatiable desire for foreign wives.

In fact, all of the letters from Amenhotep III, as well as many of the quotes attributed to him in other letters, were at least in part about women.[14] In another letter to Kadashman-Enlil, the pharaoh seems to have been much calmer.[15] He was getting ready for the arrival of the Babylonian princess: "I am preparing everything possible before the arrival of your messenger who is bringing your daughter. When your messenger returns, I will send (them) to [yo]u." The third of Amenhotep III's letters was to the king of Arzawa in western Anatolia.[16] Here the king was positively friendly, sending a messenger to take a good look at another promised princess with the message, "Let us see the daughter whom they will offer to my majesty in marriage."[17]

In the letters that the pharaohs sent to their vassals, they didn't give their names, so it's hard to determine which king was the author. But it's a good guess that those asking about women came from Amenhotep III rather than from the later reign of his son. "Prepare your daughter for the king" he wrote to one vassal, and "Send extremely beautiful female cupbearers in whom there is no defect" he asked of another.[18] The vassals did their part to make the king happy: "herew[ith I s]end my daughter to the [pa]lace, [t]o the king," wrote one vassal, presumably to Amenhotep III.[19] And more orders flowed in for women to be sent to Egypt: "Moreover, the king, my lord, has sent orders to me and I am heeding (them). I heed all the orders of the king, my lord. I herewith:...[send] 10 women."[20]

Amenhotep III's pursuit of foreign princesses probably arose in part from his desire to maintain the peace and prosperity of his era. The more princesses he married, the more royal fathers-in-law he had who would send him gifts and who would support him (and not fight against him). But one has the sense that he might have had other motivations. Those "extremely beautiful female cupbearers"—forty of them, all paid for—had nothing to do with diplomacy.

For about ten years Artatama I of Mittani must have sent gifts and messengers to Amenhotep III as he had previously to Thutmose IV, but Artatama seems not to have sent a new princess to the Egyptian harem. His daughter who had married Thutmose IV was still there, so perhaps a new princess was not yet needed.

Around 1382 BCE, a decade after Amenhotep III had become king, his friend Artatama I of Mittani died. Amenhotep III probably mourned him (a requirement for allied kings), even though they had almost certainly never met. According to the rules of alliance, he was duty bound to support Artatama's chosen heir. This proved to be a son named Shuttarna II, who might have been older than his ally the pharaoh—he already had grown children.[21] His accession seems to have been uncomplicated.

The era of friendship between Amenhotep III and Shuttarna II was remembered fondly by Shuttarna II's son in later years. He wrote, "My father loved you, and you in turn loved my father."[22] And Amenhotep III was very generous with his gold: "You sent my father much gold. You sent him large gold jars and gold jugs. You se[nt him] gold bricks."[23] The Egyptians had even honored a Mittanian goddess when Shuttarna II sent her there.[24] Of course, nostalgia is a tricky thing. The letters that passed between Shuttarna II and Amenhotep III are gone, so we have no way of knowing what the truth of their alliance was, but it seems likely that the friendship was authentic and the gifts lavish.

It's odd, though, that Amenhotep didn't brag in his inscriptions on the walls of his palaces and temples about the peace he perpetuated through diplomacy. He clearly benefited from it, and seems to have been actively pursuing alliances around the Mediterranean and the Near East. But the only list of his allies on his official inscriptions was in a collection of place names where Babylonia, Alashiya, Arzawa, Hatti, and Mittani were inscribed on a statue base, each with the picture of a bound prisoner above it. There is no indication that these were allies; the images of prisoners almost suggest that these were conquered lands and subject peoples.[25]

Nevertheless, Amenhotep III was apparently keen to cement his ties with Shuttarna II by proposing a new dynastic marriage. If we are to believe the Mittanian view of things, Shuttarna II (just like his father before him) needed some persuading. Supposedly, when Amenhotep III wrote to propose a marriage to Shuttarna's daughter "he wrote three, four times, but he did not give her. When he wrote five, six times, only under such pressure did he give her."[26] But this might be a fiction; the marriage suited both men. Shuttarna II's daughter, who had the thoroughly Hurrian name of Kilu-Hepa, was soon betrothed to Amenhotep III.

Kilu-Hepa was not just another face in Amenhotep's harem; she was an important wife, perhaps second only in importance to Tiy. She was the only wife who warranted her own commemorative scarab to celebrate her marriage to the king (Tiy's scarab hadn't been specifically about her marriage). Kilu-Hepa's scarab inscription noted that the wedding took place in the king's tenth year, at which point he must have been around twenty-two years old. The first half of the inscription was taken up with epithets of the pharaoh and his Great Wife; Amenhotep was the "son of Ra" and "Ruler of Thebes, who is granted life," and Tiy was "the Great King's-Wife…who liveth."[27] Tiy's parents were even named on the scarab—there was no mistaking that Tiy was still the Great Wife, in spite of the celebrations around Kilu-Hepa's arrival.[28]

The second half of the scarab read, "Marvels brought to his majesty…: Kirgipa (Kilu-hepa)…the daughter of the chief of Naharin (Mittani)…, Satirna (Shuttarna)…; (and) the chief of her harem-ladies, (viz.,) 317 persons."[29] The "marvels" brought from Mittani no doubt included more than the 317 "harem-ladies." Kilu-Hepa's dowry must have been significant, befitting the daughter of a great king. This marriage must have been thoroughly satisfactory to Amenhotep, something to brag about. Those 317 attendants—all speaking Hurrian and sharing a common culture—would have helped Kilu-Hepa feel more at home in Egypt.

Three other commemorative scarabs tell us a bit more about Amenhotep III's personal life as a young man, since they were all produced in the first eleven years of his reign.[30] One scarab describes how in Amenhotep III's second year, as a teenager, he had an adventure. A messenger came to tell him that "there are wild bulls upon the desert of the region of Shetep."[31] Amenhotep arranged for a boat to take him downstream to Shetep, traveling through the night, so that he arrived there "in peace…at the time of morning." He excitedly mounted his chariot to go bull hunting, but he wasn't alone. His

The scarab distributed by Amenhotep III
with a hieroglyphic inscription describing
and celebrating his marriage to Mittanian
princess Kilu-Hepa. (©Trustees of the
British Museum)

"whole army [was] in back of him." Before the hunt began, the king asked his
men to build an enclosure around the herd, with a ditch to make it impossible
for them to escape (and to make the hunt a little more assured of success). He
claimed to have killed fifty-six bulls on his first day of hunting. Then he took
four days off "to rest his horses" and on the fifth day killed another forty bulls.
In this inscription he sounded very much like his grandfather Amenhotep
II, the one who shot arrows through copper targets. Another scarab had him
hunting even fiercer prey: lions, 102 of them.[32] This type of physical prowess
was just what a pharaoh needed, even if he didn't plan on doing any military
campaigning. He was the image of health and vigor. One last scarab was distributed widely; this one touchingly described a gift that he gave to his beloved
wife Tiy—he had an artificial lake constructed for her enjoyment.[33] The king
himself was "rowed in the royal barge" on the lake at the opening ceremony.

Amenhotep III ended up ruling for thirty-eight years and is one of the
best-known pharaohs in all of Egyptian history. His image and stories must

have seemed omnipresent to a fourteenth-century Egyptian. Wherever one went, in or near Memphis or Thebes (his two capital cities), Amenhotep's statues and buildings were there. As his mortuary temple was constructed, the Egyptian peasants must have marveled at the immense size of the two statues of Amenhotep that graced its entrance. They were carved out of two massive blocks of brown quartzite, each weighing 720 tons, and they still stand fifty feet high, towering over the fields round about.[34] His mortuary temple was unlike anything Egypt had seen before. In an inscription on the building, Amenhotep wrote, "His majesty's heart was pleased with making many great monuments, the like of which never existed before since the primeval time of the two lands."[35] Ever since his reign, the two giant statues have stood as mute witness to the incomparable wealth and power of the king.

We know little about Shuttarna II of Mittani during the same era (other than from the nostalgic memories of his son). Only one known text is dated to his reign, a contract drawn up "in the presence of Shuttarna, the king" found at the site of Umm el-Marra in Syria.[36] It's a prosaic affair, recording the fact that a man had manumitted some slaves and given property to one of them.[37] To seal it, Shuttarna used the cylinder of his illustrious predecessor Shaushtatar II. This contract doesn't tell us much, beyond the fact that Shuttarna took an interest in judicial affairs concerning his subjects. Perhaps Shuttarna II, like Amenhotep III, instigated building projects across his empire. In any event, he doesn't seem to have been at war.

### Assassinations and Broken Ties

After Shuttarna II had been on the throne for some years, tragedy struck the royal family of Mittani. First, sometime around 1372, the king died, and must have been mourned by his subjects. His son Artashumara took the throne, but after only a short time, the new king was murdered. Did the assassin hope to usurp the throne? What had Artashumara done to anger this man? Did the king have any inkling of what might happen? Kilu-Hepa, in Egypt, must have been heartbroken when she heard about the deaths of her father and then, much more unexpectedly, her brother.

In spite of the alliance with Egypt, Amenhotep III doesn't seem to have sent troops to make sure that Artashumara's chosen heir (if he had even identified one yet) took the throne after the murder. On the other hand, the pharaoh might have threatened military action, because the assassin didn't usurp power. Instead, Artashumara's younger brother was made king. He was just a boy, thrust into kingship by the man who had killed his brother. He had a right to the Mittanian throne but was too young to be able to rule on his own. His name was Tushratta, and he became one of the most interesting characters of this colorful age. But in the early years of his reign he must have been traumatized by the violent death in his family, and no doubt fearful for his own life.

The man who had murdered Tushratta's brother appointed himself regent to the young king. It's quite possible that young Tushratta simply acquiesced to this man's wishes in order to preserve his own life. One of those wishes was for Tushratta to cut off all his contacts with Egypt, even though the pharaoh was married to Tushratta's sister. Indeed, the assassin cut Tushratta off from any people who might have threatened the regent's hold over him; Tushratta later lamented that "he would not permit friendship with anyone who loved me."[38]

Once Tushratta grew to adulthood he must have been filled with rage at the man who had killed his brother and who had controlled his life and his kingdom during his childhood. He had this man, and his accomplices, put to death. He wrote, "I . . . was not remiss about the unseemly things that had been done in my land, and I slew the slayers of Arta[sh]umara, my brother, and everyone belonging to them."

Tushratta's troubles weren't over, though. The Hittite king, perhaps believing that the violence within the royal family of Mittani might have weakened and distracted the king, seized the opportunity and attacked. But the Hittites themselves were weak at this time, and Tushratta was able to lead the Mittanian forces to victory against them. As Tushratta put it, "[the god] Teshup, my lord, gave him into my hand, and I defeated him." With bravado (and hyperbole, one guesses) that would have been worthy of Amenhotep II, he added, "There was not one of them who returned to his own country." Mittani and Hatti might both have had separate peace agreements with Egypt, but they seem not to have agreed to an alliance with one another. The kings of Mittani were always looking over their shoulders—over the Taurus Mountains—and worrying about Hatti. And, in spite of their loss to Mittani, the Hittites retained control over the valuable seaports and mountain passes of Kizzuwatna. Nevertheless, the economy of Mittani doesn't seem to have suffered too much. Tushratta's wealth was legendary in later years. His son wrote that "Tushratta, my father, built a palace and filled it with riches."[39]

### Keliya's Mission to Egypt

Once he had dealt with the Hittites and was finally in a position to act for himself, Tushratta was anxious to renew the ties that had traditionally bound his forebears as "brothers" to the kings of Egypt. He decided to send a formal delegation to Amenhotep III. Tushratta no doubt wondered whether his sister, and perhaps even his aunt, were still alive there, and he wanted the support and prosperity that a strong alliance with Egypt would bring.

Tushratta must have thought long and hard before choosing whom to send to Egypt to represent him on his first mission. The man he ultimately chose was named Keliya. This eminent person was variously described as a "magnate," "envoy," and "chief minister" by Tushratta, so "messenger" (although also used to refer to him) is much too humble a term. The title "messenger" (*mar shipri* in Akkadian) was used to refer to anyone who traveled for the king, from the highest ambassadors to the lowliest couriers.[40] Keliya's brother and uncle also both worked as "messengers" for the king, so it's likely that he came from a long line of civil servants and scribes.[41] He must have held administrative positions in Mittani for years—he was already a chief minister when first sent to Egypt. Keliya was to be accompanied on his expedition by another man, named Tunip-ibri. Tunip-ibri makes no other appearance in the records, and we don't know what happened to him after this. But for Keliya, this was the beginning of a remarkable phase of his career. The letters don't say how old he was (Syrians and Mesopotamians seem not to have cared, or even known, what exact age they were), but he was fit enough to travel to Egypt many times over the coming years, so he was perhaps between twenty and thirty when he traveled there first.

Keliya and Tunip-ibri were to take a message for the pharaoh with them on their long journey to Egypt, a letter that Tushratta had dictated to a scribe (perhaps to Keliya himself). The letter wasn't a long one; it would have fit easily in Keliya's hand.[42] In it, Tushratta gave a quick history of the first years of his reign; his country's struggles, including the murder of his brother; and his recent battles against the Hittites. He made only two requests of the Egyptian king: friendship and the exchange of messengers. The two were of course interwoven; kings who were friends regularly sent messengers back and forth between their courts. Tushratta asked that Keliya and Tunip-ibri be allowed to return quickly and that Egyptian messengers be sent to Mittani.

Perhaps Keliya had been to Egypt before, back in the days of Shuttarna II, or perhaps it was Tunip-ibri who had previous experience with Egyptian etiquette and customs. It's likely that one of them was chosen for his expertise in this matter. The letter tells us that the two men also were to travel with some of the booty from Tushratta's war with Hatti—a chariot and a pair of horses, along with two attendants, a man and a woman. Tushratta added five more chariots and five teams of horses to the expedition, all to be presented as gifts to the Egyptian king.

Each of the chariots would have been a two-wheeled marvel, with spoked wheels and elaborate decoration. Such chariots represented the latest in military technology. They were light and maneuverable and effective in battle. The old style of chariot, which trundled along on solid wheels, had been replaced rapidly right across the Near East once the new chariots had been introduced.

The chariots that were being given to the Egyptian king would each have required a charioteer; these men no doubt joined the traveling party to Egypt as well. Keliya and Tunip-ibri probably also brought along grooms for the horses and a number of troops for protection.[43] Wrapped up somewhere among the goods and provisions that they packed for the journey were some small presents from the king for Kilu-Hepa, his sister: a set of toggle-pins, a set of earrings, and a ring, all made of gold, and a container of scent—perhaps a perfume that would remind her of home.[44]

The delegation probably also carried a passport: a sealed clay tablet with a message like this one, which was found in Egypt:

> To the kings of Canaan, servants of my brother: Thus the king: I herewith send Akiya, my messenger, to speed posthaste to the king of Egypt, my brother. No one is to hold him up. Provide him with safe entry into Egypt and hand (him) over to the fortress commander of Egypt. Let [him] go on immediately, and as far as his presents are concerned, he is to owe nothing.[45]

The men were supposed to present this passport if stopped along the way. It was intended also to prevent them from having to pay taxes (and perhaps bribes) on the presents they were carrying.[46]

Tushratta no doubt sent his men off in great style.[47] As the delegation left, citizens might have lined the dusty streets of Washshukkanni, Tushratta's capital, to see the horses and chariots, the Hittite slaves, and the Mittanian dignitaries. But after they had left, there was nothing Tushratta could do to influence the expedition. He simply had to go about his normal business, hoping to hear of a favorable response from the Egyptian king when his men returned, at least three months hence.[48]

Keliya's delegation could not have traveled very fast, in spite of the horses and chariots that they were taking with them. Some of the men (along with the one woman, a Hittite captive) must have walked almost the whole way. Roads, if they existed at all, were unpaved, and some areas would have been hard to traverse. Horses weren't only used to pull chariots, they were also ridden, but they were probably considerably smaller than horses are today.[49] A single messenger on horseback could have traveled a great deal faster than a whole caravan like the one that Keliya and Tunip-ibri were leading.[50]

After weeks of travel, when Keliya and Tunip-ibri at last arrived at the border of Egypt, they were "handed over to the fortress commander," as the passport indicated. No doubt someone among their group spoke Egyptian; he would have explained their mission to the commander and translated for the Mittanians. Such people were regularly employed in diplomatic discussions. One man, Hane, was described in a later letter as being an Egyptian interpreter who traveled to Mittani.[51]

They would probably have been placed under the hospitable but firm control of Amenhotep III's guards. They could no longer move freely, as they had in Mittani and Canaan, but traveled at the will of the Egyptian king. They would have continued south to the capital of Thebes in a sailing vessel, the winds allowing the boat to move against the current.[52] As they sailed, the delegation finally got a rest after their long trek.

Keliya and Tunip-ibri eventually reached the palace of the Egyptian king in Thebes. It was a vast seventy-five-acre complex on the west bank of the Nile, called "the palace of the dazzling Aten."[53] Their boat probably docked at the north end of the compound in the palace's harbor, which was shaped like a giant "T," a mile and a half on each side. From there, they followed a processional way into the palace area. They passed a vast temple to Amen and continued on to the south, through a town for the support staff of the palace. Amenhotep III had only moved his court to Thebes from Memphis a short time before, in 1362—maybe just a year before this mission—so everything in the compound would have been pristine and new, the walls gleaming white. The messengers turned to the left beyond the officials' quarters and passed the double walls into the palace of the king. They would have been shown to their quarters there.

How long did they have to wait to be allowed an audience with the Egyptian king? The letters don't say. Throughout their time in Egypt, the Mittanian delegation would have been treated very well. Just like the Old Babylonian envoys visiting the court of Hammurabi, these envoys could expect to attend a banquet at which the king would be present. They were the eyes and ears of their sovereign, and the pharaoh seems to have wanted to make a powerful impression.

In all the courts to which envoys traveled, the kings showed them what they wished their brother king could see, they said what they wanted the partner king to hear, and they fed the messengers in a style fitting a king, so that the messengers would report home that the brother king's realm was rich and glorious and that the king himself was impressive and generous. The messengers returned home not just to read the words of the allied king in the letters they carried, but to talk. They told their kings everything about how they had been treated, and they answered all his questions.

Both Keliya and Tunip-ibri would have received gifts of precious metals and clothes from the Egyptian king, gifts that they apparently could keep for

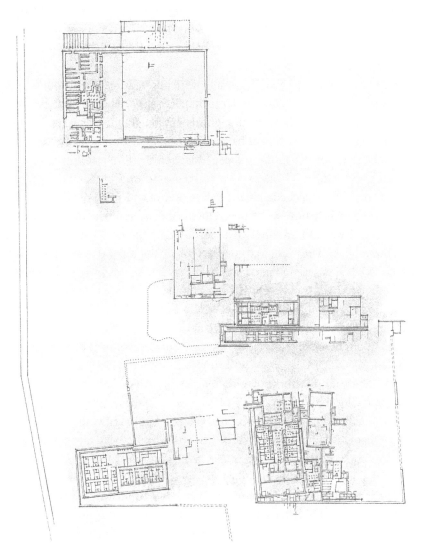

Plan of the excavated parts of the palace compound of Amenhotep III in Thebes.
The royal palace is at the bottom right of the plan, the temple of Amen at the top left,
with servants quarters in between. (© Duncan Baird Publishers, London)

themselves, separate from those that were to be taken to their king.[54] In a letter about a different encounter, Amenhotep III said that he gave messengers
"silver, gold, oil, solemn garb, every sort of finery."[55] Being a messenger was
a lucrative profession.

They might have met with some of the pharaoh's high officials before
their audience with the king. The meetings would have been formal and

intimidating. According to an ancient text, Amenhotep III's vizier "sat on a throne of judgment, a mat on the floor, a mat above him, a pillow behind his back, a pillow under his feet, [a hat] on his head, a scepter in his hand" when listening to official business.[56]

When finally Keliya and Tunip-ibri were allowed into the throne room, their experience was probably similar to that of Sinuhe, who had written about his audience with the pharaoh (though his autobiography was written a few centuries earlier). He wrote that he "was summoned. Ten men came and ten men went to usher me to the palace. I touched my forehead to the ground between the sphinxes."[57] This was before coming into the king's presence, but was a sign of respect outside the palace. Keliya and Tunip-ibri then might have washed their hands and removed their sandals, in preparation for seeing the king, and waited in a quiet area.[58] Sinuhe continued: "The Companions who showed me into the pillared court set me on the way to the reception hall. I found His Majesty upon the Great Throne set in a recess (paneled) with fine gold." If anything, Amenhotep III's reception hall was probably even grander and more gold-encrusted than the palace in Sinuhe's time. The throne itself might have been made of shining white gold.[59]

The room was painted brightly, like most of the rooms in the palace. The tiled floor on which the envoys walked was decorated with images of enemy captives. The walls (like those of other rooms) might have had bands of rosettes in red and blue bordering scenes of papyrus marshes, complete with wild geese and fish. As the men approached the pharaoh, they would have bowed also to Queen Tiy, the king's Chief Wife, who was probably present near the king. She knew all about the letters that came and went from the palace, suggesting that she was there when they were read aloud.[60]

The letter that Keliya carried with him was a complete communication; the sentences in this letter had been carefully phrased, apparently to make the right impression on the Egyptian king and to convince him to renew the alliance.[61] The letter began, like all Akkadian letters, with an instruction to the person who was to read it aloud. As in earlier eras, when kings wrote about the letters, they referred to "hearing" them rather than reading them.[62] (The pharaoh probably heard the Akkadian version but didn't understand until the translation into Egyptian.) "Say to Nibmuareya, the k[ing of Egypt], my brother: Thus Tushratta, the king of [M]ittani, your brother."[63] Tushratta could presume to call the pharaoh a brother—an ally—because of the long-standing relationship between their two lands, even though he had been out of contact with the pharaoh ever since he took the throne (and that was, of course, through no fault of his own). He was also the pharaoh's brother-in-law, as he reminded Amenhotep at the beginning of the letter, right after asking about the health of the pharaoh himself. "For Kilu-Hepa (his sister) may all go well," he wrote. Then he added a wish for the prosperity of his ally's court and king-dom, using a standard formula: "For your household, for your wives, for your sons, for your magnates, for your warriors, for your horses, for your chariots, and in your country, may all go very well." Kilu-Hepa came up again later in the letter, as Tushratta laid out the reasons why the pharaoh should "seek friendship" with him: "My father loved you, and you in turn loved my father. In keeping with his love, my father [g]ave you my sister."

Keliya continued to read the rest of the letter, which featured Tushratta's appeal for a renewal of the old alliance, and he might have put extra emphasis on the sentences at the end: "May my brother let them [Keliya and Tunip-ibri] go promptly so they can report back to me promptly, and I hear the greeting of my brother and rejoice. May my brother seek friendship with me, and may my brother send his messengers to me that they may bring my brother's greetings to me and I hear them."

Amenhotep would have asked questions after the letter had been read, per-haps about the fate of the murdered Mittanian king Artashumara or the details of the war with the Hittites. Keliya, like messengers in earlier ages, had some freedom to provide an interpretation of his king's message when he was ques-tioned. He was, after all, substituting for Tushratta himself. It would not have been practical to send a note back home to the king asking for advice about some point of negotiation or protocol at this point—months would have passed before an answer arrived. Keliya had to trust himself (and be trusted by Tushratta) to make the strongest case for the renewal of the Egyptian-Mittanian alliance.

*Mending Fences*

Although we don't know what conversation took place between Keliya and Amenhotep III, an example of the delicate way in which an envoy could influ-ence a king without causing offense is seen in a letter sent by King Burna-buriash II of Babylon to the pharaoh.

Burna-buriash was an ill-tempered king, to judge from his letters, always quick to take offense and to assume the worst from the behavior of his allies. He worried constantly about appearances and about keeping up with the neighbors. When his daughter was to marry the Egyptian king, Burna-buriash wouldn't let her go unless she could travel in a style appropriate to the daugh-ter of a great king, with a large escort. Burna-buriash was horrified that "[M]y neighboring kings [would say], 'They have transported the daughter of a great king [t]o Egypt in 5 char[iots']."[64]

More than any of the other great kings, Burna-buriash II wanted the pharaoh to think that his land was just as rich as Egypt. All the kings must have known, based on the reports from their messengers, that Egypt was far wealthier than their own lands, and several of them commented (with no small amount of jealousy) that gold lay around like dirt in the streets of Egypt, so why didn't the Egyptian king send more? But it would have hurt Burna-buriash's pride to suggest that he was poorer than Akhenaten: "as I am told, in my brother's country everything is available and my brother needs absolutely nothing. Furthermore, in my country everything too is available and I for my part nee[d] absolutely nothing."[65] Of course, he still wanted luxury goods from Egypt, in spite of such protestations. When the Egyptian king failed to send a greeting gift, on one occasion, Burna-buriash didn't send one either, in protest. But he felt that he had to add that this wasn't because he couldn't afford to: "I am one for whom nothing is scarce, and you are one for whom nothing is scarce."[66] We really are equals, he was saying. But perhaps the Egyptian king thought that he protested too much.

In any event, an Egyptian envoy arrived in Babylon on one occasion, only to find that the self-absorbed king was ill. One can imagine Burna-buriash holding court from his bed, unable to get up, but perhaps taking comfort in the many messages that were flowing in from local dignitaries all wishing for his speedy recovery.

The Egyptian envoy was an important man and deserved an appropriate reception. Burna-buriash would normally have hosted the banquet to celebrate his arrival, but he was unable to do so. He described his dilemma in a letter to the pharaoh, writing that "I have not been well, and so on no occa[sion] has [the Egyptian] messenger eaten food and [drunk] spirits [in my com]pany."[67]

The envoy had brought a letter from the pharaoh, but, not surprisingly, it made no mention of Burna-buriash's poor health. Burna-buriash was outraged at the pharaoh's insensitivity and seems to have had a temper tantrum, directed at the Egyptian messenger. He shouted at him: "Has my brother (the pharaoh) not hea[rd] that I am ill? Why has he sho[wn] me no concern? Why has he sent me no messenger here and visi[ted me]?"

This was an odd question, since the Egyptian king obviously *had* sent a messenger, and it was to this man that the tirade was addressed. But apparently what Burna-buriash wanted was a special envoy with a specific "Get well" message. The Egyptian envoy thought on his feet and replied soothingly: "(Egypt) is not a place close by so your brother can hear (about you) and send you greetings. The country is far away. Who is going to tell your brother so he can immediately send you greetings?" The envoy wisely assured Burna-buriash that of course the pharaoh would have sent good wishes had he known about the Babylonian king's illness: "Would your brother hear that you are ill and still not send you his messenger?"

Burna-buriash seems not to have been persuaded. With his constant fear of being snubbed by the pharaoh, his first instinct was still to believe that the Egyptian king was ignoring him. And yet the thing that struck him most in the envoy's explanation was the idea that Egypt was a long way away. It sounded like a fabricated excuse. He replied, disbelievingly, "For my brother, a great king, is there really a faraway country and a close-by one?" This is what he reported of the conversation in his letter to the pharaoh, and we have no reason to doubt him. The Egyptian messenger would no doubt have fulfilled his job as a witness and would have told the pharaoh if the conversation had been misrepresented.

The whole conversation is a little strange. Burna-buriash must have known that each time he sent off a messenger to Egypt it took at least four months for that man to return home, even if he wasn't detained at all. He must have heard from his messengers that they traveled the entire time and went through all kinds of countryside and encountered dangers en route. At least, one would have thought so. But the Egyptian messenger's statement seems to have been a revelation to Burna-buriash.

The Egyptian messenger again spoke carefully, finding not just a way to excuse his own king's apparently rude breach of etiquette, but also to bring in supporting evidence that Burna-buriash would have to believe. He replied, "Ask your own messenger whether the country is far away and as a result your brother did not hear (about you) and did not send (anyone) to greet you."

Burna-buriash agreed to this and called in his own messenger, who corroborated the Egyptian man's words. Burna-buriash had to concede that this was not a case of rude and insensitive behavior but of ignorance. He wrote to the pharaoh: "Now, since I asked my own messenger and he said to me that the journey is far, I was not angry (any longer), I said no [more]." It must have been a relief to the two messengers to have been excused from the king's presence, having successfully defused the situation.

As to whether Burna-buriash really was so clueless about the distance of Babylonia from Egypt—who knows? The whole exchange (and the fact that he reported it in a letter to the pharaoh) seems like something of an elaborate dance designed to make the pharaoh aware of Burna-buriash's annoyance and to be sure not to lose face.[68] The conversation probably did take place as it was described, showing that the messengers had played two of their roles well—as eyewitnesses and as mediators—and that they had soothed the king's ire.

The kings did have a tendency to argue. Many, if not most, of the Amarna letters between the great kings had an angry tone to them.[69] The kings were demanding and impatient with one another. Sometimes they complained about crimes that had been committed against their own messengers or merchants in their ally's land, or they expressed annoyance about their ally's failure to live up to their expectations.[70] The "brother" king had failed, for example, to send an invitation to a festival or (and this was the most common complaint) hadn't sent extravagant enough gifts. It seems that the kings' posturing was quite formalized and anticipated, and not at all belligerent.[71] The tone was necessary so that neither the king sending the letter nor the king receiving it could be construed to be the weaker of the two. The envoys had the tricky job of not seeming to overstep their own limited authority as subordinates, but also to not in any way suggest that the king for whom they worked was subordinate to the king whose court they were visiting. They also, understandably, wanted to avoid being penalized for the messages they brought, and the temptation to stretch the truth must have been pretty powerful.

When they gave in to such temptations, though, and misrepresented the words of a king, messengers could cause diplomatic crises. At one point Amenhotep III wrote to the Babylonian king that "I have quarreled because of your messengers....The first time the messengers went off to [y]our f[ather], and their mouths told lies. The next time they went off [and] they told lies to you." He continued, "Your messengers...I swear that they have not served you, and so they go on telling lies in order to escape your punishment."[72] Amenhotep III reprimanded the Babylonian envoys by refusing to give them the expected gifts that came to messengers, and he seems to have been equally stingy in his gifts to the Babylonian king, sending just one gift in six years—a sign, perhaps, of his enmity toward the messengers.[73] As far as Amenhotep was concerned, the Babylonian messengers were unworthy of their position; they were "nobodies" (and included one man whom he described as an assherder), and he asked the Babylonian king "Why don't you send me a dignitary of yours who can tell you the truth?"[74]

### Keliya's Return to Mittani

Keliya faced no such animosity from Amenhotep III, but he still might have had to wait for the pharaoh's response to Tushratta's letter. Keliya seems (at least sometimes) to have been the one who wrote down the pharaoh's words in the letter back to his master; this is suggested by the fact that in a later letter, Tushratta wrote to Amenhotep's wife Tiy that "you yourself [sa]id to Keliya" and then he quoted the words of the Egyptian letter he had received. Again translation must have been involved, but it isn't known whether a translator in the Egyptian court spoke the pharaoh's words in Akkadian for Keliya to write down, or if someone on the Mittani team served this purpose, or if Keliya did the translation himself. Probably the letter was read back to the pharaoh to ensure that it reflected what he wanted to say. It might then have been recopied so that the version that went back to Mittani was free from errors or corrections.

Ideally, the messengers were allowed to travel home soon after meeting with the pharaoh. According to a Babylonian king, this was the traditional way: "my father would send a messenger to you, and you would not detain him for long. You qui[ck]ly sent him off, and you would also send here to my father a beautiful greeting-gift."[75]

Keliya obviously hoped for this. He must have known, though, that it didn't always happen. Sometimes the king waited a long time before responding and allowing the messengers to return home.[76] The wait could last days, weeks, months, even years. The king of Babylon complained to Amenhotep "I sent a messenger to you, you have detained him for six years."[77] In six years of detention, a messenger would have become very familiar with the culture of his hosts, presumably learning to speak Egyptian during the time. The pharaoh would have supported him, and he would have lived comfortably. There's very little evidence to suggest that a detained messenger of an ally was punished or even put to work.[78] He was a guest of the palace. He wouldn't have been lonely, either, since a small community of people from his land was probably in residence at any given time—artists, specialists, merchants, other messengers, and the attendants of foreign princesses.[79]

Sinuhe's story described what it was like to live as a guest of the king (though clearly with a higher rank than that of a foreign ambassador): "Fine things were in [the house to which I was assigned], a cooling room in it, and representations of the horizon (perhaps wall frescoes). Valuables of the treasury were in it, vestments of royal linen were in every apartment, and first-grade myrrh....I was outfitted with fine linen and rubbed with the finest oil. I passed the night on a bed....Meals were brought from the palace three and four times a day."[80]

Ending such a detention was not in the hands of the messenger. Sometimes the delay was simply because some gift or letter wasn't ready to be sent; other times the king was punishing his ally, tit for tat, for not sending back his own messenger, or in protest about some action taken.[81] The detained man, even while living in luxury, must have missed his family and friends at home. He had a high rank, but wasn't free to do as he wished. Tushratta wrote on a different occasion, "What are messengers? Unless they are birds, are they going to fly and go away?"[82] Clearly not. They stayed, caged in a foreign country, until allowed to go home. But Keliya got his wish on that first trip: Amenhotep III sent him promptly back to Mittani.

Returning home, the envoys could face many perils, according to the letters, much as in earlier times. One of their worst worries was the heat, and messengers seem to have avoided traveling at the height of summer. On one occasion, Burna-buriash excused himself for sending just a small gift to the pharaoh because "the journey is difficult, water cut off, and the weather ho[t]...As soon as the weather improves," the king continued, "my next messenger to come I will have bring many beautiful greeting-gifts to my brother."[83] The kings weren't always considerate in this regard, however. In a later letter, an Assyrian king seems to have complained to the pharaoh that his messengers were sent from Egypt during the hottest season, when they could have faced dehydration or heat stroke: "Why should messengers be made to stay constantly out in the sun and so die in the sun?"[84] In the summer in the Near East, the temperature can reach 120 degrees Fahrenheit in the shade. The air seems to become thicker, and walking through it feels like pushing through a hot curtain. No doubt the messengers rested through the hottest hours in whatever shade they could find, and walked around dawn and in the evenings. When there was a full moon, they probably traveled at night. It would have been far more comfortable to travel in winter or spring, when the temperatures averaged in the sixties and seventies Fahrenheit.

If the messengers survived the weather, they still had to avoid being robbed or attacked.[85] Sometimes these raids came from rebel groups. In one letter the king refers to "pursuing Suteans" who put his messengers in "mortal danger."[86] But at other times the robbers were officials who, ostensibly at least, were subjects of Egypt. Burna-buriash wrote to the pharaoh to accuse two Egyptian subjects—a mayor of Damascus and another "[gov]ernor of yours in vassalage"—of robbing the Babylonian messenger on two separate occasions.[87] In another letter, he accused two other officials, also in Canaan (which "is your country," as the Babylonian king noted) of robbing and killing merchants who had been traveling with his messenger (though the messenger had, luckily for him, left his traveling companions in order to go to Egypt before this incident took place). In each case, the king named witnesses who could be brought forward to confirm his account and asked that the messenger be compensated for his losses. In the case of the murdered merchants, the Babylonian king directed the pharaoh to "Put to death the men who put my servants [to] death, and so avenge their blood." He worried that if this did not happen, "they are going to kill again, be it a caravan of mine or of your own messengers, and so messengers between us will thereby be cut off."[88] That was a real worry; the envoys had to be able to get through safely in order for the alliance to continue.

Keliya arrived home with good news for Tushratta. Amenhotep III had agreed to renew his ties with Mittani. Tushratta was overjoyed: "I rejoiced very,

very much, saying, 'Certainly there is this between us: we love (each other) very, very much, and between us let there be friendship.' "[89] At right around the same time—perhaps even before Keliya returned—Tushratta received a new directive from the pharaoh. The Egyptian king wrote: "Send your daughter here to be my wife and the mistress of Egypt."[90] This message arrived in Washshukkanni in the hands of Amenhotep's envoy, a man named Mane. So the two families would be joined by yet another dynastic marriage.

Tushratta would have held a celebratory feast, known as a *kimru* feast, to welcome the messengers and to celebrate the renewed alliance with Egypt.[91] It seems to have been traditional to invite all the "foreign guests" at the Mittani court to the feast, along with Tushratta's own nobles, and to display the greeting gifts that had been sent by the pharaoh.[92] This was a chance for the king to show off his new riches and to publicly address the Egyptian ambassador. "[W]hen...Mane br[ought] what my brother had dispatched [as] my gift, I assembled my entire land and my nobles, as many as there are...And I addressed Mane: 'All...that my brother dispatched...they may be satisfactory.' "[93] This event must have been an exciting moment for the messengers; not only had they been rewarded with valuable gifts by the pharaoh, but now they were lauded for their efforts by Tushratta as well. The success of their mission was visible to all the guests in the glittering gold objects they had brought back with them and the offer of marriage from the pharaoh.

The Mesopotamians and Syrians seem to have had fewer rules of etiquette at their official meals than did the Egyptians, which must have been a relief to Keliya. In Egypt the Mittanian envoy would have been on his best behavior, perhaps reminded by Mane of the advice of an old Egyptian text. At a meal held by "someone who is greater than you, accept what he serves when it is placed in front of you. Look only at what is right in front of you....You should speak only when he addresses you....You should laugh only when he laughs."[94] These rules must have made for quiet, respectful banquets in Egypt. Things seem to have been a little more relaxed in Mittani. Ever since the beginning of civilization in Syria and Mesopotamia, the people had loved banquets; they show up as scenes on cylinder seals and clay plaques from as early as the third millennium. Typically, several people were shown drinking through reeds or copper tubes from a clay pot (containing beer) while musicians performed. These must have been loud, social occasions, and the food had to be festive as well, going far beyond the typical breads and vegetables of a meal at home.

There are no records of a Mittanian banquet, nor have rules been preserved for how one was supposed to behave, but we know quite a lot about the Syro-Mesopotamian cuisine. A few recipes even survive for broths and cooked poultry.[95] Tushratta, like Zimri-Lim of Mari centuries earlier, must have employed many chefs, bakers, and brewers in his palace, and they would probably have pulled out all the stops for the banquet to celebrate the renewed friendship with Egypt. The banquet would have included many different types and flavors of breads—the Mesopotamian staple—along with a plentiful supply of beer. The beer was often cut with water, and although beer was the main beverage among all people, there are few references to drunkenness. Meat (including poultry, lamb, and beef) was poached or roasted; vegetables were boiled; and many of the savory dishes were flavored with onions, garlic, mint, leeks, and a number of spices. The chefs would have served cheeses and fresh fruit as well, along with pastries sweetened with dates and honey. The king made sure that none of his guests left hungry and that they returned to their families and homelands telling stories of his generosity and of the delicious food they had eaten at his court. According to Tushratta, he held a celebration every time his messengers returned with a letter from the pharaoh: "Any day that I hear the greetings of my brother, that day I make a festive occasion."[96] These celebrations almost certainly included banquets every time.

Once the festivities were over, Tushratta sent Keliya back to Egypt with a new letter, asking Amenhotep to send gold, and lots of it: "May my brother treat me [ten times] better than he did my father, and may he send me much gold that has not been worked." He also readily agreed to Amenhotep's proposal of a marriage to his daughter—saying "Of course!"—and he noted that he had taken the Egyptian envoy Mane to see the daughter that he had in mind for the marriage.[97]

And with that, the alliance was renewed. Envoys bearing letters and gifts once again became a regular sight on the long roads from Mittani to Egypt, and the two kings began preparing for the royal marriage.

## Tushratta: A Pious and Affectionate Man

Tushratta's personality comes through vividly in his letters to the pharaoh, ten of which survive, almost all of them long and heartfelt. One might have expected him to have been hardened by the horrendous experiences of his childhood: the violent death of his brother and his own (unwilling) support of the plans of the murderer, followed by the violent retribution that he took when the time was right. But his letters to the Egyptian king reveal him to have been a gentle, pious, emotional man. No doubt he was pragmatic, and he certainly didn't mince his words when he felt that he had been wronged, but an attractive personality shines through the letters nonetheless.

Tushratta often mentioned how he felt about his brother the pharaoh. To hear him tell it, he wholeheartedly adored the Egyptian king, and the feeling was mutual. Many of his letters started with the statement that the Egyptian king was someone "whom I love and who loves me."[98] The same relationship went back through previous generations: "My father loved you, and you in turn loved my father."[99] This was not just a scribal convention. Had it been, the letters from other great kings would be just as effusive. But the Babylonian kings expressed no love for the Egyptian king, nor did the kings of Assyria or Alashiya. They wrote of friendship and alliance. Tushratta professed more. True, the kings had never met, but, in Tushratta's view, their love for one another overcame that minor obstacle.

Lacking letters from Amenhotep III to Tushratta, we can't know whether he was equally demonstrative in his affections, but it seems unlikely. The Egyptian kingdom was completely secure, whereas Mittani was beginning to face uncertain times. Tushratta seems to have feared that the Hittites might attack his land again.[100] Having a strong ally in Egypt was crucial for Tushratta.

Tushratta was also the only one of the great kings who, in his messages, regularly called on the gods for their support. In letters to the pharaoh from other kings, the gods were, oddly, conspicuous in their absence, but Tushratta trusted his gods Teshup, Shaushka, and Shimige so much that he mentioned them all the time. His references to them seem natural and almost conversational, as though he couldn't imagine claiming any achievement without crediting divine help. For example, when he won a victory against the Hittite king early in his reign, it was not his own doing but took the help of Teshup. It also seems to have been second nature to Tushratta to ask the gods for assistance with any fervent wish. Strikingly, and thoughtfully, he called on not only his own god or goddess but also Amen (spelled "Aman" in cuneiform), the great god of New Kingdom Egypt. In one of Tushratta's early letters, he voiced three separate prayers to the Hurrian and Egyptian gods.

Egypt, of course, had no need for a storm god like Teshup, since it had no storms. There, the chief gods were Amen, the god of the city of Thebes, and Ra, the omnipresent god of the sun. Tushratta knew this god well; he was identical with Shimige, his own sun god (there being only one sun). In fact, in one letter, Tushratta referred to Shimige as the god of the Egyptian king, not even changing the name to Ra.[101]

### Ambassadors, at Home in Both Worlds

The lands tied together by alliances were much more distant from one another than had been true of the smaller allied kingdoms in Hammurabi's time, and they were richer and more powerful as well. These factors combined to make the role of the ambassadors even more important than in the past.

Many of the expeditions between Mittani and Egypt were led by the Mittanian envoy Keliya or the Egyptian envoy Mane, or both of them together. The letters that are preserved from their journeys show that Keliya visited Egypt at least four times, and that Mane visited Mittani at least three times, twice being detained there for months if not years. When Amenhotep III died, to be replaced on the throne by his son Akhenaten, Keliya and Mane continued to carry the letters to and from Tushratta.

Over time Tushratta increasingly referred to Keliya and Mane as a team. At one point he wanted to reassure Amenhotep III regarding some malicious gossip. He told the pharaoh to consult Keliya and Mane in order to find out the truth: "the words that Keliya and Mane say about me or about my land, they are true and right."[102] Similarly, Tushratta reminded Queen Tiy that "Keliya and Mane know" about the contents of the letters that had passed between himself and Amenhotep III.[103]

The two men traveled together, and the fact that their names appeared so often as a pair suggests that they were also friends.[104] We can only guess what language they spoke to one another as they walked side by side, day after day. Perhaps it was Akkadian, the language of the letters they carried (though the native language of neither of them). Both would have spoken the language with an accent, while making minor grammatical mistakes that are also found in the letters they wrote and read.

Mane and Keliya were not the only envoys who carried messages and goods between Egypt and Mittani; the letters mention several others. It was normal for officials from both countries to travel together, but sometimes the delegation sent by Tushratta was made up of only Mittanians, and sometimes Tushratta even sent back the Egyptian messengers without a Mittanian escort.[105]

The Egyptian queen, Tiy, had her own messengers, and she maintained a separate diplomatic relationship with Yuni, the queen of Mittani—Tushratta's chief wife. The messengers carrying the queens' letters seem to have traveled with Keliya and Mane, or with the other men taking messages to and from Egypt and Mittani. Unfortunately, none of their letters to one another were found at Amarna, but Tushratta mentioned this separate queens' correspondence when he wrote to Tiy: "May your own messengers g[o] regularly with the messengers of [the pharaoh]...to Yuni, my wife, and may the messen[gers o]f Yuni, my wife, [g]o regula[rly] to [you]."[106]

Over time, Tushratta seems to have become more and more pleased with the work of Mane. Of all the Egyptians, he was the Mittanian king's favorite.

Once Tushratta wrote emphatically to Amenhotep, "Any other envoy, may my brother not send. May he send only Mane. If my brother does not send Mane and sends someone else, I do not want him, and my brother should know it. No! May my brother send Mane!"[107] Elsewhere in the same letter he remarked that "Mane, your envoy, is very good; there does not exist a man like him in all the world."[108] Having never met the Egyptian king in person, Tushratta's image of the Amenhotep III and his land must have been formed through his impressions of the Egyptian envoys. A later Hittite ruler writing to the Egyptian king was clear about this situation: "Though we great kings are brothers, the one has never seen the other. It is our messengers who come and go between us."[109] So Mane was the ideal ambassador: he had impressed the Mittanian king and was considered to be completely trustworthy.

It seems that Keliya and the other men from Mittani were, at least initially, overawed by the wealth of Egypt, perhaps even exaggerating a little when they reported back to their king: "They (perhaps the messengers) said 'In Egypt, gold is more plentiful than dirt.... Whatever is needed is in Egypt more plentiful than dirt, [and] anyone can give anyone (else) so many things [that] they are beyond calculation.'"[110] Of course, since they had stood in the rooms described in Amenhotep III's inscriptions, with their walls and doors of gold and their floors of silver, the Mittanian messengers might have had trouble finding adequate words to describe the opulence.

Mane and the other Egyptian messengers were probably less fulsome in their praise of Mittani when they met with their kings after a trip there. If gold was the standard by which the wealth of a king was measured, the Egyptian king was far ahead of his allies. He controlled gold mines in Nubia and the Eastern Desert, whereas the other kings were dependent on Egypt for their gold. But the contrast between palaces would not have been quite as dramatic as one might think from what is left of them today. Tushratta's palace hasn't been found, of course, but it would have been built of mud brick, so the archaeological remains, even if they are found, will be uninspiring. Mud brick doesn't age well. It turns into mud.

On the evidence of provincial palaces and of palaces from eras before and after that of Tushratta, we can guess that his palace was a sprawling complex of rooms and courtyards. Perhaps the walls weren't actually covered with gold, but they would have been brightly painted or hung with elaborate textiles. Storage magazines contained grain, oil, and beer in vast quantities. A throne room with a dais for the throne itself would have been reached from a courtyard, and the furnishings would have been of the finest materials the king could obtain. To judge from the list of objects sent as a dowry with Tushratta's daughter when she eventually married the pharaoh, his wealth was nothing to sneeze at. These palaces and throne rooms—in Egypt and in Mittani—must have become familiar to Keliya and Mane over the years as they journeyed regularly from one country to the other.

As for the messages carried by the envoys, they were quite different from the earlier ones found at Mari. Whereas the Old Babylonian kings fretted in their letters to one another over movements of troops, defections of vassals, and contested border towns, the Amarna kings were preoccupied with royal marriages, expensive gifts, and breaches of etiquette. Warfare was scarcely mentioned, and threats of military retaliation were unheard of. This was a time of peace. Although the letters are frustratingly short on details about the political events of the time, this very fact shows just how effective the diplomatic system had proved to be.

### CHAPTER NINE

# Diplomatic Marriages

*"We, between us, are one, the Hurrian land
and the land of Egypt"*

*Preparations for Tadu-Hepa's Marriage*

When Tushratta took the Egyptian envoy Mane to see the princess whom he had selected to marry Amenhotep III, Mane "praised her greatly." Tushratta promised the pharaoh that he would get her safely to Egypt and hoped that the gods would "make her the image of my brother's desire."[1] But Tushratta was probably only in his early twenties at the time; he had only recently thrown off the oppressive rule of his regent, and it's almost impossible that any of his daughters was yet grown. But he wouldn't have wanted to say no to Amenhotep's proposal. His reply was "Of course I will give her," and, though he must have been decades younger than the pharaoh, he promptly started referring to himself as Amenhotep's "father-in-law."[2] The daughter he had chosen was named Tadu-Hepa, and Tushratta seems to have been very attached to her.

It would be hard to overstate the centrality of diplomatic marriages in international relationships by this time.[3] The Amarna letters give us much more information about these marriages than we have for any other period of ancient Near Eastern history. The letters provide fascinating details: the stages of the negotiations, the vast quantity of gifts exchanged, the kings' emotions and strategies, and even the words of one princess before her marriage. It does seem that an alliance wasn't seen as entirely complete until the kings were related by marriage, as true family members, not just fictitious "brothers." At that point, they said, their lands were united.

Mane, on returning to Egypt, probably did praise Tadu-Hepa, but perhaps told the pharaoh that the girl was still quite young. The Egyptian king seems to have required that his wives be "women" before marriage. The Babylonian King Kadashman-Enlil I wrote about his daughter on another occasion that "she has become a woman; she is nubile" and therefore could now be taken to Egypt to marry the king.[4] Perhaps Amenhotep wanted to be sure that his wives could bear children right away. But it was not unheard of in the ancient Near East for young girls to be "married" while continuing to live with their parents, waiting until they were older to consummate the marriage.[5] Amenhotep III himself might well have been less than fourteen years old when he married Tiy. In any event, Tushratta must have been pleased when he could write in another letter, perhaps a few years after Mane had first seen his daughter, that "she has become very mature, and … has been fashioned according to my brother's desire."[6]

This issue of "my brother's desire" seems to have been important. Amenhotep III wanted the woman chosen as his wife to be beautiful. Not only had Mane been sent to see the girl and give his assessment of her for the pharaoh, Tushratta also wrote, in all four letters that led up to the sending of Tadu-Hepa, "May (the gods) Shaushka and Aman make her the image of my brother's desire."[7]

Mane came back to Mittani, some time after Tushratta had given the go-ahead for the marriage, to carry out the negotiations and to anoint the princess by pouring oil on her head.[8] Although this act had its roots in Syria and Mesopotamia and wasn't an Egyptian tradition, the pharaoh was willing to go along with it.[9] It marked a crucial point in an engagement and is mentioned in other Amarna letters and in laws from around the same time in Assyria.[10]

The Assyrian laws provide us with a picture of the events involved in marriages between commoners during this era. Royal marriages were based on the same principles, but took place on a much grander scale. The main ideas hadn't changed since the Old Babylonian period, but some of the details were slightly different. The engagement agreement for commoners was between the father of the bride and the father of the groom, not between the married couple themselves. For a royal marriage of a ruling king, the father of the groom was obviously dead, since he had been the former king, so it was the groom—the king himself—who negotiated with the father of the bride. As part of the marriage, the groom's father (or in this case the groom himself) was required to bring a bridal gift to his fiancée's father. Among ordinary people this could include "lead, silver, gold," along with grain and sheep, food and drink.[11] In a royal marriage, the bridal gift was of spectacular size and value. This bride-wealth belonged to the woman's family even if her husband later divorced her.[12] The woman also received a dowry from her father, which she could pass on to her children.[13] The exchange of gifts was only part of the engagement; the families also participated in a ceremony that could include an elaborate banquet. It was at this point that the bride was anointed with oil by her new father-in-law.[14]

The anointing ceremony, even among commoners, marked the moment when the woman was considered a member of her husband's family, though she could still live with her father.[15] One law stated that if "the son to whom (his father) assigned the wife either dies or flees, he shall give her in marriage to whichever of his remaining sons he wishes."[16] That is, after the anointing took place, the husband's family controlled the woman's future; they could even marry her to a different man within the family if they chose.

Tadu-Hepa's marriage preparations followed the same course. Needless to say, Mane was not Amenhotep's father, but since the king himself could not travel to Mittani to anoint the bride, his trusted official took on the role. The anointing must have been a solemn occasion. From then on, Tadu-Hepa was considered to be Amenhotep's wife, even though she had not yet met him.

### Bride-wealth and Dowries: Wealth "Beyond Measure"

The marriage agreement between Tadu-Hepa's father Tushratta and Amenhotep III was now confirmed, and the preparation of the marriage gifts got underway in earnest. Three sets—vast hoards, really—of gifts were put together in honor of the occasion. The first was a bridal gift that Amenhotep sent to Tushratta. The second was Tadu-Hepa's dowry, which Tushratta set about assembling; a list that seems to represent the dowry was found at Amarna. The third was a collection of gifts that Tushratta made directly to Amenhotep at the same time, which was also recorded in a list.

Mane seems to have brought some of the bride-wealth from Amenhotep with him when he came to Mittani the second time; Tushratta later described it as being "beyond measure, ri[v]alling in height heaven and earth."[17] Amenhotep sent a letter with the bride-wealth; according to Tushratta, it read, "These goods that I have sent now are nothing, and my brother is not to complain. I have sent nothing. These goods that I have now sent you, I have sent to you with this understanding that, when my brother hands over my wife whom I have asked for, and they bring her here and I see her, then I will send you ten times more than this."[18] Ten times more than an amount that was already "beyond measure"? No wonder Tushratta had been so quick to agree to a royal marriage.

Although no inventory of the bride-wealth sent by Amenhotep to Tush-ratta was found at Amarna, we can still get a sense of the riches that Tushratta must have received. A later list of presents sent by Amenhotep's successor Akhenaten to the king of Babylon "when he (the Babylonian king) gave his daughter to him" might have been similar.[19] The wealth involved was staggering. The gold objects alone added up to a weight of 1,200 minas (pounds) plus a few shekels. At modern prices this amount of gold would be worth over fifteen million dollars.

The 1,200 minas of gold weren't in bullion, though. They were fashioned into hundreds of objects, including jewelry, goblets, containers, boxes, and knives, along with much larger gold-plated items: four chariots, two beds, six thrones, three chairs, and even "one ship, of cedar, overlaid with gold, along with all its gear, and six small ships that one tows."[20] These seem to have been full-size ships that could be sailed on the river. They must have been dismantled for transport to Babylonia, since there was no way to sail there.

Three items on the list must have particularly pleased the Babylonian king: "one large statuette that is overlaid with gold, of the king...one female figurine, overlaid with gold, of the king's wife, one female figurine, overlaid with gold, of the king's daughter." We know that Tushratta hoped for similar statues of himself and his daughter, Tadu-Hepa, though they didn't arrive with the first shipment of the bride-wealth.

The list of objects sent as bride-wealth from Egypt continued with silver items, over 130 of them, ranging in size from a sieve to a throne. Many were bowls and vessels of various kinds. Again the scribes helpfully totaled it all: 292 minas and three shekels of silver. Then on to the bronze category, which featured over 300 objects, including 170 mirrors, seventy-three razors, and ninety-two ladles, in total 860 minas, twenty shekels of bronze. The list went on and on, through textiles (1,092 individual items), stone vessels full of "sweet oil" (over 1,000), empty stone vessels (163 of those), and various items made of ivory, from combs to animal-shaped vessels (over 500). Altogether, Akhenaten sent over 3,300 objects from Egypt to Babylonia. As it happens, Akhenaten was known for being stingier than his father, so one can scarcely imagine the wealth that Tushratta was to have received as Tadu-Hepa's bridal gift from Amenhotep III.

It took Tushratta at least six months to get his gifts for Amenhotep III organized after Mane arrived to take the princess back to Egypt with him. He kept Mane in Mittani while the dowry and the separate gifts for Amenhotep III were being finished, but sent another Egyptian messenger back to let the pharaoh know that the marriage would go ahead.[21] Oddly, this time he phrased his agreement to the match as a double negative, "I did not [say],

'I will [no]t give her."[22] The pharaoh sent the messenger back to Mittani again, as quickly as it was possible to travel, with yet more gold—four sacks full. The messenger got back to Mittani after just three months away.

It's possible that at this point Princess Tadu-Hepa wrote to Amenhotep III herself. There's a letter in the Amarna archive from a Babylonian princess who seems to have been in the same position as Tadu-Hepa—awaiting the time when she would be sent to marry the pharaoh, though in her case it would have been Akhenaten.[23] Perhaps it was considered good etiquette for the princess to make direct contact with her future husband once the arrangements for her marriage had been formalized. The letter was in Babylonian handwriting, suggesting that the princess was still in Babylon and using Babylonian scribes, and she invoked the gods of her father, which also hints that she hadn't left home yet.

The letter is badly broken, but enough survives to give a sense that this was a very different letter from the missives normally sent by the kings. The princess did not write at all as the pharaoh's equal; instead she wrote: "Say to my lord: Thus the princess." The greeting "my lord" was a typical way, in Akkadian, for a royal princess to greet her husband, the king. She continued with an abbreviated version of the standard greeting in royal letters: "For you, your chariots, the m[e]n a[nd]...may all go well." The king seems to have been on a campaign or expedition when the princess wrote, since she expressed her wishes for his safe return to his palace: "May the gods of Burna-buriash (the princess's father) accompany you. March in safety, and safely push on so you will see your house (again)."

After a long broken section she added a note that "my messenger brings (you) colored cloth" and, as if as an afterthought, added some of the rest of the usual greeting that generally went at the beginning of a letter: "For your cities and your household may all go well." It seems as though the princess wasn't quite sure of the conventions of royal correspondence and had puzzled over what to say. The last line from her is a little hard to make sense of, but one possible translation reads, "Do no[t] wo[rr]y, or you will have made me sad." This kind of emotional appeal isn't seen in the letters between kings, and it might have been intended to endear her to her future husband. Unlike the earlier princesses of Mari in their correspondence, she referred to the king throughout most of the letter as "you" rather than as "my lord." This might have been a gesture of familiarity. Tadu-Hepa's letter to Amenhotep III, if she wrote one, probably was similar; it's also quite possible that she sent him a small gift of her own, just like the Babylonian princess.

Tushratta was determined to make both his personal gift to Amenhotep and Tadu-Hepa's dowry a worthy match for the bride-wealth he had just received, and even more impressive than the "marvels" that Princess Kilu-Hepa had brought to Egypt as a gift from Tushratta's father two decades before. He told the pharaoh to consult his records and to find the tablets that listed the dowries of his sister Kilu-Hepa and of his aunt, who had been married to Thutmose IV, to compare them with what he was sending, "and may my brother hear that the dowry is very extensive, that it is splendid, that it is befitting my brother."[24]

The gifts that Tushratta sent to Amenhotep, which were separate from Tadu-Hepa's dowry, were carefully listed on a four-column tablet, about the size of a large coffee table book, covered in tiny cuneiform writing. The list ends with the statement "It is all of these wedding gifts, of every sort, that Tushratta, the king of Mittani, gave to Nimmureya, the king of Egypt, his brother and his son-in-law. He gave them at the same time that he gave Tadu-Hepa, his daughter, to Egypt and to Nimmureya to be his wife."[25] This last statement suggests that the gifts were sent at the same time that Tadu-Hepa traveled to Egypt. The list was probably viewed as necessary so that Amenhotep could check that every item arrived properly; the tablet must have traveled with the gifts.

As in the case of the bride-wealth from Egypt, the gifts from Mittani were almost all manufactured goods; no raw materials were sent. Tushratta seems to have been particularly proud of the horses and chariots that he sent to the pharaoh. The horses were right at the top of the list: "4 beautiful horses that run (swiftly)," along with a gold-covered chariot.[26] Such horses must have been highly prized by both kings, and they would have been decked out in the finest trappings. Among the other gifts were necklaces for the horses, bridles, blinkers, reins, a halter, and a whip, many of them inlaid with gold and silver. For the king's use Tushratta sent richly ornamented weapons, including several made of iron (which was very rare at this time) and other ceremonial objects, all of them inlaid with gold and sometimes silver as well.[27] Tushratta also sent jewelry and clothing for the pharaoh (including several pairs of shoes, some studded with gold, and most with accompanying leggings "of shaggy wool," which, one suspects, might have been of little use in the heat of Egypt).

There were thousands of arrows among the presents. Each one of these had been made by hand, of course, representing hours of work by a skilled artisan. Javelins followed in the list, and spears, and suits of armor; these weren't ceremonial but practical gifts. Vessels and bowls of silver and bronze were destined for the palace. Tushratta's scribes were meticulous. They listed everything—a single wooden spoon deserved a mention, as did a bedspread.

The scribes carefully weighed and recorded every shekel of gold and silver used in the gifts, from 320 shekels of gold used to decorate the chariot to just

The cuneiform tablet that lists Tushratta's gifts to Amenhotep
III on the occasion of the marriage of his daughter, Tadu-hepa,
to the pharaoh. (Bildarchiv Preussischer Kulturbesitz/Art
Resource, NY)

two shekels of gold used to inlay a chest. Altogether, the total came to almost
800 shekels of gold and 600 shekels of silver. That sounds like a great deal,
until one realizes that it is equivalent to only thirteen minas of gold and ten
minas of silver, a fraction of the 1,200 minas of gold objects and 292 minas of
silver objects that the Egyptian king sent in his bridal gift for the Babylonian

princess. The Egyptian gift of gold was about ninety-two times greater than the gift to Egypt from Mittani. But this is hardly surprising, since gold had to be imported to Mittani from Egypt in the first place.

Over a hundred of the objects from Tushratta were made of fabric of various kinds, including garments, bedspreads, and other cloths. Given the fact that the kingdoms of Syria had specialized in spinning and weaving wool and linen for over a thousand years, these were probably very fine textiles. Each one might well have taken months to produce and must have been worth much more than their prosaic translations might suggest.

Tadu-Hepa's dowry was laid out on a separate tablet, even larger and more impressive than the list of gifts for Amenhotep III, which probably traveled to Egypt at the same time.[28] The columns on the tablet were neatly bordered with perfectly straight double lines, and double lines separated each line of script as well. The scribe who produced the list couldn't have made it more beautiful; each sign was carefully drawn and aligned perfectly with matching signs in the lines above and below.[29] The objects on this list, unlike the gifts for the pharaoh, were for Tadu-Hepa's own use and would have continued to belong directly to her, even after her marriage. They also differ greatly from the gifts for the pharaoh. There were no weapons, armor, or horses. Instead, we find earrings, toggle pins, necklaces, rings, and bracelets, many of them made of gold and lapis lazuli. The princess was given dozens of combs, garments, wooden chests, blankets, and vessels of various materials.

Some of the objects in Tadu-Hepa's dowry were specified as being for her attendants. Her "two principal ladies-in-waiting" received jewelry that included 521 shekels (almost nine pounds) of gold.[30] Her other servants, the dowry-women and male attendants, also were outfitted well, with silver foot bracelets and toggle pins for the women and gold bracelets for the men. Altogether, the dowry included almost 1,500 items, and the gold on them weighed over 2,500 shekels (forty-two pounds), several times more than the gold sent to the pharaoh as his gift.

### Tushratta's Hopes

Once the goods to be sent to Egypt were prepared, they must have been packed carefully into any number of Egyptian wagons and chariots (perhaps the same ones that had brought the bride-wealth), and the princess left Mittani, with all the riches being sent to Egypt and accompanied by a large force of Egyptian soldiers. The Babylonian King Burna-buriash II claimed (perhaps inflating the numbers somewhat) that 3,000 soldiers escorted his sister when she married

Amenhotep III; Tadu-Hepa probably benefited from a similar party to the one Burna-buriash mentioned.[31] According to Tadu-Hepa's dowry list, she also took with her 300 attendants (270 women and thirty men), all of whom would have needed to be fed and provided with shelter at night along the way as they journeyed to Egypt.[32]

The lives of each one of those anonymous courtiers changed forever when they left Washshukkanni. It's a safe bet that almost none of them, from the princess herself to her lowliest maid, ever returned home again. Only the messengers among them would go back and forth now. In a way, her attendants were as tied to Tadu-Hepa as she was to the pharaoh; their new homes would be over a thousand miles away from Mittani, in a land they had never visited before, where almost all of the social rules and expectations were different from those at home. Perhaps, though, they could hope that Tadu-Hepa's quarters at the Egyptian palace would feel like a little patch of Mittani in the foreign land, where everyone spoke Hurrian, her chefs cooked familiar food, and her attendants made her feel at home. Many of her aunt's 317 Mittanian attendants were probably still alive as well, so the Egyptian court would not be an entirely alien place. Perhaps she was even provided with rooms decorated in the Mittanian fashion, just as Thutmose III had built a Minoan-style palace perhaps for a foreign wife from Crete.

Tushratta seems to have been moved by his daughter's departure; he wrote a letter to Amenhotep that was probably sent right after she left, in which he prayed for her safety; "May (the gods) Shimige and Shaushka go before her," he wrote, and "May my brother rejoice on t[hat] day" when she arrived in Egypt.[33] "May Shimige and Shau[shka] grant my brother a great blessing, exquisi[te] joy." Tushratta also commended the Egyptian envoys, Mane and the interpreter Hane, who had seen through all the negotiations and preparations for the marriage; he wrote that he had "exalted [them] like gods" and "given them many presents and treated them very kindly, for their report was excellent." He continued, "In everything about them, I have never seen men with such an appearance."

The act of just getting Tadu-Hepa and her entourage to Egypt must have taken months and cost a fortune. When the wedding procession passed through a town en route, it would have been reason enough for the residents to leave their fields and workshops and line the road. At night, soldiers must have kept watch in shifts over the dowry and gifts to avoid losing anything to thieves or bandits. The journey must have been uncomfortable, but no doubt every effort was made to ease Tadu-Hepa's discomfort.

It's hard to imagine how cut off Tushratta must have felt from his daughter during her journey, and from the momentous events that would take place in Egypt when she arrived. The farther away the princess traveled, the longer it would have taken for any news of her to reach her father, even if messengers had left the caravan every day with letters for the king. Not for at least six weeks after her triumphant arrival in Thebes would he have heard any word of what had happened there.

Even while the princess was still on her way to Egypt, Tushratta sent another letter, a long, rambling epistle written in his native language of Hurrian. Maybe his Akkadian-speaking scribes were all on the journey with Tadu-Hepa or already in Egypt ready to receive her, so he had only Hurrian scribes to record his words.

The messenger who carried this letter to Egypt doesn't seem to have been encumbered even by a greeting gift for the pharaoh—at least none seems to be mentioned. He could have traveled much faster than the plodding royal caravan of soldiers and horses, gifts, dowry, and attendants accompanying the princess, and bypassed them, so that the letter, sent after the princess's party left Mittani, arrived before they reached Egypt.

When the Mittanian messenger arrived at the palace in Egypt with this letter, one can imagine the pharaoh looking anxiously at the clay tablet in the envoy's hands. The tablet was enormous—over eighteen inches tall and eleven inches wide, with over 493 lines of text in four long columns. Most letters from great kings were about six inches tall. This one was six times longer than any other known Amarna letter written to an Egyptian king by any king of Babylon, Alashiya, Hatti, or Assyria. And why, the pharaoh must have thought, wasn't it in Akkadian? Egyptian scribes couldn't have been expected to read Hurrian.[34] Amenhotep III presumably had to trust that the Mittanian messenger gave him an accurate translation.

As he began to listen to the letter, Amenhotep III would have been struck by Tushratta's hopes for the future and his profound belief that their two lands would be more than just allies; they would be unified as a result of the imminent marriage. Tushratta had written that "we, between us, are one, the Hurrian land and the land of Egypt... I am the k[ing] of the land of Egypt, and my brother is the ki[ng] of the Hurrian land."[35]

Although this sounds incredible, Tushratta had said something like it before. When the marriage preparations were still in progress he had speculated about this future time, the moment when Tadu-Hepa would arrive in Egypt. He had written then that "they will bring her to my brother. On t[hat] day shall Hanigalbat (yet another term for Mittani) and Egypt be [one]."[36]

The marriage of Tushratta's daughter to the pharaoh was marked by such a mind-boggling transfer of wealth that some scholars have suggested that the princess was just another commodity (albeit a very valuable one) in the luxury gift exchange between the two lands. But Tushratta clearly didn't see it this way. To his eyes, once his daughter arrived safely in Egypt his dynasty would once again be joined to the Egyptian dynasty (as it had been in his father's and grandfather's times) and the countries thereby united. Tushratta wasn't alone in this understanding of the purpose of diplomatic marriage. A century later, a Hittite queen voiced exactly the same hopeful idea as her daughter prepared to marry the pharaoh: "Now I know that Egypt and Hatti will become a single country.... You, as son-in-law, [will take] my daughter [in marriage]."[37]

It's not clear that the pharaohs would have agreed that their land and those of their allies had become "a single country" as a result of the royal marriages, but this, even more than a greed for gold, was evidently foremost in the minds not just of Tushratta but of other kings who arranged marriages for their daughters. In surviving sources that mention marriages between the royal houses of Hatti and Mittani, between Hatti and Babylonia, between Babylonia and Assyria, and between Babylonia and Elam, such material concerns as the size of the dowry or the bridal gift were rarely even mentioned. If royal wives really were just commodities to be traded, one would expect to see the women discussed in terms of their value. Instead, they continued to play a part in creating (or trying to create) unity between the two states. In a later treaty with Mittani that included the marriage of his daughter, the Hittite king Suppiluliuma expressed this idea clearly (though by this time, Mittani's status had diminished—this was not a treaty between equals): "Prince Shattiwaza shall be king in the land of Mittani, and the daughter of the King of Hatti shall be queen in the land of Mittani.... In the future...the Hittites shall not do evil to the Mittanians; [the Mittanians] shall not do evil to the Hittites."[38] The royal couple became the living symbol of the treaty between the two states.

As the pharaoh continued to listen to Tushratta's letter, he might have been a little taken aback by the Mittanian king's presumption. In the letter Tushratta gave the pharaoh directions as to what to do when the princess arrived:

> When she comes, my brother will see her...And again my brother will see a dowry.... And the entire land may my brother assemble, and may all other lands and the nobles (and) all envoys be present. And they may show his dowry to my brother, and they may spread out everything in the view of my brother.[39]

You can almost see Tushratta daydreaming here, thinking of all the wealth that he had just packed off to Egypt and imagining "the entire land" of Egypt assembling to admire it. He was very proud of having put together such a vast quantity of treasure, an amount so considerable that Tushratta believed that "with just a single dispatch of mine I have done ten times as much" for Amenhotep III as his own grandfather or father ever did for Egypt.

But then, after lines and lines of fond assurances of friendship, the tone of the letter changed somewhat and Tushratta began to gripe, as almost all the kings did on a regular basis, that the pharaoh wasn't sending him as much wealth as he had before. In this case he felt that he had received less than King Shuttarna II, his father: "my brother has not given to me the equivalent of what he dispatched to my father." So Tushratta came up with some concrete suggestions for what he would like as a gift: "Of my sister, the wife of my brother, may m[y brothe]r erect a mo[lt]en gold image"—this was, of course, Kilu-Hepa. Oddly enough, though, Tushratta never mentioned this statue again in other letters. Perhaps Amenhotep III sent it right away so he didn't need to, or perhaps Tushratta didn't really care about it.

The statue that he really wanted was one of his daughter Tadu-Hepa. "I have requested from my brother a molten gold image of my daughter," he wrote. This doesn't seem to have been an unusual request; long before this, Shamshi-Adad planned to send gold statues of himself and his ally on the occasion of a diplomatic marriage.[40] Akhenaten later sent a statue to the Babylonian king of his daughter as part of her bride-wealth. In his letter Tushratta started daydreaming again, this time about what people would say when they saw this statue: "Before earth and before the heavens are the words spoken. As they should be spoken, so shall it be ... 'This gold image is Tadu-Hepa, the daughter of Tushratta, the lord of Mittani, whom he gave as wife of Immureya, the lord of Egypt. And Immureya made a molten gold image and full of love dispatched it to Tushratta.'" (Immureya was one of the many different ways that Tushratta's scribes tried to render Nibmaatre—Amenhotep III's throne name.) Several lines of this column are now unreadable; they probably included Tushratta's request for a statue of himself as well, because later he wrote that he had asked "for statues of solid cast gold, one of myself and a second statue, a statue of Tadu-Hepa, my daughter."[41]

After the four long columns of his rambling musings, a final thought had crossed Tushratta's mind, just in case there was any doubt: "And this wife of my brother whom I have given, this (woman) is pure. And may my brother know it." It was crucial, in Assyrian law soon after this, that a woman be a virgin at the time of her marriage, and the same was certainly true in Mittani as well. Tushratta wanted Amenhotep to know that Tadu-Hepa was chaste; the pharaoh could be sure that any children born to his new bride were his own. Tushratta closed his letter with many more lines about the love shared by the two kings: "And between us we wish to love one another in brotherly fashion and close attachment. As man loves Shimige (the sun god) on seeing him, so do we want, between us, to love one another." It seems that Tushratta relished this moment, and he looked back on it wistfully later. It proved to be the high point of his relationship with Egypt.

Amenhotep III seems not to have taken offense at Tushratta's requests, and he wrote back, perhaps even before his new Mittanian bride had arrived, to let Tushratta know that he would be happy to send the gold statues that the Mittanian king had requested. Better still, he wrote, "Don't talk of giving statues just of solid cast gold. I will give you ones made also of lapis lazuli. I will give you, too, along with the statues, much additional gold and (other) goods beyond measure."[42] (At least, these are the words that Tushratta attributed to Amenhotep III; the original letter is lost.) The Mittanian king was thrilled; what a true friend and fond brother the pharaoh had proven to be.

### Tadu-Hepa's Arrival

The arrival of the princess in Thebes was marked by a day of celebration. Tushratta later said that Amenhotep III "made that day a festive occasion along, too, with his country."[43] This might have meant that workers had the day off and that people feasted and danced. One can imagine music and entertainment in the streets, and religious ceremonies giving thanks to the gods. Amenhotep III, at this point in his reign, held festivals on a regular basis; perhaps he enjoyed the huge national sense of jubilation that accompanied them. He had waited until his thirtieth year on the throne for his first jubilee, as was traditional, but then held two more jubilees soon after, in his thirty-fourth and thirty-seventh years.[44] We don't know exactly what the wedding celebration for Tadu-Hepa was like, but it might have resembled a jubilee. For these events, new buildings were constructed and gifts were given by and to the king.[45] The tomb of one of the king's scribes included a relief sculpture showing the king at one of his jubilees; long lines of officials were depicted, receiving gifts from the king, who was seated. The description read, "Appearance of the king upon the great throne, to reward the chiefs of the South and North."[46]

In the same way, gifts were given to officials when Tadu-Hepa married Amenhotep III. Tushratta later remembered, "He sent back all my messengers that were in residence [to]...the quarters that [were established] for Tadu-Hepa, and there was not [a single one] among them who went in and [to whom he did not g]ive [something]."[47] This must have been a grand day for the Mittanian delegation. The first treat was that they got to see Tadu-Hepa's quarters, which were no doubt magnificent. The pharaoh would have wanted the messengers to tell Tushratta how well appointed his daughter's rooms were. Tadu-Hepa's apartments probably were among the royal women's rooms that opened onto the great audience hall in the palace.[48] The almost identical suites each consisted of five large rooms. The walls of some of the women's rooms were painted with delicate flowers, birds, and red and white calves, and Tadu-Hepa's rooms would have been furnished with cushions and wall hangings of the finest fabrics, beds and chairs inlaid with gold and ivory, and many of the precious items from her dowry. The second high point of the day for the messengers was that each of them received a gift, over sixteen pounds of gold in the case of Keliya, the highest ranking of the Mittanian officials (this, it should be noted, was more than all the gold in Tushratta's gifts to the pharaoh).

Tadu-Hepa herself received a large amount of gold from the pharaoh, which she seems to have displayed for the messengers.[49] Her dowry probably was put on view for public admiration, too; gifts were usually displayed publicly, and the dowry was something that Amenhotep would have wanted his people to see. Tushratta probably imagined that their reaction would be to be amazed at the wealth of the Mittanian king, but Amenhotep might instead have suggested that this was tribute from Mittani that reflected the pharaoh's own greatness.

To Tushratta's mind, one of the best things of all, during this happy time, was that Amenhotep seems to have been delighted with the princess; when he saw her, according to Tushratta, "he rejoiced v[ery], very much!"[50] Presumably Amenhotep III sent a letter to Tushratta once Tadu-Hepa had settled in, and it was from this letter that Tushratta knew the details of his daughter's arrival. Amenhotep probably indeed found her to be "the image of his desire," just as Tushratta had prayed, to judge from his rejoicing. (The pharaoh wasn't always so complimentary in referring to his wives. He was reported to have said about a Babylonian princess, "The girl he (her father) gave me is not beautiful"—though when the words were quoted back to him, he denied having said them.[51])

So Amenhotep III began to plan the next part of his gift to his "brother"— the solid gold statues of Tadu-Hepa and Tushratta that he had promised. (Presumably these were idealized images, since Amenhotep's artists would never have seen Tushratta.) The pharaoh gathered together the whole team of Mittanian messengers who were in Egypt so that they could witness the process of making the statues. Tushratta later wrote that "every one of my messengers that were staying in Egypt saw the gold for the statues with their own eyes."[52] They also saw the casting take place, supposedly done by the pharaoh himself (one suspects that this was an embellishment on Tushratta's part, since metallurgy probably wasn't one of Amenhotep's areas of expertise). Tushratta wrote that Amenhotep III "himself recast the statues in the presence of my messengers, and he made them entirely of pure gold."

The statues were finished and ready to be sent to Mittani. The messengers seem to have written to Tushratta to let him know, and to tell him that the pharaoh, as he put it, "showed much additional gold, which he was sen[d]ing to me.... goods beyond measure.... And my messengers did see with their own eyes!" Tushratta must have looked forward to the arrival of his daughter's image in gold, along with the one of himself. He no doubt had already planned where he would display them once they arrived. They might have been planned for a temple in Washshukkanni; temples were the usual places for royal statues.[53] Or perhaps they were to be set up on a platform or in a niche in some part of the palace in Washshukkanni where any visiting vassals or ambassadors would be sure to see them and would comment appreciatively. Here would be concrete evidence of Tushratta's close relationship to the Egyptian king for all to admire. He probably also thought, perhaps a little greedily, of the wealth represented by the statues (and all that additional gold).

### Death of the Pharaoh

Just two years after the marriage, around 1353 BCE, tragedy struck. Amenhotep III died. He had been on the throne for thirty-eight years, but was probably only about fifty years old at the time of his death. He had only recently married Tadu-Hepa, and relations with Mittani were strong and affectionate. Tushratta was devastated, weeping and refusing to eat or drink. "On that day I took neither food nor water. I grieved, [saying, "Let ev]en me be dead, or let 10,000 be dead in my country, and in my [brother]'s [country] 10,000 as well, [but] let [my brother, whom I lov]e and who loves me, be alive as long as heaven and earth."[54] Tushratta must have wondered what would happen to his daughter and to his relationship with Egypt. He had another worry as well: the solid gold statues had not yet arrived.

If the mummy that bears Amenhotep III's name really was him, by the time he died he was almost bald, obese, and suffering from abscesses in his mouth.[55] His dental problems were so bad that he was completely missing his front teeth, and his back teeth were a mess; he must have had tremendous pain when eating.[56] Perhaps Tadu-Hepa wasn't terribly upset to find that she would now be joining the harem of a younger man (with better dentition), Amenhotep III's son Amenhotep IV.[57] But for Tushratta, the best days of his relationship with Egypt were over. Amenhotep IV proved to be very different from his father.

## A Network of Family Ties

Throughout the Amarna period, the Egyptian kings still refused to send daughters to their allies; they would only agree to receive them.[58] Tushratta doesn't seem to have questioned the arrangement—he never asked for an Egyptian princess in return when he sent Tadu-Hepa. The pharaoh must have bragged to his Egyptian officials that all the apparently lesser kings had sent their daughters to marry him as a sign of their submission to him, but Tushratta and the Babylonian kings (and others, no doubt) could brag, in turn, that they were the fathers-in-law of the pharaoh. Anthropologists have studied this phenomenon in many cultures, and it is generally more common, when women marry outside of their social group, for the group that provides the wives (the Mittanians and Babylonians, in this instance) to be considered superior to the group that receives wives.[59] But the pharaoh didn't view things this way; as far as he was concerned, the women were a form of tribute. Fortunately, all the kings could therefore see themselves as having "won," according to the values of their own societies, in the marriage negotiations with Egypt.

A Babylonian king did break with tradition at one point, though. He tried asking for an Egyptian princess to marry, but he was immediately rebuffed—such an idea was unthinkable to the pharaoh. The Babylonian king was astounded that the pharaoh had refused his request point-blank. After all, he was willing to send his own daughter to Egypt. Since he came from a part of the world where marrying off daughters to foreign kings was a sign of power, perhaps he had imagined that the pharaoh would welcome this opportunity.

The Babylonian king was then struck by an ingenious idea: if the pharaoh wouldn't budge, perhaps he'd be willing to lie a little. Who would be any the wiser if a woman showed up in the Babylonian court just claiming to be an Egyptian princess? He proposed this to the pharaoh: "grown daughters, beautiful women, must be available. Send me a beautiful woman as if she were [you]r daughter. Who is going to say, 'She is no daughter of the king!'?"[60] But once again the pharaoh chose to insult him, as he saw it, by not sending any Egyptian woman at all. For the pharaoh, the effect would be the same whether he sent a real daughter or a fake one; he would have looked weak.

Royal wives were sent not only to Egypt during this era, they were married off to kings all over the Near East. A Babylonian king wrote to Amenhotep III about "my daughters who are married to neigh[bor]ing kings."[61] Where did these daughters reside? Perhaps a Babylonian princess was already ensconced at the court of Tushratta in Mittani, or in Elam or in Hatti. Another Babylonian king, Kurigalzu I, had sent one of his daughters to marry an Elamite king, and his son, Burna-buriash II, later sent a daughter to marry a Hittite king, Suppi-luliuma.[62] Burna-buriash's own son then married an Assyrian princess.[63] That same Hittite king, Suppiluliuma, later had his daughter marry a son of Tush-ratta, who ruled Mittani (or what was left of it) after the death of his father.[64]

In later decades a Hittite king was married to two princesses, one from Babylonia and one from the Levantine kingdom of Amurru. Interestingly, these princesses were chosen not by the king himself but by his rather self-important mother, who wrote that "I took each daughter of a great king, though a foreigner, as daughter-in-law."[65] She said that she did this for a particular reason: not for the good of Hatti, nor in order to enhance the status of her son, nor to strengthen the alliances with the other countries, but "as a source of praise for me before the people of Hatti." She imagined the messengers, or even the royal "brothers or sisters," of the princess who would arrive "in splendor to the daughter-in-law," and reflected on the effect of these splendid visitors: "is this not also a source of praise for me?"

No matter what the motivation for such marriages, the result was a web of relationships among the great kings that spread widely throughout their capital cities. It seems that every great king was the father-in-law or son-in-law or brother-in-law of at least one or two others. Burna-buriash II of Babylon alone was, at various times in his life, the brother-in-law and father-in-law of the king of Egypt, the father-in-law of the king of Hatti, and the father-in-law of a princess of Assyria. Similar relationships must have tied the other allied courts together. The kings formed a real brotherhood.

## The Roles of the Foreign Princesses

What was life like for foreign princesses living in the courts of their fathers' allies? It's tempting to imagine that they had the same kinds of responsibilities that the princesses of Mari had taken on four hundred years earlier—writing to their fathers about affairs of state and helping their husbands in an administrative capacity—but the truth seems to have been somewhat different, at least in Egypt. Although life for the foreign wives of the pharaoh was no doubt luxurious, their position in the court was not as exalted as their fathers probably hoped. Tadu-Hepa must have had to find her way among all the wives and concubines and all their attendants at court, and it is possible that she rarely saw the king. Amenhotep III sometimes had been unable even to identify which of his wives was which.

On one occasion, the pharaoh couldn't confirm to the Babylonian king Kadashman-Enlil that the king's sister was still alive; the pharaoh seems to have forgotten which of his wives she might be. A letter from Amenhotep III to Kadashman-Enlil is full of justifications for this error, and the scene it describes is almost comical. The pharaoh had asked Kadashman-Enlil for one of his daughters as a new bride and the Babylonian king seems to have written back to say that he first wanted to hear how his sister, who was already married to the pharaoh, was doing. So he sent some messengers to Egypt, presumably to talk with the older Babylonian princess. Unfortunately, none of these messengers knew the princess personally. Kadashman-Enlil must have assumed that the pharaoh would remember which wife was his sister (or at least which was Babylonian) and would send her out to speak with the Babylonian messengers when they asked. Instead, Amenhotep seems to have brought all his wives into the hall and said to the messengers, "Here is your mistress who stands before you."[66] They were stumped; the women didn't speak, so they couldn't tell which one spoke Akkadian (or perhaps Kassite), and they had no idea what the princess looked like.

The messengers reported back to Kadashman-Enlil when they returned to Babylonia that they thought they had seen his sister, but he retorted that the woman they described could have been "the daughter of some poor man, or of some Kaskean, or the daughter of some Hanigalbatean (that is, Mittanian), or perhaps someone from Ugarit." The "daughter of some Hanigalbatean" could have been Tadu-Hepa's aunt, Kilu-Hepa, who was living at the Egyptian court by this time, and it's quite possible that Amenhotep did indeed also have wives from Ugarit, the rich port city in the Levant, and from Kaska, a land to the north of Hatti. They were all foreign women, in the pharaoh's eyes, and he didn't even claim to have known which was which. The messengers couldn't be completely sure whether the king's sister "is alive or she is dead."

Amenhotep III didn't seem to be embarrassed at not being sure of the health or even the identity of this princess. Instead, he blamed Kadashman-Enlil for not sending "a dignitary of yours who knows your sister, who could speak with her and identify her." He also wrote that he had no reason to cover up her death had she died. But he didn't affirm that she was alive either. Some scholars have suggested that he knew perfectly well which of his wives the messengers were looking for, but was keeping the Babylonian princess from talking with them because she would have told them the truth about her situation in the court, and her tale might have discouraged the Babylonian king from sending his daughter to marry the pharaoh.[67] But it's also possible that he honestly didn't know which wife was originally from Babylon.

The kings had clear expectations of how their daughters would be treated in their husbands' courts. A king regularly sent messengers to his daughter with gifts for her, and he could expect that the daughter would send gifts back, presumably from her husband's treasury. In this, too, Amenhotep III seems to have failed to hold up his end of the bargain. In one letter, Kadashman-Enlil described to the pharaoh how his other daughters were regarded in foreign courts where they lived: "if my messengers [go] there, they speak with th[em, and they bri]ng me a greeting gift." The princesses, he implied, were available to the messengers (not unidentifiable in a crowd of wives like his sister in Egypt), and they had access to wealth with which to give presents to their fathers. Amenhotep almost laughed at this, mocking Kadashman-Enlil for writing it and accusing him of greed: "Undoubtedly [your neigh]boring kings are [ri]ch (and) mighty. Your daughters can acquire something from them and send (it) to you. But what does she have, your sister who is with me? But should she make some acquisition, I will send (it) to you!"⁶⁸

The pharaoh might have touched on a sensitive topic there; how much of the kings' willingness to send their daughters to Egypt was based in materialism or greed? They knew they would receive a huge amount of bride-wealth when they did so. But to hear the pharaoh tell it, the gifts from the princesses living in Egypt dried up after the marriage; foreign royal wives in Egypt apparently weren't supplied with presents that could be sent to their fathers (though such presents were perhaps common in other lands).

The messengers from their fathers must have done more than bring gifts and formal letters to the princesses. They would also have brought news from home, which was no doubt very welcome. Perhaps they could even take letters back from the princesses themselves. There's no direct evidence of this from Amarna, but we know that Queen Tiy wrote to Tushratta's wife, so royal wives (or at least the chief wives) were allowed to have their own messengers.

On the whole, though, the power of a foreign princess seems to have been more symbolic than real in her husband's court. The princesses, like Tadu-Hepa, were married with much ceremony, then they moved into their husbands' palaces and disappeared from the limelight.

On the other hand, children born as a result of diplomatic marriages probably took the throne more often than one might expect. Kings almost always cited their fathers' names in their inscriptions, to show their legitimacy, but rarely did they name their mothers. A king whose parents were from two different royal families might have been ideally suited to rule and to continue the diplomatic contacts with the land of his mother. He might even have been bilingual, having learned his mother's language as a child. He might also have had a real sympathy, even affection, for the land of his maternal ancestors, even if he hadn't visited there.

But on one occasion a king went overboard in this feeling of connection. Long after the Amarna period, an Elamite king in the twelfth century BCE wrote a letter to a Kassite king in which he claimed the right to rule Babylonia because he counted several Kassite princesses among his maternal ancestors (he was even married to a Kassite princess himself).[69] Needless to say, he wasn't successful in his request.

In another case, a man who was the son of a local king and a foreign princess seems to have been rejected and overthrown, perhaps precisely because of his parentage. Burna-buriash II's grandson, Kara-hardash, became king of Babylon around 1333 BCE, at the end of the Amarna period; he was half Assyrian and half Babylonian, the child of the royal marriage between Burna-buriash's son and the daughter of the Assyrian leader Ashur-uballit. But his lineage didn't end up unifying the two lands; instead, he was deposed by Kassite soldiers and replaced with a man of no royal connection at all.[70] Many scholars assume that Kara-hardash must have been murdered (though the sources don't say so), because his now elderly Assyrian grandfather, Ashur-uballit, felt compelled to invade Babylonia in retribution.[71] The Assyrian king killed the usurper and replaced him with a prince of royal Babylonian blood. This was clearly not the outcome that Ashur-uballit had in mind when he first sent his daughter to Babylonia.[72]

Tushratta might have cherished a secret desire that Tadu-Hepa would give birth to a son who would become pharaoh someday, especially since the new king, Akhenaten, had only daughters with his chief wife when he took the throne. But if he did, Tushratta was too diplomatic to say so directly in his letters. He simply continued to hope for brotherhood and love.

### Akhenaten: "Is This Love?"

The many authors who have written about King Akhenaten have reached such radically different conclusions that it is impossible to sum him up neatly, other than to say that he was entirely unique among pharaohs. Did he rule for a while as coregent with his father, or did he not take the throne until after Amenhotep III's death? Was he a pacifist who ignored the empire because he didn't believe in war, or a military man who enlisted the army in suppressing revolts? Was he a theologically inspired monotheist or a pragmatic politician? Did he marry one or more of his daughters and have children with them?[73] Did he regard himself as a god equal to the god of the sun or was the sun god the only god, in his eyes? Did his wife, Nefertiti, rule as his coregent? Where is Akhenaten's mummy?

These and many other questions remain unresolved about Akhenaten, but, fortunately, on a number of facts historians are in agreement. One is that he wasn't initially chosen as Amenhotep III's successor. An older brother named Thutmose was the first crown prince; he died before his father. Another point of agreement is that Akhenaten started his reign under the name of Amenhotep (IV) and the earliest depictions of him were fairly conventional. Perhaps, to start with, his officials and his subjects thought that he would follow the (unwritten) rules and be a typical pharaoh. Gradually, though, through the first years of his reign, he grew more and more eccentric in his behavior, administration, and beliefs. Typical he was not.

The pharaoh's name, Amenhotep, wasn't just a legacy from his predecessors; it also honored the god Amen. The pharaoh seems to have become increasingly disenchanted with the cult of Amen and more and more devoted to the god that his father had venerated, the disc of the sun. He referred to this god by the baroque title of "The living one, Ra-Horus of the horizon who rejoices in the horizon in his identity of light which is in the sun-disc," or simply "the Aten," the abbreviated version of this god's name.[74] The pharaoh even changed his birth name from Amenhotep to Akhenaten, which meant "he who acts effectively on behalf of the Aten," thereby removing Amen's offensive name from his own.[75] (The name by which the king was regularly addressed remained Neferheprure-Wanre, which meant "Beautiful is the being of Ra; the unique one of Ra"; it was rendered as Naphurureya in the cuneiform version of the Amarna letters.[76]) His animosity toward Amen was such that he even stopped endowing Amen's huge temple at Karnak, refusing to make offerings to that venerable god and dedicating all the offerings to Aten instead.

Akhenaten held his first jubilee festival in just his second or third year on the throne, not waiting thirty years as had been traditional. He seems to have seen this as a festival for his dead father and for his new god Aten, rather than his own jubilee. Still, it was an odd thing to do.

Stranger still, he decided in around his fifth year that Thebes and Memphis just wouldn't do as capital cities; he needed a brand new one, one with no connection to Amen. Akhenaten chose the site now known as Tell El-Amarna and named it Akhetaten, meaning "horizon of the Aten." He set builders to work there as fast as they could, so that the large new city might have been inhabitable just two or three years after work started on it. When Akhetaten was founded, the king traveled there in a magnificent chariot made of electrum, a natural alloy of gold and silver, and, according to his own inscription, "he filled the Two Lands with his loveliness."[77] To mark the founding of the city, he made a huge offering to Aten "consisting of bread, beer, oxen, calves, cattle, fowl, wine, gold, incense, [and] all beautiful flowers."[78]

There were to be no temples to Amen here, just to the Aten. And these temples didn't have dark holy places that concealed divine statues; there were no statues of the Aten at all, just the presence of the glorious sun itself, worshiped outside in sunny courtyards. Aten wasn't even depicted as a human or animal, like most other Egyptian gods, but as a simple round sun disc with rays emanating from it. In relief sculptures of the king praising Aten, the rays of the sun often ended in hands holding symbols of life and power, which they placed before Akhenaten himself.

And those images of the king? They didn't follow the careful, mathematical conventions of Egyptian art that had been perfected over thousands of years. The king wasn't made to look heroic and perfect. Instead, many of the images look to modern eyes almost like caricatures, with wildly thin necks and long swooping foreheads and huge eyes. The king also often had himself portrayed with wide hips and female breasts. Some scholars believe that he was afflicted with a medical condition that gave him a very feminine figure and a long skull, others propose that he chose to have himself portrayed in a feminine way because he wanted to be seen as both father and mother of his country. Much of the art of the time seems to have been done quickly, almost impressionistically. It was like nothing produced in Egypt before. Indeed, the whole era of Akhenaten's reign was like nothing Egypt had ever seen before.

The Egyptians weren't particularly fond of innovation or change. If order and tradition were the ideal, then change was chaotic and unpredictable and scary. Some Egyptians must have been nervous about all these radical departures from tradition, but their voices were silenced during his reign. Akhenaten was, after all, the pharaoh, and his words and actions were, by definition, right and just. High officials and priests might have muttered their disapproval to one another privately while still following the king's program.

Many officials seem to have been loyal to him, though, perhaps in part because of the generous gifts he bestowed on them. A scene on the walls of the tomb of one official, Merire, shows the tomb owner receiving gold collars from the pharaoh's attendants, in the pharaoh's presence, and it records Akhenaten's speech: "Put gold at his throat and at his back, and gold on his legs, because of his hearing the teaching of Pharaoh."[79] Many of Akhenaten's other officials also included in their tombs scenes of themselves receiving gold treasures from the pharaoh; he seems to have won their allegiance in much the same way that pharaohs traditionally won the allegiance of their foreign allies—with gold. On the other hand, several of the tombs also included hymns of worship to Aten on those same walls. The men may have been convinced of the truth of Akhenaten's teachings.

The belief in Aten's supreme power seems to have been quite sincere on Akhenaten's part (while also having the added benefit of weakening the power of the formerly very influential priests of Amen) and perhaps was also held by his closest relatives and administrators. It seems, however, to have found few converts beyond this immediate inner circle. Quite possibly, almost none of Akhenaten's reforms reached down to the level of the peasants or perhaps even the craftsmen and merchants. They might well have gone on worshiping the gods that were most important to them, regardless of the king's idiosyncratic beliefs. The religion of the common people seems to have revolved around gods that had an impact on their daily life, such as fertility gods and the god of the Nile, rather than around the state gods like Amen. These people still worked the fields, spilled water into their irrigation canals, sailed the Nile, constructed buildings, made pots, wove linen, paid taxes, and did all the other things that kept the land running smoothly just as they had always done, regardless of who was king.

Akhenaten wasn't some sort of raving fanatic; he seems to have had a plan behind all his actions and was able to maintain a tight hold on the land. This suggests that he had the active support of the military, and he may well even have led a campaign or two during his reign.

He was also affectionate as father to his six daughters and as husband to his wife Nefertiti. Relief sculptures show him sitting opposite his wife and kissing their little girls; such domestic scenes were unprecedented in royal art before his time.

Nefertiti was a powerful queen; Akhenaten named her in his inscriptions as often as his father had named Queen Tiy. Ever since Pharaoh Hatshepsut, the Egyptian royal family had been full of powerful women. Nefertiti performed some of the rituals that had traditionally been the sole province of the king and seems to have been just as devoted to Aten as was her husband. But, no doubt to her dismay, she didn't give birth to any sons who could inherit the throne from their father.

Akhenaten had other wives, though. He maintained a harem that included not only Princess Tadu-Hepa from Mittani but also the daughter of a Babylonian king and a number of other princesses. These women might well have borne him sons, but they did not appear in domestic scenes and seem to have been unimportant to Akhenaten in comparison with Nefertiti. Whether this was distressing to Tadu-Hepa is impossible to know. But at least her father was still devoted to her. Tushratta always mentioned her in his letters to Akhenaten, addressing her in the opening section of each letter, right after he had addressed the king and the king's mother, Tiy. He wrote "for Tadu-Hepa...may all go well," and sometimes he sent her greeting gifts of jewelry, "sweet oil," or clothing from home.[80]

## The Gold Statues

When Akhenaten first came to the throne, Tushratta was optimistic that he would maintain all his father Amenhotep's alliances and mirror his father's generosity. On learning that Akhenaten was to become pharaoh, Tushratta claimed to have happily spoken the words "Nimmureya (Amenhotep III), [my brother], is not dead. [Naphure]ya (Akhenaten), his oldest son, [now exercises kingship] in his place. Not[hing whatso]ever is going to be cha[ng]ed from the way it was before."[81] In fact, things might be even better than before, he thought. He recalled that "Tiy, his mother…is alive, and she will expose before Naphureya…the fact that" he and Amenhotep III "always loved (each other) very, very much," and he believed that the love between the two kings was "going to become ten times gr[ea]ter [th]an what there was" with Amenhotep III.

Tushratta knew those gold statues that Amenhotep III had promised were ready to be sent. Akhenaten would surely fulfill his father's obligation and would send them; now Tushratta just had to wait for them to arrive. He had heard descriptions of these beautiful statues from his messengers. Since the Egyptians weighed every shekel of gold or silver or copper in any object, Tushratta probably had a good idea of their size and value.

Finally the day came when the Mittanian and Egyptian messengers arrived back from Egypt with the first letter from Akhenaten to Tushratta and, more importantly, with a gift for Tushratta. The statues were coming at last. Keliya's and Mane's caravan must have been visible from the tallest point in Washshukkanni long before the men got there, giving plenty of time for the preparation of an appropriate welcome.

The palace officials gathered to meet the messengers. But when the statues were unloaded and unwrapped, Tushratta had a horrible shock: "my brother sent me statues (made) of wood." The gold plate that covered them didn't fool Tushratta for a moment. He had—to his mind—been robbed. "So I became angry…I became extremely hostile," he wrote to Akhenaten. Tushratta turned and addressed the assembled magnates, reminding them that "My ancestors…[always showed great love] to his (Akhenaten's) ancestors," and he presumably tried to impress on them how cruelly he had been treated by this new king. Worse yet, Akhenaten didn't send all the other goods that his father had promised; Tushratta wrote to Akhenaten that "you have reduced (them) greatly."[82]

And from then on, Tushratta could barely finish a thought in any letter to Akhenaten without demanding, once again, that the real statues be sent. The hated "plated [statues] of wood" came up over and over, in three letters, always to be compared with the longed-for "statues of solid chased gold" that were still in Egypt.[83]

Even the pharaoh's mother, Tiy, became involved in this controversy. She seems to have sent the ambassador, Keliya, back to Mittani, early in Akhenaten's reign, with a message for Tushratta, asking him to support her son as he had previously supported Amenhotep III. She wrote: "And now you are the one that must not forget your [l]ove for Mimmu[reya], your brother. Increase (it) f[or] Naphurre[y]a and maintain (it) for hi[m]."[84] After the ignominious arrival of the plated gold statues, Tushratta wrote back to her. He said he had, indeed, loved Akhenaten (Naphurreya), showing "ten times—much, much—more love to Naphurreya," but then, of course, her son had failed to send the solid gold statues. "Is this love?" Tushratta asked. So he begged Tiy to help him: "Let [Nap]hurreya give me statues of sol[id] gold!"

Tushratta's obsession with the statues might have reflected a deeper worry. Perhaps Akhenaten didn't regard Mittani as important anymore. Perhaps Tushratta's status as a "great king" was in jeopardy. The statues certainly were somewhere in Egypt; enough witnesses had seen them that this couldn't have been denied. But lacking the prior relationship with Tushratta that his father had enjoyed, Akhenaten seems to have thought the statues too valuable to send, or Tushratta too unimportant to receive them.

When the Amarna letters from Mittani ceased around 1350 BCE (long before the last letters from the other kingdoms), Tushratta was still alive, still protesting his love for Akhenaten, and still waiting, perhaps in vain, for the arrival of the solid gold statues. If the statues ever did arrive, it is highly unlikely that they are lying in the ground somewhere awaiting the future archaeologists who will eventually locate the Mittanian capital city. Unless Tushratta took the statues to his grave with him, and unless that tomb somehow escaped being robbed, the gold of the statues was certainly melted down and reused. It may well still be in circulation today—most ancient gold is, since it never tarnishes or decomposes.

What happened to Tadu-Hepa during her years in the Egyptian court after the letters from Mittani came to an end? She probably adopted an Egyptian name after her marriage, under which she would be unrecognizable to us. She may well have been the mother of princes and princesses with Akhenaten, and she almost certainly was buried in Egypt after she died. There is one intriguing theory about her fate, though it can't be proven: namely, that Tadu-Hepa might have been the same woman as Kiya, a wife of Akhenaten who had a brief happy moment as "greatly beloved wife of the king."[85] She gave birth to at least one daughter, and perhaps other children as well. If one of these had been a son, Akhenaten would presumably have been overjoyed. At last he had an heir. This might account for Kiya's moment of glory, when she enjoyed a high status in the court. Not only did she warrant the special title of "greatly beloved wife," she was also the recipient of a fabulous coffin and other funerary equipment.[86] Kiya's luck didn't last, however. Her coffin was defaced (literally—the face was torn off) and her name was scratched off it. It was altered and eventually used by someone else. She disappeared from the records, and her fate is unknown.

As Akhenaten gradually distanced himself from Tushratta, perhaps Tadu-Hepa (whether or not she was the same person as Kiya) suffered as well, losing her status at the court. The king who eventually inherited the throne from Akhenaten was a boy referred to as "the King's bodily son, his beloved Tutankhaten."[87] This boy (known to us under his later name of Tutankhamen) was not Kiya's son, however, nor was he the son of Nefertiti. His mother, according to recent DNA studies, was a previously unknown wife of Akhenaten: the king's own sister. And Tutankhamen, in turn, married his half-sister. After Tadu-Hepa, the royal marriages between Mittani and Egypt came to an end.

CHAPTER TEN

# Luxury Goods from Everywhere

*"The gold is much. Among the kings there*
*are brotherhood, amity, peace, and good relations"*

*Gift-Giving between the Great Kings*

King Burna-buriash II of Babylonia thought he knew well the benefits of membership in the great king brotherhood. He put it succinctly in a letter to the pharaoh: "From the time my ancestors and your ancestors made a mutual declaration of friendship, they sen[t] beautiful greeting-gifts to each other, and refused no request for anything beautiful."[1] Ideally, a great king could ask another great king to send him luxury objects and he would kindly give them; then the first king would reciprocate. This was what had frustrated Tushratta so much about those gold statues; Akhenaten had acted as though he simply didn't understand the rules.[2]

Luxury goods were often referred to in the same breath (or at least within a line or two) as friendship and brotherhood in the letters. In the eyes of the kings in Syria and Mesopotamia, their alliances and their intermarriages had united their countries, and therefore the resources of one king belonged, in a way, to his allies as well. Four hundred years before the Amarna kings, in the Old Babylonian period, King Ishhi-Addu of Qatna had emphasized this when he was appalled about the paltry gift of tin he had received from his ally in exchange for much more valuable horses. He had written, "This house is your house. What is missing in your house (that) a brother does not grant a request to a brother?"[3] In an ideal family relationship, brothers shared a "house" and gave freely to one another, so the great kings, as brothers, should do the same.[4]

Tushratta of Mittani had this in mind when he wrote, generously, to the pharaoh, "I will give ten times more than what my brother asks for. This country is my brother's country, and this house is my brother's house."[5] Perhaps the pharaoh didn't quite understand the implications of this when he withheld the statues; it was, after all, a Syrian and Mesopotamian convention.

Gifts had always been important in diplomatic correspondence, but by the time of the Amarna letters it almost seemed as though the alliances existed solely so that the kings could acquire luxury goods. This wasn't the case— there were many other reasons for alliances to flourish—but the allure of exotic wares that were unavailable at home was powerful. Just about every letter was accompanied by valuable presents.[6]

Many goods that had previously reached the Near Eastern kings as a result of trade with distant lands—places outside the diplomatic circle of Mesopotamia and Syria—now arrived as luxury gifts from brother kings. As the diplomatic circle had grown to include Egypt, Hatti, and other eastern Mediterranean lands, it seems that the center of the gift exchange had shifted westward as well. Perhaps, though, this phenomenon is an illusion, just a reflection of the fact that the written evidence is largely from Egypt. The prospect of presents of Egyptian gold certainly appears to have tantalized the other kings. It doesn't seem that the pharaohs had any equivalent obsession with gifts from any of the other lands.

On the other hand, the idea that the goods sent from one king to another were unconditional "gifts" is a little laughable. No king sent valuable objects to another without the expectation of receiving something in return—often something, in fact, that he had specifically asked for; Burna-buriash's statement makes that clear. The value of the gifts would have been hard to determine, though; was a finely worked and inlaid ebony chair worth more or less than a lump of lapis lazuli? These objects had no prices attached to them, so there was plenty of room for argument and hurt feelings.

Some gifts were sent in response to specific requests; others seem to have been selected spontaneously. The term for greeting gifts in Akkadian was *shulmanu*, a word related to the term for "peace" or "well-being."[7] This was what they were supposed to inspire; they smoothed relations between the courts and demonstrated the value of the alliances and the strength of the brotherhood between the kings.

But there was another kind of gift as well, one that caused much more anxiety. Such gifts involved significant quantities of raw materials that had, for all practical purposes, been ordered by a king from his ally with the promise that a shipment of a local product on a similar scale would be sent in return. Most of the Amarna letters that mention such large shipments pertained to unworked gold from Egypt, but it's likely that other goods, such as silver, copper, and horses, might have been viewed in a similar way and requested from other kings.[8]

## Greeting Gifts

The great kings usually saved the ends of their letters for a listing of the greeting gifts that they were sending.[9] Each of the great kings had his own specialties in the greeting gifts he offered. The king of Hatti probably had control of the only source of silver in the region, lapis lazuli mostly came from Babylonia and Assyria (having arrived there from Afghanistan), while Mittani specialized in fine jewelry.[10] The rings, earrings, and toggle pins were usually of gold; the necklaces were often made of gold, lapis lazuli, and semiprecious stones known as *hulalu*. Chariots and horses came to Egypt from all across the Near East; the kings of Assyria, Babylonia, and Mittani all provided them.[11] Other gifts were mentioned as well, such as objects made of wood from Babylonia; sweet oil and scent, along with bows and arrows, from Mittani; and textiles from Babylonia and Mittani.[12] Male and female servants were also sometimes sent as gifts.[13]

Although the Amarna letters between the great kings don't mention that they sent any specialists to one another, letters found at Hatti discuss several physicians and conjurers who were sent to Hatti from Egypt and from Babylonia, along with two sculptors who traveled from Babylonia to Hatti.[14] The king of Ugarit asked the pharaoh to give him a physician because there weren't any in Ugarit.[15] Likewise, the Minoan fresco painters who had decorated the palace at Avaris during the time of Thutmose III were certainly not the only craftsmen who set up shop outside their own lands. Other artisans traveled to foreign courts and learned new techniques and styles, or copied objects and motifs from the beautiful gifts that were sent between the kings. After their time of service in the foreign court, where they were treated well, provided with gifts and houses, and regarded as celebrities of a kind, the craftsmen and other specialists were supposed to be sent right back home; they were not permanent "gifts" to the other king.[16] In reality, though, they were often detained, and could run into difficulties when they wanted to go home. One Babylonian physician even died in Hatti.[17] Probably it was something of a mixed blessing for a man like this to be asked to travel to the court of another great king. No doubt it was a prestigious assignment, but the men must have worried about ever seeing their families again.

Curiously enough, the gifts from the great kings to Egypt didn't include glass. It may be that it was seen as a cheaper substitute for lapis lazuli and therefore inappropriate as a greeting gift for a great king. Glass was, instead, available within the Egyptian empire, in Canaan. Several letters from Egyptian vassals refer to the pharaoh ordering shipments of glass from Canaanite cities, including places that are familiar from the Bible, such as Acco, Ashkelon, and Lachish (though this was before the arrival of the Israelites in those cities).[18]

Tin is missing from the international letters too, though it was needed in order to make bronze and had been a principal commodity traded by the Assyrians in the Old Babylonian period. Perhaps it too wasn't considered enough of a luxury to serve as a gift. (After all, in the Old Babylonian period, the king of Qatna had been very put out at receiving tin from the king of Ekallatum.) Unworked stone for statues, jars, or mace heads is also missing among the gifts, perhaps because it was heavy and difficult to transport overland; besides, most of the preserved letters were written to the pharaoh, and he had abundant sources of good stone in his own land. Pots were only mentioned if they contained something valuable, such as sweet oil or scent; pottery apparently wasn't valuable enough to serve as a gift by itself.

Carnelian isn't listed, either, among the greeting gifts. The Indus Valley civilization of Meluhha had been the main source of carnelian for Mesopotamia and Syria in the past, and it had long since collapsed. Finds of carnelian are rare throughout the Near East in this era, though it showed up among the goods that the pharaoh put together to pay for forty female cupbearers from one of his vassals in the Levant.[19]

For his part, the Egyptian king sometimes sent unworked gold to his allies as a "greeting gift," though it was not always as warmly appreciated as he might have hoped. The rather morose king of Babylon, Kadashman-Enlil I, at one point received thirty minas (pounds) of gold from Amenhotep III—an impressive amount for a greeting gift—but he complained that it was the only greeting gift he had received from Egypt in six years and that the gold "looked like silver."[20] The pharaoh made up for it later. He cheerily wrote to Kadashman-Enlil that "I have [just] heard that you have built some n[ew] quarters" and that he was sending along "some furnishings for your house" as a greeting gift.[21] These included four beds, ten chairs, and ten footrests, all made of ebony and inlaid with over ten minas of gold.

The biggest greeting gift of all from the pharaoh (at least among those recorded in the surviving letters) didn't go to one of the other great kings. At a time when Hatti was weak, Amenhotep III entered into negotiations with the leader of another Anatolian power, King Tarhundaradu of Arzawa. Perhaps the pharaoh thought that Arzawa might take Hatti's place in the brotherhood of great kings. He wanted to marry one of Tarhundaradu's daughters and had sent a messenger to see the princess who had been chosen and to anoint her

with oil. This messenger brought along an immense greeting gift from Amenhotep III: twenty minas of gold in a sack, 317 linen textiles, ten containers of
sweet oil, thirteen inlaid ebony chairs, and 100 beams of ebony.[22] Given that
the princess was being anointed and that therefore the marriage was almost
certainly going ahead, this "greeting gift" was also probably a down payment
on the bride-wealth that would be coming later.

The other kings could occasionally be almost this generous in their greeting gifts. Tushratta of Mittani once sent, with a single letter to Amenhotep
III, an inlaid gold goblet; two gold and lapis lazuli necklaces; ten chariots, each
with a team of horses; and thirty men and women.[23] Most of the time, though,
the great kings' greeting gifts were more modest.

The great kings anticipated that their *shulmanu* greeting gifts would warm
the heart of the pharaoh and encourage him to send more extravagant shipments with lots of unworked gold. They also anticipated that he would ask
for other luxury goods in exchange. In one letter the Babylonian king complained to the pharaoh that "you have not sent me a single beautiful greeting-
gift," but just a few lines later discussed the "twenty minas of gold that were
brought here" by the Egyptian messenger.[24] Apparently this large amount of
gold didn't count as a greeting gift this time.

### Large Shipments of Gold

In eleven of the Amarna letters, the leaders of the great powers wrote to the
pharaoh to request "much gold." They almost all did it—Tushratta of Mittani,
Kadashman-Enlil I and then Burna-buriash II of Babylonia, Ashur-uballit of
Assyria, and even a Hittite prince.[25]

Why did they want all this gold? It was always for a good reason, they protested. Vital building projects were in the works, and gold was simply essential. In one letter, Burna-buriash II of Babylonia virtually demanded gold for
a temple that he was building: "At the moment my work on a temple is extensive, and I am quite busy with carrying it out. Send me much gold."[26]

His predecessor, Kadashman-Enlil I, had been in even more of a hurry to
receive as much gold as possible in order to "finish the work I am engaged on."[27]
He needed it right away, specifying that it should be sent "in all haste, either
in the month of Tammuz (June-July) or in the month of Ab (July-August)."[28]
He even went so far as to state that he had no other use for gold: "Once I have
finished the work I am engaged on, what need will I have of gold?"[29] The
pharaoh probably had trouble believing the Babylonian king's next sentence,
though: "Then you could send me 3,000 talents (180,000 pounds) of gold,

and I would not accept it." Perhaps what Kadashman-Enlil was implying here was that it would be unthinkable for him to accept gold from Egypt unless it was destined for a specific project. It wasn't that he was poor, or in any other way inferior to the Egyptian king, he just had this particular need at this particular time.[30] He also knew Amenhotep III well. What the Egyptian king really wanted was a Babylonian princess, so Kadashman-Enlil threatened not to send his daughter to Egypt if the gold didn't arrive in time.

Tushratta of Mittani wanted his gold statues from Akhenaten because Amenhotep III had promised them as a greeting gift. But the unworked gold that he pestered Akhenaten about was for a construction project of his own: "may my brother give me much gold that has not been worked for the mausoleum."[31] He too associated this larger request with a dynastic marriage, as he explained in another letter: "the gold that I ask for from my brother is meant for a double purpose: one, for the mausoleum, and the other, for the bride-price."[32] Tushratta recognized that a transaction on this scale could cause problems between the countries, but he earnestly hoped that things would go well: "May the gold that I ask for not become a source of distress to my brother, and may my brother not cause me distress." He, as usual, was happy to send anything at all in return: "Whatever my brother needs for his house, let him write and take (it). I will give ten times more than what my brother asks for."

Strikingly, though, the exact amount of gold needed for these building projects was never specified. Perhaps it would have been in poor taste to name an exact quantity; it might have seemed too much like an invoice.

Whatever gold the pharaoh sent would be melted down and transformed into the ornamentation for the relevant building that was under construction. The pharaoh sometimes seems not to have understood this, sending instead beautiful gold objects crafted by Egyptian artists. Tushratta had once asked Amenhotep III for "very great quantities [of] gold that has not been worked" but had been disappointed: "My brother has sent the gold.... Still, it has been worked."[33]

When King Ashur-uballit of Assyria later joined the brotherhood of great kings, he learned the diplomatic rules from his neighbors and approached the pharaoh with an appropriate greeting gift (two chariots, two white horses, and a lapis lazuli seal) before asking for a large quantity of gold. In his case it was a palace that was in need of beautification: "I am engaged in building a new palace. Send me as much gold as is needed for its adornment."[34] The Assyrian king might have revealed his naiveté in these matters when he went on to hint at a possible amount that the pharaoh might send. He noted that "when Ashur-nadin-ahhe, my ancestor, wrote to Egypt, twenty talents of gold were sent to him."[35] He claimed that the king of Mittani had received the same amount. If this was even close to the truth, one can see why the kings were so keen to maintain their relationships with Egypt; twenty talents was equivalent to around 1,200 pounds.

### Problems with the Gold Shipments

The Egyptian kings seem rarely if ever to have satisfied their allies' desire for gold for their building projects. Burna-buriash II of Babylonia was repeatedly frustrated in this regard. At one point he was in the middle of construction on his temple and was anticipating a sizeable quantity of gold from Egypt. But only a greeting gift of gold arrived, and a small one at that. "My brother has now sent me 2 minas of gold as my greeting gift." You can hear his dismay as he continued: "Now, if gold is plentiful, send me as much as your ancestors (sent), but if it is scarce, send me half of what your ancestors (sent). Why have you sent me 2 minas of gold? At the moment my work on a temple is extensive, and I am quite busy with carrying it out."[36] What could he do with just two minas?

In the face of such a disappointing gift, a king had a challenge—how could he let the pharaoh know that he was upset without alienating him? In spite of his oversized ego and tendency to take offense, Burna-buriash II was a skillful diplomat when it came to such situations. On another occasion Akhenaten had sent him considerably more unworked gold, forty minas this time, and Burna-buriash had sent it to be melted down for use on his current building project. In the kiln, the truth was revealed: it wasn't pure gold. Burna-buriash wrote that "when I pu[t] the 40 minas of gold that were brought to me into a kiln, not (even) [10, I sw]ear, appear[ed]."[37] The Babylonian king might well have suspected Akhenaten of trying to cheat him, but he wisely didn't come out and say so. Instead, he created an excuse for Akhenaten: "Certainly my brother did not check the earlier (shipment of) gold that my brother sent to me. It was only a deputy of my brother who sealed and sent it to me."[38] The pharaoh himself would never have knowingly sent an alloy instead of pure gold, he asserted; it must have been the work of a corrupt official.

But then, some time later, the same thing happened again. The gold sent by the pharaoh once more wasn't pure: "the 20 minas of gold that were brought here were not all there. When they put it into the kiln, not 5 minas of gold appeared."[39]

Perhaps, like Ashur-uballit of Assyria, Burna-buriash had in mind that the pharaoh would eventually send him as much as 1,200 minas of gold. Each time he sent a mission to Egypt with the same request for "much gold," it would take months before the messenger came back bearing the gold that the king needed, if any of it came at all. And Burna-buriash wasn't asking for a handout—like Tushratta and the other kings, he was quite willing to provide compensation: "Send me much gold," he wrote. "And you for your part, whatever you want from my country, write me so that it may be taken to you."[40]

This was the best way, of course. Burna-buriash didn't know what the pharaoh needed right now, and without guidance he might send something that was either less valuable than the "much gold" that he wanted or of no interest to the pharaoh. He hoped that the Egyptian king would send a wish list—maybe a number of chariots and teams of horses and a large quantity of lapis. In his very first letter to Akhenaten, Burna-buriash had impressed upon him that he needed to know what Akhenaten wanted: "Wri[te me] for what you want from my country so that it may be taken to you, and I will write you for what I want from your country so that it may be taken [to me]."[41] He wrote this several times, but as far as we know, Akhenaten never replied with a clear request.[42]

Burna-buriash, on the other hand, became more and more specific in his own demands. He always wanted "much gold," of course, but he also started listing other objects; he wanted a sculpture of a "wild animal, land or aquatic, lifelike, so that the hide is exactly like that of a live animal."[43] It sounds like a classified ad; he knew exactly what he wanted. He would even have been willing to take a secondhand sculpture: "if there are some old ones already on hand, then as soon as … my messenger reaches you, let him immediately, posthaste, borrow chariot[s] and get here."[44] In another letter he asked for "trees … to be carved from ivory and colored," along with "matching plants of the countryside" that would be "carved, colored, and taken to me."[45] He must have wanted these sculptures for particular rooms in his palace or temple, and presumably he had already seen some Egyptian workmanship like them or had been told that they existed in Egypt by his messengers. The very foreignness of the art would have made it all the more valuable and desirable.

In his quest for Egyptian gold, Burna-buriash II even sent presents to "the mistress of the house" in the pharaoh's court.[46] Perhaps he hoped that she would put in a good word for him and would convince her husband to do his part in the larger gift exchange and send "much gold" for the Babylonian building project.

But he didn't have much luck, no matter whom he tried to influence. In one letter he targeted a daughter of Akhenaten, named Mayatu: "having heard (about her), I send to her as her greeting gift a necklace of cricket-(shaped) gems, of lapis lazuli, 1,048 their number."[47] This was an extravagant present.

Each of those beads had been meticulously crafted by palace artisans, drilled, shaped and polished, and carefully strung; there were probably many strands of the fine blue beads. This surely would turn Mayatu's head and she would feel obliged to lobby her father to send Burna-buriash the goods he wanted, right? Apparently not. In a later letter Burna-buriash lamented "[I know] that Mayatu alone did nothing for me...and showed no concern for me," and as far as we know she didn't get another present from him.[48] Whether or not Burna-buriash ever received the amount of gold he wanted for his building project is unknown. It doesn't seem likely.

Tushratta had similar problems. Once, during the reign of Amenhotep III, Tushratta gathered together all his foreign guests, apparently to show off the gold he had just received from Egypt. This was presumably at a banquet after the arrival of the messengers. The reaction of the foreign guests was far from what he had hoped for, however, as they surveyed the gold bars or ingots. They said "Are all of these gold? They do not lo[ok (like gold)]."[49] These guests kept twisting the knife; they said "In Egypt, gold is more plent[iful] than dirt. Besides, my brother loves you very much. (But) if there be someone whom he loves, then he would not giv[e] such things to him." Tushratta took the hint and replied to his guests (or at least claimed that he did), "I cannot say [be]fore you, as I am used to sa[ying], 'My [brother], the king of Egypt, loves me very, very much.'" The implication was clear: if the pharaoh had loved him he would have sent him enough gold to have impressed his foreign guests. Tushratta said so even more bluntly later in the letter; he asked the gods to "grant that my brother show his love for me, that my brother glorify me before my country and before my foreign guests" by sending gold.

Several of the kings seem to have believed that there had been a glorious time in the past when gold had flowed to their lands from Egypt. Tushratta hounded Akhenaten for his failure to live up to his father's example in the matter of the gold statues, but even before Akhenaten came to the throne, Tushratta seems to have had a childhood memory of his father receiving much more gold from Amenhotep III than had come his way. He wistfully wrote to Amenhotep that "You sent him (Tushratta's father) large gold jars and gold jugs. You se[nt him] gold bricks as if they were (just) the equivalent of copper."[50] But later, when Akhenaten had taken the throne and was holding back the gold statues that Tushratta so dearly wanted, suddenly Amenhotep III had become the model of generosity: "[Your father] sent me [much gold]; there were four sacks [full of gold that he sent me]." And he wasn't making this up. He encouraged the pharaoh to check with his own envoy: "May my brother ask [Haa]mashshi, his messenger."[51] Perhaps it's true that gold flowed more readily from Egypt early in the reign of Amenhotep III, or perhaps the earlier amounts had become inflated in the wistful memories of the great kings.

Visitors to the monumental buildings in Babylonia, Mittani, and Assyria—to the temples, palaces, and mausoleums—must have been impressed by the gold that glinted on the walls and doors, and by the Egyptian-style statues of animals and plants and the finely carved ebony furniture inlaid with gold, silver, and ivory. All of it announced each king's power and wealth. It's significant, though, that the kings seem to have been unable simply to purchase the gold that they needed. They had to wheedle it out of the often uncooperative king of Egypt.

### Copper from Alashiya

Amenhotep III had only one real request when writing to most of the great kings: he wanted to marry their daughters. The greeting gifts that they sent were nice, of course, and Mittanian or Babylonian horses and chariots certainly could come in useful, but it was princesses that he was collecting.

The same does not seem to have been true of his relationship with Alashiya, the island of Cyprus. Nowhere in the eight letters from the king of Alashiya to Egypt was there any mention of marriage or princesses. The letters were all business, because the Egyptian king wanted something very specific from Alashiya: copper. Egypt needed a lot of copper to make bronze tools, utensils, armor, weapons, and vessels—more copper, apparently, than could be mined within Egypt or the Sinai.

The copper mentioned in the Alashiyan king's letters was usually weighed in talents (one talent equaling sixty pounds). At ancient sites, copper is, in fact, found in talent-sized ingots. Each was shaped, for easy carrying, into a rectangle with extensions at each corner (known to excavators as an "oxhide ingot" because of its coincidental resemblance to a stretched-out oxhide).[52] These have been found as far west as Sardinia and as far east as Babylonia. Like today's oil-rich states, Alashiya was lucky in its natural resources. The kingdom of Alashiya didn't need to be large to be wealthy.

This gave the king of Alashiya a certain amount of bargaining power that the great kings lacked. Once a great king had sent a daughter to marry the pharaoh, he had played his hand and had to just hope (and plead) that the Egyptian king would continue to send gold for his various projects and that the pharaoh might want something else (besides a princess) in return. Egypt always needed more copper, so the king of Alashiya could hold out for more goods, and he was certainly demanding.

Alashiya had been a trading partner with other kingdoms in the Near East ever since the era of Hammurabi and Zimri-Lim. Over time, Alashiyan copper had become more popular than copper from Magan. With the wealth that came from the copper trade, the villages of Alashiya had grown into towns with elaborate public buildings. These towns were fortified with thick masonry walls, perhaps because of internal battles among different regions of the island.[53] To judge from analysis of the clay used to write the Alashiya letters, the capital city was probably near the Troodos Mountains, which was also the region where copper was mined.[54] With wealth also came administration; the Alashiyans used a writing system known to us as Cypro-Minoan, which is still undeciphered. Some of their scribes even learned the cuneiform script that they needed for writing letters from the king of Alashiya to the pharaoh. If any other documents were written in cuneiform, they haven't yet been found.

Who lived on the island? The Alashiyans weren't Greeks—Greek invaders didn't arrive there until a few hundred years later, around the eleventh century BCE.[55] To judge from the names of the Alashiyan people that show up in texts from other places, the towns were cosmopolitan, with residents from all over the Near East, speaking Hittite, Hurrian, Egyptian, and Canaanite.[56]

Alashiya had escaped being drawn into one of the larger empires that surrounded it, but it was, geographically, right in the heart of the Near East, closer to Hatti and Mittani than Egypt. Sailors on a boat traveling north from Egypt to the wealthy port cities of Syria might have seen the hills of Alashiya off to the west, just fifty-seven miles from the coast. Part of the Alashiyan king's cockiness might have come from his conviction that the king of Egypt wouldn't stand a chance of adding Alashiya to his empire. The pharaoh had no navy, and his fighters were accustomed to battles in chariots, not boats.

By the reign of Amenhotep III, Alashiya was a significant place, more than just a source of copper for the other lands. The Alashiyan king was an active participant in diplomacy as well as trade.

Alashiya's king was an interesting character, and quite unlike the pharaoh's other correspondents. For one thing, he seemed averse to mentioning anyone's name in his letters. He never addressed the Egyptian king by name (so we don't know which, if any, of the letters were to Amenhotep III and which were to Akhenaten or even to later kings), he didn't give his own name, and he didn't name his messengers. He didn't even identify a man whose possessions he wanted the pharaoh to return from Egypt. He wrote that "a man from [Alashiya] has died in Egypt, and [his] thing[s] are in your country, though his son and wife are with me. So, my brother, loo[k to] the things of the Alashiya people and hand them over, my brother, to the charge of my messenger."[57] (Let the pharaoh figure out for himself which man from

Alashiya had died in Egypt.) The only exception to this strange omission is a list of names on one letter.[58] The king of Alashiya asked the king of Egypt to expel three men and let two others go. Presumably, in such a specific situation names were unavoidable.

He also never used the term "great king" in referring to himself, presumably because he wasn't one. All the other major kings who wrote to Egypt—the kings of Hatti, Mittani, Babylonia, and later Assyria—reminded pharaoh that they too were great kings, but not so the king of Alashiya. And yet he wrote to the pharaoh as "my brother" as though they were equals, and he was certainly higher in rank than Egypt's vassals, who groveled constantly in their letters.[59] The king of Alashiya was sometimes quite high-handed with the pharaoh. At one point he asked forthrightly, "Moreover, why have you not sent me oil and linen?" and in another letter he demanded payment for timber that he had sent: "My brother, [give me] the payment due."[60] He could be just as demanding as the great kings.

Unlike Tushratta, the king of Alashiya seems to have been not the least bit fond of the king of Egypt. There were no assertions of love, or even of friendship. He was as surly as Kadashman-Enlil I of Babylon. The closest he got to a kind word (other than in the required and formulaic wishes for well-being at the beginning of each letter) was in his first letter to a king who had just taken the throne (this was probably Akhenaten): "[A]nd year by ye[ar] let my messenger go [into your presence], and, on you[r part], year by year, your messenger should come from [your] pre[sence] into my presence."[61] His relationship with the pharaoh was defined in terms of messengers going back and forth between the kings.

The king of Alashiya was also given to hyperbole. When a disease struck his country, he wrote that the god of pestilence "is now in my country; he has slain all the men of my country, and there is not a (single) copper-worker."[62] The fact that all the men in Alashiya had not in fact died was given away just a few lines later when he noted that "men of my country keep speaking with m[e] about my timber that the king of Egypt receives from me."[63]

In other ways, though, the king of Alashiya was familiar with the usual rules of royal correspondence. He had his scribes write in Akkadian; he addressed his letters in the traditional way; he sent messengers to the Egyptian court and expected them to be returned to him promptly (and complained when they were detained); he sent greeting gifts of a few talents of copper, along with ivory and boxwood, and, like all the kings, came up with convoluted excuses as to why he hadn't sent more.[64]

Also like the great kings, he wanted lots of precious metal from Egypt, but, surprisingly, it wasn't gold that he asked for. The Alashiyan king wrote that he hoped the pharaoh would send him "silver in very great quantities...and then I will send you, my brother, whatever you, my brother, request."[65] Why would he have asked the pharaoh for silver? It wasn't native to Egypt. The king of Alashiya could have turned to his northern neighbor in Hatti and found a much better source. And why didn't he ask the pharaoh for gold? He could hardly have been ignorant of Egypt's wealth in gold, since his messengers must have told him that gold was the main luxury good produced in Egypt. Perhaps silver was simply the term that he was using to mean "wealth."[66]

The Alashiyan king had other requests from Egypt, too: beds, linens, oil, horses, and "one of the experts in vulture augury."[67] This in spite of the fact that Egypt was usually a recipient, not a giver, of horses, and doesn't seem to have had a field of divination that pertained to vultures at all.[68] If he wasn't simply ignorant of Egypt's available resources, perhaps the Alashiyan king knew that a foreign specialist was residing at the pharaoh's court and wanted that man in particular (his aversion to using names has already been noted—he might well have had someone specific in mind even though he didn't name him). Or perhaps the king of Alashiya needed a number of luxury items and had only the king of Egypt to request them from; it could be that he wasn't in direct communication with the lands from which silver, horses, and vulture divination experts usually came. The pharaoh might have been willing to send the Alashiyan king just about anything he needed if he could provide a ready and extensive supply of copper. And that he usually could do; as many as 100 talents of copper (6,000 pounds) were mentioned in one letter.[69]

We're left with a bit of a mystery surrounding this unnamed king. Alashiya was just an island state, not an empire like Egypt, Mittani, or Hatti or a major kingdom like Babylonia. The pharaoh doesn't seem to have objected to being called "brother" by the king of Alashiya, but this man was not a member of the great king brotherhood. In some ways, he seems to have been a bit of a loose cannon: unfriendly, accusatory, but then promptly conciliatory as well, and surprisingly uninformed on the luxury goods available in the home of his ally.

## A Shipwrecked Load of Luxury Goods

Some time around 1300 BCE, a cargo ship left Alashiya for Greece. Its crew included three or four Canaanite merchants.[70] They had just stopped in Alashiya to pick up over 450 ingots of copper totaling about ten tons, perhaps part of a gift from the king of Alashiya to one or more of his allies.[71] The merchants would have been used to the rigors of life at sea. Their boat traveled on a regular circular route around the eastern Mediterranean, mostly hugging the seashore. They traveled from Canaan to Cyprus, westward along the southern Anatolian coast to Greece and Crete, then south across the open Mediterranean to Libya, east along the North African coast to Egypt, and north to Canaan again—about 1,500 miles in total.[72] With all the stops along the way, and allowing for bad weather from time to time, the whole voyage must have taken many months.[73]

Their ship was sturdily built out of fine cedar, with a wickerwork fence around the deck; it had sails and complicated rigging that the sailors must have been adept at climbing and controlling, even in rough seas. The ship was about forty-five feet long and could hold as much as twenty tons of cargo.[74] Its Canaanite crew had few luxuries on board—some oil lamps for light at night, plain bowls for their meals, and a set of knucklebones for entertainment. They ate bread, olives, almonds, pine nuts, and dried figs, along with fish, when they had a chance to catch some. When the sea was calm they cast nets out, or used harpoons and fishhooks to procure their dinner.

The chief merchant, a rich man who was probably in charge of the ship, carried an impressive-looking Canaanite sword with a fine ebony and ivory hilt. The other three merchants had daggers, and all of the merchants owned sets of balance weights. These came in various sizes so that the merchants could weigh out silver or other materials at the conclusion of a transaction. The chief merchant kept a collection of scrap gold and silver on board, probably for use in paying for goods for his crew. Included among the gold fragments were some precious objects, a scarab bearing the name of Queen Nefertiti among them.[75] It was all hoarded away together in a secure bag or a box.

The sailors and merchants weren't alone on this part of the journey, from Alashiya to the Aegean. The ship also had at least two passengers on board, Mycenaean ambassadors from Greece. They were traveling in style. They had their own fine Mycenaean jugs and cups to drink from, five sharp razors to shave with, and three short bronze knives. They wore strands of beads made of amber (from the Baltic region), quartz, and faience as jewelry, and each man had a stamp seal that he used to identify his goods. Unlike the merchants, the Mycenaeans didn't have a set of weights with them. They weren't traveling for commerce; these were diplomats.[76] Now they were heading home, perhaps from Alashiya. Some of the copper on board might have been a greeting gift for their own king from the king of Alashiya. They might even have had a letter from him for their king.

As the ship sailed out of the harbor in northern Alashiya, perhaps the sky was clear and a good wind was blowing. The cargo was safely stored below-decks. In addition to the copper ingots, which were lined up neatly in four rows and stacked as much as twelve deep in the center of the boat, there were many other valuable goods in the hold: tin ingots (one ton of those, from Afghanistan); over 700 pounds of glass ingots, mostly of a vivid deep blue, from Canaan; and innumerable Canaanite jars and pots, at least half of them containing terebinth resin, which was used in scented oils and incense. There were some special items as well, in smaller quantities, perhaps for use as luxury gifts: eighteen ebony logs from Africa; fourteen hippopotamus teeth; an ivory tusk; three ostrich eggshells; a yellow pigment called orpiment; murex shells; copper, tin, and wood containers; thousands of tiny faience beads in a jar; and some bolts of cloth. The boat also contained some spices—black cumin, coriander, safflower, and sumac—along with olives and pomegranates.[77]

The Mycenaean ambassadors probably looked forward to seeing their homeland again. They anticipated seeing the golden hills in the distance, the sun-parched grass looking like soft carpet between rocks. Patches of olive trees and vines surrounded small harbor towns of blocky houses painted white and blue.[78] The cargo ship would pull in at one of these towns, sailing between smaller boats that stayed close to shore. Oarsmen manned such boats, rowing belowdecks while travelers sat in comfort beneath striped canopies, talking and watching dolphins that swam alongside. The sailors on the cargo ship would set down one of their many stone anchors when they reached port, and the Mycenaean ambassadors would go ashore on the last leg of their journey home. Messengers might have been waiting to greet them and to help them transport the greeting gifts from Cyprus to their king.

But the ship never made it to Greece. A bad storm must have blown up as the men were sailing close to a rocky cliff in southern Anatolia; the wind and waves battered the ship. In what was no doubt a terrifying moment, the ship began to take on water, and it sank to the bottom, taking its valuable cargo with it. Some or even all of the crew might have been able to swim to shore, though—it was only sixty yards away.

As word got back to Alashiya that the ship was lost, the king probably cursed his luck. All that copper, ten tons of it, the work of hundreds of miners and smelters, worth a fortune.... gone. No king in Greece or Egypt would receive the copper now and feel obligated to reciprocate with an equivalent gift. Perhaps the Mycenaean ambassadors, if they survived, were able to eventually return home on another boat, but bereft of their possessions.

The cargo and all the personal effects of the crew and the passengers lay on the sea floor for over 3,000 years until, in 1982, their ship was rediscovered. From 1984 to 1994, teams of underwater archaeologists excavated the boat—called the Uluburun shipwreck after the cape where it was found—and recovered all the valuable objects from the cargo hold, as well as the cups, swords, and even food of the crew. No bodies were found in the wreckage,

A diver excavating a row of copper ingots from the
hull of the Uluburun shipwreck. (Institute of Nautical
Archaeology)

either because the men had made it to safety or because sharks and other
predators long ago removed their remains.

One crew member had left behind his folding wooden writing tablet—the
two pages would have had wax inserts on which to write, though they're lost
now. One wonders what words were written on it, and in what language. If
the Mycenaean ambassadors were carrying a letter written on wax or clay from
the king of Alashiya to their own king, it would long since have disintegrated
in the sea.

The cargo gives us just a glimpse into all that wealth that is mentioned
almost offhandedly in the letters to pharaoh. When the king of Alashiya in
one letter noted that he was sending 100 talents of copper, a donkey-hide, and
some *habannatu* jars full of "sweet oil" to the pharaoh, this is probably the type
of boat that would have carried those goods to Egypt.[79]

## The Puzzle of Mycenae

Mycenae, the apparent destination of the Alashiyan gift, was not as integrally tied into the network of diplomatic relationships as the other Amarna period powers. No letters from a Mycenaean king showed up among the Amarna correspondence. And yet it was not for lack of wealth—Mycenae was a very rich place—nor even for lack of contact.

The Minoan traders and artists of Crete from Thutmose III's time had by now largely been subsumed into the civilization of the Mycenaean Greeks. The Mycenaeans adopted some of the best ideas of the Minoans, such as their writing system (which they modified to write their own Greek language in a script known as Linear B), and some of the shapes and designs of their pottery and wall paintings. But where the Minoans had preferred images of dolphins and landscapes on their walls and vases, the Mycenaeans often painted shields and chariots. In death, the faces of the Mycenaean kings were adorned with lifelike gold masks that portrayed their full beards (very different from the clean-shaven Minoans), and they were armed with weapons to use in the afterlife.[80] By the fourteenth century BCE, fortification walls surrounded their cities.[81] The stone blocks of the walls were so huge and so exactly placed that later Greeks could scarcely believe they had been built by mere humans; they called the walls Cyclopean, imagining them to be the work of a race of superhuman Cyclopes. The Mycenaean people were not afraid of war; they seem to have welcomed it. In the *Iliad* and the *Odyssey,* Homer later remembered the Mycenaeans as the brave fighters of the Trojan War. The stories were mostly fiction, but some of the details have proved to be accurate. Even helmets made of boars' tusks, which Homer mentions, have been found on Mycenaean sites and in some of their images of warriors.

Greece was short on agricultural land and long on shoreline, so the Mycenaeans, like the Minoans before them, looked at the Mediterranean as a highway to other places where they might enrich themselves. They spread out around the Aegean, settling in Crete and other islands and establishing colonies on the Western Anatolian coast.[82]

But the Mycenaeans seem not to have taken to the sea with quite the enthusiasm of the Minoans.[83] Their images don't show up on Egyptian tombs. They seem to have depended on others, like the Canaanite merchants of the Uluburun ship, to transport their goods abroad and to bring foreign materials to Greece. Artisans in a glass workshop in the Greek city of Tiryns and others in an ivory workshop in Mycenae both used raw materials from Canaan.[84] Mycenaean artists also made use of imported stone, ivory, carnelian, and lapis lazuli in their artworks.

The Mycenaeans perhaps knew something of the lands of the great kings as well. In a Mycenaean palace in the Greek city of Thebes was found a hoard of beads and cylinder seals from foreign lands, including lapis lazuli seals of outstanding workmanship from Kassite Babylonia, Mittani, and Hatti.[85] Some of the seals had been reworked by Cypriot artists, so they probably had arrived in Greece from Cyprus rather than directly from the courts of the great kings themselves. They may well have been royal gifts.[86] An early royal tomb at Mycenae included a stag made from silver from the Taurus Mountains.[87] It too might have been a luxury gift, in this case from the king of Hatti or another Anatolian monarch.

By the mid-fourteenth century, Mycenaean wine and perfumed oil were being exported in striped stirrup jars to cities all over the Levant, Cyprus, and Egypt.[88] Mycenaean potters even made ceramics in distinctive shapes just for their trading partners. The Mycenaeans manufactured textiles in vast amounts, according to the Linear B tablets—600 women were employed as weavers by the palace at Pylos alone—and these fabrics might also have been exported abroad.[89]

The Egyptian kings knew a lot about Greece. Amenhotep III listed Aegean place names on a statue, almost as though they were subject to him, which they weren't.[90] It's possible that the list instead records the travels of Egyptian ambassadors who had been sent by the pharaoh perhaps to pursue trade relationships with the various Mycenaean cities.[91] Amenhotep III seems to have seen the Aegean as part of his world, right alongside his vassal states, the lands of the other great kings, and the African kingdoms with which he traded.

Few Mycenaean pots have been found in Hatti, but the Hittites had a powerful impact on Mycenaean defensive architecture. The similarities are so striking that it is almost as though Hittite advisors had shown up with plans and engineers to help the Greeks design their fortification walls and city gates.[92]

So why wasn't the king of Mycenaean Greece a participant in the diplomatic network of the Amarna letters? It's puzzling. Of course, there's only one letter from the king of the Hittites in the archive, and he was definitely a great king. There were certainly more, but they've been lost. Maybe Mycenaean letters existed too, but weren't brought to Amarna when Akhenaten moved the capital city; or maybe they weren't found by the peasants who uncovered most of the letters, and are still in the ground somewhere; or maybe they were among the group of cuneiform letters from Amarna that were broken and lost soon after their discovery. Back in the reign of Thutmose III, before the brotherhood of great kings had formed, a delegate from Tanaja had sent gifts to the pharaoh.[93] This was almost certainly in Greece. Perhaps they continued to do so.

One probable answer is that there simply wasn't a single "king of Greece," that the Mycenaeans had not one king but many, which would account for their absence from the great king brotherhood. After all, Greece wasn't unified in Classical times either; the city-states were independent of one another, often fiercely so. In the time of the Near Eastern great kings each Mycenaean city had its own palace. Those heavy fortification walls around the cities, and the chariots on their pots, might have been in defense against one another rather than against foreigners. The Greek cities of Mycenae and Tiryns are so close together that modern tourists can easily visit both in a single morning, and yet they might well not have been in the same Mycenaean kingdom. If this is true, then some of the Mycenaean kingdoms were no larger than the smallest Canaanite vassal states of Egypt, and the pharaoh wouldn't have given them a second thought, except to obtain whatever luxury goods their merchants might have had to offer.

It's also possible, as some scholars have suggested, that the Greeks thought of writing as just an organizational tool (all the documents found in Linear B are administrative), and that they relied on the talents of bards to recall their literature.[94] Perhaps it initially didn't occur to the kings to write letters.

We tend to think of Greece as always having been important because, in its later incarnation, it played such a starring role in the development of civilization in the west. It's surprising to realize that the great kings of Egypt, Mittani, Babylonia, and Hatti would never have guessed that their own languages would be lost for centuries while that of the Mycenaeans would never be forgotten, nor that the descendants of the warlike inhabitants of a land at the edge of their world would create such a brilliant civilization as that of Classical Greece.

But before we leave Mycenaean Greece, there is one other piece to its puzzle. The Hittite kings mentioned many minor kingdoms in their records; western Anatolia was littered with them. One of these kingdoms has intrigued scholars for decades: it was called Ahhiya or Ahhiyawa, and it showed up in a few Hittite records from the early fourteenth to the late thirteenth century.[95] It seems that it wasn't within Anatolia; one had to go by sea to get there. Sometimes the Ahhiyawan leaders were allied with the Hittites; at other times they were helping with rebellions against the Hittites. Their history is impossibly spotty; it has been pulled together from fragmentary references in just a couple of dozen texts. But that name—Ahhiyawa. To the people who first deciphered Hittite texts, it looked a little like Achaea, one of the ancient names for Greece, and it still does. In fact, most scholars now think that Ahhiyawa was Greek.

In some of the texts, leaders from Ahhiyawa seem to have been recruiting or kidnapping men and women in western Anatolia, perhaps to bring them back to Greece to work as forced laborers on the many Mycenaean construction projects and as textile workers in the palaces. The Linear B tablets from Mycenaean cities don't say anything about diplomacy, but they do list workers from Aegean islands and from western Anatolia.[96] Often, the kings of Ahhiyawa helped Anatolian kings rebel against Hatti, to the annoyance of the Hittite king. A letter found at Hattusa was written by a Hittite king to a king of Ahhiyawa to complain about just such a situation. It must have been a copy kept for the Hittite files, since presumably the original was sent to Greece.

If Ahhiyawa was a name for Greece, does this mean that Greece was unified under a single king? Or was Ahhiyawa the name of just one of the Mycenaean kingdoms, the most powerful one? The latter seems most likely, and the most powerful of the kingdoms was Mycenae itself.

Mycenae was small, but wealthy enough that its kings could afford to be buried in immense beehive-shaped "tholos" tombs built of massive blocks of stone. The tombs were robbed long before they were the subject of modern excavations, but they no doubt were packed with extravagant gifts for the kings, just as the shaft graves of earlier Mycenaean kings had been. Mycenae's city gate was surmounted by a striking triangular sculpture, over nine feet in height, of two lions, perhaps the heraldic symbol of the kingdom or of its dynasty.

In late texts, long after the time of the Amarna letters, the Hittite king Hattusili III called the king of Ahhiyawa "my brother," and there's a most intriguing Hittite document that listed the great kings. In it, the Hittite king wrote that "the kings who are my equals in rank are the King of Egypt, the King of Babylonia, the King of Assyria, and the King of Ahhiyawa."[97] But the scribe who wrote this text thought better of it before the clay was even dry, and he crossed out the king of Ahhiyawa.[98] It wasn't a great power, not on the scale of Hatti, Babylonia, Assyria, or Egypt, but it played an important role in the politics and economics of the eastern Mediterranean region. Ahhiyawa seems even to have participated in the usual gift exchanges. One letter to Hattusili III mentioned "the gift of the king of Ahhiyawa."[99]

If it turns out that the Greeks were participants in the diplomatic system and some cuneiform letters are eventually found at one of the palaces in Mycenaean Greece, or if a letter from an Ahhiyawan king is found in Egypt or one of the other great powers, then we'll know much more. For now, Ahhiyawa is an intriguing side note to the story of the brotherhood of great kings.

In the Amarna period, distant lands continued to provide the Near Eastern kings with luxuries. Afghanistan was still apparently outside of the network of kings, connected with the Near East only by trade, helping feed the insatiable appetite for tin and lapis lazuli. The Baltic region, far off in northern Europe, now provided amber for jewelry, not only to the Mycenaeans but to Egypt, Cyprus, Alalakh, and Ugarit.[100] Visible within the warm amber beads one could sometimes make out tiny insects, trapped in what had once been tree sap. The trade route that brought the amber to Greece passed through farming villages and dense forests and over mountain ranges. One wonders whether the Europeans had heard rumors of the staggering wealth and huge cities of the great powers to the south.

People at a much greater distance from the Near East also felt ripples of its influence around this time. By 1200 BCE, two-wheeled chariots were being used in China by the Shang dynasty kings to conquer their enemies. There is little doubt that this was an innovation from outside. Just as in the Near East, the lightweight horse-drawn chariot rode along on two wheels, spoked rather than solid ones. But the technology wasn't identical. One can't posit chariot salesmen from Hatti or Mittani crossing the Asian continent with their latest models to sell to the Chinese. The wheels of Chinese chariots had more spokes than the western version, and the axle was located in the center, not the rear of the box.[101] The design had been adapted, probably as a result of being copied repeatedly by people in any number of communities spread out across Asia. Any technology that provided an advantage in battle would have been emulated by enemies as much as by allies. The spread of the battle chariot across the continent had taken centuries.

From the perspective of the peoples of Syria and Mesopotamia, the rest of their world must have seemed much closer than in the time of Hammurabi and Zimri-Lim. Distant Dilmun was now controlled by the Kassite Babylonians. Egypt was not only in contact with the Syrians and Mesopotamians but was a firm ally. Goods that came through Egypt from Nubia or Punt were widely available. Alashiya was an ally too, and merchants, and probably envoys, even traveled to and from Greece. The balance of power between the great kings brought about a peace that allowed for vast amounts of wealth, both in raw materials and manufactured goods, to be transported safely from one land to another by land and sea. The artists copied ideas from one another, bringing about an international style in art that paralleled the international spirit of the age.[102]

Perhaps someday a royal tomb of Burna-buriash II will be discovered and found to contain his favorite Egyptian animal and tree sculptures. Or the royal tomb of Tushratta will prove to hold those gold statues from Egypt that he waited so impatiently for. And it's just as likely that Amenhotep III's tomb (before it was robbed) included Babylonian lapis beads, Mittanian necklaces, and Alashiyan bronzes.

This spirit of peace, prosperity, and international cooperation was about to face a challenge, however. A king came to power in Hatti with a different agenda altogether. He wanted to expand his empire, and to his mind, if one of the other Great Powers had to fall in order for him to realize his ambition, so much the better.

CHAPTER ELEVEN

# A Crisis in the Brotherhood

*"My father became hostile"*

### Tushratta's Worries

On the happy occasion of his daughter's marriage to Amenhotep III, around 1355 BCE, Tushratta's mind wasn't wholly at ease. Although he gloried in the peace that he enjoyed with Egypt—"in our lands, peace prevails"—he was still troubled.[1] He worried openly in his letter to the pharaoh about the security of his own land and of Egypt and about some unnamed enemy. Oddly enough, he seemed to suggest that the threat to Egypt was more imminent. He brought it up first and volunteered to send help: "If only an enemy of my brother did not exist! But should in the future an enemy invade my brother's land, (then) my brother writes to me, and the Hurrian land, armor, arms, . . . and everything concerning the enemy of my brother will be at his disposition." But he must have been wrong; there was no real threat to Egypt proper. It was surrounded by deserts and it controlled large stretches of Nubia to the south and the Levant to the north. So perhaps Tushratta worried about a threat to the Egyptian holdings in Canaan. He certainly worried even more for his own land: "But should, on the other hand, there be for me an ene[my]—if only he did not exist!—I will write to my brother, and my brother will dispatch . . . [from] the land of Egypt, armor, arms, . . . and everything concerning my enemy." If his land were invaded, he would love to know that Egyptian forces would materialize to support him.

The identity of this enemy was no mystery; it haunted him throughout his reign: the land of Hatti. When Tushratta had first written to Amenhotep

III, he had included an account of a Hittite incursion into his land and of his victory over them: "When the enemy advanced against [my] country, Teshup, my lord, gave him into my hand, and I defeated him. There was [n]ot one of them who return[ed] to his own country."

Hatti had a long history by now. It had been about 250 years since the Hittite king Mursili I had led the Hittite troops against Babylon, and about 400 years since Assyrian merchant colonies had flourished in Anatolian cities. Even then, the Anatolian cities had been very old; Hatti was an ancient and rich civilization.

The heart of the kingdom was the region of the central Anatolian plateau, home to many Hittite cities. It was a place of extremes, with blazing hot, dry summers and intensely cold winters. Blizzards could blow in and wrap the thick stone and brick walls of the temples and palaces in snow, confining the people to their homes. But the winter days could also be dry, though bitterly cold.

Hattusa, the capital, was in an area of rocky steppe, with deep craggy valleys and high city walls protecting it from the incursions of the enemies nearby to the north, the Kaska people. The sky over Hattusa was often a clear blue flecked with white clouds, the mountains to the south a gray purple line on the horizon. Forests surrounded the capital back then, though the forests are gone now, and the Hittites used the oak and pine timber in their buildings. A lot of wood was also certainly used up in keeping fires going in the hearths all winter, though it must have seemed to the Hittites that their forests could never be exhausted. Seven springs provided an ample supply of fresh water for the city.

In some ways, though, Hattusa was an odd choice for the capital. It was at the far northern edge of the Hittite empire, and cut off from easy access to much of the land, even within Anatolia, by high hills and mountains. The city seems to have looked north, rather than south. And yet it suited the kings well enough; they ruled from Hattusa for centuries.

Excavators have been working at Hattusa for over a century, since 1906, and have unearthed palaces, temples, houses, streets, and the city's vast and well-designed fortification system. They've also found thousands of cuneiform documents written on clay tablets, much like those from Syria and Mesopotamia, some of them still stacked up in order, right where they were when the palaces and temples burned down, with clay labels from the shelves still preserved next to them. The Hittites used cuneiform both to write the international language of Akkadian and for their own language of Hittite. They also wrote on wood, but the wooden tablets have long since disintegrated. Among the clay tablets are some—treaties, letters, edicts, and annals—that give us the

Hittite perspective on their history, including the time of Tushratta, who was always seen as an enemy.[2]

### Suppiluliuma's Determination to Isolate Tushratta

For several years after Tushratta's early battle against Hatti, that land seems to have been quiet, which allowed Tushratta some peace—even if it was a worried peace. Amenhotep III in Egypt had been less worried; he thought that Hatti was no longer a great power, and even approached the western Anatolian land of Arzawa as a new ally, believing that in Hatti "everything is finished and the country Hattusa is shattered," and so it had seemed.[3] The capital city of Hattusa had even burned down around 1360 BCE.[4] But King Tudhaliya II, who had come to the Hittite throne just a few years into Tushratta's reign, seemed determined to change Hatti's fortunes. He launched a series of campaigns around Anatolia to expand his kingdom, many of them led by his warrior son, Prince Suppiluliuma.

So when Tushratta wrote to Amenhotep III about his worries concerning possible enemies, Hatti was almost certainly on his mind. After Amenhotep's death, Tushratta's letters to Akhenaten took on an increasingly desperate air. It wasn't just the missing gold statues that bothered him; he was worried that someone was maligning him in the Egyptian court. He wrote to reassure Akhenaten of his love and to demand love in return: "Just as your father always showed love to me, so now may my brother always show love to me. And may my brother listen to nothing from anyone else."[5] But Akhenaten seemed to be deaf to his entreaties.

Around 1344 BCE, after Akhenaten had ruled Egypt for about nine years, a big change took place in Hatti. Tudhaliya II died and Suppiluliuma I came to the Hittite throne.[6] Suppiluliuma was one of the great kings of Hittite history; he ruled for at least twenty-two years, and he seems to have outlived almost all his contemporaries who are known from the Amarna archive: Akhenaten and Tutankhamen in Egypt, Tushratta in Mittani, Burna-buriash II in Babylonia, and probably Ashur-uballit of Assyria.

Whereas in Babylonia and Assyria scribes created lists of kings' names in order, with the lengths of their reigns, no such lists survive from Hatti or Mittani. We know that Suppiluliuma was a contemporary of Tushratta and that he outlived him, because his interactions with both Tushratta and his successor are mentioned in Suppiluliuma's treaties. We know quite a lot about Suppiluliuma's achievements—he wasn't shy about recording them in the prologues to his treaties—and his son and successor also authored a long text about his

father (called by its author "The Manly Deeds of Suppiluliuma"). But it's difficult to place the Amarna letters into the chronology of Suppiluliuma's life.

Once Suppiluliuma took power, it was clear that he was going to be a
force to be reckoned with in the Near East. Perhaps Hatti had briefly slipped
out of the great king brotherhood, but it was back. Suppiluliuma wasn't just a
"great king." Like the pharaoh, he referred to himself as "the Sun." Never for
a moment does he seem to have entertained the thought of being allied with
Tushratta. To his mind, Mittani had robbed Hatti of lands in northern Syria,
and he was determined to get them back. He developed a strategy that threatened to undo the whole network of peaceful diplomatic interaction that the
other lands had nurtured. Ironically, diplomacy was central to this strategy.

Although Suppiluliuma is considered one of the great Hittite kings, he
was a cutthroat, power-hungry man. He was obsessed with expanding his
empire and initially was unafraid to deceive or hurt others in order to attain
his goals. Even the way in which he had come to power was distasteful (even
to his own son, who wrote about it). Suppiluliuma's father had died and Suppiluliuma had not been designated as his successor, although he had a lot of
military support, having already led the army to a number of victories. One of
his brothers, another Tudhaliya (known as Tudhaliya the Younger), was made
the new king, so, according to Suppiluliuma's son, "the princes, the noblemen, the commanders of the thousands, the officers...and all [the infantry]
and chariotry of Hattusa swore an oath to him. My father also swore an oath
to him."[7]

An oath was not something to take lightly in the ancient Near East; people believed that the gods would severely punish anyone who broke an oath.
But Suppiluliuma did so anyway. He "mistreated Tudhaliya" and "all [the
princes, the noblemen], the commanders of the thousands, and the officers
of Hattusa [went over] to" Suppiluliuma, "[they seized] Tudhaliya, and they
killed [Tudhaliya]." Even if Suppiluliuma did not kill his brother with his own
hands, he was obviously both the instigator and the beneficiary of the assassination; he even executed those of his brothers who had supported Tudhaliya
so that he would have no rivals for the throne.

Suppiluliuma soon went on the offensive, not directly against Mittani, but
against two lands that were closely allied with Mittani, lands that were physically near Mittani as well.[8] It was as though he was already spoiling for a fight
with Tushratta.

He wasn't antagonistic towards the other great kings, however. His attitude towards Egypt was, at least to start with, positively friendly. He later wrote
a letter to a pharaoh who succeeded Akhenaten that reflects back on a time
early in his reign when he first communicated with Egypt. His comments

prove that he was a full member of the great king brotherhood, was thoroughly familiar with their diplomatic conventions, and enjoyed a good relationship with Egypt during Akhenaten's reign.[9]

Suppiluliuma wrote that the pharaoh had been the one to renew the old alliance between their lands, with Akhenaten writing to Suppiluliuma "Let us establish only the most friendly relations between us." The Hittite king was delighted to comply, sending messengers and greeting gifts. These seem to have been reciprocated generously by Akhenaten; Suppiluliuma wrote that "my own request, indeed, that I made to...[Akhenaten], he never refused; he gave me absolutely everything."[10]

And yet while Akhenaten was apparently willing to send rich gifts to Hatti, he was still routinely ignoring Tushratta in Mittani. He was now failing to send Egyptian messengers regularly.[11] He held back Tushratta's messengers and put them in detention, and he complained that Mittanian messengers had broken the law in Egypt but then failed to follow up with a description of their crimes so that Tushratta could punish them.[12] In desperation Tushratta pleaded "Now may my brother esta[bl]ish the natu[re of their crime], and I will treat [them] j[ust as] my brother wants them treated."[13] Tushratta so badly wanted to be favored in Akhenaten's eyes that he was even willing to grovel, claiming that "[My love for] my [brother] is ten times greater than what we always had with Nimmureya, your father" (although this was blatantly not true).[14] It didn't work.

Tushratta's last letter to Akhenaten was written on a great doorstop of a tablet, just as monumental in size as the Hurrian one he had sent to Amenhotep III when Tadu-Hepa had been on her way to Egypt. It too was over eighteen inches tall and eleven inches wide (though at least it was in Akkadian, this time)—and in it Tushratta reviewed his long relationship with Egypt, fondly recalling how well he had been treated by Amenhotep III in years gone by. But now everything had changed. He brought up the gold statues six separate times in the letter—they seemed to symbolize to him everything that had gone wrong. He assured the pharaoh (and perhaps himself) that as soon as Akhenaten sent the Mittanian messengers home, bringing those statues with them, normal relations would be restored. Tushratta would then "send Keliya, and...a large mission to my [bro]ther."[15] But he complained that "my brother has given me no information [with regard to the re]quests that I have made."[16] He could, it seems, feel his Egyptian ally slipping away from him. Tushratta was shut out of Akhenaten's affections even as the power of his Hittite enemy was growing.

Akhenaten might well have guessed that Suppiluliuma was likely to attack Mittani, and he must have wanted to make sure that the Hittite king didn't assume that he would side with Tushratta. The pharaoh presumably wanted his own cities in Canaan to be spared any attack, hence his willingness to be an ally to Hatti. And Suppiluliuma may have had a similar motivation in warming up to Egypt; he'd rather not face Egyptian troops as well as those of Mittani when he attacked in northern Syria. No doubt he didn't underestimate Tushratta's forces; one of his predecessors had faced them before and had lost.

So perhaps Suppiluliuma now had Egypt on his side, and Akhenaten's cold shoulder to Tushratta was a result. Suppiluliuma chose not to invade Mittani right away, but first to isolate Tushratta from all the great kings.

Suppiluliuma approached Burna-buriash II in Babylonia about establishing an alliance, and, only about two years after Suppiluliuma had come to power, they confirmed their treaty with a marriage between Burna-buriash's daughter and the Hittite king.[17] One small problem with this was that Suppiluliuma was already married. His queen Henti was the mother of at least five sons and had, up to that time, been a woman of great importance.[18] Apparently the terms of Suppiluliuma's agreement with Babylon included a clause specifying that Burna-buriash's daughter would take over the position of queen; Henti seems to have been unceremoniously banished. One has the sense that Suppiluliuma was not going to let anything get in the way of his plans for undermining Mittani. He was using the diplomatic machinery of the great kings as well as anyone—sending messengers to foreign courts, negotiating diplomatic marriages, presumably exchanging valuable gifts and formalizing treaties—but his goal seems to have been not to assure peace but to strengthen his own hand for a coming war against Mittani.

The Babylonian princess took the name Tawananna after marrying Suppiluliuma, and she became the reigning queen of Hatti, a powerful position in which she had some joint responsibilities with Suppiluliuma for administering the palace. Her stepson Mursili (Suppiluliuma's son and successor) seems to have loathed her. The descriptions we have of her come from him. He accused her of performing black magic, giving away royal riches, and introducing unwelcome Babylonian customs to the Hittite court. He later even accused her of murdering (through magic) his own beloved wife.[19]

Suppiluliuma's last strategic move was to seek out and cultivate a man named Artatama, who might have been Tushratta's own brother. He was living in exile but he claimed the right to the throne of Mittani—Tushratta's throne.[20] Suppiluliuma referred to Artatama as "king of the land of Hurri" (even though that was Tushratta's title), and he and Artatama "made a treaty with one another."[21] The treaty hasn't been found, but it presumably mandated that Artatama would take over the throne of Mittani after Suppiluliuma had conquered the land and killed Tushratta. It's unclear whether Artatama had any delusions that his kingdom might end up being independent of Hatti.

### The Hittites Attack Mittani

By the time that Suppiluliuma had ruled Hatti for a few years, Tushratta must have been extremely nervous. His kingdom had, in the time of Thutmose III, been feared as a threat to its neighbors, but had since settled into the role of peaceful ally. Now Tushratta must have sat talking with his high officials, looking for a way to counter the Hittite threat.

To the southwest, Egypt, his sometime friend, was now Hatti's ally. Even if Egypt was still ostensibly on his side, it had been weakened by Akhenaten's religious reformation and would probably not send troops. To the southeast, Babylon's King Burna-buriash II was not only allied to Hatti, he was Suppiluliuma's father-in-law. Within Mittani, an Assyrian leader named Ashur-uballit had been ruling as his vassal in the east for almost as long as Tushratta himself had been on the throne. Tushratta must have known that Ashur-uballit was looking for a way to break free from Mittanian control. And even some of Tushratta's other subjects probably supported Artatama's claim to his throne. Tushratta may have had no real allies at all. It was not at all obvious how Tushratta could prevail if Suppiluliuma decided to attack.

Not surprisingly, the attack came quickly. Suppiluliuma set out on a campaign into Mittani soon after his treaty had been formalized with Artatama, supposedly because he had been provoked by Tushratta. He had been on the throne for only four or five years, but he'd prepared for this war extensively.[22] It's unclear what Tushratta did to bring on this attack, since Suppiluliuma wrote that "Tushratta called for attention from the great king, King of Hatti, Hero," that is, himself.[23] There's a fragmentary text mentioning that the king of Mittani attacked a country called Nuhashi, which had been allied with Hatti. The text isn't dated, but perhaps this was the time when the attack took place. Maybe Tushratta wanted to create a buffer between his empire and that of the Hittites. In any event, Suppiluliuma felt that he had to "turn his attention," as he put it, to Tushratta, and to "plunder the lands of the west bank of the River (Euphrates)."

Tushratta was infuriated. These lands beyond the Euphrates were subject to him; the Hittite king had no right to go marauding through his lands stealing sheep and cattle from his subjects. So he sent a messenger to Suppiluliuma, protesting forcefully but not threatening military action: "Why are you plundering on the west bank of the Euphrates? If you plunder on the west bank of the Euphrates, then I too will plunder the lands on the west bank of the Euphrates.... If you plunder them, what will I do to them? If a lamb, or a kid of my land is... I will cross over from the east bank of the Euphrates."

He presumably was threatening to retaliate by doing the same thing to the Hittite lands beyond the river that were being done to his. This sounds like a pretty mild reaction—you steal my sheep, I'll steal yours. When Tushratta's envoy arrived in Hattusa with this message he perhaps even had directions from Tushratta to negotiate with Suppiluliuma to attempt to avoid a conflict. Tushratta seems to have been much more interested, by this time, in enjoying his life of peace and prosperity than in going to war. He had "built a palace and filled it with riches" and really wanted to get his hands on those gold statues he'd been promised to add to the decor, but he doesn't seem to have been involved in a war of any size since his battle against the Hittites at the beginning of his reign.[24] And now that his alliance with Egypt had weakened, largely through Akhenaten's neglect, he was probably less anxious than ever to face the Hittites on the battlefield.

But Suppiluliuma was in no mood to negotiate. He had a list of grievances against Mittani, most of which dated back to his father's reign, and he wanted vengeance. He called Tushratta's mild protest "presumptuous," but boasted that "I maintained my pride before him."[25]

Pride seems to have been a big concern for Suppiluliuma; he had to show that he was not an equal like the other kings but a "hero." The Egyptian king once had the gall (in Suppiluliuma's eyes) to name himself first in a letter to Suppiluliuma. We don't have this letter, but the Hittite king wrote back to protest. It seems his pride had been wounded: "And now, as to the tablet that [you sent me], why [did you put] your name over my name?... My brother, did you write [to me] with peace in mind? And if [you are my brother], why have you exalted [your name], while I, for [my part], am tho[ught of as] a corpse?"[26] This seems like a silly overreaction—no other great king seems to have even noticed the order of the names in a letter beyond what was traditional practice—but Suppiluliuma was always quick to perceive an insult or a slight.

Tushratta's "presumptuousness" was, apparently, reason enough for Suppiluliuma to go far beyond plundering the areas west of the Euphrates. He set out to retake all the north Syrian lands that he felt had been stolen from Hatti in his father's time.

He managed it, too. Each time he drew up a treaty with one of the lands he reconquered, he included a historical introduction recounting how the treaty came about. The introductions are full of the names of cities and vassal kingdoms that he brought back under Hittite rule during this one dramatic yearlong campaign around 1340 BCE. An ancient Mittanian or Hittite reading or hearing these lists of place names would have been able to conjure them up in his mind; perhaps one was famous for its textiles and another for its glass production. One might have been known for its cooler weather in summer and another for its tyrannical ruler. But to us they are mostly just names of places not yet found: Isuwa, Kurtalissa, Arawanna, Zazisa, Kalasma, Timana, and on and on.

Finally Suppiluliuma made it to Washshukkanni, Tushratta's capital, and some scholars assume that he conquered the city. But he didn't say so himself, and if he had conquered it, we probably would have heard about it. "I reached the city of Washshukkanni in search of plunder," he wrote. "I brought to Hatti the cattle, sheep, and horses of the district of Shuta (where Washshukkanni was located) along with its possessions and its civilian captives."[27] If he was hoping to meet Tushratta there in a pitched battle for his capital and his crown, he was disappointed: "King Tushratta fled. He did not come against me for battle."

In fact, as far as we know, the two kings never crossed paths, in spite of the fact that Suppiluliuma put all the blame for his war on Tushratta. He repeated his assertion again later in a treaty, as though convincing himself as well as his reader of the fact: "Because of the presumptuousness of King Tushratta, I plundered all these lands in one year and brought them to Hatti."

By saying that Tushratta fled, Suppiluliuma gives the impression that he had been victorious over Mittani, but that wasn't the case. Tushratta was still the king there, and none of the lands in central Mittani defected to the Hittite cause. Suppiluliuma continued his year of marching and plundering by heading out of Mittani proper and traveling west to retake some of Tushratta's prize vassal kingdoms between the Euphrates and the Mediterranean.

## Ugarit Sides with Hatti

He started with the region near Aleppo, which, over two centuries before, had been conquered by the Hittite king Mursili I on his way to attack Babylon. Suppiluliuma thought he might be able to muster some support in the area, so he wrote to Niqmaddu II, the king of Ugarit, promising him a "favor" if he would attack his neighbors. This letter was found in the excavations at Ugarit.[28] It's quite possible that if the other cities he attacked were excavated, similar documents would be found there too. Suppiluliuma seems to have used the diplomatic system of messengers and treaties in much the same way that Hammurabi and Zimri-Lim used them back in the eighteenth century, as a way to rally allies and to limit the amount of actual fighting that his troops had to do.

Ugarit had been within the Egyptian sphere of influence, though not directly subject to Egypt, since around 1400 BCE. Excavations have taken place there for more than seventy-five years, providing hundreds of cuneiform documents and making it one of the best known of the Levantine cities.[29] It was one of the northernmost cities under Egyptian hegemony, situated in a fertile valley right on the Mediterranean coast. It had a perfect mild Mediterranean climate: lots of warm, sunny days, but enough rainfall to make irrigation unnecessary. The people of Ugarit grew wheat and barley, olives, grapes, pistachios, and almonds, and the nearby hills and mountains provided good stone for construction, along with pine and cedar trees.[30]

The craftsmen of this region had also figured out how to make a vivid red-purple dye from the shells of a sea snail called the murex. Not only was the color brighter than most natural dyes, it didn't require the use of a dye fixative in order to be stable. Murex-dyed fabric kept its startling color even when washed or left in the sun.[31] But it was time-consuming and expensive to produce; thousands of shells produced only a few ounces of dye. Only the wealthy and powerful could afford purple clothing, and it became the color of royalty all around the Mediterranean.

Just 800 yards from the town was a fine port, which Ugarit controlled and profited from. Boats from many different lands moored there—from Egypt, Canaan, Alashiya, and the Aegean. At the highest point of the tell in Ugarit, where the streets were already sixty-five feet above the surrounding land, was a temple to the god Baal with a tower that would have stood almost sixty feet high.[32]

This landmark was visible from the sea and must have helped sailors find their way into the port. Some ships' crews—perhaps those who arrived safely at the end of troubled voyages—dedicated stone anchors to the god in thanks. Seventeen such anchors were found in the temple.[33] (The boats brought luxury goods from their lands of origin and exchanged them for purple-dyed cloth, among other local products.)

Besides the sea trade, merchant caravans arrived overland from Mittani, Hatti, and Babylonia. As a result of all this commerce, Ugarit's population comprised a microcosm of the international community: documents were found there written in Egyptian, Akkadian, Sumerian (long a dead language but still used for literary works), Hurrian, Hittite, Ugaritic (the local language), and even Cypro-Minoan.[34] People speaking all these languages (except Sumerian) must have mingled in the streets and marketplaces. Ugarit was truly cosmopolitan. In some ways, it was the city that most typified the international spirit of the age.

The palace at Ugarit looked fit for a great king, even though the local king was only a "servant" of the king of Egypt. The palace was famous among the vassals of Egypt and was held up as a standard against which to compare other palaces. One mayor wrote to the pharaoh that "there is no mayor's residence like that of the residence in Tyre. It is like the residence in Ugarit."[35] The Ugarit palace covered over three acres and was built of finely cut stone, as well as wood and other materials.[36] Over 100 rooms were grouped around six courtyards on the first floor alone, and twelve stairways led to at least one upper floor.[37] It had a huge throne room, administrative offices, a garden, a tiled rectangular shallow pool, painted walls, a sewer system, and wells. The director of excavations, Marguerite Yon, was particularly taken with a room that was separated from the pathway around the garden only by two large pillars, evoking, as she put it, "an enjoyable life of leisure and festivities" as diners sat in the shade of the airy room, presumably enjoying a view of the trees in the garden.[38]

In one room, near the garden and the pillared room, excavators found several artifacts that hint at the opulent lifestyle of the royal family and of their close ties to Egypt. Two ivory panels from a bed were made locally but were strongly influenced by Egyptian art.[39] In the same room were found other precious items: a small pedestal table, an ivory horn, a small ivory head of a man—it was inlaid with gold, silver, and bronze—and a copy of Amenhotep III's cartouche announcing his marriage to Queen Tiye.[40]

Clearly, Ugarit was a rich place, but it did not support a large or powerful military. Although it was within the sphere of influence of the pharaoh in Egypt, the Amarna letters show that the city enjoyed a lot of independence.

When the kings of Ugarit wrote to the pharaoh, it was with an odd mix of humility and assertiveness. A letter from King Niqmaddu II, probably to Akhenaten, is a good example.[41] He started the letter, as did the Egyptian vassals, in all humility. The pharaoh was "the Sun, my lord," Niqmaddu was "your servant."[42] He didn't presume to use the term "brother" or even "son," and he wrote that he fell "at the feet of the king, the Sun, my lord." The rest of the short letter, in contrast, could almost have been written by a great king. Niqmaddu put in a wish for the pharaoh's well-being that vassals didn't use, though the great kings did: "May all go well for the king, the Sun, my lord, [h]is househ[old], his ch[ief wife], for his (other) wives" and so on (of course, a fellow great king wouldn't have called the pharaoh "my lord"). And he had a request of the pharaoh: he needed two palace attendants from Nubia and a physician. In exchange, Niqmaddu sent a greeting gift of some kind (the description of it is broken). But Ugarit's wealth and strategic location weren't adequate to place him in the brotherhood of great kings, and he still looked to the pharaoh as his "lord."

Ugarit is noteworthy for many reasons, among them some remarkable myths that were found among the documents, reflecting the beliefs of the Canaanites. The Ugaritian scribes also employed a unique script to write their local language. It used cuneiform wedges and was written on clay tablets, but the signs were unlike those of Akkadian, and each sign stood for just one consonant, resulting in an alphabet of 30 letters. Unlike in normal cuneiform, the script did not record vowels. It took the Greeks, a few hundred years later, to think of adding vowels to their alphabet as separate symbols. It's odd that the Ugaritian scribes didn't think of this for themselves, because normal cuneiform had individual signs for each of the vowels used in Akkadian—"a," "e," "i," and "u." (The Greek alphabet didn't derive from the one at Ugarit but from the later Phoenician alphabet, which did not have a cuneiform origin.)

In writing to Niqmaddu II of Ugarit, therefore, and appealing to him for help in his Syrian campaign, Suppiluliuma must have known that he might upset relations with Egypt. But the letter to Niqmaddu was not belligerent; it was perfectly respectful and civil, if a little disingenuous. Suppiluliuma pretended that the lands of Nuhashi and Mukish were being hostile to him, rather than vice versa. He promised the king of Ugarit that he'd be happy to send troops to help Niqmaddu fight his neighbors if the king needed them, but he didn't make any threats if Niqmaddu turned down his offer.

Niqmaddu seems to have found the offer of assistance to be attractive. Maybe he had originally thought that his state, which was famous for its rich trade and cosmopolitan living, would somehow be immune from the conflict and could function like some sort of ancient version of Switzerland. But now he realized that he needed the powerful protection from Hatti.[43] Perhaps, like Tushratta, he had found Akhenaten to be an unhelpful correspondent and he didn't trust him to send support if Hatti attacked. But once Niqmaddu had chosen to side with Suppiluliuma, his state was perhaps even more vulnerable than before.

A Mittanian war leader named Aki-Teshup and his allies, all of them opposed to the Hittite campaign, "assembled their troops; captured cities in the interior of the land of Ugarit; oppressed (?) the land of Ugarit; carried off subjects of Niqmaddu, king of the land of Ugarit, as civilian captives; and devastated the land of Ugarit."[44] This local war must have been terrifying for the Ugaritians; their land had never had much of a military, and the king was probably caught by surprise at the attack.

Niqmaddu quickly sent off a messenger to Suppiluliuma, who was campaigning nearby: "May Your Majesty, Great King, my lord, save me from the hand of my enemy! I am the subject of Your Majesty, Great King, my lord. To my lord's enemy I am hostile, [and] with my lord's friend I am at peace. The kings are oppressing(?) me!"[45] That was just what Suppiluliuma wanted to hear. He quickly sent a contingent of troops, along with "princes and noblemen" to Ugarit, and they were able to regain control of the land for Niqmaddu, who thanked them with gifts of silver, gold, and bronze.

Niqmaddu then traveled north and east to the city of Alalakh, where Suppiluliuma was staying with his troops, to work out the terms of a treaty between Hatti and Ugarit. It was a generous treaty in some ways; Niqmaddu would not be a Hittite vassal, though his land was to be protected by Hatti, and there were no curses included in the clauses to scare him into complying. On the other hand, though it wasn't included in the treaty, he had to start paying tribute to Hatti—a lot of tribute: dozens of minas of gold, along with many linen garments and hundreds of shekels of the red-purple wool for which Ugarit was famous.[46]

### More Conquests by Hatti

Meanwhile, Suppiluliuma turned his attention to the other cities of northwestern Syria, including those that had ganged up on Ugarit. Did the king of Aleppo send a messenger to his overlord, Tushratta in Mittani, asking for military reinforcements? He probably did, but the Hittites overpowered him nonetheless.

Where were the Mittanian forces anyway? We don't have copies of any of Tushratta's treaties, or lists of his deeds, in the way that we do for Suppiluliuma. Other than his letters to Egypt, the only documents that mention Tushratta were written by his enemy, who was in no mood to make him look good. Perhaps he did sent forces to help his vassals.

Some other leaders of cities in the region started appealing to Suppiluliuma for peace terms, perhaps realizing that Tushratta wasn't sending much help and seeing the relatively generous treatment that Niqmaddu of Ugarit had received. Other leaders joined forces to fight against Hatti under Aki-Teshup. His brother had surrendered to Suppiluliuma, but Aki-Teshup took the offensive, supposedly thinking (though one wonders how Suppiluliuma knew this) "[Let] us fight with the Great King, King of Hatti."[47] Messengers must have been hurrying between the cities in the region with letters to and from the local kings. It took a lot of nerve to stand up to the Hittite army without the support of the army of their own, absent, great king of Mittani, but they chose to do it anyway. And they were defeated.

Excavations at the major city of Qatna in Syria show that it, too, fell to Suppiluliuma during this campaign. The palace burned and walls collapsed.

Debris from the upper story fell to the lower story, and debris from the lower story fell yet lower, into a corridor that led down to a royal tomb. Some of the destroyed walls and floors were knocked into a huge well on the ground floor. Excavators found wood in the well shaft, great logs of cedar, and thousands of fragments of paintings from palace walls. These had been done in the most fashionable technique, in an Aegean style.[48] Tablets from a royal archive room mention some of the luxuries of the palace—objects made of gold and lapis lazuli, and elaborate furniture, all the products of a more peaceful time— which Suppiluliuma's troops no doubt took as booty.

Suppiluliuma's military successes and the devastation they caused must have been discussed everywhere, among messengers traveling from Babylonia to Egypt, for example, or in the courts of the Egyptian-controlled cities to the south in Canaan. In cities near the conflicts, people must have talked across their rooftops in the evenings and at the markets during the day. Should our king give in to the Hittites or hold out? What will happen to us? Should we flee to stay with distant relatives in Egyptian-controlled areas to the south—surely the great king of Hatti won't touch those?

### Hittite Campaigns in Egyptian Territory

Suppiluliuma did end up tangling with two other lands that had close ties to Egypt, in addition to Ugarit. These altercations might well have led to a major war against Egypt itself had Akhenaten been more interested in protecting his empire. The region around Kadesh (also called Kinza) was still subject to Egypt, and Suppiluliuma initially had no intention of attacking it. He said so specifically: "I did not seek to attack the land of Kinza."[49] But he claimed that he was attacked by its king and forced into battle. He won, and took the king of Kadesh, along with the whole royal family, back to Hatti with him. Later, though, a prince of Kadesh, Aitakkama, was allowed to return home to rule as a Hittite vassal.[50]

The land of Amurru lay to the south of Kadesh along the coast of what is now Lebanon. It was a vassal state of Egypt, but by this time was functioning more or less independently.[51] The Amarna letters from Akhenaten's vassals in Syria include many from leaders of cities in the region pleading for help in controlling Amurru, but the pharaoh seems to have been unresponsive. Besides, the wily leader of Amurru, a man named Aziru, wrote his own letters to the pharaoh, portraying himself as a loyal vassal: "Now may the king, my lord, know that I am [your] servant forever. I do not deviate from the orders of my lord." Who was Akhenaten to believe? Which of the leaders in the region were really loyal to him? Aziru was worried about the Hittite troops of Suppilu-liuma and asked for Egyptian reinforcements: "If the king of Ha[tti advances] for war against me, the king, my lord, should give me...troops and chariots [t]o help me, and I will guard the land of the king, my lord."[52] But Akhen-aten and Suppiluliuma had not become open enemies, although their alliance must have been severely strained; if Akhenaten armed the land of Amurru against the Hittites, he might have faced a war against his ally Suppiluliuma.

So the pharaoh sent a letter to Aziru asking him to come to Egypt. He had a lot of suspicions about Aziru that he laid out in his letter. Aziru had betrayed other Egyptian vassals, he had avoided going to Egypt in the past, and he had become friendly with the new ruler of Kadesh, a Hittite vassal: "The two of you take food and strong drink together.... Why do you act so? Why are you at peace with a ruler with whom the king is fighting?"[53] Eating a meal together was clear evidence of an alliance; one never sat down to eat with an enemy.[54] In fact, contrary to what he wrote, Akhenaten wasn't actually fighting with the king of Kadesh. That was one of the problems for his vassals in Syria; if Kadesh had been captured by the Hittites without help coming from Egypt, could they expect help if Suppiluliuma turned towards them?

Aziru went to Egypt, as commanded, and was detained there for a year.[55] But when he returned to Amurru he decided that he would be better off in the Hittite camp than staying loyal to Akhenaten. According to the treaty that Suppiluliuma imposed on him, Aziru "came up from the gate of Egyptian territory, and knelt [down]" at the feet of Suppiluliuma "and became a vassal," apparently of his own accord.[56]

This loss of both Kadesh and Amurru to the Hittites might have driven the pharaoh to react; he could have sent troops to the Levant to fight directly against the Hittites, and a region-wide war of Egyptians, Hittites, and Mit-tanians might have erupted for control of the Levantine lands. It didn't happen, though. Perhaps messengers were still passing between Suppilu-liuma and Akhenaten, and they were able to avoid an open conflict through diplomatic means.

### How Suppiluliuma Saw His Successes

One might assume that Suppiluliuma's own descriptions of his wars during this yearlong campaign in Syria would be full of bloodshed, with tales of the number of dead and descriptions of cruel treatments of the local leaders, espe-cially those who rebelled with Aki-Teshup. Suppiluliuma, of course, had had his brother killed so that he could take the throne, so he wasn't squeamish about such things. But, for all his bluster, Suppiluliuma doesn't seem to have wanted to brag about killing enemy troops. He always said that he "overpowered" the troops and the lands "and returned [them] to Hatti."[57] The rebellious kings, including Aki-Teshup, were not killed or tortured but were captured and taken to Hatti. On their long march north to the Hittite capital they must have been fed and allowed rest along the way. It seems to have been a point of pride for Suppiluliuma that his civilian prisoners were well treated. His son later wrote that during his father's wars, "The civilian captives who [were carried off] from the land of the enemy survived; none died." On the other hand, this might largely have been Suppiluliuma's choice of how to portray himself. When Mursili wrote about his father's deeds, he didn't shy away from recording the violence of the wars and the treatment of enemy soldiers; frequently he wrote that the gods "marched before my father (so that)...the enemy troops died en masse."[58]

Suppiluliuma boasted that this first campaign to Syria had been a complete success, and to a great extent this seems to have been true. He had recaptured the lands in Syria that had long ago been subject to Hatti and, in doing so, had severely weakened Mittani. His son later reiterated the same theme: "because...the enemy had taken [borderlands] of Hatti [my father...] repeatedly defeated them. He took back the borderlands of Hatti which [the enemy had taken]. He [settled] them anew [with Hittites]."[59] He had even expanded the empire to the south at the expense of the Egyptian empire. But in fact he had not succeeded in conquering Mittani, and even in western Syria, one crucial city in the borderlands had kept the Hittites at bay—Carchemish, one of the great Syrian strongholds on the Euphrates.[60]

Carchemish, like many Syrian cities, had been occupied for over a thousand years by this time. It was mentioned all the way back in the Ebla archives and was allied with Mari in the time of Zimri-Lim. The tell there is still impressive, and tantalizing; the site hasn't ever been excavated properly (it's now on land used by the Turkish military and is off-limits to archaeologists).[61] Its archives may still be preserved and untouched underground. The site is now just to the north of the border between Syria and Turkey, a situation not unlike its ancient one, where it stood, for the time being, between Mittani and Hatti as the westernmost outpost of Mittani.

### Strains in the Brotherhood of Great Kings

After Suppiluliuma's first war in Syria, the international brotherhood of great kings must have been strained almost to the breaking point. Babylonia was uninvolved militarily in the conflict, but Burna-buriash II was probably still on the throne there, and he was allied with Hatti by marriage. On the other hand, Mittani had been attacked in the west, and none of Tushratta's brother kings had come to his aid. Particularly galling to him must have been the failure of Egypt to help him; surely if Amenhotep III had still been alive he would have come to his friend's aid? Worse yet, in the eastern half of Tushratta's empire Assyria seems to have taken advantage of the chaos and achieved its independence from Mittani. Ashur-uballit I proclaimed himself "king of Assyria," which was a new title.[62] At this moment, the whole region could have splintered apart and the bold experiment in international relations could have come to an ignominious end.

But the ideal of the international brotherhood still seems to have kept a hold on the imaginations of the kings. Ashur-uballit I had a new, big kingdom; far from wanting to go it alone, he wanted to join the prestigious brotherhood. So he sent a letter to "the king of E[gypt]" (probably Akhenaten) with a greeting gift.[63] He didn't ask for anything—not for a present in return, not for status as a great king—just for his messenger to be allowed to return home. His message must have been received well and his messenger sent back with a positive response, because within a few years he had joined the brotherhood. In the only other Amarna letter that is preserved from Ashur-uballit, he called himself "great king," referred to the Egyptian king as "my brother," complained that the pharaoh hadn't sent him enough gold, and worried about the treatment of his messengers.[64] He sounded just like the other great kings who came before him.

Egypt, meanwhile, had weathered the loss of two of its vassal states to Hatti and had survived the movement of the capital city to Akhetaten and the closing of the temple to Amen-Ra in Thebes. But now, around 1336 BCE, it faced a new upheaval—the death of its eccentric, though arguably brilliant, pharaoh, Akhenaten. His son Smenkhare might have been ruling with him for a short time, and Smenkhare now took the throne alone, marrying his half sister, one of Akhenaten's daughters.[65]

If the brotherhood was to continue, the change of ruler made it necessary for the other great kings to renew their ties with Egypt. Suppiluliuma was quick to do so, in spite of his previously shaky relationship with Akhenaten: "Now, my brother, [yo]u have ascended the throne of your father, and just as your father and I were desirous of peace between us, so now too should you and I be friendly with one another.... Let us be helpful to each other," he wrote to Smenkhare.[66]

With his letter, Suppiluliuma sent a greeting gift of two silver rhytons in animal shapes and two silver disks, weighing a total of eighteen minas. He asked the new pharaoh to send some presents that had been promised by his father before he died—two gold statues, two silver statues, and a large piece of lapis lazuli. He sounded a little like Tushratta as he expressed his impatience about this: "Why, my brother, have you held back the presents that your father made to me when he was al[iv]e?"[67]

But Smenkhare seems to have ruled for less than a year, so Suppiluliuma might well have been sending another messenger soon afterwards to carry his good wishes to Smenkhare's successor, Tutankhaten (and perhaps to pester him about the gold and silver statues as well). Tutankhaten was only about nine years old, but he was hastily married off to another of the daughters of Akhenaten and Nefertiti, a woman named Ankhesenpaaten.[68]

### Tutankhamen: A Young Pharaoh Ruling at a Crucial Moment

This was, of course, the famous King Tut, the best known of all Egyptian kings, but his modern fame might have surprised him. He was far from the most important king of the New Kingdom; he just had the good fortune to be the only one whose tomb was not ransacked and emptied in antiquity. When it was excavated in 1922, the tomb's riches captured the imagination of a whole generation, and the objects continue to attract tourists to the Cairo Museum and to draw record-breaking crowds every time they are shown in museums outside Egypt. One can only wonder what the furnishings of the tomb of a truly powerful king such as Amenhotep III might have been like. Akhenaten probably made sure that his father took to his grave far more wealth than he had, for example, given to Burna-buriash II as bride-wealth for his daughter, and even that consisted of thousands of precious objects, including hundreds made of pure gold and silver.

Tutankhaten wasn't old enough to rule alone when he took the throne in 1336 BCE, and his advisors weren't at all enamored of the changes that had taken place in Akhenaten's reign. Within a couple of years they had convinced Tutankhaten to change his name. His original name honored the god Aten, Akhenaten's god, but Amen was the state god once again, so the king became Tutankhamen. His wife went from being Ankhesenpaaten to Ankhesenamen. The advisors also convinced the young king to move the capital city back to Thebes and to abandon Amarna, which he did very quickly; none of the letters in the Amarna archive was written after his first or second year. The advisors to Tutankhamen also seem to have been anxious to win back the lands that had been lost to Suppiluliuma. They began to prepare for a campaign against Kadesh and the Hittites.

The years from 1336 to 1327 seem to have been surprisingly quiet. Or perhaps that's an illusion that comes from a shortage of evidence, because the

Amarna letters stop when Tutankhamen moved the capital back to Thebes, and there's also a big gap in the text that recorded the "Manly Deeds of Suppiluliuma." If the kings of Mittani, Hatti, Babylonia, Assyria, and Alashiya continued to write to him (which they probably did) the letters haven't been found. Meanwhile, Tutankhamen was growing up and gradually taking on more responsibilities as pharaoh. Tushratta was still alive, perhaps attempting to rebuild Washshukkanni in the wake of Suppiluliuma's raid. Burna-buriash II of Babylon died around 1333 and was succeeded by Kurigalzu II. Ashur-uballit I was aiming for closer ties with Babylonia. And Suppiluliuma was preparing for a second war in Syria.

The apparent calm of nine years didn't last. Starting in 1327 BCE, a series of events changed the map of the Near East and nearly created an empire larger than any that had existed before. Tutankhamen, now in his late teens, might have been moving towards becoming a new Thutmose III, active in campaigns, perhaps, and ready to rebuild Egyptian power in the Levant. He sent troops to Kadesh to attempt to bring it back within Egyptian control. Mursili II, Suppiluliuma's son, wrote concerning this time that "Egyptian troops and chariots came to the land of Kinza, which my father had conquered, and attacked the land of Kinza (Kadesh)."[69]

King Tutankhamen shows his military skill as he fights a group of Nubians from his chariot. This image was on a chest that was a funerary gift for the king. (Scala/Art Resource, NY)

Meanwhile, Tushratta was also preparing for another battle against the Hittites in the same region, apparently in order to defend Carchemish and perhaps to win back some of the lands he had lost. In Mursili's account of his father's reign, "The Manly Deeds of Suppiluliuma," the seventh tablet first gives accounts of some battles near Hattusa against the neighboring Kaska peoples and then follows events back into Syria. The Hurrians, probably Mittanian troops, attacked Hittite forces near Carchemish. Theirs was an impressive force: "they were superior to the troops and chariots of Hatti who were there." The Hittite king and his son were both absent, having left only six hundred men and chariots while they met together in another town.

Suppiluliuma sent generals and troops to the land of Amka, where Kadesh was located: "[t]hey went to attack Amka and brought civilian captives, cattle and sheep back to my father." This makes it sound as though the Hittite forces weren't entirely successful in reconquering the town, since there's no specific mention of a victory.

So here was almost the whole Near East poised on the brink of a major war, Hatti against Mittani and Egypt against Hatti. And Assyria was flexing its muscles as well, doubtless interested in capturing some of Mittani's lands if that state collapsed. Although Tushratta didn't personally lead the Mittanian forces in Syria, he was apparently still alive in Mittani. Artatama II (the pretender to the Mittani throne) was allied with Suppiluliuma and waiting for his chance to be king. Suppiluliuma, having defeated the Hurrians, was getting ready to besiege Carchemish.

But right at this crucial moment, the young pharaoh Tutankhamen died. Mursili II of Hatti picks up the story: "When the people of Egypt heard of the attack on Amka, they were afraid. And since their lord Nibhururiya (Tutankhamen) had just died, the Queen of Egypt who was the king's wife sent a messenger to my father." The boy king had not even reached his twenties. Recent studies of his mummy show that he wasn't murdered; he probably died of natural causes—perhaps he caught the flu, or suffered from an infection when he broke his leg.[70]

His wife (and half-sister) Ankhesenamen was still alive, perhaps the sole surviving child of Akhenaten. What was she to do? So much was going on in Egypt and its empire—the reestablishment of the cult of Amen-Ra, the attempted reconquest of Kadesh...and now no one was in charge. Not that no one *wanted* to be in charge; there were some very ambitious men in and around the court who would have loved to take the reins and push Egypt forward, but they weren't members of the royal family. Of course there was one way that such a man could become a member of the royal family: he could marry the widowed queen.

### The Egyptian Queen's Unprecedented Offer to Suppiluliuma

According to Mursili II, Suppiluliuma's successor, Queen Ankhesenamen then did an absolutely remarkable thing—she took the fate of Egypt in her own hands when she "sent a messenger to my father," the Hittite king. It wasn't simply a note to let him know of the pharaoh's death, but a letter informing Suppiluliuma of a plan that she had hatched.[71] The messenger must have left Egypt hurriedly to travel to Suppiluliuma, who was near Carchemish at the time, with the queen's message. This is what she wrote: "My husband has died, and I have no son. They say you have many sons. If you will give me one of your sons, he will become my husband. I do not wish to choose a subject of mine and make him my husband . . . I am afraid."[72]

Throughout this era, royal women had their marriages arranged for them by their fathers. Some princesses were sent away to distant lands to marry their fathers' allies; Egyptian princesses, though, could never marry foreigners. Here was a member of the Egyptian royal family asking for a royal spouse from a foreign land, as so many kings had done before, but it was a queen who was writing, and the royal spouse would presumably become pharaoh of Egypt. This was unheard of.

On the other hand, it makes sense. Since the time of Amenhotep II almost a hundred years before, the great kings had written to and thought about one another as brothers. Their courts were international meeting places full of foreign wives and attendants and children with ties to the lands of both their parents. Even though the Amarna letters don't say so, there were almost certainly Hittite princesses in the Egyptian court, and there probably had been such princesses for decades; there simply aren't many letters from Hatti in the Amarna archive as evidence.

Ankhesenamen probably wasn't thinking of Suppiluliuma as a foreign king, even though his troops were, right at that time, engaged against Egyptian troops. She was thinking of him as the "brother" of her husband and of her father, one of the wide extended family of royals that spread across the Near East. And it was true that he had many adult sons (a fact she might have learned from some Hittite woman living at her court); we know of five of them by name, and there were probably many more. Faced with the option of marrying a power-hungry Egyptian commoner or a Hittite prince, she chose a union with a son of Suppiluliuma. Amenhotep III had said, some years before, "From time immemorial no daughter of the king of Egypt is given to anyone."[73] Ankhesenamen knew she had to marry, but she was going to choose who that man would be, and it would be a son of a member of the great king brother-hood. She was decisive, but fearful nonetheless. If one of her husband's ambi-tious advisors got wind of her plan, she might find herself married off to him before the Hittite king even had time to reply.

One might wonder why she hadn't written to the king of Babylon or Mit-tani or Assyria—at least her land wasn't fighting them. But Mittani was weak, and the other lands were far away; Suppiluliuma, on the other hand, was in Carchemish, much closer than Babylon. Besides, as she had noted, he was known to have many grown sons; that was crucial.

Suppiluliuma was dumbfounded after he heard the messenger's letter. He must have made accommodations for the messenger in the army camp near Carchemish, and told him to wait for an answer. Then he called a council of his advisors, told them the situation and said in amazement, "Nothing like this has ever happened to me in my whole life."[74] His mind must have been reeling. It sounded like the best proposal that had ever been made to him. What more could he ask for? To have his son ruling as pharaoh would effec-tively stretch the Hittite Empire right around the Eastern Mediterranean. But no doubt his advisors were wary—after all they were in the middle of a battle with Egypt for the city of Kadesh. This sounded to some of them like a trap. So Suppiluliuma sent his own chamberlain to Egypt. He told him privately, "Go bring back the true story to me. Maybe they are trying to deceive me. Maybe (in fact) they do have a son of their lord. Bring back the true story to me." He probably sent the Egyptian messenger back with his chamberlain, but perhaps he didn't reveal to that man that he mistrusted the Egyptian queen.

Time passed. The Hittites were able to finally take Carchemish after an eight-day siege, and Suppiluliuma put another of his sons on the throne there as king. It was to become one of the most important Hittite cities anywhere in the empire. Then Suppiluliuma took a break; he went "back into the land of Hatti and spe[nt] the winter in the land of Hatti." In winter he couldn't have hoped to do much fighting, and messengers would be hard put to get through to Hattusa because of the harsh weather.

So it wasn't until spring that his chamberlain came back from Egypt, accompanied by the Egyptian messenger Hani and carrying an angry letter from the Egyptian queen. She had written, "Why did you say 'they deceive me' in that way? If I had a son, would I have written about my own and my land's embarrassing predicament to a foreign land? You did not believe me and have dared to speak this way to me." But her fury didn't make her any less anxious to marry a Hittite prince; she went on to reiterate her first letter, almost word for word: "My husband has died, and I have no son. I do not wish to take one of my subjects and make him my husband." She reassured Suppiluliuma that she hadn't written to any other great kings, even though they might have seemed friendlier at that time: "I have written to no other land, only to you. They say you have many sons. Well then, give me one of them." And she added a final sentence that must have made Suppiluliuma catch his breath, if only he could believe her, "To me he will be a husband, but in Egypt he will be king."

There stood Hani, the Egyptian messenger, before him. Suppiluliuma railed at him, voicing all his suspicions about this unprecedented request. "[Y]ou suddenly did me evil," he said to Hani, addressing him as though he were the embodiment of the whole land of Egypt, "You [came (?)] and attacked the man of Kinza (Kadesh) whom I had [taken away (?)] from the king of Hurri-land (Mittani)." And although the queen was asking for his son to become king, "[h]e will probably become a hostage, and you will not make him [king]." Suppiluliuma's worries were justified; recent events between Egypt and Hatti hardly inspired confidence. Hani then had to use all his skills as a diplomat in representing his queen's request and assuring Suppiluliuma of her honesty. His speech, as recorded by Mursili II, simply repeated what was in the letter. This seems unlikely and may reflect the fact that Mursili wasn't present for the speech and didn't know exactly what Hani said. The Egyptian messenger must have elaborated beyond the text of the letter, because somehow he was able to convince Suppiluliuma of his, and his queen's, sincerity.

"Then my father asked for the tablet of the treaty again," wrote Mursili II. This was the treaty that had first bound Egypt and Hatti together, an ancient document that must have been carefully stored in the palace archives. The fact that Suppiluliuma asked for it "again" suggests that this wasn't the first time he had consulted it. As someone, probably his own chamberlain, "read aloud the tablet before them," it reminded Suppiluliuma "how they remained on friendly terms with one another." One can imagine Suppiluliuma attentively listening to the words on the old tablet as his chamberlain read; perhaps he paced the room or knitted his hands together, or stopped the chamberlain at some points to ask for clarification. This promised to be the most important decision of his reign. If all went well, a new era might begin with something much more than an alliance between two great powers. A single Hittite-Egyptian empire might result, and with no bloodshed in its creation.

Finally, Suppiluliuma was convinced. He would do it. He spoke to the people in the room, which certainly included Hani and the Hittite chamberlain, but probably many of his advisors as well: "Hatti and Egypt have been friends a long time. Now this too on our behalf has taken place between t[hem]. Thus Hatti and Egypt will keep on being friends."

Suppiluliuma put his trust in the century of friendship between the two lands that had come before. Here he was seeing beyond his individual alliances with specific Egyptian kings to realize that the real relationship was between kingdoms; it was something that was more than personal.

The next part of the "Deeds" text is broken. We know, though, that Suppiluliuma selected his son Zannanza to marry the Egyptian queen and to become pharaoh. This could not have been a secret; Mursili II doesn't mention any attempt to hide the forthcoming marriage. Perhaps the lands even drew up a treaty. A later text presents the request for a king as coming not from the queen but from the whole people: "When the Egyptians became frightened, they came and actually asked my father for his son for kingship."[75] The same text suggests that the prince had an Egyptian escort, saying that "they took him off" to Egypt, "they" being the Egyptians. Perhaps, like the princesses who had married pharaohs in the past, Zannanza was accompanied by Egyptian troops and carried gifts with him—the bride-wealth for his new queen.

But something went terribly wrong. When Mursili's text resumes, Zannanza had been killed and Suppiluliuma was devastated. "He began to lament for [Zanna]nza, [and] to the god[s . . .] he spoke [th]us: 'O gods, I did [them no h]arm, [yet] the people of Egy[pt d]id [this to me].'"[76] His animosity about the attack on Kadesh was reignited, and he ranted that "they have (also) [attacked] the frontier of my land." Suppiluliuma seems to have believed that it was the Egyptian people as a whole who had killed his son, not a particular faction.

In his fury Suppiluliuma put aside all fond thoughts about the long friendship that had existed with Egypt, and he went on a rampage. In a prayer, Mursili II wrote, "My father became hostile, went to Egyptian territory, and attacked Egyptian territory. He killed the infantry and chariotry of Egypt."[77]

A new pharaoh took the throne in Egypt, but he wasn't a member of the royal family—there were no male heirs left, as Ankhesenamen had bemoaned. He was a man named Ay, an elderly courtier who had served under Akhenaten. Ay sent a messenger with a letter to Suppiluliuma, apparently trying to sooth that king's ire, to call upon their "brotherhood" as great kings, and to assure him that he, Ay, wasn't responsible for Zannanza's death. Suppiluliuma, however, was unconvinced.[78] A draft of an angry response to the letter was found in his archive in Hattusa.[79] Suppiluliuma launched a new war against Syria, including the territories there that Egypt controlled. It was to last much longer than his first Syrian war—five long years.

By 1326 BCE, the Near East was very different from the place that it had been when Suppiluliuma took the throne just eighteen years earlier. The peace had proved far more fragile than the great kings might have thought, especially when confronted with the ambitions of Suppiluliuma to reclaim lands that he thought were rightfully his. But it wasn't just Suppiluliuma's doing; small events had cascaded out of control. Now the dynasty of Amenhotep III had ended in Egypt, and there was no clear legitimate ruler. What had been eastern Mittani was now independent under Assyrian kings, and the west was subject to Hatti. Mittani was no longer a great power, and blood was being shed on battlefields across Syria and Canaan.

It might have seemed that a restoration of order was beyond reach, that the era of the brotherhood of great kings was over. The travels of the international messengers must have grown more perilous during this time, as battles raged in the Levant and the great kings grew increasingly antagonistic towards one another. But the messengers still got through, and they were still accorded audiences with the kings. Throughout this chaos, the mechanisms of diplomacy must have still been present, if hidden, waiting for a time when peaceful relationships might resume. Eventually they did, and the whole international apparatus was resurrected—greeting gifts, diplomatic marriages, treaties, ambassadors, and all.

CHAPTER TWELVE

# The End of an Empire and
# the Restoration of Peace

*"My ancestors and your ancestors made
a mutual declaration of friendship"*

### The Death of Tushratta

Tushratta had survived so much. He had been in serious danger since 1344 BCE, when Suppiluliuma had taken the Hittite throne, but seventeen years later the Mittanian king still lived on. He might have been almost sixty years old, having been on the throne for about forty-five years, by the time that Tutankhamen died in 1327 and Suppiluliuma's son Zannanza was killed.[1] Tushratta's kingdom had shrunk dramatically during that time; the Hittites had taken the lands west of the Euphrates, including, most recently, Carchemish, and Tushratta had lost the eastern half of his empire when the Assyrian declared their independence. But at least Washshukkanni and the lands around it were still his.

Finally, though, Tushratta's luck ran out. He was not killed in battle; he was assassinated. It wasn't even an agent sent by Suppiluliuma who killed him. The Hittite records tell us tersely that Tushratta was murdered by one of his own sons, and that the pretender, Tushratta's rival Artatama II, came to power as a result. Which son was the murderer and what were his motives? The texts don't say.[2] The Mittanian people must have been shocked as the news spread out from the capital.

A messenger probably hurried from Mittani to Egypt to inform the pharaoh of the murder, and to let Tadu-Hepa know the sad news about her father (always supposing she was still alive herself). Another messenger hastened to Suppiluliuma, who must have been delighted, knowing that his protégé, Artatama, would soon be taking the throne in Mittani as Artatama II and that the Hittite king would now have an ally in Mittani. After all, he had a treaty with Artatama. But things did not go as he had hoped.

Artatama II seems to have completely abandoned his treaty with Hatti when Mittani finally fell into his hands. Suppiluliuma had probably expected Artatama's messenger to bring a second letter confirming their alliance. Instead he received a very different message. Word came of the looting of Washshukkanni by the new king, with the wealth hemorrhaging eastward to Assyria and to Assyria's northern neighbor, the land of Alshi. Shuttarna III, the son of Artatama II, who seems to have taken over from his father almost immediately, forwarded vast amounts of wealth to Assyria, sending them "silver and gold, and the caldrons of silver from the bath house" and returning the gold and silver door that Shaushtatar of Mittani had captured from Assyria decades before.[3] Shuttarna "exhausted the house of the king of the land of Mittani, together with its treasures and its riches. He filled it with dirt. He destroyed the palace and exhausted the households of the Hurrians."[4] Shuttarna even "threw himself down before the Assyrian…and gave him his riches as a gift." Worse yet, he handed Mittanian noblemen over to Assyria to be killed. The elderly King Ashur-uballit had probably died a couple of years before, so that a new king, Enlil-nirari, was on the Assyrian throne. He treated these captured Mittanian noblemen with a brutality that had not been seen before in this era, as far as we know: "They were turned over and impaled in the city of Taite." The Assyrians were later to get a notorious reputation for such cruelty, but it was new and certainly terrifying at this time.

The Hittite king must have been worried by all this news. He had no doubt longed for Tushratta's fall, but not in such a way that the result would strengthen Assyria rather than himself.

Aki-Teshup, the Mittanian leader who had led the resistance to Suppiluliuma during his earlier campaign in Syria and who had remained loyal to Mittani throughout the Hittite incursions into the Levant, tried to flee from the chaos in his homeland to Babylonia. He took 200 chariots (and presumably at least 200 charioteers) with him, but even Babylonia wasn't a safe haven: "the King of Babylonia took away for himself the 200 chariots and all the possessions of Aki-Teshup. He made Aki-Teshup assume the same rank as his chariot warriors. He conspired to kill him."[5] Whether or not Aki-Teshup was actually killed, the cold—mortally dangerous, even—reception he met in Babylonia might have had something to do with the turmoil that Babylon was going through at the time. The new king of Babylonia, Kurigalzu II, had been put on the throne by Ashur-uballit of Assyria just a few years before, but now his counterpart in Assyria, Enlil-nirari, had turned against Babylon.[6] Aki-Teshup must have wondered if there was anywhere to which he could safely escape.

Meanwhile, Suppiluliuma had decided that the new leader of Mittani, Shuttarna III, was no ally of his, and so he now proclaimed himself the protector of Mittani against the ravages of Shuttarna. Suppiluliuma announced that he would send relief to Mittani: "I, King of Hatti, had the palace officials bring them cattle, sheep, and horses."[7] He also rewrote history somewhat. It appeared that he had never attacked Mittani, never plundered Washshukkanni (though his boast of having done so appeared, only a few lines earlier, in the very same text in which he claimed that he hadn't): "Until now I, Great King, Hero, King of Hatti, have not crossed to the east bank, and have not taken even a blade of straw or a splinter of wood of the land of Mittani." He was now the friend of Mittani and the enemy of its illegitimate king. But he needed an alternate ruler there, someone who could claim the throne in place of Shuttarna III.

In Kizzuwatna, and recently also in Carchemish, Suppiluliuma had installed two of his own sons as rulers, but he decided not to try to have a Hittite prince rule Mittani. Mittani had been a great power and an enemy of Hatti, and its people might have rebelled if he had imposed a Hittite prince on them as their king. Suppiluliuma needed someone with a legitimate claim to the throne who would be supported by his subjects but willing to do the bidding of the Hittite king.

As it happens, the very man was at that moment fleeing from Mittani after an attempt on his life by Shuttarna III. His name was Shattiwaza and he was a Mittanian prince, son of Tushratta, brother of Tadu-Hepa, and as legitimate an heir to the throne of Mittani as one could hope for. He might even have tried to take the throne after the assassination of his father, but had been unsuccessful. When forced to flee, he didn't think to head to Hatti. Why should he? Hatti had been the main enemy of his father Tushratta. Instead he had joined the Mittanian war leader Aki-Teshup and escaped down the Euphrates to the south, to Babylonia.

Unfortunately he found himself just as unwelcome there as Aki-Teshup. Prince Shattiwaza barely escaped with his life. According to his account, the Babylonian king "would have killed me...but I escaped from his hands and called upon the gods of His Majesty, Suppiluliuma."[8] In this new, ever more hostile world, his father's long-time enemy now seemed to be Shattiwaza's one possible ally.

### A Mittanian Prince Flees to Hatti

Shattiwaza probably didn't have time to send a messenger to Hatti and to wait for his response to see if he would be welcome there. He simply sped back north as fast as he could, going beyond Mittani this time, hoping that he would be given refuge and support by Suppiluliuma. The journey from the flat fields of Babylon to the forested rocky highlands of Hattusa was over 750 miles as the crow flies and considerably farther on foot. It would have taken him at least six weeks to get there. But he wasn't encumbered by much of an entourage, and he had lost almost all his personal possessions: "I had only three chariots, two Hurrians, two other attendants, who set out with me, and a single outfit of clothes—which I was wearing—and nothing else." He probably didn't look much like a prince as he pushed his exhausted team to travel as many miles as they could each day, his clothes growing ever dirtier, his beard and hair more ragged.

When he reached the Marassantiya River (now the Kizil Irmak) near Hattusa, Suppiluliuma was there to meet him; the Hittite king must have received advance word of his arrival. Shattiwaza would have been nervous about his reception, not sure whether Suppiluliuma would welcome him or treat him as an enemy. Shattiwaza fell at his feet. What a relief it must have been when the Hittite king, as he put it, "took me by the hand and rejoiced over me." After a saga that had taken him from surviving an assassination attempt in Mittani to another planned attempt on his life in Babylon, he was finally safe and in the heartland of what was now a powerful ally.

The two men sat down for a long discussion, with Suppiluliuma asking many questions about the situation in Mittani. He questioned Shattiwaza "at length about all the customs of the land of Mittani." Suppiluliuma then offered Shattiwaza a deal; he said, "If I conquer Shuttarna and [the troops of] the land of Mittani, I will not reject you but will adopt you as my son. I will stand by you and place you on the throne of your father. And the gods know My Majesty, Suppiluliuma, Great King, King of Hatti, Hero, Beloved of the Storm-god. He never goes back on the words which issue from his mouth." So this was the proposal for Shattiwaza to consider: if he accepted Suppiluliuma's support, and if the Hittites conquered Shuttarna, Shattiwaza would become a son, not a brother, to Suppiluliuma—he would not be one of the brotherhood of great kings. And, for now, the agreement was oral, not in the form of a written treaty. Perhaps Shattiwaza was disappointed at the proposed demotion to "son," but at least he had the support of the Hittites and the promise that he would take his father's throne if the usurper Shuttarna was defeated. And although the treaty was not yet in writing, Suppiluliuma had invoked the gods to say that he would not go back on his word. Shattiwaza made up his mind and agreed to the terms, replying "If you, my lord, will give me life, and the gods will stand by me, then…let me stand as his (Artatama's) designated successor, and let me rule the land of Mittani. Shuttarna treated the lands badly, but I will never do anything for ill." Shattiwaza was to become Suppiluliuma's son in more ways than one; Suppiluliuma also promised to give him one of his daughters as his wife.

The Hittite king seems to have made a public pronouncement about his new relationship with Shattiwaza and with Mittani. He proclaimed,

> The Storm-god has decided his legal case. As I have taken up Shattiwaza, son of King Tushratta, in my hand, I will seat him upon the throne of his father, so that the land of Mittani, the great land, does not go to ruin. I, Great King, King of Hatti, have given life to the land of Mittani for the sake of my daughter. I took up Shattiwaza, son of Tushratta, in my hand, and I gave him a daughter in marriage.[9]

Shattiwaza, in his disheveled state, still didn't look the part of the future king of Mittani, and he owned next to nothing, so Suppiluliuma "took pity" on him, in Shattiwaza's words, and gave him traveling gear suitable for a prince: "chariots mounted with gold, chariot horses with armor" for battle, "a tent of linen" for camping while on campaign, servants, "festive garments" to wear, and two gold and silver vessels and matching cups for his meals, along with a silver wash basin.

### The Capture of Mittani

Now that an agreement had been reached, Shattiwaza still had to claim his throne, so military preparations got under way at once. Shattiwaza hurried back to Syria, but without Suppiluliuma, because his campaign against Shuttarna was to be fought with the help of Suppiluliuma's son Piyassili, the king of Carchemish, rather than with the great king himself.[10]

Shuttarna III in Mittani, hearing of these preparations, called on his ally the king of Assyria for military assistance. The text describing these events tells us that Shattiwaza and Piyassili crossed the Euphrates and fought against a couple of western Mittanian cities, while Assyrian troops besieged Washshukkanni. When Shattiwaza and Piyassili heard this, they marched with their troops towards Washshukkanni, anticipating at any moment the arrival of Assyrian troops to fight against them. "The Assyrians, however, were not to be seen again. They did not come against us in battle."[11] And there, frustratingly, the text breaks off, leaving us to guess about the circumstances of Shattiwaza's and Piyassili's victory over Shuttarna.

The important part, though, is that they were victorious, and Shattiwaza was able to take his proper place as king of Mittani. Suppiluliuma was true to his word, and a treaty was drawn up between the two kings. In fact, two treaties were drawn up, one written by Suppiluliuma imposing terms on Shattiwaza, the other ostensibly written by Shattiwaza, as though he had come up with the idea of the treaty subjecting himself to the Hittite king. The latter was probably a face-saving document for Mittanian consumption; both treaties seem to have been the work of the Hittite chancellery.[12]

### The Treaty between Suppiluliuma of Hatti and Shattiwaza of Mittani

The treaties have been found in multiple copies, in both Hittite and Akkadian (which was the usual written language used in Mittani). One copy of Suppiluliuma's version of the treaty, written in Hittite but with Hurrian handwriting, was probably created right at the meeting at which the treaty was drawn up. A Mittanian scribe must have made a copy of the Hittite version, presumably to take home for the archives in Washshukkanni, but it somehow stayed in Hattusa, where it was found.[13] The treaty negotiations must have taken place in Hattusa, with Suppiluliuma, Shattiwaza, and their officials debating the provisions perhaps for days before the final versions were produced.[14]

Shattiwaza's version of the treaty hardly warrants the term "treaty" at all—it was missing all the provisions.[15] It simply gave a historical outline that justified Shattiwaza's partnership with Hatti and then moved right on to the list of divine witnesses (from both lands), the curses on Shattiwaza if he were to break the treaty, and the blessings he would receive if he observed the treaty.

Suppiluliuma's version was the real treaty, and it was strongly slanted in his favor. True, Shattiwaza did not become an outright vassal to Hatti, but his land certainly wasn't independent anymore.

The provisions of the Suppiluliuma-Shattiwaza treaty were relatively simple, compared to treaties that the Hittite king imposed on his vassals. The provisions began with a paragraph about succession, which made two things very clear. One placed Shattiwaza into a clearly specified family relationship with the king: "In the future Prince Shattiwaza shall be a brother and equal [to my sons], and the sons of Prince Shattiwaza—his sons and grandsons [...]—shall be brothers and equals to my grandsons."[16] The other showed that the Hittite princess whom Shattiwaza would marry was much more than an item of exchange, she was the reason for Shattiwaza's new status as son of Suppilu-liuma, her position was unassailable, and she would rule with him:

> Prince Shattiwaza shall be king in the land of Mittani, and the daughter of the King of Hatti shall be queen in the land of Mittani. Concubines will be allowed for you, Shattiwaza, but no other woman shall be the greater than my daughter. You shall allow no other woman to be her equal, and no one shall sit as an equal beside her. You shall not degrade my daughter to second rank. In the land of Mittani she shall exercise queenship.

Suppiluliuma had repeated the same basic idea about his daughter four times in different ways here, just in case there was any doubt. Shattiwaza's position seems to have depended on her.

One item in this paragraph pertained not to the king's own behavior, but to that of his subjects: "In the future the Mittanians shall indeed not plan rebellion against Prince Shattiwaza, against my daughter, the queen, [against his sons], or against his grandsons." This part of the treaty was with all the Mittanian people, rather than just with their king. This same idea continues into the next paragraph, which calls on all the people of both lands to overcome their old hostilities towards one another: "In the future... the Hittites shall not do evil to the Mittanians; [the Mittanians] shall not do evil to the Hittites." Obviously the treaty could not have been confirmed by every subject of each king, but the kings (especially Shattiwaza) had the obligation to persuade their subjects of the rightness of the treaty, and presumably to prosecute any rebels who tried to undermine it.

This same paragraph specified that "as someone is the enemy of the land of Mittani, [he shall be] the enemy [of Hatti]" and vice versa, and that they would also share alliances. A missing section of the treaty discussed their military obligations to one another. Often in treaties the two states agreed both to defend one another against external enemies and to come to one another's aid in the case of internal rebellion; this might have been the case here.

The next paragraph, about fugitives, is broken in some annoying spots. The preserved words of the first sentence are "If a fugitive flees from Hatti... return...." The second sentence is "If a fugitive of the land of Mittani,... the King of Hatti will not seize him and return him." Presumably this was not a situation in which the kings had the same obligations to one another—in the first sentence the missing words almost certainly noted that the king of Mittani had to return Hittite fugitives to Hatti, whereas we see that the Hittite king did not have to return Mittanian fugitives to Mittani. Fugitives seem to have been a big problem in the ancient Near East—just about every peace treaty that has been found included a prominent clause about them. Presumably, if someone had broken the law in his own land and feared arrest or private retribution, he would often try to cross into another kingdom and seek protection there. Allies did not allow this; it was a sign of hostility to harbor fugitives from another state. Hatti's insistence on keeping Mittanian fugitives doesn't imply that Suppiluliuma would provide a safe haven for such men, who "will belong to Hatti." Instead, it implies that their trials would take place there at some sort of Mittanian embassy in Hatti, called here "the household which Prince Shattiwaza is establishing in Hatti," which would take charge of the fugitives.

A long section of the Hittite-Mittanian treaty was taken up with clearly designating the borders between the two lands. This made the Euphrates the new western frontier of Mittani, awarding all the former Mittanian lands to the west of the river to Suppiluliuma's son, Piyassili, the ruler of Carchemish. This must have been a tough concession for Shattiwaza; in the peace talks he might have tried demanding more. These were contested lands but they had long been subject to Mittani and no doubt many of the people there were still strongly attached to Mittani. There were Hurrian leaders from this region, like Aki-Teshup, who had fled to Babylon when the Hittites took control of northern Syria (if he was still alive)—leaders who might try instigating rebellion against Hatti. But Shattiwaza had little bargaining power. According to the treaty, Piyassili was owed these lands because "he crossed the Euphrates with Shattiwaza and penetrated to the city of Irrite." Without Suppiluliuma and Piyassili, Shattiwaza would have had no kingdom at all.

The final provision confirmed the fact that Shattiwaza was not a great king: "You shall not again act independently, nor transgress your treaty, nor shall you seek further territories for yourselves." The clause reiterated the fact that Shattiwaza was now on a par with Suppiluliuma's son, Piyassili, the king of Carchemish, with whom he had defeated Shuttarna: "Piyassili and Shattiwaza are bound to one another in brotherhood."

Apparently the two "brothers" would meet in person from time to time; Shattiwaza could summon Piyassili to one of his cities, and Piyassili could summon Shattiwaza to Carchemish. Their capitals were close enough to one another that they didn't need to depend only on messengers to communicate between them. This would have been an advantage; the two men had fought side by side and were now brothers-in-law and brother kings, both of them subject to Suppiluliuma. Strategizing together in person would have been much more productive than using messengers. But each man would be vulnerable when he left his land, especially given the old animosities between Hatti and Mittani, so the treaty added clauses to protect them, both from one another and from others. When Piyassili came to Mittani, "Shat-tiwaza shall not plan any evil against Piyassili, his brother, and he may not cause another man to undertake evil against Piyassili," and when Shattiwaza came to Carchemish, "Piyassili shall not plan any evil matter or malicious-ness against Shattiwaza."

As Shattiwaza considered the situation, perhaps in the evenings when the men took a break from negotiations and he could pause to reflect, he must have concluded that the treaty was a good one, even though he would end up much less powerful than his father Tushratta had been. At least Mittani would have survived, if diminished in size and power, and Shattiwaza would be its rightful king.

Once the negotiations were complete, the treaty needed to be confirmed. This confirmation and pledge to uphold the treaty took the form of a solemn oath sworn by both kings before a long list of divine witnesses—gods and goddesses of both lands. It seems that the gods were "summoned" to "stand and listen and be witnesses." This presumably took place in a temple of one of the Hittite gods, and the room must have seemed crowded, filled to the raf-ters with gods (though not all their physical statues could have been present). Seventy deities of Hatti were named, invoked alongside all the other unnamed ones: "the mountain-dweller gods, the mercenary gods, all the male deities and female deities of Hatti, the male deities and female deities of the land of Kizzuwatna, the deities of the Netherworld," and, just for good measure, all the natural features of the land: "the mountains, the rivers, the sea, the Euphrates, heaven and earth, the winds, the clouds." Representing Mittani were twenty-five named local gods as well as groups of ancient Indo-Aryan Mitra-gods, Varuna-gods, and Nasatya-gods, "the deities of heaven, and the deities of earth." Just about every god of both lands could be subsumed under the many categories of gods listed here. Together, these gods would—accord-ing to the beliefs of both parties—enforce the treaty.[17]

After the oath had been sworn, duplicates were made of the tablets and taken to great temples of the two lands for safekeeping. One was "deposited before the Sun-goddess of Arinna" in Hatti, "since the Sun-goddess of Arinna governs kingship and queenship." Another was taken to Mittani and "depos-ited before the Storm-god, Lord of the *kurinnu* of Kahat." Shattiwaza was required to assemble his people on a regular basis to remind them (and him-self) of the terms of the treaty: "It shall be read repeatedly, for ever and ever, before the king of the land of Mittani and before the Hurrians." Obviously he couldn't bring all the Hurrians to one place, but his officials and governors needed to hear it. No one could break the tablet, change its words, or hide it, because the gods knew its contents.

The lists of gods were followed by a curse on not only Shattiwaza but on all his people, if they broke the oath. The gods would "destroy you [and] you Hurrians, together with your land, your wives, and your possessions." The people would "have no progeny," and would live in "poverty and destitution," while Shattiwaza himself would be subject to the gods' particular ire: "they shall overthrow your throne.... shall snap you off like a reed...you shall be eradicated. The ground shall be ice, so that you will slip. The ground of your land shall be a marsh...so that you will certainly sink and be unable to cross. You, Shattiwaza, and the Hurrians shall be the enemies of the Thousand Gods. They shall defeat you."

There was no equivalent paragraph cursing Suppululiuma if he broke the oath; the onus was entirely on Shattiwaza. Even in the version of the treaty that was supposedly in Shattiwaza's own words, there is no discussion of penalties if the Hittites didn't keep their end of the bargain. Instead, Shattiwaza called even more disasters upon himself and his kingdom if he broke the treaty:

> as a fir tree when it is felled has no more shoots, like this fir tree let me, Shattiwaza, together with any other wife whom I might take, and us Hurrians...like the fir tree have no progeny. As the water of a drainpipe never returns to its place, let us, like the water of a drain-pipe not return to our place.... If we do not observe this treaty and oath, the gods, lords of the oath, shall destroy us.

There was just one small group of people that was exempted (and very clearly exempted) from this curse: Suppululiuma's daughter and her children with Shattiwaza. It was only "your progeny by another wife whom you might take" who would be "eradicated from the earth"; Shattiwaza's progeny by the Hittite princess would be safe.[18] After all, Suppululiuma would hardly have agreed to an oath that might have caused death and suffering to his daughter and grandchildren.

But if Shattiwaza and the Hurrians obeyed the treaty, then everything would be fine—better than ever, in fact—because the gods would "protect you, Shattiwaza, together with your wife, [daughter of the King] of Hatti, her sons and grandsons, and you Hurrians, together with your wives and your sons, and [together with your land]." Mittani would "prosper and expand," and Shattiwaza would be accepted as the legitimate king by all his people: "the Hurrians shall accept you for kingship for eternity."[19]

Here is the classic contrast between chaos and order—disobeying the treaty would bring upon the Mittanians death, destruction, infertility, loss of authority, and displacement; obeying it would bring them prosperity, fertility, and legitimate authority for the king. The people really believed in the power of the gods to bring this all about; if the oath invoked it, it would happen.

With the conclusion of this treaty, a measure of order was to return to this corner of the Near East, at least for a short while. The kings of Mittani and Hatti were now members of a single family, through marriage and treaty, though no longer as equals. Shattiwaza would obey Suppiluliuma and Suppiluliuma would protect Shattiwaza.

Meanwhile, Suppiluliuma was fighting elsewhere. His second Syrian war raged for over five years. Now that Mittani was in his grasp, Suppiluliuma targeted his anger and aggression at Egypt. He wanted revenge for the death of his son Zannanza. As his son Mursili put it, "My father became hostile, went to Egyptian territory, and attacked Egyptian territory. He killed the infantry and chariotry of Egypt."[20] He also fought in numerous Syrian cities, burning many of them before moving on to the next.

Although Suppiluliuma was victorious in his battles against Egyptian states in the Levant, these battles proved to be his own undoing. The Hittite troops brought Egyptian prisoners of war back to Hatti, and those POWs brought with them a disease that spread as a plague throughout the land. "[T]he plague broke out among the prisoners of war, and they [began] to die in great numbers. When the prisoners of war were carried off to Hatti, the prisoners of war introduced the plague into Hatti, and from that time people have been dying in Hatti."

We don't know which plague this was, but it killed indiscriminately, rich and poor alike. The Hittites had no concept how diseases spread, of course, so the people quite reasonably concluded that they were being punished by the gods.

### The Death of Suppiluliuma

Then, in 1322 BCE, the seemingly undefeatable King Suppiluliuma himself died of this plague, as did the crown prince who succeeded him for less than a year. Mursili II, a royal prince who had never been in line for the throne, became king and watched helplessly as the plague ravaged the Hittite empire for over twenty years.[21]

When, in desperation, Mursili II asked the gods what had brought this plague on his people, he was told by an oracle that it had been caused by his father's actions. Suppiluliuma had broken two oaths, and had therefore incited the wrath of the gods. First he had broken the oath he took to his brother and had him assassinated in order to become king himself, and second, he had broken the oath in the ancient treaty with Egypt, the one that had forged their first alliance over a century before. Mursili wrote that although the Hittites and the Egyptians had been put under oath by the Storm-god of Hatti, the Hittites came to repudiate (the agreement) and suddenly the Hittites transgressed the oath.... It was ascertained (through an oracle) that the cause of the anger of the Storm-god of Hatti, my lord, was the fact that (although) the...deities were in the temple of the Storm-god of Hatti, my lord, the Hittites on their own suddenly transgressed the word (of the oath).

Mursili begged the gods repeatedly for mercy, reminding them that he didn't deserve punishment: "[the sin] did not take place in my time. [Rather, it took place] in the time of my father.... I kneel down to you and [cry out]: 'Have mercy!' Listen to me, O Storm-god, my lord. Let the plague be removed from Hatti." His desperation is evident in the prayers he wrote to the gods to try to get them to put an end to the misery. "I cannot master the turmoil of my heart," he wrote. "I can no longer master the anguish of my body." In time, and after tremendous losses suffered by families all across Hatti, the plague diminished.

Mursili II renewed his father's treaties with vassals in northern Syria, receiving the oaths of the kings of Amurru and Ugarit.[22] But in his ninth year on the throne, he had to deal with Egyptian attacks on Amurru, the strategic Syrian kingdom claimed by Hatti that had been subject to both Egypt and Mittani at various times in the past. Mursili II summed up Amurru's troubled history: "It was the king of the land of Hanigalbat (Mittani) who took the land of Amurru away from the king of the land of Egypt, and then my father (Suppiluliuma) defeated the king of the land of Amurru."[23]

During this crisis, envoys still passed back and forth between the Egyptian and Hittite courts. King Haremhab of Egypt (a former army general whose name was spelled as 'Arma'a in cuneiform) at one point sent his envoy Zirtaya to Hattusa with a message for Mursili II, but Mursili II would not let him return home. King Haremhab then sent another messenger with an angry letter to the Hittite king: "Since Zirtaya is my servant, [giv]e h[im back to me]!" Mursili was unmoved; one of his vassals, a man named Tetti, was being detained in Egypt. He would hold Zirtaya until that vassal was returned. "An[d you]?" He wrote back. "Wh[y] did you [not g]ive Tetti back to me?" Just as in the earlier Amarna period, the kings were using detention of messengers to try to force one another's hands. This time it seems to have resulted in a diplomatic stalemate: "Then 'Arma'a remained totally quiet, [and] said [nothing] at all! [So] we were [not] on good terms with one another. We were [not] at all on [goo]d terms."[24] Each king held a valuable hostage in his court and was unwilling to make any concessions. The relationship between the two great powers of Egypt and Hatti was worse than ever.

In the meantime, Mursili II was unable to hold onto Mittani. Its king, Shattiwaza, took advantage of the crisis caused by the plague in Hatti and abandoned his position as a "son" of the Hittite king. But this didn't mark a new era of greatness for Mittani. Shattiwaza's successor, Shattuara I, took on his eastern neighbor, Assyria, "becoming hostile" and doing "evil things," in the words of the Assyrian king, Adad-nirari. This did not, however, result in Mittani regaining control over Assyria. Instead, Adad-nirari wrote that "I captured him [the king of Mittani] and brought him to my city Ashur.... I made him take an oath and let him go back home. Annually, as long as he lived I received his tribute in Ashur."[25] For the next few decades Mittani was regularly ravaged by the Assyrian army, probably because the Mittanian kings repeatedly rebelled against Assyria and attempted to regain their independence. By the mid-thirteenth century, Mittani was gone. What had been its western half (west of the Euphrates) was part of the Hittite empire, and what had been the eastern half (east of the Euphrates) was part of Assyria.[26]

## The Brotherhood of Great Kings in Harmony Again

Mursili II died around 1282, but the hostility between Egypt and Hatti didn't die with him. Throughout the first decades of the thirteenth century they regularly sparred over territory. Within the borders of the empires, though, the lands were prospering. Ugarit, Amurru, and Carchemish flourished in Syria under Hittite rule, and the Hittites built a new capital city called Tarhuntassa, closer to the center of their kingdom.

Egypt was in the capable hands of a new dynasty of pharaohs—the Nineteenth—all descended from a general who had taken the name Seti I. One remarkable pharaoh dominated almost the whole of the thirteenth century. This was Ramesses II, whose sixty-seven-year reign was one of the highpoints of Egyptian history. He too built a new capital city, and named it Per-Ramesse after himself.

In 1275 BCE, the armies of Egypt and Hatti finally clashed. Thousands of soldiers on both sides fought near the city of Kadesh, which had so often been the site of hostilities. This time the great kings themselves led their armies. Ramesses II was enormously proud of this battle and often recounted it in texts and images in Egypt. Oddly enough, though, he doesn't seem to have won—Kadesh remained in Hittite hands. If Ramesses didn't actually lose the battle, then one can only conclude that the kings fought to a draw. This proved to be a good outcome for both Egypt and Hatti. Convinced that neither could hope to overcome the other, they eventually agreed to a peace treaty. Messengers and ambassadors traveled back and forth between Hatti and Egypt negotiating all the provisions, just as they had done so many times before in Near Eastern history. Sixteen years after the battle, the kings swore oaths to abide by the treaty. After another thirteen years, in 1245 BCE, a marriage was arranged between a Hittite princess and Ramesses II.[27] The princess was dispatched for Egypt with a large retinue and an extravagant dowry, and these two great powers were at peace once more.

The Hittite kings settled comfortably into this new, relatively peaceful era. They were less belligerent than Suppiluliuma I had been. They kept up a regular correspondence with the other great kings—the kings of Babylonia and Egypt—just as before. Many of their letters have been found in the excavations at Hattusa.[28] Ambassadors had the same responsibilities, the kings once again sent gifts and complained about any appearance of unequal treatment, and princesses traveled long distances to marry their fathers' allies.

The letters that they sent one another were a little more worldly-wise, though, than the Amarna letters had been. The kings were now much more likely to mention their armies and to worry about possible military threats while also still fretting about gifts and marriages. Assyria was not quite a full member of the brotherhood, perhaps because its kings were much more aggressive than the others. When an Assyrian king wrote to the Hittite king calling him "brother," he received a very cold response: "What is this, brotherhood? For what reason should I write to you about brotherhood?...Do those who are not on good terms customarily write to one another about brotherhood?.... you shall not keep writing to me [about brotherhood] and great kingship. [It is not my] wish."[29] But for the most part the kings were able to keep Assyria in check and to enjoy the benefits of their alliance. As a Hittite king wrote to the king of Babylon, "When your father and I established friendly relations and became affectionate brothers, we did not become brothers for a single day. Did we not establish brotherhood and friendly relations in perpetuity?"[30] In the end, the real victor was not any one of the great powers, it was the idea of brotherhood.

# Epilogue

To men and women living in the mid-thirteenth century BCE, civilization must have seemed just as old and established at it seems to us today, perhaps even more so. To their minds, the origins of cities had not been thousands of years in the past (as they actually were) but hundreds of thousands of years. The Sumerian King List told them that the earliest kings had ruled for 385,200 years—and that was before the mythical flood. They believed that more than 30,745 additional years passed between the flood and the reign of Sargon of Akkad.[1]

For as long as anyone could remember, messengers had traveled between the capitals of the great kingdoms, and between the lesser ones as well. They would have been a familiar sight on the roads: men of different nationalities walking together, accompanied by armed guards, and always keeping a cuneiform letter from one king to another safely stowed among their belongings. Sometimes they traveled with horses or chariots, sometimes with large and ostentatious gifts, sometimes even with princesses and hundreds of attendants. The messengers could be simple couriers or esteemed high officials. They made their journeys during peacetime and during war. They were always needed.

The earliest records of "brotherhood" and diplomatic missions coincide with the earliest records of organized warfare, as though the two were, at least initially, inextricably linked. (People had, of course, been fighting for long before writing was invented, but state-organized warfare was something different.) Having formal allies seems to have become essential to all ancient kings. Some explanations for the brotherhood of kings that emerged have been posed here, such as the economic benefit of obtaining luxury goods through exchange, the pragmatic desire to have as many allies as possible, and the way in which family relations (even fictional ones) created order out of chaos. Other possible explanations are beyond the scope of this work, though interesting to wonder about. Evolutionary psychologists might say that theirs was an example of "kinship selection"—that one way to explain benevolent behavior towards people who were really strangers was that it became necessary to see them as relatives.[2] And perhaps, speculating further, the lavish gift-giving that characterized the relationships could be analyzed not only as an exchange of luxury goods that increased each king's wealth but as a demonstration of power. Each king tried to make himself look good (and the other kings look less good) by giving the biggest and most expensive gifts. Whatever the reason, the urge to join the community of brothers was undeniably strong.

Initially, the kings seem to have used diplomacy to accumulate allies in order to fight against one another, as well as to acquire luxury goods that weren't available at home. The desire for luxury goods didn't change, but, for a few centuries in the late second millennium BCE, peace and brotherhood, not military strength, became the goals of diplomacy. During the Amarna period, the letters were mostly about gifts, ambassadors, and marriages, with almost no discussion of war at all. This is probably, in part, because the lands of the great kings were too far away from one another for the types of constant battles that took place in Hammurabi's time. But diplomacy had also been separated from war. The peace treaties seem to have been effective, so that the kingdoms were usually at peace.

Meanwhile, another change had taken place. Distant lands came in contact with one another first through indirect trade, then through direct trade, then through diplomatic contact, and finally as treaty-bound allies. For example, the peoples of Anatolia first extracted obsidian from their volcanic landscape and distributed it (presumably through middlemen) to Mesopotamia and other regions. Later, in the early second millennium BCE, the Assyrian merchants traveled to Anatolia and set up direct trade relationships. Later still, in the sixteenth century BCE, the Babylonian king Agum-kakrime negotiated with the Anatolian Hittites for the return of the statues of the Babylonian city gods, and by the Amarna Age, Mesopotamian princesses married Hittite kings, treaties confirmed their alliances, and envoys traveled back and forth between the courts.

Over time, more and more of the world (at least the Near Eastern world) was seen as familiar and predictable in its behavior. The more foreigners one saw on the roads—traders, envoys, itinerant craftsmen, translators, couriers, and so on—the less alien they must have seemed. Artists adopted motifs from other lands, and the royal families became increasingly international. Everyone involved in this system seems to have benefited in some way.

It all eventually came to an end during the twelfth century BCE, but not because of a tyrant managing to overthrow the diplomatic system, or even because of the aggressiveness of the Assyrian kingdom. All the major powers, one after another, fell or went into decline. Mycenaean and Hittite cities were abandoned or burned, Ugarit and other Canaanite cities were destroyed, Kassite Babylonia was conquered by the Elamites, the Assyrian kingdom shrank in size and importance, and even New Kingdom Egypt eventually collapsed. The cause of this crisis has been the subject of many books. Suffice to say that it was probably largely natural in origin—climate change, famine, or disease (or a combination of all three) set off a series of events that proved unstoppable.

The brotherhood of great kings didn't recover. Small, relatively weak kingdoms dominated the Near East for more than two hundred years. And then, in the late tenth century BCE, Assyrian kings of the so-called Neo-Assyrian period began to create a new kind of empire, one that aimed to control the whole known world. They fought almost constantly and had no desire to acknowledge any other kingdom as an equal as they swallowed up much of the Near East. Other powers that had not been conquered by the Assyrians did, however, continue to stay in diplomatic contact with one another and sometimes tried to use diplomatic means to deal with Assyria itself. For example, the Egyptian kings sent gifts to the Assyrian kings in the eighth century BCE and later established an alliance with Lydia.[3] The new era of empires had little room for expressions of love and friendship among kings. Just one great power existed at a time, and it dominated all the rest. First it was Assyria, then Babylonia, then Persia, then Macedonian Greece, then Rome. But even these great powers inspired those threatened by them to form alliances and to communicate through ambassadors; a group of Greek states standing up against Persia seem to have communicated with Lydians and Egyptians in the sixth century BCE. Many other examples could be cited. Chances are they used many of the same diplomatic strategies that had been used in earlier centuries.[4]

This book has barely scratched the surface of its topic. Each event, city, and character touched on could be expanded into an entire book, and, indeed, each of them has been studied and written about by a great many scholars. The materials from Ebla, Mari, Nuzi, Ugarit, Alalakh, Amarna, and so on are the topics of vast bibliographies of studies, written over decades. The interpretations given here are not the only ones. As with any field of history, scholars can use the same evidence to argue for somewhat different conclusions. In exploring the ancient Near East, historians have plenty of room to disagree with one another because there are so many gaps in our documentation. To get a sense of the puzzles faced by ancient Near Eastern scholars, one could imagine a future historian trying to understand the influences and connections between the American and French Revolutions. Now imagine that same historian working on the same topic but with little evidence for the exact dates of either event, no list of the order of the American presidents, and uncertainty as to which revolution happened first. It would not be an easy task.

In coming years, the narrative laid out in this book no doubt will prove wrong in some places, maybe many. That is one occupational hazard, but also a great source of excitement, in writing ancient Near Eastern history. Excavations take place every year, and the finds sometimes upset long-held assumptions. For example, in the last few weeks of writing this book (but, fortunately, not too late to be included) came word of the late Old Babylonian letter fragment found at a Hyksos site in Egypt, showing that written contacts between the two lands took place considerably earlier than had been thought. Such dramatic discoveries happen all the time. It's something of an act of hubris to publish a reconstruction of the ancient events based on today's knowledge when we will no doubt know a great deal more from tomorrow's excavations. Still, the importance of the material and of the era make it worth the risk.

Perhaps future excavations in Syria will provide us with a list of Mittanian kings and the lengths of their reigns, which might well reveal that the estimated dates given here are wrong. Perhaps a treaty between Egypt and Mittani will materialize that will demonstrate for certain who was the first Egyptian king to agree to join the international diplomatic community. Perhaps cuneiform letters will be found in Greece that show one of its kings to have been a full member of the brotherhood of great kings. Perhaps an actual copy of the letter from the Egyptian queen to Suppiluliuma will give us her name and the name of her husband, thereby resolving that particular dispute. Historians can only look forward to and welcome such finds, even if they prove us wrong in our current hypotheses.

It is also possible that other finds will reveal connections that no one has dared to propose, because of the lack of evidence to date—Mittanian conquests far beyond what had been thought, maybe, or Mesopotamian traders physically traveling to Afghanistan, or marriages between the dynasties of Ebla and Hamazi. These seem highly unlikely now (and may remain so), but one suspects that the ancient peoples traveled much more and had more contacts with distant lands than we currently know about.

For the ancient Near East, scholars have no ancient storyteller to provide us with a big narrative, in the way that Herodotus and Thucydides did for ancient Greek history or that Livy, Tacitus, and others did for Roman history. Had this person existed, he might have told us which victories the Babylonians believed were their greatest, which Syrian kings treated their allies evenhandedly, how the Egyptians coped with the religious reforms of the Amarna Age, and so on. But even without the guidance of an ancient writer who lived through the events, it is still clear that there are some big stories to be told about the ancient Near East. One of them is the topic of this book: how the people of the ancient lands discovered one another, traded with one another, sometimes fought one another, and resolved their differences to mutual satisfaction.

Over the course of the centuries that separate the ancient world from our own, diplomacy reemerged, either reborn from the embers of the original Near Eastern system or entirely reinvented. The basic ideals were the same: ambassadors traveled and negotiated tirelessly in order to bring leaders closer together, while kings arranged marriages and sent extravagant gifts to one another, and sometimes, as a result, avoided war.[5]

The Near East is often described as the birthplace of law, home to the earliest cities, and the "cradle of civilization." It was also home to the first diplomats and to the first kings to discover the benefits of peaceful coexistence.

# Abbreviations

| | |
|---|---|
| A. | Registration number for texts found at Mari |
| *AAAS* | *Annales Archéologiques Arabes Syriennes* |
| AHK | Texts in Edel 1994 |
| *AJA* | *American Journal of Archaeology* |
| *AJSL* | *American Journal of Semitic Languages* |
| AO | Tablets in the collection of the Louvre |
| AOAT | Alter Orient und Altes Testament |
| ARET | Texts from Ebla published in the series Archivi Reali di Ebla, Testi |
| ARM | Texts from Mari published in the series Archives Royales de Mari |
| *ARRIM* | *Annual Review of the Royal Inscriptions of Mesopotamia* |
| *BASOR* | *Bulletin of the American Schools of Oriental Research* |
| *CAD* | *Chicago Assyrian Dictionary* |
| EA | Designation of tablets in the Amarna archive as listed in Moran 1992 |
| CUSAS | Cornell University Studies in Assyriology and Sumerology |
| HDT | Texts in Beckman 1999 |
| *JAOS* | *Journal of the American Oriental Society* |
| *JCS* | *Journal of Cuneiform Studies* |
| *JEA* | *Journal of Egyptian Archaeology* |
| *JESHO* | *Journal of the Economic and Social History of the Orient* |
| *JNES* | *Journal of Near Eastern Studies* |

| | |
|---|---|
| KBo | Texts in *Keilschrifttexte aus Boghazköi* |
| Ki | Kish texts in Cooper 1986 |
| KUB | Texts in *Keilschrifturkunden aus Boghazköi* |
| La | Lagash texts in Cooper 1986 |
| LAPO | Littératures anciennes du Proche-Orient |
| LEM | Texts in Michalowski 1993 |
| LH | Laws of Hammurabi |
| MAL | Middle Assyrian Laws |
| MARI | *Mari, annales de recherches interdisciplinaires* (Paris: Éditions Recherche sur les Civilisations, 1982–1997) |
| *NABU* | *Nouvelles Assyriologiques Brèves et Utilitaires* |
| RAI | Rencontre Assyriologique Internationale |
| RIM | Royal Inscriptions of Mesopotamia |
| *RLA* | *Reallexikon der Assyriologie* |
| SCCNH | Studies on the Civilization and Culture of Nuzi and the Hurrians |
| SH | Registration number for texts found at Shemshara |
| *SMEA* | *Studi Micenei ed Egeo-Anatolici* |
| Sumer 14 | Texts in Goetze 1958 |
| TM | Registration number for texts found at Ebla |
| UET | Ur Excavations, Texts |
| Ur | Ur texts in Cooper 1986 |
| Urk IV | Texts in Sethe and Helck, 1955–1958 |
| VAT | Tablets in the Staatliche Museen zu Berlin |
| *ZA* | *Zeitschrift für Assyriologie und verwandte Gebiete* |

# Notes

INTRODUCTION

1. Arielle P. Kozloff, Betsy M. Bryan, et al., *Egypt's Dazzling Sun: Amenhotep III and His World* (Cleveland: Cleveland Museum of Fine Arts, 1992), 59.

2. Dominique Collon, *First Impressions: Cylinder Seals in the Ancient Near East* (London: British Museum Publications, 1987), 62–65.

3. EA 23: William L. Moran (ed. and trans.), *The Amarna Letters* (Baltimore and London: Johns Hopkins University Press, 1992), 61.

4. EA 23: Moran 1992, 61.

5. EA 23: Moran 1992, 61–62.

6. This sentence is not phrased as a question in the original (there were no question marks in cuneiform) and could have been read instead as "Shaushka is a goddess of mine, she is not a goddess of my brother." If so, Tushratta might have been reminding Amenhotep III of the need to send her back to him: Carlo Zaccagnini, "Patterns of Mobility among Ancient Near Eastern Craftsmen," *JNES* 42 (1983), 255.

7. Piotr Bienkowski and Alan Millard (eds.), *Dictionary of the Ancient Near East* (Philadelphia: University of Pennsylvania Press, 2000), 15.

8. A. H. Sayce, "The Discovery of the Tel El-Amarna Tablets," *AJSL* 33 (1917), 89–90.

9. Kofi A. Annan, "The Meaning of International Community," United Nations Information Service, December 30, 1999. Available at http://www.unis.unvienna.org/unis/pressrels/1999/sg2478.html.

10. See the section on Further Reading for a discussion of some of the major scholars and their works in this field.

CHAPTER ONE

1. Lucio Milano, "Ebla: A Third Millennium City-State in Ancient Syria," in *Civilizations of the Ancient Near East,* vol. 2, edited by Jack M. Sasson et al. (New York: Scribner's, 1995), 1226.

2. Paolo Matthiae, "Ebla and the Early Urbanization of Syria," in *Art of the First Cities: The Third Millennium* B.C. *from the Mediterranean to the Indus,* edited by Joan Aruz (New Haven and London: Yale University Press, 2003), 165; Alfonso Archi, "Ebla Texts," in *The Oxford Encyclopedia of Archaeology in the Near East,* vol. 2, edited by Eric M. Meyers (Oxford and New York: Oxford University Press, 1997), 185.

3. Alfonso Archi, "Trade and Administrative Practice: The Case of Ebla," *Altorientalische Forschungen* 20/1 (1993), 47.

4. Milano 1995, 1225–1226; Archi 1993, 46–47.

5. Archi 1993, 49; Archi 1997, 186.

6. Paolo Matthiae, "Ebla," in Meyers 1997, vol. 2, 180.

7. Although houses have not yet been excavated at Ebla for this period, the layout of the city probably resembled that of Mari during the same era, for which see Jean-Cl. Margueron, *Mari: Metropole de l'Euphrate au IIIe et au debut du IIe millénaire av. J.-C.* (Paris: Picard, 2004), chaps 8 and 9.

8. Matthiae 2003, 166 and fig. 44.

9. LEM 96: Piotr Michalowski, *Letters from Early Mesopotamia* (Atlanta, Ga.: Scholars Press, 1993), 64. The letter was written to King Shulgi of Ur in the twenty-first century BCE, around three centuries after Irkab-damu, and describes Apillasha, a high commissioner. Presumably, a king's appearance would have been even more spectacular when he greeted visitors.

10. Aruz 2003, objects 115a–f, pp. 175–177.

11. Aruz 2003, object 114, p. 174.

12. For an image of this statue, see Aruz 2003, object 88, pp. 148–149; distance from Mari to Ebla: Aruz 2003, 178.

13. Aruz 2003, object 115c, p. 176.

14. Amalia Catagnoti, "Ebla," in Raymond Westbrook, *A History of Ancient Near Eastern Law,* vol. 1 (Leiden and Boston: Brill, 2003), 233; Alfonso Archi and Maria Giovanna Biga, "A Victory over Mari and the Fall of Ebla," *JCS* 55 (2003), 9.

15. This description is based on two small statues of royal women, probably queens, which were recently excavated in Ebla. See Marco Merola, "Royal Goddesses of a Bronze Age State," *Archaeology* 61/1 (2008). Available at http://www.archaeology.org/0801/trenches/goddesses.html.

16. Matthiae 2003, 166–167. For the total number of tablets: Daniel C. Snell, "Syria-Palestine in Recent Research," in *Current Issues in the History of the Ancient Near East,* edited by Mark W. Chavalas (Claremont, Calif.: Regina Books, 2007), 123.

17. Matthiae 2003, 166; Archi and Biga 2003, 6–7.

18. Archi and Biga 2003; Archi 2008, 3; see also Piotr Michalowski, "Third Millennium Contacts: Observations on the Relationships between Mari and Ebla," *JAOS* 105 (1985), 297.

19. Archi 1997, 185.

20. Piotr Michalowski, "Sumerian Literature: An Overview," in Sasson et al. 1995, vol. 4, 2281.

21. Michalowski 1995, 2281.

22. Archi 1993, 43.

23. Matthiae 2003, 167.

24. Alfonso Archi, "More on Ebla and Kish," in *Eblaitica,* vol. 1. edited by C. H. Gordon et al. (Winona Lake, Ind.: Eisenbrauns, 1987), 128.

25. Alfonso Archi, "The Royal Archives of Ebla," in *Ebla to Damascus: Art and Archaeology of Ancient Syria,* edited by Harvey Weiss (Seattle and London: University of Washington Press, 1985), 142–144.

26. Milano 1995, 1222.

27. ARET VII 115: Archi and Biga 2003, 4.

28. TM.75.G.1405: Archi and Biga 2003, 5.

29. Some southern Mesopotamian cities had fortification walls by 3100 BCE: Susan Pollock, *Ancient Mesopotamia: The Eden that Never Was* (Cambridge and New York: Cambridge University Press, 1999), 5. The Syrian site of Terqa had a three-ring fortification system almost seventy feet thick by 2700 BCE: Mark W. Chavalas, "Terqa and the Kingdom of Khana," *Biblical Archaeologist* 59/2 (1996), 93.

30. Archi 1997, 185.

31. The text of the grant can be found in Milano 1995, 1227; Archi and Biga 2003, 10.

32. William W. Hallo, "The Road to Emar," *JCS* 18 (1964), 57–88. The latter route was described in an itinerary from a later period. It was a longer journey (around 394 miles rather than around 260 miles straight down the river), but it went around the region controlled by Mari, so it might have been used by the Ebla kings when Mari was hostile.

33. The reign of Enna-Dagan of Mari, who wrote the letter, fell almost entirely within the reign of Irkab-damu of Ebla: Archi and Biga 2003, 4, 6.

34. This is known as the Enna-Dagan letter: Michalowski, 1993, text 3, pp. 14–18; Archi and Biga 2003, 1.

35. Milano 1995, 1226; Archi 1997, 185–186; Archi and Biga 2003, 2.

36. Archi and Biga 2003, 3.

37. Archi and Biga 2003, 10.

38. Archi and Biga 2003, 10.

39. LEM 2: Michalowski 1993, 13–14. The location of Hamazi is not certain (Michalowski 1993, 13). The city of Kish was thought to have been occupied by Hamazi in the twenty-fifth century (Petr Charvát, "The Kish Evidence and the Emergence of States in Mesopotamia," *Current Anthropology* 22 [1981], 687). But an Early Dynastic king who "vanquished Hamazi" proves not to have been from Kish (Ki 6 note 2: Jerrold S. Cooper, *Presargonic Inscriptions. Sumerian and Akkadian Royal Inscriptions* I, The American Oriental Society Translation Series, vol. 1 [New Haven: American Oriental Society, 1986], 21)—he is unknown from any other inscription. In any event, Hamazi is usually thought to have been to the northeast of Mesopotamia, perhaps about the same distance from Ebla as Kish. Others put it in northern Iran (William H. Shea, "The Form and Significance of the Eblaite Letter to Hamazi," *Oriens Antiquus* 23 [1984],

143; Raymond Cohen, "Reflections on the New Global Diplomacy: Statecraft 2500 BC to 2000 AD," in *Innovation in Diplomatic Practice,* edited Jan Melissen [New York: St. Martin's, 1999], 3). But it's possible that the letter refers to another city by the name of Hamazi that was closer to Ebla. A much later document mentions a governor of Hamazi along with gods who were worshiped in the region near Ebla: Maria Giovanna Biga, review of Marcel Sigrist, *Neo-Sumerian Texts in the Royal Ontario Museum,* vol. 1: *The Administration at Drehem, JAOS* 121 (2001), 168.

40. Michalowski 1985, 294.

41. Cohen 1999, 3; Shea 1984, 1556; Bertrand Lafont, "International Relations in the Ancient Near East: The Birth of a Complete Diplomatic System," *Diplomacy and Statecraft* 12/1 (2001), 40.

42. LEM 2: Michalowski 1993, 13–14.

43. For example, Cohen 1999, 3.

44. Aruz 2003, 239.

45. Shea 1984, 154–155.

46. "The Curse of Agade": James B. Pritchard (ed.), *Ancient Near Eastern Texts Relating to the Old Testament* (Princeton, N.J.: Princeton University Press, 1969), 650.

47. "*abu* A" in CAD A, vol. 1, 67–73. For an overview of the family metaphors used between allies see Mario Liverani, "The Great Powers' Club," in Cohen and Westbrook 2000, 18–19.

48. Raymond Westbrook, "Introduction," in *A History of Ancient Near Eastern Law,* vol. 1, edited by Raymond Westbrook (Leiden and Boston: Brill, 2003), 83; Raymond Westbrook, "International Law in the Amarna Age," in Cohen and Westbrook 2000, 29–30.

49. "*ahu* A, B" in CAD A, vol. 1, 195–210.

50. Jerrold Cooper, "International Law in the Third Millennium," in Westbrook 2003, 245; Benjamin R. Foster, "Water under the Straw: Peace in Mesopotamia," in *War and Peace in the Ancient World,* edited by Kurt A. Raaflaub (Blackwell, 2007), 67; Archi and Biga 2003, 10; Maria Giovanna Biga and Francesco Pomponio, "Elements for a Chronological Division of the Administrative Documentation of Ebla," *JCS* 42 (1990), 199.

51. TM.75.G.2420: E. Sollberger "The So-Called Treaty Between Ebla and 'Ashur.'" *Studi Eblaiti* III 9–10 (1980), 129–147. An image of the tablet can be found in Weiss 1985, catalogue no. 80, p. 171, described on p. 173. An excerpt from the treaty is included in Milano 1995, 1228. See also the discussion in Cohen 1999, 5.

52. One possibility is that it was located at Tell Chuera, which features a major city from this era, with a substantial palace: Archi and Biga 2003, 10; Winfried Orthmann, "Tell Chuera" in Meyers 1997, vol. 1, 491–492.

53. Sollberger 1980, 147.

54. Sollberger 1980, 136, 146.

55. Sollberger 1980, 144.

56. All the remaining quotes from the treaty are from Milano 1995, 1228.

57. Archi and Biga 2003, 10.

58. TM.75.G.2464: Archi and Biga 2003, 10–11.

59. Archi and Biga 2003, 10–11.

60. Cooper 2003, 246.

61. Archi and Biga 2003, 10–11.

62. La 5.3: Cooper 1986, 58; Cooper 2003, 244. For translations and discussions of all the documents associated with this rivalry, see Jerrold S. Cooper, *Reconstructing History from Ancient Inscriptions: The Lagash-Umma Border Conflict* (Malibu, Calif.: Undena, 1981).

63. Ur 5.1: Glenn Magid, "Sumerian Early Dynastic Royal Inscriptions," in Mark W. Chavalas, *The Ancient Near East* (Blackwell, 2006), 6, 10.

64. Magid 2006, 6.

65. Béatrice André-Salvini, "Tello (Ancient Girsu)," in Aruz 2003, 69.

66. Cooper 1983, 46. See discussion in Gary Beckman, "Hittite Treaties and the Development of the Cuneiform Treaty Tradition," in *Der deuteronomistischen Geschichtswerke: Redaktions- und religionsgeschichtliche Perspektiven zur "Deuteronomismus"-Diskussion in Tora und Vorderen Propheten,* edited by Markus Witte et al. (Berlin and New York: Walter de Gruyter, 2006), 292.

67. La 5.1: Cooper 1986, 55.

68. M. G. Biga, "Femmes de la famille royale d'Ebla," in *La femme dans le Proche-Orient antique,* RAI 33, edited by J.-M. Durand (Paris: A.D.P.F. 1987), 41–47; Catagnoti 2003, 232–233.

69. Biga 1987, 45.

70. Biga 1987, 47.

71. Biga 1987, 45.

72. Catagnoti 2003, 232–233.

73. TM.75.G.2283: Archi and Biga 2003, 28. It's possible that these items were a gift from the king of Kish rather than from Ebla: Catagnoti 2003, 233.

74. Catagnoti 2003, 232.

75. Archi and Biga 2003, 28.

76. Biga 1987, 46.


CHAPTER TWO

1. Archi 1993, 49.

2. Archi 1993, 54–55.

3. Archi 1993, 49–50.

4. For example, a human-headed bull: Aruz 2003, object 111.

5. Steatite: for example, Aruz 2003, objects 108, 109, 111. Lapis lazuli: for example, Matthiae 2003, 166; Aruz 2003, objects 116a–c.

6. Aruz 2003, objects 116a–c.

7. Archi and Biga 2003, 29–35.

8. For a full description of these objects, with images, see Aruz 2003, 139–147.

9. P. R. S. Moorey, *Ur 'of the Chaldees': A Revised and Updated Edition of Sir Leonard Woolley's Excavations at Ur* (Ithaca, N.Y.: Cornell University Press, 1982), 124.

10. William W. Hallo, "Women of Sumer," in *The Legacy of Sumer,* edited by Denise Schmandt-Besserat (Malibu, Calif.: Undena, 1976), 28 and n. 41.

11. "Sumerian King List," translated by Piotr Michalowski: Chavalas 2006, 81–85.

12. Gonzalo Rubio, "From Sumer to Babylonia: Topics in the History of Southern Mesopotamia," in Chavalas 2007, 14–15.

13. Christopher Woods, "Bilingualism, Scribal Learning, and the Death of Sumerian," in *Margins of Writing, Origins of Cultures,* Oriental Institute Seminars, 2, edited by Seth L. Sanders (Chicago: Oriental Institute of the University of Chicago, 2006), 101–103.

14. Susan Pollock, "Ur," in Meyers 1997, vol. 5, 289.

15. Woolley believed that the attendants had died willingly, but recent research shows that the deaths were violent: John Noble Wilford, "At Ur, Ritual Deaths That Were Anything but Serene," October 26, 2009.

16. The same board game, known as "twenty squares," was played as far west as Cyprus and to the north in Anatolia: "Board Games" in Joan Aruz (ed.), *Beyond Babylon: Art, Trade, and Diplomacy in the Second Millennium* B.C. (New Haven and London: Yale University Press, 2008), 151.

17. See Moorey's chapter on "The 'Royal' Tombs of the Early Dynastic Period," in Moorey 1982, 51–103.

18. Frances Pinnock, "Ebla and Ur: Exchanges and Contacts between Two Great Capitals of the Ancient Near East," *Iraq* 68 (2006), 85–98.

19. Pinnock 2006, 85–89.

20. Archi 2003, 45, 49.

21. Archi 1993, 49.

22. Carnelian: Aruz 2003, 243. Gold: Aruz 2003, object III, 172–173; D. T. Potts, "The Gulf: Dilmun and Magan," in Aruz 2003, 310. Lapis lazuli: Joan Aruz, "Art and Interconnections in the Third Millennium B.C.," in Aruz 2003, 242; Maurizio Tosi and C. C. Lamberg-Karlovsky, "Pathways Across Eurasia," in Aruz 2003, 347.

23. Hallo 1964, 63.

24. Tosi and Lamberg-Karlovsky 2003, 347.

25. Andrew M. T. Moore, "Syria and the Origins of Agriculture," in Weiss 1985, 55.

26. The land and city of Akkad are also known as Agade and Akkade. Akkad will be used here because it is the most widely used form.

27. "The Sargon Birth Legend," translated by Christopher Morgan: Chavalas 2006, 24.

28. "Inscription of Sargon: Foundation of the Akkadian Empire (2.89)," translated by Burkhart Kienast: William W. Hallo and K. Lawson Younger Jr., *The Context of Scripture,* vol. 2 (Leiden and Boston: Brill, 2003), 243.

29. W. Hinz, "Elams Vertrag mit Naram-Sin von Akkade," *ZA* 58 (1967), 66–96.

30. W. Hinz, "Persia c. 2400–1800 B.C.," in *Cambridge Ancient History,* vol. 1, part 2, ed. I. E. S. Edwards et al. (Cambridge: Cambridge University Press, 1971), 651.

31. "Sargon of Agade," translated by A. Leo Oppenheim: Pritchard 1969, 268.

32. "Curse of Agade," translated by Samuel N. Kramer: Pritchard 1969, 648. Imports from Meluhha: W. Sallaberger, W. and A. Westenholz, *Mesopotamien: Akkade-Zeit und Ur III-Zeit* (Freiburg: Universitätsverlag Freiburg 1999), 102.

33. Potts 2003, 307.

34. Aruz 2003, 239. The civilization is often referred to as Harappan, after a major city, or as the Indus Valley culture. For a discussion of recent scholarship concerning Dilmun, Magan, and Meluhha, see Rubio 2007, 20–22.

35. Jesper Eidem and Flemming Hojlund, "Trade or Diplomacy? Assyria and Dilmun in the Eighteenth Century BC," *World Archaeology* 24/3 (1993), 441–448.

36. Potts 2003, 307.

37. D. T. Potts, "Distant Shores: Ancient Near Eastern Trade with South Asia and Northeast Africa," in Sasson et al. 1995, vol. 3, 1453; Shereen Ratnagar, *Trading Encounters: From the Euphrates to the Indus in the Bronze Age* (New Delhi: Oxford University Press, 2004), 53, 126.

38. This king was named Urnanshe. La 1.2, 1.5. 1.17, 1.20, 1.22–23, 1.25: Cooper 1986, 22–30.

39. Joan Aruz, "'Intercultural Style' Carved Chlorite Objects," in Aruz 2003, 325–345.

40. Eidem and Hojlund 1993, 446.

41. Potts 1995, 1454–1456.

42. Potts 2003, 308.

43. "The standard inscription of Manishtusu," translated by Benjamin Studevent-Hickman: Chavalas 2006, 19. Although Manishtusu didn't name Magan as the enemy, it is likely, based on parallel evidence in the reign of Naram-Sin: Potts 1995, 1455.

44. "The standard inscription of Manishtusu": Chavalas 2006, 19.

45. "The standard inscription of Manishtusu": Chavalas 2006, 19.

46. Van De Mieroop 2007, 67.

47. Benjamin R. Foster, "Naram-Sin in Martu and Magan," *ARRIM* 8 (1990) 25–44; D. T. Potts, "'The Plant for the Heart Grows in Magan...': Redefining Southeastern Arabia's Role in Ancient Western Asia," *Australian Archaeology* 48 (1999), 38.

48. Jonathan Mark Kenoyer, "The Indus Civilization," in Aruz 2003, 378–379.

49. Kenoyer 2003, 393–395.

50. Aruz 2003, 243; D. T. Potts, *Mesopotamian Civilization: The Material Foundations* (London: The Athlone Press, 1997), 265.

51. Rubio 2007, 22; Henri-Paul Francfort, *Fouilles de Shortughaï: Recherches sur l'Asie centrale protohistorique*, vol. 1 (Paris: Diffusion de Boccard, 1989), 392: Pearls have been found at Ashur, Kish, Eshnunna, Abu Salabikh, Nippur, Ur, and Susa.

52. Potts 1997, 264.

53. Potts 1995, 1456; Potts 1997, 257, 260 gives evidence for zebu, water buffalo, and elephants in Mesopotamian art during this era. There is no evidence for how the animals were transported: Sallaberger and Westenholz, 1999, 102.

54. Simo Parpola, Asko Parpola, and Robert H. Brunswig, Jr., "The Meluhha Village: Evidence of Acculturation of Harappan Traders in Late Third Millennium Mesopotamia?" *JESHO* 20/2 (1977), 130. See also Julian Reade, "Assyrian King Lists,

the Royal Tombs of Ur, and Indus Origins," *JNES* 60 (2001), 27–28. Reade believes that the Middle Chronology (used widely, including in this book) is too high and that the dates of the Royal Tombs of Ur should be considerably later than 2500 BCE. The dates of the Indus Valley material are unchanged in his interpretation, however.

55. Kenoyer 2003, 393, object 279.

56. Francfort 1989, 393, 459–460.

57. Ratnagar 2004, 62.

58. Tosi and Lamberg-Karlovsky 2003, 349.

59. Andrew Lawler, "Middle Asia Takes Center Stage," *Science* 317 (2007), 586–590.

60. Parpola et al. 1977, 131.

61. Parpola et al. 1977, 131; Francfort 1989, 391.

62. Aruz 2003, 409, 411.

63. Francfort 1989, 392.

64. Aruz 2003, 241.

65. Aruz 2003, 408.

66. See Dominique Collon, *First Impressions: Cylinder Seals in the Ancient Near East* (London: British Museum Publications, 1987), Seals 95–101, pp. 32–33 for Mesopotamian examples.

67. Aruz 2003, 408, objects 300b and 300c.

68. Francfort 1989, 392.

69. For many examples of cylinder seals from this era, see "Period II: City States 3000–2334 BC," in Collon 1987, 20–31.

70. Tosi and Lamberg-Karlovsky 2003, 348.

71. Examples of lapis lazuli seals from the Early Dynastic period, before Sargon, can be seen in Collon 1987: Seal 52, pp. 22–23; Seals 84, 86, 92, and 93, pp. 30–31.

72. G. Herrmann and P. R. S. Moorey, "Lapislazuli. B. Archäologisch," *RLA* vol. 6 (1980), 490; Ratnagar 2004, 186.

73. Mitchell S. Rothman, "Tepe Gawra," in Meyers 1997, vol. 5, 184; Herrmann and Moorey 490.

74. Francfort 1989, 459.

75. "Enmerkar and the Lord of Aratta," translated by Thorkild Jacobsen, in Hallo and Younger 2003, vol. 1, 548.

76. Carlo Zaccagnini, "Ideological and Procedural Paradigms in Ancient Near Eastern Long Distance Exchanges: The Case of Enmerkar and the Lord of Aratta," *Altorientalische Forschungen* 20/1 (1993), 38; Ratnagar 2004, 191.

77. Zaccagnini 1993, 38–42.

78. Francfort 1989, 394.

79. Michel Al-Maqdissi, "The Development of Trade Routes in the Early Second Millennium B.C.," in Aruz 2008, 42.

80. Peter M. M. G. Akkermans and Glenn M. Schwartz, *The Archaeology of Syria: From Complex Hunter-Gatherers to Early Urban Societies (ca. 16,000–300 BC)* (Cambridge: Cambridge University Press, 2003), 240.

81. Martha Sharp Joukowsky, "Byblos," in Meyers 1997, vol. 1, 391.

82. "The Report of Wenamon": William Kelly Simpson, *The Literature of Ancient Egypt*, 3rd ed. (New Haven and London: Yale University Press, 2003), 119.

83. Matthiae 2003, 166.

84. Gabriella Scandone Matthiae, "Les rapports entre Ebla et l'Égypte à l'Ancien et au Moyen Empire," in *Egyptology at the Dawn of the Twenty-First Century,* vol. 2, edited by Zahi Hawass (Cairo, New York: American University in Cairo Press, 2003) 487–488.

85. Aruz 2003, object 161, p. 253. The missing parts of the inscription were reconstructed based on a duplicate but more complete object found in Saqqara in Egypt. The description in Aruz 2003 gives the name of the last king of Ebla as Ibbi-Zikir, but this was the name of King Ishar-damu's minister: Archi and Biga 2003, 7.

86. Aruz 2003, object 111, pp. 172–173.

87. Scandone Matthiae 2003, 488; Aruz 2003, 241.

88. Robert R. Stieglitz, "Long-Distance Seafaring in the Ancient Near East," *Biblical Archaeologist* 47/3 (1984), 136.

89. Kasia Szpakowska, *Daily Life in Ancient Egypt* (Malden, Mass.: Blackwell, 2008), 132.

90. Beatrix Midant-Reynes, *The Prehistory of Egypt,* translated by Ian Shaw (Malden, Mass.: Blackwell, 2000), 196.

91. Midant-Reynes 2000, 219.

92. Midant-Reynes 2000, 238.

93. Stieglitz 1984, 135.

94. Holly Pittman, "Constructing Context: The Gebel el-Arak Knife: Greater Mesopotamian and Egyptian Interaction in the Late Fourth Millennium B.C.E.," in *The Study of the Ancient Near East in the 21st Century,* edited by Jerrold S. Cooper and Glenn M. Schwartz (Winona Lake, Ind.: Eisenbrauns, 1996), 10. Examples of scholars who believe it to be fake are cited by Midant-Reynes 2000, 238.

95. Pittman 1996, 10.

96. Kathryn A. Bard, "The Emergence of the Egyptian State," in *The Oxford History of Ancient Egypt,* edited by Ian Shaw (Oxford and New York: Oxford University Press, 2000), 66; see p. 55 for a drawing of the tomb painting.

97. Bard 2000, 66.

98. Pittman 1996, 16.

99. For an overview of the Uruk period, see Guillermo Algaze, *The Uruk World System: The Dynamics of Expansion of Early Mesopotamian Civilization* (Chicago: University of Chicago Press, 1993).

100. Pittman 1996, 17.

101. James P. Allen, "Egypt and the Near East in the Third Millennium B.C.," in Aruz 2003, 251.

102. Aruz 2003, 244.

103. Aruz 2003, 247–248.

104. Archi and Biga 2003, 12–13.

105. Archi 2008, 4.

106. Archi and Biga 2003, 16.

107. This description is based on plaques and inlayed scenes from Mari (Margueron 2004, Figs. 278–282, pp. 290–293), the Standard of Ur (see Aruz 2003, object 52, pp. 97–100), and the Stela of the Vultures (see Aruz 2003, Figs. 52 and 53, pp. 190–191).

108. Archi and Biga 2003, 17.

109. TM.75.G.12450: Archi and Biga 2003, 18

110. Archi and Biga 2003, 29.

111. This argument is made by Archi and Biga 2003, 35.

### CHAPTER THREE

1. "The Kaiser Right in Lauding Hammurabi," *New York Times*, April 26, 1903.

2. "Hammurabi's Code," *New York Times*, Feb. 20, 1904.

3. "Bible and Babel—Professor Delitzsch and the Old Testament," *New York Times*, Jan. 21, 1906.

4. Bill T. Arnold and David B. Weisberg, "A Centennial Review of Friedrich Delitzsch's 'Babel und Bibel' Lectures," *Journal of Biblical Literature* 121 (2002), 441–457.

5. C. H. W. Johns, *The Oldest Code of Laws in the World* (Edinburgh: T. & T. Clark, 1903).

6. For example, Micheline Ishay, *The History of Human Rights: From Ancient Times to the Globalization Era* (Berkeley: University of California Press, 2004), 19.

7. For example, "Earliest Law Code Is Now at Yale," *New York Times*, Jan. 29, 1915.

8. This was either King Ur-Namma or his son Shulgi. The laws are found in Martha T. Roth, *Law Collections from Mesopotamia and Asia Minor*, 2nd ed. (Atlanta, Ga.: Scholars Press, 1997), 15–21.

9. Roth 1997, 23–70.

10. Two excellent biographies of Hammurabi have been published in the past few years: Marc Van De Mieroop, *King Hammurabi of Babylon: A Biography* (Malden, Mass.: Blackwell, 2005), and Dominique Charpin, *Hammu-rabi de Babylon* (Paris: Presses Universitaires de France, 2003).

11. Georges Dossin, "Les archives épistolaires du palais de Mari," *Syria: Revue d'art oriental et d'archéologie* 19 (1938), 114.

12. "The Sumerian King List," translated by Piotr Michalowski: Chavalas 2006, 84.

13. Elizabeth Carter and Matthew W. Stolper, *Elam: Surveys of Political History and Archaeology* (Berkeley and Los Angeles: University of California Press, 1984), 16–22.

14. "The Marriage of Martu," in Herman L.J. Vanstiphout. *The Marriage of Martu* (unpublished manuscript, 1998), available at *The Electronic Text Corpus of Sumerian Literature*, http://etcsl.orinst.ox.ac.uk/cgi-bin/etcsl.cgi?text=t.1.7.1#.

15. Anne Porter, "You Say Potato, I Say... Typology, Chronology and the Origins of the Amorites," in *Sociétés humaines et changement climatique à la fin du troisième millénaire: une crise a-t-elle eu lieu en haute Mésopotamie?*, edited by Catherine Kuzucuoglu and Catherine Marro (Paris: Diffusion de Boccard, 2007), 105–107.

16. P. Villard, "Shamshi-Adad and Sons," in Sasson et al. 1995, vol. 2, 881.

17. Evelyn Klengel-Brandt, "Babylon," in Meyers 1997, vol. 1, 252.

18. Jean-Claude Margueron, "Mari," in Aruz 2008, 27–29.

19. Innumerable works have been written about Mari and its archives. Most are in French, because a French team has directed the excavations there. Jean-Cl. Margueron, *Mari: Métropole de l'Euphrate au IIIe et au début du IIe millénaire av. J.-C.* (Paris: Picard, 2004) is detailed and includes over 500 illustrations. In English, a short overview is available in Bienkowski and Millard 2000, 189–190. A brief description of the archaeological remains is found in Kay Kohlmeyer, "Mari (Tell Hariri)," in Weiss 1985, 194–197, and in Akkermans and Schwartz 2003, 313–316. The events of the last two years of Zimri-Lim's reign are reconstructed in detail in chap. 2 of Wolfgang Heimpel, *Letters to the King of Mari* (Winona Lake, Ind.: Eisenbrauns, 2003), 37–163.

20. Daniel E. Fleming, *Democracy's Ancient Ancestors: Mari and Early Collective Governance* (Cambridge and New York: Cambridge University Press, 2004), 230.

21. Fleming 2004, 231–234.

22. Bertrand Lafont, "Relations internationales, alliances et diplomatie au temps des royaumes amorrites," in *Amurru 2: Mari, Ébla et les Hourrites: Dix ans de travaux, deuxième partie,* edited by Jean-Marie Durand and Dominque Charpin (Paris: Éditions Recherche sur les Civilisations, 2001), 232–233; Gary M. Beckman, "Hittite Treaties and the Development of the Cuneiform Treaty Tradition," in *Der deuter-onomistischen Geschichtswerke: Redaktions- und religionsgeschichtliche Perspektiven zur "Deuteronomismus"-Diskussion in Tora und Vorderen Propheten,* edited by Markus Witte et al. (Berlin and New York: Walter de Gruyter, 2006), 281.

23. See Heimpel 2003, 64–163 for details of these alliances as they concerned the kingdom of Mari.

24. Heimpel 2003, 48.

25. An overview of the diplomatic system in this era is found in Dominique Charpin, "Histoire politique du Proche-Orient amorrite (2002–1595)," in *Mesopotamien: Die altbabylonische Zeit,* Dominque Charpin, Dietz Otto Edzard, and Marten Stol (Göttingen: Academic Press Fribourg, 2004), 293–304.

26. The Mari letters have been published, in cuneiform and translated into French, in the series *Archives Royales de Mari* (Paris: Éditions Recherche sur les Civilisations, 1950 ff.), and in more recent French translations in three volumes of *Les documents épistolaires du palais de Mari,* LAPO 16–18 (Paris: Éditions Recherche sur les Civilisations,1988–1990). English translations of several hundred of the letters can be found in Heimpel 2003.

27. ARM 2 21: Heimpel 2003, 472.

28. Van de Mieroop 2005, 66.

29. Charpin 2004, 294.

30. ARM 26 384: Heimpel 2003, 332.

31. ARM 27 161: Heimpel 2003, 467.

32. Christopher M. Monroe, "Money and Trade," in *A Companion to the Ancient Near East,* edited by Daniel C. Snell (Malden, Mass.: Blackwell, 2007), 177.

33. Jesper Eidem, "International Law in the Second Millennium: Middle Bronze Age," in Westbrook 2003, 751.

34. Charpin 2004, 293–294.

35. Eidem 2003, 751; Lafont 2001 "International Relations," 50.

36. Charpin 2004, 293.

37. Charpin 2004, 294.

38. Archi 1993, 57.

39. Charpin 2004, 294.

40. Lafont 2001 "International Relations," 48.

41. ARM 2 76: Jack M. Sasson, "Thoughts of Zimri-Lim," *Biblical Archaeologist* 47/2 (1984), 116–117.

42. ARM 2 76: Sasson 1984, 117.

43. ARM 26 449: Heimpel 2003, 372–374.

44. Lafont 2001 "International Relations," 47.

45. Lafont 2001, "International Relations" 47.

46. Charpin 2004, 295.

47. ARM 26 449: Heimpel 2003, 372–374.

48. Jesper Eidem and Jørgen Læssøe, *The Shemshara Archives 1: The Letters* (Copenhagen, Denmark: The Royal Danish Academy of Sciences and Letters, 2001), 33.

49. ARM 26 449: Heimpel 2003, 373; the king of Elam was viewed as higher ranking than Hammurabi at this time: Heimpel 2003, 38.

50. Amanda H. Podany, "Preventing Rebellion through the Creation of Symbolic Ties of Kinship in Syria and Mesopotamia during the Second Millennium BCE," in *Rebellions and Peripheries in the Cuneiform World*, American Oriental Series, vol. 91, edited by Seth Richardson (American Oriental Society, 2010), 45–72.

51. Eidem 2003, 751.

52. Charpin 2004, 296.

53. ARM 28 49: Jack M. Sasson, "'Babylon and Beyond': Remarks on the Occasion of a Symposium." Unpublished comments presented at the Metropolitan Museum of Art, Dec. 19, 2008. Cited with permission.

54. ARM 5 20: Pritchard 1969, 628–629.

55. Ali Abou Assaf "Mishrifeh," in Meyers 1997, vol. 4, 35–36.

56. See Qatna website at www.qatna.org for photos and maps.

57. Peter Pfälzner, "The Royal Palace at Qatna: Power and Prestige in the Late Bronze Age," in Aruz 2008, 219.

58. Pzälzner 2008, 220. See the picture of the statues, Figure 72 on p. 218.

59. ARM 5 20 translated by William L. Moran: Pritchard 1969, 628.

60. Charpin 2004, 296.

61. ARM 5 20: Pritchard 1969, 629.

62. All quotes from this letter are found in ARM 26 384: Heimpel 2003, 332–333.

63. LEM 2: Michalowski 1993, 14.

64. Jean Bottero, *The Oldest Cuisine in the World: Cooking in Mesopotamia*, translated by Teresa Lavender Fagan (Chicago and London: University of Chicago Press, 2004), 19.

65. D. D. Luckenbill, "Old Babylonian Letters from Bismya," *American Journal of Semitic Languages and Literatures* 32/4 (1916), 276.

66. YOS 2 15: A. Leo Oppenheim, *Letters from Mesopotamia* (Chicago and London: University of Chicago Press, 1967), 86.

67. For a discussion of treaties, see Donald L. Magnett, "The Function of the Oath in the Ancient Near Eastern International Treaty," *American Journal of International Law* 72 (1978), 815–829.

68. LH 7: Roth 1997, 82.

69. LH 128: Roth 1997, 105.

70. Eidem 2003, 747, 750.

71. This is found in ARM 26 404: Heimpel 2003, 343–346. Analysis of the letter is in Heimpel 2003, 133–135; Eidem 2003, 748.

72. ARM 26 404: Heimpel 2003, 344.

73. One of the two vassals was higher in rank than the other. To him Zimri-Lim was an "elder brother," to the other he was "father," as reflected in this statement.

74. A list of references to the sacrifice of a donkey is found in Lafont 2001 "Relations Internationales," 263–266.

75. Charpin 2004, 300.

76. All quotes regarding this treaty are from ARM 26 404: Heimpel 2003, 343–345.

77. A. 96: Francis Joannès, "Le traité de vassalité d'Atamrum d'Andarig envers Zimri-Lim de Mari," in *Marchands, diplomates et empereurs. Etudes sur la civilisation mésopotamienne offertes à Paul Garelli*, edited by Dominque Charpin and Francis Joannès (Paris: Editions Recherche sur les Civilisations, 1991), 169; Foster 2007, 67.

78. SH 809: Eidem and Læssøe 2001, 71.

79. SH 886: Eidem and Læssøe 2001, 76.

80. Charpin 2004, 301.

81. Lafont 2001 "International Relations," 54.

82. A. 361: Dominique Charpin, "Un traité entre Zimri-Lim de Mari et Ibâl-pî-El II d'Ešnunna," in Charpin and Joannès 1991, 141–145; Charpin 2004, 301–302; Foster 2007, 68.

83. Charpin 2004, 301–302.

84. Charpin 2004, 302.

85. Charpin 2004, 303, Eidem 2003, 748–749.

86. Eidem 2003, 748–749; Lafont 2001, 260.

87. A. 2730: Heimpel 2003, 509.

88. Text 71: Eidem and Læssøe 2001, 53.

89. Lafont 2001, 312.

90. Lafont 2001, 313.

91. In contrast, Egyptian kings did regularly marry their sisters, and didn't approve of royal princesses marrying out of the immediate family.

92. SH 874, Eidem and Læssøe, 2001, 131.

93. Raymond Cohen and Raymond Westbrook, *Amarna Diplomacy: The Beginnings of International Relations* (Baltimore: Johns Hopkins University Press, 2000), 230.

94. For example, Haya-Sumu, who was married to two of Zimri-Lim's daughters, and who wrote: "To Zimri-Lim speak! Your son Haya-Sumu (says)": ARM 28 81 = ARM 2 62: Heimpel 2003, 502.

95. Giorgio Buccellati and Marilyn Kelly-Buccellati, "Tar'am-Agade, Daughter of Naram-Sin, at Urkesh," in *Of Pots and Pans: Papers on the Archaeology and History of Mesopotamia and Syria presented to David Oates in Honor of his 75th Birthday*, edited by L. Al-Gailani Werr et al. (London: Nabu Publications 2002), 11–31; Andrew Lawler, "Who Were the Hurrians?" *Archaeology* 61 (2008), 49.

96. Elizabeth Carter and Matthew W. Stolper, *Elam: Surveys of Political History and Archaeology* (Berkeley and Los Angeles: University of California Press, 1984), 16–22.

97. Lafont 2001 "Relations internationales," 313–314 gives a list of all the Mari princesses and their husbands. At least ten of them were married to other kings, and at least one was a priestess.

98. For details of the marriage process, see F. Abdallah, "La femme dans le royaume d'Alep au XVIIIe siècle av. J.-C.," in Durand 1987, 13–15; Jean-Marie Durand, "Documents pour l'histoire du royaume de Haute-Mesopotamie II," *MARI* 6 (1990), 280–288.

99. Karen Rhea Nemet-Nejat, *Daily Life in Ancient Mesopotamia* (Westport, Conn.: Greenwood, 1998), 133.

100. Bertrand Lafont, "Les filles du roi de Mari," in Durand 1987, 118–119.

101. Abdallah 1987, 14.

102. The dress of a goddess figure found at Mari is probably characteristic of women's attire: see Weiss 1985, object 90, pp. 226–227.

103. This description is based on a statuette of a Mari princess in the Louvre: AO 17554: *De Sumer à Babylone: Collections du Louvre* (Brussels: Crédit Communal de Belgique, 1983), object 109, p. 104.

104. Lafont 2001 "Relations internationales," 315; Jean-Marie Durand, *Les documents épistolaires du palais de Mari,* vol. 3, LAPO 18 (1990), 277.

105. ARM 10 34+: Heimpel 2003, 491–492, discussed on pp. 80–81.

106. ARM 10 84: Heimpel 2003, 492–493.

107. These marriages have been discussed in several publications, including Heimpel 2003, 80–81; Bertrand Lafont, "The Women of the Palace at Mari," in *Everyday Life in Ancient Mesopotamia,* edited by Jean Bottero, translated by Antonia Nevill (Baltimore: Johns Hopkins University Press, 2001), 127–140; Jean-Marie Durand, "Trois études sur Mari," *MARI* 3 (1984), 162–172; Dominique Charpin, *Archives Épistolaires de Mari* 1/2, ARM 26/2, Paris: Éditions Recherche sur les Civilisations, 1988, 43–46; Nele Ziegler, *La population féminine des palais d'après les archives royales de Mari: Le Harem de Zimri-Lim,* Florilegium Marianum IV, Memoires de NABU 5 (Paris: Société pour l'étude du Proche Orient Ancient, 1999), 64.

108. Heimpel 2003, 71–80.

109. ARM 26 315: Heimpel 2003, 298.

110. ARM 26 239: Heimpel 2003, 268.

111. ARM 26 314: Heimpel 2003, 297.

112. ARM 26 312: Heimpel 2003, 296.

113. ARM 26 352: Heimpel 2003, 312.

114. ARM 10 32: Heimpel 2003, 292, 491.

115. ARM 10 33: Heimpel 2003, 491.

116. ARM 10 32: Heimpel 2003, 490.

117. ARM 26 315: Heimpel 2003, 298.

118. All quotes in this paragraph are from ARM 10 32: Heimpel 2003, 491.

119. ARM 10 33: Heimpel 2003, 491.

120. ARM 10 34: Heimpel 2003, 492.

121. Eidem 2003, 751.

122. Foster 2007, 67.

123. Lafont 2001 "International Relations," 42.

124. These activities are described in the names that he gave to the years of his reign.

125. Hammurabi, year 30, in which he "overthrew the army of Elam which had mobilized Subartu, Gutium, Eshnunna and Malgium en masse from the border of Marhashi…": Malcolm J. A. Horsnell, *The Year-Names of the First Dynasty of Babylon,* vol. 2, *The Year-Names Reconstructed and Critically Annotated in Light of their Exemplars* (Hamilton, Ont.: McMaster University Press, 1999), 139.

126. Hammurabi, year 33 ("overthrew in battle the army of Mari and Malgium, subjugated Mari and its villages…") and year 35 ("destroyed the (great) wall of Mari and the (wall of) Malgium"): Horsnell 1999, vol. 2, 146–147, 151.

127. Jack M. Sasson, "The King and I: A Mari King in Changing Perspectives." *JAOS* 118 (1998), 461.

128. Pritchard 1969, 268.

129. Code of Hammurabi. Prologue: Roth 1997, 76–80.

130. Roth 1997, 76–81.

131. Roth 1997, 133.

132. Van de Mieroop 2005, 123.

CHAPTER FOUR

1. Foster 2007, 67.

2. ARM 27 83, 84: Heimpel 2003, 439–440.

3. Kenoyer 2003, 380–381.

4. Francfort 1989, 391.

5. Reade 2001, 28 notes that some "post-Urban" towns in the region continued to exist until 1700 BCE.

6. Tosi and Lamberg-Karlovsky 2003, 349.

7. "Gudea Statue B," translated by Richard Averbeck: Chavalas 2006, 48.

8. Potts 1997, 266.

9. Parpola et al. 1977, 131.

10. Parpola et al. 1977, 134 ff; the tablets are dated to the thirty-fourth year of king Shulgi of Ur: Potts 1995, 1457.

11. Francfort 1989, 391.

12. ARM 27 161: Heimpel 2003, 466.

13. ARM 27 161: Heimpel 2003, 467.

14. Sumer 14 pl. 23 No. 47: cited in Oppenheim 1967, 87.

15. Juris Zarins, "Oman," in Meyers 1997, vol. 4, 185.

16. Potts 1999, 39–40.

17. Aruz 2003, object 304, pp. 426–427.

18. "Gudea Statue B": Averbeck 2006, 49.

19. Potts 1999, 39. Potts even maintains that the Ur III kings might have ruled Magan directly for a while.

20. Potts 1995, 1456.

21. A. Leo Oppenheim, "The Seafaring Merchants of Ur," *JAOS* 74/1 (1954), 13; Rathnagar 2004, 107.

22. UET III 751: Oppenheim 1954, 13.

23. Oppenheim 1954, 15.

24. Eidem and Højlund 1993, 445–446.

25. Eidem and Højlund 1993, 446.

26. Potts 1995, 1454; Oppenheim 1954.

27. Moorey 1982, 204; Sir Leonard Woolley, *Joint Expedition of the British Museum and of the Museum of the University of Pennsylvania to Mesopotamia,* vol. 7, *Old Babylonian Period* (London: British Museum Publications, 1976), 124–125.

28. We know this because when a house was sold, no address was given on the sale contract. Instead, the house was identified as being next to the houses of Mr. X on one side and of Mr. Y on the other, and sometimes of Mr. Z whose house was at the back.

29. In some versions of the Mesopotamian flood story, such as the Atrahasis epic, the gods decided to wipe out humankind because they were tired of all the noise they made.

30. Moorey 1982, 203–204.

31. Potts 1995, 1454.

32. UET V 796: Oppenheim 1954, 10.

33. Ratnagar 2004, 53.

34. UET V 81: Oppenheim 1954, 10–11.

35. Oppenheim 1954, 11.

36. "Inscription of Shamshi-Adad, king of Ekallatum (1796–1775 BC)," translated by Frans van Koppen: Chavalas 2006, 102.

37. "Inscription of Shamshi-Adad": Chavalas 2006, 102.

38. Ronald Lamprichs, "Aššur," in Meyers 1997, vol. 1, 226.

39. "Inscription of Shamshi-Adad": Chavalas 2006, 102.

40. Eidem and Højlund 1993, 443–444.

41. Potts 1995, 1454.

42. Klaas R. Veenhof, "Kanesh: An Anatolian Colony in Anatolia," in Sasson et al. 1995, vol. 2, 864.

43. Mogens Trolle Larsen, "The Old Assyrian Merchant Colonies," in Aruz 2008, 70.

44. Veenhof 1995, 860.

45. Larsen 2008, "Old Assyrian Merchant Colonies," 71.

46. Larsen 2008, "Old Assyrian Merchant Colonies," 72.

47. Veenhof 1995, 866.

48. Larsen 2008, "Old Assyrian Merchant Colonies," 72.

49. Larsen 2008, "Old Assyrian Merchant Colonies," 71.

50. "Kanesh," in Bienkowski and Millard 2000, 163–164.

51. Larsen 2008, "Old Assyrian Merchant Colonies," 71.

52. Larsen 2008, "Old Assyrian Merchant Colonies," 72.

53. Veenhof 2005, 861.

54. Veenhof 1995, 866.

55. Some of the letters relating to Kunnaniya can be found, translated into French, in Cécile Michel, *Correspondance des marchands de Kanish* (Paris: Les éditions du Cerf, 2001), 493–499, letters 377–385.

56. Larsen 2008, "Old Assyrian Merchant Colonies," 72.

57. Mogens Trolle Larsen, "The Middle Bronze Age," in Aruz 2008, 15.

58. Larsen 2008, "Old Assyrian Merchant Colonies," 72.

59. VAT 9249: Veenhof 1995, 862.

60. K. R. Veenhof, *Aspects of Old Assyrian Trade and Its Terminology* (Leiden and Boston: Brill 1972), 98.

61. Larson 2008, "Middle Bronze Age," 15.

62. Monroe 2007, 180.

63. Veenhof 1995, 868–870.

64. Gary Beckman, "Mesopotamians and Mesopotamian Learning at Hattuša," *JCS* 35 (1983), 100.

65. Trevor Bryce, *Life and Society in the Hittite World* (New York and Oxford: Oxford University Press, 2002), 8.

66. Heimpel 2003, 13; Jack M. Sasson, "Zimri-Lim Takes the Grand Tour," *Biblical Archaeologist* 47/4 (1984), 246–251.

67. A detailed account of this trip is found in Sasson 2008, "Texts, Trade, and Travelers," 95–100. Sasson 2008, "Babylon and Beyond."

68. See the translation of A. 1270: Jack M. Sasson in Aruz 2008, 4.

69. Sasson 2008, "Texts, Trade, and Travelers," 100.

70. Heimpel 2003,12; a reference to copper from Alashiya is found in the Mari documents: A. Bernard Knapp, "Bronze Age Mediterranean Cultures and the Ancient Near East, Part 2," *Biblical Archaeologist* 55/3 (1992), 123.

71. A. 1270 in Aruz 2008, 4; A. Bernard Knapp, "Bronze Age Mediterranean Cultures and the Ancient Near East, Part 1," *Biblical Archaeologist* 55/2 (1992), 67; Amelie Kuhrt, *The Ancient Near East c. 3000–330 BC*, vol. 1 (London and New York: Routledge, 1995), 101.

72. Wolf-Dietrich and Barbara Niemeier, "Minoan Frescoes in the Eastern Mediterranean," in Cline and Harris-Cline 1998, 93; Sasson 2008, "Texts, Trade, and Travelers,"100. Alahtum was probably the earlier name for the town of Alalakh, where such frescoes were found by excavators. Aruz 2008, 123.

73. Barbara Niemeier and Wolf-Dietrich Niemeier, "Aegean Frescoes in Syria-Palestine: Alalakh and Tel Kabri," in Susan Sherratt (ed.) *The Wall Paintings of Thera: Proceedings of the First International Symposium, Petros M. Nomikos Conference Center, Thera, Hellas, 30 August–4 September 1997*, vol. 2 (Piraeus: Petros M. Nomikos and the Thera Foundation, 2000), 763–802.

74. Neimeier and Neimeier 2000, 802.

75. Sasson 2008, "Texts, Trade, and Travelers," 96.

76. Sasson 2008, "Texts, Trade, and Travelers,"100.

77. Aruz 2008, 123.

78. Larsen 2008, "Middle Bronze Age,"15.

79. F. Matz, "The Maturity of Minoan Civilization," in I. E. S. Edwards et al. (eds.), *Cambridge Ancient History,* vol. 2 part 1: *History of the Middle East and Aegean Region c. 1800–1380 B.C.,* 3rd ed. (Cambridge: Cambridge University Press, 1973), 141–164.

80. Andrew Robinson, *Lost Languages: The Enigma of the World's Undeciphered Scripts* (London, New York, Sydney, Toronto: BCA, 2002), 182–199.

81. Robinson 2002, 185.

82. Philip P. Betancourt, "Middle Minoan Objects in the Near East," in Cline and Harris-Cline 1998, 8.

83. Holley Martlew, "Minoan and Mycenaean Technology as Revealed through Organic Residue Analysis," in Janine Bourriau and Jacke Phillips (eds.), *Invention and Innovation: The Social Context of Technological Change 2, Egypt, the Aegean and the Near East, 1650–1150 BC* (Oxford: Oxbow Books, 2004), 128.

84. Knapp 1992, part 1, 65; Oliver Dickinson, *The Aegean Bronze Age* (Cambridge: Cambridge University Press, 1994), 238.

85. Eric H. Cline, *Sailing the Wine-Dark Sea: International Trade and the Late Bronze Age Aegean* (B.A.R. International Series 591, Oxford: Tempus Reparatum, 1994), 27, 126–128 nos. D3–12.

86. A. Bernard Knapp, "Island Cultures: Crete, Thera, Cyprus, Rhodes, and Sardinia," in Sasson et al. 1995, 1438–1439; 1446–1447.

87. Gae Callender, "The Middle Kingdom Renaissance (c. 2055–1650 BC)," in *Oxford History of Ancient Egypt,* edited by Ian Shaw (Oxford and London: Oxford University Press, 2000), 178.

88. Szpakowska 2008, 91. Although the most famous and largest of the pyramids were constructed during the Egyptian Old Kingdom, the Middle Kingdom kings were also usually buried in pyramids. Theirs were smaller and less well made, and many of them now look like piles of rubble.

89. Eric H. Cline, "The Nature of the Economic Relations of Crete with Egypt and the Near East during the Late Bronze Age," in *From Minoan Farmers to Roman Traders: Sidelights on the Economy of Ancient Crete,* edited by Angelos Chaniotos et al. (Wiesbaden: Franz Steiner Verlag, 1999), 124.

90. Cline 1999, 118.

91. R. N. L. Barber, review of *Aegean Painting in the Bronze Age* by Sara A. Immerwahr, *Classical Review* 41/2 (1991), 429; Janice L. Crowley, *The Aegean and the East: an Investigation into the Transference of Artistic Motifs between the Aegean, Egypt and the Near East in the Bronze Age* (Jonsered, Sweden: Paul Åströms, 1989).

92. Cline 1999, 117, 123; Aruz 2008, 59.

93. Cline 1999, 118, 123; Joan Aruz, "The Aegean and the Orient: The Evidence of Stamp and Cylinder Seals," in Cline and Harris-Cline 1998, 302.

94. Aruz 2008, object number 17. The document is from Tell Sianu.

95. J. D. Muhly, "Cyprus," in Meyers 1997, vol. 2, 92.

96. Thomas Schneider, "Egypt and the Levant," in Aruz 2008, 61.

97. Lafont 2001, "Relations internationales," 270; Sasson 2008, "Texts, Trade, and Travelers," 100.

98. Callender 2000.

99. W. K. Simpson, "Papyrus Lythgoe: A Fragment of a Literary Text of the Middle Kingdom from El-Lisht," *Journal of Egyptian Archaeology* 46 (1960), 67.

100. Schneider 2008, 61; Suzy Hakiman, "Byblos," in Aruz 2008, 49.

101. All Sinuhe quotes are from "Sinuhe," translated by Miriam Lichtheim in Hallo and Younger 2003, vol. 1, 77–82.

102. Callender 2000, 167.

103. "The boundary stela of Senwosret III," in R. B. Parkinson, *Voices from Ancient Egypt: An Anthology of Middle Kingdom Writings* (Norman: University of Oklahoma Press, 1991), 45.

104. Paolo Matthiae, "Ebla," in Aruz 2008, 35.

105. K. S. B. Ryholt, "Hotepibre, a Supposed Asiatic King in Egypt with Relations to Ebla," *BASOR* 311 (1998), 1–6.

106. Matthiae 2008, 38–39.

107. "Sensationelle Ausgrabung: Ältestes ägyptisches Keilschriftdokument gefunden," Universität Wien website: http://public.univie.ac.at/index.php?id=6576&no_cache=1&tx_ttnews[tt_news]=9759.

108. Chavalas 1996, 97–99; Giorgio Buccellati and Marilyn Kelly-Buccellati, "Terqa: The First Eight Seasons." *AAAS* 33/2 (1983), 47–67.

109. Chavalas 1996, 97.

110. Peter V. Lape, "Political Dynamics and Religious Change in the Late Pre-Colonial Banda Islands, Eastern Indonesia," *World Archaeology* 32/1 (2000), 141. Lape notes that some scholars do not think that the spices found at Terqa were in fact cloves. Further research is underway on this issue: Giorgio Buccellati, personal communication.

111. Andrew Lawler, "Bridging East and West," *Science* 325 (2009), 940–943.

112. Elizabeth Wayland Barber, *The Mummies of Ürümchi* (New York and London: W. W. Norton, 1999), 71–76, and plate 9.

113. Andrew Lawler, "Millet on the Move," *Science* 325 (2009), 942–943.

CHAPTER FIVE

1. Dominique Charpin, "The History of Ancient Mesopotamia: An Overview," in Sasson et al. 1995, vol. 2, 817; Stephanie Dalley, *Babylonian Tablets from the First Sealand Dynasty in the Schøyen Collection*, CUSAS, vol. 8 (Bethesda, Md.: CDL Press, 2009), 8.

2. H. Gasche, *Le Babylonie au 17e siècle avant notre ère: approche archéologique, problèmes et perspectives*, MHEM 1 (Ghent, Belgium: University of Ghent, 1989), 134–141.

3. Samsuiluna, year 9; Abi-eshuh, year 3: Malcolm J. A. Horsnell, *The Year-Names of he First Dynasty of Babylon*, vol. 2, *The Year-Names Reconstructed and Critically Annotated in Light of their Exemplars* (Hamilton, Ont.: McMaster University Press, 1999), 192, 245.

4. Amanda H. Podany, *The Land of Hana: Kings, Chronology, and Scribal Tradition* (Bethesda, Md.: CDL Press, 2002), 55–56; Olivier Rouault, "Cultures locales et influences extérieures: le cas de Terqa," *SMEA* 30 (1992), 253.

5. Samsuditana year names: Horsnell 1999, vol. 2, 359–383.

6. Years 8, 12, 13: statues of himself; year 11: statue carrying a curved staff of gold; year 15: leading a contingent of soldiers; year 17: marching; year 21: on a throne of gold; year 24?: holding a scepter; year 25?: holding a lamb as a gift; year 27?: holding a scepter of justice: Horsnell 1999, vol. 2, 359–383.

7. Statues of individuals were placed in temples in order to pray constantly on behalf of the person depicted: Nemet-Nejat 1998, 188. This was probably also true of the kings' statues that were placed in temples.

8. Samsuditana, year 1; Horsnell 1999, vol. 2, 359.

9. J. C. Macqueen, "The History of Anatolia and of the Hittite Empire: An Overview," in Sasson et al. 1995, vol. 2, 1086.

10. Ann C. Gunter, "Ancient Anatolia," in Meyers 1997, vol. 1, 127.

11. Labarna is only known from later inscriptions. Hittite tradition had him as a patriarch who adopted Hattusili I as his son and successor, but some scholars are not convinced that he existed: Macqueen 1995, 1089.

12. "The Proclamation of Telepinu," translated by Th. P. J. van den Hout: Hallo and Younger 2003, vol. 1, 194.

13. Billie Jean Collins, "Hattušili I, The Lion King," *JCS* 50 (1998) 15.

14. Annals II 48–III 9: Trevor Bryce, *The Kingdom of the Hittites* (Oxford: Clarendon Press, 1998), 82.

15. Macqueen 1995, 1089.

16. Giorgio Buccellati and Marilyn Kelly-Buccellati, "Urkesh, the First Hurrian Capital," *Biblical Archaeologist* 60 (1997), 77–97.

17. Cord Kühne, "Imperial Mittani: An Attempt at Historical Reconstruction," in Owen and Wilhelm 1999, 207–208.

18. Annals III 29–40: Bryce 1998, 84.

19. Macqueen 1995, 1089.

20. "The Proclamation of Telipinu": Hallo and Younger 2003, vol. 1, 195.

21. A document dating to the reign of Samsuditana has been found at Terqa, suggesting that it was under Babylonian control: Olivier Rouault, "Les relations internationales en Mésopotamie du nord: techniques d'expansion et stratégies de survie," in E. Frézouls and A. Jacquemin (eds.), *Les relations internationals: Actes du Colloque de Strasbourg 15–17 juin 1993* (Paris: Diffusion de Boccard, 1995), 103. For an overview of the history of Hana, see Podany 2002, 32–74.

22. Olivier Rouault, "Terqa et sa region (6e–1er millénaires av. J.-C.): Recherches récentes," *Akkadica* 122 (2001), 9. It is unclear where Kuwari's reign fits with respect to the other kings of this region: Podany 2002, 42–43.

23. "The Proclamation of Telipinu"; Hallo and Younger 2003, vol. 1, 195.

24. Kühne 1999, 211.

25. Although the capture of these statues isn't mentioned by Telipinu, it is clear that they were taken, because a later Babylonian king had to bring them back.

26. Bryce 2002, 59.

27. There's some question about the source for the Hittite cuneiform script, since the forms of the cuneiform signs they adopted are not identical to either the Assyrian or Babylonian script of the era; they more resemble the script of the earlier Old Akkadian period: Beckman 1983, 100.

28. Dalley 2009, 4.

29. Podany 2002, 57–69.

30. For detailed information about Kassite sources, see J. A. Brinkman, *Materials and Studies for Kassite History,* vol. 1 (Chicago: The Oriental Institute of the University of Chicago, 1976). For an overview of Kassite history, see Walter Sommerfeld, "The Kassites of Ancient Mesopotamia: Origins, Politics, and Culture," in Sasson et al. 1995 vol. 2, 917–930.

31. Sommerfeld 1995, 917. After the end of the Kassite dynasty, a scribe recorded 48 Kassites words and their Akkadian equivalents on a tablet. The Kassite words are typical of those found in personal names: British Museum tablet number 93005 in Erle Leichty and Albert Kirk Grayson, *Catalogue of the Babylonian Tablets in the British Museum,* vol. VII: *Tablets from Sippar 2* (London: British Museum, 1987), 157.

32. L. Sassmannshausen, "The Adaptation of the Kassites to the Babylonian Civilization," in *Languages and Cultures in Contact: At the Crossroads of Civilizations in the Syro-Mesopotamian Realm, RAI 42,* edited by K. van Lerberghe and G. Voet (Leuven: Uitgeverij Peeters en Departement Oosterse Studies, 1999), 409–424.

33. Brinkman 1976, 35.

34. "Agum-Kakrime and the Return of Marduk": Benjamin R. Foster, *Before the Muses: An Anthology of Akkadian Literature,* vol. 1, 2nd ed. (Bethesda, Md.: CDL Press, 1996), 274–278.

35. "Agum-Kakrime": Foster 1996, vol. 1, 275.

36. HL 32: Roth 1997, 87.

37. HL 32: Roth 1997, 87.

38. All quotes from the Agum-kakrime inscription are found in Foster 1996, vol. 1, 275–276.

39. Agum-Kakrime's inscription was copied in later years, and it is the copy that survives; no doubt it was preserved because people were interested in this tale of the gods' return from exile. Some scholars have doubted that the text is authentic and have suggested that it might be an invention of scribes centuries later, but that seems unlikely. For one thing, Agum was the name of at least one Kassite king, and the historical details in the text ring true; for example that he brought the gods home from Hana rather than Hatti—this was indeed the time when Hana was thriving, which a later author might not have known. Even small features of the text, such as the signs used, are appropriate to the early Kassite time, but not to a later era. The document is a copy but must be an accurate one.

40. "Marduk Prophecy": Foster 1996, vol. 1, 302.

41. Macqueen 1995, 1090.

42. Brinkman 1976, 101.

CHAPTER SIX

1. The dates of Egyptian kings are debated; I am following the chronology given in Catherine H. Roehrig (ed.), *Hatshepsut: From Queen to Pharaoh* (New Haven and London: Yale University Press, 2005), 6.

2. David O'Connor, "Thutmose III: An Enigmatic Pharaoh," in *Thutmose III: A New Biography*, edited by Eric H. Cline and David O'Connor (Ann Arbor: University of Michigan Press, 2006), 13.

3. "The Hymn to the Aten": Simpson 2003, 282.

4. "The Craft of the Scribe: Papyrus Anastasi I," translated by James P. Allen: Hallo and Younger, vol. 3, 2003, 12.

5. "The Hardships of a Soldier's Life" Papyrus Anastasi IV, 9, 4–10, 1: Simpson, 2003, 441.

6. O'Connor 2006, 12–13. See Donald B. Redford, "A Gate Inscription from Karnak and Egyptian Involvement in Western Asia during the Early 18th Dynasty," *JAOS* 99 (1979), 276 for a list of the other source material regarding this campaign. Margaret S. Drower, "Syria ca. 1550–1400 B.C.," in Edwards et al. 1973, 432.

7. Redford 1979, 275–276.

8. Miriam Lichtheim, *Ancient Egyptian Literature*, vol. 2 (Berkeley and Los Angeles: University of California Press, 1976), 15 n. 9.

9. Redford 1979, 275.

10. Redford 1992, 153.

11. Redford 1979, 275.

12. Mario Liverani, *International Relations in the Ancient Near East* (Basingstoke, U.K.: Palgrave, 2001), 34–35.

13. Redford 1979, 274.

14. Redford 1979, 276.

15. Simpson 2003, 441.

16. Freu 2008, 6.

17. Kizzuwatna was often allied with the Hittites, but around 1450 BCE was brought under the control of the kings of Mittani: Macqueen 1995, 1090.

18. Abou Assaf 1997, 300. The modern excavations can be seen online at http://www.fecheriye.de.

19. Yuval Goren, Israel Finkelstein, and Nadav Na'aman, *Inscribed in Clay: Provenance Study of the Amarna Tablets and Other Ancient Near Eastern Texts* (Tel Aviv: Emery and Claire Yass Publications in Archaeology, 2004), 44.

20. These tablets comprise one from Nuzi, three from Alalakh, two from Nawar (Tell Brak), one from Umm el-Marra, two from Tell Bazi, and seven from Terqa: Freu 2008, 6–7; Rouault 1992, 254.

21. See the chart of the kings of Mittani and Egypt in Jacques Freu, "Note sur les sceaux des rois de Mitanni/Mittani," *NABU* 2008 No. 1 (March), 8.

22. "The Autobiography of Idrimi," translated by Tremper Longman III: Hallo and Younger 2003, vol. 1, 479.

23. Jacques Freu, *Histoire du Mitanni* (Paris: Collection Kubaba, éditions L'Harmattan. 2003), 34.

24. Von Dassow suggests that the inscription was made to look old. It might have been produced soon after Idrimi's reign or as much as a century later: Eva von Dassow, *State and Society in the Late Bronze Age: Alalaḫ under the Mittani Empire*, SCCNH 17 (Bethesda, Md.: CDL Press, 2008), 32–33.

25. "The Autobiography of Idrimi": Hallo and Younger 2003, vol. 1, 479.

26. Gernot Wilhelm, "The Kingdom of Mitanni in Second-Millennium Upper Mesopotamia," in Sasson et al. 1995, vol. 2, 1247; von Dassow 2008, 44.

27. Freu 2003, 35, von Dassow 2008, 43.

28. Wilhelm 1995, 1247.

29. This was the time between the relatively strong reign of King Telipinu of Hatti, who came to the throne around 1525, and a resurgence of Hittite power under Tudhaliya I about a century later: Macqueen 1995, 1090.

30. All quotes from Idrimi are from "The Autobiography of Idrimi": Hallo and Younger 2003, vol. 1, 479.

31. "Autobiography of Idrimi": Hallo and Younger 2003, vol. 1, 480.

32. von Dassow 2008, 34.

33. After 1500 Kizzuwatna had a treaty with Hatti, and around 1450 Mittani took control of Kizzuwatna; the Hittites then reestablished a treaty with Kizzuwatna, but by around 1420 it had switched back to an alliance with Mittani: Macqueen 1995, 1090–1091.

34. HDT 2: Beckman 1999, 18. This Tudhaliya was, for some time, referred to as Tudhaliya II, for example in Gary Beckman, *Hittite Diplomatic Texts*, 2nd ed. (Atlanta, Ga.: Scholars Press, 1999), xiv. He was even called Tudhaliya I/II: Bryce 1998, 132–133. But he is now generally referred to as Tudhaliya I, for example in Beckman 2000, 26. Although he certainly ruled in the fifteenth century, the dates of his reign are debated. Beckman and Bryce have Tudhaliya I taking the throne around 1400: Beckman 1999, xiv; Bryce 2002, xi. Macqueen puts his accession at "about 1450" (Macqueen 1995, 1090), Freu at 1425 (Freu 2003, 74). This book uses the date of 1425, though it may be wrong by several years, since the evidence is inconclusive.

35. Freu 2003, 17.

36. HDT 2: Beckman 1999, 19.

37. Rouault 1992, 254.

38. For an analysis of the transformed relationship between Egypt and the Near East during this period, see William J. Murnane, "Imperial Egypt and the Limits of Power," in Cohen and Westbrook 2000, 101–103.

39. O'Connor 2006, 10; Liverani 2001, 31.

40. John Baines, "Contextualizing Egyptian Representations of Society and Ethnicity," in Cooper and Schwartz 1996, 363.

41. "Amenemhet": Simpson 2003, 419. Kush was the more ancient name for Nubia.

42. For an overview of the issues surrounding the Hyksos, see Donald B. Redford, *Egypt, Canaan, and Israel in Ancient Times* (Princeton, N.J.: Princeton University Press, 1992), 98–122, and Janine Bourriau, "The Second Intermediate Period," in Shaw 2000, 185–217.

43. "Inscription of the Speos Artemidos" by Hatshepsut: first part from Bourriau 2000, 201, second part from James Henry Breasted, *Ancient Records of Egypt,* vol. 2 (New York: Russell and Russell, 1906), 125–126.

44. Manetho, *Aegyptiaca,* frag. 42, quoted in Redford 1992, 98.

45. "Sensationelle Ausgrabung: Ältestes ägyptisches Keilschriftdokument gefunden," Universität Wien, available at http://public.univie.ac.at/index.php?id=6576 &no_cache=1&tx_ttnews[tt_news]=9759

46. Roehrig 2005, 7.

47. Redford 1992, 148.

48. Cline and O'Connor 2006, Plates: Figure 1.3.

49. William C. Hayes, "Egypt: Internal Affairs from Thutmosis I to the Death of Amenophis III," in Edwards et al., 1973, 316.

50. Betsy M. Bryan, "The 18th Dynasty Before the Amarna Period," in Shaw 2000, 238.

51. Ann Macy Roth, "Models of Authority, Hatshepsut's Predecessors in Power," in Roehrig 2005; O'Connor 2006, 5.

52. Bryan 2000, 238.

53. W. Vivian Davies, "Egypt and Nubia: Conflict with the Kingdom of Kush," in Roehrig 2005, 52–53.

54. Ann Macy Roth, "Hatshepsut's Mortuary Temple at Deir el-Bahri: Architecture as Political Statement," in Roehrig 2005, 149.

55. All quotes from the Punt expedition captions are from "The Punt Reliefs": Breasted 1906, vol. 2, 107–113.

56. Edward Bleiberg, *The Official Gift in Ancient Egypt* (Norman, Okla.: University of Oklahoma, 1996), 24–25.

57. Breasted 1906, vol. 2, 107.

58. "Harkhuf": Simpson 2003, 411.

59. Andrew Martin, "Found: Egypt's Lost Queen," *The Times,* July 13, 2007.

60. Peter Popham, "Broken Tooth Provides the Key to Solving the Riddle of Hatshepsut," *The Independent,* June 28, 2007.

61. Donald B. Redford, "The Northern Wars of Thutmose III," in Cline and O'Connor, 2006, 329–330.

62. Redford 2006, 327.

63. Redford 2006, 328, 330.

64. "Papyrus Lansing: A Schoolbook": Lichtheim 1976, vol. 2, 172.

65. All quotes regarding this campaign are in Urk IV, 645–667: "From the annals of Thutmose III": Lichtheim 1976, vol. 2, 30–32.

66. "Papyrus Lansing": Lichtheim 1976, vol. 2, 172.

67. "The Annals of Thutmose III," translated by James K. Hoffmeier: Hallo and Younger, vol. 2, 2003, 12–13.

68. "The Annals of Thutmose III": Hallo and Younger, vol. 2, 2003, 12–13.

69. "Papyrus Lansing": Lichtheim 1976, vol. 2, 172.

70. Redford 2006, 332.

71. Urk IV 610–619: "The Poetical Stela of Thutmose III": Lichtheim 1976, vol. 2, 36.

72. Christine Lilyquist, "Egypt and the Near East: Evidence of Contact in the Material Record," in Roehrig 2005, 61.

73. Urk IV 696–703: "The Annals in Karnak," translated by John A. Wilson: Pritchard 1969, 239–240; "Gebel Barkal Stela of Thutmose III," translated by James K. Hoffmeier: Hallo and Younger, vol. 2, 2003, 15.

74. Redford 2006, 333.

75. Drower 1973, 455.

76. Redford 1996, 333; Redford 1992, 159.

77. Wilhelm 1995, 1248.

78. The next group of quotes is from "Gebel Barkal Stela of Thutmose III": Hallo and Younger, vol. 2, 2003, 15.

79. "The Annals in Karnak": Pritchard 1969, 239–240.

80. Redford 2006, 333–334.

81. Redford 1992, 162.

82. Manfred Bietak, "Egypt and the Aegean: Cultural Convergence in a Thutmoside Palace at Avaris," in Roehrig 2005, 75–76.

83. Bietak 2005, 80.

84. Bietak 2005, 76.

85. Manfred Bietak, "Minoan Artists at the Court of Avaris (Tell el-Dab'a)," in Aruz 2008, 131.

86. Objects from the tomb are shown in Aruz 2008, 254–258.

87. Bietak 2005, 79.

88. Bietak 2008, 131.

89. This is assuming that Avaris was now known as Perunefer, as Bietak argues: Bietack 2005, 80.

90. Niemeier and Niemeier 2000, under the subheading "The Fresco Paintings from Tel Kabri and Alalakh within the Eastern Mediterranean Koine"; Bleiberg 1996, 109–110.

91. The Egyptian term for tribute was *inw*: Bleiberg 1996, 109–110.

92. Joan Aruz, "Painted Palaces," in Aruz 2008, 123.

93. Drower 1973, 457; Redford 1992, 160; Freu 2003, 66.

94. Redford 2006, 336.

95. For example, Wilhelm 1995, 1248.

96. Redford 2006, 336.

97. Pinhas Artzi, "The Rise of the Middle-Assyrian Kingdom, according to El-Amarna Letters 15 & 16," in Pinhas Artzi (ed.), *Bar-Ilan Studies in History* (Ramat-Gan, Israel: Bar-Ilan University Press, 1978), 31. Note that an earlier reference to an embassy from Assyria in Thutmose's year 24 might be a scribal error: see Redford 2006, 343 n. 27.

98. "Eighth campaign": Breasted 1906, vol. 2, 204.

99. When a pharaoh noted that a foreign king had sent him tribute, this was not necessarily a sign that he ruled over that king's land. It could be, as here, just that the pharaoh's status was acknowledged there: Bleiberg 1996, 114.

100. Breasted has this arriving in his forty-first year: "Sixteenth Campaign": Breasted 1906, vol. 2, 213.

101. Freu 2003, 59.

102. Freu 2003, 58–59 believes that the treaty could have been drawn up in the time of Thutmose III. Macqueen also puts the treaty at around the same time, in the reign of Hittite king Tudhaliya I, who Macqueen has taking power around 1450 BCE. If Tudhaliya I came to power in 1425, which is more likely, the treaty would have been drawn up in the reign of Amenhotep II. Other reasons for putting it in Amenhotep II's reign are discussed in chapter 7.

103. Redford 2006, 335.

104. Peter F. Dorman, "The Early Reign of Thutmose III: An Unorthodox Mantle of Coregency," in Cline and O'Connor 2005, 58.

105. Peter F. Dorman, "The Destruction of Hatshepsut's Memory: The Proscription of Hatshepsut," in Roehrig 2005, 267–269.

106. Freu 2008, 6; Freu 2003, 70. Freu makes a convincing argument for there having been two Mittani kings named Shaushtatar.

107. A. Kirk Grayson, *Assyrian Rulers of the Third and Second Millennia BC (to 1115 BC)*, RIM Assyrian Periods, A:1 (Toronto: University of Toronto Press 1987), 333.

108. Freu 2008, 6.

109. The seal is found on two contracts from Nawar (Brak) dating to kings Tushratta and Artashumara, on two contracts from Basiru (Tell Bazi) dating to kings Artatama and Shaushtatar II, on a contract from Umm el-Marra dating to Shutarna II, and on an otherwise undated letter from Nuzi: Freu 2008, 7.

110. Freu 2008, 7.

111. HDT 6B: Beckman 1999, 49.

112. Freu 2003, 66.

113. Liverani 2008, 161.

114. Akkermans and Schwartz 2003, 354.

115. Akkermans and Schwartz 2003, 355.

116. EA 22: Moran 1992, 51–57.

117. Akkermans and Schwartz 2003, 353.

118. Akkermans and Schwartz 2003, 346.

119. Freu 2003, 22.

120. Wilhelm 1995, 1247.

121. Freu 2008, 6.

122. HDT 6A: Beckman 1999, 47.

123. Freu 2003, 22.

124. Freu 2008, 6. One recent proposed decipherment of Linear A suggests that the Minoans on Crete also spoke a language related to Sanskrit, but this had not received much support among scholars: Hubert La Marle, *Linéaire A*, tome 3: *L'Histoire et la vie de la crête Minoënne* (Paris: Geuthner, 1998). On the other hand, the name of the Homeric hero Meriones, who came from Crete, has been seen as identical to the Mittanian title *maryannu*: Martin West, *The East Face of Helicon: West Asiatic Elements in Greek Poetry and Myth* (New York and Oxford: Oxford University Press, 1999), 612 n. 81. My thanks to Sarah Morris for this observation and citation.

125. Wilhelm 1995, 1247; Freu 2003, 20.

126. Kühne 1999, 208, 211.

127. The date of this letter has been discussed extensively. Although it bears a seal of Shaushtatar, this same seal was used by his successors: Diana L. Stein, "A Reappraisal of the 'Sauštatar Letter' from Nuzi," *ZA* 79/1 (1989) 38. Freu 2008 believes, though, that the letter could have been sent during the reign of Shaushtatar II.

128. H 146: E. A. Speiser, "A Letter of Shaushtatar and the Date of the Kirkuk Tablets," *JAOS* 49 (1929), 271.

129. Olof Pedersen, *Archives and Libraries in the Ancient Near East 1500–300 B.C.* (Baltimore: CDL, 1998), 28.

130. Brigitte Lion, "Les archives privées d'Arrapkha et de Nuzi," in D.I. Owen and G. Wilhelm (eds.), *Nuzi at Seventy-Five,* SCCNH 10 (Bethesda, Md.: CDL Press, 1999), 48.

131. Plan in Pedersen 1998, 29

132. Diana L. Stein, "Nuzi," in Meyers 1997, 173.

133. Stein 1997, "Nuzi,"173.

134. Martha A Morrison, "The Family of Šilwa-Tešub *mar šarri,*" *JCS* 31 (1979), 4–5.

135. Morrison 1979, 3–29.

136. Maynard Paul Maidman, "Nuzi: Portrait of an Ancient Mesopotamian Provincial Town," in Sasson et al. 1995, vol. 2, 942.

137. Morrison 1979, 3.

138. Stein 1989, 46.

139. Maidman 1995, 941–942.

140. An illustration of one of these wall paintings can be found in Roehrig 2005, 63, Fig. 23.

141. All from Maidman 1995, 935–936.

142. Akkermans and Schwartz 2003, 331–333.

143. Maidman 1995.

144. Freu 2003, 68.

145. Eva von Dassow, "Archives of Alalakh IV in Archaeological Context," *BASOR* 338 (2005), 51–52.

146. Edward L. Greenstein, "Alalakh Texts," in Meyers 1997, vol. 1, 59–61.

147. Diana L. Stein, "Alalakh," in Meyers 1997, vol. 1, 55–59; Akkermans and Schwartz 2003, 333–335.

148. Stein 1997, "Alalakh," 55–59.

149. N. Na'aman, "Syria at the Transition from the Old Babylonian Period to the Middle Babylonian Period," *UF* 6 (1974), 272.

150. "The Agreement Between Ir-Addu and Niqmepa (AT 2)," translated by Richard S. Hess: Hallo and Younger 2003, vol. 2, 329–331, originally published by D. J. Wiseman, *The Alalakh Tablets* (London: British Institute of Archaeology at Ankara, 1953), 29.

151. Liverani 2001, 124. For an extensive discussion of vassal treaties in Hatti, which were similar to Syrian vassal treaties, see Amnon Altman, *The Historical Prologue of the Hittite Vassal Treaties: An Inquiry into the Concepts of Hittite Interstate Law* (Ramat-Gan: Bar-Ilan University Press, 2004).

152. Liverani 2001, 124.

153. Liverani 2001, 40.

154. Liverani 2001, 134.

155. EA 51: Moran 1992, 122; Ellen F. Morris, "Bowing and Scraping in the Ancient Near East: An Investigation into Obsequiousness in the Amarna Letters," *JNES* 65 (2006), 194.

156. Meir Malul, *Studies in Mesopotamian Legal Symbolism,* AOAT 221 (Kevelaer, Neukirchen-Vluyn, Germany: Verlag Butzon & Bercker, Neukirchener Verlag, 1988), 176.

157. Liverani 2001, 128.

CHAPTER SEVEN

1. Peter Der Manuelian, "The End of the Reign and the Accession of Amenhotep II," in Cline and O'Connor 2006, 416.

2. Der Manuelian 2006, 423.

3. "The Great Sphinx Stela of Amenhotep II at Giza": Lichtheim 1976, vol. 2, 41.

4. "Buried Monarchs Seen Again," *New York Times,* May 1, 1898.

5. G. Elliot Smith, *Catalogue Général Antiquités Égyptiennes du Musée du Caire: The Royal Mummies* (Cairo: Imprimerie de l'Institut français d'archéologie orientale, 1912), 36.

6. Urk IV 1343–44: Redford 1992, 230.

7. Breasted 1906, vol. 2, 304.

8. Most scholars agree that the first campaign was in the seventh year (e.g., Betsy M. Bryan, "The Egyptian Perspective on Mittani," in Cohen and Westbrook 2000, 76), but some put it in his third year (e.g., Freu 2003, 65).

9. Quotes from Amenhotep II's inscription are from "The Memphis and Karnak Stelae of Amenhotep II," translated by James K. Hoffmeier: Hallo and Younger 2003, vol. 2, 20–22.

10. James M. Weinstein, "The Egyptian Empire in Palestine: A Reassessment," *BASOR* 241 (1981), 13.

11. Redford 1992, 163.

12. Bryan 2000, 252.

13. "Amada and Elephantine stelae": Breasted 1906, vol. 2, 313.

14. "The Great Sphinx Stela of Amenhotep II at Giza": Lichtheim 1976, vol. 2, 41.

15. "The Memphis and Karnak Stelae of Amenhotep II": Hallo and Younger 2003, vol. 2, 20.

16. Freu 2003, 72.

17. "The Memphis and Karnak Stelae of Amenhotep II": Hallo and Younger 2003, vol. 2, 21.

18. "The Memphis and Karnak Stelae of Amenhotep II": Hallo and Younger 2003, vol. 2, 22 and note 47.

19. For example, Weinstein 1981, 14; J. K. Hoffmeier, *Egypt in Israel: The Evidence for the Authenticity of the Exodus Tradition* (New York and Oxford: Oxford University Press, 1997), 113.

20. "The Great Sphinx Stela of Amenhotep II at Giza": Lichtheim 1976, vol. 2, 40–41.

21. "The Memphis and Karnak Stelae of Amenhotep II": Hallo and Younger 2003, vol. 2, 22.

22. Bryan 2000, 252.

23. Bryan 1998, 33–34.

24. Urk IV 1326: Redford 1992, 164. An alternative translation given by Bryan has the chiefs there not "to seek the peace" but "to request offering gifts": Bryan 2000, 253.

25. Redford 1992, 161, 164.

26. Betsy M. Bryan, "Antecedents to Amenhotep III," in *Amenhotep III: Perspectives on His Reign,* edited by David O'Connor and Eric H. Cline (Ann Arbor: University of Michigan Press, 1998), 34.

27. Bryan 1998, 33.

28. Bryan 2000, 250.

29. The issue of whether Mittani and Egypt reached a peace agreement in the reign of Amenhotep II has been discussed extensively, starting with Horst Klengel, *Geschichte Syriens im 2. Jahrtausend v.u.Z, vol. 1, Nordsyrien* (Berlin: Akademie Verlag, 1965), 39, and Cord Kühne, *Die Chronologie der internationalen Korrespondenz von El-Amarna* (Kevelaer: Butzon and Bercker, 1973), 20 n. 85.

30. Redford 1992, 164.

31. Redford 1992, 165.

32. Bryce 1998, 105–109.

33. Gary Beckman, "Hittite Chronology," *Akkadica* 119–120 (2000), 26.

34. "The Proclamation of Telipinu," translated by Th. P. J. van den Hout: Hallo and Younger 2003, vol. 1, 196.

35. Freu 2008, 7. Dates for the Hittite kings are not at all certain. For example, Macqueen writes that Telipinu came to power right before 1500 (Macqueen 1995, 1090), while Bryce gives his dates as 1525–1500 (Bryce 2002, xi). Bryce's dates are followed in this case.

36. Redford 1992, 163.

37. All quotes from the Kizzuwatna treaty are from HDT 2: Beckman 1999, 18–24.

38. Freu 2003, 74; Bryce 1998, 133–137.

39. Macqueen 1995, 1090–1091. Wilhelm 1995, 1249 refers to this king as Tudhaliya II.

40. Some religious rituals seem to have required the presence of gods from other cities or kingdoms. This was true of the New Year's Festival in Babylon, which is best known from the first millennium BCE. The goddess Shaushka also visited Egypt from Mittani (see Introduction).

41. "The Memphis and Karnak Stelae of Amenhotep II": Hallo and Younger 2003, vol. 2, 21.

42. EA 15: Moran 1992, 38.

43. Redford 1992, 164.

44. In several of the later Amarna letters, kings expressed this sentiment, for example in EA 19: "In my brother's country [Egypt], gold is as plentiful as dirt": Moran 1992, 44.

45. This is found in almost all the Amarna letters from the Egyptian vassals, EA 45–378: Moran 1992.

46. Redford 1992, 164.

47. Bryan 2000, 253.

48. Samuel A. Meier, "Diplomacy and International Marriages," in Cohen and Westbrook 2000, 171.

49. EA 4: Moran 1992, 8.

50. "The Great Sphinx Stela of Amenhotep II at Giza": Lichtheim 1976, vol. 2, 40.

51. "The Great Sphinx Stela of Amenhotep II at Giza": Lichtheim 1976, vol. 2, 41.

52. These are the most common gifts from Mittani in the Amarna letters: EA 16–29.

53. "The Great Sphinx Stela of Amenhotep II at Giza": Lichtheim 1976, vol. 2, 42.

54. Redford 1992, 165.

55. These aspects of "customary international law" are discussed by Gary Beckman, "International Law in the Second Millennium: Late Bronze Age," in Westbrook 2003, 765–768.

56. Beckman has noted that the great powers of this period probably all followed procedures similar to those recorded in the treaties that have been found in Hatti: Beckman 2003, 759.

57. HDT 2: Beckman 1999, 17–26; the core of this treaty was written when Hatti and Kizzuwatna were equal partners, though later additions put Hatti in the superior position: Beckman 1999, 17.

58. Quotes from the Kizzuwatna treaty are from HDT 2: Beckman 1999, 19–24.

59. HDT 1: Beckman 1999, 12.

60. Wilhelm 1995, 1250.

61. EA 8: Moran 1992, 16–17.

62. Brinkman 1976, 169–172.

63. Synchronistic History I 1'–4', ABC Chronicle no. 21: Brinkman 1976, 169.

64. EA 10: Moran 1992, 19–20.

65. Bryan 1998, 36 and note 45.

66. "Plague Prayers of Muršili II," translated by Gary Beckman: Hallo and Younger 2003, vol. 1, 158.

67. Macqueen 1995, 1091.

68. Beckman 2003, 761.

69. Beckman 2003, 763.

70. Sherine El Menshawy, "The Protocol of the Ancient Egyptian Royal Palace," in *Egyptology at the Dawn of the Twenty-First Century*, vol. 2, edited by Zahi Hawass and Lyla Pinch Brock (Cairo: American University in Cairo Press, 2004), 401.

71. El Menshawy, 401–402.

72. Redford 1992, 230.

73. Urk IV 1343–44: Bryan 1998, 37. A different translation is given by Redford: "[the destroyer of] Naharin, the one that laid waste to Hatti": Redford 1992, 230.

74. Bryan 1998, 37.

75. Roehrig 2005, 6.

76. Freu 2008, 8.

77. Bryan 1998, 42.

78. Bryan 1998, 54.

79. Bleiberg 1996, 94.

80. EA 29: Moran 1992, 93.

81. Bryan 1998, 52.

82. Meier 2000, 171.

83. For images of many of the Amarna letters, go to "The El-Amarna letters at the Vorderasiatisches Museum of Berlin" at www.amarna.ieiop.csic.es/maineng.html.

84. Moran 1992, xvi. Another thirty-two texts found at Amarna were literary: Aruz 2008, 169.

85. See Moran 1992, xxxiv–xxxix for the chronology of the letters.

86. Liverani 2000, 21.

### CHAPTER EIGHT

1. Lawrence Berman, "Overview of Amenhotep III and His Reign," in O'Connor and Cline 1998, 9. The date is given as 1390 in Roehrig 2005, 7.

2. Modern scholars have often referred to the great kings of this era as a "club," but a "brotherhood" seems the more fitting term, since it reflects their own terminology and the idea of a club is anachronistic for this time.

3. EA 31: Moran 1992, 101.

4. His name was written by his own scribes as "Nibmuarea" in cuneiform in a later letter to the king of Babylon: Moran 1992 EA1, 1.

5. Although they are often called "marriage" scarabs, the inscription doesn't actually mention the marriage. Hayes 1973, 339.

6. Urk IV 1665–66: Berman 1998, 11.

7. "Stela of Amenhotep III": Lichtheim 1976, vol. 2, 44–45.

8. Kozloff, Bryan, et al. 1992, 36.

9. Kozloff, Bryan, et al. 1992, 33.

10. Kozloff, Bryan, et al. 1992, 5, 76.

11. "Stela of Amenhotep III": Lichtheim 1976, vol. 2, 44, 47.

12. EA 1: Moran 1992, 2.

13. EA1: Moran 1992, 2.

14. Kozloff, Bryan, et al. 1992, 58.

15. EA 5: Moran 1992, 10–11.

16. EA 31: Moran 1992, 101.

17. EA 31: Moran 1992, 101.

18. EA 99, EA 369: Moran 1992, 171, 366.

19. EA 187: Moran 1992, 268–269.

20. EA 64: Moran 1992, 135.

21. Freu 2008 gives the dates 1375–1355 for Shuttarna II, but this must be wrong, since he was already on the throne in Amenhotep III's tenth year, 1381.

22. EA 17: Moran 1992, 41.

23. EA 19: Moran 1992, 44.

24. EA 23: Moran 1992, 61.

25. Eric Cline, "The World Abroad: Amenhotep III, the Aegean, and Anatolia," in O'Connor and Cline 1998, 241.

26. EA 29: Moran 1992, 93.

27. "Marriage with Kirgipa": Breasted 1906, vol. 2, 347–348.

28. Berman 1998, 13.

29. "Marriage with Kirgipa": Breasted 1906, vol. 2, 347–348.

30. Kozloff, Bryan, et al. 1992, 67–68.

31. "Wild Bull-Hunt Scarab": Kozloff, Bryan, et al. 1992, 70.

32. Kozloff, Bryan, et al. 1992, 67.

33. "The Commemorative Scarabs": Breasted 1906, vol. 2, 343–349; Kozloff, Bryan, et al. 1992, 67–70.

34. Kozloff, Bryan, et al. 1992, 4.

35. Boundary stela from his mortuary temple: Kozloff, Bryan, et al. 1992, 33.

36. Jerrold Cooper, Glenn Schwartz, and Raymond Westbrook, "A Mittani-Era Tablet from Umm el-Marra," in General Studies and Excavations at Nuzi 11/1, SCCNH 15, edited by David I. Owen and Gernot Wilhelm (Bethesda, Md.: CDL Press 2005), 46.

37. Cooper, Schwartz, and Westbrook 2005, 48–51.

38. The following three quotes are all from EA 17: Moran 1992, 41–42.

39. HDT 6B: Beckman 1999, 49. Some scholars think the attack by the Hittites that Tushratta mentioned took place around 1344, when Suppiluliuma came to the throne: for example, Bryce 1998, 169–170. This would be much too late, however, since Amenhotep III was already dead by 1344.

40. Trevor Bryce, Letters of the Great Kings of the Ancient Near East: The Royal Correspondence of the Late Bronze Age (London and New York: Routledge, 2003), 63.

41. EA 29: Moran 1992, 96.

42. EA 17: Moran 1992, 41–42.

43. EA 20: Moran 1992, 48 mentions "all my brother's troops who accompanied Mane." This probably reflects a normal practice.

44. EA 17: Moran 1992, 41–42.

45. EA 30: Moran 1992, 100.

46. Liverani 2000, 22–23.

47. As mentioned for Mane in EA 24: Moran 1992, 70.

48. A very fast return trip between the lands took three months: EA 29: Moran 1992, 93. More common, though, was for the round trip to take a whole year: Liverani 2000, 21–22.

49. Kim Benzel, "The Horse in the Ancient Near East," in Aruz 2008, 155; M. A. Littauer and J. H. Crouwel, Wheeled Vehicles and Ridden Animals in the Ancient Near East (Leiden: E.J. Brill, 1979), 96.

50. Liverani 2001, 73.

51. EA 21: Moran 1992, 50.

52. Amenhotep III moved the capital to Thebes in his twenty-ninth year. Previously, it had been in Memphis: Kozloff, Bryan, et al. 1992, 38. The delegation from Tushratta probably arrived in his thirtieth year.

53. For a description of the palace, see Joann Fletcher, *Chronicle of a Pharaoh: The Intimate Life of Amenhotep III* (New York: Oxford University Press, 2000), 128–135.

54. EA 29: Moran 1992, 93.

55. EA 1: Moran 1992, 2.

56. Norman de Garis Davis, *The Tomb of Rekh-mi-rē' at Thebes,* I (New York: Arno Press, 1943), 88, quoted in "Did Diplomatic Immunity Exist in the Ancient Near East?" by David Elgavish, *Journal of the History of International Law* 2 (2000), 79 n. 30.

57. "Story of Sinuhe": Simpson 2003, 64.

58. El Menshawy 2004, 400–401.

59. El Menshawy 2004, 403.

60. In a later letter, Tushratta commented to Tiy that she knew about the "things that I would write and say to...your husband, and the things that...your husband would always write and say to me": EA 26: Moran 1992, 84.

61. In one letter to the king of Babylon, Amenhotep quoted an earlier letter, explaining "These are the words that you sent me on your tablet," (EA 1: Moran 1992, 1), which suggests that the letters were read aloud verbatim as written.

62. For example, EA 17: Moran 1992, 42; "I listened to its words": EA 20: Moran 1992, 47.

63. All quotes from this letter are from EA17: Moran 1992, 41–42.

64. EA 11: Moran 1992, 21.

65. EA 7: Moran 1992, 13.

66. EA 10: Moran 1992, 19.

67. All quotes from this letter are from EA 7: Moran 1992, 13.

68. Liverani notes that Burna-buriash must have known how distant Egypt was from Babylonia, and that he used this dispute as a reason to bargain and argue with the pharaoh: Liverani 2000, 19.

69. Liverani 2001, 65.

70. Liverani 2001, 60.

71. Liverani 2001, 41.

72. EA 1: Moran 1992, 2.

73. EA 3: Moran 1992, 7.

74. EA 1: Moran 1992, 1.

75. EA 3: Moran 1992, 7.

76. On the detention of messengers, see Elgavish 2000, 74–77.

77. EA 3: Moran 1992, 7.

78. On at least one occasion, however, a king put the messenger of his enemy in chains, though this was described as being "not according to custom": Elgavish 2000, 76.

79. Liverani 2001, 76.

80. "Story of Sinuhe": Simpson 2003, 65–66.

81. For example, EA 20: Moran 1992, 47.

82. EA 28: Moran 1992, 91.

83. EA 7: Moran 1992, 13–14.

84. EA 16: Moran 1992, 39.

85. See Elgavish 2000, 77–78.

86. EA 16: Moran 1992, 39.

87. EA 7: Moran 1992, 14.

88. EA 8: Moran 1992, 16.

89. EA 19: Moran 1992, 44.

90. EA 19: Moran 1992, 43–44.

91. EA 27: Moran 1992, 89.

92. EA 20: Moran 1992, 48 EA 24: Moran 1992, 65; EA 27: Moran 1992, 89.

93. EA 24: Moran 1992, 65.

94. "Maxims of Ptahhotep": Simpson 2003, 133.

95. Bottero 2004, 25–35.

96. EA 27: Moran 1992, 87.

97. EA 19: Moran 1992, 44.

98. EA 23: Moran 1992, 61.

99. EA 17: Moran 1992, 41.

100. Pinhas Artzi, "The Diplomatic Service in Action: The Mittani File," in Cohen and Westbrook 2000, 209.

101. EA 24: Moran 1992, 64.

102. EA 24: Moran 1992, 69.

103. EA 26: Moran 1992, 84.

104. EA 24: Moran 1992, 70; EA 29: Moran 1992, 94–96.

105. Bryce 2003, 65.

106. EA 26: Moran 1992, 85.

107. EA 24: Moran 1992, 70.

108. EA 24: Moran 1992, 66.

109. AHK 53 15′–16′ : 138–139: Bryce 2003, 63.

110. EA 20: Moran 1992, 48; it's not entirely clear that the "they" mentioned here were messengers.

CHAPTER NINE

1. Both quotes: EA 19: Moran 1992, 43–44.

2. EA 29: Moran 1992, 93; EA 19: Moran 1992, 43.

3. For diplomatic marriage during the Amarna period, see especially Alan R. Schulman, "Diplomatic Marriage in the Egyptian New Kingdom," *JNES* 38 (1979), 177–193; Meier 2000.

4. EA 3: Moran 1992, 7.

5. Nemet-Nejat 1998, 135.

6. EA 20: Moran 1992, 47.

7. EA 19: Moran 1992, 43–44; EA 20: Moran 1992, 47; EA 21: Moran 1992, 50; EA 24: Moran 1992, 66–67. EA 24 is in Hurrian and phrased slightly differently.

8. EA 29: Moran 1992, 93.

9. Bryce 2003, 108 n. 2.

10. Amarna references: EA 11, Moran 1992, 21–22; EA 31: Moran 1992, 101; Middle Assyrian law references: MAL A 42, 43: Roth 1997, 169; Malul 1988, 161.

11. MAL A 30, 31: Roth 1997, 164–165.

12. MAL A 38: Roth 1997, 167.

13. MAL A 29: Roth 1997, 163–164.

14. MAL A 43: Roth 1997, 169.

15. See Sophie Lafont, "Middle Assyrian Period," in *A History of Ancient Near Eastern Law,* vol. 1, edited by Raymond Westbrook (Leiden: Brill 2003), 535–536; Malul 1988, 176.

16. MAL A 43: Roth 1997, 169.

17. EA 29: Moran 1992, 93.

18. EA 27: Moran 1992, 87.

19. EA 14: Moran 1992, 34 and n. 1.

20. All quotes from the list of bride-wealth are from EA 14: Moran 1992, 27–34.

21. EA 20: Moran 1992, 47.

22. EA 29: Moran 1992, 93.

23. All quotes from the princess's letter are from EA 12: Moran 1992, 24.

24. EA 24: Moran 1992, 67.

25. EA 22: Moran 1992, 57.

26. EA 22: Moran 1992, 51.

27. Iron could not yet be forged, so it was a brittle metal that was of little use in battle. Its rarity made it particularly valuable, however, for ornamental objects.

28. EA 25: Moran 1992, 72–81.

29. A picture of this tablet can be seen in Aruz 2008, object 118, p. 196.

30. EA 25: Moran 1992, 78–79.

31. EA 11: Moran 1992, 21.

32. EA 25: Moran 1992, 81.

33. Quotes from this letter are all from EA 21: Moran 1992, 50.

34. The letter, EA 24 (Moran 1992, 63–71), is something of a blessing and a curse for modern scholars. It's a blessing in that it's by far the longest surviving text in Hurrian and has provided all kinds of information about the grammar and vocabulary of that poorly understood language. But it's a curse in being so difficult to understand. The standard translation is littered with words in italics whose meaning is uncertain, and ellipses fill sections that are simply not understood.

35. EA 24: Moran 1992, 65.

36. EA 20: Moran 1992, 47.

37. HDT 22E: Beckman 1999, 135.

38. HDT 6A: Beckman 1999, 44–45.

39. All quotes from this letter are from EA 24: Moran 1992, 63–71.

40. Text 71: Eidem and Læssøe. 2001, 53.

41. EA 27: Moran 1992, 87.

42. EA 27: Moran 1992, 87.

43. EA 29: Moran 1992, 93.

44. Kozloff, Bryan, et al. 1992, 38.

45. Kozloff, Bryan, et al. 1992, 40–41.

46. "Jubilee celebrations": Breasted 1906, vol. 2, 350.

47. EA 29: Moran 1992, 93.

48. See the figure on page 203 of chapter 8 for a plan of the palace complex. The great hall with the women's quarters opening off it is in the bottom right hand corner of the plan.

49. EA 29: Moran 1992, 93.

50. EA 29: Moran 1992, 93.

51. EA 1: Moran 1992, 2.

52. The following three quotes are from EA 27: Moran 1992, 86–89.

53. In earlier times, kings such as Naram-Sin and Samsuditana set up statues of themselves in temples, either in vassal lands or in cities within their empires, as evidence of their power over these regions. Tushratta was not a vassal of the pharaoh, of course, and the statues he was receiving were of himself and his daughter, so he probably had more flexibility in where he placed the statues.

54. EA 29: Moran 1992, 94.

55. Smith 1912, 50.

56. Stephanie Pain, "Why the Pharaohs Never Smiled," *New Scientist* 187 (2005), 36–39. Note, though, that not all Egyptologists believe this was his mummy: see Edward F. Wente, review of *Das Ende der Amarnazeit: Beiträge zur Geschichte und Chronologie des Neuen Reiches* in *JNES* 42/4 (1983), 316.

57. At this point he was still known as Amenhotep—he is referred to as Amenhotep IV until he changed his name.

58. Schulman 1979, 180.

59. Kevin Avruch, "Reciprocity, Equality, and Status-Anxiety in the Amarna Letters," in Cohen and Westbrook 2000, 163.

60. EA 4: Moran 1992, 8–9.

61. EA 1: Moran 1992, 2.

62. Francois Vallat, "Susa and Susiana in Second Millennium Iran," in Sasson et al. 1995, vol. 2, 1029; Bryce 2003, 18.

63. Artzi 1978, 40.

64. HDT 6A, 6B: Beckman 1999, 42–54.

65. The three quotes from this text are from HDT 22E: Beckman 1999, 132–135.

66. All the quotes from this letter are from EA 1: Moran 1992, 1–5.

67. Bryce 2003, 110.

68. EA 1: Moran 1992, 2.

69. Vallat 1995, 1029–1030.

70. Brinkman 1976, 166–172; Liverani 2001, 132.

71. For example, Bryce 2003, 111.

72. Kuhrt 1995, vol. 1, 352.

73. Wente 1983, 315–318; Nicholas Reeves, *Akhenaten: Egypt's False Prophet* (London: Thames and Hudson, 2001), 161.

74. Van Dijk 2000, 275.

75. Van Dijk 2000, 277.

76. "The Tell el-Amarna Landmarks": Breasted 1906, vol. 2, 395 and note b.

77. "The Tell el-Amarna Landmarks": Breasted 1906, vol. 2, 396.

78. "The Tell el-Amarna Landmarks": Breasted 1906, vol. 2, 396.

79. "The Tell el-Amarna Tombs": Breasted 1906, vol. 2, 407.

80. EA 26: Moran 1992, 84.

81. This and the next five quotes are from EA 29: Moran 1992, 92–98.

82. EA 27: Moran 1992, 87.

83. EA 26: Moran 1992, 85; EA 27: Moran 1992, 87–88; EA 29: Moran 1992, 94–97.

84. All the quotes in this paragraph are from EA 26, Moran 1992, 84–85.

85. Bryce 2003, 113; Reeves 1988, 100–101; Reeves 2001, 159–160.

86. Reeves 1988, 101.

87. Van Dijk 2000, 278.

CHAPTER TEN

1. EA 9: Moran 1992, 18: the letter was probably written to Tutankhamen.

2. See Liverani 2000, 23–26 on the basic features of gift exchanges in the Amarna period.

3. "The God of My Father," translated by G. Dossin, in Pritchard 1969, 629.

4. For a discussion of the concept of "house" in Syria and Mesopotamia, see David Schloen, *The House of the Father as Fact and Symbol: Patrimonialism in Ugarit and the Ancient Near East* (Winona Lake, Ind.: Eisenbrauns, 2001).

5. EA 19: Moran 1992, 44–45.

6. Of the twenty-six international letters between the great kings of Egypt, Babylonia, Mittani, Hatti, and Assyria that have survived completely enough for interpretation, only two were not originally accompanied by valuable presents, according to the texts of the letters. The letters that were not accompanied by gifts were EA 1 (Moran 1992, 1–5) from Egypt to Babylonia and EA 28 (Moran 1992, 90–92) from Mittani. EA 29 (Moran 1992, 92–99) was also not apparently accompanied by a greeting gift, but it was sent at the same time as the vast dowry of Tadu-Hepa and the marriage gifts sent by Tushratta to Amenhotep III, which must have made a greeting gift unnecessary.

7. Artzi 1978, 37.

8. Liverani has asserted that silver was not given as a gift because it was used as money at this time, and giving money would have been in bad form: Mario Liverani, "The Late Bronze Age: Materials and Mechanisms of Trade and Cultural Exchange," in Aruz 2008, 166. On the other hand, the Hittite king sent silver objects to the pharaoh, and the king of Alashiya requested silver from the pharaoh.

9. This was true of letters from Babylonia, Mittani, and Hatti. The kings of Assyria and Alashiya mentioned their greeting gifts earlier in the letters.

10. There are few letters from Hatti. Silver objects were sent along with letter EA 41 (Moran 1992, 114). Both the letters from Assyria (EA 15 and EA 16: Moran 1992, 37–41) and almost all the letters from Babylonia (EA 2: Moran 1992, 6; EA 7, EA 8, EA 9, EA 10, EA 11: Moran 1992, 12–23) refer to gifts of lapis lazuli. Jewelry is mentioned as a gift in Mittani letters (EA 17, EA 19, EA 20, EA 21, EA 26, EA 27, and EA 29: Moran 1992, 42, 45, 48, 50, 85, 89, 97) as well as in both the inventories of gifts from Mittani (EA 22. EA 25: Moran 1992, 51–61, 72–84).

11. Chariots and horses from Assyria (all references are to Moran 1992): EA 15 (p. 38) EA 16 (p. 39); from Babylonia: EA 3 (p. 7), EA 9 (p. 18); from Mittani: EA 17 (p. 42), EA 19 (p. 45). Horses alone from Babylonia: EA 2 (p. 6, though chariots might have been mentioned in the broken section of the text), EA 7 (p. 13).

12. Wooden objects from Babylonia: EA 2: Moran 1992, 6; sweet oil, bows and arrow from Mittani: (all in Moran 1992): EA 17 (p. 42), EA 26 (p. 85), EA 27 (p. 89), EA 29 (p. 97); textiles from Babylonia: EA 12; textiles and garments from Mittani: EA 27 (p. 89), EA 29 (pp. 97–98).

13. From Mittani: EA 17 (p. 42), EA 19 (p. 45); from Babylon: EA 3 (p. 7); from Hatti: EA 44 (p. 117).

14. Zaccagnini 1983, 250–251. See also Louise A. Hitchcock, "'Who Will Personally Invite a Foreigner, Unless He Is a Craftsman?': Exploring Interconnections in Aegean and Levantine Architecture," in Laffineur and Greco 2005, 691–699.

15. EA 49: Moran 1992, 120–121.

16. Zaccagnini 1983, 254.

17. Zaccagnini 1983, 253.

18. Acco: EA 235 (+) 327: Moran 1992, 293; Ashkelon: EA 323: Moran 1992, 351–352; Lachish: EA 331: Moran 1992, 335.

19. Liverani 2008, 163.

20. EA 3: Moran 1992, 7.

21. EA 5: Moran 1992, 11.

22. EA 31: Moran 1992, 101.

23. EA 19: Moran 1992, 45.

24. EA 10: Moran 1992, 19.

25. Tushratta: (all in Moran 1992) EA 19 (pp. 44–45), EA 20 (p. 48), EA 24 (pp. 65, 68), EA 27 (p. 89), EA 29 (p. 97); Kadashman-Enlil I: EA 4: Moran 1992, 9; Burna-buriash II: (all in Moran 1992) EA 7 (p. 14), EA 9 (p. 18), EA 11 (p. 22); Ashur-uballit: EA 16: Moran 1992, 39; Hittite prince: EA 44: Moran 1992, 117.

26. EA 9: Moran 1992, 18.

27. EA 4: Moran 1992, 9.

28. EA 4: Moran 1992, 9.

29. EA 4: Moran 1992, 9.

30. Liverani 2008, 166.

31. EA 29: Moran 1992, 92–99.

32. This and the next four quotes are from EA 19: Moran 1992, 44–45.

33. EA 19: Moran 1992, 44.

34. EA 16: Moran 1992, 39.
35. EA 16: Moran 1992, 39.
36. EA 9: Moran 1992, 12.
37. EA 7: Moran 1992 14.
38. EA 7: Moran 1992, 14.
39. EA 10: Moran 1992, 16.
40. EA 9: Moran 1992, 18.
41. EA 6: Moran 1992, 12.
42. EA 7: Moran 1992, 13–14.
43. EA 7: Moran 1992, 14; EA 10: Moran 1992, 19.
44. EA 10: Moran 1992, 19.
45. EA 11: Moran 1992, 21.
46. EA 11: Moran 1992, 22.
47. EA 10: Moran 1992, 19.
48. EA 11: Moran 1992, 22.
49. All quotes in this paragraph are from EA 20: Moran 1992, 48.
50. EA 19: Moran 1992, 44.
51. EA 27: Moran 1992, 88.
52. James D. Muhly, "Cyprus," in Meyers 1997, vol. 2, 93.
53. A. Bernard Knapp, "Alashiya, Caphtor/Keftiu, and Eastern Mediterranean Trade: Recent Studies in Cypriote Archaeology and History," in *Journal of Field Archaeology* 12 (1985), 247.
54. Goren, Finkelstein, and Na'aman 2004, 72–73.
55. Muhly 1997, 90.
56. Knapp 1995, 1435.
57. EA 35: Moran 1992, 107–108.
58. EA 37: Moran 1992, 107.
59. Artzi claims that "brother" had the meaning of "business partner" in the case of Alashiya: Artzi 1978, 29 n. 5.
60. EA 34: Moran 1992, 106; EA 35: Moran 1992, 107.
61. EA 33: Moran 1992, 104.
62. EA 35: Moran 1992, 107.
63. EA 35: Moran 1992, 107.
64. EA 33: Moran 1992, 104. In one letter the greeting gift was five talents of copper and five teams of horses (EA 37: Moran 1992, 110), in another it was "five (talents) of copper, three talents of fine copper, one piece of ivory, one (beam) of boxwood, one (beam) for a ship" (EA 40: Moran 1992, 113). In a third letter, it was 500 [shekels] of copper" (EA 35: Moran 1992, 107); see Liverani 2008, 167.
65. EA 35: Moran 1992, 107–108.
66. Zaccagnini notes that "silver" could also mean "price" or "(equivalent) value": Carlo Zaccagnini, "The Interdependence of the Great Powers," in Cohen and Westbrook 2000, 146.
67. EA 35: Moran 1992, 107.
68. Moran 1992, 109 note 6.

69. EA 34: Moran 1992, 105–106.

70. A log on board the ship has been dated by dendrochronology to 1305 BCE. It was presumably cut not long before the ship sailed: George F. Bass, "Sailing between the Aegean and the Orient," in Cline and Harris-Cline 1998, 184. Regarding the makeup of the crew, see Cemal Pulak, "Who Were the Mycenaeans Aboard the Uluburun Ship?" in Laffineur and Greco 2005, 295–310.

71. Cemal Pulak, "The Uluburun Shipwreck and Late Bronze Age Trade," in Aruz 2008, 290–291, 304.

72. Pulak 2008, 298.

73. Knapp notes, "Various 16th century [CE] records indicate that crossing the Mediterranean from north to south could take from one to two weeks; from east to west—or vice versa—two to three months." He observes that the same journey in the Bronze Age probably took a similar amount of time: A Bernard Knapp, "Mediterranean Bronze Age Trade: Distance, Power and Place," in Cline and Harris-Cline 1998, 193–194.

74. Pulak 2008, 302.

75. Pulak 2008, 297.

76. Pulak 2008, 302.

77. Pulak 2008, 290–297.

78. An image of such an Aegean harbor town is seen in the miniature frieze from the West House in Thera: Aruz 2008, 124–125. See analysis in Sarah P. Morris, "A Tale of Two Cities: The Miniature Frescoes from Thera and the Origins of Greek Poetry," AJA 93 (1989), 511–535. Although the cargo ship sailed over a hundred years after the frieze was painted, it's likely that such a scene would not have changed much.

79. EA 34: Moran 1992, 105–106.

80. Bryce 2006, 95.

81. Aruz 2008, 274.

82. Bryce 2006, 99.

83. Trevor Bryce, The Trojans and their Neighbours: An Introduction (London and New York: Routledge, 2006), 98; Bass 1998.

84. Aruz 2008, 274.

85. Aruz 2008, 282–284.

86. Bass 1998, 189.

87. Robert B. Koehl, "Aegean Interactions with the Near East and Egypt during the Late Bronze Age," in Aruz 2008, 270.

88. Koehl 2008, 271.

89. For a description of Mycenaean textile production at Pylos, see Marc Van De Mieroop, The Eastern Mediterranean in the Age of Ramesses II (Malden, Mass.: Blackwell, 2007) 153–156.

90. Kozloff, Bryan, et al. 1992, 57.

91. Eric H. Cline, "Amenhotep III and the Aegean: A Reassessment of Egypto-Aegean Relations in the 14th Century B.C.," Orientalia 56 (1987), 1–36.

92. Koehl 2008, 271.

93. A. Margherita Jasink, "Mycenaean Means of Communication and Diplomatic Relations with Foreign Royal Courts," in Laffineur and Greco 2005, 59 n. 1.

94. Jasink 2005, 67.

95. Bryce 2006, 101.

96. Bryce 2006, 102.

97. HDT 17: Beckman 1999, 106; Koehl 2008, 271.

98. Beckman 1999, 124, n. 23.

99. KBo II 11: Jasink 2005, 61.

100. George F. Bass, "A Bronze Age Shipwreck at Ulu Burun (Kaš): 1984 Campaign," *AJA* 90/3 (1986), 286; amber beads were also found in Tutankhamen's tomb: Annie Caubet, "The International Style: A Point of View from the Levant and Syria," in Cline and Harris-Cline 1998, 106.

101. Edward L. Shaughnessy, "Historical Perspectives in the Introduction of the Chariot into China," *Harvard Journal of Asiatic Studies* 48 (1988), 228.

102. Marian Feldman, *Diplomacy by Design: Luxury Arts and an "International Style" in the Ancient Near East, 1400–1200 BCE* (Chicago: University of Chicago Press, 2005).

CHAPTER ELEVEN

1. All quotes in this paragraph are from EA 24 iii: Moran 1992, 69. The sequence of events in this chapter and the next are much debated, since they are reconstructed from a number of different Hittite, Egyptian, and Mittanian sources, most of which don't include dates.

2. Kurt Bittel, *Hattusha: The Capital of the Hittites* (New York: Oxford University Press, 1970), 3–23.

3. EA 31: Moran 1992, 101.

4. Andreas Müller-Karpe, "The Hittite Empire," in Aruz 2008, 171.

5. EA 28: Moran 1992, 91.

6. Some scholars attribute as many as forty years to Suppiluliuma's reign: for example, Kuhrt 1995, 252. I am following Bryce's persuasive arguments for dating his reign from 1344 to 1322: Trevor R. Bryce, "Some Observations on the Chronology of Šuppiluliuma's Reign," *Anatolian Studies* 39 (1989): 19–30.

7. "Plague Prayers of Mursili II": Hallo and Younger 2003, vol. 1, 156.

8. Bryce suggests that this campaign might have been the one that Tushratta referred to as his victory against the Hittites in his first letter (EA 17) after taking the throne, written to Amenhotep III: Bryce 1998, 170. This is unlikely, however, since Suppiluliuma seems to have come to power during the reign of Akhenaten, and EA 17 was written several years before Amenhotep III's death.

9. EA 41: Moran 1992, 114; Suppiluliuma used a strange spelling for the name of the king to whom he was writing: Huriy[a]. This could have represented Naphurureya (Akhenaten), Nibhurureya (Tutankhamen), or Anahururiya (Smenkhare). Scholars debate this, but Smenkhare seems the most likely.

10. EA 41: Moran 1992, 114.

11. EA 26: Moran 1992, 84.

354 NOTES TO PAGES 269–277

12. EA 28, Moran 1992, 91, EA 29: Moran 1992, 96–97.

13. EA 29: Moran 1992, 96–97.

14. EA 29: Moran 1992, 92.

15. EA 29: Moran 1992, 97.

16. EA 29: Moran 1992, 96.

17. Bryce 1989, 28, 30.

18. Bryce 1998, 172–174.

19. Harry A. Hoffner, Jr., "A Prayer of Muršili II about His Stepmother," *JAOS* 103 (1983), 187–192.

20. Van De Mieroop 2007, 31–32. This man's name, Artatama, is the same as that of Tushratta's father, so it is likely that he was from the same family, though the texts don't specify that he was Tushratta's brother.

21. HDT 6A: Beckman 1999, 42.

22. Bryce 1998, 174–177.

23. This and the following three quotes are from HDT 6A: Beckman 1999, 42–48.

24. HDT 6B: Beckman 1999, 48–49.

25. HDT 6A: Beckman 1999, 42.

26. EA 42: Moran 1992, 115–116.

27. Quotes from this text are all from HDT 6A: Beckman 1999, 43.

28. HDT 19: Beckman 1999, 125–126.

29. Pedersen 1998, 68–80.

30. Marguerite Yon, "Ugarit: History and Archaeology," trans. S. Rosoff, in *Anchor Bible Dictionary,* vol. 6, edited by David Noel Freedman (New York: Doubleday, 1992), 698.

31. Elizabeth J. W. Barber, "Textiles," in Meyers 1997, vol. 5, 192.

32. Marguerite Yon, "Ugarit," in Meyers 1997, 260.

33. Yon 1997, 260.

34. W. H. Van Soldt, "The Palace Archives at Ugarit," in *Cuneiform Archives and Libraries,* 30th RAI, edited by Klaas R. Veenhof (Istanbul: Nederlands Historisch-Archaeologisch Instituut, 1986), 196 n. 2; Michael Astour, "Ugarit and the Great Powers," in *Ugarit in Retrospect: 50 Years of Ugarit and Ugaritic,* edited by Gordon D. Young (Winona Lake, Ind.: Eisenbrauns, 1981), 23.

35. EA 89: Moran 1992, 162.

36. Yon 1997, 259.

37. Yon 2006, 38.

38. Yon 2006, 43.

39. Yon 2006, 136–137.

40. Yon 2006, 129.

41. EA 49: Moran 1992, 120.

42. EA 49: Moran 1992, 120.

43. Beckman 2006, 282 notes that neutrality was impossible for a lesser state.

44. HDT 4: Beckman 1999, 34.

45. HDT 4: Beckman 1999, 34–35.

46. IIDT 28A: Beckman 1999, 166–167.

47. HDT 6A: Beckman 1999, 43.

48. Peter Pfälzner, "The Royal Palace at Qatna: Power and Prestige in the Late Bronze Age," in Aruz 2008, 220.

49. HDT 6A: Beckman 1999, 43–44.

50. Bryce 1998, 176.

51. Introduction to HDT 5: Beckman 1999, 36.

52. EA 157: Moran 1992, 243.

53. EA 162: Moran 1992, 249.

54. EA 162 n. 6: Moran 1992, 250.

55. Bryce 1998, 188.

56. HDT 5: Beckman 1999, 37.

57. For example, HDT 6A: Beckman 1999, 43.

58. "Deeds of Suppiluliuma": Hallo and Younger 2003, vol. 1, 187.

59. "The Plague Prayers": Hallo and Younger 2003, vol. 1, 156.

60. Bryce 1998, 176.

61. J. D. Hawkins, "Carchemish," in Meyers 1997, vol. 1, 423–424.

62. EA 15: Moran 1992, 38; Artzi 1978, 28, 30.

63. EA 15: Moran 1992, 38.

64. EA 16: Moran 1992, 38–39.

65. The issue of a possible coregency of Akhenaten and Smenkhare is much debated among Egyptologists: Jared L. Miller, "Amarna Age Chronology and the Identity of Nibhururiya in the Light of a Newly Reconstructed Hittite Text," *Altorientalische Forschungen* 34 (2007), 257.

66. EA 41: Moran 1992, 114. See note 10.

67. EA 41: Moran 1992, 114.

68. The argument has been made that he might have been Nefertiti's seventh child: Marc Gabolde, "La parenté de Toutânkhamon," *Bulletin de la Société Française d'Égyptologie* 155 (2002), 32–48.

69. All the quotes from the "Deeds of Suppiluliuma" are from Hallo and Younger 2003, vol. 1, 189–190.

70. Thomas H. Maugh II, "Infection, Not a Rival, May Have Dealt the Fatal Blow to King Tut," *Los Angeles Times,* March 9, 2005.

71. A vast number of studies have been written about this episode. For a list of them, see the bibliography in Jared L. Miller, "Amarna Age Chronology and the Identity of Nibhuruiya in the Light of a Newly Reconstructed Hittite Text," *Altorientalische Forschungen* 34 (2007), 290–293. The major question is whether the queen who wrote to Suppiluliuma was the widow of Tutankhamen or of Akhenaten. The proponents of both theories are very adamant and each group has plenty of evidence to support them, though neither is completely proven. The king's name was written as "Nibhururiya" in the Hittite text, a reasonable cuneiform approximation of Nebkheprure, Tutankhamen's throne name. Akhenaten's name was usually written as Naphurureya in cuneiform. Several recent studies have made strong arguments for the idea that it was Akhenaten who had died (see especially Miller 2007, 252–293, and Theo P. J. van den Hout, "Der Falke und das Kücken: der neue Pharao und der hethitische Prinz?" *ZA* 84 (1994), 60–88), but, as the authors admit, they cannot answer all the questions. For example, Akhenaten did have a son—Tutankhamen—who might

even have been Nefertiti's son. It's unlikely that Nefertiti would have worried about a "servant" taking the throne. And in his ninth year Mursili II was sending envoys to the court of Haremhab in Egypt (see below, chapter 12, note 24). Haremhab seems to have been king at that time. If it had been Nefertiti who wrote to Suppiluliuma, this would not allow enough years for Tutankhamen's reign. The date of Mursili's accession is based on a solar eclipse in his tenth year (one took place on June 5, 1312). This is only possible if it was Tutankhamen's widow who wrote to Suppiluliuma. The other arguments for it having been Tutankhamen who died, as followed in this book, are laid out in Trevor R. Bryce, "The Death of Niphururiya and Its Aftermath," *Journal of Egyptian Archaeology* 76 (1990), 97–105.

72. "Deeds of Suppiluliuma": Hallo and Younger 2003, vol. 1, 190.

73. EA 4: Moran 1992, 8–9.

74. The quotes regarding the Egyptian queen's request are all from the "Deeds of Suppiluliuma": Hallo and Younger 2003, vol. 1, 190–191.

75. "Plague Prayers of Mursili I": Hallo and Younger 2003, vol. 1, 158.

76. "Deeds of Suppiluliuma": Hallo and Younger 2003, vol. 1, 191.

77. "Plague Prayers of Mursili I": Hallo and Younger 2003, vol. 1, 158.

78. Jacobus Van Dijk, "The Amarna Period and the Later New Kingdom," in Shaw 2000, 292–293.

79. KUB XIX 20 +: van den Hout 1994, 64–70; see also Bryce 1998, 198, n. 106.


## CHAPTER TWELVE

1. This is a longer span of time for Tushratta's reign than most scholars estimate, but it seems likely. The king took the throne as a child, and ruled for several years under the domination of his brother's assassin. By c. 1355 BCE, Tushratta's daughter was old enough to marry Amenhotep III. If she was thirteen at the time, and he had been seventeen when she was born (to take the minimum likely number of years), he would have been thirty in 1355, hence born no later than 1385. In 1326, the likely year of his death, he would have been at least fifty-nine years old. He might have been a few years older, perhaps in his early sixties.

2. Some scholars believe that it was Shuttarna III, son of Artatama II, who killed Tushratta; for example, Van De Mieroop 2007, 31. For the sequence of events in the reigns of Tushratta and Suppiluliuma at this period, see Bryce 1998, 195–199.

3. HDT 6B: Beckman 1999, 49. The date of Tushratta's death is debated. Some scholars put it at 1335 BCE (e.g., Freu 2003), but Carchemish was in Hittite hands shortly after Tushratta's death and the Hittites did not take Carchemish until after the death of Tutankhamen, so Tushratta must have died after 1327 BCE.

4. All the quotes in this paragraph are from HDT 6B: Beckman 1999 text 6B, 49.

5. HDT 6B: Beckman 1999, 49.

6. Kurigalzu II's reign followed very short reigns by two men, both of whom were killed: Ashur-uballit's grandson, Karahardash, who was assassinated, and his usurper, Nazi-bugash, who was then executed by Ashur-uballit before Kurigalzu II took the throne: Kuhrt 1995, vol. 1, 352. The names of the Assyrian and Babylonian kings who were ruling at the time of Tushratta's death are not given in the sources.

Some scholars believe that Ashur-uballit I and Burna-buriash II were still ruling at this time: Van De Mieroop 2007, 31–34.

7. Quotes in this paragraph are to HDT 6A: Beckman 1999, 44.

8. This and the next five quotes are from HDT 6B: Beckman 1999, 49–51.

9. HDT 6A: Beckman 1999, 44.

10. This king was also known in other texts as Sharri-kushuh.

11. HDT 6B: Beckman 1999 text 6B, 51.

12. Intro to HDT 6: Beckman 1999, 41.

13. G. M. Beckman, "Some Observations on the Suppiluliuma-Šattiwaza Treaties," in *The Tablet and the Scroll: Near Eastern Studies in Honor of William W. Hallo,* edited by Mark E. Cohen et al. (Bethesda, Md.: CDL Press, 1993), 56.

14. For an analysis of international treaties in the Amarna period, see Westbrook 2000, 36–41.

15. HDT 6B: Beckman 1999, 48–54.

16. All quotes from this treaty (the next seventeen quotes) are from HDT 6A: Beckman 1999, 44–45.

17. Westbrook 2000, 30–31.

18. HDT 6B: Beckman 1999, text 6B, 52.

19. HDT 6A: Beckman 1999, 48.

20. This and the next four quotations are all from "Plague Prayers": Hallo and Younger 2003, vol. 1, 157–158.

21. The date of Mursili's accession to the throne is based on a reference to a solar omen in his tenth year. A solar eclipse took place in 1312 BCE: Miller 2007, 288 (though Miller discounts this evidence).

22. HDT 8 and HDT 9, Beckman 1999, 59–69.

23. KUB 19.15+KBo 50.24: Miller 2007, 253.

24. KUB 19.15+KBo 50.24: Miller 2007, 253. Miller argues that this text refers to a time before Haremhab was king, when he was commanding troops in Canaan for Tutankhamen. Miller notes that Mursili did not use the term for "king" with reference to Haremhab. It seems more likely, though, that this exchange was between equals—two great kings—since there was obviously no deference on the part of either one to the other, and Mursili II notes that "it was I who took the [land] of Amurru away from you." It is unlikely that he would say this to anyone but the king. Perhaps he was unwilling to use the term "king" because Haremhab was not related to the previous royal family and had taken the throne that Mursili believed should have been occupied by his brother Zannanza. The exchange of envoys and letters between the two men is so familiar that the obvious conclusion is that they were both great kings.

25. Adad-nirari inscription: A. Kirk Grayson, *Assyrian Rulers of the Third and Second Millennium BC,* RIM Assyrian Periods, vol. 1 (Toronto: University of Toronto Press, 1987), 183–184.

26. Van De Mieroop 2007, 34–35.

27. For the dates, see Beckman 2000, 23.

28. The diplomatic correspondence is found in Beckman 1999, 125–152.

29. HDT 24A: Beckman 1999, 147.

30. HDT 23: Beckman 1999, 139.

EPILOGUE

1. Michalowski 2006.

2. Jim Holt, "Good Instincts: Why Is Anyone an Altruist?" *New York Times Magazine,* March 9, 2008, 11–12.

3. Alan Lloyd, "Egyptians Abroad in the Late Period," in *Travel, Geography and Culture in Ancient Greece, Egypt and the Near East,* edited by Colin Adams and Jim Roy (Oakville, CT: Oxbow Books, 2007), 34–36.

4. Lloyd 2007, 36.

5. See, for example, Jonathan Wright, *The Ambassadors* (London: HarperPress, 2006).

# Further Reading

This work is based on the research of dozens of scholars. They might not agree with all my conclusions—the interpretations are mine (unless footnotes note otherwise)—but I am indebted to them for their many books, essays, articles, and text translations. Readers who are interested in learning more may want to consult the following works.

A number of excellent books have been written in recent years giving overviews of all of ancient Near Eastern history, such as *A History of the Ancient Near East* by Marc Van De Mieroop (2nd ed. 2007) and *The Ancient Near East c. 3000–330 BC* (in two volumes) by Amélie Kuhrt (1995). Books about specific civilizations include *Civilizations of Ancient Iraq* by Benjamin R. Foster and Karen Pollinger Foster (2009), *The Kingdom of the Hittites* by Trevor Bryce (1998), *The Oxford History of Ancient Egypt,* edited by Ian Shaw (2000), *Canaanites* by Jonathan Tubb (1998), *The Aegean Bronze Age* by Oliver Dickinson (1994), and *Ancient Cities of the Indus Valley Civilization* by Jonathan M. Kenoyer (1998). Studies of daily life can be found in *Life in the Ancient Near East* by Daniel C. Snell (1997), *Daily Life in Ancient Mesopotamia* by Karen Rhea Nemet-Nejat (1998), and *Daily Life in Ancient Egypt* by Kasia Szpakowska (2008).

Some encyclopedias and volumes of collected essays include contributions by some of the top scholars in the relevant fields. Notable among these are *Civilizations of the Ancient Near East* (in four volumes), edited by Jack M. Sasson and others (1995); *A Companion to the Ancient Near East,* edited by Daniel C. Snell (2005); and *The Babylonian World,* edited by Gwendolyn Leick (2009).

Some recent museum exhibits relevant to the topic of this book have been accompanied by catalogues that are both accessibly written and beautifully illustrated. These include *Egypt's Dazzling Sun: Amenhotep III and His World* by Arielle P. Kozloff, Betsy M. Bryan, and others (1992), which was produced for an exhibition organized by the Cleveland Museum of Fine Art; *Syria: Land of Civilizations* by Michel Fortin (1999),

for an exhibition organized by the Musée de la civilisation de Québec; and three catalogues for exhibits organized by the Metropolitan Museum of Art in New York: *Art of
the First Cities: The Third Millennium B.C. from the Mediterranean to the Indus*, edited by
Joan Aruz (2003); *Hatshepsut: From Queen to Pharaoh*, edited by Catherine H. Roehrig
(2005); and, most recently, *Beyond Babylon: Art, Trade, and Diplomacy in the Second
Millennium B.C.*, edited by Joan Aruz and others (2008).

For the study of ancient international relations before the Amarna period, some
of the most important work is found in journal articles and essays (for example, in the
collections and museum catalogues listed above) rather than books. The Italian scholars Paolo Matthiae and Alfonso Archi have written extensively on the foreign relations
of Ebla. For southern Mesopotamia during the same period, see, for example, articles
by Jerold Cooper and Piotr Michalowski. Much of what has been written about Mari in
the Old Babylonian period has been published in French (and occasionally in English)
by scholars Dominique Charpin, Bertrand Lafont, and Jean-Marie Durand. American
scholars Jack M. Sasson and Daniel Fleming have also contributed a great deal to Mari
studies.

Raymond Westbrook's research spans both the Old Babylonian and Amarna
periods, with a particular focus on international law (see especially the book that he
coedited in 2000 with Raymond Cohen called *Amarna Diplomacy*). The same wide
chronological span is found in the work of Gary M. Beckman, who has specialized in
the study of Hittite treaties and other aspects of diplomacy. The Amarna period has
been chronicled and analyzed by many other scholars, such as Mario Liverani (see
his 2001 book *International Relations in the Ancient Near East, 1600–1100 BC*), Trevor
Bryce (*Letters of the Great Kings of the Ancient Near East*, 2003), Donald Redford (*Egypt,
Canaan, and Israel in Ancient Times*, 1992), A. Bernard Knapp (who studies the Aegean
and Cyprus); and Eric H. Cline and David O'Connor (*Amenhotep III: Perspectives on His
Reign*, 1998). Other scholars who have explored long-distance contacts in the ancient
Near East include Daniel Potts, Carlo Zaccagnini, Marian Feldman (see her 2005 study
*Diplomacy by Design*), and Marc Van De Mieroop (his 2007 book *The Eastern Mediter-
ranean in the Age of Ramesses II* also includes much information about the era before
Ramesses II).

Most of the ancient documents used in this study have been translated into English and are available in books and articles. Books that include a wide variety of documents from the ancient Near East include *The Context of Scripture* (in three volumes),
edited by William W. Hallo and K. Lawson Younger (2003); *The Ancient Near East*,
edited by Mark W. Chavalas (2006); and *Ancient Near Eastern Texts*, edited by James B.
Pritchard (1969). Egyptian documents are translated in *Ancient Egyptian Literature* (in
three volumes) by Miriam Lichtheim (1976), *The Literature of Ancient Egypt* by William
Kelly Simpson (2003), and *Ancient Records of Egypt* (in five volumes) by James Henry
Breasted (1906). Mesopotamian literary works can be found in *Before the Muses* (two
volumes) by Benjamin R. Foster (1996) and *Myths from Mesopotamia* by Stephanie
Dalley (1989). Various Mesopotamian letters are translated in *Letters from Mesopotamia*
by A. Leo Oppenheim (1967) and *Letters from Early Mesopotamia* by Piotr Michalowski
(1993). Several hundred Mari letters are translated into English in *Letters to the King
of Mari* by Wolfgang Heimpel (2003). For the Amarna correspondence, along with

a commentary, see *The Amarna Letters* by William L. Moran (1992). For Hittite treaties and letters, and a valuable analysis of them, see *Hittite Diplomatic Texts* by Gary M. Beckman (1999). For laws from Mesopotamia and Hatti, see *Law Collections from Mesopotamia and Asia Minor* by Martha T. Roth (1997).

Paul Collins, *From Egypt to Babylon* (2008), chapters 4–11, gives an excellent overview of international relations in the period after that which is covered by this book, from 1300 to 500 BCE, including the collapse of the great powers and the growth of empires.

# Bibliography

Abdallah, F. "La femme dans le royaume d'Alep au XVIIIe siècle av. J.-C." In Durand 1987, 13–15.

Abou Assaf, Ali. "Fakhariyah, Tell." In Meyers 1997, vol 2, 300.

Akkermans, Peter M. M. G., and Glenn M. Schwartz. *The Archaeology of Syria: From Complex Hunter-Gatherers to Early Urban Societies (ca. 16,000–300 BC)*. Cambridge: Cambridge University Press, 2003.

Algaze, Guillermo. *The Uruk World System: The Dynamics of Expansion of Early Mesopotamian Civilization*. Chicago: University of Chicago Press, 1993.

Al-Maqdissi, Michel. "The Development of Trade Routes in the Early Second Millennium B.C." In Aruz et al. 2008, 42–43.

Allen, James P. "Egypt and the Near East in the Third Millennium B.C." In Aruz 2003, 251–253.

Altman, Amnon. *The Historical Prologue of the Hittite Vassal Treaties: An Inquiry into the Concepts of Hittite Interstate Law*. Ramat-Gan: Bar-Ilan University Press, 2004.

André-Salvini, Béatrice. "Tello (Ancient Girsu)." In Aruz 2003, 68–69.

Annan, Kofi A. "The Meaning of International Community." United Nations Information Service, December 30, 1999. Available at http://www.unis.unvienna. org/unis/pressrels/1999/sg2478.html

Archi, Alfonso. "The Royal Archives of Ebla." In *Ebla to Damascus: Art and Archaeology of Ancient Syria*, ed. Harvey Weiss, 140–148. Seattle and London: University of Washington Press, 1985.

———."More on Ebla and Kish." In *Eblaitica*, vol. 1., ed. C. H. Gordon et al., 125–140. Winona Lake, Ind.: Eisenbrauns, 1987.

———."Trade and Administrative Practice: The Case of Ebla," *Altorientalische Forschungen* 20/1 (1993): 43–58.

———."Ebla Texts." In Meyers 1997, vol. 2, 184–186.

————."Considerations on a Delivery of Spearheads from Ebla." *JCS* 60 (2008): 1–5.

Archi, Alfonso, and Maria Giovanna Biga. "A Victory over Mari and the Fall of Ebla." *JCS* 55 (2003): 1–44.

*Archives Royales de Mari.* Paris: Éditions Recherche sur les Civilisations, 1950 ff.

Arnold, Bill T., and David B. Weisberg. "A Centennial Review of Friedrich Delitzsch's 'Babel und Bibel' Lectures." *Journal of Biblical Literature* 121 (2002): 441–457.

Artzi, Pinhas. "The Rise of the Middle-Assyrian Kingdom, according to El-Amarna Letters 15 & 16." In *Bar-Ilan Studies in History,* ed. Pinhas Artzi, 25–41. Ramat-Gan, Israel: Bar-Ilan University Press, 1978.

————."The Diplomatic Service in Action: The Mittani File." In Cohen and Westbrook 2000, 205–211.

Aruz, Joan. "The Aegean and the Orient: The Evidence of Stamp and Cylinder Seals." In Cline and Harris-Cline 1998, 301–309.

————(ed.). *Art of the First Cities: The Third Millennium B.C. from the Mediterranean to the Indus.* New Haven and London: Yale University Press, 2003.

————."Art and Interconnections in the Third Millennium B.C." In Aruz 2003, 239–250.

————."'Intercultural Style' Carved Chlorite Objects." In Aruz 2003, 325–345.

————."Painted Palaces." In Aruz et al. 2008, 123.

Aruz, Joan, et al. (eds.). *Beyond Babylon: Art, Trade, and Diplomacy in the Second Millennium B.C.* New Haven and London: Yale University Press, 2008.

Astour, Michael. "Ugarit and the Great Powers." In *Ugarit in Retrospect: 50 Years of Ugarit and Ugaritic,* ed. Gordon D. Young, 3–29. Winona Lake, Ind.: Eisenbrauns, 1981.

Averbeck, Richard, Benjamin Studevent-Hickman, and Piotr Michalowski. "Late Third Millennium BCE Sumerian Texts." In Chavalas 2006, 47–87.

Avruch, Kevin. "Reciprocity, Equality, and Status-Anxiety in the Amarna Letters." In Cohen and Westbrook 2000, 154–164.

Baines, John. "Contextualizing Egyptian Representations of Society and Ethnicity." In Cooper and Schwartz 1996, 339–384.

Barber, Elizabeth. J. W. "Textiles." In Meyers 1997, vol. 5, 192.

————.*The Mummies of Ürümchi.* New York and London: W. W. Norton, 1999.

Barber, R. N. L. Review of *Aegean Painting in the Bronze Age* by Sara A. Immerwahr, *Classical Review* 41/2 (1991): 429–31.

Bard, Kathryn A. Review of *From Egypt to Mesopotamia: A Study of Predynastic Trade Routes* by Samuel Mark. *American Antiquity* 63/4 (1998): 720–721.

————."The Emergence of the Egyptian State." In Shaw 2000, 61–88.

Bass, George F. "A Bronze Age Shipwreck at Ulu Burun (Kaš): 1984 Campaign." *AJA* 90/3 (1986): 269–296.

————."Sailing between the Aegean and the Orient." In Cline and Harris-Cline 1998, 183–189.

Beckman, Gary M. "Mesopotamians and Mesopotamian Learning at Hattuša." *JCS* 35 (1983): 97–114.

————."Some Observations on the Suppiluliuma-Šattiwaza Treaties." In *The Tablet and the Scroll: Near Eastern Studies in Honor of William W. Hallo,* ed. Mark E. Cohen et al., 53–57. Bethesda, Md.: CDL Press, 1993.

————. *Hittite Diplomatic Texts,* 2nd ed. Atlanta, Ga.: Scholars Press, 1999.

————. "Hittite Chronology." *Akkadica* 119–120 (2000): 19–32.

————. "International Law in the Second Millennium: Late Bronze Age." In Westbrook 2003, vol. 1, 753–774.

————. "Hittite Treaties and the Development of the Cuneiform Treaty Tradition." In *Der deuteronomistischen Geschichtswerke: Redaktions- und religionsgeschichtliche Perspektiven zur "Deuteronomismus"-Diskussion in Tora und Vorderen Propheten,* ed. Markus Witte et al., 279–301. Berlin and New York: Walter de Gruyter, 2006.

Benzel, Kim. "The Horse in the Ancient Near East." In Aruz et al. 2008, 155.

Berman, Lawrence. "Overview of Amenhotep III and His Reign." In O'Connor and Cline 1998, 1–25.

Betancourt, Philip P. "Middle Minoan Objects in the Near East." In Cline and Harris-Cline 1998, 5–13.

"Bible and Babel—Professor Delitzsch and the Old Testament." *New York Times,* Jan. 21, 1906.

Bienkowski, Piotr and Alan Millard (eds.). *Dictionary of the Ancient Near East.* Philadelphia: University of Pennsylvania Press, 2000.

Bietak, Manfred. "Egypt and the Aegean: Cultural Convergence in a Thutmoside Palace at Avaris." In Roehrig 2005, 75–81.

————. "Minoan Artists at the Court of Avaris (Tell el-Dabᶜa)." In Aruz et al. 2008, 131.

Biga, Maria Giovanna. "Femmes de la famille royale d'Ebla." In Durand 1987, 41–47.

————. Review of *Neo-Sumerian Texts in the Royal Ontario Museum,* vol. 1: *The Administration at Drehem* by Marcel Sigrist. *JAOS* 121 (2001): 167–168.

Biga, Maria Giovanna, and Francesco Pomponio. "Elements for a Chronological Division of the Administrative Documentation of Ebla." *JCS* 42 (1990): 179–201.

Bittel, Kurt. *Hattusha: The Capital of the Hittites.* New York: Oxford University Press, 1970.

Bleiberg, Edward. *The Official Gift in Ancient Egypt.* Norman and London: University of Oklahoma Press, 1996.

Bottero, Jean. *The Oldest Cuisine in the World: Cooking in Mesopotamia.* Translated by Teresa Lavender Fagan. Chicago and London: University of Chicago Press, 2004.

Bourriau, Janine. "The Second Intermediate Period." In Shaw 2000, 185–217.

Breasted, James Henry. *Ancient Records of Egypt.* 5 vols. New York: Russell and Russell, 1906.

Brinkman, John. *Materials and Studies for Kassite History,* vol. 1: *A Catalogue of Cuneiform Sources Pertaining to Specific Monarchs of the Kassite Dynasty.* Chicago: Oriental Institute of the University of Chicago, 1976.

Bryan, Betsy M. "Antecedents to Amenhotep III." In O'Connor and Cline 1998, 27–62.

————. "The Egyptian Perspective on Mittani." In Cohen and Westbrook 2000, 71–84.

————. "The 18th Dynasty Before the Amarna Period." In Shaw 2000, 218–271.

Bryce, Trevor. "Some Observations on the Chronology of Šuppiluliuma's Reign." *Anatolian Studies* 39 (1989): 19–30.

————. "The Death of Niphururiya and Its Aftermath." *JEA* 76 (1990): 97–105.

————. *The Kingdom of the Hittites.* Oxford: Clarendon Press, 1998.

————.*Life and Society in the Hittite World.* New York and Oxford: Oxford University Press, 2002.

————.*Letters of the Great Kings of the Ancient Near East: The Royal Correspondence of the Late Bronze Age.* London and New York: Routledge, 2003.

————.*The Trojans and their Neighbours: An Introduction.* London and New York: Routledge, 2006.

Buccellati, Giorgio and Marilyn Kelly-Buccellati. "Terqa: The First Eight Seasons." *AAAS* 33/2 (1983): 47–67.

————."Urkesh, the First Hurrian Capital," *Biblical Archaeologist* 60 (1997): 77–97.

————."Tar'am-Agade, Daughter of Naram-Sin, at Urkesh." In *Of Pots and Pans: Papers on the Archaeology and History of Mesopotamia and Syria presented to David Oates in Honor of his 75th Birthday,* ed. L. Al-Gailani Werr et al., 11–31. London: Nabu Publications 2002.

"Buried Monarchs Seen Again," *New York Times,* May 1, 1898.

Callender, Gae. "The Middle Kingdom Renaissance (c. 2055–1650 BC)." In Shaw 2000, 148–183.

Carter, Elizabeth, and Matthew W. Stolper. *Elam: Surveys of Political History and Archaeology.* Berkeley and Los Angeles: University of California Press, 1984.

Catagnoti, Amalia. "Ebla." In Westbrook 2003, vol. 1, 232–233.

Caubet, Annie. "The International Style: A Point of View from the Levant and Syria." In Cline and Harris-Cline 1998, 105–113.

Charpin, Dominique. *Archives Épistolaires de Mari* 1/2. ARM 26/2. Paris: Éditions Recherche sur les Civilisations, 1988.

————."Un traité entre Zimri-Lim de Mari et Ibâl-pî-El II d'Ešnunna." In Charpin and Joannès 1991, 139–166.

————."The History of Ancient Mesopotamia: An Overview." In Sasson et al. 1995, vol. 2, 807–829.

————.*Hammu-rabi de Babylon.* Paris: Presses Universitaires de France, 2003.

————."Histoire politique du Proche-Orient Amorrite (2002–1595)." In *Mesopotamien: Die altbabylonische Zeit* by Dominique Charpin, Dietz Otto Edzard, and Marten Stol, 25–480. Göttingen: Vandenhoeck & Ruprecht, 2004.

Charpin, Dominique and Francis Joannès (eds.). *Marchands, diplomates et empereurs. Etudes sur la civilisation mésopotamienne offertes à Paul Garelli.* Paris: Éditions Recherche sur les Civilisations, 1991.

Charvát, Petr. "The Kish Evidence and the Emergence of States in Mesopotamia." *Current Anthropology* 22 (1981): 686–688.

Chavalas, Mark W. "Terqa and the Kingdom of Khana." *Biblical Archaeologist* 59/2 (1996) 90–103.

————.(ed.) *The Ancient Near East.* Malden, Mass.: Blackwell, 2006.

————.(ed.) *Current Issues in the History of the Ancient Near East.* Claremont, Calif.: Regina Books, 2007.

Cline, Eric H. "Amenhotep III and the Aegean: A Reassessment of Egypto-Aegean Relations in the 14th Century B.C." *Orientalia* 56 (1987): 1–36.

————.*Sailing the Wine-Dark Sea: International Trade and the Late Bronze Age Aegean.* B.A.R. International Series 591. Oxford: Tempus Reparatum, 1994.

————."The World Abroad: Amenhotep III, the Aegean, and Anatolia." In O'Connor and Cline 1998, 236–250.

————."The Nature of the Economic Relations of Crete with Egypt and the Near East during the Late Bronze Age." In *From Minoan Farmers to Roman Traders: Sidelights on the Economy of Ancient Crete*, ed. Angelos Chaniotos et al., 115–144. Wiesbaden: Franz Steiner Verlag, 1999.

Cline, Eric H., and Diane Harris-Cline (eds.). *The Aegean and the Orient in the Second Millennium: Proceedings of the 50th Anniversary Symposium, Cincinnati, 18–20 April, 1997*. Aegaeum 18. Liège: Université de Liège, 1998.

Cline, Eric H., and David O'Connor. *Thutmose III: A New Biography*. Ann Arbor: University of Michigan Press, 2006.

Cohen, Raymond. "Reflections on the New Global Diplomacy: Statecraft 2500 BC to 2000 AD." In *Innovation in Diplomatic Practice*, ed. Jan Melissen, 1–20. Basingstoke, U.K.: Palgrave Macmillan, 1999.

Cohen, Raymond and Raymond Westbrook (eds.). *Amarna Diplomacy: The Beginnings of International Relations*. Baltimore, Md.: Johns Hopkins University Press, 2000.

Collins, Billie Jean. "Hattušili I, The Lion King." *JCS* 50 (1998): 15–20.

Collins, Paul. *From Egypt to Babylon: The International Age 1550–500 BC*. Cambridge, Mass.: Harvard University Press, 2008.

Collon, Dominique. *First Impressions: Cylinder Seals in the Ancient Near East*. London: British Museum Publications, 1987.

Cooper, Jerrold S. *Reconstructing History from Ancient Inscriptions: The Lagash-Umma Border Conflict*. Malibu, Calif.: Undena, 1981.

————.*Presargonic Inscriptions. Sumerian and Akkadian Royal Inscriptions* I. The American Oriental Society Translation Series, vol. I. New Haven: American Oriental Society, 1986.

————."International Law in the Third Millennium." In Westbrook 2003, vol. 1, 241–251.

Cooper, Jerrold S., and Glenn M. Schwartz (eds.). *The Study of the Ancient Near East in the 21st Century*. Winona Lake, Ind.: Eisenbrauns, 1996.

Cooper, Jerrold, Glenn Schwartz, and Raymond Westbrook. "A Mittani-Era Tablet from Umm el-Marra." In *General Studies and Excavations at Nuzi* 11/1, SCCNH 15, ed. David I. Owen and Gernot Wilhelm 41–56. Bethesda, Md.: CDL Press, 2005.

Crowley, Janice L. *The Aegean and the East: an Investigation into the Transference of Artistic Motifs between the Aegean, Egypt, and the Near East in the Bronze Age*. Jonsered, Sweden: Paul Åströms, 1989.

Dalley, Stephanie. *Babylonian Tablets from the First Sealand Dynasty in the Schøyen Collection, CUSAS*, vol. 8. Bethesda, Md.: CDL Press, 2009.

Davies, Norman de Garis. *The Tomb of Rekh-mi-rē'at Thebes*, I. New York: Arno Press, 1943.

Davies, W. Vivian. "Egypt and Nubia: Conflict with the Kingdom of Kush." In Roehrig 2005, 49–56.

De Martino, Stefano. "A Tentative Chronology of the Kingdom of Mittani from its Rise to the Reign of Tušratta." In *Mesopotamian Dark Age Revisited*, ed. Hermann

Hunger and Regine Pruzsinszky, 35–42. Vienna: Verlag der Österreichischen Akademie der Wissenschaften, 2004.

Der Manuelian, Peter. "The End of the Reign and the Accession of Amenhotep II." In Cline and O'Connor 2006, 413–429.

*De Sumer à Babylone: Collections du Louvre.* Brussels: Crédit Communal de Belgique, 1983.

Dickinson, Oliver. *The Aegean Bronze Age.* Cambridge: Cambridge University Press, 1994.

Dorman, Peter F. "The Early Reign of Thutmose III: An Unorthodox Mantle of Coregency." In Cline and O'Connor 2005, 39–68.

———."The Destruction of Hatshepsut's Memory: The Proscription of Hatshepsut." In Roehrig 2005, 267–269.

Dossin, Georges. "Les archives épistolaires du palais de Mari." *Syria: Revue d'art oriental et d'archéologie* 19 (1938): 105–126.

Drower, Margaret S. "Syria ca. 1550–1400 B.C." In Edwards et al., 1973, 417–525.

Durand, Jean-Marie. "Trois études sur Mari." *MARI* 3 (1984): 127–180.

———.(ed.) *La femme dans le Proche-Orient antique.* RAI 33. Paris: A.D.P.F. 1987.

———."Documents pour l'histoire du royaume de Haute-Mésopotamie II." *MARI* 6 (1990): 280–288.

———.*Les documents épistolaires du palais de Mari,* vol. 3, LAPO 18. Paris: Éditions Recherche sur les Civilisations, 1990.

"Earliest Law Code Is Now at Yale," *New York Times,* Jan. 29, 1915.

Edel, Elmar. *Die ägyptisch-hethitische Korrespondenz aus Boghazköi in babylonischer und hethitischer Sprache.* Opladen, Germany: Westdeutscher Verlag, 1994.

Edwards, I. E. S., et al. (eds.). *Cambridge Ancient History,* vol. 2 part 1: *History of the Middle East and Aegean Region c. 1800–1380 B.C.* 3rd ed. Cambridge: Cambridge University Press, 1973.

Eidem. Jesper. "International Law in the Second Millennium: Middle Bronze Age." In Westbrook 2003, vol. 1, 748–752.

Eidem, Jesper, and Flemming Højlund. "Trade or Diplomacy? Assyria and Dilmun in the Eighteenth Century BC." *World Archaeology* 24/3 (1993): 441–448.

Eidem, Jesper, and Jørgen Læssøe. *The Shemshara Archives 1: The Letters.* Copenhagen: Royal Danish Academy of Sciences and Letters, 2001.

"The El-Amarna Letters at the *Vorderasiatisches Museum* of Berlin." Available at www.amarna.ieiop.csic.es/maineng.html

Elgavish, David. "Did Diplomatic Immunity Exist in the Ancient Near East?" *Journal of the History of International Law* 2 (2000): 73–90.

El Menshawy, Sherine. "The Protocol of the Ancient Egyptian Royal Palace." In *Egyptology at the Dawn of the Twenty-First Century,* vol. 2, ed. Zahi Hawass and Lyla Pinch Brock, 400–406. Cairo: American University in Cairo Press, 2004.

Feldman, Marian H. *Diplomacy by Design: Luxury Arts and an "International Style" in the Ancient Near East, 1400–1200 BCE.* Chicago: University of Chicago Press, 2005.

Fleming, Daniel E. *Democracy's Ancient Ancestors: Mari and Early Collective Governance.* Cambridge and New York: Cambridge University Press, 2004.

Fletcher, Joann. *Chronicle of a Pharaoh: The Intimate Life of Amenhotep III*. Oxford and New York: Oxford University Press, 2000.

Fortin, Michel. *Syria: Land of Civilizations*. Trans. Jane Macaulay. Québec: Musée de la Civilisation, 1999.

Foster, Benjamin R. "Naram-Sin in Martu and Magan." *ARRIM* 8 (1990): 25–44.

———.*Before the Muses: An Anthology of Akkadian Literature*, 2 vols., 2nd ed. Bethesda, Md.: CDL Press, 1996.

———."Water under the Straw: Peace in Mesopotamia." In *War and Peace in the Ancient World*, ed. Kurt A. Raaflaub, 66–80. Malden, Mass.: Blackwell, 2007.

Foster, Benjamin R., and Karen Pollinger Foster. *Civilizations of Ancient Iraq*. Princeton and Oxford: Princeton University Press, 2009.

Francfort, Henri-Paul. *Fouilles de Shortughaï: Recherches sur l'Asie centrale protohisto-rique,* vol. 1. Paris: Diffusion de Boccard, 1989.

Freu, Jacques. *Histoire du Mitanni,* Paris: Collection Kubaba, éditions L'Harmattan. 2003.

———."Note sur les sceaux des rois de Mitanni/Mittani" *NABU* 2008: 1 (March) 5–9.

Gabolde, Marc. "La parenté de Toutânkhamon." *Bulletin de la Société Française d'Égyptologie* 155 (2002): 32–48.

Gasche, H. *La Babylonie au 17e siècle avant notre ère: approche archéologique, problèmes et perspectives.* Mesopotamian History and Environment, Memoirs 1. Ghent, Belgium: University of Ghent, 1989.

Goetze, A. "Fifty Old Babylonian Letters from Harmal," *Sumer* 14 (1958): 3–78.

Goren, Yuval, Israel Finkelstein, and Nadav Na'aman. *Inscribed in Clay: Provenance Study of the Amarna Tablets and Other Ancient Near Eastern Texts.* Tel Aviv: Emery and Claire Yass Publications in Archaeology, 2004.

Grayson, A. Kirk. *Assyrian Rulers of the Third and Second Millennia BC (to 1115 BC)*, RIM Assyrian Periods, A:1. Toronto: University of Toronto Press, 1987.

Greene, John T. *The Role of the Messenger and Message in the Ancient Near East*. Atlanta, Ga.: Scholars Press, 1989.

Greenstein, Edward L. "Alalakh Texts." In Meyers 1997, vol. 1, 59–61.

Gunter, Ann C. "Ancient Anatolia." In Meyers 1997, vol. 1, 127–131.

Hakiman, Suzy. "Byblos." In Aruz et al. 2008, 49–50.

Hallo, William W. "The Road to Emar." *JCS* 18 (1964): 57–88.

———."Women of Sumer." In *The Legacy of Sumer*, ed. Denise Schmandt-Besserat, 23–40. Malibu, Calif.: Undena, 1976.

Hallo, William W., and K. Lawson Younger, Jr. *The Context of Scripture,* 3 vols. Leiden and Boston: Brill, 2003.

"Hammurabi's Code." *New York Times,* Feb. 20, 1904.

Hawass, Zahi and Lyla Pinch Brock (eds.). *Egyptology at the Dawn of the Twenty-First Century,* 3 vols. Cairo, New York: American University in Cairo Press, 2003.

Hawkins, J. D. "Carchemish." In Meyers 1997, vol. 1, 423–424.

Hayes. William C. "Egypt: Internal Affairs from Tuthmosis I to the Death of Amenophis III." In Edwards et al. 1973, 313–416.

Heimpel, Wolfgang. *Letters to the King of Mari*. Winona Lake, Ind.: Eisenbrauns, 2003.

Herrmann, G., and P. R. S. Moorey. "Lapislazuli. B. Archäologisch." *RLA* vol. 6 (1980): 489–492.

Hinz, W. "Elams Vertrag mit Narōm-Sîn von Akkade." *ZA* 58 (1967): 66–103.

———. "Persia c. 2400–1800 B.C." In *Cambridge Ancient History* vol. 1, part 2, ed. I. E. S. Edwards et al., 644–680. Cambridge: Cambridge University Press, 1971.

Hitchcock, Louise A. "'Who Will Personally Invite a Foreigner, Unless He Is a Craftsman?': Exploring Interconnections in Aegean and Levantine Architecture." In Laffineur and Greco 2005, 691–699.

Hoffmeier, J. K. *Egypt in Israel: The Evidence for the Authenticity of the Exodus Tradition.* New York and Oxford: Oxford University Press, 1997.

Hoffner, Harry A., Jr. "A Prayer of Muršili II about His Stepmother." *JAOS* 103 (1983): 187–192.

Holmes, Y. Lynn. "The Messengers of the Amarna Letters." *JAOS* 95 (1975): 376–381.

Holt, Jim. "Good Instincts: Why Is Anyone an Altruist?" *New York Times Magazine*, March 9, 2008, 11–12.

Horsnell, Malcolm J. A. *The Year-Names of the First Dynasty of Babylon*, vol. 2, *The Year-Names Reconstructed and Critically Annotated in Light of Their Exemplars*. Hamilton, Ont.: McMaster University Press, 1999.

Ishay, Micheline. *The History of Human Rights: From Ancient Times to the Globalization Era*. Berkeley: University of California Press, 2004.

Jasink, A. Margherita. "Mycenaean Means of Communication and Diplomatic Relations with Foreign Royal Courts." In Laffineur and Greco 2005, 59–67.

Joannès, Francis. "Le traité de vassalité d'Atamrum d'Andarig envers Zimri-Lim de Mari." In Charpin and Joannès 1991, 167–175.

Johns, C. H. W. *The Oldest Code of Laws in the World*. Edinburgh: T. & T. Clark, 1903.

Joukowsky, Martha Sharp. "Byblos." In Meyers 1997 vol. 1, 390–394.

Kenoyer, Jonathan Mark. *Ancient Cities of the Indus Valley Civilization*. Karachi, Pakistan: Oxford University Press, 1998.

———. "The Indus Civilization." In Aruz 2003, 377–406.

Klengel, Horst. *Geschichte Syriens im 2. Jahrtausend v.u.Z*, vol. 1, *Nordsyrien*. Berlin: Akademie-Verlag, 1965.

Klengel-Brandt, Evelyn. "Babylon." In Meyers 1997, vol. 1, 251–256.

Knapp, A. Bernard. "Alashiya, Caphtor/Keftiu, and Eastern Mediterranean Trade: Recent Studies in Cypriote Archaeology and History." *Journal of Field Archaeology* 12 (1985): 231–250.

———. "Bronze Age Mediterranean Island Cultures and the Ancient Near East, Part 1." *Biblical Archaeologist* 55/2 (1992): 52–72.

———. "Bronze Age Mediterranean Cultures and the Ancient Near East, Part 2." *Biblical Archaeologist* 55/3 (1992): 112–128.

———. "Island Cultures: Crete, Thera, Cyprus, Rhodes, and Sardinia." In Sasson et al. 1995, vol. 3 (1995): 1433–1449.

———. "Mediterranean Bronze Age Trade: Distance, Power and Place." In Cline and Harris-Cline 1998, 193–205.

Koehl, Robert B. "Aegean Interactions with the Near East and Egypt during the Late Bronze Age." In Aruz et al. 2008, 270–272.

Kohlmeyer, Kay. "Mari (Tell Hariri)." In Weiss 1985, 194–197.

Kozloff, Arielle P., Betsy M. Bryan, et al. *Egypt's Dazzling Sun: Amenhotep III and His World.* Cleveland: Cleveland Museum of Fine Art, 1992.

Kühne, Cord. *Die Chronologie der internationalen Korrespondenz von El-Amarna.* Kevelaer, Neukirchen-Vluyn, Germany: Butzon & Bercker, 1973.

———."Imperial Mittani: An Attempt at Historical Reconstruction." In Owen and Wilhelm 1999, 203–221.

Kuhrt, Amelie. *The Ancient Near East c. 3000–330 BC,* vol. 1. London and New York: Routledge, 1995.

Laffineur, Robert, and Emanuele Greco (eds.). *Emporia: Aegeans in the Central and Eastern Mediterranean.* Aegaeum 25. Liège: Université de Liège, 2005.

Lafont, Bertrand. "Les filles du roi de Mari." In Durand 1987, 113–123.

———."The Women of the Palace at Mari." In *Everyday Life in Ancient Mesopotamia,* ed. Jean Bottero, tr. Antonia Nevill, 127–140. Baltimore: Johns Hopkins University Press, 2001.

———."Relations internationales, alliances et diplomatie au temps des royaumes amorrites." In *Amurru 2: Mari, Ebla et les Hourrites: Dix ans de travaux, deuxieme partie,* ed. Jean-Marie Durand and Dominque Charpin, 213–327. Paris: Editions Recherche sur les Civilisations, 2001.

———."International Relations in the Ancient Near East: The Birth of a Complete Diplomatic System." *Diplomacy and Statecraft* 12:1 (2001): 39–60.

Lafont, Sophie. "Middle Assyrian Period." In Westbrook 2003, vol. 1, 521–563.

Lamprichs, Ronald. "Aššur." In Meyers 1997, vol. 1, 225–228.

Lape, Peter V. "Political Dynamics and Religious Change in the Late Pre-Colonial Banda Islands, Eastern Indonesia." *World Archaeology* 32/1 (2000): 138–155.

Larsen, Mogens Trolle. "The Old Assyrian Merchant Colonies." In Aruz et al. 2008, 70–73.

———."The Middle Bronze Age." In Aruz et al. 2008, 13–17.

Lawler, Andrew. "Middle Asia Takes Center Stage." *Science* 317 (2007): 586–590.

———."Who Were the Hurrians?" *Archaeology* 61 (2008): 46–52.

———."Bridging East and West." *Science* 325 (2009): 940–943.

———."Millet on the Move." *Science* 325 (2009): 942–943.

Leemans, W. F. *Foreign Trade in the Old Babylonian Period as Revealed by Texts from Southern Mesopotamia.* Leiden: Brill, 1960.

Leichty, Erle and Albert Kirk Grayson. *Catalogue of the Babylonian Tablets in the British Museum,* vol. VII: *Tablets from Sippar 2.* London: British Museum, 1987.

Leick, Gwendolyn. *The Babylonian World.* London and New York: Routledge, 2009.

Lichtheim, Miriam. *Ancient Egyptian Literature,* 3 vols. Berkeley: University of California Press, 1976.

Lilyquist, Christine. "Egypt and the Near East: Evidence of Contact in the Material Record." In Roehrig 2005, 60–67.

Lion, Brigitte. "Les archives privées d'Arrapha et de Nuzi." In Owen and Wilhelm 1999, 35–62.

Littauer, M. A., and J. H. Crouwel. *Wheeled Vehicles and Ridden Animals in the Ancient Near East.* Leiden: E.J. Brill, 1979.

Liverani, Mario. "The Great Powers' Club." In Cohen and Westbrook 2000, 15–27.

———. *International Relations in the Ancient Near East, 1600–1100 BC.* Basingstoke, U.K.: Palgrave, 2001.

———. "The Late Bronze Age: Materials and Mechanisms of Trade and Cultural Exchange." In Aruz et al. 2008, 161–168.

Lloyd, Alan. "Egyptians Abroad in the Late Period." In *Travel, Geography and Culture in Ancient Greece, Egypt and the Near East,* ed. Colin Adams and Jim Roy, 31–43. Oakville, CT: Oxbow Books, 2007.

Luckenbill, D. D. "Old Babylonian Letters from Bismya." *American Journal of Semitic Languages and Literatures* 32/4 (1916): 270–292.

Macqueen, J. C. "The History of Anatolia and of the Hittite Empire: An Overview." In Sasson et al. 1995, vol. 2, 1085–1011.

Magid, Glenn. "Sumerian Early Dynastic Royal Inscriptions." in Chavalas 2006, 4–16.

Magnetti, Donald L. "The Function of the Oath in the Ancient Near Eastern International Treaty." *American Journal of International Law* 72, no. 4 (1978): 815–829.

Maidman, Maynard Paul. "Nuzi: Portrait of an Ancient Mesopotamian Provincial Town." In Sasson et al. 1995, vol. 2, 931–947.

Malul, Meir. *Studies in Mesopotamian Legal Symbolism.* AOAT 221. Kevelaer, Neukirchen-Vluyn, Germany: Butzon & Bercker, Neukirchener Verlag, 1988.

"Map of the World" at the British Museum, available at www.britishmuseum.org/explore/highlights/highlight_objects/me/m/map_of_the_world.aspx

Margueron, Jean-Cl. *Mari: Metropole de l'Euphrate au IIIe et au debut du IIe millénaire av. J.-C.* Paris: Picard, 2004.

———. "Mari" in Aruz et al. 2008, 27–29.

Martin, Andrew. "Found: Egypt's Lost Queen." *The Times,* July 13, 2007.

Martlew, Holley. "Minoan and Mycenaean Technology as Revealed through Organic Residue Analysis." In *Invention and Innovation: The Social Context of Technological Change 2, Egypt, the Aegean and the Near East, 1650–1150 BC,* ed. Janine Bourriau and Jacke Phillips, 121–148. Oxford: Oxbow Books, 2004.

Matthiae, Paolo. "Ebla (Tell Mardikh)." In Weiss 1985, 134–139.

———. "Ebla." In Meyers 1997, vol. 2, 180–184.

———. "Ebla and the Early Urbanization of Syria." In Aruz 2003, 165–168.

———. "Ebla." In Aruz et al. 2008, 34–41.

Matz, F. "The Maturity of Minoan Civilization." In Edwards et al. 1973, 141–164.

Maugh, Thomas H. II. "Infection, Not a Rival, May Have Dealt the Fatal Blow to King Tut." *Los Angeles Times,* March 9, 2005.

Meier, Samuel A. *The Messenger in the Ancient Semitic World.* Harvard Semitic Monographs 45. Cambridge, Mass.: Harvard Semitic Museum, 1989.

Meier, Samuel A. "Diplomacy and International Marriages." In Cohen and Westbrook 2000, 165–173.

Melissen, Jan (ed.). *Innovation in Diplomatic Practice.* Basingstoke, U.K.: Palgrave Macmillan, 1999.

Merola, Marco. "Royal Goddesses of a Bronze Age State." *Archaeology* 61/1 (2008), available online at http://www.archaeology.org/0801/trenches/goddesses.html.

Meyers, Eric M. *The Oxford Encyclopedia of Archaeology in the Near East*. 5 vols. Oxford and New York: Oxford University Press, 1997.

Michalowski, Piotr. "Third Millennium Contacts: Observations on the Relationships between Mari and Ebla." *JAOS* 105 (1985): 293–302.

———.*Letters from Early Mesopotamia*. Atlanta, Ga.: Scholars Press, 1993.

———."Sumerian King List." in Chavalas 2006, 81–85.

Michel, Cécile. *Correspondance des marchands de Kanish*. Paris: Les éditions du Cerf, 2001.

Midant-Reynes, Beatrix. *The Prehistory of Egypt,* tr. Ian Shaw. Malden, Mass.: Blackwell, 2000.

Milano, Lucio. "Ebla: A Third Millennium City-State in Ancient Syria." In Sasson et al. 1995, vol. 2, 1219–1230.

Miller, Jared L. "Amarna Age Chronology and the Identity of Nibhuruiya in the Light of a Newly Reconstructed Hittite Text." *Altorientalische Forschungen* 34 (2007): 252–293.

Monroe, Christopher M. "Money and Trade." In Snell 2007, 171–184.

Moore, Andrew M. T. "Syria and the Origins of Agriculture." In Weiss 1985, 50–57.

Moorey, P. R. S. *Ur 'of the Chaldees': A Revised and Updated Edition of Sir Leonard Woolley's Excavations at Ur*. Ithaca, N.Y.: Cornell University Press, 1982.

Moran, William L. *The Amarna Letters*. Baltimore and London: Johns Hopkins University Press, 1992.

Morgan, Christopher. "Late Traditions Concerning Sargon and Naram-Sin." In Chavalas 2006, 22–44.

Morris, Ellen F. "Bowing and Scraping in the Ancient Near East: An Investigation into Obsequiousness in the Amarna Letters." *JNES* 65 (2006): 179–195.

Morris, Sarah P. "A Tale of Two Cities: The Miniature Frescoes from Thera and the Origins of Greek Poetry." *AJA* 93 (1989): 511–535.

Morrison, Martha A. "The Family of Šilwa-Tešub *mâr šarri*." *JCS* 31 (1979): 3–29.

Muhly, James D. "Cyprus." In Meyers 1997, vol. 2, 89–96.

Müller-Karpe, Andreas. "The Hittite Empire." In Aruz et al. 2008, 170–172.

Murnane, William J. "Imperial Egypt and the Limits of Power." In Cohen and Westbrook 2000, 101–111.

Na'aman, N. "Syria at the Transition from the Old Babylonian Period to the Middle Babylonian Period." *Ugarit Forschungen* 6 (1974): 265–274.

Nemet-Nejat, Karen Rhea. *Daily Life in Ancient Mesopotamia*. Westport, Conn.: Greenwood, 1998.

Niemeier, Barbara, and Wolf-Dietrich Niemeier. "Minoan Frescoes in the Eastern Mediterranean." In Cline and Harris-Cline 1998, 69–98.

———."Aegean Frescoes in Syria-Palestine: Alalakh and Tel Kabri." In *The Wall Paintings of Thera: Proceedings of the First International Symposium, Petros M. Nomikos Conference Center, Thera, Hellas, 30 August–4 September 1997*, vol. 2, ed. Susan Sherratt, 763–802. Piraeus, Greece: Petros M. Nomikos and the Thera Foundation, 2000.

O'Connor, David. "Thutmose III: An Enigmatic Pharaoh." In Cline and O'Connor 2006, 1–38.

O'Connor, David, and Eric H. Cline (eds.). *Amenhotep III: Perspectives on His Reign.* Ann Arbor: University of Michigan Press, 1998.

Oppenheim, A. Leo. "The Seafaring Merchants of Ur." *JAOS* 74/1 (1954): 6–17.

———.*Letters from Mesopotamia.* Chicago and London: University of Chicago Press, 1967.

Orthmann, Winfried. "Tell Chuera." In Meyers 1997, vol. 1, 491–492.

Owen, David I., and Gernot Wilhelm. *Nuzi at Seventy-Five,* SCCNH 10. Bethesda, Md.: CDL Press, 1999.

Pain, Stephanie. "Why the Pharaohs Never Smiled." *New Scientist* 187 (2005): 36–39.

Parkinson, R. B. *Voices from Ancient Egypt: An Anthology of Middle Kingdom Writings.* Norman: University of Oklahoma Press, 1991.

Parpola, Simo, Asko Parpola, and Robert H. Brunswig Jr. "The Meluhha Village: Evidence of Acculturation of Harappan Traders in Late Third Millennium Mesopotamia?" *JESHO* 20/2 (1977): 129–165.

Pedersen, Olof. *Archives and Libraries in the Ancient Near East 1500–300 B.C.* Baltimore: CDL Press, 1998.

Pfälzner, Peter. "The Royal Palace at Qatna: Power and Prestige in the Late Bronze Age." In Aruz et al. 2008, 219–221.

Pinnock, Frances. "Ebla and Ur: Exchanges and Contacts between Two Great Capitals of the Ancient Near East." *Iraq* 68 (2006): 85–98.

Pittman, Holly. "Constructing Context: The Gebel el-Arak Knife: Greater Mesopotamian and Egyptian Interaction in the Late Fourth Millennium B.C.E." In Cooper and Schwartz 1996, 9–32.

Podany, Amanda H. *The Land of Hana: Kings, Chronology, and Scribal Tradition.* Bethesda, Md.: CDL Press, 2002.

———."Preventing Rebellion through the Creation of Symbolic Ties of Kinship in Syria and Mesopotamia during the Second Millennium BCE." In *Rebellions and Peripheries in the Cuneiform World,* American Oriental Series vol. 91, ed. Seth Richardson, 45–72. New Haven, Conn.: American Oriental Society, 2010.

Pollock, Susan. "Ur." In Meyers 1997, vol. 5, 288–291.

———.*Ancient Mesopotamia: The Eden that Never Was.* Cambridge and New York: Cambridge University Press, 1999.

Popham, Peter. "Broken Tooth Provides the Key to Solving the Riddle of Hatshepsut." *The Independent,* June 28, 2007.

Porter, Anne. "You Say Potato, I Say…Typology, Chronology and the Origins of the Amorites." In *Sociétés humaines et changement climatique à la fin du troisième millé-naire: une crise a-t-elle eu lieu en haute Mésopotamie?* Ed. Catherine Kuzucuoglu and Catherine Marro, 69–115. Paris: Diffusion de Boccard, 2007.

Potts, D. T. "Distant Shores: Ancient Near Eastern Trade with South Asia and Northeast Africa." In Sasson 1995 et al., vol. 3, 1451–1463.

———.*Mesopotamian Civilization: The Material Foundations.* London: The Athlone Press, 1997.

———."'The Plant for the Heart Grows in Magan…': Redefining Southeastern Arabia's Role in Ancient Western Asia." *Australian Archaeology* 48 (1999): 35–41.

———."The Gulf: Dilmun and Magan." In Aruz 2003, 307–308.

Pritchard, James B. (ed.). *Ancient Near Eastern Texts Relating to the Old Testament,* 3rd ed. with supplement. Princeton, N.J.: Princeton University Press, 1969.

Pulak, Cemal. "Who Were the Mycenaeans Aboard the Uluburun Ship?" In Laffineur and Greco 2005, 295–310.

———."The Uluburun Shipwreck and Late Bronze Age Trade." In Aruz et al. 2008, 289–305.

Raaflaub, Kurt A. *War and Peace in the Ancient World.* Malden, Mass.: Blackwell, 2007.

Ratnagar, Shereen. *Trading Encounters: From the Euphrates to the Indus in the Bronze Age.* New Delhi: Oxford University Press, 2004.

Reade, Julian. "Assyrian King Lists, the Royal Tombs of Ur, and Indus Origins." *JNES* 60 (2001): 1–29.

Redford, Donald B. "A Gate Inscription from Karnak and Egyptian Involvement in Western Asia during the Early 18th Dynasty." *JAOS* 99 (1979): 270–287.

———.*Egypt, Canaan, and Israel in Ancient Times.* Princeton, N.J.: Princeton University Press, 1992.

———."The Northern Wars of Thutmose III." In Cline and O'Connor 2006, 325–343.

Reeves, C. Nicholas. "New Light on Kiya from Texts in the British Museum." *JEA* 74 (1988): 91–101.

———.*Akhenaten: Egypt's False Prophet.* London: Thames and Hudson, 2001.

Robinson, Andrew. *Lost Languages: The Enigma of the World's Undeciphered Scripts.* London: BCA, 2002.

Roehrig, Catherine H. (ed.). *Hatshepsut: From Queen to Pharaoh.* New Haven and London: Yale University Press, 2005.

Roth, Ann Macy. "Models of Authority, Hatshepsut's Predecessors in Power." In Roehrig 2005, 9–14.

———."Hatshepsut's Mortuary Temple at Deir el-Bahri: Architecture as Political Statement." In Roehrig 2005, 147–151.

Roth, Martha T. *Law Collections from Mesopotamia and Asia Minor,* 2nd ed. Atlanta, Ga.: Scholars Press, 1997.

Rothman, Mitchell S. "Tepe Gawra." In Meyers 1997, vol. 5, 183–186.

Rouault, Olivier. "Cultures locales et influences extérieures: le cas de Terqa." *SMEA* 30 (1992): 247–256.

———."Les relations internationales en Mésopotamie du nord: techniques d'expansion et stratégies de survie." In *Les relations internationales: Actes du Colloque de Strasbourg 15–17 juin 1993,* ed. E. Frézouls and A. Jacquemin, 95–106. Paris: Diffusion de Boccard, 1995.

———"Terqa et sa region (6e–1er millénaires av. J.-C.): Recherches récentes." *Akkadica* 122 (2001): 1–26.

Rubio, Gonzalo. "From Sumer to Babylonia: Topics in the History of Southern Mesopotamia." In Chavalas 2007, 5–51.

Ryholt, K. S. B. "Hotepibre, a Supposed Asiatic King in Egypt with Relations to Ebla." *BASOR* 311 (1998): 1–6.

Sallaberger, W., and A. Westenholz. *Mesopotamien: Akkade-Zeit und Ur III-Zeit.* Freiburg, Germany: Universitätsverlag Freiburg, 1999.

Sassmannshausen, L. "The Adaptation of the Kassites to the Babylonian Civilization." In *Languages and Cultures in Contact: At the Crossroads of Civilizations in the Syro-Mesopotamian Realm, RAI* 42, ed. K. van Lerberghe and G. Voet, 409–424. Leuven: Uitgeverij Peeters en Departement Oosterse Studies, 1999.

Sasson, Jack M. "Thoughts of Zimri-Lim." *Biblical Archaeologist* 47/2 (1984): 110–120.

———. "Zimri-Lim Takes the Grand Tour." *Biblical Archaeologist* 47/4 (1984): 246–251.

———. "The King and I: A Mari King in Changing Perspectives." *JAOS* 118 (1998): 453–470.

———. "Texts, Trade, and Travelers." In Aruz et al. 2008, 95–100.

———. " 'Babylon and Beyond': Remarks on the Occasion of a Symposium." Unpublished comments presented at the Metropolitan Museum of Art, Dec. 19, 2008.

Sasson, Jack M., et al. (eds.). *Civilizations of the Ancient Near East.* 4 vols. New York: Scribner's, 1995.

Sayce, A. H. "The Discovery of the Tel El-Amarna Tablets." *AJSL* 33 (1917): 89–90.

Scandone Matthiae, Gabriella. "Les rapports entre Ebla et l'Égypte à l'Ancien et au Moyen Empire." In Hawass 2003, 487–493.

Schemm, Paul. "Egypt to Soon Announce King Tut DNA Test Results." *Washington Post*, January 31, 2010.

Schloen, David. *The House of the Father as Fact and Symbol: Patrimonialism in Ugarit and the Ancient Near East.* Winona Lake, Ind.: Eisenbrauns, 2001.

Schneider, Thomas. "Egypt and the Levant." In Aruz et al. 2008, 61–62.

Schulman, Alan R. "Diplomatic Marriage in the Egyptian New Kingdom," *JNES* 38 (1979): 177–193.

Sethe, Kurt, and Wolfgang Helck (eds.) *Urkunden des ägyptischen Altertums IV: Urkunden der 18. Dynastie*, 1–16. Leipzig: J.C. Hinrichs, 1906–1909; 17–22. Berlin: Akademie, 1955–1958.

Shaughnessy, Edward L. "Historical Perspectives in the Introduction of the Chariot into China." *Harvard Journal of Asiatic Studies* 48 (1988): 189–237.

Shaw, Ian (ed.). *The Oxford History of Ancient Egypt.* Oxford and New York: Oxford University Press, 2000.

Shea, William H. "The Form and Significance of the Eblaite Letter to Hamazi," *Oriens Antiquus* 23 (1984): 143–158.

Simpson, William Kelly. "Papyrus Lythgoe: A Fragment of a Literary Text of the Middle Kingdom from El-Lisht." *JEA* 46 (1960): 65–70.

———. *The Literature of Ancient Egypt*, 3rd ed. New Haven and London: Yale University Press, 2003.

Smith, G. Elliot. *Catalogue Général Antiquités Égyptiennes du Musée du Caire: The Royal Mummies.* Cairo: Imprimerie de l'Institut français d'archéologie orientale, 1912.

Snell, Daniel C. *Daily Life in the Ancient Near East.* New Haven and London: Yale University Press, 1997.

———. *A Companion to the Ancient Near East.* Malden, Mass.: Blackwell, 2007.

———. "Syria-Palestine in Recent Research." In Chavalas 2007, 113–149.

Sollberger, E. "The So-Called Treaty Between Ebla and 'Ashur.' " *Studi Eblaiti* III 9–10 (1980): 129–155.

Sommerfeld, Walter. "The Kassites of Ancient Mesopotamia: Origins, Politics, and Culture." In Sasson et al. 1995, vol. 2, 917–930.

Speiser, E. A. "A Letter of Saushshatar and the Date of the Kirkuk Tablets." *JAOS* 49 (1929): 269–275.

Stein, Diana L. "A Reappraisal of the 'Sauštatar Letter' from Nuzi." *ZA* 79/1 (1989): 36–60.

———."Nuzi." In Meyers 1997, vol. 4, 173.

———."Alalakh." In Meyers 1997, vol. 1, 55–59.

Stieglitz, Robert R. "Long-Distance Seafaring in the Ancient Near East." *Biblical Archaeologist* 47/3 (1984): 134–142.

Szpakowska, Kasia. *Daily Life in Ancient Egypt*. Malden, Mass.: Blackwell, 2008.

"The Kaiser Right in Lauding Hammurabi," *New York Times,* April 26, 1903.

Tosi, Maurizio, and C. C. Lamberg-Karlovsky. "Pathways across Eurasia." In Aruz 2003, 347–350.

Tubb, Jonathan N. *Canaanites*. London: British Museum Press, 1998.

Vallat, Francois. "Susa and Susiana in Second Millennium Iran." In Sasson et al. 1995, vol. 2, 1023–1033.

Van De Mieroop, Marc. *A History of the Ancient Near East*. Malden, Mass.: Blackwell, 2004.

———.*King Hammurabi of Babylon: A Biography*. Malden, Mass.: Blackwell, 2005.

———.*The Eastern Mediterranean in the Age of Ramesses II*. Malden, Mass.: Blackwell, 2007.

van den Hout, Theo P. J. "Der Falke und das Kücken: der neue Pharao und der hethitische Prinz?" *ZA* 84 (1994): 60–88.

Van Dijk, Jacobus. "The Amarna Period and the Later New Kingdom." In Shaw 2000, 272–313.

Van Koppen, Frans. "Old Babylonian Period Inscriptions." In Chavalas 2006, 88–106.

Van Soldt, W. H. "The Palace Archives at Ugarit." In *Cuneiform Archives and Libraries,* 30th RAI, ed. Klaas R. Veenhof, 196–204. Istanbul: Nederlands Historisch-Archaeologisch Instituut, 1986.

Vanstiphout, Herman L. J. *The Marriage of Martu*. Unpublished manuscript, 1998. Available at *The Electronic Text Corpus of Sumerian Literature,* http://etcsl.orinst. ox.ac.uk/cgi-bin/etcsl.cgi?text=t.1.7.1#.

Veenhof, Klaas R. *Aspects of Old Assyrian Trade and Its Terminology*. Leiden: Brill, 1972.

———."Kanesh: An Anatolian Colony in Anatolia." In Sasson et al. 1995, vol. 2, 859–871.

Villard, P. "Shamshi-Adad and Sons." In Sasson et al. 1995, vol. 2, 873–883.

von Dassow, Eva. "Archives of Alalakh IV in Archaeological Context." *BASOR* 338 (2005): 1–69.

———.*State and Society in the Late Bronze Age: Alalah under the Mittani Empire*. SCCNH 17. Bethesda, Md.: CDL Press, 2008.

Weinstein, James M. "The Egyptian Empire in Palestine: A Reassessment," *BASOR* 241 (1981): 1–28.

Weiss, Harvey (ed). *Ebla to Damascus: Art and Archaeology of Ancient Syria.* Seattle and London: University of Washington Press, 1985.

Wente, Edward F. Review of *Das Ende der Amarnazeit: Beiträge zur Geschichte und Chronologie des Neuen Reiches* by Rolf Krauss. *JNES* 42 (1983): 315–318.

West, Martin. *The East Face of Helicon: West Asiatic Elements in Greek Poetry and Myth.* New York and Oxford: Oxford University Press, 1999.

Westbrook, Raymond. "International Law in the Amarna Age." In Cohen and Westbrook 2000, 28–41.

———.*A History of Ancient Near Eastern Law,* vol. 1. Leiden and Boston: Brill, 2003.

———."Introduction: The Character of Ancient Near Eastern Law." In Westbrook 2003, vol. 1, 1–90.

Wilhelm, Gernot. "The Kingdom of Mitanni in Second-Millennium Upper Mesopotamia." In Sasson et al. 1995, vol. 2, 1243–1254.

Wiseman, D. J. *The Alalakh Tablets.* London: British Institute of Archaeology at Ankara, 1953.

Woods, Christopher. "Bilingualism, Scribal Learning, and the Death of Sumerian." In *Margins of Writing, Origins of Cultures,* Oriental Institute Seminars, 2, ed. Seth L. Sanders, 91–120. Chicago: Oriental Institute of the University of Chicago, 2006.

Woolley, Sir Leonard. *Joint Expedition of the British Museum and of the Museum of the University of Pennsylvania to Mesopotamia,* vol. 7: *Old Babylonian Period.* London: British Museum Publications, 1976.

Wright, Jonathan *The Ambassadors.* London: HarperPress, 2006.

Yon, Marguerite. "Ugarit: History and Archaeology." Tr. S. Rosoff. In *Anchor Bible Dictionary,* vol. 6, ed. David Noel Freedman, 695–706. New York: Doubleday, 1992.

———."Ugarit." In Meyers 1997, 260.

———.*The City of Ugarit at Tell Ras Shamra.* Winona Lake, Ind.: Eisenbrauns, 2006.

Zaccagnini, Carlo. "Patterns of Mobility among Ancient Near Eastern Craftsmen." *JNES* 42 (1983): 245–264.

———."Ideological and Procedural Paradigms in Ancient Near Eastern Long Distance Exchanges: The Case of Enmerkar and the Lord of Aratta." *Altorientalische Forschungen* 20/1 (1993): 34–42.

———."The Interdependence of the Great Powers." In Cohen and Westbrook 2000, 141–153.

Zarins, Juris. "Oman." In Meyers 1997 vol. 4, 184–187.

Ziegler, Nele. *La population féminine des palais d'après les archives royales de Mari: Le Harem de Zimri-Lim.* Florilegium Marianum IV, Memoires de NABU 5. Paris: Société pour l'étude du Proche Orient Ancien, 1999.

# Index

Page numbers followed by "f" denote figures and maps.

Abarsal
and treaty with Ebla, 29–32, 82, 182
Abi-ili, 93
Acco, 184f–185f, 246
Adab, 66f, 91
Adad-nirari, 303
Advisors, 4, 69, 74, 145, 282, 286
Aegean region, 42f
and Egypt, 260
and Hittites, 170
and Mediterranean trade, 256, 274
and Mycenaean settlements, 259, 262
See also Kaptara, Mycenae
Afghanistan, 13
as possible source of gold, 43
as source of lapis lazuli, 14, 43, 54, 245, 262–263
as source of tin, 106, 257, 262–263
Africa, 142, 256–257, 260
Agum-kakrime, Kassite king of Babylonia, 126–129, 131, 306, 333 n. 39
Aha-arshe, official from Mari, 32
Ahhiyawa (Greece), 261–262
Ahmose, king of Egypt, 140–141
Ahmose, wife of King Thutmose I, 140, 141

Ahmose, first soldier in the time of King Thutmose I, 132–133
Ahmose, second soldier in the time of King Thutmose I, 133
Aitakkama, prince of Kadesh, 278
Akhenaten, king of Egypt, 236–237
and Alashiya, 254
and Amarna, 8–9, 191, 237–238, 260
and art, 238
and Assyria, 281
and Babylon, 206, 220, 221, 228, 249–250
daughters of, 281, 282, 284
death of, 281
and Hatti, 268–269, 279, 281, 353 n. 8, 355–356 n. 71
and Mittani, 8–9, 214, 236, 239, 240–242, 243, 248, 251, 267, 269–270, 272
and Nefertiti, 239
and religion, 237, 239, 271
and Ugarit, 275–276
and vassal kings, 278–279
Akhetaten. See Amarna
Aki-Teshup, Mittanian leader, 276–277, 279–280, 292–293, 298

Akkad, 25f
  referring to southern Mesopotamia,
    91, 106
  as Sargon's capital, 44–48, 94, 318 n. 26
Akkadian art, 50
Akkadian empire, 45, 63
Akkadian language, 266
  in Alalakh, 160
  in Alashiya, 254
  and Amorite, 68
  as common diplomatic language, 5, 7,
    10, 15, 89, 169, 175–176, 178, 204
  and cuneiform, 276
  in Hatti, 125, 266
  in Mittani, 296
  names in, 49
  spoken by envoys, 214
  in Sumer, 39
  terms, 29, 72, 85, 104, 200, 211, 244
  in Ugarit, 274
  used by Kassites, 126, 234
Alalakh, 66f
  in the Amarna period, 263, 277
  Idrimi, king of, 136–137
  in the Old Babylonian period,
    108–109, 111
  in the sixteenth and fifteenth centuries
    BCE, 134, 159–160, 180, 182
  as source of gifts to Thutmose III, 149
Alashiya (Cyprus), 66f
  in the Amarna period, 186–187, 191,
    193, 195, 263, 274
  in Old Babylonian period, 108
  as source of copper, 110, 111, 252–255,
    256–259
Aleppo, 66f
  contested between Hatti and Mittani,
    170
  as homeland of Idrimi, 135, 137
  in the Old Babylonian period, 65,
    107–108
  in sixteenth century BCE, 122–123
  and Suppiluliuma, 273, 277
Alliances
  in Amarna, 199, 265, 268, 270,
    294–295, 301
  in Early Dynastic period, 27–28, 32, 33
  in Old Babylonian period, 74, 89
  in sixteenth and fifteenth centuries
    BCE, 137, 186
Alphabet, Phoenician, 276

Alshi, 184f–185f, 292
Amarna, 184f–185f
  as capital, 8, 237–238, 282
  overview of period, 191
Amarna letters
  from Canaan, 278
  current locations of, 9
  discovered, 9–10
  international, 186–187, 216
  shape and size, 226
  tone of, 207–208
  See also letters
Amaz, 66f, 87
Ambassadors. See messengers
Amber, 256, 263, 353 n. 100
Amen, Egyptian god of Thebes, 177, 213,
    237, 282
  temple of, 6, 202, 237
Amenhotep II, king of Egypt, 163–169,
    164f, 172–179, 180–183
Amenhotep III, king of Egypt, 6–8,
    191–198, 197f, 202–205, 217–231,
    233–235, 240, 247, 251–253, 265, 267
Amenhotep IV, king of Egypt.
    See Akhenaten
Amen-Ra, 193, 281, 284
Amka, 284
Amminaia, queen of Arrapkha, 156–158
Amorites
  and Hyksos, 139
  kingdoms, 68, 70, 112
  language, 68, 126
  myths about, 68
Amurru, 184f–185f, 233, 278–279, 302,
    303
Amut-pi-El, king of Qatna, 65
Anatolia, 42f
  in Amarna period, 246, 261
  and Mesopotamia, 306
  in Old Babylonian period, 103–107,
    121–122, 125
  See also Hatti, Hittites
Anatolian Plateau, 103, 105, 121, 125, 138
  geography and climate of, 266
Anchors, 257, 274
Andarig, 66f, 86
Animal contest scene, 41f, 50, 55, 54
Ankhesenpaaten/Ankhesenamen, wife
    of King Tutankhamun, 282, 284,
    285, 288
Annan, Kofi, 10–11

Anointment,
  in hygiene, 113
  in marriages, 161, 218–219, 246, 247
Antioch, 25f, 26
Aphek, 166, 184f–185f
Arabia, 46, 54, 125
Aratta, 51
Archaeology, 43, 46, 51, 52, 54, 59, 99,
    105, 110, 111, 114–115, 138, 140, 148,
    153, 159, 257, 266, 274, 280, 308
Archives
  in Amarna, 8, 186, 282
  in Babylon, lost, 69
  in Carchemish, possible, 280
  conditions of preservation, 60, 70, 135
  in Ebla, 21–23, 57, 59
  in Hattusa, 187, 266, 287–288
  in Kanesh, 104–105
  in Mari, 70, 90, 93
  in Mittani, possible, 5, 134, 152
  in Nuzi, 159
  in Qatna, 278
  in Ugarit, 187
Armanum, 58
Arrapkha, 156–160, 182, 184f–185f
Arrows
  in archery, 164
  as royal gifts, 222, 245
  in warfare, 57, 165
Art
  Akkadian, 49–50
  Egyptian, 54, 144, 238–239, 275
  international style, 263
  Minoan, 56, 110, 148
Artists. See artisans
Artashumara, King of Mittani, 198, 205
Artatama I, king of Mittani, 183, 186,
    192, 195
Artatama II, king of Mittani,
  ascension to power of, 291–292
  identity of, 354 n. 20, 356 n. 2
  and support from Suppiluliuma,
    270–271, 284
Artisans, 41, 107, 114, 153
  arrow makers, 222
  artists, 55, 67, 139, 148–149, 230, 263,
    307
  bead makers, 48–49, 251
  cylinder seal makers, 50, 260
  dye manufacturers, 274
  exchanged between kings, 108

glass workers, 259
ivory workers, 259
metalworkers, 101, 254, 248
  on statues of gods, 128
stone workers, 43
textile workers, 159, 262
traveling, 148–149, 245–246
wall painters, 108–109, 148–149, 157
Arzawa, 184f–185f, 186, 187, 191, 193,
    194, 246–247, 267
Asha, official from Mari, 32
Ashkelon, 184f–185f, 246
Ashur (city), 66f, 102, 103–106, 156,
    303
Ashur-nadin-ahhe, king of Assyria, 248
Ashur-uballit, king of Assyria
  and Amarna great kings, 174, 247,
    248, 267, 281
  and Babylon, 236, 293, 357 n. 6
  death of, 292
  and independence from Mittani, 271,
    281, 283
Assassinations, 170, 198, 268, 288, 291
Assuwa, 149
Assyria, 66f
  in Amarna period, 191, 245, 281, 284,
    289, 292, 295, 304
  conquered by Mittani, 152, 174
  control over Mittani, 303
Aten, Egyptian god of the disk of the
    sun, 193, 202, 237–239, 282
Attendants
  to accompany a princess, 34, 39, 88,
    196, 209, 224–226, 233
  to accompany envoys, 102
  as a gift, 200, 275
  of a king, 238, 294
  in Royal Tombs of Ur, 40
Avaris, 184f–185f
  Eighteenth Dynasty palaces in,
    148–149, 245
  as Hyksos capital, 139, 140
Ay, king of Egypt, 288
Ayadaragalama, king of the Sealand, 125
Aziru, leader of Amurru, 278–279

Baal, chief god of the Canaanites, 274
Babylon, 66f
  attack on, 121, 123–125
  extent of kingdom, 120
  after Hammurabi, 119–120

Babylon, (*continued*)
 in reign of Hammurabi, 14, 63–65,
  68–69, 71–75, 81, 90, 103, 109, 114
 in sixteenth century BCE, 125, 129
Babylonia, 184f–185f
 in Amarna period, 191, 206–208, 245,
  263, 280–281, 292–293, 304
 and Assyria, 233, 236
 and early New Kingdom Egypt, 167
 and Elam, 232, 235–236
 and Hatti, 233, 270
 and New Kingdom Egypt, 194, 205,
  232, 248
Bad-tibira, 25f, 33
Bahrain. *See* Dilmun
Banquets
 description of, 211–212
 for envoys, 8, 73, 202, 206, 251
 in marriage preparations, 219
Barley, 19, 40, 79, 113, 152–153, 274
Bathrooms, 69, 148, 158, 292
Beads, 38, 40, 48–49, 86, 97, 98, 110,
 250–251, 256–257, 260, 263, 264
Beards, 6, 21, 67, 69, 77, 113, 259
Beer. *See* drink
Bible, 44, 63–65, 246
Bietak, Manfred, 148
Blood relations between allies, 83
Boats
 in Akkadian period, 45–49
 in Amarna period, 6, 220, 274,
 in Crete, 56, 149
 in Early Dynastic period, 46
 in Egypt, 53, 54, 55, 112, 131,
  142–143, 147, 148, 196, 202, 253
 and Idrimi, 135
 in Old Babylonian period, 75, 85, 96,
  98–99, 101, 111, 123
 Uluburun shipwreck, 255–258
 in Ur III period, 98
Booty
 from Babylon, 124
 from Canaan, 146, 166
 from Hatti, 137
 from Magan, 47
 from Mari, 58
 from Mittani, 133, 166, 273,
  292
 from Qatna, 278
British Museum, 3, 9–10

Bronze, 14, 21, 37, 43, 57, 85, 88, 94, 98,
 99, 111, 115, 116, 153, 181, 220, 222,
 252, 256, 264, 275, 277
Brother, as hierarchical term
 Akkadian term for, 29
 in Amarna period, 194, 204, 254, 255,
  262, 281, 304, 351 n. 59
 in Early Dynastic period, 27–28, 32, 33, 59
 in early New Kingdom, 173
 in Old Babylonian period, 77
 use of term, 10, 29, 70
Brotherhood
 in Amarna period, 10, 187, 191, 261,
  280, 288, 298, 304
 in Early Dynastic period, 27, 33
 general use of term, 11
 in Old Babylonian period, 93
 reasons for, 306
 in sixteenth century BCE, 129
 Sumerian term for, 33
Buffalo, water, 45, 48, 49
Buildings, construction of, 193, 229, 248
Bulls, hunting, 196–197
Burials
 rituals, 40
 *See also* tombs
Burna-buriash I, Kassite king of
 Babylonia, 129
Burna-buriash II, king of Babylonia
 daughter's letter, 221
 daughter's marriage, 224–225
 death of, 283
 description of, 205
 and envoys, 206–207, 210
 and gift-giving 243–244, 247,
  249–251
 grandson of, 236
 and Hatti, 270–271, 281
 son's marriage, 233
Byblos, 42f
 description of, 52–53
 Egyptian relationship with, 52–54, 56,
  112, 131, 139, 182

Calcite, vase of, 38
Canaan, 66f
 cities destroyed in, 307
 Egyptian relationship with, 112–114,
  138–139, 144–149, 161, 166, 173, 177,
  186, 193, 210, 265, 270

language of, 253
  merchants from, 255–257, 259, 274
  and Mittani, 134, 201
  religious beliefs of, 155, 276
  as source of glass, 246
Caravans, 52, 79–80, 103, 107, 201, 210,
    226, 240, 274
Carchemish, 25f
  in Early Dynastic period, 26
  Hittite attack on and conquest of, 286,
    291, 293, 356 n. 3
  in Hittite empire, 303
  in Mittani, 280, 284–285
  Piyassili, king of, 295, 298–299
Carnelian
  from Dilmun, 101
  as luxury good, 94, 152
  Meluhha as source of, 43, 48–49, 96
  objects made of, 14, 38, 40, 102, 246, 259
Cattle, 113, 146, 166, 271, 273, 293
Cedar, 52–53, 56, 102, 128, 132, 220, 256,
    274
Celebrations, 229, 237
Ceramics, 55, 105, 110, 121, 153, 158–159,
    246, 257, 259, 260
Chaos
  at end of Mittani kingdom, 281, 292
  Hyksos period and, 139
  Mesopotamian and Syrian conception
    of, 29, 173, 300, 306
Chariots
  to accompany princesses, 89, 224
  in China, 263
  depictions in art, 58f, 164f, 259, 283f
  description of, 200–201
  as gifts, 5, 174, 200, 220, 222, 245,
    247, 248
  as loot captured in battle, 132–133, 146,
    166, 200, 292
  Mittani as source of, 153, 178
  as transport, 136, 173, 183, 237, 250,
    292, 294
  use in archery and hunting, 164f, 196
  use in warfare, 33, 57–58, 145, 263,
    279, 283–284, 283f, 288, 295
  warriors, 292, 301
Chastity, in brides, 228
Children, 21, 29, 106, 113, 126, 140, 142,
    146, 158, 194, 235
China, 13, 95f, 115–116, 263

Chlorite, 46, 49
Chronology, ix, 65, 268, 319–320
    n. 54, 334 n. 1, 352 n. 70, 353 n. 1
Cilician Gates, 66f, 122, 138
Climate
  in Babylonia, 210
  change in, 307
  in Hatti, 286
  in Mittani, 152
  in Sumer, 40
  in Ugarit, 274
Clothing
  Canaanite, 113
  in dowries, 85, 153, 224
  in Early Dynastic period, 20, 21, 22,
    39, 40, 58, 67
  Egyptian, 6, 209
  as gifts, 58, 178, 202, 222, 224, 239,
    295, 202, 222, 295
  for gods, 7, 128, 172
  of Mittanian envoy, 6
  in the Old Babylonian period, 73, 77,
    85–86, 86f
  purple dyed, 274
  as rations, 72
  of soldiers, 57
  symbolic gestures with, 75, 89
  as trade goods, 110
  as tribute, 277
  in Yanghai, 116
Colonies
  Mycenaean, 250
  Old Assyrian, 103–107, 121, 123, 266
  Uruk period, 55–56
Community, International 13–15, 119,
    126, 187, 274
  end of, 307
  United Nations definition of, 10
Contracts, 60, 80, 105, 135, 138, 151,
    158, 198
Copper
  from Alashiya, 110–111, 252–258
  from Anatolia, 43
  from Dilmun, 46, 97, 101, 103
  from Egypt, 53, 112, 143
  from Magan, 47, 97–99
  needed for bronze, 14, 94, 152
  objects made of, 38, 40, 44, 49, 98,
    164, 181, 183, 197, 211
  in oxhide ingots, 164f, 252, 258f

Coral, 101
Crete. *See* Kaptara
Cuneiform, 89
    adoption of, in Ebla and Mari, 23
    adoption of, in Hatti, 121
    alphabetic, 276
    uses for, 23
Cuneiform tablets, 4f, 223f
    administrative, 55, 67
    descriptions of, 3, 21, 29, 222, 224,
        226, 269
    dictionaries, 23
    earliest, 22–23
    lists of kings, 267
    map, 35f, 36
    types of, 11
    *See also* contracts, letters, treaties
Curses, 29
    in treaties, 30–31, 82–83, 160, 181,
        277, 296, 300
Cylinder seals. *See* seals, cylinder
Cypro-Minoan
    language, 274
    script, 253
Cyprus. *See* Alashiya

Dagan, Syrian god of Middle Euphrates,
    45, 58
Damascus, 184f–185f, 210
Dancers, 73, 143
Delitzsch, Friedrich, 64
Dilbat, 66f, 91
Dilmun (Bahrain), 42f
    in Akkadian empire, 45–46, 48
    in Kassite kingdom, 263
    in Old Babylonian period, 69, 98,
        101–103
    in reign of Gudea, 97–98
    resources of, 99
    trade with, 103
Diorite, 47, 52, 97–98
Diplomacy
    in Akkadian period, 45
    in the Amarna period, 15
    earliest recorded, 27
    in Early Dynastic period, 14, 26, 33–34,
        57, 59–60
    essential characteristics, 10, 270, 289
    evidence for, 71, 187
    in the fifteenth century BCE, 169
    goals of, 306

in Old Babylonian period, 14, 70–83,
    93, 119
in the sixteenth century BCE, 125, 127,
    129
and Suppiluliuma, 273
*See also* messengers, negotiations,
    treaties
Divination and diviners, 74, 81, 108, 128,
    135, 255, 301–302, 357 n. 21
Divorce, 88–89, 219
Dogs, 142
Donkeys
    hide of, as a gift, 258
    as pack animals in trade, 14, 103, 104
    to pull chariots, 57–58
    sacrificed, 82
Dowry
    in Amarna period, 219
    for an Ebla princess, 34
    for a Hittite princess, 304
    for a Mari princess, 85
    for a Mittani princess, 153, 183, 196,
        215, 219–222, 224–227, 230
    in Old Babylonian period, 83–84, 85
Dreams, 82
Drink
    abstaining from, 231
    beer, 19, 142, 211, 212, 215, 237
    as bridal gift, 218
    cups for, 110, 256
    for gods, 237
    for travelers, 113
    in treaty ceremony, 82
    water, 30, 132, 144
    wine, 19, 110, 146, 182, 237, 260
Dusigu, wife of King Irkab-damu, 21, 32
Dutum, official from Mari, 32
Dye, purple, 110, 274

Ea-nasir, Dilmun trader, 98–101, 111, 114
Eanatum, king of Lagash, 33
Early Dynastic kingdoms. *See* Ebla,
    Emar, Hamazi, Kish, Lagash, Mari,
    Nagar, Sumer,
Eastern Desert, 53, 184f–185f, 215
Ebla, 25f
    archive at, 22, 24
    buildings in, 20
    and diplomatic relations with Hamazi,
        26–28, 31, 59, 79
    destruction of, 22, 35, 57–59

diplomatic conventions in, 34
distant contacts with, 36, 41, 43, 51–53, 56, 105
and Egypt, 114
economy of, 19, 37–38, 41, 51
excavation of, 38
extent of kingdom, 22
formation of tell at, 20
language of, 23–24, 39
and Mari, 24, 26, 32, 37, 57–58
palace in, 20
and peace with other kingdoms, 24
population of, 19
Sargon's conquest of, 45
setting of, 19
and treaty with Abarsal, 29–32, 82, 182
warfare in, 26, 57–58
workers in, 19
Egypt, 42f
  in Amarna period, 6–9, 191–199, 202–205, 213–216, 236–239, 263, 278–279, 281–283
  and Babylonia, 194, 205, 232, 248
  climate and resources, 53–54
  earliest contacts with Mesopotamia, 54–56
  in early New Kingdom, 131–134, 139–151, 161, 163–169, 172–179, 180–186
  and Ebla, 52–53
  geography of, 139
  and Hatti, 285–287, 304
  in Hyksos period, 139–140
  language of, 7, 274
  and Mittani, 196, 211
  in Middle Kingdom, 110, 111–114
  Old Kingdom, 52–54
Eighteenth Dynasty, 141, 148, 150, 163, 193
Ekallatum, 65, 66f, 69, 76, 84, 101, 246
Elam
  and Babylon, 67–68, 74–75 90, 121, 307
  and Mari, 87, 89, 94
  as market for lapis lazuli, 97
  marriage with Babylon, 232, 235
  marriage with Ur, 67
  treaty with Naram-Sin, 45
Electrum, 142, 237
Elephants, 45, 48, 133
Emar, 25f, 26, 77

Empires
  Akkadian  45, 67, 105
  Egyptian, 140–141, 143, 147, 163, 167, 192, 198, 236, 280, 284
  Hammurabi's, 90, 115, 119
  Hittite, 264, 266, 268, 280, 286, 301, 303
  Mittanian, 135, 137, 151–152, 156–160, 172, 178, 271, 281, 291
  Neo-Assyrian, 307
  Shamshi-Adad's  102
Enlil, king of the Mesopotamian gods, 33, 102
Enlil-nirari, king of Assyria, 292–293
Enmetena, king of Lagash, 33–34
Envoys. See messengers
Esagila, temple of Marduk, 124, 127–128
Eshnunna, 65, 66f, 84
Etiquette, 15, 70, 73, 182, 207, 216, 221
Euphrates River, 25f
  ancient map of, 35, 36
  and Egypt, 131, 133, 146, 147
  flood, 120
  geography, 39–40
  and Hatti, 122, 271–273, 291, 295, 303
  and locations of cities, 22, 26, 77, 280
  and locations of kingdoms, 68–69, 120, 122, 125, 134, 303
  as travel route, 54, 72, 76, 293

Faience, 153, 192, 256, 257
Families
  as model for other relationships, 28–29, 84, 243
Farmers, 19, 68, 115, 116, 153, 159, 166, 259
Father
  meanings of Akkadian term for, 29
  king as, 29, 68, 70
Fields, 85, 115, 120, 132, 152
Floods, 47, 120, 305, 328 n. 29
Food and eating, 39, 212
  abstaining from, 231
  dining room, 275
  in Egypt, 209
  for envoys, 31, 52, 73, 206
  in families, 79–80, 157, 218
  as indicating an alliance, 279
  for ship's crew, 256–257
  for strangers, 112
  as traded items, 46, 98, 142
  See also banquets

"Friends" as allies, 7, 179–187, 269, 276, 281, 287, 304
"Friendship," 199, 205, 211, 243
fruit trees, 113
Furniture, 20, 40–41, 69, 85, 178, 252, 278
  beds, 89, 146, 209, 220, 230, 246, 255, 275
  chairs, 220, 230, 246, 247
  chests, 223, 224, 283
  footrests, 246
  tables, 275

Games, 40, 256, 318 n. 16
Gifts
  for allies, after victory, 57
  of artisans and specialists, 245, 275
  complaints about, 208, 228, 240, 249–252, 281
  for gods, 94, 120
  for kings, Amarna period, 5, 8, 15, 195, 200, 201, 206, 211, 219–224, 223f, 229, 234–235, 243–258, 260, 262, 269, 275, 277, 295
  for kings, Early Dynastic period, 26–28
  for kings, early New Kingdom, 149–150, 167
  for kings, Old Babylonian period, 76–77, 82, 102–103, 108
  for kings, from vassals, 166
  for messengers, 8, 73, 76, 182, 229–230
  for officials, 238
  for princesses, 35
  public display of, 78, 211
  requests for, 250–251, 254–255, 269, 282
  rules concerning, 171
  for servants, 224
  between siblings, 79–80
Giza, 52
Glass, 153, 245–246, 257, 259
Goats
  herding, 68, 115–116, 153
  hunting, wild, 183
  in lists, 158
  in ritual, 82
Gods and goddesses
  as arbiters, 81, 295
  captured in war, 122, 124, 129, 152

of cities, 39
of commoners, 239
families of, 28–29
gifts for, 94, 237, 274
inflicting injury, 88
kings' relation to, 8, 147, 302
in legends, 51
in letters, 213, 221, 225
movement of, 5, 341 n. 40
needs of, 172
in oaths, 138, 268
as owners of land, 39
roles in treaties, 30, 32, 33, 45, 82–83, 181, 296, 299
sent to allies, 5, 83, 195
shared in Syria and Mesopotamia, 89
in war, 145, 199, 280
See also divination and diviners
Gold, 241
  abundance, in Egypt, 206, 215
  as booty, 146, 166
  as building decoration, 102, 152, 193, 204, 247–249
  in dowry, 85, 224
  Egypt as source of, 43, 53, 110
  as gifts, 98, 195, 220–224, 230, 238, 246–247, 277
  for gods' adornment, 128
  kings' desire for, 244
  large shipments of, 247–252
  Meluhha as source of, 96
  Nubia as source of, 139
  objects made of, 37, 38, 40, 41, 56, 58, 101, 114, 115, 121, 145, 146, 150, 204, 220, 222, 224, 278, 292
  as payment, 256
  statues of, 84, 98, 228–231, 240–242, 269
  in trade, 103–104
  as tribute, 26, 37, 145, 277
  unworked, 248–249
  value of, 37–38
"Great King," 78, 170, 178, 241, 254, 262, 268, 281
Greece
  Ahhiyawa as ancient name of, 261–262
  artistic influence from, 157
  destination of trade, 255–257, 259, 263
  and diplomacy, 260–261
  and Egypt, 260

envoys from, 256, 263
geography of, 259
sent gifts, 149
*See also* Mycenae
Guards
for booty, 146
for messengers, 28, 72, 174
for kings, 112
Gudea, king of Lagash, 96–98

Haamashshi, 251
Hairstyles, 6, 20–22, 67, 86
Halpa. *See* Aleppo
Hama, 25f, 26
Hamazi, 25f, 27–31, 34, 53, 79, 315 n. 39
Hammurabi, king of Babylon, 64f
as an Amorite, 68
appearance, 67
career of, 90–91, 103, 120
early reign, 65
laws of, 63–65, 90–91, 127
personality of, 71–72
Hana, 66f, 123, 125, 128, 333 n. 39
Hane, interpreter from Egypt, 202, 225
Hani, ambassador from Egypt, 286–287
Hanigalbat, 226, 302
*See also* Mittani
Harappa, 42f, 47
Haremhab, king of Egypt, 302, 357 n. 24
Hathor, Egyptian goddess, 53, 157
Hatshepsut, king of Egypt,
Avaris during era of, 148–149
proscription of, by Thutmose III,
150–151
reign of, 6, 141–144
Hatti, 66f
in Amarna period, 191, 199, 245,
266–269, 270–273, 276–282,
284–289
and early New Kingdom Egypt, 167, 182
and Egypt, 302–304
geography of, 266
and Kassites, 127–129
and Mittani, 169, 265, 294–301, 303
in sixteenth and fifteenth centuries
BCE, 170
as source of silver, 245, 260
*See also,* Hittites, Hattusa
Hattic language, 107
Hattusa, 66f, 121, 187, 191, 262, 267,
268, 284, 288, 294, 296, 302, 304

description of, 266
Hattusili I, king of Hatti, 121–122, 125,
137, 155, 332 n. 11
Hattusili III, king of Hatti, 262
Haya-Sumu, king of Ilan-Sura, 87–89,
107
Heliopolis, 167, 184f–185f
Henti, wife of Suppiluliuma, queen of
Hatti, 270
Hepat, Hurrian goddess, 155
Herodotus, Greek historian of the
Persian War, 308
Hierakonpolis, 42f, 55
Hierarchy
in society, 153–154
in state relationships, 29, 68,
70, 79
Hieratic script, 8, 11
Hieroglyphic script, Egyptian, 11–12, 52,
112, 114, 133, 197
Hieroglyphic script, Minoan 109
Hindu Kush Mountains, 42f, 43, 46,
49–51, 96, 116
History, ancient
popular view of, 12
Hittites
attack on Babylon, 15, 121, 123–124
civilization of, 121
documents, 261
empire, expansion of, 184f–185f, 268,
272, 280
kings, 121–124
language, 107, 121, 253, 266,
274, 296
origin, 107
*See also* specific Hittite kings, Hattusa,
Hatti, warfare, treaties
Homer, 259
Horses
in China, 263
as gifts, 5, 27, 50, 77–78, 174, 178,
200–201, 222, 243, 245, 247, 248,
250, 255, 293
in hunting and sport, 163, 178, 183,
197
in lists, 158
mentioned in greetings, 7, 205
in Mittani, 153–154, 178
as spoils of war, 133, 200, 273
as transport, 135, 201
in warfare, 57, 132–133, 145, 295

Houses
  in Aegean, 257
  allied kings as sharing a common, 74,
    78, 243–244
  concept of, 349
  in Egypt, 209
  for envoys, 73, 245
  location defined legally, 328 n. 28
  in Mesopotamia and Syria, 89,
    99–101, 115, 137, 153, 157–158
  palace as, 69, 89, 183, 221, 246, 248,
    250, 292
  private, in Anatolia, 103, 105–106
  in Punt, 142
  purchase of, 80
Hotepibre, king of Egypt, 114
Hurrian
  gods, 154–155, 213
  land, 265
  language, 5, 7, 253, 274
  peoples, 122–124, 132, 135–136,
    154–156, 226, 284, 292, 294,
    298–300
  See also Mittani
Hygiene, 69, 148, 157, 158
Hyksos, 139–140, 142

Ibal-pi-El, king of Eshnunna, 65, 71
Ibubu, steward of King Irkab-damu, 27,
Idrimi, vassal king of Mittani, king of
    Alalakh, 135–138, 136f, 159, 160
Ila, official from Mari, 32
Illness, 81, 144, 206–207, 231, 254,
    301–303, 307
Immureya. See Amenhotep III
Inanna, Mesopotamian goddess of love,
    44, 180
Inbatum, daughter of King Zimri-Lim,
    86–87
Incense, 54, 142, 237, 257
India, 43, 44, 95f, 154
Indo-European languages, 107, 154
Indonesia, 115
Indus Valley. See Meluhha
Indus Valley script, 47, 49
Inscriptions, royal, 11, 12, 23, 24, 33, 46, 52,
    90, 126, 127, 128, 143, 151, 168, 194
Iran, 48–50, 55, 67, 96, 154
Irkab-damu, king of Ebla, 13–14, 19–22,
    24, 26–29, 32, 52

iron, 222, 347 n. 27
Irrite, 184f–185f, 298
Isfet, 139
Ishar-damu, king of Ebla, 21, 32, 52–53, 57
Ishqi-Mari, king of Mari, 20–21
Ishhi-Addu, king of Qatna, 76–80, 243
Ishme-Dagan, king of Ekallatum, 69,
    71–72, 76–80, 84, 101
Ishtar, 44, 180
Isin, 65, 66f
Ivory
  from Alashiya, 254
  from Dilmun, 46, 101
  as gifts, 220
  from Magan, 98
  from Meluhha, 48–49, 101
  objects made of, 38. 40, 54, 230, 250,
    256, 275
  from Punt, 54, 142
  tusk, 257
  workshop, 259

Jewelry, 48, 86, 97, 115, 121, 152, 263
  in burials, 40
  in dowries, 34, 85, 153
  as gifts, 37, 178, 220, 222, 224, 239,
    245, 247, 150, 256, 350 n. 10
  for gods and goddesses, 172
  hoarded, 38
  worn by kings, 67
  worn by princesses, 86
Journeys. See travel
Jubilee celebration, 229, 237
Judicial system, 60
  See also laws

Ka (soul), 182
Kadashman-Enlil I, king of Babylonia,
    194, 218, 233–235, 246–248
Kadesh, 66f
  battle of, 303
  and Egypt, 144, 278–279, 283–284,
    286–288
  and Mittani, 134
Kakmum, 82
Kanesh, 66f, 103–106, 121
Kaptara (Minoan Crete), 42f
  art, 108–109, 148–149, 157, 259, 278
  civilization of, 56, 109
  and Egypt, 110, 148–149, 177, 225, 245

language, 338 n. 124
and the Levant, 13, 110–111
and Mediterranean trade, 256
and Mycenaeans, 259
scripts of, 109
seafarers from, 109–111, 259
*See also* Aegean
Kara-hardash, king of Babylonia, 236
Kara-indash, king of Babylonia, 180–181
Karnak, 150, 167, 184f–185f, 237
Kaska, 184f–185f, 234, 266, 284
Kassite
conquest of, 307
kingdom, 263
kings, 125–129, 236
language, 126, 234
people, 120, 121, 124–125, 156, 236
*See also* Burna-buriash II, Kadashman-
Enlil I, Kurigalzu I, Kurigalzu II,
Keftiu. *See* Kaptara
Keliya, ambassador from Mittani, 4–8,
200–205, 208–209, 210–212,
214–216, 230, 240–241, 269
Keshdut, princess of Ebla, 34–35
Khabur River, 22, 134, 152, 184f–185f
Khafra, king of Egypt, 52
Kilu-Hepa, princess of Mittani, 196–198,
201, 205, 222, 228, 234
King
as chosen by gods, 120
as divine, 45, 193
as father of the state, 29
as lawgiver, 90
as shepherd of the people, 90
titles of, 33, 101–102, 281
as tribal leader in Syria, 70
as war leader, 33, 69, 90
*See also* specific kings
King List, Sumerian, 38–39, 67, 305
Kirkuk, 158
Kirum, daughter of King Zimri-Lim,
88–89, 107
Kish, 22, 23, 25f, 34–36, 44, 57
Kiya, wife of King Akhenaten, 241–242
Kizzuwatna, 184f–185f
on Assyrian trade route, 105
contested between Mittani and Hatti,
134, 137–138, 161, 170–171, 179–180,
199, 293, 299, 334 n. 17, 335 n. 33
description of, 137–138

Knossos, 149, 184f–185f
Krishna, 44
Kunnaniya, Anatolian wife of an
Assyrian trader, 106
Kura, Syrian god of Ebla, 32
Kurigalzu I, king of Babylonia, 232
Kurigalzu II, king of Babylonia, 283, 293,
357 n. 6
Kurushtama, 181
Kush. *See* Nubia
Kutu, 91
Kuwari, king of Terqa, 123

Labarna, king of Hatti, 121, 332, n. 11
Lachish, 184f–185f, 246
Lagash, 25f, 33, 46, 96
Land
grants 151, 156
purchase of, 39
Languages. *See* Akkadian, Amorite,
Canaan, Cypro-Minoan, Ebla, Egypt,
Hattic, Hittite, Hurrian, Indo-
European, Kassite, Sanskrit,
Semitic, Sumerian, Ugarit
Lapis lazuli,
description of, 50
in dowry, 153
as gifts, 5, 150, 174, 178, 229, 248,
250, 282
as item of trade, 53–54
in jewelry, 20, 224, 245, 247, 250
objects made of, 14, 38, 40, 41, 49, 98,
101, 128, 259, 278
in room decoration, 102, 193
seals made of, 41f, 260
as sign of wealth, 14, 94
as tribute, 145
source of, 38, 43, 49, 50–51, 54,
96–97, 116, 245, 263
unworked, 38
Larsa, 33, 65, 66f, 68, 91, 96, 100
Laws
Assyrian, 218
death penalty, 210
early precursors of, 31
Hammurabi's 63–65, 80, 90
Near East as birthplace of,
309
Ur III period, 67
Lebanon, 42f, 56, 102, 278

Legends and myths
  about Amorites, 68
  of Aratta, 51
  of Sargon's birth, 44
  of Trojan War, 259
  at Ugarit, 276
Letters
  from Ebla to Hamazi, 27
  from Ebla to Abarsal, 31
  from Egypt to Babylonia, 194, 234
  from Egypt to Hatti, 284–287
  greeting formula in, 6–7, 171, 174, 175,
    205, 221, 275
  from Hatti to Ugarit, 276
  to Mari, 69, 86, 88
  from Mari to Babylon, 74
  from Mittani to Arrapkha, 156–157
  from Mittani to Egypt, 4–8, 4f,
    204–205, 225–229, 269, 347 n. 34
  from Princess of Babylonia to Egpyt,
    221
  process of writing, 4–5, 8
  from Qatna to Ekallatum, 77–78
  reading aloud of, 6–7, 74, 87,
    204–205, 226
Levant, 42f, 108, 110, 111–113, 131, 133,
    139, 141, 192, 234, 246, 260, 265,
    279, 283, 289, 292, 301
  See also Canaan, Lebanon, Syria
Libya, 184f–185f, 256
Linear A script, 109, 338 n. 124
Linearn B script, 109, 259, 261–262
Lions, 20, 50, 54, 183, 192, 197, 262
Literacy, 10, 23
Loans, 105–106, 158
Love, between allies, 6–7, 195, 213, 228,
    240–241, 251, 267
Lower Sea (Persian Gulf), 38, 45, 46, 54,
    89, 90, 98, 106, 119
Lu-Enlilla, seafarer, 98–99, 101
Lugalkiginedudu, king of Uruk, 33

Magan (Oman), 42f
  in Akkadian period, 45–48
  in the Old Babylonian period,
    98–99, 111
  in reign of Gudea, 97–98
  in Ur III period, 98
Maluku, Indonesia, 95f, 115
Mane, ambassador from Egypt, 211–212,
    214–216, 217–220, 240

Manetho, historian of Egypt, 139
Manishtusu, king of Akkad, 47, 97
Manium, lord of Magan, 47
Marassantiya River (Kizil Irmak),
    184f–185f, 294
Marduk, Mesopotamian god of Babylon,
    120, 124, 126–129
Mari, 25f
  cities in Old Babylonian kingdom of, 93
  in Early Dynastic period, 20, 22–24,
    26, 32
  geography of, 39
  Old Babylonian period destruction of,
    70, 90
  palace of, 69–70, 90
  trade beyond, 94
  treasure of Ur, 38
Marriage
  age at, 218
  bridewealth, 218–220
  conventions in, 186
  creating unity between lands, 217,
    226–227, 233
  goals, 227
  of officials, 113
  perception of, 232
  royal, in Akkadian empire, 84
  royal, in Amarna period, 194–196,
    205, 211, 217–242, 248, 270,
    285–287, 295, 304
  royal, in Early Dynastic period, 34–35,
    38–39, 59
  royal, in early New Kingdom period,
    148, 177, 182, 183
  royal, in Old Babylonian period, 83–89
  royal, in Ur III, 67, 84
  stages of, 218–219
Maryanni, chariot warriors, 153–154
Mayatu, a daughter of Akhenaten, 250–251
Mediterranean Sea, 13, 25f, 45, 52, 54, 56,
    77, 107, 110, 111, 148, 159, 180, 244,
    255–257, 259, 262
Megiddo, 144–145, 184f–185f
Meluhha (Indus Valley), 42f
  in Akkadian period, 45–51
  decline of, 96
  in Old Babylonian period, 94–96
  in Ur III period, 96
Mcluhhans in Mesopotamia, 49, 96
Memphis, 165, 167, 173, 184f–185f, 198,
    202, 237

Menkheperurue. *See* King Thutmose IV
Merchants, 49
    in Amarna period, 210, 255–256, 274
    Assyrian, in Anatolia, 103–107
    in Hatti, 129
    from Kaptara, 108
    in Old Babylonian period, 63, 94, 99
    protection for, 31
    ransomed prisoners, 127
    in Ur III period, 98–99
    before writing, 51
Mesanepadda, king of Ur, 38
Mesopotamia, 25f
    chaos and order, in 29, 173, 300, 306
    climate of, 40
    gods and goddesses in, 33, 40, 44, 64,
        89, 102, 120, 124, 126–129, 154, 180
    houses in, 89, 99–101, 115, 137, 153,
        157–158
    resources of, 39–40
    roads from, 52, 76
    scribes in, 23
    travel in, 54
    worldview of, 36, 263
    writing invented in, 22
    *See also* Sumer, Akkad, Babylon,
        Babylonia, Assyria
Messengers
    in Akkadian period, 49
    annual visits to courts by, 186, 254
    banquets for, 202
    on boats, 256
    commendation of, 225
    defusing crises, 206–207, 271
    description of embassy to Egypt,
        200–205, 208, 210–212
    detention of, 209, 269, 302
    in Early Dynastic period, 27–28, 31, 57
    in early New Kingdom, 150, 167–168
    as eyewitnesses, 207, 230–231, 234
    gifts for, 32, 73, 202–203, 208, 229–230
    house for, 72
    information gathering by, 286
    in legends, 51
    in negotiations, 45, 71, 74–76, 81–83,
        127, 218–219, 272, 285, 304
    in Old Babylonian period, 70–76,
        81–83, 86–87
    passports for, 201–202
    from princesses and queens, 86–87,
        214

to princesses, 235
    as prisoner of war, 173
    provisions for, 31, 72–73
    reliability of, 194, 208, 214
    role in Amarna period, 214–216
    rules concerning, 171
    on trading mission, 142
    travel, 113, 210–211
    treatment of, 72
Metallurgy, 55
    *See also* bronze, copper, gold, silver, tin
Minoan Crete. *See* Kaptara
Mittani, 184f–185f
    in Amarna period, 4–6, 191–192, 196,
        198–202, 208–216, 265, 267,
        269–270, 271–273, 274, 276–277,
        281, 284, 289
    decline of, 291–301, 303
    and Egypt, 167–168, 196, 211
    evidence for history of, 135
    expansion of empire, 155–156
    founding of, 129
    geography and climate of, 152–153
    and Hatti, 170–171, 233, 295
    religion, 155
    resources of, 152–153
    in sixteenth and fifteenth centuries
        BCE, 132, 134–138, 150–161
    *See also,* treaties, warfare, Hurrian,
        names of specific kings
Mohenjo Daro, 42f, 47
Monkeys, 45, 48, 68, 142
Months, 22, 247
Monuments, *see* stelas and buildings
Moses, 44, 63–64
Mudbricks, 55, 72
Mukish, 184f–185f, 276
Mummies, 52, 116, 143–144, 165, 231
Murex shells, 110, 257, 274
Mursili I, king of Hatti, 121–123, 126,
    137, 156, 169–170, 266, 273
Mursili II, king of Hatti, son of
    Suppiluliuma, 270, 280, 283–285,
    287–288, 301–303, 357 n. 21,
    357 n. 24
Musical instruments, 40, 41
Musicians, 73, 108, 211, 229
Mycenae, 184f–185f, 259–263

Nagar, 22, 35, 36, 57
Naharin. *See* Mittani

names, personal, 154
Nanna, Mesopotamian moon god, 40
Napata, 166, 184f–185f
Naphurureya, *See* Akhenaten
Naram-Sin, king of Akkad, 45, 47, 58–59, 63, 67, 84, 348 n. 53
Nazi-bugash, 357 n. 6
Nebmaatra. *See* Amenhotep III
Neferheprure-Wanre. *See* Akhenaten
Nefertiti, wife of King Akhenaten, 236, 239, 256, 282, 355–356 n. 71
Negotiation, 33, 81–83, 85, 127–128, 178, 299
   *See also* messengers, treaties
*New York Times*, 40, 63
Nibhururiya. *See* Tutankhamen
Nibmuareya. *See* Amenhotep III
Nile, 6, 9, 42f, 54, 113, 132, 139, 140, 141, 177, 179, 202, 239
Nineteenth Dynasty, 303
Nineveh, 7
Ninmetabarri, princess of Mari, 38–39
Niqmaddu II, king of Ugarit, 273, 275–277
Nubia, 9, 42f, 114, 131, 139, 142, 147, 150, 161, 165, 166, 177, 182, 192–194, 215, 263, 265, 275, 283f, 335 n. 41
Nuhashi, 184f–185f, 271, 276
Nuzi, 134, 157–160, 184f–185f

Oasis towns
   in Iran, 43, 49
   Tadmor, in Syria, 76
Oath
   to a king, 268
   as part of a treaty, 32, 33, 81–83, 137, 161, 171, 299, 304
   punishment for breaking, 30, 268, 301–302
Obsidian, 43, 105, 306
Oil (cedar, olive, perfumed, sesame)
   anointment with, 35, 113, 161, 218–219
   as food, 79
   in hygiene, 209
   lamps, 52, 155, 256
   for mummification, 52
   in gifts for messengers, 203
   offering to gods, 32, 58–59
   production of, 19, 110, 113
   in rations, 72, 157
   as a royal gift, 103, 178, 220, 239, 245, 246, 247, 254–255, 258
   storage of, 215
   for trade, 98, 260
   in wall decoration, 102
Okheperkare. *See* Thutmose I
Old Babylonian kingdoms, 65, 68, 94
Old Babylonian period, 63–67, 68–91, 93–94, 96–97, 98–116, 119–124
Oman. *See* Magan
onagers, 57
oracles. *See* divination and diviners
Order, desire for social, 29, 36, 67, 139, 173, 238, 289, 300–301, 306
Orontes Valley, 76
Ostrich eggshells, 257
Oxen, 40

Paharrashe, in Arrapkha, 157
Pakistan, 48
   *See also* Meluhha
Palaces
   at Alalakh, 160
   in Assyria, 248
   at Avaris, 148–149
   at Babylon, missing, 69
   at Byblos, 52
   at Ebla, 20
   in Egypt, 183
   in Greece, 261
   at Kanesh, 104
   at Mari, 69–70, 90, 109
   in Kaptara, 109
   at Nuzi, 158
   in Sumer, 39
   at Thebes, 202–204, 203f, 229–230
   of Tushratta, missing, 199, 215
   at Ugarit, 275
Palmyra. *See* Tadmor
panthers, 142
Parattarna I, king of Mittani, 134–138, 154, 156, 160
Pastoralists, 68
Peace
   in Amarna period, 4, 10, 15, 193, 195–196, 216, 263–265, 272, 276–277, 279, 281, 306, 341 n. 24
   between Early Dynastic kingdoms, 24, 28, 58

in the Early New Kingdom 167–169,
   172–178, 183
and the gods, 172–173
in the Hyksos period, 140
between Old Babylonian kingdoms,
   71, 90–91
related terms, 244
treaties, 10, 14, 16, 32, 36, 57–59, 71,
   82–83, 129, 168, 179, 199,
   297–298, 303, 306
Pearls, 48–49, 99, 319 n. 51
Pepi I, king of Egypt, 52–53
Pepi II, king of Egypt, 143
Perfume, 53, 110, 178, 201, 260
Per-Ramesse, 303
Persian Gulf, 42f
   See also, Lower Sea
Peshgaldaramesh, king of the Sealand, 125
Phalanx, 57
Physicians, 108, 245, 275
Piyassili, king of Carchemish, 295–296,
   298–299
Plague. See illness
Polygamy, 87
Polytheism, 39
Priests and priestesses, 5, 85, 239
Princes, 71, 145–146, 157, 166, 193–194,
   268, 277, 293
Princesses, 15,
   in Amarna period, 194–195, 217–236,
      239, 246–248, 270, 285, 296–297,
      300
   in Early Dynastic period, 34–35, 38–39
   in early New Kingdom, 141, 148–149,
      177, 186
   in Old Babylonian period, 84–88, 86f
   in the thirteenth century BCE, 304
   in Ur III period, 67
Prisoners of war, 58, 122, 127–128, 133,
   137, 146–147, 165, 166, 173, 183, 273,
   276, 278, 280, 292, 301
Protocol, 27, 70–76, 77, 187
Punt, 95f
   in New Kingdom, 142–143, 149, 177,
      263
   in Old Kingdom, 53–54, 143
Puzur-Ashur III, king of Assyria, 129
Puzurum, Terqa resident, 115
Pylos, 184f–185f, 260
Pyramids, 12, 52–53, 110, 150, 330 n. 88

Qatna, 66f
   in Amarna period, 277–278
   in Old Babylonian period, 65, 76–79,
      84, 108
Queens, 35, 40, 86, 141, 142, 227, 297
   See also specific queens

Ra, Egyptian god of the sun, 139, 145,
   146, 167, 193, 196, 213, 237
Rainfall, 132, 139, 155, 274
Ramesses II, king of Egypt, 303–304
Ransom of prisoners, 127
Red Sea, 42f, 53, 54, 55
Religion. See gods and goddesses,
   temples, divination and diviners
Retjenu, 133
Resources
   control of, 56
   in Dilmun, 99
   in Egypt, 53–54
   in Mesopotamia, 39–40
   in Mittani, 152–153
Rim-Sin, king of Larsa, 65, 68, 100
Rivers, use for irrigation and farming,
   39–40
   See also Nile, Euphrates, Tigris, Orontes
Roads
   in Canaan, 145
   to Egypt, 112
   from Mediterranean to Mesopotamia,
      52, 76
   safety on, 104
   in Ur, 99
Romulus and Remus, 44
Royal inscriptions, 11–12, 23, 24, 33, 46,
   52, 90, 126–128, 151, 152, 168

Sacrifices
   donkey, 82
   human, 40
Samsuditana, king of Babylon, 120–121,
   123–124
Sanskrit, 154, 338 n. 124
Sardinia, 252
Sargon, king of Akkad, 44–49, 58, 63, 65,
   67, 90, 97, 102, 106, 119, 122, 305
Sar-i Sang, 42f, 50
Sarpanitum, Mesopotamian goddess of
   Babylon, 124, 126–128
Scarabs, 110, 192, 196–197, 197f, 256, 275

Schools, 23, 125
Scribes, 10, 22–24, 60, 71, 89, 125, 206,
    220, 222, 229, 253, 267, 276
  in a dowry, 85
  roles in palace, 20
  training, 23
Sealand Dynasty, First, 125
Seals, 38
  cylinder, 3, 41f, 49–50, 111, 135, 151,
    153, 156, 159, 160, 198, 201, 211,
    248, 260
  cylinder, in Aegean region, 56
  cylinder, in Egypt 55–56
  Meluhhan, 46, 47, 49, 50, 96
  Mycenaean, 256
  See also scarabs
Semitic languages, 22, 29, 39, 126
Senusret I, 113
Seti I, king of Egypt, 303
Shahr-i Sokhta, 42f, 49
Shamash, Mesopotamian sun god, 64f,
    128, 154
Shamshi-Adad, king of Upper
    Mesopotamia, 68–69, 71, 76, 84,
    101–103, 228
Sharon, Valley of, 173
Sharrukin. See Sargon, king of Akkad
Sharruwa, author of the autobiography
    of Idrimi, 135
Shashuri, wife of Shilwa-Teshup,
    157–158
Shattiwaza, king of Mittani, 227,
    293–301, 303
Shattuara I, king of Mittani, 303
Shaushtatar II, king of Mittani, 151–153,
    159, 165, 169–176, 178, 182
  seal of, 151
Shaushka, Hurrian goddess of love and
    war, 5–8, 155, 213, 218, 225, 313 n. 6,
    341 n. 40
Shaving, 20–21, 256, 259
Sheep
  as booty, 146, 273, 284
  in dowry, 34
  as gift, 218, 293
  herding, 19, 22, 68, 115–116, 153
  in lists, 158
  stealing of, 80, 271–272
Shetep, 196
Shilwa-Teshup, prince of Arrapkha,
    157–159

Shimatum, daughter of King Zimri-Lim,
    87–88
Shimige, Hurrian god of the sun, 155,
    213, 225, 229
Shimurrum, 82
Ships. See boats
Shiptu, wife of King Zimri-Lim, 86
Shortughaï, 42f, 49, 51
Shubat-Enlil, 66f, 69
Shulgi, 67, 98, 314 n. 9
Shusharra, 66f, 84
Shushim. See Susa
Shuttarna II, king of Mittani, 195–196,
    198, 200, 228, 344 n. 21
Shuttarna III, king of Mittani, 292–296,
    298, 356 n. 2
Silver
  in administrative texts, 37
  from Anatolia, 43, 105, 245
  as booty, 152, 166
  as bridal gift, 218, 220
  as decoration, 102, 193
  in dowries, 85, 153, 224
  as gifts for envoys, 72–73, 76, 203
  as a medium of exchange, 23, 78, 80,
    94, 97, 101, 106, 256
  from Meluhha, 48
  mines in Magan, 47
  objects made of, 32, 37, 38, 40, 121,
    146, 260, 275, 282
  as payment to soldiers, 72
  royal gifts of, 32, 150, 222–223, 255,
    277, 281–282, 292, 295,
    349–350 n. 8
  stolen, 80
  Sumerian term for, 37
  traded for, 46, 103–104
  as tribute, 26, 146
  value of, 37–38
Silk Road, 116
Sim'alites, 70
Sinai, 5, 144, 177, 184f–185f, 252
Sin-ilishu, Meluhha interpreter, 49
Sinuhe, Egyptian official, 112–114
Sippar, 26, 66f, 73, 75, 91
Slave
  in a dowry, 85
  in Egypt, 166
  employed in farming, 158
  employed in palaces, 69
  manumission of, 198

prisoners of war, 140, 201
purchase of, 80
as term for subordinate, 31
Smenkhare, king of Egypt, 281–282,
    353–354 n. 9, 355 n. 65
Soldiers
    in Amarna period, 5, 7, 174, 201, 225,
        236, 276–277, 279–280, 283–284,
        288, 294–295, 301, 357 n. 24
    in Early Dynastic period, 21f, 57–58, 58f
    in early Mittani, 135, 137, 154, 156
    in early New Kingdom Egypt, 131–134,
        140, 142, 144–148
    in Old Babylonian period, 70, 72, 75,
        85, 90, 107, 123, 127
    in the sixteenth century BCE, 122–124,
        127, 266
    in the thirteen century BCE, 303
Somalia. See Punt
Son, lesser king as, 70
Sphinx, Great, 52, 150, 164, 177
Spices, 110, 114–115, 257, 331 n. 110
Statues, 38, 282
    base of, 195
    found in Ebla, 38
    gifts of, 37,
    of gods and goddesses, 5–7, 82–83,
        122, 124, 128, 299, 306
    gold, promised by Amenhotep III,
        228–231, 240–241, 243–244. 248,
        251, 267, 269, 272
    of kings, 20, 45, 47, 64, 67, 77, 84,
        97–98, 120, 135–136, 136f, 146, 151,
        193, 198, 220, 238
    in tombs, 40
Stela of the Vultures, 33
Stelas, 64, 133, 147, 165–166, 182
Stone
    for building, 40
    bowls, 41, 110
Storms, 155, 257
Storm-god of Hatti, Hittite god, 181, 302
Strait of Hormuz, 42f, 46, 48
Succession of kings, 195, 296
Sudan. See Nubia
Suicide, threatened, 88
Sumer, 33, 38, 51
Sumerian language, 23–24, 39, 89, 274
    terms in, 33, 37
Sun Goddess of Arinna, chief deity of
    the Hittites, 122, 181, 299

Suppiluliuma, king of Hatti 267–273,
    277–288, 292–301, 355–356 n. 71
Susa, 66f, 97
Syria
    in Amarna period, 191–192, 196,
        198–202, 208–216, 265, 267,
        269–270, 271–273, 274, 276–277,
        281, 284, 289
    climate, 40
    description of, 132
    in Early Dynastic period, 19–32, 34–36
    geographic importance, 13
    in Old Babylonian period, 69–70
Syrian desert, 66f, 68, 76

Tacitus, 308
Tadmor/Palmyra, 66f, 76
Tadu-Hepa, princess of Mittani, 7, 149,
    217–231, 233–235, 239, 241–242
Taite, 292
Tanaja, 149, 260
Tarut, island of, 46
Tarhundaradu, king of Arzawa, 246
Tarhuntassa, 303
Taurus Mountains, 42f, 43, 103, 105, 121,
    122, 199, 260
Tawananna, Hittite queen, 270
Taxes, 11, 23, 77, 104, 159, 167, 201
Tel Kabri, 66f, 108
Tell
    at Carchemish, 280
    formation of, at Ebla, 20
    at Kanesh, 104
    in Mittani, 152
    at Qatna, 76
    at Ugarit, 274
Tell Fakhariyah, 134
Telipinu, king of Hatti, 121–125, 170
Temples
    decoration of, 96, 97, 102, 128, 249
    dedicated to a king, 193
    descriptions of, 230, 274
    Egyptian, 55
    as home to city god or goddess, 39–40,
        122
    kings' statues in, 45, 120
    improvement of, 90, 102
    merchants working for, 101
    mortuary, 6, 151, 194, 198
    as site of treaty, 32
Tents, 68, 132, 142, 295

Tepe Gawra, 42f, 51
Terebinth resin, 257
Terqa, 57, 114–115, 120, 123, 138,
    315 n. 29, 331 n. 110, 332 n. 21
Teshup, Hurrian storm god, 155, 181,
    199, 213, 266
Tetti, vassal of Mittani, 302
Textiles
    as gifts, 35, 220, 221, 224, 247
    as cargo, 257
    manufacture of, 19, 158–159, 260
    records of, 22
    in trade, 51, 53, 98, 101, 103, 106, 110
    as tribute, 277
Thebes (Egypt), 6, 140, 166, 184f–185f,
    196, 198, 202, 203, 213, 226, 229,
    237, 281–283, 345 n. 53
Thebes (Greece), 260
Throne room, 6, 69, 204, 215, 275
Thucydides, 308
Thutmose I, king of Egypt, 131–135,
    137–141, 146, 147, 148, 151, 156, 161
Thutmose II, king of Egypt, 141, 151
Thutmose III, king of Egypt, 138, 141,
    143–152, 161, 163, 165, 167, 169, 171,
    177, 192, 225, 245, 259, 260, 271,
    338 n. 102
Thutmose IV, king of Egypt, 183,
    186–187, 195, 222
Tigers, 50
Tigris River, 14, 15, 26, 68, 102, 134,
Timber. See wood, in construction
Tin, 14, 46, 77–79, 94, 96, 98, 103–107,
    108, 110–111, 123, 125, 152, 177, 243,
    246, 257, 263
Tira-Il, scribe of Irkab-damu, 27
Tirukkeans, 82
Tiryns, 184f–185f, 259, 261
Tiy, wife of King Amenhotep III,
    192–193, 196–197, 204, 208, 214,
    218, 235, 239, 240–241
Tombs
    in Dilmun, 98–99
    in Egypt, 54–55, 132, 148, 165, 229,
        238, 282
    in Greece, 260, 262
    robbed, 97
    royal, at Ur, 40–41, 48, 58f, 318 n. 15
Trade
    in Akkadian empire, 44–54
    in Amarna period, 15

development of, 306
    in Early Dynastic period, 14, 36, 43, 53,
        56–57
    in early New Kingdom Egypt, 142
    evidence for, 105
    in Middle Kingdom Egypt, 112
    in Old Babylonian period, 14
    before writing, 43–44, 51
    See also merchants
Traders. See merchants
Translators
    in Akkadian period, 49
    in Amarna period, 7, 175, 202, 208,
        225
    in Early Dynastic period, 28, 39
    in Old Babylonian period, 108
Travel
    around the Mediterranean, 255–257
    difficulties of, 43, 210
    from Anatolia to Babylon, 123
    from Ashur to Anatolia, 103
    from Babylon to Hatti, 294
    from Dilmun to Shubat-Enlil, 102–103
    from Egypt to Canaan, 112
    from Egypt to the Euphrates, 131–132
    from Magan to Ur, 98
    from Mari to the Mediterranean, 107
    from Mari to Sippar, 75–76
    from Meluhha to Akkad by sea, 48
    from Meluhha to Akkad by land, 49
    from Mesopotamia to Egypt, 54
    from Mittani to Egypt, 5–6
    from Mittani to Thebes, 201–202,
        224–226
Treaties
    in Amarna period, 11
    Babylonia-Assyria, 181
    Babylonia-Egypt, 180
    clauses, 297–299
    consulted later, 287
    Ebla-Abarsal, 29–32
    Ebla-Hamazi, possible, 28, 31
    Ebla-Mari, 32, 57
    Hatti-Egypt 181, 287, 303–304
    Hatti-Kizzuwatna, 170, 179–180
    Hatti-Mittani, 227, 270, 296–301
    Hatti-Ugarit, 277
    Hittite, earliest, 129
    Lagash with other kingdoms, 33
    negotiated, 296
    in Old Babylonian period, 80–83, 137

placed in temples, 32, 299
procedures, 342 n. 56
with vassals, 136–137, 302
written copies, 181
Tribute, 26, 71, 102–103, 142, 145, 149,
     150, 161, 277, 337 n. 99
Troodos Mountains, 184f–185f, 253
Troops. *See* soldiers
Tudhaliya I, king of Hatti, 138, 170–171,
     179, 181, 335 n. 29, 335 n. 34,
     338 n. 102
Tudhaliya II, king of Hatti, 267
Tudhaliya the Younger, successor to
     Tudhaliya II, king of Hatti, 268
Tukrish, 66f, 102–103
Tunip-ibri, envoy from Mittani, 200–205
Turquoise, 49, 53, 112, 143, 145
Tushratta, king of Mittani
     and Akhenaten, 4–9, 239–242,
          269–270
     and Amenhotep III, 217–231, 247, 251,
          265
     death of, 291, 356 n. 3
     early reign, 199–201
     length of reign, 356 n. 1
     personality, 212–213
     and Suppiluliuma, 267, 270–273, 281,
          283–284
Tutankhaten/Tutankhamen, king of
     Egypt, 282–284, 283f, 355–356 n. 71
Tuttul, 66f, 91
Tyre, 184f–185f, 275

Ugarit, 66f
     in Amarna period, 180, 187, 234, 245,
          263
     description of, 273–276
     destruction of, 307
     language of, 274
     in Old Babylonian period, 77, 108–111
     relationship with Hatti, 276–277, 302,
          303
Ugi, man in Arrapkha, 157
Uluburun shipwreck, 184f–185f,
     257–259, 258f
     description of the voyage
          before  255–257
Umm el-Marra, 184f–185f, 198
Umma, 33
United Nations, 10–11, 16
Upper Sea. *See* Mediterranean

Ur
     description of, 38–40, 99–101
     and Ebla, 41
     in Old Babylonian period, 91, 100f
     royal tombs at, 40–41, 48, 58
     and trade, 43, 47, 49, 98–101, 103
     and Uruk, 33
Ur III period, 65, 67–68, 71, 84, 96, 98,
     101, 119
Urkesh, 84, 155
Ur-Namma, 67
Uruk (city), 33, 51, 91, 180
Uruk period, 55–56

Vassals
     freedoms of, 158, 160
     rebellions of, 79, 279
     relationships with overlords, 70, 76, 87,
          89, 107–108, 135, 156, 175, 194–195
     treaties between, 160
     treaties with overlords, 31, 81–83,
          136–137, 160, 171, 278, 279
Viceroys, 69, 77, 182, 293
Vizier, in Egypt, 112, 204

Wagons, 27–28, 40, 89, 224
Walls, fortification, 24, 104, 259, 260,
     266, 315 n. 29
Wall decorations, 193
Wall paintings, 69, 108–109, 148–149,
     157, 158, 209, 230, 259, 275, 278
Warfare, 280, 305
     in Akkadian period, 45
     Early Dynastic, 33–34, 57, 59
     Egypt v. Kinza, 283
     Egypt v. Mittani, 131–133, 138, 144,
          146–148, 165, 183
     Egypt v. Nubia, 142, 192
     Hatti and Mittani v. Shuttarna III,
          295–296
     Hatti in Anatolia, 267
     Hatti v. Amurru, 279
     Hatti v. Babylon, 121–122
     Hatti v. Carchemish, 286
     Hatti v. Egypt 288, 301, 303
     Hatti v. Syria, 170
     Hatti v. Kadesh 284
     Hatti v. Kinza, 278
     Hatti v. Mittani, 271–273, 277–278
     Hatti v. Mittani's allies, 268
     Hatti v. Syria, 288

Warfare (*continued*)
  Mittanian expansion, 135–137
  Mittani v. Assyria, 152
  Mittani v. Hatti, 199
  Mittani v. Ugarit, 276–277
  in Old Babylonian period, 90–91
  Trojan War, 259
  before writing, 24
  *See also* soldiers
Washshukkanni, 134, 152, 156,
    184f–185f, 201, 211, 225, 231,
    240, 273, 283, 291–293,295, 296
Weapons, 37, 40, 57–58, 94, 110, 153,
    165, 166, 222, 256, 265
Weddings
  royal, 34–35, 85, 161, 196, 225, 229
Weights and measures, 22, 46, 67, 96,
    99, 104, 256
Wheat, 40, 115–116, 152, 274
Wheel
  on chariots, 153, 200–201, 263
  invention of, 55
Wine. *See* drink
Windows, 6, 52, 72, 90
Witchcraft, 87, 270
Witnesses, 60, 80, 89, 210
Wives, royal
  in Amarna period, 194, 218, 227,
    233–234, 239
  beauty of, 218, 230
  in early New Kingdom Egypt, 177
  at Ebla, 21
  in Old Babylonian period, 107
  roles of, 233, 270
  *See also* specific royal wives
Wood
  for construction, 40, 266, 274, 275,
    278
  for fires, 266
  as loans, 158
  in luxury furniture, 20
  from Meluhha, 96
  objects in dowries, 224
  objects as royal gifts, 26, 150, 222,
    245, 254
  from Punt, 142
  statues of, 240–241
  in trade, 46, 48, 54, 257

writing tablets made of, 258, 266
Wool
  in economy, 19, 153
  as gifts, 222, 224
  as items of trade, 46, 98, 153
  as rations, 72, 157
  as tribute, 277
Woolley, Sir Leonard, 40, 99
Workers, palace, 19, 69, 260, 262
Worldview, 306–307
  Babylonian, 206–207
  Egyptian, 138
  Hittite, 125
  Mesopotamian, 36, 263
  in Old Babylonian period, 89
Writing
  adopted in Anatolia, 103
  invention of, 55
  wooden tablet for, 258, 266
  *See also* alphabet, Cuneiform,
    Cuneiform tablets, Cypro-Minoan,
    Hieratic, Hieroglyphs (Egypt),
    Hieroglyphs (Crete), Indus Valley,
    Linear A (Crete), Linear B (Crete)

Xinjiang province, 95f, 115

Ya'ilanum, 82
Yamhad, 65, 66f, 73, 84, 107–108, 122
Yansib-Addu, official of King Zimri-Lim,
    73–76
Yarim-Lim, king of Yamhad, 65
Year-names, ix, 34, 90, 120
Yon, Marguerite, 275
Yumras-El, king of Abi-ili, 93
Yuni, queen of Mittani, Tushratta's chief
    wife, 214

Zagros Mountains, 49, 68, 134, 156
Zannanza, prince of Hatti, 288, 291, 301,
    357 n. 24
Zebu, 48, 49
Ziggurats, 67
Zimri-Lim, king of Mari, 13–14, 69–76,
    79, 81–82, 84–90, 93, 94, 96–97,
    107–109
Zippasna, 122, 128
Zirtaya, 302

Lightning Source UK Ltd.
Milton Keynes UK
UKHW021836300123
416202UK00006B/400

9 780195 313987